Public Records Online

The National Guide to Private & Government Online Sources of Public Records

©2001 By Facts on Demand Press
1971 East Fifth Street, Suite 101
Tempe, AZ 85281
(800) 929-3811
www.brbpub.com

Public Records Online

The National Guide to Private & Government Online Sources of Public Records

©2001 By Facts on Demand Press
1971 East Fifth Street, Suite 101
Tempe, AZ 85281
(800) 929-3811

ISBN: 1-889150-21-5
Cover Design by Robin Fox & Associates
Edited by Michael L. Sankey, James R. Flowers Jr., and Peter J. Weber.
Second Printing, August 2001 (revised)

Cataloging-in-Publication Data

        Public Records Online : the national guide to private & government online sources of public records / [edited by Michael L. Sankey, James R. Flowers, Jr., and Peter J. Weber] – 3rd rev. ed.

        p. cm. – (Online ease)

        1. Electronic public records – United States -- Directories 2. Information services industries – United States – Directories I. Sankey, Michael L., 1949- II. Flowers, James R. (James Robert) 1973- III. Weber, Peter J. (Peter Julius), 1952- IV. Series.

        JK468.P76P83 2000
        352.3'87'0973

                QB100-700981

Contents

Section II - Government Sources   57

Section III - Private Company Sources 311

Forward

"Public Records" often conveys an image of a complex, almost mysterious source of information that is inaccessible, difficult to find, and likely to be of interest only to private investigators and reporters. This view could not be further from the *truth*!

Indeed, the use of public records is one of the fundamental principles of our democratic society.

Have you ever—

☑   obtained a driver's license?

☑   applied for a voter registration card?

☑   borrowed money for your business?

☑   set up a corporation?

☑   purchased a home or a vehicle?

☑   been involved in a court matter?

If so, you have not only become involved in the "public record information trail," but probably left an online trace.

The Doorway to Online Public Records

Today, there are literally thousands of public records and public information sources accessible by anyone with a computer and a modem. With this rapid growth, it becomes necessary for online users to understand what information is available and what information is not, to know how the information is gathered and stored, and to know who "has" the information and where it is located.

This book is your key to opening the door to online public records information. Whether you surf the World Wide Web, connect via modem to a court's computer system or utilize a company's dial-up system, *Public Records Online* is your gateway to the world of online records research.

The information you desire is probably out there somewhere. You need only find its particular "trail." To that end, this book has been designed to be your tour guide when traveling the trail of online information. With this book in hand, you've made the first step on your trip. Now, we suggest that you read the beginning chapters to fully prepare you for your journey. Once you're familiar with the cyber scenery, you'll need only to scan the chapters and sources to find the right "trail" to take.

Our goal is to provide you with a complete primer—so you can understand what you need, where it might be, and how to access that information like a pro.

Equipped with the information contained in these pages, you can find the facts, gain access to the information you need and even track your own "trail."

Good hunting!

A Public Records Primer

The Information Trail

Modern society has become extremely dependent on information. Information is, indeed, the life load of most business and personal interaction. Government and private industry require record keeping to regulate, license, and hire or fire. Individuals need public information for managing personal affairs and meeting one's responsibilities as citizens.

Nearly all individuals and business entities create a trail of information that is a history of daily life. You could say that the trail starts with a birth certificate, a Social Security Number or articles of incorporation. The trail extends past the death certificate or record of dissolution into, virtually, infinite time. These many records—some accessible, some accessible with restrictions, and some inaccessible—create and embellish an identity. Finding and staying "on the trail" of accurate discovery takes knowledge and persistence. Thankfully, computers and the Internet now allow us to examine these trails where they exist online.

Whether you are new at searching public records or not, there are a myriad of issues that must be considered and questions that must be answered if you are to become an effective, efficient user of the online tools now available.

Finding information is not an easy process; *Public Records Online* aims to make it so. *Public Records Online* reveals where records are kept, outlines access requirements and gives searching hints so that you can explore the depths of the public record industry.

Information – Public or Private?

Let's define the types of records held by government or by private industry from the viewpoint of a professional record searcher.

Definition of Public Records

Public records are records of **incidents** or **actions** filed or recorded with a government agency for the purpose of notifying others—the "public"—about the matter. These incidents can be court actions, filings at a county recorder's office, or marriages. The strict **definition** of **public records** is—

"Those records maintained by government agencies that are open without restriction to public inspection, either by statute or by tradition."

The **deed** to your house recorded at the county recorder's office is a public record. It is a legal requirement that you "record it" with the county recorder. Anyone requiring details about your property may review or copy the documents. According to the above definition, if access to a record held by a government agency is restricted in some way, or if a private company holds the record, it is not a public record.

However, this does not take into consideration the **accessibility paradox**. For example, in some states access to a specific category of records is severely restricted, and consequently records are not public, while the very same category of records may be 100% open in other states. Among these categories are criminal histories, motor vehicle records, and worker's compensation records.

> **Editor's Tip:** Just because records are maintained in a certain way in your state or county do not assume that any other county or state does things the same way that you are used to.

Public Information

Your **telephone listing** in the phone book is an example of public information; it is not public record information. Public information is furnished freely by people and businesses. The use of public information contributes to the flow of commercial and private communications. While this is an important distinction, it is important to keep in mind certain pieces of information can appear both in public records and public information. **Therefore, this book makes an effort to cover many sources of public information as well as public records**.

Personal Information

Any information about a person or business that the person or business might consider private and confidential in nature, such as your **Social Security Number**, is personal information. Such information will remain private to a limited extent unless you disclose it to some outside entity that could make it public. **Often, personal information may be found in either public records or in public information.**

Many people confuse these three categories, lump them into one, and wonder how "Big Brother" accumulated so much information about them. The distinctions are important. Consider as fact that much of this information is given **willingly**.

There are two ways that personal information can enter the public domain— voluntary and statutory. In a **voluntary** transaction, you **share** personal information of your own free will. In a **statutory** transaction, you **disclose** personal information because the law **requires** it.

The increasing conflict between privacy advocates and commercial interests is driving legislation that would apply more and more **restrictions** on the **dissemination of personal information**—the same personal information which, in fact, is willingly shared by most people and companies in order to participate in our market economy.

The Benefits of Public Records

Public records are meant to be used for the benefit of society. Whether you are a business owner, a reporter, an investigator, or even a father trying to check on your daughter's first date, you can access public records to meet your needs. As a member of the public, you or someone in authority is entitled to review the public records held and established by government agencies.

Here are a few basic examples of the benefits of public records and public record searching:

For your family & friends

- discover whether a long lost friend is alive and well;
- determine if your spouse is hiding assets;
- learn whether a neighbor is also a child molester.

For your business

- find out if a prospective employee is falsifying a resume;
- ascertain whether a potential business partner is legitimate;
- determine if a new client is a risk or is likely to pay promptly.

For your community

- learn if a bus driver has one or more DUIs;
- find out if a public official is also a convicted felon;
- determine whether 911 and the fire department know where you live.

Where to Obtain Public Records

There are two places you can find public records—

♦ at a **government agency**

♦ within the database of a **private company**

Government agencies keep or maintain records in a variety of ways. While many state agencies and highly populated county agencies are computerized, many still use microfiche, microfilm, and paper storage of files and indexes. Agencies that have converted to computer have not necessarily placed complete file records on their system; they are more apt to include only an index, pointer, or summary data to the computerized files. Again, be aware that certain records may be available without restriction in one state or county, yet be restricted in another.

Private enterprises develop their databases in one of two ways: they buy the records in bulk from government agencies, or they send personnel to the agencies to compile this information by using a copy machine or keying into a laptop computer. The database is then available for internal use, for resale online, or is accessible in some other form. This book contains profiles of the nation's elite private vendors of public record information.

> **Editor's Tip:** Public records purchased and/or compiled by private companies for resale purposes must follow the same access and restriction regulations as the related government jurisdiction.

How to Obtain Public Records

Whether it is a public record or not, there are two ways to obtain a piece of information:

♦ Look it up or obtain it yourself;

♦ Have someone else look it up for you.

In the world of public records and public information, you may be able to look it up - or "do the search" - yourself under these circumstances:

1. The information is available in your own geographic area, and you can retrieve it in-person;

2. The information is available by written request;

3. The information can be obtained over the telephone;

4. **The information is available online or on CD-ROM.**

The purpose of this book is to examine #4 above. These pages reflect which government agencies offer online access to their public record databases, and which elite private companies compile and maintain their own proprietary databases of public record information.

Fees & Charges for Accessing Public Records

Public records are not necessarily free of charge—certainly not if they are maintained by private industry. Remember, public records are records of incidents or transactions. Among these incidents can be civil or criminal court actions, recordings, filings or occurrences such as speeding tickets or accidents. **It costs money** (time, salaries, supplies, etc.) **to record and track these events**. Common charges found at the government level for non-online access include copy fees (to make copies of the document), search fees (for clerical personnel to search for the record), and certification fees (to certify the document as being accurate and coming from the particular agency). These fees can vary from $.10 per page for copies to a $15.00 or more search fee for court personnel to do the actual look-up. Some government agencies will allow you to walk in and view records at no charge, many times from a "counter terminal." Yet fewer will release information over the phone without a fee.

Online access of government-held records usually costs less money on a per record basis than non-online. A key to purchasing public records online direct from some government agencies is the **frequency of usage requirements**. Many agencies require a minimum amount of requests per month or per session. Certainly, it does not make economic sense to spend a lot of money on programming and set-up fees if you intend on ordering only five records per month. You would be better off to do the search by more conventional methods (mail, visit in person) or hire a search vendor. Going direct online to the source is not always the least expensive option!

When private enterprise is in the business of maintaining a public records database, it generally does so to offer these records for resale based on volume of usage. However, government agencies have one price per category, regardless of the number of requests. One exception is when government agencies sell database lists in bulk, in which case prices are on a "per thousand records" basis.

Finding Online Sources of Public Records

Over the past twenty years, public record information has been compiled into vast computer databases. As mentioned previously, these databases are being compiled by the government and by private enterprise. Searching online for what you need is a challenge; you must utilize the appropriate online resource, gather the information you want, and use it effectively.

Government Online Sources

For the purposes of this book, the term "government" refers to every level of government from city/township through county/parish and state, up to and including the federal level. All levels collect data and, provided the law allows, will provide you with access.

Some agencies provide a higher degree of online access than others. Typical state government agencies offer extensive online access include secretary of state offices (corporate records, Uniform Commercial Code records) and department of motor vehicle offices (driver and vehicle records). Federal court records are virtually all online. However, finding real estate, assessor, civil and criminal information online directly from a local or state government agency can be difficult. A few states, among them Alabama, Maryland, Oregon, Utah, and Washington, provide their court records online to the public from a statewide system. A few scattered county courts that have implemented their own local remote online systems. And, the Internet is not a major component (see page 9).

Private Online Sources

Private companies have been more aggressive than government agencies in making this computerized information available online. By buying or collecting indexes from government agencies, private companies combine data in ways that are generally more useful to the public. For a fee, these companies make their information available to individuals and other companies through an **online** connection or on **CD-ROM**. Chances are if the information you seek is not available online from the government, it may be obtained from a private company.

> **Editor's Tip:** There are over 165 private companies offering online access to their proprietary database(s) of public record information. The competition is overlapping due to an enormous amount of sharing and wholesaling of data between vendors and resellers.

The next chapter reviews 26 categories of public records and public information. The index pages found at the beginning of the Private Company Sources Section is a good place to start to find a particular company for a specific type or category of public record.

Searching on the Internet

Fact: less than 15% of the 20,000 government locations in the US, profiled in BRB Publications' *Sourcebook to Public Record Information,* offer free online access to the public record and public information. But the good news is that there's a definite trend for more government sites to be placed on the 'Net. This is especially true for the records held by the secretary of state offices, and by the county recorder and assessor offices.

Needless to say, there are plenty of great government web sites offering valuable information, forms, explanations of policies and procedures, lists of locations of offices and personnel, etc. The Government Sources Section includes web addresses with the profiled agencies, when appropriate.

Probably the best trend involving the Internet and public record access is that the Internet is replacing many of the costly dial-up access systems. When fees or subscriptions are required to obtain a record, the switchover to the Internet has helped reduce or do away with the access fee charges

Other Searching Methods

When all methods of online access fail for a particular record search, it may be necessary to physically retrieve the records you want. In such cases, utilizing a public record retriever, someone who is in the business of retrieving records and providing copies for a fee, is probably the most efficient method.

> **Editor's Tip:** In the event of such a necessity, refer to the Public Record Retriever Network (PRRN) found at www.brbpub.com/prrn. This web site lists reputable retrieval firms and contact information by state, county and type of record.

Online Information Categories

The following pages examine the 26 general categories of records considered either public record, public information or restricted information (such as credit reports). Although there are more general ways to categorize this information, such as court records instead of civil or criminal records, such generalizations tend to mask important variations in how certain type of records are subject to access restrictions.

In considering these alphabetically listed summaries, keep the following points in mind:

♦ Very little of what you may perceive as government record information is truly open to the general public. Even the seemingly most harmless information is subject to restrictions somewhere in the US. On the other hand, what you may think of as highly confidential information is likely public information somewhere.

♦ Simply because your state or county has certain rules, regulations and practices regarding the accessibility and content of public records, does not mean that another state or county adheres to the same rules.

Addresses & Telephone Numbers

Basic locator information about a person or organization

This category of online information may be obtained from either government or private sources.

As the most elementary of public information categories, addresses and telephone numbers are no longer considered restricted information by most people. Even though you have an unlisted telephone number, it still can be found if you have listed that number on, for example, a voter registration card or magazine subscription form.

> **Editor's Tip:** To access this type of information from government agencies beyond a single look-up, you must normally purchase the data on magnetic tapes, disks, or cartridges, but rarely will you find it available online.

Some government agencies offer customized lists for sale. Typical types of agencies include those holding motor vehicle, voter registration, corporation filings, or business license records.

Private companies develop databases of addresses and telephone numbers in two ways. They may do this in the normal course of business, such as phone companies, credit card companies, or credit bureaus. Or, they may purchase and merge government and/or private company databases to create their own database. They then sell this "new database" online in a batch format, perhaps on CD-ROM. These companies must be careful to follow any restrictions that government agencies may place on the release of the data. For example, Experian collects information about vehicle owners to supply vehicle manufacturers with address and telephone data for vehicle recalls. Experian also sells information from that same database for direct marketing purposes, but only if state regulations permit.

The Internet is filled with people-finder sites; most search engines have one, which is an excellent way to do a national white-pages search.

Aviation Records

Records about pilots and ownership & registration of aircraft

Pilots are licensed and aircraft is registered with the Federal Aviation Association (FAA) whose web site is <u>www.faa.gov</u>.

For a list of private companies offering access to pilot and aircraft records, go to page 314.

Bankruptcy

Case information about people and businesses that have filed for protection under the bankruptcy laws of the United States.

Only federal courts handle bankruptcy cases.

The federal government offers online access to bankruptcy records through its PACER system. Turn to page 29 for details on this relatively inexpensive access mode.

Several private companies compile their own bankruptcy databases with names and dates - and make this information available online.

Corporate & Trade Names

Registration information about corporations and other business entities

Each state maintains basic information about businesses that register with them for the purpose of making their business name public and protecting its uniqueness. A number of states offer this information online. In fact, there is a trend for state agencies to use the **Internet** as a means to provide this information. BRB Publication's web site at www.brbpub.com is an excellent source to check for new sites.

As in many other categories, private companies purchase and/or compile a database for resale via online. Fees are based on volume.

The amount of business information collected by government agencies varies widely from state to state. Much, but not all, of the information collected by government agencies is open to public inspection. For example, annual reports are not available in some states, yet may be available for a fee in others.

Credit Information

Records derived from financial transactions of people or businesses

Private companies *maintain* **this information; government agencies only** *regulate* **access.**

Availability of certain credit information about individuals is restricted by law, such as the federal Fair Credit Reporting Act. Even more restrictive laws apply in many states. Major credit companies prefer to sell credit information online. High volume, ongoing requesters pay in the $2.00 per record range for credit reports.

> **Editor's Tip:** Keep in mind that a business' credit information is not restricted by law and is fully open to anyone who requests (pays for) it.

Criminal History

Information about criminal activities, taken primarily from court records, is often combined into a central state database and always available from local courts

Criminal history information has probably the most diverse treatment of all categories of public record. All states maintain some type of central database of information about arrest and criminal court activity. 15 states consider this information open public record, while 6 states consider it closed. The remaining 30 states impose various types of restrictions on access to criminal information. In most states, criminal court information is openly accessible from the local court where the arraignments, preliminary hearings and/or trials took place. One open source of information about criminal activities is the newspaper, freely and openly accessible in any public library and searchable online through various services.

Three states (Colorado, Michigan, & Texas) offer the public online access to a central criminal record repository. However, a number of states maintain a central repository of court records open to online access, as you will find in the Government Sources Section.

Another source of criminal record information is from state corrections (prison) agencies. However, this information is not available online, and can be incomplete.

> **Editor's Tip:** The only truly national criminal database is the FBI's NCIC file, but it is not open to the public.

Very few private companies purchase local records to create databases for resale. Their "online access" of criminal record information usually involves 24-48 hour service, unless they are connected to one of the state court systems, such as in Washington or Maryland.

Driver & Vehicle Information

Information about licensed drivers and registered motor vehicles of all types

All states maintain records of drivers, vehicle registrations, and vehicle owners. Some private companies buy records from permitting states and offer commercial access to name, address and vehicle data.

Driver history, accident reports, and vehicle information, which traditionally have been open public record in most states, are subject to federal legislation. The Drivers' Privacy Protection Act (DPPA) required each state to impose at least a minimum set of restrictions on access to that information.

All states offer an electronic means to obtain some type of motor vehicle information, usually by online access or magnetic tape. 36 states offer online retrieval to approved accounts. Access is not always immediate; some states require a wait of up to four hours before retrieving the data. In many instances, a minimum order requirement must be agreed to before an online access account is permitted.

Editor's Tip: Driver history (MVR) information can be ordered online from many search firms throughout the country. However, only a handful of companies have the ability to directly access multiple state DMVs. Most public record search firms and specialty firms buy MVRs from one of these companies and then resell them to clients.

Vessel title and registration information is usually maintained by the same state agency responsible for vehicle records, but not as often is it found online. Some of these state agencies also hold lien information on vessels, but usually lien records should be searched where Uniform Commercial Code recordings are maintained. **Aviation** records must be searched at the federal level or through private companies.

Education & Employment

Information about an individual's schooling, training, education, and jobs

Learning institutions maintain their own records of attendance, completion, and degree/certification granted. Employers will confirm certain information about former employees.

Education and employment information is an example of private information that becomes public by voluntary disclosure. As part of your credit record, this information would be considered restricted. However if, for example, you disclose this information to *Who's Who*, it becomes public information.

Environmental

Information about hazards to the environment

There is little tradition and less consistency in laws regarding how open or restricted information is at the state and local (recorder's office) levels.

Most information about hazardous materials, soil composition, and even OSHA inspection reports is, in fact, public record.

Finding online access to this type of information at the government level is difficult. However, a few private companies compile and maintain databases of environmental information.

Legislation & Regulations

Laws and regulations at all levels of government

This information is always open public record.

Each state's legislative branch makes this information available, although records older than 2 years are harder to find. This category of information is increasingly finding its way onto **Internet** sites maintained by the state legislatures.

A number of private companies market a customized search-and-retrieval product of pending legislation and regulatory information. Access includes online and CD-ROM products.

Licenses, Registrations & Permits

Registration of individuals and businesses with government agencies
related to specific professions, businesses, or activities

Basic information about registrants, including address and status, is generally public record from state agencies and licensing boards. Some boards consider that their data should not be open to public inspection. Others boards will sell their entire database to commercial marketing vendors.

Also, there is significant variation in the extent of information that each state or local agency will disclose from a particular record. Some will release addresses, phone numbers, present place of employment, and current status. Other agencies will only give you "yes or no" responses.

To find this information online or on CD-ROM, you must turn to the private sector. A good example of a vendor with this type of information available is Merlin Information Systems or BRB Publication's *The Sourcebook of State Public Records* (call 800-929-3811 for information) wherein over 5,000 state agencies are listed.

Litigation & Civil Judgments

Information about civil litigation in municipal, state, or federal courts

Actions under federal laws are found at US District Courts. Actions under state laws are found within the state court system at the county level. Municipalities also have courts where information may be kept. Litigation and judgment information is often collected by commercial database vendors.

> **Editor's Tip:** The traditional general rule says that what goes on in a courtroom is public record. However, some types of court proceedings, such as juvenile cases, are closed. Judges may close or seal any portion of any case record at their discretion.

As with criminal information, there are a few state court systems and some local courts that offer online access. There are a number of private companies who create databases of this information for online access by their clients. These companies have the option of purchasing a tape from the government agency or sending personnel with laptop computers to manually gather case information at the court house.

Medical

Information about an individual's medical status and history

Medical records are summarized in various repositories that are accessible only to authorized insurance, legal, and other private company personnel.

Medical information is neither public information nor closed record. Like credit information, it is not meant to be shared with anyone, unless you give authorization. Only those who have the proper authority are able to access the information online.

Military Service

Information about individuals who are or were in military service

Each military branch maintains its own records. Much of this, such as years of service and rank, is open public record. However, some details in the file of an individual may be subject to access restrictions—approval by the subject may be required. For further information regarding this subject, the *Armed Forces Locator Guide* by MIE Publishing (800-937-2133) is recommended.

Occupational Licenses

Records from state licensing boards and business registrations

While some state agencies consider this information private and confidential, most agencies freely release at least some basic data over the phone, by mail or online. There is a definite trend as more and more state licensing boards are offering free access via the Internet. Over 1,800 sites are listed in this book.

Real Estate & Assessor

Information about the ownership, transfer, value and mortgaging of real property

The county (or parish) recorder's office is the legal source. Traditionally, real estate records are public so that everyone can know who owns any given property. Liens on real estate must be public record so potential buyers know all the facts about whether the title is clear.

The real estate industry needs quick access to this information. Most communities have a local multiple listing service (MLS) showing records of sales. This is generally available online. Many title companies and abstract companies will buy a "plant" from the local recorder's office. This is usually in a microfiche or microfilm format and is updated on a regular basis.

A number of private companies purchase entire county record files and create their own database for commercial purposes. This information is generally sold online or in some form of bulk medium such as magnetic tape.

SEC & Other Financial Data

Information on publicly and privately held businesses

The Securities and Exchange Commission is the public repository for information about publicly held companies, which are required to share their material facts with existing and prospective stockholders. The common online access mode is through the government's EDGAR system (see page 46 for further details).

Non-publicly held companies, on the other hand, are not required to be "open" to public scrutiny, so their financial information is public information only to the extent that the company itself decides to disclose it.

There are private companies who compile this information and make it available online, on CD-ROM, or in book format.

Social Security Numbers

The most extensively used individual identifier in the US

There is a persistent myth that a Social Security Number (SSN) is private information. The truth is that individuals gave up the privacy of that number by writing it on a voter registration form, using it on a driver's license number (in eight states), or by any of a myriad of other voluntary disclosures made over the years. It is probable that one can find the Social Security Number of anyone (along with at least an approximate birth date) with ease.

The sale of record information containing Social Security Numbers is illegal unless the purchaser is in compliance with the Fair Credit Reporting Act (FCRA). This has drastically affected the automated distributors of public record documents, and private investigators that routinely accessed "credit headers" (basic information without credit data obtained from credit bureaus).

For more information about FCRA and SSNs, visit the Federal Trade Commission Site at www.ftc.gov.

Tax & Other Involuntary Liens

Liens filed by the government and others against individuals and businesses without their consent

Liens are filed, according to a state's law, either at a state agency or county recorder's office. Some states require filing at both locations.

Mortgages and UCC liens are voluntary liens accepted by a borrower in order to obtain financing. Involuntary liens, on the other hand, arise by action of law against a person or business owing a debt that would otherwise be unsecured. The federal and state governments file tax liens when there is a failure to pay income or withholding taxes. Another example: a contractor can file a mechanic's lien to be first in line to receive payment for materials used on a job.

States that offer online access to corporate records generally make their lien records available online also. While there is less likelihood of finding this information online at the local government level, a limited number of local recorder offices make the information available online.

Editor's Tip: Liens are a very competitive arena for private companies offering online access. There are several nationwide databases available as well as a number of strong regionally-oriented companies who offer this information online to their clientele.

Tenant

History information about people who rent

This, like credit history, is another example of a combination of public and proprietary information collected by private businesses for the purpose of tracking an element of personal life important to an industry—in this case the housing rental industry.

These records are often shared within the industry on a restricted online basis according to disclosure rules set by the companies themselves.

Trademarks, Patents & Copyrights

Protection of intellectual property and proprietary ideas

The state agency controlling trademarks and service marks is generally at the same location as corporate records. The Lanham Act provides for a trademark registration system mandated by the federal government. The federal government controls copyrights and patents. Several private companies maintain online searchable databases of trademarks, service marks, and patents.

The filing for public review of trademarks and patents is designed to protect these assets from copying.

Uniform Commercial Code

Transactions that are secured by personal property

As with tax liens, Uniform Commercial Code (UCC) recordings are filed either at the state or county level, according to each state's law. Some states require dual filing.

UCC filings are to personal property what mortgages are to real property. They are in the category of financial records that must be fully open to public scrutiny so potential lenders are given notice about which assets of the borrower have been pledged.

UCC filings can be found online from a number of state agencies, and access via the Internet is increasing.

A number of private companies have created their own databases for commercial resale. As with tax liens, this is a very competitive arena. There are nationwide database companies available as well as a number of strong, regionally-oriented companies who offer this information online to their clientele.

Vessel Records

Information about vessel ownership and registration

Except for the larger ocean liners, which are regulated by the US Coast Guard, this is a state agency function. Many times the same agency that oversees vehicle records also oversees vessel records. When this occurs, the release of records is governed by the degree that the state complies with DPPA.

Vital Records

Birth, death, marriage, and divorce information

Most states have central repositories for each of these four types of vital records. In some states divorce records are maintained at the county level, but the state maintains a searchable index.

State regulations vary regarding which of these four types of records are public and which are subject to restrictions. States impose approval or use restrictions similar to those imposed by schools with regard to access to student transcript information.

> **Editor's Tip:** Finding online access to vital records from either government agencies or private companies is rare. Some agencies do offer access to an index, but the documents themselves are not available online.

Voter Registration

Information on the application to become a registered voter

Voter registration applications are maintained at the local level. Generally, they are a public record accessible by anyone. This makes them an important source, for instance, of the real signature of a person or of an **unlisted** telephone number. At the state level, many states aggregate the local information into a central database.

Access to many state-held databases is restricted to non-commercial use. However, one third of the states have set no restrictions on the use of voter registration records, including information gathered that otherwise would be considered private such as a Social Security Number or unlisted telephone number.

Several privates companies purchase databases from states wherein voter registration information is "open," and make that data available online. Profiles of these companies are included in this book.

Workers' Compensation Records

Work related injury claims and case history

Each state has a board or commission responsible for these records.

Access to this information is generally restricted to those who have a direct interest in the case. Due to federal legislation, only seven states now consider their Workers Compensation records to be unrestricted open public record. Few offer the information online.

Several companies purchase and combine entire state databases to create a proprietary database for resale, which may be available online.

Searching Hints— Court Records

What You Will Find in the Courthouse

Before signing up for every court online access available, you should be familiar with certain court basics! Whether it is filed in federal, state, or municipal court, each case is subject to a similar processing. Determining the exact location of case records depends upon: (1) the county where the subject is located; (2) the specific court structure of that state or district; and (3) the types of cases.

Criminal

In **criminal cases**, the plaintiff is a government jurisdiction, which brings the action against the defendant under one of its statutes. Criminal cases are categorized as *felonies* or *misdemeanors*. A general rule to distinguish these is: usually a felony may involve a jail term of one year or more, whereas a misdemeanor may only involve a monetary fine and/or short jail terms.

Civil

A **civil case** usually commences when plaintiffs file a *complaint* against defendants with a court. The defendants respond to the complaint with an *answer*. After this initial round, literally hundreds of activities may occur before the court issues a judgment. These activities can include revised complaints and their answers, motions of various kinds, and discovery proceedings including depositions to establish the documentation and facts involved in the case. All of these activities are listed on a **docket sheet**.

Civil cases are categorized as *tort*, *contract*, and *real property* rights. Torts include but are not limited to *automobile accidents, medical malpractice and product liability* cases. Actions for small money damages, typically under $3,000, are known as *small claims*.

Other

Other types of cases that frequently are handled by separate courts or divisions of courts include *juvenile*, *domestic relations*, and *probate* (wills and estates).

In **bankruptcy cases**, there is neither defendant nor plaintiff. Instead, the debtor files voluntarily for bankruptcy protection against creditors, or the creditors file against the debtor in order to force that debtor into involuntary bankruptcy.

State Court Structure

The vast majority of court cases in the United States are filed within the state court system at the county level. The secret to determining where a state court case and its records are located is to understand how the court system is structured within each state. The general structure of all states' court systems has four levels:

- ◆ Limited Jurisdiction Courts
- ◆ General Jurisdiction Courts
- ◆ Intermediate Appellate Courts
- ◆ Appellate Courts

Most cases originate in general or limited jurisdiction courts. General jurisdiction courts usually handle a full range of civil and criminal litigation. These courts usually handle felonies and larger civil cases.

Limited Jurisdiction courts come in two varieties. First, many limited jurisdiction courts handle smaller civil claims (usually $10,000 or less), misdemeanors, and pretrial hearing for felonies. Second, some of these courts, sometimes called special jurisdiction courts, are limited to one type of litigation, such as Court of Claims in New York, which only handles liability cases against the state.

The two highest court levels hear cases on appeal from the trial courts only. Opinions of these appellate courts are of interest primarily to attorneys who need legal precedent information for new cases. Once a lower court issues a judgment, either party may appeal the ruling to an appellate division or court. In the case of a monetary decision or award, the winning side can usually file the judgment as a lien with the county recorder. The appellate division usually deals only with the legal issues and not with the facts of the case.

Some states, Iowa for instance, have consolidated their general and limited jurisdiction court structure into one combined court system. In other states, there is a further distinction between state-supported courts and municipal courts. In New York, for example, nearly 1,500 justice courts handle local ordinance and traffic violations, including DWI cases.

Searching State Courts Online

Online searching is generally limited to a copy of the courts' docket sheets. The docket sheet contains the basics of the case: name of court, including location (division) and the judge assigned; case number and case name; names of all plaintiffs and defendants/debtors; names and addresses of attorneys; and nature and cause of action. Information from cover sheets and from documents filed as a case goes forward is also recorded on the docket sheet. While docket sheets differ somewhat in format, basic information contained on a docket sheet is consistent from court to court. Docket sheets are used in both the state court systems and the federal court system.

Most courts are computerized in-house, which means that the docket sheet data is entered into a computer system of the courthouse itself. Checking a courthouse's computer index is the quickest way to find if case records exist online.

Not a large number of state courts provide electronic access to their records. In Alabama, Maryland, Minnesota, New Mexico, Oregon, Washington, and Wisconsin where "statewide" online systems are available, you still need to understand (1) the court structure in that state, (2) which particular courts are included in their online system, and (3) what types of cases are included. Without proper consideration of these variables, these online systems are subject to misuse, which can lead to disastrous consequences like failing to discover that an applicant for a security guard position is a convicted burglar.

Maryland has a two-tiered structure with higher courts named "Circuit Courts" and the lower courts called "District Courts," but their online system includes the District Courts and *only 3 Circuit Courts.* Since the courts with online records do handle most preliminary hearing and some felony cases, it has been suggested that a name search in the online system is adequate to discover all criminal cases. However, it is possible for a felony case to be brought before a higher court only. A full criminal search of courts in Maryland would require manual searches of all the Circuit Courts as well as through the District Court online system.

If Records Are Not Available Online

If you need copies of case records, court personnel may make copies for you for a fee, or you may be able to make copies yourself if the court allows. Also, court personnel may certify the document for you for a fee. Perhaps due to a shortage of staff or fear of litigation, some courts that previously would conduct searches of criminal records on behalf of the public are no longer making that service available. Typically, these courts do one of two things. In some states, such as Kentucky, the courts refer the searcher to a state agency that maintains a database combining individual court records (which may not be very current). In other states, such as Nebraska, the courts simply refuse to conduct searches, leaving the searcher with no choice but to use a local retrieval firm or other individual to conduct the search on his or her behalf.

Internet Access to State Court Systems

Although there are a handful of state (local county) courts profiled in this book that provide Internet access to case index information, most sites charge fees. However, there is a growing wealth of information available on the Internet about state court structure and rules, as well as higher court opinions. A good place to start is www.ncsc.dni.us/court/sites/courts.htm. This site is maintained by the National Center for State Courts (NCSC) and includes Internet addresses for state-level information and for many local court locations as well. NCSC publications are the definitive source of information about the structure of state court systems and for state court statistics.

A second locator site is the Villanova Center for Information Law and Technology at http://vls.law.vill.edu/library.

There is an excellent list available of courts with records accessible via the Internet. This list is maintained on a web page found at www.brbpub.com.

Federal Court Structure

The Federal Court system includes three levels of courts, plus some special courts, described as follows—

Supreme Court of the United States

The Supreme Court of the United States is the court of last resort in the United States. It is located in Washington, DC, where it hears appeals from the United States Courts of Appeals and from the highest courts of each state.

United States Court of Appeals

The United States Court of Appeals consists of thirteen appellate courts that hear appeals of verdicts from the courts of general jurisdiction. They are designated as follows:

The Federal Circuit Court of Appeals hears appeals from the US Claims Court and the US Court of International Trade. It is located in Washington, DC.

The District of Columbia Circuit Court of Appeals hears appeals from the district courts in Washington, DC as well as from the Tax Court.

Eleven geographic **Courts of Appeals**—each of these appeal courts covers a designated number of states and territories. The chart on the pages 31-32 lists the circuit numbers (1 through 11) and location of the Court of Appeals for each state.

United States District Courts

The United States District Courts are the courts of general jurisdiction, or trial courts, and are subdivided into two categories—

The District Courts are courts of general jurisdiction, or trial courts, for federal matters, excluding bankruptcy. Essentially, this means they hear cases involving federal law and cases where there is diversity of citizenship. Both **civil** and **criminal** cases come before these courts.

The Bankruptcy Courts generally follow the same geographic boundaries as the US District Courts. There is at least one bankruptcy court for each state; within a state there may be one or more judicial districts and within a judicial district there may be more than one location (division) where the courts hear cases. While civil lawsuits may be filed in either state or federal courts depending upon the applicable law, all bankruptcy actions are filed with the US Bankruptcy Courts.

Special Courts/Separate Courts

The Special Courts/Separate Courts have been created to hear cases or appeals for certain areas of litigation demanding special expertise. Examples include the US Tax Court, the Court of International Trade and the US Claims Court.

How Federal Trial Courts are Organized

At the federal level, all cases involve federal or US constitutional law or interstate commerce. The task of locating the right court is seemingly simplified by the nature of the federal system—

♦ All court locations are based upon the plaintiff's county of domicile.

♦ All civil and criminal cases go to the US District Courts.

♦ All bankruptcy cases go to the US Bankruptcy Courts.

However, a plaintiff or defendant may have cases in any of the 500 court locations, so it is really not all that simple to find them.

There is at least one District and one Bankruptcy Court in each state. In many states there is more than one court, often divided further into judicial districts— e.g., the State of New York consists of four judicial districts, the Northern, Southern, Eastern and Western. Further, many judicial districts contain more than one court location (usually called a division).

The Bankruptcy Courts generally use the same hearing locations as the District Courts. If court locations differ, the usual variance is to have fewer Bankruptcy Court locations.

How Federal Trial Courts are Organized

Case Numbering

When a case is filed with a federal court, a case number is assigned. This is the primary indexing method. Therefore, in searching for case records, you will need to know or find the applicable case number. If you have the number in good form already, your search should be fast and reasonably inexpensive.

You should be aware that case numbering procedures are not consistent throughout the Federal Court system: one judicial district may assign numbers by district while another may assign numbers by location (division) within the judicial district or by judge. Remember that case numbers appearing in legal text citations may not be adequate for searching unless they appear in the proper form for the particular court.

All the basic civil case information that is entered onto docket sheets, and into computerized systems like PACER (see page 29), starts with standard form JS-44, the Civil Cover Sheet, or the equivalent.

Docket Sheet

As in the state court system, information from cover sheets, and from documents filed as a case goes forward, is recorded on the **docket sheet**, which then contains the case history from initial filing to its current status. While docket sheets differ somewhat in format, the basic information contained on a docket sheet is consistent from court to court. As noted earlier in the state court section, all docket sheets contain:

- ◆ Name of court, including location (division) and the judge assigned;
- ◆ Case number and case name;
- ◆ Names of all plaintiffs and defendants/debtors;
- ◆ Names and addresses of attorneys for the plaintiff or debtor;
- ◆ Nature and cause (e.g., US civil statute) of action;
- ◆ Listing of documents filed in the case, including docket entry number, the date and a short description (e.g., 12-2-92, #1, Complaint).

Assignment of Cases

Traditionally, cases were assigned within a district by county. Although this is still true in most states, the introduction of computer systems to track dockets has led to a more flexible approach to case assignment, as is the case in Minnesota and Connecticut. Rather than blindly assigning all cases from a county to one judge, their districts are using random numbers and other logical methods to balance caseloads among their judges.

This trend may appear to confuse the case search process. Actually, the only problem that the searcher may face is to figure out where the case records themselves are located. Finding cases has become significantly easier with the wide availability of PACER from remote access and on-site terminals in each court location with the same district-wide information base.

Computerization

Traditionally, cases were assigned within a district by county. Although this is still true in most states, the introduction of computer systems to track dockets has led to a more flexible approach to case assignment, as is the case in Minnesota and Connecticut. Rather than blindly assigning all cases from a county to one judge, their districts are using random numbers and other logical methods to balance caseloads among their judges.

This trend may appear to confuse the case search process. Actually, the only problem that the searcher may face is to figure out where the case records themselves are located. Finding cases has become significantly easier with the wide availability of PACER from remote access and on-site terminals in each court location with the same district-wide information base.

Computerized Indexes are Available

Computerized courts generally index each case record by the names of some or all the parties to the case—the plaintiffs and defendants (debtors and creditors in Bankruptcy Court) as well as by case number. Therefore, when you search by name you will first receive a listing of all cases in which the name appears, both as plaintiff and defendant.

Electronic Access to Federal Courts

Numerous programs have been developed for electronic access to Federal Court records. In recent years the Administrative Office of the United States Courts in Washington, DC has developed three innovative public access programs: VCIS, PACER, and ABBS. The most useful program for online searching is PACER.

PACER

PACER, the acronym for Public Access to Electronic Court Records, provides docket information online for open cases at all US Bankruptcy courts and most US District courts. Cases for the US Court of Federal Claims are also available. The user fee is $.60 per minute. Each court controls its own computer system and case information database; therefore, there are some variations among jurisdictions as to the information offered.

A continuing problem with PACER is that each court determines when records will be purged and how records will be indexed, leaving you to guess how a name is spelled or abbreviated and how much information about closed cases your search will uncover. A PACER search for anything but open cases cannot take the place of a full seven-year search of the federal court records available by written request from the court itself or through a local document retrieval company. Many districts report that they have closed records back a number of years, but at the same time indicate they purge docket items every six months.

Sign-up and technical support is handled at the PACER Service Center in San Antonio, Texas (800) 676-6856. You can sign up for all or multiple districts at once. In many judicial districts, when you sign up for PACER access, you will receive a PACER Primer that has been customized for each district. The primer contains a summary of how to access PACER, how to select cases, how to read case numbers and docket sheets, some searching tips, who to call for problem resolution, and district specific program variations.

The most impressive change in Federal Courts record access is the expansion of the PACER System. It covers all 190 Bankruptcy Court Districts and all but 8 of the 300 Civil/Criminal Court Districts.

Before Accessing PACER,
Search the "National" US Party/Case Index

It is no longer necessary to call each court in every state and district to determine where a debtor has filed bankruptcy, or if someone is a defendant in Federal litigation. National and regional searches of district and bankruptcy filings can be made with one call (via modem) to the US Party/Case Index.

The US Party/Case Index is a national index for U.S. district, bankruptcy, and appellate courts. This index allows searches to determine whether or not a party is involved in federal litigation almost anywhere in the nation.

The US Party/Case Index provides the capability to perform national or regional searches on party name and Social Security Number in the bankruptcy index, party name and nature of suit in the civil index, and party name in the criminal and appellate indices.

The search will provide a list of case numbers, filing locations and filing dates for those cases matching the search criteria. If you need more information about the case, you must obtain it from the court directly or through that court's individual PACER system.

You may access the US Party/Case Index by dialup connection or via the Internet. The Internet site for the US Party/Case Index is http://pacer.uspci.uscourts.gov. The toll-free dial-up number for the US Party/Case Index is 800-974-8896. For more information, call the PACER service center at 800-676-6856.

In accordance with Judicial Conference policy, most courts charge a $.60 per minute access fee for this service. Persons desiring to use this service must first register with the PACER Service Center at 1-800-676-6856. For more information on the U.S. Party/Case Index, please contact the PACER Service Center at 1-800-676-6856.

ECF

Electronic Case Files (ECF) is a prototype system that focuses on the filing of cases electronically. This service initially introduced in January 1996 enables participating attorneys and litigants to electronically submit pleadings and corresponding docket entries to the court via the Internet thereby eliminating substantial paper handling and processing time. ECF permits any interested parties to instantaneously access the entire official case docket and documents on the Internet of selective civil and bankruptcy cases within these jurisdictions.

It is important to note, that when you search ECF you are ONLY searching cases that have been filed electronically. You must still conduct a search using PACER if you want to know if a case exists.

RACER

RACER stands for Remote Access to Court Electronic Records. Accessed through the Internet, RACER offers access to the same records as PACER. At present, searching RACER is free, but there are plans to make it a fee-based system.

Miscellaneous Online Systems

Many courts have developed their own online systems. The Bankruptcy Courts for the Eastern District of Virginia have an elaborate system accessible for free and available on their web site. In addition to RACER, Idaho's Bankruptcy and District Courts have more searching options available on their web site. Likewise, the Southern District Court of New York offers CourtWeb, which provides information to the public on selected recent rulings of those judges who have elected to make information available in electronic form.

VCIS

Another system worth mentioning is **VCIS** (Voice Case Information System). Nearly all of the US Bankruptcy Court judicial districts provide **VCIS**, a means of accessing information regarding open bankruptcy cases by merely using a touch-tone telephone. There is no charge. Individual names are entered last name first with as much of the first name as you wish to include. For example, Carl R. Ernst could be entered as ERNSTC or ERNSTCARL. Do not enter the middle initial. Business names are entered as they are written, without blanks. BRB Publications has books available with all the VCIS numbers listed (800-929-3811).

Federal Records Centers & The National Archives

After a federal case is closed, the documents are held by Federal Courts themselves for a number of years, then stored at a designated Federal Records Center (FRC). After 20 to 30 years, the records are then transferred from the FRC to the regional archives offices of the National Archives and Records Administration (NARA). The length of time between a case being closed and its being moved to an FRC varies widely by district. Each court has its own transfer cycle and determines access procedures to its case records, even after they have been sent to the FRC.

When case records are sent to an FRC, the boxes of records are assigned accession, location and box numbers. These numbers, which are called case locator information, **must be obtained from the originating court in order to retrieve documents from the FRC.** Some courts will provide such information over the telephone, but others require a written request. This information is now available on PACER in certain judicial districts. The Federal Records Center for each state is listed as follows:

State	Circuit	Appeals Court	Federal Records Center
AK	9	San Francisco, CA	Anchorage (Some temporary storage in Seattle)
AL	11	Atlanta, GA	Atlanta
AR	8	St. Louis, MO	Fort Worth
AZ	9	San Francisco, CA	Los Angeles
CA	9	San Francisco, CA	Los Angeles (Central & Southern) San Francisco (Eastern & Northern)
CO	10	Denver, CO	Denver
CT	2	New York, NY	Boston
DC		Washington, DC	Washington, DC

State	Circuit	Appeals Court	Federal Records Center
DE	3	Philadelphia, PA	Philadelphia
FL	11	Atlanta, GA	Atlanta
GA	11	Atlanta, GA	Atlanta
GU	9	San Francisco, CA	San Francisco
HI	9	San Francisco, CA	San Francisco
IA	8	St. Louis, MO	Kansas City, MO
ID	9	San Francisco, CA	Seattle
IL	7	Chicago, IL	Chicago
IN	7	Chicago, IL	Chicago
KS	10	Denver, CO	Kansas City, MO
KY	6	Cincinnati, OH	Atlanta
LA	5	New Orleans, LA	Fort Worth
MA	1	Boston, MA	Boston
MD	4	Richmond, VA	Philadelphia
ME	1	Boston, MA	Boston
MI	6	Cincinnati, OH	Chicago
MN	8	St. Louis, MO	Chicago
MO	8	St. Louis, MO	Kansas City, MO
MS	5	New Orleans, LA	Atlanta
MT	9	San Francisco, CA	Denver
NC	4	Richmond, VA	Atlanta
ND	8	St. Louis, MO	Denver
NE	8	St. Louis, MO	Kansas City, MO
NH	1	Boston, MA	Boston
NJ	3	Philadelphia, PA	New York
NM	10	Denver, CO	Denver
NV	9	San Francisco, CA	Los Angeles (Clark County) San Francisco (Other counties)
NY	2	New York, NY	New York
OH	6	Cincinnati, OH	Chicago, Dayton (Some bankruptcy)
OK	10	Denver, CO	Fort Worth
OR	9	San Francisco, CA	Seattle

State	Circuit	Appeals Court	Federal Records Center
PA	3	Philadelphia, PA	Philadelphia
PR	1	Boston, MA	New York
RI	1	Boston, MA	Boston
SC	4	Richmond, VA	Atlanta
SD	8	St. Louis, MO	Denver
TN	6	Cincinnati, OH	Atlanta
TX	5	New Orleans, LA	Fort Worth
UT	10	Denver, CO	Denver
VA	4	Richmond, VA	Philadelphia
VI	3	Philadelphia, PA	New York
VT	2	New York, NY	Boston
WA	9	San Francisco, CA	Seattle
WI	7	Chicago, IL	Chicago
WV	4	Richmond, VA	Philadelphia
WY	10	Denver, CO	Denver

GU is Guam, PR is Puerto Rico, and VI is the Virgin Islands.

According to some odd logic, the following Federal Records Centers are located somewhere else:

Atlanta—East Point, GA; Boston—Waltham, MA; Los Angeles—Laguna Niguel, CA; New York—Bayonne, NJ; San Francisco—San Bruno, CA

Searching Hints —
Recorded Documents
at County Agencies

Types of Records Available

A multitude of information can be found at the county, parish or city recorders' offices. Recorded documents include:

- ◆   Real Estate Transactions

- ◆   Uniform Commercial Code (UCC) Filings

- ◆   All liens, including State and Federal Tax Liens

Descriptions of these categories of records appear on pages in the previous chapter.

The County Rule

The County Courts and Recording Offices section in each state chapter presents detailed instructions and searching hints. Where to search for **recorded documents** usually isn't a difficult problem to overcome in everyday practice. In most states, these transactions are recorded at one designated recording office in the county where the property is located.

We call this the "**County Rule.**" It applies to types of public records such as real estate recordings, tax liens, Uniform Commercial Code (UCC) filings, vital records, and voter registration records. However, as with most government rules, there are a variety of exceptions, which are summarized here.

The Exceptions

The five categories of exceptions to the County Rule (or Parish Rule, if searching in Louisiana) are listed below (the details are listed in the chart to follow)—

- ♦ Special Recording Districts (AK, HI)

- ♦ Multiple Recording Offices (AL, AR, IA, KY, ME, MA, MS, TN)

- ♦ Independent Cities (MD, MO, NV, VA)

- ♦ Recording at the Municipal Level (CT, RI, VT)

- ♦ Identical Names—Different Place (CT, IL, MA, NE, NH, PA, RI, VT, VA)

The Personal Property Problem and the Fifth Exception

The real estate recording system in the US is self-auditing to the extent that you generally cannot record a document in the wrong recording office. However, many documents are rejected for recording because they are submitted to the wrong recording office. There are a number of reasons why this occurs, one of which is the overlap of filing locations for real estate and UCC.

Finding the right location of a related UCC filing is a different and much more difficult problem from finding a real estate recording. In the majority of states, the usual place to file a UCC financing statement is at the Secretary of States office—these are called **central filing states**. In the **dual** and **local filing** states, the place to file, in addition to the central filing office, is **usually** at the same office where your real estate documents are recorded. However, where there are identical place names referring to two different places, it becomes quite confusing, so hence, the fifth exemption.

The County Rule—Exceptions Chart

Each of these five categories of recording exceptions is summarized below by state.

AL	Four counties contain two separate recording offices. They are Barbour, Coffee, Jefferson, and St. Clair.
AK	The 23 Alaskan counties are called boroughs. However, real estate recording is done under a system that was established at the time of the Gold Rush (whenever that was) of **34 Recording Districts**. Some of the Districts are identical in geography to boroughs, such as the Aleutian Islands, but other boroughs and districts overlap. Therefore, you need to know which recording district any given town or city is located in.

AR	Ten counties contain two separate recording offices. They are Arkansas, Carroll, Clay, Craighead, Franklin, Logan, Mississippi, Prairie, Sebastian, and Yell.
CT	There is **no county recording** in this state. All recording is done at the city/town level. Lenders persist in attempting to record or file documents in the counties of Fairfield, Hartford, Litchfield, New Haven, New London, Tolland, and Windham related to property located in other cities/towns because each of these cities/towns bears the same name as a Connecticut county.
HI	All recording is done at one central office.
IL	Cook County has separate offices for real estate recording and UCC filing.
IA	Lee county has two recording offices.
KY	Kenton County has two recording offices. Jefferson County has a separate office for UCC filing.
LA	Louisiana counties are called **Parishes**. One parish, St. Martin, has two non-contiguous segments.
ME	Aroostock and Oxford counties have two separate recording offices.
MD	The City of Baltimore has its own separate recording office.
MA	Berkshire and Bristol counties each has three recording offices. Essex, Middlesex and Worcester counties each has two recording offices. Cities/towns bearing the same name as a county are Barnstable, Essex, Franklin, Hampden, Nantucket, Norfolk, Plymouth, and Worcester. UCC financing statements on personal property collateral are submitted to cities/towns, while real estate recording is handled by the counties.
MS	Ten counties contain two separate recording offices. They are Bolivar, Carroll, Chickasaw, Harrison, Hinds, Jasper, Jones, Panola, Tallahatchie, and Yalobusha.
MO	The City of St. Louis has its own recording office.
NE	Fifteen counties have separate offices for real estate recording and for UCC filing.
NH	Cities/towns bearing the same name as a county are Carroll, Grafton, Hillsborough, Merrimack, Strafford, and Sullivan. UCC financing statements on personal property collateral are submitted to cities/towns, while real estate recording is handled by the counties.
NV	Carson City has its own recording office.

PA	Each county has a separate recording office and prothonotary office. UCC financing statements on personal property are submitted to the prothonotary, and real estate documents are submitted to the recorder.
RI	There is **no county recording** in this state. All recording is done at the city/town level. Lenders persist in attempting to record or file documents in the counties of Bristol, Newport, and Providence related to property located in other cities/ towns because each of these cities/towns bears the same name as a Rhode Island county.
TN	Sullivan County has two separate recording offices.
VT	There is **no county recording** in this state. All recording is done at the city/town level. Lenders persist in attempting to record or file documents in the counties of Addison, Bennington, Chittenden, Essex, Franklin, Grand Isle, Orange, Rutland, Washington, Windham, and Windsor related to property located in other cities/towns because each of these cities/towns bears the same name as a Vermont county. Adding to the confusion, there are four place names in the state that refer to both a city and a town: Barre, Newport, Rutland, and St. Albans.
VA	There are 41 independent cities in Virginia. Twenty-seven have separate recording offices. The following 15 share their filing offices with the surrounding county:

INDEPENDENT	
CITY	*FILE IN*
Bedford	Bedford County
Covington	Alleghany County
Emporia	Greenville County
Fairfax	Fairfax County
Falls Church	Arlington or Fairfax County
Franklin	Southhampton County
Galax	Carroll County
Harrisonburg	Rockingham County
Lexington	Rockbridge County
Manassas	Prince William County
Manassas Park	Prince William County
Norton	Wise County
Poquoson	York County
South Boston	Halifax County
Williamsburg	James City County

Online Searching For Asset/Lien Records

A growing number of county government jurisdictions provide online access to recorded documents and they can be found in the Government Sources Section. Many are fee sites, but the number of free sites available via the Internet is increasing.

Keep in mind there are a number of private companies who compile and maintain these records and offer them for resale, and they offer the most comprehensive source. Look for a list of these companies in the Index portion of the **Private** Company Sources Section.

Also, the BRB Publications site at www.brbpub.com has an updated list of county agencies offering free access to records over the Internet.

Searching Hints — State Agencies

Types of Records Available

Each state has government agencies that maintain records in each of the following categories—

Criminal Records	Sales Tax Registrations
Corporation Records	Workers' Compensation Records
Limited Partnership Records	Marriage Records
Limited Liability Company Records	Divorce Records
Trademark, Trade Name	Birth Records
Fictitious or Assumed Names	Death Records
Uniform Commercial Code Filings	Driver Records
Federal Tax Liens	Vehicle & Ownership Records
State Tax Liens	State Investigated Accident Reports
Vessel Records	Certain Occupational Licensing

Certain of these categories are more apt to offer online access, and some rarely do. For definitions, descriptions and comments about online accessibility of these categories see the Online Information Categories section starting on page 10.

Each state chapter in the Government Sources Section begins with the state's web site as well as those of the Attorney General and the State Archives. These are excellent starting points to answer questions about topics or agencies not covered in this book.

State Agency Public Record Restrictions Table

Codes

O	Open to Public
R	Some Access Restrictions (Requesters Screened)
N/A	Not Available to the Public
F	Special Form Needed
S	Severe Access Restrictions (Signed Authorization, etc.)
L	Available only at Local Level

State	Criminal Records	UCC Records	Worker's Comp	Driver Records [2]	Vehicle Records [2]	Vessel Records	Voter Reg. [3]
Alabama	S	O,F	S	S	S	O	L
Alaska	R	O,F	R	S	R	S	O
Arizona	S	O,F	S	S	S	R	L
Arkansas	S	O,F	O	S	R	O	L
California	N/A,L	O,F	R	S	S	S	L
Colorado	R	O,F	S	S	S	R	O
Connecticut	O	O,F	S	S	S	R	L
Delaware	S	O,F	S	S	S	S	O
Dist. of Columbia	S,F	O,F	S	S	S	N/A	O
Florida	O	O,F	S	S	S	R	L
Georgia	S	L,F₁	S	S	S	O	O
Hawaii	O	O,F	S	S	N/A	R	L
Idaho	R	O,F	S	S	S	S	L
Illinois	S,F	O,F	O	S	S	O	L
Indiana	S,F	O,F	S	S	R	R	L
Iowa	O	O,F	O	S	S	L	O
Kansas	R,F	O,F	R	S	S	R	L
Kentucky	S	O	R	S	S	O	O
Louisiana	S	L,F₁	R	S	S	O	L
Maine	O	O,F	R	S	S	O	Table
Maryland	S	O,F	O	S	S	O	L
Massachusetts	R	O,F	R	S	S	O	L
Michigan	O	O,F	R	S	S	S	L
Minnesota	R	O,F	S	S	S	O	L
Mississippi	N/A,L	O,F	R	S	S	O	L
Missouri	O	O,F	R	S	S	R	L
Montana	O	O,F	S	S	R	R,F	O

State	Criminal Records	UCC Records	Worker's Comp	Driver Records [2]	Vehicle Records[2]	Vessel Records	Voter Reg.[3]
Nebraska	O	O,F	O	S	S	S	L
Nevada	S	O,F	S	S	S	O	L
New Hampshire	S	O,F	S	S	S	S	L
New Jersey	S,F	O,F	O,F	S	S	S	L
New Mexico	S	O	S	S	S	S	L
New York	L	O,F	S	S	S	S	L
North Carolina	N/A,L	O,F	S	S	S	O	L
North Dakota	S	O,F	S	S	S	O	L
Ohio	S,F	O	O	S	S	O	O&L
Oklahoma	O	O,F	O	S	S	S	O&L
Oregon	O	O,F	S	S	S	O	L
Pennsylvania	R,F	O,F	S	S	S	N/A	L
Rhode Island	S,L	O,F	S	S	S	R	L
South Carolina	O	,O,F	S	S	S	O	O
South Dakota	S,F	O,F	S	S	S	R	L
Tennessee	N/A,L	O,F	S	S	S	O	L
Texas	O	O,F	S,F	S	S	R	L
Utah	N/A,L	O,F	S	S	S	R	L,R
Vermont	N/A,L	O,F	S	S	S	S	L
Virginia	S,F	O,F	S	S	S	R	L
Washington	O	O,F	S	S	S	S	L
West Virginia	S,F	O,F	S	S	S	R	L
Wisconsin	O	O,F	S	S	S	O	L
Wyoming	S,F	O,F	S	S	S	O	L

1	=	Georgia and Louisiana UCCs are filed locally, but a state central index is available.
2	=	These categories -- Driver and Vehicle -- indicate restriction codes based on the assumption that the requester is "the general public." In general, these records are open ("O") to employers, their agents, the insurance industry and other permissible users as defined by DPPA.
3	=	This category, Voter Registration, indicates most record searching requires going to the local county or municipality. However, many state election agencies will sell customized voter lists statewide or for multiple counties.

Searching State Occupational Licensing Boards

Using the Licensing Section

Each state's "State Level . . . Occupational Licensing" section indicates when verification may be accomplished for free via the Internet. This section lists the occupation and the corresponding URL.

The Privacy Question

While some agencies consider this information private and confidential, most agencies freely release at least some basic data over the phone or by mail.

Our research indicates that many agencies appear to make their own judgments regarding what specifically is private and confidential in their files. For example, although most agencies will not release an SSN, 8% do. On the other side, 45% of the agencies indicate that they will disclose adverse information about a registrant, and many others will only disclose selected portions of the information.

In any event, the basic rule to follow when you contact a licensing agency is to ask **for the specific kinds of information available.**

What Information May Be Available

An agency may be willing to release part or all of the following—

- ◆ Field of Certification
- ◆ Status of License/Certificate
- ◆ Date License/Certificate Issued
- ◆ Date License/Certificate Expires
- ◆ Current or Most Recent Employer
- ◆ Social Security Number

- ◆ Address of Subject

- ◆ Complaints, Violations or Disciplinary Actions

Searching Tip—
Distinguish the Type of Agency

It is important to note that there are five general types of licensing agencies. When you are verifying credentials, you should be aware of what distinguishes each type, which in turn could alter the questions you ask.

Private Certification

Private Licensing and Certification—requires a proven level of minimum competence before license is granted. These professional licenses separate the true "professions" from the third category below. In many of these professions, the certification body, such as the American Institute of Certified Public Accountants, is a private association whereas the licensing body, such as the New York State Education Department, is the licensing agency. Also, many professions may provide additional certifications in specialty areas.

State Certification

State Licensing & Certification—requires certification through an *examination* and/or other *requirements supervised* directly *by the state* rather than by a private association.

By Individual

Individual Registration—required if an individual intends to offer specified products or services in the designated area, but does not require certification that the person has met minimum requirements. An everyday example would be registering a handgun in a state that does not require passing a gun safety course.

By Business

Business Registration—required if a business intends to do business or offer specified products or services in a designated area, such as registering a liquor license. Some business license agencies require testing or a background check. Others merely charge a fee after a cursory review of the application.

Special Permits

Permits—give the grantee specific permission to do something, whether it is to sell hot-dogs on the corner or to put up a three story sign. Permits are usually granted at the local level rather than the state level of government.

Other Forms of Licensing & Registration

Although the state level is where much of the licensing and registration occurs, you should be aware of other places you may want to search.

Local Government Agencies

Local government agencies at both the **county** and **municipal levels** require a myriad of business registrations and permits in order to do business (construction, signage, etc.) within their borders. Even where you think a business or person, such as a remodeling contractor, should have local registrations you want to check out, it is still best to start at the state level.

County Recording Office & City Hall

If you decide to check on local registrations and permits, call the offices at both the county—try the **county recording office**—and municipal level—try **city hall**—to find out what type of registrations may be required for the person or business you are checking out.

Like the state level, you should expect that receiving basic information will only involve a phone call and that you will not be charged for obtaining a status summary.

Professional Associations

As mentioned above, many professional licenses are based on completion of the requirements of professional associations. In addition, there are *many professional designations* from such associations that *are not recognized as official licenses by government*. Other designations are basic certifications in fields that are so specialized that they are not of interest to the states, but rather only to the professionals within an industry. For example, if your company needs to hire an investigator to check out a potential fraud against you, you might want to hire a CFE—Certified Fraud Examiner—who has meet the minimum requirements for that title from the Association of Certified Fraud Examiners.

Other Information Available

Mail Lists & Databases

Many agencies make their lists available in reprinted or computer form, and a few maintain online access to their files. If you are interested in the availability of licensing agency information in bulk (e.g. mailing lists, magnetic tapes, disks) or online, call the agency and ask about formats that are available.

Compilation by Vendors

A number of private vendors also compile lists from these agencies and make them available online or on CD-ROM. We do not suggest these databases for credential searching because they may not be complete, may not be up to date, and may not contain all the information you can obtain directly from the licensing agency. However, these databases are extremely valuable as a general source of background information on an individual or company that you wish to do business with.

Searching Hints — Other Federal Agencies

EDGAR

EDGAR, the Electronic Data Gathering Analysis, and Retrieval system was established by the Securities and exchange Commission (SEC) to allow companies to make required filing to the SEC by direct transmission. As of May 6, 1996, all public domestic companies are required to make their filings on EDGAR, except for filings made to the Commission's regional offices and those filings made on paper due to a hardship exemption.

EDGAR is an extensive repository of US corporation information and it is available online.

What is Found on EDGAR?

Companies must file the following reports with the SEC:

- ◆ 10-K, an annual financial report, which includes audited year-end financial statements.

- ◆ 10-Q, a quarterly report, unaudited.

- ◆ 8K - a report detailing significant or unscheduled corporate changes or events.

- ◆ Securities offering and trading registrations and the final prospectus.

The list above is not conclusive. There are other miscellaneous reports filed, including those dealing with security holdings by institutions and insiders. Access to these documents provides a wealth on information.

How to Access EDGAR Online

EDGAR is searchable online at: www.sec.gov/edgarhp.htm. LEXIS/NEXIS acts as the data wholesaler or distributor on behalf of the government. LEXIS/NEXIS sells data to information retailers, including it's own NEXIS service.

There is an additional number of companies found in the Company Information Category Index (see page 309) that may very well offer online access to EDGAR. Many of these companies have compiled data prior to May 1996 and offer proprietary databases of SEC and other company documents.

Aviation Records

The Federal Aviation Association (FAA) is the US government agency with the responsibility of all matters related to the safety of civil aviation. The FAA, among other functions, provides the system that registers aircraft, and documents showing title or interest in aircraft. Their web site, at www.faa.gov, is the ultimate source of aviation records, airports and facilities, safety regulations, and civil research and engineering.

The Aircraft Owners and Pilots Association is the largest organization of its kind with a 340,000 members. Their web site is www.aopa.org and is an excellent source of information regarding the aviation industry.

Three other excellent sources are *Jane's World Airlines* at www.janes.com; the Insured Aircraft Title Service at www.insuredaircraft.com; and the excellent web site http://theaviationhub.com.

Military Records

This topic is so broad that there can be a book written about it, and in fact there is! *The Armed Forces Locator Directory* from MIE Publishing (800-937-2133) is an excellent source. The author, Lt. Col. Richard S Johnson, covers every conceivable topic regarding military records.

The Privacy Act of 1974 (5 U.S.C. 552a) and the Department of Defense directives require a written request, signed and dated, to access military personnel records. For further details, visit the NPRC site listed below.

Internet Sources

There are a number of great Internet sites that provide valuable information on obtaining military and military personnel records as follows:

www.nara.gov/regional/mpr.html This is the National Personnel Records Center (NPRC), maintained by the National Archives and Records Administration. This site is full of useful information and links.

www.army.mil	The official site of the US Army
www.af.mil	The official site of the US Air Force
www.navy.mil	The official site of the US Navy
www.usmc.mil	The official site of the US Marine Corps
www.ngb.dtic.mil	The official site of the National Guard
www.uscg.mil	The official site of the US Coast Guard

Searching Hints — Using a Private Vendor

Hiring Someone to Obtain the Record Online

There are five main categories of public record professionals: distributors and gateways; search firms; local document retrievers; investigative firms; and information brokers. The Private Company Indexes and Profiles sections of this book contain information on over 140 of these companies.

In the interest of presenting an all-encompassing overview, the five categories are described below—

1. Distributors and Gateways (Proprietary Database Vendors)

Distributors are automated public record firms who combine public sources of bulk data and/or online access to develop their own database product(s). Primary Distributors include companies that collect or buy public record information from its source and reformat the information in some useful way. They tend to focus on one or a limited number of types of information, although a few firms have branched into multiple information categories.

Gateways are companies that either compile data from or provide an automated gateway to Primary Distributors. Gateways thus provide "one-stop shopping" for multiple geographic areas and/or categories of information.

Companies can be both Primary Distributors and Gateways. For example, a number of online database companies are both primary distributors of corporate information and also gateways to real estate information from other Primary Distributors

2. Search Firms

Search firms are companies that furnish public record search and document retrieval services through outside online services and/or through a network of specialists, including their own employees or correspondents (see Retrievers below). There are three types of Search Firms.

Search Generalists offer a full range of search capabilities in many public record categories over a wide geographic region. They may rely on gateways, primary distributors and/or networks of retrievers. They combine online proficiency with document retrieval expertise.

Search Specialists focus either on one geographic region—like Ohio—or on one specific type of public record information—like driver/vehicle records.

Application Specialists focus on one or two types of services geared to specific needs. In this category are pre-employment screening firms and tenant screening firms. Like investigators, they search many of the categories of public records in order to prepare an overall report about a person or business.

3. Local Document Retrievers

Local document retrievers use their own personnel to search specific requested categories of public records usually in order to obtain documentation for legal compliance (e.g., incorporations), for lending, and for litigation. They do not usually review or interpret the results or issue reports in the sense that investigators do, but rather return documents with the results of searches. They tend to be localized, but there are companies that offer a national network of retrievers and/or correspondents. The retriever or his/her personnel goes directly to the agency to look up the information. A retriever may be relied upon for strong knowledge in a local area, whereas a search generalist has a breadth of knowledge and experience in a wider geographic range.

The 650+ members of the **Public Record Retriever Network (PRRN)** can be found, by state and counties served, at www.brbpub.com/prrn. This organization has set industry standards for the retrieval of public record documents and operates under a Code of Professional Conduct. Using one of these record retrievers is an excellent way to access records in those jurisdictions that do not offer online access.

4. Private Investigation Firms

Investigators use public records as tools rather than as ends in themselves, in order to create an overall, comprehensive "picture" of an individual or company for a particular purpose. They interpret the information they have gathered in order to identify further investigation tracks. They summarize their results in a report compiled from all the sources used.

Many investigators also act as Search Firms, especially as tenant or pre-employment screeners, but this is a different role from the role of Investigator per se, and screening firms act very much like investigators in their approach to a project. In addition, an investigator may be licensed, and may perform the types of services traditionally thought of as detective work, such as surveillance.

> **Editor's Tip:** A great source to find licensed private investigators is www.investigatorsanywhere.com.

5. Information Brokers

There is one additional type of firm that occasionally utilizes public records. **Information Brokers** (IB) gather information that will help their clients make informed business decisions. Their work is usually done on a custom basis with each project being unique. IB's are extremely knowledgeable in online research of full text databases and most specialize in a particular subject area, such as patent searching or competitive intelligence. The Association of Independent Information Professionals (AIIP), at www.aiip.org, has over 750 experienced professional information specialist members from 21 countries.

Which Type of Vendor is Right for You?

With all the variations of vendors and the categories of information, the obvious question is; "How do I find the right vendor to go to for the public record information I need?" Before you start calling every interesting online vendor that catches your eye, you need to narrow your search to the **type** of vendor for your needs. To do this, ask yourself the following questions—

What is the Frequency of Usage?

If you have on-going, recurring requests for a particular type of information, it is probably best to choose a different vendor then if you have infrequent requests. Setting up an account with a primary distributor, such as Metromail, will give you an inexpensive per search fee, but the monthly minimum requirements will be prohibitive to the casual requester, who would be better off finding a vendor who accesses or is a gateway to Metromail.

What is the Complexity of the Search?

The importance of hiring a vendor who understands and can interpret the information in the final format increases with the complexity of the search. Pulling a driving record in Maryland is not difficult, but doing an online criminal record search in Maryland, when only a portion of the felony records are online, is not so easy.

Thus, part of the answer to determining which vendor or type of vendor to use is to become conversant with what is (and is not) available from government agencies. Without knowing what is available (and what restrictions apply), you cannot guide the search process effectively. Once you are comfortable knowing the kinds of information available in the public record, you are in a position to find the best method to access needed information.

What are the Geographic Boundaries of the Search?

A search of local records close to you may require little assistance, but a search of records nationally or in a state 2,000 miles away will require seeking a vendor who covers the area you need to search. Many national primary distributors and gateways combine various local and state databases into one large comprehensive system available for searching. However, if your record searching is narrowed by a region or locality, an online source that specializes in a specific geographic region like Superior Information Services in NJ, may be an alternative to a national vendor. Keep in mind that many national firms allow you to order a search online, even though results cannot be delivered immediately and some hands-on local searching is required.

Of course, you may want to use the government agency online system if available for the kind of information you need.

Ten Questions to Ask an Online Vendor
(Or a Vendor Who Uses Online Sources)

The following discussion focuses specifically on automated sources of information because many valuable types of public records have been entered into a computer and, therefore, require a computer search to obtain reliable results. The original version of this article was authored by **Mr. Leroy Cook**, Director of ION and The Investigators Anywhere Resource Line (www.investigatorsanywhere.com). Mr. Cook has graciously allowed us to edit the article and reprint it for our readers.

1. Where does he or she get the information?

You may feel awkward asking a vendor where he or she obtained the information you are purchasing. The fake Rolex watch is a reminder that even buying physical things based on looks alone—without knowing where they come from—is dangerous.

Reliable information vendors *will* provide verification material such as the name of the database or service accessed, when it was last updated, and how complete it is.

It is important that you know the gathering process in order to better judge the reliability of the information being purchased. There *are* certain investigative sources that a vendor will not be willing to disclose to a you. However, that type of source should not be confused with the information that is being sold item by item. Information technology has changed so rapidly that some information brokers may still confuse "items of information" with "investigative reports." Items of information sold as units are *not* investigative reports. The professional reputation of an information vendor is a guaranty of sorts. Still, because information as a commodity is so new, there is little in the way of an implied warranty of fitness.

2. How long does it take for the new information or changes to get into the system?

Any answer *except* a clear, concise date and time or the vendor's personal knowledge of an ongoing system's methods of maintaining information currency is a reason to keep probing. Microfiche or a database of records may have been updated last week at a courthouse or a DMV, but the department's computer section may also be working with a three-month backlog. In this case, a critical incident occurring one month ago would *not* show up in the information updated last week. The importance of timeliness is a variable to be determined by you, but to be truly informed you need to know how "fresh" the information is. Ideally, the mechanism by which you purchase items of information *should* include an update or statement of accuracy—as a part of the reply—*without* having to ask.

3. What are the searchable fields?
Which fields are mandatory?

If your knowledge of "fields" and "records" is limited to the places where cattle graze and those flat, round things that play music, you *could* have a problem telling a good database from a bad one. An MVR vendor, for example, should be able to tell you that a subject's middle initial is critical when pulling an Arizona driving record. You don't have to become a programmer to use a computer and you needn't know a database management language to benefit from databases, *but* it is very helpful to understand how databases are constructed and (*at the least*) what fields, records, and indexing procedures are used.

As a general rule, the computerized, public-record information world is not standardized from county to county or from state to state; in the same way, there is little standardization within or between information vendors. Look at the system documentation from the vendor. The manual should include this sort of information.

4. How much latitude is there for error (misspellings or inappropriate punctuation) in a data request?

If the vendor's requirements for search data appear to be concise and meticulous, then you're probably on the right track. Some computer systems will tell (or "flag") an operator when they make a mistake such as omitting important punctuation or using an unnecessary comma. Other systems allow you to make inquiries by whatever means or in whatever format you like—and then tell you the requested information has *not* been found. In this instance, the desired information may *actually* be there, but the computer didn't understand the question because of the way in which it was asked. It is easy to misinterpret "no record found" as "there is no record." Please take note that the meanings of these two phrases are quite different.

5. What method is used to place the information in the repository and what error control or edit process is used?

In some databases, information may be scanned in or may be entered by a single operator as it is received and, in others, information may be entered *twice* to allow the computer to catch input errors by searching for non-duplicate entries. You don't have to know *everything* about all the options, but the vendor selling information in quantity *should*.

6. How many different databases or sources does the vendor access and how often?

The chance of obtaining an accurate search of a database increases with the frequency of access and the vendor's/searcher's level of knowledge. If he or she only makes inquiries once a month—and the results are important—you may need to find someone who sells data at higher volume. The point here is that it is usually better to find someone who specializes in the type of information you are seeking than it is to utilize a vendor who *can* get the information, but actually specializes in another type of data.

7. Does the price include assistance in interpreting the data received?

A report that includes coding and ambiguous abbreviations may look impressive in your file, but may not be too meaningful. For all reports, except those you deal with regularly, interpretation assistance can be *very* important. Some information vendors offer searches for information they really don't know much about through sources that they only use occasionally. Professional pride sometimes prohibits them from disclosing their limitations—until *you* ask the right questions.

8. Do vendors "keep track" of requesters and the information they seek (usage records)?

This may not seem like a serious concern when you are requesting information you're legally entitled to; however, there *is* a possibility that your usage records could be made available to a competitor. Most probably, the information itself is *already* being (or will be) sold to someone else, but you may not necessarily want *everyone* to know what you are requesting and how often. If the vendor keeps records of who-asks-what, the confidentiality of that information should be addressed in your agreement with the vendor.

9. Will the subject of the inquiry be notified of the request?

If your inquiry is sub rosa or if the subject's discovery of the search could lead to embarrassment, double check! There are laws that mandate the notification of subjects when certain types of inquires are made into their files. If notification is required, the way in which it is accomplished could be critical.

10. Is the turnaround time and cost of the search made clear at the outset?

You should be crystal clear about what you expect and/or need; the vendor should be succinct when conveying exactly what will be provided and how much it will cost. Failure to address these issues can lead to disputes and hard feelings.

These are excellent questions and concepts to keep in mind when reviewing the vendor profiles found in the Private Company Sources Section.

Government Sources

How to Read the State Chapters

Each State Chapter Contains:

- ◆   Addresses and phone numbers of the Governor, Attorney General, State Archives, and State Legislation.

- ◆   Useful state **facts**, including the official state Internet site.

- ◆   Detailed **examinations** of **state level agencies** that offer online access to their records.

- ◆   Profiles of the federal **Bankruptcy and US District Courts,** including the a breakdown of which counties are assigned to which geographic district. Special attention is given to PACER.

- ◆   Analysis of the **structure and organization** of all of the county courts and the county recording offices, including **search hints** and typical costs of record searching.

- ◆   **Profiles** of the **county level courts and recording offices** that do offer online access.

| Capital: | Montgomery | Home Page | www.state.al.us |

Montgomery County

| Time Zone: | CST | Attorney General | www.ago.state.al.us |

| Number of Counties: | 67 | Archives | www.archives.state.al.us |

State Level...Major Agencies

Criminal Records

Alabama Department of Public Safety, A.B.I., Identification Unit, PO Box 1511, Montgomery, AL 36102-1511 (Courier: 2720 A Gunter PK Dr W, Montgomery, AL 36109); 334-395-4340, 334-395-4350 (Fax), 8AM-5PM.

Online: The State Court Administration provides records over its State Judicial Online System (SJIS) at www.alacourt.org. The SJIS contains criminal records from all county courthouses. Access to this statewide system, which is used by the courts as well as the public, requires a $150 setup fee plus a $50 per month for unlimited access. The system is open 24 hours daily. Call Cheryl Lenoir at 334-242-0300 for more information.

Corporation Records, Limited Partnership Records, Limited Liability Company Records, Limited Liability Partnerships, Trade Names, Trademarks/Servicemarks

Secretary of State, Corporations Division, PO Box 5616, Montgomery, AL 36103-5616 (Courier: 11 S Union St, Ste 207, Montgomery, AL 36104); 334-242-5324, 334-242-5325 (Trademarks), 334-240-3138 (Fax), 8AM-5PM.

www.sos.state.al.us

Online: Two systems are available. The commercial online system is called STARPAS. It functions 24 hours a day, 7 days a week. The initial set-up fee is $36 and access costs $.30 per minute. Call 602-542-0685 for a sign-up package. The web site has free searches of corporate and UCC records. Search individual files for Active Names at http://arc-sos.state.al.us/CGI/SOSCRP01.MBR/INPUT.

Uniform Commercial Code, Federal Tax Liens, State Tax Liens

UCC Division, Secretary of State, PO Box 5616, Montgomery, AL 36103-5616 (Courier: 11 S Union St, #207, Montgomery, AL 36104); 334-242-5231, 8AM-5PM.

www.sos.state.al.us/sosinfo/inquiry.cfm

Online: The agency has UCC information available to search at the web address, there is no fee. Corporation data is also available.

Driver Records

Department of Public Safety, Driver Records-License Division, PO Box 1471, Montgomery, AL 36102-1471 (Courier: 502 Dexter Ave, Montgomery, AL 36104); 334-242-4400, 334-242-4639 (Fax), 8AM-5PM.

www.ador.state.al.us/motorvehicle/MVD_MAIN.html

Online: Alabama offers real time batch processing access via the AAMVAnet 3270 Terminal Connection. There is a minimum order requirement of 500 requests per month. Fee is $5.75 per record. Requesters must provide their own connection device and terminal emulation software. Generally, requests are available 30 minutes after request transmission.

Legislation Records

Alabama Legislature, State House, 11 S Union St, Montgomery, AL 36130-4600; 334-242-7826 (Senate), 334-242-7637 (House), 334-242-8819 (Fax), 8:30AM-4:30PM.

www.legislature.state.al.us

Online: There is a free service on the Internet for bill text and status. The commercial access system is called "ALIS" and provides state code, bill text, bill status, voting history, statutory retrieval, and boards/commission information. The initial fee is $400 plus $100 per month. You must sign up for 12 months. The fees entitle you to unlimited usage 24 hours a day, 7 days a week. For details, call Angela Sayers at 334-242-7482.

State Level...Occupational Licensing

Architect	www.alarchbd.state.al.us/rostersearch/rostersearch.asp
Attorney	www.alabar.org/Database_search/dirSearch.cfm
Forester	http://home.earthlink.net/~pbsears/foresters.html
Home Inspector	www.sos.state.al.us/sosinfo/inquiry.cfm
Insurance Agent	www.aldoi.org/Agents/dirSearch.cfm
Insurance Company	www.aldoi.org/examiners/dirSearch.cfm
Medical Doctor	www.albme.org/verification.htm
Notary Public	www.sos.state.al.us/sosinfo/inquiry.cfm
Nursing Home Administrator	www.alboenha.state.al.us/logon.html
Optometrist	www.odfinder.org/LicSearch.asp
Public Accountant-CPA	www.asbpa.state.al.us
Real Estate Salesperson/Agent/Broker	www.arec.state.al.us/search/search.asp
Social Worker	www.abswe.state.al.us/Lic_Search/search.asp

County Level...Courts, Recorders & Assessors

Director of Courts, 300 Dexter Ave, Montgomery, AL, 36104; 334-242-0300; www.alacourt.org

Editor's Note: A commercial online system is available over the Internet or through the Remote Access system of the State Judicial Information System (SJIS). Access is designed to provide "off-site" users with a means to retrieve basic case information and to allow a user access to any criminal, civil, or traffic record in the state. The system is available 24 hours per day. There is a $150 setup fee, and the monthly charge is $50 for unlimited access Call Cheryl Lenoir at 334-242-0300 for add'l information. The Alabama legal information web site offers commercial access to appellate opinions. For more information, go to http://alacourt.org. Also, a private firm offers access to these records; they may be contacted at www.alacourt.com

Tuscaloosa County
Real Estate, Liens, UCC, Grantor/Grantee, Probate, Marriage
www.tuscco.com
Online access to the records database is available free at www.tuscco.com/RecordsRoom/Records.htm. Also included are searches for mortgages, incorporations, bonds, discharges, and exemptions.

Federal Courts in Alabama...

US District Court - Middle District of Alabama

Home Page: www.almd.uscourts.gov
PACER: Sign-up number is 800-676-6856. Access fee is $.60 per minute. Case records are available back to 1994. New records are available online after 1 day.
Dothan Division Counties: Coffee, Dale, Geneva, Henry, Houston.
Montgomery Division Counties: Autauga, Barbour, Bullock, Butler, Chilton, Coosa, Covington, Crenshaw, Elmore, Lowndes, Montgomery, Pike.
Opelika Division Counties: Chambers, Lee, Macon, Randolph, Russell, Tallapoosa.

US Bankruptcy Court - Middle District of Alabama

Home Page: www.almb.uscourts.gov
PACER: Sign-up number is 800-676-6856. Access fee is $.60 per minute. Toll-free access: 888-247-9272. Local access: 334-223-7486. Case records are available back to case 89-02000. Records are purged every 6 months. New civil records are available online after 2-3 days.
Montgomery Division Counties: Autauga, Barbour, Bullock, Butler, Chambers, Chilton, Coffee, Coosa, Covington, Crenshaw, Dale, Elmore, Geneva, Henry, Houston, Lee, Lowndes, Macon, Montgomery, Pike, Randolph, Russell, Tallapoosa.

US District Court - Northern District of Alabama

Home Page: www.alnd.uscourts.gov
PACER: Sign-up number is 800-676-6856. Access fee is $.60 per minute. Case records are available back to 1994. Records are purged every 18 months. New records are available online after 1 day.
PACER Internet Access: http://pacer.alnd.uscourts.gov.
Birmingham Division Counties: Bibb, Blount, Calhoun, Clay, Cleburne, Greene, Jefferson, Pickens, Shelby, Sumter, Talladega, Tuscaloosa.
Florence Division Counties: Colbert, Franklin, Lauderdale.
Gadsden Division Counties: Cherokee, De Kalb, Etowah, Marshall, St. Clair.
Huntsville Division Counties: Cullman, Jackson, Lawrence, Limestone, Madison, Morgan.
Jasper Division Counties: Fayette, Lamar, Marion, Walker, Winston.

US Bankruptcy Court - Northern District of Alabama

Home Page: www.alnb.uscourts.gov
PACER: Sign-up number is 800-676-6856. Access fee is $.60 per minute. Toll-free access: 800-689-7645. Local access: 256-238-0456. Use of PC Anywhere v4.0 suggested. Case records are available back to October 31, 1976. New civil records are available online after 1 day.
Anniston Division Counties: Calhoun, Cherokee, Clay, Cleburne, De Kalb, Etowah, Marshall, St. Clair, Talladega.
Birmingham Division Counties: Blount, Jefferson, Shelby.
Decatur Division Counties: Colbert, Cullman, Franklin, Jackson, Lauderdale, Lawrence, Limestone, Madison, Morgan. The part of Winston County North of Double Springs is handled by this division.
Tuscaloosa Division Counties: Bibb, Fayette, Greene, Lamar, Marion, Pickens, Sumter, Tuscaloosa, Walker, Winston. The part of Winston County North of Double Springs is handled by Decatur Division.

US District Court - Southern District of Alabama

Home Page: www.als.uscourts.gov
PACER: Sign-up number is 800-676-6856. Access fee is $.60 per minute. Toll-free access: 800-622-9392. Local access: 334-694-4672. Case records are available back to 1993. New records are available online after 1 day.
PACER Internet Access: http://pacer.alsd.uscourts.gov.

Mobile Division Counties: Baldwin, Choctaw, Clarke, Conecuh, Escambia, Mobile, Monroe, Washington.
Selma Division Counties: Dallas, Hale, Marengo, Perry, Wilcox.

US Bankruptcy Court - Southern District of Alabama

Home Page: www.alsb.uscourts.gov
PACER: Sign-up number is 800-676-6856. Access fee is $.60 per minute. Toll-free access: 800-622-9392. Local access: 334-441-5638. Case records are available back to 1993. New civil records are available online after 1 day.
Mobile Division Counties: Baldwin, Choctaw, Clarke, Conecuh, Dallas, Escambia, Hale, Marengo, Mobile, Monroe, Perry, Washington, Wilcox.

Editor's Choice for Alabama

Here are some additional sites recommended for this state.

Attorney General Opinions
     www.ago.state.al.us/opinion.cfm
Constitution Text
     www.legislature.state.al.us/CodeOfAlabama/Constitution/1901/Constitution1901_toc.ht
County Election Officials Directory
     www.sos.state.al.us/cf/election/borjop1.cfm
Elections Database
     http://arc-sos.state.al.us/
Felony Fugitives Directory
     www.gsiweb.net/abiweb_scripts/fugitive_list.idc
Land Records Database
     http://userdb.rootsweb.com/landrecords/
Legislative Acts Database
     http://arc-sos.state.al.us
Missing Persons Directory
     www.gsiweb.net/abiweb/missing_frame.html
Office of the Governor - Staff Contacts Listing
     www.governor.state.al.us/office/main-contact.html
Sex Offenders Database
     www.gsiweb.net/so_doc/so_index_new.html
State Law Search Form
     www.legislature.state.al.us/Search/SearchText.htm
Supreme Court Opinions
     www.wallacejordan.com/decision.htm
Vital Records Request Forms (Paper)
     www.alapubhealth.org/vital/vitalrcd.htm

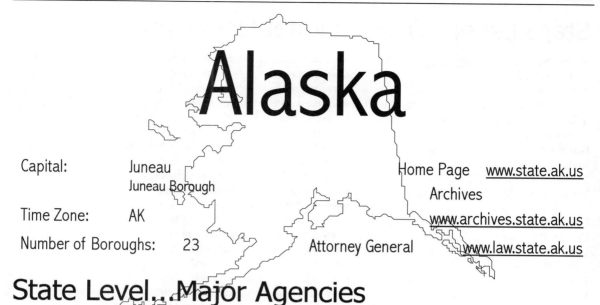

Capital:	Juneau	Home Page	www.state.ak.us
	Juneau Borough	Archives	
Time Zone:	AK		www.archives.state.ak.us
Number of Boroughs:	23	Attorney General	www.law.state.ak.us

State Level...Major Agencies

Corporation Records, Trademarks/Servicemarks, Fictitious Name, Assumed Name, Limited Partnership Records, Limited Liability Company Records, Limited Liability Partnership Records

Corporation Section, Department of Community & Econ Dev, PO Box 110808, Juneau, AK 99811-0808 (Courier: 150 Third Street Rm 217, Juneau, AK 99801); 907-465-2530, 907-465-3257 (Fax), 8AM-5PM.

www.dced.state.ak.us/bsc/corps.htm

Online: At the web site, one can access status information on corps, LLCs, LLP, LP (all both foreign and domestic), registered and reserved names, as well as trademark information. There is no fee.

Driver Records

Division of Motor Vehicles, Driver's Records, 2760 Sherwood Lane #B, Juneau, AK 99801; 907-465-4361 (Motor Vehicle Reports Desk), 907-465-4363 (Licensing), 907-465-5509 (Fax), 8AM-5PM.

www.state.ak.us/dmv

Online: Online access costs $5.00 per record. Inquiries may be made at any time, 24 hours a day. Batch inquiries may call back within thirty minutes for responses. Search by the first four letters of driver's name, license number and date of birth. At present, there is only one phone line available for users; you may experience a busy signal.

Legislation Records

Alaska State Legislative Affairs Agency, Legislative Information Office, 120 4th St #111-State Capitol, Juneau, AK 99801-1182; 907-465-4648, 907-465-2864 (Fax), 8AM-5PM.

www.legis.state.ak.us

Online: All information, including statutes, is available on the Internet. At the main web site, click on "Bills."

State Level...Occupational Licensing

Acupuncturist.. www.dced.state.ak.us/occ/search3.htm
Architect... www.dced.state.ak.us/occ/search3.htm
Athletic Promoter.. www.dced.state.ak.us/occ/OccStart.cfm
Athletic Trainer .... www.dced.state.ak.us/occ/OccStart.cfm
Attorney... www.alaskabar.org/422.cfm
Audiologist/Hearing Aid Dealer www.dced.state.ak.us/occ/search3.htm
Bail Bond .... www.dced.state.ak.us/ins/apps/InsLicStart.cfm
Barber.. www.dced.state.ak.us/occ/search3.htm
Boxer... www.dced.state.ak.us/occ/OccStart.cfm
Boxing & Wrestling Related Occupation www.dced.state.ak.us/occ/search3.htm
Chiropractor... www.dced.state.ak.us/occ/search3.htm
Collection Agency/Operator www.dced.state.ak.us/occ/search3.htm
Concert Promoter www.dced.state.ak.us/occ/search3.htm
Construction Contractor www.dced.state.ak.us/occ/search3.htm
Dental Hygienist www.dced.state.ak.us/occ/search3.htm
Dentist... www.dced.state.ak.us/occ/search3.htm
Dietitian/Nutritionist....................................... www.dced.state.ak.us/occ/OccStart.cfm
Electrical Administrator www.dced.state.ak.us/occ/search3.htm
Engineer www.dced.state.ak.us/occ/search3.htm
Examining Physician, Boxing............................ www.dced.state.ak.us/occ/search3.htm
Geologist www.dced.state.ak.us/occ/search3.htm
Guide Outfitter (Hunting) www.dced.state.ak.us/occ/search3.htm
Hairdresser & Cosmetologist............................ www.dced.state.ak.us/occ/search3.htm
Hearing Aid Dealer www.dced.state.ak.us/occ/search3.htm
Independent Adjuster .... www.dced.state.ak.us/ins/apps/InsLicStart.cfm
Insurance Occupation .... www.dced.state.ak.us/ins/apps/InsLicStart.cfm
Insurance Producer.. www.dced.state.ak.us/ins/apps/InsLicStart.cfm
Lobbyist.. www.state.ak.us/local/akpages/ADMIN/apoc/lobcov.htm
Managing General Agent .... www.dced.state.ak.us/ins/apps/InsLicStart.cfm
Marine Pilot.. www.dced.state.ak.us/occ/search3.htm
Marital & Family Therapist............................... www.dced.state.ak.us/occ/OccStart.cfm
Mechanical Administrator www.dced.state.ak.us/occ/search3.htm
Medical Doctor/Surgeon.................................. www.dced.state.ak.us/occ/search3.htm
Midwife.. www.dced.state.ak.us/occ/OccStart.cfm
Mortician-Embalmer www.dced.state.ak.us/occ/search3.htm
Naturopathic Physician (Naturopathic Doctor).... www.dced.state.ak.us/occ/search3.htm
Nurse... www.dced.state.ak.us/occ/search3.htm
Nurse (RN & LPN)-Nurse Anesthetist............... www.dced.state.ak.us/occ/search3.htm
Nurses' Aide... www.dced.state.ak.us/occ/search3.htm
Nursing Home Administrator www.dced.state.ak.us/occ/search3.htm
Occupational Therapist/Assistant www.dced.state.ak.us/occ/search3.htm
Optician... www.dced.state.ak.us/occ/search3.htm
Optometrist.. www.dced.state.ak.us/occ/search3.htm
Osteopathic Physician www.dced.state.ak.us/occ/search3.htm
Paramedic.. www.dced.state.ak.us/occ/search3.htm
Pharmacist www.dced.state.ak.us/occ/search3.htm

Physical Therapist/Assistant.............................. www.dced.state.ak.us/occ/search3.htm
Physician Assistant www.dced.state.ak.us/occ/search3.htm
Podiatrist www.dced.state.ak.us/occ/search3.htm
Professional Counselor..................................... www.dced.state.ak.us/occ/OccStart.cfm
Psychologist & Psychological Assistant www.dced.state.ak.us/occ/search3.htm
Public Accountant-CPA..................................... www.dced.state.ak.us/occ/OccStart.cfm
Real Estate Agent & Broker www.dced.state.ak.us/occ/search3.htm
Real Estate Appraiser....................................... www.dced.state.ak.us/occ/search3.htm
Referee .... www.dced.state.ak.us/occ/OccStart.cfm
Reinsurance Intermediary Broker .... www.dced.state.ak.us/ins/apps/InsLicStart.cfm
Reinsurance Intermediary Manager .... www.dced.state.ak.us/ins/apps/InsLicStart.cfm
Residential Contractor...................................... www.dced.state.ak.us/occ/search3.htm
Social Worker .... www.dced.state.ak.us/occ/OccStart.cfm
Surplus Line Broker... www.dced.state.ak.us/ins/apps/InsLicStart.cfm
Surveyor www.dced.state.ak.us/occ/search3.htm
Underground Storage Tank Worker/Contractor... www.dced.state.ak.us/occ/search3.htm
Veterinarian.. www.dced.state.ak.us/occ/search3.htm
Veterinary Technician www.dced.state.ak.us/occ/search3.htm
Wrestler.. www.dced.state.ak.us/occ/OccStart.cfm

County Level...Courts, Recorders & Assessors

Office of the Administrative Director, 303 K St, Anchorage, AK, 99501; 907-264-0547;
www.alaska.net/~akctlib/homepage.htm

Editor's Note: There is no internal or external online statewide judicial computer system available.

Fairbanks District in Fairbanks North Star Borough
Real Estate
www.co.fairbanks.ak.us
Access to the City of Fairbanks Property database is available for free online at www.co.fairbanks.ak.us/database/aurora/default.asp.

Juneau District in Juneau Borough
Real Estate
www.juneau.org/cbj/main.htm
Access to City of Juneau Property Records database is available free online at www.juneau.lib.ak.us/assessordata/assessor.asp. Also includes link access to Juneau rentals data and the Records home

Kenai District in Kenai Peninsula Borough
Assessor
www.dnr.state.ak.us/ssd/recoff/default.htm
Access to Kenai Peninsula Borough Assessing Department Public Information Search Page is available free at www.borough.kenai.ak.us/assessingdept/Parcel/SEARCH.HTM.

Federal Courts in Alaska...

US District Court - District of Alaska

Home Page: www.akd.uscourts.gov
PACER: Sign-up number is 800-676-6856. Access fee is $.60 per minute. Toll-free access: 888-271-6212. Local access: 907-271-6212. Case records are available back to 1987. Records are purged every 6 months. New records are available online after 1 day.
Anchorage Division Counties: Aleutian Islands-East, Aleutian Islands-West, Anchorage Borough, Bristol Bay Borough, Kenai Peninsula Borough, Kodiak Island Borough, Matanuska-Susitna Borough, Valdez-Cordova.
Fairbanks Division Counties: Bethel, Fairbanks North Star Borough, North Slope Borough, Northwest Arctic Borough, Southeast Fairbanks, Wade Hampton, Yukon-Koyukuk.
Juneau Division Counties: Haines Borough, Juneau Borough, Prince of Wales-Outer Ketchikan, Sitka Borough, Skagway-Hoonah-Angoon, Wrangell-Petersburg.
Ketchikan Division Counties: Ketchikan Gateway Borough.

Nome Division Counties: Nome.

US Bankruptcy Court - District of Alaska

Home Page: www.akb.uscourts.gov
PACER: Sign-up number is 800-676-6856. Access fee is $.60 per minute. Toll-free access: 888-878-3110. Local access: 907-271-2695, 907-271-2696, 907-271-2697, 907-271-2698, 907-271-2699. Case records are available back to July 1991. Records are purged 6 months. New civil records are available online after 2 days.
PACER Internet Access: http://pacer.akb.uscourts.gov.
Anchorage Division Counties: All boroughs and districts in Alaska.

Editor's Choice for Alaska

Here are some additional sites recommended for this state.

Administrative Code Search Form
> http://touchngo.com/lglcntr/aacsearch.htm
Appeals Court Opinions
> www.alaska.net/~akctlib/ap.htm
Codes Text
> http://bpc.iserver.net/codes/fairbank/index.htm
Codes Text
> www.borough.kenai.ak.us/assemblyclerk/Assembly/BoroCode/SearchTools/CodeIntro.ht
Constitution Text
> www.gov.state.ak.us/ltgov/akcon/table.html
Public Notices Database
> http://notes.state.ak.us/pn/pubnotic.nsf
State Employee Contact Information Database
> www.state.ak.us/local/whtpage1.html
Statutes Text
> www.touchngo.com/lglcntr/akstats/statutes.htm
Supreme Court Opinions
> http://touchngo.com/sp/spsearch.htm

Capital:	Phoenix Maricopa County	Home Page	www.state.az.us
Time Zone:	MST (no DST)	Archives	www.dlapr.lib.az.us/ archives
Number of Counties:	15	Attorney General	www.attorney_general. state.az.us

State Level...Major Agencies

Corporation Records, Limited Liability Company Records

Corporation Commission, 1300 W Washington, Phoenix, AZ 85007; 602-542-3026 (Status), 602-542-3285 (Annual Reports), 602-542-3414 (Fax), 8AM-5PM.

www.cc.state.az.us

Online: The web site provides free access to all corporation information.

Uniform Commercial Code, Federal Tax Liens, State Tax Liens

UCC Division, Secretary of State, State Capitol, West Wing, 7th Floor, Phoenix, AZ 85007; 602-542-6178, 602-542-7386 (Fax).

www.sosaz.com

Online: UCC records can be searched for free over the web site. Searching can be done by debtor, secured party name, or file number. From this site you can also pull down a weekly microfiche file of filings (about 10 megabytes).

Driver Records

Motor Vehicle Division, Record Services Section, PO Box 2100, Mail Drop 539M, Phoenix, AZ 85001-2100 (Courier: Customer Records Services, 1801 W Jefferson, Rm 111, Phoenix, AZ 85007); 602-255-0072, 8AM-5PM.

www.dot.state.az.us/MVD/mvd.htm

Online: Arizona's online system is interactive and open 24 hours daily. Fee is $3.00 per record. This system is primarily for those requesters who are exempt. For more information call 602-712-7235.

Vehicle Ownership, Vehicle Identification

Motor Vehicle Division, Record Services Section, PO Box 2100, Mail Drop 504M, Phoenix, AZ 85001-2100 (Courier: Customer Records Services, 1801 W Jefferson, Rm 111, Phoenix, AZ 85007); 602-255-0072, 8AM-5PM.

www.dot.state.az.us/MVD/mvd.htm

Online: Online access is offered to permissible users. Fee is $3.00 per record. The system is open 24 hours a day, seven days a week. For more information, call 602-712-7235.

Legislation Records

Arizona Legislature, State Senate - Room 203, 1700 W Washington, Phoenix, AZ 85007 (Courier: Senate Wing or, House Wing, Phoenix, AZ 85007); 602-542-3559 (Senate Information), 602-542-4221 (House Information), 602-542-3429 (Senate Fax), 602-542-3550 (Senate Resource Ctr), 602-542-4099 (Fax), 8AM-5PM.

www.azleg.state.az.us

Online: Most information, beginning with 1997, is available through the Internet (i.e. bill text, committee minutes, committee assignments, member bios, etc.). There is no fee.

State Level...Occupational Licensing

Advance Fee Loan Broker	www.azbanking.com/Lists/ALB_List.HTML
Architect	www.btr.state.az.us
Assayer	www.btr.state.az.us
Attorney	www.azbar.org/MemberFinder
Bank	www.azbanking.com/Lists/BA_List.HTML
Bank	www.azbanking.com/Lists/BA_List.HTML
Behavioral Health Emergency Service	www.hs.state.az.us/als/databases/index.html
Behavioral Health Residential	www.hs.state.az.us/als/databases/index.html
Behavioral Outpatient Clinic	www.hs.state.az.us/als/databases/index.html
Charity	www.sosaz.com/scripts/Charity_Search_engine.cgi
Collection Agency	www.azbanking.com/Lists/CA_List.HTML
Commercial Mortgage Banker	www.azbanking.com/Lists/CBK_List.HTML
Consumer Lender	www.azbanking.com/Lists/CL_List.HTML
Contractor	www.rc.state.az.us/AZROCLicenseQuery
Court Reporter	www.supreme.state.az.us/cr/CRcertlist2001.htm
Credit Union	www.azbanking.com/Lists/CU_List.HTML
Day Care Establishment	www.hs.state.az.us/als/databases/index.html
Debt Management	www.azbanking.com/Lists/DM_List.HTML
Engineer	www.btr.state.az.us
Escrow Agent	www.azbanking.com/Lists/EA_List.HTML
Geologist	www.btr.state.az.us
Hearing Aid Dispenser	www.hs.state.az.us/als/databases/index.html
Home Inspector	www.btr.state.az.us
Landscape Architect	www.btr.state.az.us
Liquor Producer	www.azll.com/query.html
Liquor Retail Co-Operative/Agent/Manager	www.azll.com/query.html
Liquor Wholesaler	www.azll.com/query.html
Lobbyist	www.sosaz.com/scripts/lobbyist_engine.cgi
Marriage & Family Therapist	http://aspin.asu.edu/~azbbhe/directory/listing.html
Medical Doctor	www.docboard.org/az/df/azsearch.htm
Money Transmitter	www.azbanking.com/Lists/MT_List.HTML
Mortgage Banker	www.azbanking.com/Lists/BK_List.HTML
Mortgage Broker	www.azbanking.com/Lists/MB_List.HTML
Motor Vehicle Dealer & Sales Finance	www.azbanking.com/Lists/MVD_List.HTML
Notary Public	www.sosaz.com/scripts/Notary_Search_engine.cgi
Optometrist	www.odfinder.org/LicSearch.asp

Pawn Shop...www.azbanking.com/Lists/DPC_List.HTML
Physician Assistant ....www.docboard.org/az/df/azsearch.htm
Physician Assistant ....www.docboard.org/az/df/azsearch.htm
Premium Finance Company...............................www.azbanking.com/Lists/PF_List.HTML
Pre-Need Funeral Trust Company ....www.azbanking.com/Lists/PFT_List.HTML
Professional Counselor......................................http://aspin.asu.edu/~azbbhe/directory/listing.html
Property Tax Agent..www.appraisal.state.az.us/Directory/taxagent.html
Psychologist..www.goodnet.com/~azbpe/dir.html
Public Accountant-CPA & PA...........................www.acancy.state.az.us/Aug%2000%20CPA%20LIST.htm
Public Accounting Firm-CPA & PA...................www.acancy.state.az.us
Real Estate Appraiser..www.appraisal.state.az.us/Directory/appr1.html
Sales Finance Companies..................................www.azbanking.com/Lists/SF_List.HTML
Social Worker...http://aspin.asu.edu/~azbbhe/directory/listing.html
Substance Abuse Counselor ....http://aspin.asu.edu/~azbbhe/directory/listing.html
Surveyor ....www.btr.state.az.us
Telemarketing Firm ....www.sosaz.com/scripts/TS_Search_engine.cgi
Trust Company ....www.azbanking.com/Lists/TC_List.HTML
Trust Divisions (of Chartered Fin. Institutions) .. www.azbanking.com/Lists/TD_List.HTML

County Level...Courts, Recorders & Assessors

Administrative Office of the Courts, Arizona Supreme Court Bldg, 1501 W Washington, Phoenix, AZ, 85007; 602-542-9301; www.supreme.state.az.us

Editor's Note: A system called ACAP (Arizona Court Automation Project) is implemented in over 100 courts. Mohave County is not a part of ACAP. ACAP is, fundamentally, a case and cash management information processing system. When fully implemented ACAP will provide all participating courts access to all records on the system. Current plans call for public availability later in 2001. Access will be over the Internet. For more information, call Tim Lawler at 602-542-9614.

The Maricopa and Pima county courts maintain their own systems, but will also, under current planning, be part of ACAP. These two counties provide limited online access to the public.

Apache
Real Estate, Recording
www.co.apache.az.us/Recorder/index.htm
Online access to the Apache County Recorder Query Index is available free at www.co.apache.az.us/Recorder/index/query.asp.

Maricopa
Civil Cases, Criminal Records
www.superiorcourt.maricopa.gov
Online access is available free at www.superiorcourt.maricopa.gov/docket/public_new.html. Case file can be printed. Search by name or case number.
Real Estate, Liens
http://recorder.maricopa.gov
Access is available by direct dial-up or on the Internet. Dial-up access requires one-time set-up fee of $300 plus $.06 per minute. Dial-up hours are 8am-10pm M-F, 8-5 S-S. Records date back to 1983. For additional information, contact Linda Kinchloe at 602-506-3637. Also, access to the County Recorder's database is available free at http://recorder.maricopa.gov/recdocdata. Records go back to

1983. Also, access to the Assessor database is available free at www.maricopa.gov/assessor/default.asp. Residential data is available. Also, perform name/parcel/property tax lookups free

Mohave
Real Estate, Grantor/Grantee, Liens, Assessor
www.co.mohave.az.us
Online access to the Recorder's System is available free at http://216.173.151.223/splash.jsp. Registration and password is required. Also, online access to the Assessor's property database is available free (no registration) at www.co.mohave.az.us/1moweb/depts_files/assessor_files/assessdata.asp. A sales history database is also here. Also, the treasurer's tax sale parcel search is available at www.co.mohave.az.us/1moweb/depts_files/treasure_files/about_treasure.htm.

Pima
Civil Cases, Criminal Records
http://jp.co.pima.az.us
Online access is free through the Internet site. You can search docket information for civil, criminal or traffic cases by name, docket or citation number.
Assessor, Real Estate, Lien, Recording
www.recorder.co.pima.az.us
Online access to the recorder's Research Records database is available free at www.recorder.co.pima.az.us/research.html. Click "Enter Here" and use the word "public" for user name and password. Also, records on the Pima County Tax Assessor database are available free online at www.asr.co.pima.az.us/apiq/index.html. Also, a name/parcel/property tax lookup may be performed free on the SBOE site at www.sboe.state.az.us/cgi-bin/name_lookup.pl. Also, search by parcel number on the Treasurer's tax inquiry database at www.to.co.pima.az.us/inquiry.html.

Yavapai
Assessor, Real Estate, Recordings
www.co.yavapai.az.us/departments/recorder/RecorderMain.asp
Online access to the recording office iCRIS database is available free at http://icris.co.yavapai.az.us/splash.jsp. Records from 1976 to present; images from 1986 to present. Also, assessor and land records on the County Geographic Information Systems (GIS) database are available free online at www.co.yavapai.az.us/departments/gis/gisOnlineApps.asp. To search, choose a "session" In the "Locate Property Information" box.

Federal Courts in Arizona...

US District Court - District of Arizona

Home Page: www.azd.uscourts.gov
PACER: Sign-up number is 800-676-6856. Access fee is $.60 per minute. Toll-free access: 888-372-5707. Local access: 602-514-7113. Case records are available back to 1992. Records are purged every 12 months. New records are available online after 1-3 days.
PACER Internet Access: http://pacer.azd.uscourts.gov.
Phoenix Division Counties: Gila, La Paz, Maricopa, Pinal, Yuma. Some Yuma cases handled by San Diego Division of the Southern District of California.
Prescott Division Counties: Apache, Coconino, Mohave, Navajo, Yavapai.
Tucson Division Counties: Cochise, Graham, Greelee, Pima, Santa Cruz. The Globe Division was closed effective January 1994, and all case records for that division are now found here.

US Bankruptcy Court - District of Arizona

Home Page: www.azb.uscourts.gov
PACER: Sign-up number is 800-676-6856. Access fee is $.60 per minute. Toll-free access: 800-556-9230. Local access: 602-640-5832. Use of PC Anywhere v4.0 suggested. Case records are available back to 1986. Records are purged every six months. New civil records are available online after 1 week.
Electronic Filing: Searching of electronically filed cases is NOT currently available online. Electronic filing information is available online at http://ecf.azb.uscourts.gov.
Phoenix Division Counties: Apache, Coconino, Maricopa, Navajo, Yavapai.
Tucson Division Counties: Cochise, Gila, Graham, Greenlee, Pima, Pinal, Santa Cruz.
Yuma Division Counties: La Paz, Mohave, Yuma.

Editor's Choice for Arizona

Here are some additional sites recommended for this state.

Appeals Court - Open Cases (Division 1) Listing
www.apltwo.ct.state.az.us/casendx.html
Appeals Court - Open Cases (Division 2) Listing
www.apltwo.ct.state.az.us/casendx.html
Appeals Court (Division 1) Opinions
www.state.az.us/co/opidx.htm
Appeals Court (Division 2) Opinions
www.apltwo.ct.state.az.us/decis.html
Bills Database
www.azleg.state.az.us/legtext/bills.htm
Campaign Finance Database
www.sosaz.com/cfs/CampaignFinanceSearch.htm
Codes Text
www.co.pima.az.us/cob/code/c.htm
Courts & Judges Directory
www.supreme.state.az.us/info/location
Industrial Commission Homepage
www.ica.state.az.us/
Insurance Forms (Paper)
www.state.az.us/id/forms/forms.htm
Law Firms Links
http://firms.findlaw.com/firms/AZ.html
Legislator Roster Listing
www.azleg.state.az.us/members/members.htm
Name Change Forms (Paper)
www.supreme.state.az.us/selfserv/formnmchg.htm
Probate Forms (Paper)
http://forms.findlaw.com/states/azp_1.html
Sex Offenders Database
www.azsexoffender.com/
State Web Site Search Form
www.state.az.us/search.html
Statutes (Revised) Search Form
www.azleg.state.az.us/ars/ars.htm
Supreme Court Opinions
www.supreme.state.az.us/opin
Water Banking Authority Homepage
www.awba.state.az.us/
Water Resources Department Homepage
www.adwr.state.az.us/
Workforce Development Policy Office Homepage
www.azcommerce.com/workforcedevelopment.htm

Arkansas

Capital:	Little Rock Pulaski County	Home Page	www.state.ar.us
Time Zone:	CST	Attorney General	www.ag.state.ar.us
Number of Counties:	75	Archives	www.state.ar.us/ahc

State Level...Major Agencies

Corporation Records, Fictitious Name, Limited Liability Company Records, Limited Partnerships

Secretary of State, Corporation Department-Aegon Bldg, 501 Woodlane, Rm 310, Little Rock, AR 72201-1094; 501-682-3409, 888-233-0325, 501-682-3437 (Fax), 8AM-5PM.

www.sosweb.state.ar.us/corps

Online: The Internet site permits free searching of corporation records. You can search by name, registered agent, or filing number.

Trademarks/Servicemarks

Secretary of State, Trademarks Section-Aegon Bldg, 501 Woodlane, #310, Little Rock, AR 72201; 501-682-3409, 888-233-0325, 501-682-3437 (Fax), 8AM-5PM.

www.sosweb.state.ar.us/corps/trademk

Online: Searching is available at no fee over the Internet site. Search by name, owner, city, or filing number. You can also search via e-mail at corprequest@sosmail.state.as.us.

Workers' Compensation Records

Workers' Compensation Department, 324 Spring St, PO Box 950, Little Rock, AR 72203-0950; 501-682-3930, 800-622-4472, 501-682-6761 (Fax), 8AM-4:30PM M-F.

www.awcc.state.ar.us

Online: To perform an online claim search, one must be a subscriber to the Information Network of Arkansas (INA). Fee is $3.50 per claim per search. If 20 searches are reached in a month then fee goes to $2.50 per search. Records are from May 1, 1997 forward. There is an annual $50 subscriber fee to INA. For more information, visit the web site at www.state.ar.us/ina.html.

Driver Records

Department of Driver Services, Driving Records Division, PO Box 1272, Room 1130, Little Rock, AR 72203 (Courier: 1900 W 7th, #1130, Little Rock, AR 72201); 501-682-7207, 501-682-7908, 501-682-2075 (Fax), 8AM-4:30PM.

www.accessarkansas.org/dfa/driverservices/

Online: Access is available through the Information Network of Arkansas (INA). The system offers both batch and interactive service. The system is only available to INA subscribers who have statutory rights to the data. The record fee is $8.00, or $11.00 for commercial drivers. Visit www.state.ar.us/ina.html.

Legislation Records

Elections Department, State Capitol, Room 026, Little Rock, AR 72201; 501-682-5070, 501-682-3408 (Fax), 8AM-5PM.
www.arkleg.state.ar.us

Online: Probably the best way to search is through the Internet site listed above. You may also search by subject matter.

State Level...Occupational Licensing

Architect..www.state.ar.us/arch/search.html
Attorney..http://courts.state.ar.us/attylist/index.html
Bank..www.sosweb.state.ar.us/corps/bkin
Cemeteries, Perpetual Care
... www.ark.org/arsec/database/dbsearch.cgi?dbname=7&LIMIT=20&LISTALL=ON
Child Care Provider ....www.state.ar.us/childcare/search.html
Chiropractor...www.accessarkansas.org/asbce
Contractor..www.state.ar.us/clb/search.html
Cosmetologist ....www.accessarkansas.org/cos/search.php
Cosmetology Instructor.....................................www.accessarkansas.org/cos/search.php
Counselor ....www.state.ar.us/abec/search.php
Dentist/Dental Hygienist...................................www.asbde.org/RDH-Web-10-2000.PDF
Electrologist/Electrolysis Instructor ....www.accessarkansas.org/cos/search.php
Engineer ....www.state.ar.us/pels/search.html
Engineer-in-Training...www.state.ar.us/pels/search.html
Home Inspector..www.sosweb.state.ar.us/corps/homeinsp
Homebuilder...www.sosweb.state.ar.us/corps/homebldr
Insurance Agency...www.sosweb.state.ar.us/corps/bkin
Insurance Sales Agent ....www.state.ar.us/insurance/license/search.html
Investment Advisor
... www.ark.org/arsec/database/dbsearch.cgi?dbname=2&LIMIT=20&LISTALL=ON
Landscape Architect..www.state.ar.us/arch/search.html
Lobbyist...www.sosweb.state.ar.us/elect.html
Manicurist ....www.accessarkansas.org/cos/search.php
Marriage & Family Therapist............................www.state.ar.us/abec/search.php
Mortgage Loan Brokers/Companies
... www.ark.org/arsec/database/dbsearch.cgi?dbname=7&LIMIT=20&LISTALL=ON
Notary Public...www.sosweb.state.ar.us/corps/notary
Nurse - Nurse-LPN ....www.accessarkansas.org/nurse/registry/index.html
Nurse Midwife..www.accessarkansas.org/nurse/registry/index.html
Nurse-Anesthetist ....www.accessarkansas.org/nurse/registry/index.html
Optometrist..www.odfinder.org/LicSearch.asp
Public Accountant-CPA.....................................www.accessarkansas.org/asbpa
Real Estate Broker/Sales Agent.........................www.accessarkansas.org/arec/db/
Securities Agent/Broker/Dealer
... www.ark.org/arsec/database/dbsearch.cgi?dbname=7&LIMIT=20&LISTALL=ON
Social Worker ....www.state.ar.us/swlb/search/index.html
Surveyor ....www.state.ar.us/pels/search.html
Surveyor-in-Training...www.state.ar.us/pels/search.html
Teacher..www.as-is.org/directory/search_lic.html

County Level...Courts, Recorders & Assessors

Administrative Office of Courts, 625 Marshall St, Justice Bldg, Little Rock, AR, 72201; 501-682-9400; http://courts.state.ar.us/

Editor's Note: There is a limited internal online computer system at the Administrative Office of Courts.

Baxter
Assessor, Real Estate
Assessor/property records are available trough Arcountydata.com at www.arcountydata.com. Registration required; setup fee is $200 with a $.10 per minute charge.

Benton
Civil Cases, Criminal Records
www.co.benton.ar.us
Court dockets and judgments from the circuit clerk's web site are available free at http://64.217.42.130:5061.
Real Estate, Liens, Property Tax
www.co.benton.ar.us
Benton County Assessor, tax collector, and circuit court information is available free online at http://64.217.42.130:5061. Also, assessor/property records are available trough Arcountydata.com at www.arcountydata.com. Registration required; setup fee is $200 with a $.10 per minute charge.

Lee
Real Estate, Recordings
www.leeclerk.org/wb_or1
Online access to the clerk of circuit court official records/land records database is available free at the web site.

Pulaski
Assessor, Real Estate
Assessor/property records are available trough Arcountydata.com at www.arcountydata.com. Registration required; setup fee is $200 with a $.10 per minute charge.

White
Assessor, Real Estate
Assessor/property records are available trough Arcountydata.com at www.arcountydata.com. Registration required; setup fee is $200 with a $.10 per minute charge.

Federal Courts in Arkansas...

US District Court - Eastern District of Arkansas
Home Page: www.are.uscourts.gov
PACER: Sign-up number is 800-676-6856. Access fee is $.60 per minute. Toll-free access: 800-371-8842. Local access: 501-324-6190. Case records are available back to 1987-89. Records are purged every five years. New records are available online after 1 day.
Other Online Access: You can search records on the Internet using RACER. Currently the system is free and requires free registration. Simply visit www.are.uscourts.gov and click on "Case Information."
Batesville Division Counties: Cleburne, Fulton, Independence, Izard, Jackson, Sharp, Stone.
Helena Division Counties: Cross, Lee, Monroe, Phillips, St. Francis, Woodruff.
Jonesboro Division Counties: Clay, Craighead, Crittenden, Greene, Lawrence, Mississippi, Poinsett, Randolph.
Little Rock Division Counties: Conway, Faulkner, Lonoke, Perry, Pope, Prairie, Pulaski, Saline, Van Buren, White, Yell.
Pine Bluff Division Counties: Arkansas, Chicot, Cleveland, Dallas, Desha, Drew, Grant, Jefferson, Lincoln.

US Bankruptcy Court - Eastern District of Arkansas

Home Page: www.areb.uscourts.gov

PACER: Sign-up number is 800-676-6856. Access fee is $.60 per minute. Toll-free access: 800-891-6572. Local access: 501-918-6199. Case records are available back to May 1989. Records are purged every six months. New civil records are available online after 1 day.

PACER Internet Access: http://pacer.areb.uscourts.gov.

Little Rock Division Counties: Same counties as included in Eastern District of Arkansas, plus the counties included in the Western District divisions of El Dorado, Hot Springs and Texarkana. All bankruptcy cases in Arkansas prior to mid-1993 were heard here.

US District Court - Western District of Arkansas

Home Page: www.arwd.uscourts.gov

PACER: Sign-up number is 501-783-6833. Access fee is $.60 per minute. Case records are available back to September 1990. Records are purged every five years. New records are available online after 1 day.

Other Online Access: PACER via E-mail offers case information directly to your e-mailbox. Simply visit www.arwd.uscourts.gov/mailform.html and input the information you are looking for, and the system will automatically send the results to you by e-mail.

El Dorado Division Counties: Ashley, Bradley, Calhoun, Columbia, Ouachita, Union.

Fayetteville Division Counties: Benton, Madison, Washington.

Fort Smith Division Counties: Crawford, Franklin, Johnson, Logan, Polk, Scott, Sebastian.

Hot Springs Division Counties: Clark, Garland, Hot Springs, Montgomery, Pike.

Texarkana Division Counties: Hempstead, Howard, Lafayette, Little River, Miller, Nevada, Sevier.

US Bankruptcy Court - Western District of Arkansas

Home Page: www.arb.uscourts.gov

PACER: Sign-up number is 800-676-6856. Access fee is $.60 per minute. Toll-free access: 800-891-6572. Local access: 501-918-6199. Case records are available back to May 1989. Records are purged every six months. New civil records are available online after 1 day.

Fayetteville Division Counties: Same counties as included in the Western District of Arkansas except that counties included in the divisions of El Dorado and Texarkana are heard in Little Rock.

Editor's Choice for Arkansas

Here are some additional sites recommended for this state.

Appeals Court Opinions
> http://courts.state.ar.us/opinions/opmain.htm

Constitution Text
> www.arkleg.state.ar.us/data/constitution/index.html

Criminal Justice Officials & Agencies Directory
> www.acic.org/directory

Land Records (Pre-1908) Database
> http://searches.rootsweb.com/cgi-bin/arkland/arkland.pl

Missing Children Database
> http://leonardo.aristotle.net/acic/missing/missing-search.html

Supreme Court Opinions
> http://courts.state.ar.us/opinions/opmain.htm

Capital: Sacramento   Home Page   www.state.ca.us
                Sacramento County

Time Zone: PST
                                              Attorney General   http://caag.state.ca.us

Number of Counties: 58   Archives   www.ss.ca.gov/archives/
                                                                   archives.htm

State Level...Major Agencies

Corporation Records, Limited Liability Company Records, Limited Partnerships, Limited Liability Partnerships,

Secretary of State, Information Retrieval/Certification Unit, 1500 11th Street, 3rd Fl, Sacramento, CA 95814; 916-657-5448 (Corps), 916-653-3794 (LLCs), 916-653-3365 (Partnerships), 8AM-4:30PM.

www.ss.ca.gov

Online: The web site offers access to more than 2 million records including corporation, LLC, LP and LLP. Information available includes status, file number, date of filing and agent for service of process. Please note the file is updated weekly (not daily).

Uniform Commercial Code, Federal Tax Liens, State Tax Liens

UCC Division, Secretary of State, PO Box 942835, Sacramento, CA 94235-0001 (Courier: 1500 11th St, 2nd Fl, Sacramento, CA 95814); 916-653-3516, 8AM-5PM.

www.ss.ca.gov

Online: Direct Access provides dial-up searching via PC and modem. Fees range from $1-3 dollars, depending on type of search. Each page scroll is $.25. Requesters operate from a prepaid account.

Sales Tax Registrations

Board of Equalization, Account Analysis and Control, PO Box 942879, Sacramento, CA 94279-0001; 916-445-6362, 800-400-7115 (In California Only), 916-324-4433 (Fax), 8AM-5PM.

www.boe.ca.gov

Birth Certificates

State Department of Health Svcs, Office of Vital Records, PO Box 730241, Sacramento, CA 94244-0241 (Courier: 304 S Street, Sacramento, CA 95814); 916-445-2684 (Recording), 916-445-1719 (Attendant), 800-858-5553 (Fax), 8AM-4:30PM.

www.dhs.ca.gov/chs

Online: Birth records from 1905-1995 can be accessed at http://userdb.rootsweb.com/ca/birth/search.cgi. The site is maintained by a private entity, but the data is provided by the Health Service Dept.

Driver Records

Department of Motor Vehicles, Information Services, PO Box 944247, Mail Station G199, Sacramento, CA 94244-2470; 916-657-8098, 916-657-6525 (Driver Licensing), 8AM-5PM.

Online: The department offers online access, but a $10,000 one-time setup fee is required. The system is open 24 hours, 7 days a week. For more information call (916) 657-5582.

Vehicle Ownership, Vehicle Identification, Boat & Vessel Ownership, Boat & Vessel Registration

Department of Motor Vehicle, Public Contact Unit, PO Box 944247, MS-G199, Sacramento, CA 94244-2470; 916-657-8098 (Walk-in/Mail-in Phone), 916-657-7914 (Commercial Accounts), 916-657-6739 (Vessel Registration), 916-657-5583 (Fax), 8AM-5PM.

Online: Online access is limited to certain Authorized Vendors. Hours are 6 AM to midnight. Requesters are may not use the data for direct marketing, solicitation, nor resell for those purposes. A bond is required and very high fees are involved. For more information, call Sue Jefferson at 916-657-5582.

Legislation Records

California State Legislature, State Capitol, Room B-32 (Legislative Bill Room), Sacramento, CA 95814; 916-445-2323 (Current/Pending Bills), 916-653-7715 (State Archives), 8AM-5PM.

www.leginfo.ca.gov

Online: The Internet site has all legislative information back to 1993. The site also gives access to state laws.

State Level...Occupational Licensing

Acupuncturist
    www2.dca.ca.gov:8001/wllpub/plsql/wllqryna$lcev2.startup?p_qte_code=AC&p_qte_pgm_code=6500
Alarm Company/Employee
    www2.dca.ca.gov:8001/wllpub/plsql/wllqryna$lce.startup?p_qte_code=AC&p_qte_pgm_code=2420
Apprentice Training Establishment   www.dca.ca.gov/cemetery/lookup.htm
Architect   www.cab.ca.gov/Templates/querysearch.cfm
Attorney   www.calsb.org/MM/SBMBRSHP.HTM
Automotive Repair Dealer
    www2.dca.ca.gov:8001/wllpub/plsql/wllqryna$lce.startup?p_qte_code=ARD&p_qte_pgm_code=1310
Bank   www.sbd.ca.gov/directry/db.asp
Baton Training Facility/Instructor
    www2.dca.ca.gov:8001/wllpub/plsql/wllqryna$lce.startup?p_qte_code=TFB&p_qte_pgm_code=2420
Boiler, Hot Water & Steam Fitting   www.cslb.ca.gov/license+request.html
Boxer, Boxing Manager   www.dca.ca.gov/csac/directories.htm
Boxing Judge/Promoter/Matchmaker   www.dca.ca.gov/csac/directories.htm
Brake & Lamp Adjuster/Brake Station
    www2.dca.ca.gov:8001/wllpub/plsql/wllqryna$lce.startup?p_qte_code=MEC&p_qte_pgm_code=1310
Building Moving/Demolition   www.cslb.ca.gov/license+request.html
Cabinet & Mill Work Contractor   www.cslb.ca.gov/license+request.html
Cemetery, Cemetery Agent/Broker   www.dca.ca.gov/cemetery/lookup.htm
Clinical Polygraph Examiner of Convicted Sex Offenders
                         www.wordnet.net/cape/docs/certified.htm
Clinical Social Worker/Associate   www.bbs.ca.gov/weblokup.htm
Concrete Contractor   www.cslb.ca.gov/license+request.html
Continuing Education Providers   www.bbs.ca.gov/weblokup.htm
Contractor   www.cslb.ca.gov

Credit Union	www.sbd.ca.gov/directry/cu.asp
Crematory/Remains Disposer	www.dca.ca.gov/cemetery/lookup.htm
Dental Assistant	www2.dca.ca.gov:8001/wllpub/plsql/wllquery$.startup
Dental Hygienist	www2.dca.ca.gov:8001/wllpub/plsql/wllquery$.startup
Drywall	www.cslb.ca.gov/license+request.html
Earthwork & Paving	www.cslb.ca.gov/license+request.html
Educational Psychologist	www.bbs.ca.gov/weblokup.htm
Electrical (General) & Electrical Sign	www.cslb.ca.gov/license+request.html
Electronic & Appliance Repairs	www2.dca.ca.gov/wllpub/plsql/wllquery$.startup
Elevator Installation	www.cslb.ca.gov/license+request.html
Embalmer/Apprentice Embalmer	www.dca.ca.gov/cemetery/lookup.htm
Engineer, various	www.dca.ca.gov/pels/l_lookup.htm
Fencing	www.cslb.ca.gov/license+request.html
Fire Protection	www.cslb.ca.gov/license+request.html
Firearm Permit/Training Facility/Instructor	
	www2.dca.ca.gov:8001/wllpub/plsql/wllqryna$lce.startup?p_qte_code=FQ&p_qte_pgm_code=2420
Flooring & Floor Covering	www.cslb.ca.gov/license+request.html
Fumigator	www.dca.ca.gov/pestboard/lookup.htm
Funeral Director/Establishment	www.dca.ca.gov/cemetery/lookup.htm
General Building Contractor-Class B	www.cslb.ca.gov/license+request.html
General Manufactured Housing	www.cslb.ca.gov/license+request.html
Geologist	www.dca.ca.gov/geology/lookup
Geophysicist	www.dca.ca.gov/geology/lookup
Glazier	www.cslb.ca.gov/license+request.html
Horse Racing Licenses	www.chrb.ca.gov/license.htm
Hypodermic Needle & Syringe Distributor	
	www2.dca.ca.gov:8001/wllpub/plsql/wllqryna$lcev2.startup?p_qte_code=HYX&p_qte_pgm_code=7200
Industrial Loan Company/Premium	www.sbd.ca.gov/directry/pf.asp
Insulation & Acoustical Contractor	www.cslb.ca.gov/license+request.html
Insurance Adjuster/Agent/Broker	www.insurance.ca.gov/LIC/Licensestatus.htm
Insurance Company	www.insurance.ca.gov/docs/FS-CompanyProfiles.htm
Issuer of Money Orders/Payment Instr.	www.sbd.ca.gov/directry/pi.asp
Issuer of Travelers Checks	www.sbd.ca.gov/directry/tc.asp
Landscaper	www.cslb.ca.gov/license+request.html
Lathing	www.cslb.ca.gov/license+request.html
Limited Specialty (Sublicenses)	www.cslb.ca.gov/license+request.html
Lobbyist/Lobbyist Firm/Employer	www.ss.ca.gov/prd/ld/contents.htm
Locksmith/Locksmith Company	
	www2.dca.ca.gov:8001/wllpub/plsql/wllqryna$lce.startup?p_qte_code=LC&p_qte_pgm_code=2420
Marriage & Family Therapist	www.bbs.ca.gov/weblokup.htm
Masonry	www.cslb.ca.gov/license+request.html
Medical Doctor/Surgeon	www.docboard.org/ca/df/casearch.htm
Optometrist	www.optometry.ca.gov/search.asp
Ornamental Metal	www.cslb.ca.gov/license+request.html
Painter & Decorator	www.cslb.ca.gov/license+request.html
Parking & Highway Improvement	www.cslb.ca.gov/license+request.html
Pest Control Field Representative	www.dca.ca.gov/pestboard/lookup.htm
Pest Control Operator/Applicator	www.dca.ca.gov/pestboard/lookup.htm

Pharmacist/Pharmacist Intern/Pharmacy
      www2.dca.ca.gov:8001/wllpub/plsql/wllqryna$lcev2.startup?p_qte_code=RPH&p_qte_pgm_code=7200
Physician Assistant   www.docboard.org/ca/df/casearch.htm
Pipeline   www.cslb.ca.gov/license+request.html
Plasterer   www.cslb.ca.gov/license+request.html
Plumber   www.cslb.ca.gov/license+request.html
Podiatrist   www.docboard.org/ca/df/casearch.htm
Polygraph Examiner   www.wordnet.net/cape/docs/camemb.htm
Private Investigator/ Private Patrol Operator
      www2.dca.ca.gov:8001/wllpub/plsql/wllqryna$lce.startup?p_qte_code=PI&p_qte_pgm_code=2420
Psychologist
      www2.dca.ca.gov:8001/wllpub/plsql/wllqryna$lcev2.startup?p_qte_code=PSX&p_qte_pgm_code=7300
Real Estate Broker/Sales Agent   http://secure.dre.ca.gov/PublicASP/pplinfo.asp
Refrigeration   www.cslb.ca.gov/license+request.html
Repossessor Agency/Employee/Manager
      www2.dca.ca.gov:8001/wllpub/plsql/wllqryna$lce.startup?p_qte_code=RA&p_qte_pgm_code=2420
Roofing   www.cslb.ca.gov/license+request.html
Sanitation System   www.cslb.ca.gov/license+request.html
Savings & Loan Association   www.sbd.ca.gov/directry/sl.asp
Security Guard/Armored Car Guard
      www2.dca.ca.gov:8001/wllpub/plsql/wllqryna$lce.startup?p_qte_code=G&p_qte_pgm_code=2420
Sheet Metal   www.cslb.ca.gov/license+request.html
Smog Check Station/Technician
      www2.dca.ca.gov:8001/wllpub/plsql/wllqryna$lce.startup?p_qte_code=SMS&p_qte_pgm_code=1310
Solar Energy   www.cslb.ca.gov/license+request.html
Specialty Contractor-Class C   www.cslb.ca.gov/license+request.html
Steel, Reinforcing & Structural   www.cslb.ca.gov/license+request.html
Physician - Supervising   www.docboard.org/ca/df/casearch.htm
Surveyor   www.dca.ca.gov/pels/l_lookup.htm
Swimming Pool   www.cslb.ca.gov/license+request.html
Termite Control   www.dca.ca.gov/pestboard/lookup.htm
Thrift and Loan Company   www.sbd.ca.gov/directry/tl.asp
Tile - Ceramic & Mosaic   www.cslb.ca.gov/license+request.html
Trust Company   www.sbd.ca.gov/directry/trust.asp
Warm-air Heating, Ventilating & AC   www.cslb.ca.gov/license+request.html
Water Well Driller   www.cslb.ca.gov/license+request.html

County Level...Courts, Recorders & Assessors

Administrative Office of Courts, 455 Golden Gate Ave, San Francisco, CA, 94102; 415-865-4200;
www.courtinfo.ca.gov

Editor's Note: There is no statewide online computer access available, internal or external. However, a
                      number of counties have developed their own online access sytems and provide Internet
                      access at no fee. The web site contains useful information about the state court system.

Alameda
Civil Cases
www.co.alameda.ca.us/courts/index.shtml
Online access to calendars, limited civil case summaries and complex litigations are available free from the Register of

Actions/Domain Web at the web site. Search limited cases by number; litigations by case name or number.

Assessor

www.co.alameda.ca.us

Access to the Property Value and Tax Information database is available free online at www.co.alameda.ca.us/aswpinq.

Amador

Recordings, Fictitious Names, Birth, Death, Marriage

Online access to the county clerk database is available free at www.criis.com/amador/official.htm.

Butte

Real Estate, Fictitious Names, Marriage, Birth, Death, Recording

www.buttecounty.net

Online access to the County Recorder's database of official documents is free at http://clerk-recorder.buttecounty.net/election/index.html. Records go back to 1988.

Contra Costa

Civil Cases, Criminal, Probate Records

www.co.contra-costa.ca.us

There is a free remote dial-up system for civil, probate and county law records. Call 925-646-2479 for details.

Recordings, Fictitious Business Names, Marriage, Death, Birth

www.co.contra-costa.ca.us/depart/elect/Rindex.html

Recorder Office records back to 1996 is available free at www.criis.com/contracosta/srecord_current.shtml. County Birth records are at www.criis.com/contracosta/sbirth.htm. County Death records are at www.criis.com/contracosta/sdeath.htm. Fictitious Business names are at www.criis.com/contracosta/sfictitious.htm. Marriage records are at www.criis.com/contracosta/smarriage.htm.

El Dorado

Real Estate, Personal Property, Vital Statistics, Fictitious Names

www.co.el-dorado.ca.us/countyclerk

Online access to the Recorder's index is available free on the Internet at http://main.co.el-dorado.ca.us/CGI/WWB012/WWM501/R. Records go back to 1949. Official records on the County Recorder database are available free on the Internet at http://main.co.el-dorado.ca.us/CGI/WWB012/WWM501/C. Search by date range and name or document number. County vital statistics - births, deaths, non-confidential marriages, and fictitious names - are available free on the Internet at http://main.co.el-dorado.ca.us/CGI/WWB012/WWM500/C.

Fresno

Assessor, Birth, Death, Marriage, Fictitious Names

www.fresno.ca.gov/0420/recorders_web/index.htm

Recording office records on the county recorder database are available free at http://assessor.fresno.ca.gov/fresno/srecord.shtml. County Birth Records are at http://assessor.fresno.ca.gov/fresno/sbirth.htm. County death records are at http://assessor.fresno.ca.gov/fresno/sdeath.htm. Marriage records are at http://assessor.fresno.ca.gov/fresno/smarriage.htm. Search fictitious names at http://assessor.fresno.ca.gov/fresno/sfictitious.htm.

Inyo

Recordings, Fictitious Names, Birth, Death, Marriage

Online access to the county clerk database is available free online at www.criis.com/inyo/official.htm.

Kern

Assessor

www.co.kern.ca.us/recorder

Records on the County of Kern Online Assessor database are available free online at www.co.kern.ca.us/assessor/search.htm. Birth, Death, Marriage records may be purchased through vitalchek at www.vitalchek.com.

Lassen

Real Estate, Recordings

http://clerk.lassencounty.org

Online access to the county recorder database is available free at http://icris.lassencounty.org. Registration is required. Recorded documents go back to 7/1985. Vital statistics back to 7/12/1999.

Los Angeles
Civil Cases, Criminal Records
www.lasuperiorcourt.org
Online access is available at www.lasuperiorcourt.org/CivilRegister. Court location, case number, and last name are all required to search. Available for civil, small claims, and unlawful detainer records.

Assessor, Fictitious Business Names
The PDB Inquiry System is a dial-up service with a $100.00 monthly fee plus $1.00 per inquiry, also a $75 sign-up fee for 3-year dial-up. Usage fee is $6.50 per hour or 11 cents per minute. Contract must be approved. Send registration request letter, stating reason for request, to: Data Systems Supervisor II Tech Admin, LA County Assessor's, 500 W Temple St Rm 293, LA, CA 90012-2770. Further info: 213-974-3237 or visit http://assessor.co.la.ca.us/html/online.htm. Also, property and assessor information (no name searching) is available free online at http://assessor.co.la.ca.us/html/pais.cfm. Search the map or by address. Search for county Fictitious Names free online at http://regrec.co.la.ca.us/fbn/FBN.cfm.

Modoc
Recordings, Fictitious Names, Birth, Death, Marriage
Online access to the county clerk database is available free at www.criis.com/modoc/official.htm.

Monterey
Criminal Records
www.co.monterey.ca.us/court
Online access to calendars and current cases is available free online at www.co.monterey.ca.us/court/calendar.asp.

Nevada
Recording, Fictious Names, Birth, Death, Marriage
http://recorder.co.nevada.ca.us/
Online access to the county clerk database is available free at www.criis.com/nevada/official.htm.

Orange
Grantor/Grantee
Orange County Grantor/Grantee records are available free online at http://cr.ocgov.com/grantorgrantee/index.asp.

Placer
Recordings, Fictitious Names, Birth, Death, Marriage
www.placer.ca.gov/clerk/clerk.htm
Recorder office records are available free at the web site. County Birth records are at www.criis.com/placer/sbirth.htm. County Death records are at www.criis.com/placer/sdeath.htm. County Marriage records are at www.criis.com/placer/smarriage.htm. County Fictitious Business Names are at www.criis.com/placer/sfictitious.htm.

Riverside
Civil Cases, Criminal Records, Probate
www.co.riverside.ca.us/depts/courts
The Automated Case Management System is the pay system for Riverside County Superior Courts; there is a one-time fee of $225 for Internet access. Records date back to 1984 and include civil, criminal, family law, probate & traffic case information for all Riverside and Indio Courts. For further information, call 909-955-5945.

Assessor, Property Records
https://riverside.ca.ezgov.com/ezproperty
Property tax information from the County Treasurer database is available free from www.EZproperty.com on the Internet at https://riverside.ca.ezgov.com/ezproperty/review_search.jsp.

Sacramento
Civil Cases, Criminal Records
www.saccourt.com
All civil records for Sacramento County are available free on the Internet at www.saccourt.com. All criminal records for Sacramento County are available free on the Internet at www.saccourt.com.

Recordings, Fictitious Names, Birth, Death, Marriage
www.saccounty.net/index.html

Online access to the county clerk database is available free at www.criis.com/sacramento/official.htm.

San Bernardino
Recorder, Assessor, Fictitious Names
www.co.san-bernardino.ca.us
Records on the County Assessor database are available free on the Internet at www.co.san-bernardino.ca.us/tax/trsearch.asp. For automated call distribution, call 909-387-8306; for fictitious names information, call 909-386-8970. Fictitious business names are also available online at www.co.san-bernardino.ca.us/ACR/RecSearch.htm.

San Diego
Assessor, Fictitious Names
www.co.san-diego.ca.us
Records on the County Assessor/Recorder/County Clerk Online Services site are available free online at www.co.san-diego.ca.us/cnty/cntydepts/general/assessor/online.html including fictitious business names, indexes, maps, property information. Grantee/grantor index search by name for individual record data is free at http://arcc.co.san-diego.ca.us/services/grantorgrantee. Bulk data downloads are also available but require pre-payment or

San Francisco
Property Tax, Recordings, Fictitious Names, Birth, Death, Marriage
Online access to the City Property Tax database is available free at https://cityservices.sfgov.org/serv/ttx_pt. No name searching; and address or Block/lot # is required. Also, online access recording, birth, death, marriage and fictitious name records on the county clerk database is available free at www.criis.com/sanfrancisco/official.htm.

San Mateo
Property Tax, Fictitious Name
www.care.co.sanmateo.ca.us
Records on the county Property Taxes database are available free online at www.co.sanmateo.ca.us/taxcollector/online/index.htm. Search by address, city or parcel ID#. Also, records on the Fictitious Business Name Center are available free online at www.care.co.sanmateo.ca.us/frames/our_office/ceo_d.htm.

Santa Barbara
Assessor
www.sb-democracy.com
Online access to assessor online property info system (OPIS) is available free at the web site with parcel #. Records go back 10 years. Database is free to view but only subscribers will be able to download. Full access requires registration. Contact Larry Herrera for an account. herrera@co.santa-barbara.ca.us.

Shasta
Assessor
www.ci.redding.ca.us
Records on the City of Redding Parcel Search By Parcel Number Server are available free online. At the main site, look under "Online Services" to find "Property Lookup."

Solano
Civil Cases, Criminal Records
www.solanocourts.com
Online access to civil records is available free at the web site; click on "Court Connect."
Property Tax
www.solanocounty.com
Online access to the Treasurer/Tax Collector/county Clerk property database is available free at www.solanocounty.com/treasurer/propquery.asp.

Stanislaus
Recordings, Fictitious Names, Birth, Death, Marriage
http://criis.com/stanislaus/official.htm
Recorder office records are available free at www.criis.com/stanislaus/srecord_current.shtml. County Birth records are at www.criis.com/stanislaus/sbirth.htm. Death records are at www.criis.com/stanislaus/sdeath.htm. Marriage records are at

www.criis.com/stanislaus/smarriage.htm. County Fictitious Business Name records are at www.criis.com/stanislaus/sfictitious.htm.

Trinity
Vital Statistics, Fictitious Names
www.trinitycounty.org/index.html
Online access to the Recorder's vital statistics database is available free at http://halfile.trinitycounty.org. For user name, enter "vital"; leave password field empty.

Ventura
Civil Cases, Criminal Records
http://courts.countyofventura.org
Access to civil court records 10/93 to present is available free online at http://courts.countyofventura.org/case_inquir.htm. Search by defendant or plaintiff name, case number, or date. Access to criminal court records is available free online at http://courts.countyofventura.org/criminalindex.htm. There are two indices to search: Music (older cases) or Vision (newer). Search by name & DOB, or code and citation number.
Recordings, Fictitious Names, Births, Deaths, Marriage
www.ventura.org/assessor/index.html
Online access to the county clerks database is available free at www.criis.com/ventura/official.htm.

Yolo
Assessor, Birth, Death, Marriage, Fictitious Business Names
www.yolocounty.org/org/Recorder
Online access to recordings on the county clerk database is available free at www.criis.com/yolo/srecord_current.shtml. County Birth records are at www.criis.com/yolo/sbirth.htm. County Death records are at www.criis.com/yolo/sdeath.htm. Marriage records are at www.criis.com/yolo/smarriage.htm. County Fictitious Business Name records are at www.criis.com/yolo/sfictitious.htm.

Federal Courts in California...

US District Court - Central District of California

Home Page: www.cacd.uscourts.gov
PACER: Sign-up number is 800-676-6856. Access fee is $.60 per minute. Toll-free access: 800-263-9358. Local access: 213-894-3625. Case records are available back to 1993. New records are available online after 2 days.
PACER Internet Access: http://pacer.cacd.uscourts.gov.
Opinions Online: Court opinions are available online at www.cacd.uscourts.gov.
Los Angeles (Western) Division Counties: Los Angeles, San Luis Obispo, Santa Barbara, Ventura.
Riverside (Eastern) Division Counties: Riverside, San Bernardino.
Santa Ana (Southern) Division Counties: Orange.

US Bankruptcy Court - Central District of California

Home Page: www.cacb.uscourts.gov
PACER: Sign-up number is 800-676-6856. Access fee is $.60 per minute. Toll-free access: 800-257-3887. Local access: 213-894-6199. Use of PC Anywhere v4.0 suggested. Case records are available back to 1992. Records are purged once a year. New civil records are available online after 1 day.
PACER Internet Access: You can access PACER via the Internet, using webPACER. For info and software visit www.cacb.uscourts.gov.
Los Angeles Division Counties: Los Angeles. Certain Los Angeles ZIP Codes are assigned to a new location, San Fernando Valley Division, as of early 1995.
Riverside Division Counties: Riverside, San Bernardino.
Santa Ana Division Counties: Orange.
Santa Barbara (Northern) Division Counties: San Luis Obispo, Santa Barbara, Ventura. Certain Ventura ZIP Codes are assigned to the new office in San Fernando Valley.

US District Court - Eastern District of California

Home Page: www.caed.uscourts.gov
PACER: Sign-up number is 800-676-6856. Access fee is $.60 per minute. Toll-free access: 800-530-7682. Local access: 916-498-6567. Case records are available back to 1990 (some earlier). Records are purged at varying intervals. New records are available online after 1 day.
PACER Internet Access: http://pacer.caed.uscourts.gov.
Opinions Online: Court opinions are available online at www.caed.uscourts.gov.
Fresno Division Counties: Fresno, Inyo, Kern, Kings, Madera, Mariposa, Merced, Stanislaus, Tulare, Tuolumne.
Sacramento Division Counties: Alpine, Amador, Butte, Calaveras, Colusa, El Dorado, Glenn, Lassen, Modoc, Mono, Nevada, Placer, Plumas, Sacramento, San Joaquin, Shasta, Sierra, Siskiyou, Solano, Sutter, Tehama, Trinity, Yolo, Yuba.

US Bankruptcy Court - Eastern District of California

Home Page: www.caeb.uscourts.gov
PACER: Sign-up number is 800-676-6856. Access fee is $.60 per minute. Toll-free access: 800-990-8897. Local access: 916-498-5530. Case records are available back to August 1990. Records are purged every six months. New civil records are available online after 1 day.
PACER Internet Access: http://pacer.caeb.uscourts.gov/pacerhome.html.
Fresno Division Counties: Fresno, Inyo, Kern, Kings, Madera, Mariposa, Merced, Tulare. Three Kern ZIP Codes, 93243 and 93523-24, are handled by San Fernando Valley in the Central District.
Modesto Division Counties: Calaveras, San Joaquin, Stanislaus, Tuolumne. The following ZIP Codes in San Joaquin County are handled by the Sacramento Division: 95220, 95227, 95234, 95237, 95240-95242, 95253, 95258, and 95686.Mariposa and Merced counties were transferred to the Fresno Division as of January 1, 1995.
Sacramento Division Counties: Alpine, Amador, Butte, Colusa, El Dorado, Glenn, Lassen, Modoc, Mono, Nevada, Placer, Plumas, Sacramento, Shasta, Sierra, Siskiyou, Solano, Sutter, Tehama, Trinity, Yolo, Yuba. This court also handles the following ZIP Codes in San Joaquin County:95220, 95227, 95234, 95237, 95240-95242, 95253, 95258 and 95686.

US District Court - Northern District of California

Home Page: www.cand.uscourts.gov
PACER: Sign-up number is 800-676-6856. Access fee is $.60 per minute. Toll-free access: 888-877-5883. Local access: 415-522-2144. Case records are available back to 1984. Records are purged every six months. New records are available online after 1 day.
PACER Internet Access: http://pacer.cand.uscourts.gov.
San Jose Division Counties: Alameda, Contra Costa, Del Norte, Humboldt, Lake, Marin, Mendocino, Monterey, Napa, San Benito, San Francisco, San Mateo, Santa Clara, Santa Cruz, Sonoma.

US Bankruptcy Court - Northern District of California

Home Page: www.canb.uscourts.gov
PACER: Sign-up number is 800-676-6856. Access fee is $.60 per minute. Toll-free access: 888-773-8548. Local access: 415-705-3148, 415-433-0211. Case records are available back to 1993. Records are purged every six months to one year. New civil records are available online after 1 day.
PACER Internet Access: You can access PACER via the Internet, using webPACER. For info and software visit www.cacb.uscourts.gov.
Oakland Division Counties: Alameda, Contra Costa.
San Francisco Division Counties: San Francisco, San Mateo.
San Jose Division Counties: Monterey, San Benito, Santa Clara, Santa Cruz.
Santa Rosa Division Counties: Del Norte, Humboldt, Lake, Marin, Mendocino, Napa, Sonoma.

US District Court - Southern District of California

Home Page: www.casd.uscourts.gov
PACER: Sign-up number is 800-676-6856. Access fee is $.60 per minute. Toll-free access: 888-241-9760. Local access: 619-557-7138. Case records are available back to 1990. New records are available online after 1 day.
PACER Internet Access: http://pacer.casd.uscourts.gov.
Other Online Access: There is also a computer bulletin board accessible at 619-557-6779.
San Diego Division Counties: Imperial, San Diego. Court also handles some cases from Yuma County, AZ.

US Bankruptcy Court - Southern District of California

Home Page: www.casb.uscourts.gov
PACER: Sign-up number is 800-676-6856. Access fee is $.60 per minute. Toll-free access: 800-870-9972. Local access: 619-557-6875. Case records are available back to 1989. Records are purged every six months. New civil records are available online after 3 days.
PACER Internet Access: http://pacer.casb.uscourts.gov.
Electronic Filing: Only law firms and practitioners may file documents electronically. Anyone can search online; however, searches only include those cases which have been filed electronically. Use http://ecf.casb.uscourts.gov/cgi-bin/PublicCaseFiled-Rpt.pl to search. Electronic filing information is available online at http://ecf.casb.uscourts.gov.
San Diego Division Counties: Imperial, San Diego.

Editor's Choice for California

Academic Performance Database
www.openrecords.org/records/schools/california/index.html
Ballot Propositions (1911+) Database
http://holmes.uchastings.edu/cgi-bin/starfinder/0?path=calprop.txt&id=webber&pass=webber&
Ballot Propositions Database
http://holmes.uchastings.edu/Welcome.html
Business Bonds Database
www.ss.ca.gov/business/sf/bond_search.htm
Campaign Finances Database
http://prodclmtrans.ss.ca.gov/claims
Citations Database
https://www.epay-it.com/ePay-it/CitationSearch.asp
Constitution Search Form
www.leginfo.ca.gov/const.html
Death Row Inmates Listing
www.cdc.state.ca.us/issues/capital/capital9.htm
Inmates Database
http://pajis.lasd.org/ajis_search.cfm
Inmates Database
www.co.san-diego.ca.us/cnty/cntydepts/safety/sheriff/whosin.html
Missing Persons Database
http://justice.hdcdojnet.state.ca.us/missingpersons/html
Mortality Information Database
www.ehdp.com/vn/cau1-eg1/index.htm
Sheriff's Warrants Database
www.co.san-diego.ca.us/cnty/cntydepts/safety/sheriff/csb/warrantdata.html
State Law Search Form
www.leginfo.ca.gov/calaw.html
Supreme Court & Appellate Courts Listing
www.courtinfo.ca.gov/opinions
Traffic Incident Information Database
http://cad.chp.ca.gov
Vanity Plates Database
http://plates.ca.gov/search/l

Capital: Denver
Denver County

Time Zone: MST

Number of Counties: 63

Home Page www.state.co.us

Attorney General www.ago.state.co.us

Archives www.archives.state.co.us

State Level...Major Agencies

Criminal Records

Bureau of Investigation, State Repository, Identification Unit, 690 Kipling St, Suite 3000, Denver, CO 80215; 303-239-4208, 303-239-0865 (Fax), 8AM-4:30PM.

Online: There is a remote access system available called the Electronic Clearance System (ECS). This is an overnight batch system, open M-F from 7AM to 4PM. The fee is $5.50 per record. There is no set-up fee, but requesters must register. Billing is monthly. For more information, call (303) 239-4230.

Corporation Records, Trademarks/Servicemarks, Fictitious Name, Limited Liability Company Records, Assumed Name

Secretary of State, Business Division, 1560 Broadway, Suite 200, Denver, CO 80202; 303-894-2251 (Corporations), 900-555-1717 (Status-Name), 303-894-2242 (Fax), 7:30AM-5PM.

www.sos.state.co.us

Online: The Sec. of State's Business Record Search page offers free searching of corporate names and associate information at www.sos.state.co.us/pubs/business/main.htm.

Uniform Commercial Code, Federal Tax Liens, State Tax Liens

Secretary of State, UCC Division, 1560 Broadway, #200, Denver, CO 80202; 303-894-2200, 303-894-2242 (Fax), 7:30AM-5PM.

ww.sos.state.co.us

Online: There is an in-depth commercial direct dial-up service with 3 price levels. Typically, the fee is $15.00 for each UCC keyword search or $2,500.00 per 6 months of unlimited access. Search by reception # is free. Go to www.cocis.com. There is no fee to search notice of farm product liens, the sales tax by address locator, or trade names. The commercial system has filings from the state and the counties and lien records from the DMV. Registrants may also file UCCs electronically for $5.00 each.

Marriage Certificates, Divorce Records

Department of Public Health & Environment, Vital Records Section, 4300 Cherry Creek Dr S, Denver, CO 80246-1530; 303-756-4464 (Recorded Message), 303-692-2224 (Credit Card Ordering), 303-692-2234, 800-423-1108 (Fax), 8:30AM-4:30PM.

www.cdphe.state.co.us/hs/certs.asp

Online: Marriages from 1975-to present can be searched at no charge on the web at www.quickinfo.net/madi/comadi.html. Only index information (names and date) is available. You may order a certified verification for $15.00 at www.cdphe.state.co.us/hs/certs.asp. Index information only. We advise customers to order record from county where license was purchased.

Legislation Records

Colorado General Assembly, State Capitol, 200 E Colfax Ave, Denver, CO 80203-1776; 303-866-2316 (Senate), 303-866-3055 (Bill Data (if in session)), 303-866-2390 (Archives), 303-866-2904 (House), 8AM-5PM.

www.state.co.us/gov_dir/stateleg.html

Online: The web site gives access to bills, status, journals from the last two sessions, and much more.

State Level...Occupational Licensing

Acupuncturist	www.dora.state.co.us/pls/real/ARMS_Search.Set_Up
Architect/Architect Firms	www.dora.state.co.us/pls/real/ARMS_Search.Set_Up
Audiologist	www.dora.state.co.us/pls/real/ARMS_Search.Set_Up
Barber	www.dora.state.co.us/pls/real/ARMS_Search.Disclaimer_Page
Chiropractor	www.dora.state.co.us/pls/real/ARMS_Search.Set_Up
Cosmetician/ Cosmetologist	www.dora.state.co.us/pls/real/ARMS_Search.Disclaimer_Page
Credit Union	www.dora.state.co.us/Financial-Services/homeregu.html#credit
Dental Hygienist	www.dora.state.co.us/pls/real/ARMS_Search.Disclaimer_Page
Dentist	www.dora.state.co.us/pls/real/ARMS_Search.Disclaimer_Page
Electrical Contractor	www.dora.state.co.us/pls/real/ARMS_Search.Disclaimer_Page
Electrician Journeyman/Master	www.dora.state.co.us/pls/real/ARMS_Search.Disclaimer_Page
Engineer	www.dora.state.co.us/pls/real/ARMS_Search.Disclaimer_Page
Engineer-in-Training (Engineer Intern)	www.dora.state.co.us/pls/real/ARMS_Search.Disclaimer_Page
Family Therapist	www.dora.state.co.us/pls/real/ARMS_Search.Disclaimer_Page
Hearing Aid Dealer	www.dora.state.co.us/pls/real/ARMS_Search.Set_Up
Land Surveyor	www.dora.state.co.us/pls/real/ARMS_Search.Disclaimer_Page
Land Surveyor Intern	www.dora.state.co.us/pls/real/ARMS_Search.Disclaimer_Page
Lobbyist	www.sos.state.co.us/pubs/bingo_raffles/new2001lobbyist_dir.htm
Manicurist	www.dora.state.co.us/pls/real/ARMS_Search.Disclaimer_Page
Manufactured Housing Dealer	www.dola.state.co.us/doh/dealers.htm
Marriage Therapist	www.dora.state.co.us/pls/real/ARMS_Search.Disclaimer_Page
Medical Doctor	www.dora.state.co.us/pls/real/ARMS_Search.Disclaimer_Page
Midwife	www.dora.state.co.us/pls/real/ARMS_Search.Disclaimer_Page
Nurse	www.dora.state.co.us/pls/real/ARMS_Search.Disclaimer_Page
Nurses' Aide	www.dora.state.co.us/pls/real/ARMS_Search.Disclaimer_Page
Nursing Care Facility	www.hfd.cdphe.state.co.us/info.asp
Nursing Home Administrator	www.dora.state.co.us/pls/real/ARMS_Search.Disclaimer_Page
Optometrist	www.dora.state.co.us/pls/real/ARMS_Search.Disclaimer_Page
Outfitter	www.dora.state.co.us/pls/real/ARMS_Search.Disclaimer_Page
Pharmacist/Pharmacy/Intern	www.dora.state.co.us/pls/real/ARMS_Search.Disclaimer_Page
Physical Therapist	www.dora.state.co.us/pls/real/ARMS_Search.Disclaimer_Page
Physician Assistant	www.dora.state.co.us/pls/real/ARMS_Search.Disclaimer_Page
Plumber Journeyman/Master/Residential	www.dora.state.co.us/pls/real/ARMS_Search.Disclaimer_Page
Podiatrist	www.dora.state.co.us/pls/real/ARMS_Search.Disclaimer_Page
Professional Counselor	www.dora.state.co.us/pls/real/ARMS_Search.Disclaimer_Page
Psychologist	www.dora.state.co.us/pls/real/ARMS_Search.Disclaimer_Page
Public Accountant-CPA	www.dora.state.co.us/pls/real/ARMS_Search.Disclaimer_Page
Real Estate Appraiser	www.dora.state.co.us/pls/real/re_estate_home

Real Estate Broker/Salesperson........................... www.dora.state.co.us/pls/real/re_estate_home
River Outfitter .... www.dora.state.co.us/pls/real/ARMS_Search.Disclaimer_Page
Savings & Loan Association.............................. www.dora.state.co.us/Financial-Services/homeregu.html#savings
Securities Broker .... http://pdpi.nasdr.com/pdpi/disclaimer_frame.htm
Securities Dealer... http://pdpi.nasdr.com/pdpi/disclaimer_frame.htm
Social Worker .... www.dora.state.co.us/pls/real/ARMS_Search.Disclaimer_Page
Stock Broker .... http://pdpi.nasdr.com/pdpi/disclaimer_frame.htm
Veterinarian... www.dora.state.co.us/pls/real/ARMS_Search.Disclaimer_Page
Veterinary Student .... www.dora.state.co.us/pls/real/ARMS_Search.Disclaimer_Page

County Level...Courts, Recorders & Assessors

State Court Administrator, 1301 Pennsylvania St, Suite 300, Denver, CO, 80203; 303-861-1111; www.courts.state.co.us

Editor's Note: State court records - all district courts and all county courts except Denver County Court - are available on the Internet at www.cocourts.com as of 11/2000. Real-time records include civil, civil water, small claims, domestic, felony, misdemeanor, and traffic cases and can be accessed by name or case number. Court records go as far back as 1995. There is a fee for this subscription Internet access, generally $5.00 per search and there are discounts for volume users. Contact Jeff Mueller, Major Accounts, by telephone at 866-COCOURT, or by e-mail at Jeffm@cocourts.com. Note: Denver County Court civil records are available free online.

Adams
Assessor
Records from the Adams County Assessor database are available free online at www.co.adams.co.us/AssessorSearch/asrsearch.htm.

Arapahoe
Assessor
www.co.arapahoe.co.us
Records on the Arapahoe County Assessor database are available free online at www.co.arapahoe.co.us/as/ResForm.htm.

Boulder
Assessor
www.co.boulder.co.us/departments/Default.htm
Online access to the assessor's property database is available free at www.co.boulder.co.us/assessor/disclaimer.htm. Also, the county treasurer has data available electronically and on microfiche; Alpha index by owner name is $25.00 per set.

Denver
Civil Cases
www.courts.state.co.us/district/02nd/dcadmn02.htm
Online searching of the Denver County Civil Division court cases is available at www.denvergov.org/civilcourts.asp. Search by name, business name, or case number.
Assessor
www.denvergov.org
Records on the Denver City and Denver County Assessor database are available free online at www.denvergov.org/realproperty.asp.

Douglas
Assessor, Property
www.douglas.co.us/assessor
Records on the county assessor database are available free on the Internet at the web site.

Eagle

Assessor

www.eagle-county.com/frames/gov.htm

Records on the County Assessor Database are available free online at www.eagle-county.com/frames/tax.htm.

El Paso

Assessor

www.co.el-paso.co.us

Records on the county Assessor database are available free online at www.co.el-paso.co.us/assessor/asr_location/srch.htm.

Jefferson

Assessor

http://buffy.co.jefferson.co.us

Records on the county Assessor database are available free online at http://buffy.co.jefferson.co.us/cgi-bin/mis/ats/assr.

La Plata

Assessor

www.laplatainfo.com

Records on the county Assessor database are available free online at www.laplatainfo.com/search2.html.

Larimer

Property Tax, Assessor, Treasurer, Voter Records

www.larimer.co.us/assessor/query/search.cfm

Assessor records on the Larimer County Property Records database are available free at the web site. Search for County Treasurer Property Tax Records at www.co.larimer.co.us/depts/treasu/query/search.cfm. Search the County Clerk Recorder records for years 1971 to 1989 at www.co.larimer.co.us/depts/clerkr/query/arch_search.htm. Search the County Clerk Recorder records for years 1990 to present at www.co.larimer.co.us/depts/clerkr/query/search.htm. Search for County Voter records at www.co.larimer.co.us/depts/clerkr/elections/voter_inquiry.cfm.

Logan

Assessor, Real Estate

www.loganco.gov/departments.htm

Online access to the Assessor's Property Search database is available free at www.loganco-assessor.org/search.asp?.

Mesa

Assessor, Real Estate, Property Tax

www.co.mesa.co.us

Records on the county Assessor database are available free online at http://205.169.141.11/Assessor/Database/ netsearch.html. Any search is by address or parcel #. Do parcel searches at http://mcweb.co.mesa.co.us/imd/gis/autoFrame.htm. There is also a GIS-mapping search page for property information at http://198.204.117.70/maps/index.htm. Also, an interactive Voice Response System lets callers access real property information at 970-256-1563. Fax back service is available. Also, search the Treasurer's Tax Status Information database at http://205.169.141.11/Treasurer/Database/NETSearch.HTML#Top.

Park

Assessor

www.parkco.org

Records on the county Assessor database are available free online at www.parkco.org/Search2.asp? including tax information, owner, address, building characteristics, legal and deed information.

Pitkin

Assessor

http://aimwebdomain.aspen.com

Records on the county Assessor database are available free online at http://aimwebdomain.aspen.com/db/pca/pcareg1.asp.

Pueblo
Assessor, Real Estate
www.co.pueblo.co.us/index2.htm
Online access to the county assessor database is available free at http://pueblocountyassessor.org/FrontPage.html.

Routt
Real Estate, Assessor, Treasurer
www.co.routt.co.us/clerk
Records on the county Assessor/Treasurer Property Search database are available free online at
http://pioneer.yampa.com/asp/assessor/search.asp?. Records on the Routt County Clerk and Recorder Reception Search database are available free online at http://pioneer.yampa.com/asp/clerk/search.asp?.

Weld
Real Estate
www.co.weld.co.us
Online access to property information on the map server database is available at the web site. Click on the "Property Information and mapping" button then search by name.

Federal Courts in Colorado...

US District Court - District of Colorado

Home Page: www.co.uscourts.gov
PACER: Sign-up number is 800-676-6856. Access fee is $.60 per minute. Toll-free access: 888-481-7027. Local access: 303-844-3454. Case records are available back to 1990. Records are purged on a varying schedule. New records are available online after 1 day.
PACER Internet Access: http://pacer.cod.uscourts.gov.
Denver Division Counties: All counties in Colorado.

US Bankruptcy Court - District of Colorado

Home Page: www.co.uscourts.gov
PACER: Sign-up number is 800-676-6856. Access fee is $.60 per minute. Toll-free access: 888-213-4715. Local access: 303-844-0263. Case records are available back to July 1981. New civil records are available online after 1 day.
PACER Internet Access: http://pacer.cob.uscourts.gov.
Denver Division Counties: All counties in Colorado.

Editor's Choice for Colorado

Here are some additional sites recommended for this state.

> **Bills Listing**
> www.state.co.us/gov_dir/stateleg.html
> **Birth Records (19th Century) Listing**
> www.co.clear-creek.co.us/Depts/Archives/archbirt.htm
> **Constitution Text**
> http://i2i.org/SuptDocs/ColoCon/iscolocn.htm
> **Lawyers Links**
> www.lawyernet.com/members.htm

Capital:	Hartford	Home Page	www.state.ct.us
	Hartford County		
Time Zone:	EST	Attorney General	www.cslib.org/attygenl
Number of Counties:	8	Archives	www.cslib.org

State Level...Major Agencies

Corporation Records, Limited Partnership Records, Trademarks/Servicemarks, Limited Liability Company Records

Secretary of State, Commercial Recording Division, 30 Trinity St, Hartford, CT 06106; 860-509-6001, 860-509-6068 (Fax), 8:30AM-4:30PM.

www.sots.state.ct.us

Online: Click on the CONCORD option at the web site for free access to corporation and UCC records. The system is open from 7AM to 11PM. You can search by business name only.

Uniform Commercial Code, Federal Tax Liens, State Tax Liens

UCC Division, Secretary of State, PO Box 150470, Hartford, CT 06115-0470 (Courier: 30 Trinity St, Hartford, CT 06106); 860-509-6004, 860-509-6068 (Fax), 8:30AM-4PM.

www.sots.state.ct.us

Online: Records may be accessed at no charge on the Internet. Click on the CONCORD option. The system is open 7AM to 11PM.

Driver Records

Department of Motor Vehicles, Copy Records Unit, 60 State St., Wethersfield, CT 06161-1896; 860-263-5154, 8:30AM-4:30PM T,W,F; 8:30AM-7:30PM TH; 8:30AM-12:30 S.

http://dmvct.org

Online: Online access is provided to approved businesses that enter into written contract. The contract requires a prepayment with minimum hits annually. Fee is $5.00 per record. The address is part of the record. For more information, call 203-263-5348.

Vehicle Ownership, Vehicle Identification

Department of Motor Vehicles, Copy Record Unit, 60 State St, Wethersfield, CT 06161-1896; 860-263-5154, 8:AM-4:30PM T,W,TH,F.

http://dmvct.org

Online: The Department has started a pilot program for online access that is not yet open to the general business public. This program, when available to all, will have the same restrictions and criteria as described in the Driving Records Section.

Legislation Records

Connecticut General Assembly, State Library, Bill Room at State Library, 231 Capitol Ave, Bill Room, Hartford, CT 06106; 860-757-6550, 860-757-6594 (Fax), 9AM-5PM.

www.cga.state.ct.us/default.asp

Online: From the web site you can track bills, find update or status, and print copies of bills. Also, you can request via e-mail at billroom@cslib.org.

State Level...Occupational Licensing

Acupuncturist	www.state.ct.us/dph/scripts/hlthprof.asp
Alcohol/Drug Counselor	www.state.ct.us/dph/scripts/hlthprof.asp
Asbestos Professional	www.state.ct.us/dph/scripts/hlthprof.asp
Audiologist	www.state.ct.us/dph/scripts/hlthprof.asp
Auto Adjuster/Appraiser	www.ct-clic.com/RsltKey.asp
Bail Bond Agent	www.ct-clic.com/RsltKey.asp
Bank	www.state.ct.us/dob/pages/banklist.htm
Bank Branch Office	www.state.ct.us/dob/pages/branch1.htm
Bank & Trust Company	www.state.ct.us/dob/pages/bcharter.htm
Barber	www.state.ct.us/dph/scripts/hlthprof.asp
Casualty Adjuster	www.ct-clic.com/RsltKey.asp
Check Cashing Service	www.state.ct.us/dob/pages/chckcash.htm
Chiropractor	www.state.ct.us/dph/scripts/hlthprof.asp
Collection Agency/ Consumer Coll. Agency	www.state.ct.us/dob/pages/collect.htm
Cosmetologist	www.state.ct.us/dph/scripts/hlthprof.asp
Credit Union	www.state.ct.us/dob/pages/culist.htm
Debt Adjuster	www.state.ct.us/dob/pages/debtadj.htm
Dental Anes/Consciou Sedation Permittee	www.state.ct.us/dph/scripts/hlthprof.asp
Dentist/Dental Hygienist	www.state.ct.us/dph/scripts/hlthprof.asp
Dietician/Nutritionist	www.state.ct.us/dph/scripts/hlthprof.asp
Electrologist/Hypertricologist	www.state.ct.us/dph/scripts/hlthprof.asp
Embalmer	www.state.ct.us/dph/scripts/hlthprof.asp
Emergency Medical Technician	www.state.ct.us/dph/scripts/hlthprof.asp
EMS Professional	www.state.ct.us/dph/scripts/hlthprof.asp
Fraternal Agent	www.ct-clic.com/RsltKey.asp
Funeral Director/Home	www.state.ct.us/dph/scripts/hlthprof.asp
Hairdresser	www.state.ct.us/dph/scripts/hlthprof.asp
Hearing Instrument Specialist	www.state.ct.us/dph/scripts/hlthprof.asp
Homeopathic Physician	www.state.ct.us/dph/scripts/hlthprof.asp
Hypertrichologist	www.state.ct.us/dph/scripts/hlthprof.asp

Insurance Adjuster/Appraiser .... www.ct-clic.com/RsltKey.asp
Insurance Agent/Broker/Producer .... www.ct-clic.com/RsltKey.asp
Insurance Company .... www.ct-clic.com/RsltKey.asp
Insurance Consultant .... www.ct-clic.com/RsltKey.asp
Insurance Producer .... www.ct-clic.com/RsltKey.asp
Lead Planner/Project Designer/Professional .... www.state.ct.us/dph/scripts/hlthprof.asp
Lobbyist .... www.lobbyist.net/Connecti/CONLOB.htm
LPN .... www.state.ct.us/dph/scripts/hlthprof.asp
Marriage & Family Therapist .... www.state.ct.us/dph/scripts/hlthprof.asp
Massage Therapist .... www.state.ct.us/dph/scripts/hlthprof.asp
Medical Doctor .... www.state.ct.us/dph/scripts/hlthprof.asp
Medical Response Technician .... www.state.ct.us/dph/scripts/hlthprof.asp
Midwife .... www.state.ct.us/dph/scripts/hlthprof.asp
Money Forwarder .... www.state.ct.us/dob/pages/$forward.htm
Mortgage Lender/Broker; First www.state.ct.us/dob/pages/1stmtg.htm
Mortgage Lender/Broker; Secondary www.state.ct.us/dob/pages/2ndmtg.htm
MVPD Appraiser .... www.ct-clic.com/RsltKey.asp
Naturopathic Physician .... www.state.ct.us/dph/scripts/hlthprof.asp
Nurse/Nurse-LPN .... www.state.ct.us/dph/scripts/hlthprof.asp
Nurse, Advance Registered Practice .... www.state.ct.us/dph/scripts/hlthprof.asp
Nursing Home Administrator .... www.state.ct.us/dph/scripts/hlthprof.asp
Occupational Therapist/Assistant .... www.state.ct.us/dph/scripts/hlthprof.asp
Optical Shop .... www.state.ct.us/dph/scripts/hlthprof.asp
Optician .... www.state.ct.us/dph/scripts/hlthprof.asp
Optometrist .... www.state.ct.us/dph/scripts/hlthprof.asp
Osteopathic Physician .... www.state.ct.us/dph/scripts/hlthprof.asp
Paramedic .... www.state.ct.us/dph/scripts/hlthprof.asp
Physical Therapist/Assistant .... www.state.ct.us/dph/scripts/hlthprof.asp
Physician Assistant .... www.state.ct.us/dph/scripts/hlthprof.asp
Podiatrist .... www.state.ct.us/dph/scripts/hlthprof.asp
Professional Counselor .... www.state.ct.us/dph/scripts/hlthprof.asp
Psychologist .... www.state.ct.us/dph/scripts/hlthprof.asp
Public Adjuster .... www.ct-clic.com/RsltKey.asp
Radiographer .... www.state.ct.us/dph/scripts/hlthprof.asp
Reinsurance Intermediary .... www.ct-clic.com/RsltKey.asp
Respiratory Care Practitioner .... www.state.ct.us/dph/scripts/hlthprof.asp
Sales Finance Company .... www.state.ct.us/dob/pages/salefinc.htm
Sanitarian .... www.state.ct.us/dph/scripts/hlthprof.asp
Savings & Loan Association Bank .... www.state.ct.us/dob/pages/bcharter.htm
Savings Bank .... www.state.ct.us/dob/pages/bcharter.htm
Small Loan Company .... www.state.ct.us/dob/pages/smalloan.htm
Social Worker .... www.state.ct.us/dph/scripts/hlthprof.asp
Speech Pathologist .... www.state.ct.us/dph/scripts/hlthprof.asp
Subsurface Sewage Cleaner/Installer .... www.state.ct.us/dph/scripts/hlthprof.asp
Surplus Line Broker .... www.ct-clic.com/RsltKey.asp
Veterinarian .... www.state.ct.us/dph/scripts/hlthprof.asp
Viatical Settlement Broker .... www.ct-clic.com/RsltKey.asp

County Level...Courts, Recorders & Assessors

Chief Court Administrator, 231 Capitol Av, Hartford, CT, 06106; 860-757-2100; www.jud.state.ct.us

Editor's Note: The Judicial Branch provides access to civil and family records via the Internet, located online at www.jud2.state.ct.us/Civil_Inquiry. It contains assignment lists and calendars. Also, questions about the fuller commercial system available through Judicial Information Systems should be directed to the CT JIS Office at 860-282-6500. There is currently no online access to criminal records; however, criminal and motor vehicle data is available for purchase in database format.

Canterbury Town in Windham County

Assessor

Property tax records on the Assessor's database are available online at http://data.visionappraisal.com/canterburyct. Registration is required for full access; registration is free.

Chester Town in Middlesex County

Assessor

Property records on the Assessor's Taxpayer Information System database are available free online at http://140.239.211.227/chesterct. Registration is required for full access; registration is free.

Enfield Town in Hartford County

Tax Sales

Online access to the town's tax sale list is available free at www.enfield.org/Link_Tax.HTM. Use Control+F and search for name.

Fairfield County

Civil Cases, Criminal Records

See state introduction for online access info. Free access to civil case records is available on the Internet at www.jud2.state.ct.us.

Glastonbury Town in Hartford County

Property

www.glasct.org
Online access to town property information is available free on the GIS Interactive Mapping site at www.glasct.org/isa/intermaps.html. Click on "Property Information (Parcels)."

Granby Town in Hartford County

Assessor

Property tax records on the Assessor's database are available online at http://140.239.211.227/granbyct. Registration is required for full access; registration is free.

Hamden Town in New Haven County

Assessor

Property records on the Assessor's database are available free online at http://data.visionappraisal.com/hamdenct. Registration is required for full access; registration is free.

Hartford County

Civil Cases, Criminal Records

Access to civil case records is available free on the Internet at www.jud2.state.ct.us.

Lebanon Town in New London County

Assessor

Property Tax records on the Assessor's Database are available free online at http://140.239.211.227/lebanonct. Registration is required for full access; registration is free.

Litchfield County
Civil Cases, Criminal Records
Access to civil case records is available free on the Internet at www.jud2.state.ct.us.

Madison Town in New Haven County
Assessor
http://140.239.211.227/MadisonCT
Property records on the Town assessor database are available free online at http://140.239.211.227/MadisonCT. Registration is required for full access; registration is free.

Manchester Town in Hartford County
Assessor
http://140.239.211.227/manchesterCT
Property records on the Town assessor database are available free online at http://140.239.211.227/manchesterCT. Registration is required for full access; registration is free.

Middlesex County
Civil Cases
www.jud.state.ct.us/directory/direcetory/location/middlesex.htm. Access to civil case records is available free on the Internet at www.jud2.state.ct.us.

Milford City in New Haven County
Assessor
Online access to the Assessor's database for Milford is available free online at http://data.visionappraisal.com/milfordct. User ID is required; registration is free.

New Haven County
Civil Cases, Criminal Records
Access to civil case records is available free on the Internet at www.jud2.state.ct.us.

New London City in New London County
Assessor
Property tax records on the Assessor's database are available free online at http://140.239.211.227/newlondonct. Registration is required for full access; registration is free.

New London County
Civil Cases, Criminal Records
In person access limited to five names. Access to civil case records is available free on the Internet at www.jud2.state.ct.us.

North Stonington Town in New London County
Assessor
Online access to the town assessor database is available free at http://data.visionappraisal.com/NorthStoningtonCT.

Norwich City in New London County
Assessor
Property tax records on the Assessor's database are available online at http://140.239.211.227/norwichct. Registration is required for full access; registration is free.

Old Lyme Town in New London County
Assessor
Property tax records on the Assessor's database are available online at http://140.239.211.227/oldlymect. Registration is required for full access; registration is free.

Old Saybrook Town in Middlesex County
Assessor
www.oldsaybrookct.com

Property tax records on the Assessor's database are available free online at http://oldsaybrookct. Registration is required for full access; registration is free.

Pomfret Town in Windham County
Assessor
Property records on the Assessor's database are available free online at http://data.visionappraisal.com/pomfretct. Registration is required for full access; registration is free.

Stamford City in Fairfield County
Assessor, Real Estate, Personal Property
www.cityofstamford.org/Welcome.htm
Online access to the city tax assessor database is available free online at www.cityofstamford.org/Tax/main.htm. A land records index should be online in Fall, 2001.

Suffield Town in Hartford County
Assessor
Property tax records on the Assessor's database are available free online at http://140.239.211.227/suffieldct. Registration is required for full access; registration is free.

Tolland County
Civil Cases
Access to civil case records is available free on the Internet at www.jud2.state.ct.us.

Westport Town in Fairfield County
Assessor
www.ci.westport.ct.us/govt/services
Online access to the 2000 assessments database is available free at www.ci.westport.ct.us/govt/services/finance/assessor/default.asp.

Wethersfield Town in Hartford County
Assessor
Property tax records on the Assessor's database are available free online at http://140.239.211.227/wethersfieldct. Registration is required for full access; registration is free.

Willington Town in Tolland County
Property Records
www.willingtonct.org
Records on the Town of Willington Property Records database are available free online at http://univers.akanda.com/ProcessSearch.asp?cmd=Willington.

Windham County
Civil Cases
Access to civil case records is available free on the Internet at www.jud2.state.ct.us.

Windsor Town in Hartford County
Assessor, Real Estate
www.townofwindsorct.com
Online access to the Town Clerk's Recording database is available free at www.townofwindsorct.com/records.htm. Records go back to 1991; plan is to go back to 1970. Also, records on the Assessor's Taxpayer Information System database are available free online at http://140.239.211.227/windsorct. Registration is required for full access; registration is free.

Woodbridge Town in New Haven County
Assessor
www.munic.state.ct.us/woodbridge/townclerk.html
Online access to the Assessor's database for Woodbridge is available free online at http://data.visionappraisal.com/woodbridgeCT. User ID is required; registration is free.

Federal Courts in Connecticut...

US District Court - District of Connecticut

Home Page: www.ctd.uscourts.gov
PACER: Sign-up number is 800-676-6856. Access fee is $.60 per minute. Toll-free access: 800-292-0658. Local access: 203-773-2451. Case records are available back to November 1, 1991. New records are available online after 1 day.
Bridgeport Division Counties: Fairfield (prior to 1993). Since January 1993, cases from any county may be assigned to any of the divisions in the district.
Hartford Division Counties: Hartford, Tolland, Windham (prior to 1993). Since 1993, cases from any county may be assigned to any of the divisions in the district.
New Haven Division Counties: Litchfield, Middlesex, New Haven, New London (prior to 1993). Since 1993, cases from any county may be assigned to any of the divisions in the district.

US Bankruptcy Court - District of Connecticut

Home Page: www.ctb.uscourts.gov
PACER: Sign-up number is 800-676-6856. Access fee is $.60 per minute. Case records are available back to 1979. Records are purged every 6 months. New civil records are available online after 1 day.
PACER Internet Access: http://pacer.ctb.uscourts.gov.
Bridgeport Division Counties: Fairfield.
Hartford Division Counties: Hartford, Litchfield, Middlesex, Tolland, Windham.
New Haven Division Counties: New Haven, New London.

Editor's Choice for Connecticut

Here are some additional sites recommended for this state.

> **Attorney General Opinions**
> www.cslib.org/attygenl
> **Sex Offenders Database**
> www.state.ct.us/dps/Sor.htm

Delaware

Capital: Dover
                   Kent County

Time Zone: EST

Number of Counties: 3

Home Page   www.state.de.us

Archives   www.archives.lib.de.us

Attorney General   www.state.de.us/attgen

State Level...Major Agencies

Birth, Death, & Marriage Certificates

Department of Health, Office of Vital Statistics, PO Box 637, Dover, DE 19903 (Courier: William Penn & Federal Sts, Jesse Cooper Bldg, Dover, DE 19901); 302-739-4721, 302-736-1862 (Fax), 8AM-4:30PM (Counter closes at 4:20 PM).

Online: Access available at www.vitalchek.com.

Driver Records

Division of Motor Vehicles, Driver Services, PO Box 698, Dover, DE 19903 (Courier: 303 Transportation Circle, Dover, DE 19901); 302-744-2506, 302-739-2602 (Fax), 8AM-4:30PM M-T-TH-F; 12:00PM-8PM W.

www.delaware.gov/yahoo/DMV

Online: Online searching is single inquiry only, no batch request mode is offered. Searching is done by driver's license number or name and DOB. A signed contract application and valid "business license" is required. Hours are 8 AM to 4:30 PM. Access is provided through a 900 number at a fee of $1.00 per minute, plus the $4.00 per record fee. For information, call 302-744-2606.

Vehicle Ownership, Vehicle Identification

Division of Motor Vehicles, Correspondence Section, PO Box 698, Dover, DE 19903 (Courier: 303 Transportation Circle, Dover, DE 19901); 302-744-2500, 302-739-2042 (Fax), 8:30AM-4:30PM M-T-TH-F; 12-8PM W.

Online: There is an additional $1.00 per minute fee for using the on-line "900 number" system. Records are $4.00 each. The system is single inquiry mode and open from 8 AM to 4:30 PM, except on Wed. from noon to 8PM. For information, call 302-744-2606.

Legislation Records

Legislative Hall, Division of Research, PO Box 1401, Dover, DE 19903; 302-744-4114, 302-739-5318 (Archives for old bills), 800-282-8545 (In-state), 8AM-4:30PM.

www.legis.state.de.us

Online: Access information at the Internet site, no fee.

State Level...Occupational Licensing

Optometrist www.arbo.org/nodb2000/licsearch.asp

County Level...Courts, Recorders & Assessors

Administrative Office of the Courts, PO Box 8911, Wilmington, DE, 19899; 302-577-2480; http://courts.state.de.us/supreme/index.htm

Editor's Notes: Only Supreme Court Final Orders and opinions are available at the web site.

An online system called CLAD, developed by Mead Data Central and the New Castle Superior Court, is currently available in Delaware. CLAD contains only toxic waste, asbestos, and class action cases; however, based on CLAD's success, Delaware may pursue development of online availability of other public records by working in conjunction with private information resource enterprises.

New Castle City
Real Estate
Records on the City of New Castle Geographic Information System database are available free on the Internet at www.2isystems.com/newcastle/Search2.CFM

Federal Courts in Delaware...

US District Court - District of Delaware

PACER: Sign-up number is 800-676-6856. Access fee is $.60 per minute. Toll-free access: 888-793-9488. Local access: 302-573-6651. Case records are available back to January 1991. Records are purged every few years (not since 1/91). New records are available online after 2 days.
PACER Internet Access: http://pacer.ded.uscourts.gov.
Opinions Online: Court opinions are available online at www.lawlib.widener.edu/pages/deopind.htm.
Wilmington Division Counties: All counties in Delaware.

US Bankruptcy Court - District of Delaware

Home Page: www.deb.uscourts.gov
PACER: Sign-up number is 800-676-6856. Access fee is $.60 per minute. Toll-free access: 800-249-9857. Local access: 302-573-6243. Use of PC Anywhere v4.0 suggested. Case records are available back to 1991. Records are purged every four years. New civil records are available online after 1 day.
Other Online Access: You can search case records using RACER at http://206.96.0.130/wconnect/WCI.DLL?usbcn_racer~main. Searching is currently free, but a fee may be charged in the future. You may need to sign up at the main web site prior to using RACER for the first time.
Wilmington Division Counties: All counties in Delaware.

Editor's Choice for Delaware

Here are some additional sites recommended for this state.

Constitution Text
www.state.de.us/facts/constit/de_const.htm
Inmates on Death Row Listing
www.state.de.us/correct/Data/Death_Row.htm
Sex Offenders Database
www.state.de.us/dsp/sexoff/search.htm

District of Columbia

Time Zone: EST   Home Page   <u>www.washingtondc.gov</u>

State Level...Major Agencies

Driver Records

Department of Motor Vehicles, Driver Records Division, 301 "C" St, NW, Washington, DC 20001; 202-727-6761, 202-727-5000 (General), 8:15AM-4PM M-T-TH-F; 8:15AM-7:00PM W.

<u>www.dmv.washingtondc.gov/main.htm</u>

Online: Requests are taken throughout the day and are available in batch the next morning after 8:15 am. There is no minimum order requirement. Fee is $5.00 per record. Billing is a "bank" system which draws from pre-paid account. Requesters are restricted to high volume, ongoing users. Each requester must be approved and sign a contract. For more information, call (202) 727-5692.

Legislation Records

Council of the District of Columbia, 441 4th Street, Rm 714, Washington, DC 20004; 202-724-8050, 202-347-3070 (Fax), 9AM-5:30PM. <u>www.dccouncil.washington.dc.us</u>

Online: Bill text and status may be reviewed at the Internet site.

State Level...Occupational Licensing

Lobbyist.. www.lobbyist.net/Federal/FEDLOB.htm
Optometrist... www.arbo.org/nodb2000/licsearch.asp

County Level...Courts, Recorders & Assessors

Executive Office, 500 Indiana Av NW, Rm 1500, Washington, DC, 20001; 202-879-1700; <u>www.dcsc.gov</u>

Editor's Note: The Court of Appeals maintains a bulletin board system for various court notices, and can be dialed from computer at 202-626-8863. Additionally, opinions from 1/1997 to 5/2001 are listed, also memorandum opinions and judgments from 9/199 to 5/2201. The Court of Appeals has their own web site at <u>www.dcca.state.state.dc.us</u>. The Superior Court at <u>www.dcsc.gov</u> lists Administrative Orders from 1/16/2201 to 5/25/2001.

Federal Courts in District of Columbia...

US Bankruptcy Court - District of Columbia

PACER: Sign-up number is 800-676-6856. Access fee is $.60 per minute. Toll-free access: 888-289-2414. Local access: 202-273-0630, 202-273-0642. Case records are available back to 1991. Records are purged every six months. New civil records are available online after 2 days.

Capital:	Tallahassee Leon County	Home Page		www.state.fl.us
Time Zone:	EST/CST	Attorney General		http://legal.firn.edu
# of Counties:	67	Archives		http://dlis.dos.state.fl.us/barm/fsa.html

State Level...Major Agencies

Criminal Records

Florida Department of Law Enforcement, User Services Bureau, PO Box 1489, Tallahassee, FL 32302 (Courier: 2331 Phillip Rd, Tallahassee, FL 32308); 850-410-8109, 850-410-8107, 8AM-5PM.

www.fdle.state.fl.us/index.asp

Online: Criminal history information from 1967 forward may be ordered over the Department Program Internet site at www.fdle.state.fl.us. Click on "Background Checks." A $15.00 fee applies. Juvenile records from 10/1994 forward are also available. Credit card ordering will return records to your screen or via e-mail.

Corporation Records, Limited Partnership Records, Limited Liability Company Records, Trademarks/Servicemarks, Fictitious Names

Division of Corporations, Department of State, PO Box 6327, Tallahassee, FL 32314 (Courier: 409 E Gaines St, Tallahassee, FL 32399); 850-488-9000 (Telephone Inquires), 850-487-6053 (Copy Requests), 850-487-6056 (Annual Reports), 8AM-5PM.

www.sunbiz.org

Online: The state's excellent Internet site gives detailed information on all corporate, trademark, limited liability company and limited partnerships (from 01/96): fictitious names (from 01/97); and UCC records (from 01/97).

Uniform Commercial Code, Federal Tax Liens

UCC Division, Sec. of State, PO Box 5588, Tallahassee, FL 32314 (Courier: 409 E Gaines St, Tallahassee, FL 32399); 850-487-6055, 850-487-6013 (Fax), 8AM-5PM.

www.sunbiz.org

Online: The state Internet site allows access for no charge. The state also has a document image delivery system on the web site. This includes all UCC filings since 01/97 and all documents that were filed electronically since 03/95.

Driver Records

Department of Highway Safety & Motor Vehicles, Division of Drivers Licenses, PO Box 5775, Tallahassee, FL 32314-5775 (Courier: 2900 Apalachee Pky, Rm B-133, Kirkman Bldg, Tallahassee, FL 32399); 850-488-0250, 850-487-7080 (Fax), 8AM-5PM.

www.hsmv.state.fl.us

Online: Online requests an on interactive basis. The state differentiates between high and low volume users. Requesters with 5,000 or more records per month are considered Network Providers. Call 850-488-6264 to become a Provider. Requesters with less than 5,000 requests per month (called Individual Users) are directed to a Provider. A list of providers is found at the web site.

Vehicle Ownership, Vehicle Identification

Division of Motor Vehicles, Information Research Section, Neil Kirkman Bldg, A-126, Tallahassee, FL 32399; 850-488-5665, 850-488-8983 (Fax), 8AM-4:30PM.

www.hsmv.state.fl.us

Online: Florida has contracted to release vehicle information through approved Network Providers. Accounts must be approved by the state first. For each record accessed, the charge is $.50 plus the subscriber fee. Users must work from an estimated 2 1/2 month pre-paid bank. New subscribers must complete an application with the Department 850-488-6264.

Legislation Records

Office of Legislative Services, Legislative Information Services Division, 111 W Madison St, Pepper Bldg, Rm 704, Tallahassee, FL 32399-1400; 850-488-4371, 850-487-5915 (Senate Bills), 850-488-7475 (House Bills), 850-488-8427 (Session Laws), 850-921-5334 (Fax), 8AM-5PM.

www.leg.state.fl.us

Online: Their Internet site contains full text of bills and a bill history session outlining actions taken on bills. The site is updated every day at 11 PM. Records go back to 1995. There is a more extensive online information service available. This system also includes information on lobbyists. Fees are involved.

State Level...Occupational Licensing

Acupuncturist	www.doh.state.fl.us/irm00praes/praslist.asp
Air Conditioning Contractor	www.state.fl.us/oraweb/owa/www_dbpr2.qry_lic_menu
Alcohol	www.state.fl.us/oraweb/owa/www_dbpr2.qry_lic_menu
Asbestos Remover/Contractor	www.state.fl.us/oraweb/owa/www_dbpr2.qry_lic_menu
Asbestos Surveyor Consultant	www.state.fl.us/oraweb/owa/www_dbpr2.qry_lic_menu
Assisted Living Facilities	www.floridahealthstat.com/qs/owa/facilitylocator.facllocator
Athletic Agent	www.state.fl.us/oraweb/owa/www_dbpr2.qry_lic_menu
Athletic Trainer	www.doh.state.fl.us/irm00praes/praslist.asp
Attorney	www.flabar.org/newflabar/findlawyer.html
Auction Company	www.state.fl.us/oraweb/owa/www_dbpr2.qry_lic_menu
Auctioneer	www.state.fl.us/oraweb/owa/www_dbpr2.qry_lic_menu
Barber/Barber Assistant/Barber Shop	www.state.fl.us/oraweb/owa/www_dbpr2.qry_lic_menu
Building Code Administrator	www.state.fl.us/oraweb/owa/www_dbpr2.qry_lic_menu
Building Contractor/Inspector	www.state.fl.us/oraweb/owa/www_dbpr2.qry_lic_menu
Certified Nursing Assistant	www.doh.state.fl.us/irm00praes/praslist.asp
Chiropractor	www.doh.state.fl.us/irm00praes/praslist.asp
Clinical Lab Personnel	www.doh.state.fl.us/irm00praes/praslist.asp
Community Association Manager	www.state.fl.us/oraweb/owa/www_dbpr2.qry_lic_menu
Construction Businees	www.state.fl.us/oraweb/owa/www_dbpr2.qry_lic_menu
Consulting Pharmacist	www.doh.state.fl.us/irm00praes/praslist.asp
Cosmetologist, Braiders, Nail Specialists, Salons	www.state.fl.us/oraweb/owa/www_dbpr2.qry_lic_menu
Crematory	www.state.fl.us/oraweb/owa/www_dbpr2.qry_lic_menu
Dentist/Dental Assistant	www.doh.state.fl.us/irm00praes/praslist.asp
Dietician/Nutritionist	www.doh.state.fl.us/irm00praes/praslist.asp
Electrical Contractor	www.state.fl.us/oraweb/owa/www_dbpr2.qry_lic_menu
Electrologist/Electrologist Facility	www.doh.state.fl.us/irm00praes/praslist.asp
Embalmer	www.state.fl.us/oraweb/owa/www_dbpr2.qry_lic_menu
Firearms Instructor	http://licgweb.dos.state.fl.us/access/individual.html
Funeral Director, Funeral Home	www.state.fl.us/oraweb/owa/www_dbpr2.qry_lic_menu
General Contractor	www.state.fl.us/oraweb/owa/www_dbpr2.qry_lic_menu

Geologist, Geology Business .... www.state.fl.us/oraweb/owa/www_dbpr2.qry_lic_menu
Health Facility .... www.floridahealthstat.com/qs/owa/facilitylocator.facllocator
Hearing Aid Specialist www.doh.state.fl.us/irm00praes/praslist.asp
Home Health Care Agency .... www.floridahealthstat.com/qs/owa/facilitylocator.facllocator
Hospitals.. www.floridahealthstat.com/qs/owa/facilitylocator.facllocator
Insurance Adjuster/Agent/Title Agent................ www.doi.state.fl.us/Consumers/Agents_companies/Agents/index.htm
Lab Licenses.. www.floridahealthstat.com/qs/owa/facilitylocator.facllocator
Limited License Doctor.................................... www.doh.state.fl.us/irm00praes/praslist.asp
Lobbyist/Principal
    . . . www.leg.state.fl.us/Info_Center/index.cfm?Tab=info_center&submenu=1#lobbyist
Lodging Establishment...................................... www.state.fl.us/oraweb/owa/www_dbpr2.qry_lic_menu
Marriage/Family Therapist................................ www.doh.state.fl.us/irm00praes/praslist.asp
Massage Therapist/School/Facility www.doh.state.fl.us/irm00praes/praslist.asp
Mechanical Contractor .... www.state.fl.us/oraweb/owa/www_dbpr2.qry_lic_menu
Medical Doctor... www.doh.state.fl.us/irm00praes/praslist.asp
Medical Faculty Certificate www.doh.state.fl.us/irm00praes/praslist.asp
Medical Physicist... www.doh.state.fl.us/irm00praes/praslist.asp
Mental Health Counselor www.doh.state.fl.us/irm00praes/praslist.asp
Midwife.. www.doh.state.fl.us/irm00praes/praslist.asp
Naturopath... www.doh.state.fl.us/irm00praes/praslist.asp
Nuclear Radiology Physicist............................. www.doh.state.fl.us/irm00praes/praslist.asp
Nurse... www.doh.state.fl.us/irm00praes/praslist.asp
Nursing Home Administrator www.doh.state.fl.us/irm00praes/praslist.asp
Nutrition Counselor www.doh.state.fl.us/irm00praes/praslist.asp
Occupational Therapist www.doh.state.fl.us/irm00praes/praslist.asp
Optician/Optician Apprentice............................ www.doh.state.fl.us/irm00praes/praslist.asp
Optometrist.. www.doh.state.fl.us/irm00praes/praslist.asp
Orthotist/Prosthetist... www.doh.state.fl.us/irm00praes/praslist.asp
Osteopathic Physician/Limited Osteo. Physician. www.doh.state.fl.us/irm00praes/praslist.asp
Pedorthist www.doh.state.fl.us/irm00praes/praslist.asp
Pesticide Applicator Commericial/Private/Public http://doacs.state.fl.us/~aes/pstcert.html
Pesticide Dealer... http://doacs.state.fl.us/~aes/pstcert.html
Pharmacist/Pharmacist Intern www.doh.state.fl.us/irm00praes/praslist.asp
Physical Therapist/Assistant.............................. www.doh.state.fl.us/irm00praes/praslist.asp
Physician Assistant www.doh.state.fl.us/irm00praes/praslist.asp
Plumbing Contractor .... www.state.fl.us/oraweb/owa/www_dbpr2.qry_lic_menu
Polygraph Examiner... www.floridapolygraph.org/members.html
Pool/Spa Contractor .... www.state.fl.us/oraweb/owa/www_dbpr2.qry_lic_menu
Practical Nurse... www.doh.state.fl.us/irm00praes/praslist.asp
Private Investigator/Agency.............................. http://licgweb.dos.state.fl.us/access/individual.html
Psychologist/Limited License Psychologist www.doh.state.fl.us/irm00praes/praslist.asp
Public Accountant-CPA..................................... www.state.fl.us/oraweb/owa/www_dbpr2.qry_lic_menu
Real Estate Appraiser.. www.state.fl.us/oraweb/owa/www_dbpr2.qry_lic_menu
Real Estate Broker/Salesperson......................... www.state.fl.us/oraweb/owa/www_dbpr2.qry_lic_menu
Recovery Agent School/Instructor/Manager .... http://licgweb.dos.state.fl.us/access/agency.html
Recovery Agent/Agency/Intern .... http://licgweb.dos.state.fl.us/access/agency.html
Respiratory Care Therapist/Provider................... www.doh.state.fl.us/irm00praes/praslist.asp
Roofing Contractor... www.state.fl.us/oraweb/owa/www_dbpr2.qry_lic_menu
School Psychologist.. www.doh.state.fl.us/irm00praes/praslist.asp

Security Officer School .... http://licgweb.dos.state.fl.us/access/agency.html
Security Officer/Instructor .... http://licgweb.dos.state.fl.us/access/individual.html
Social Worker/Clinical www.doh.state.fl.us/irm00praes/praslist.asp
Solar Energy Contractor .... www.state.fl.us/oraweb/owa/www_dbpr2.qry_lic_menu
Speech-Language Pathologist/Audiologist www.doh.state.fl.us/irm00praes/praslist.asp
Statewide Firearms License .... http://licgweb.dos.state.fl.us/access/individual.html
Surveyor, Mapping .... www.state.fl.us/oraweb/owa/www_dbpr2.qry_lic_menu
Talent Agency .... www.state.fl.us/oraweb/owa/www_dbpr2.qry_lic_menu
Therapeutic Radiologic Physician www.doh.state.fl.us/irm00praes/praslist.asp
Tobacco Wholesale .... www.state.fl.us/oraweb/owa/www_dbpr2.qry_lic_menu
Underground Utility Contractor .... www.state.fl.us/oraweb/owa/www_dbpr2.qry_lic_menu
Veterinarian, Veterinary Establishment .... www.state.fl.us/oraweb/owa/www_dbpr2.qry_lic_menu

County Level...Courts, Recorders & Assessors

Office of State Courts Administrator, Supreme Court Bldg, 500 S Duval, Tallahassee, FL, 32399-1900; 850-922-5082; www.flcourts.org

Editor's Note:　　There is a statewide, online computer system for internal use only; there is no external access available nor planned currently. However, a growing number of courts do offer online access to the public.

Alachua
Civil Cases, Criminal Records
http://circuit8.org
The Circuit's Civil open cases can be searched free at http://circuit8.org/case/index.html by division; password required Contact court for information. The Circuit's criminal open cases can be searched free on the web at http://circuit8.org/case/index.html by division; password required. Contact court for information.

Property Appraiser, Real Estate, Liens, Vital Records
www.clerk-alachua-fl.org/clerk/pubrec.html
Online access to the Clerk of Courts recording database is available free at the web site. Records go back to 1/93. Records can be searched by name or case number. Also, search the County Property Search page free online at www.propappr-alachua-fl.org/services/search/search.asp.

Baker
Criminal Records
http://circuit8.org
Access to the circuit-wide criminal quick lookup is available at http://circuit8.org/golem/gencrim.html. Account and password is required; restricted usage.

Bay
Property Appraiser
http://bcpa.co.bay.fl.us
Property information from the County Property Assessor database is available free online at http://bcpa.co.bay.fl.us/database.htm.

Bradford
Civil Cases, Criminal Records
www.bradford-co-fla.org
Access to court records from the County Clerk should be available some time in 2001 at the web site. At present, access to the circuit-wide criminal quick lookup is available at http://circuit8.org/golem/gencrim.html. Account and password is required; restricted usage.

Brevard
Criminal Records, Property Appraiser, Real Estate, Liens, Marriage, Recordings

www.clerk.co.brevard.fl.us
Online access to county criminal court records is available free through FACTSweb at www.clerk.co.brevard.fl.us/pages/facts1.htm.
Search by name, case number or citation number. Also, Online access to the Circuit Clerk's tax lien (1981-95), land records (1995 to
present) and marriage records is free at www.clerk.co.brevard.fl.us/pages/pubrec9.htm. Also, property records are available free at
http://appraiser.co.brevard.fl.us/asp/disclaimer.asp. Search by name or map.

Broward
Civil Cases, Criminal Records, Property Appraiser, Real Estate, Liens, Recordings
www.17th.flcourts.org or www.co.broward.fl.us/records1.htm
The county clerk online fee system is being replaced by a web system. The web allows basic information free. More "Detailed
information" requires a fee; call 954-831-5654 for information. Also, Limited court records on the County Records Division Public
Search database 1978-present are available free at http://205.166.161.20/CRSearch/crSearch.asp. Also, the Circuit Clerk's recording
database is available free at www.clerk-17th-flcourts.org/bccoc/disclaimer.asp. There are civil and criminal records. Also, Property
Appraiser records are available free online at www.bcpa.net/search.htm.

Charlotte
Criminal Records
http://co.charlotte.fl.us/clrkinfo/clerk_default.htm
Online access to criminal records is available by subscription; see the web site. Original payment is $186.00 ($150 refundable) plus a
usage fee based on number of transactions. Allows printing of copies. For more information, call 941-637-2199.
Property Appraiser, Real Estate, Liens, Recordings
www.co.charlotte.fl.us
Property records are available free online at www.ccappraiser.com/record.asp. Sales records are also available here and at the tax
collector database, which is free at www.cctaxcol.com/record.asp?. Also, recordings from the county clerk database are available free
online at http://208.47.160.70. Search by book/page. Search by book/page or grantor/grantee. A subscription service (CASWEB) is
also available, which includes images, court records, recordings, etc. Bulk database record purchases, by year, are also available.

Citrus
Civil Cases, Criminal Records, Property Appraiser, Real Estate, Liens, Recordings, Marriage
www.clerk.citrus.fl.us/
Online access to the Clerk of Circuit Court records is available free at www.clerk.citrus.fl.us/offrsearch.htf. Search Marriage License
records free online at www.clerk.citrus.fl.us/marrsearch.htf. Search by first and last name. Also, Property records are available free
online at www.pa.citrus.fl.us/ccpaask.html.

Clay
Civil Cases, Criminal Records, Appraiser, Real Estate, Liens, Recordings
http://clerk.co.clay.fl.us
The county clerk of circuit court allows free online access to recording records at http://clerk.co.clay.fl.us/new_search.htm. This
replaces the commercial system. Records go back to 1990. Also, the Clay County Property Appraiser's office records are available free
at www.ccpao.com/ccpao/ccpao.asp?page=Disclaimer. Search by name, street name and number, or real estate number. Also, search
real estate and personal property free on the tax collector database at http://claycountytax.com/Tax_Searchr.

Collier
Civil Cases, Criminal Records, Property Appraiser, Real Estate, Liens, Vital Records
www.clerk.collier.fl.us
Records on the Property Appraiser database are available free online at www.collierappraiser.com/Disclaimers.asp.
Access to the County Clerk's data requires registration - the online access system has a $100.00 setup fee, a monthly $10.00 fee and a
$.05 per minute access charge. Records include court records, recordings, probate, traffic and domestic. Searching is by name for both
felony and misdemeanor records. For information, contact Judy Stephenson at 941-774-8339. Lending agency information is
available.

Columbia
Civil Cases, Criminal Records, Real Estate, Liens, Recordings, Probate
www.columbiaclerk.com
Online access to the Clerk of Circuit Courts recording database is available free at
www.columbiaclerk.com/Public_Records/public_records.html. Search by name, book/page, file number of document type. There is
only limited online access to the Clerk's court records database; search by name, file number or document type.

Dade
Civil Cases, Criminal Records
http://jud11.flcourts.org or http://jud11.flcourts.org
Two sources exist. Subscription online access to criminal records requires a $125.00 setup fee, $52.00 monthly and $.25 per minute after the first 208 minutes each month. Docket information can be searched by case number or name. Call 305-596-8148 for more information. Also, online access to civil court records on the county clerk database is available free at www.metro-dade.com/clerk/Public-Records/disclaimer.asp.

Property Appraiser, Real Estate, Liens, Recordings, Marriage Records, Tax Records
www.metro-dade.com/clerk
Three options are available. Record access to 11 databases requires an initial setup fee is $125 and a minimum monthly fee of $52 for 208 minutes of use, $.25 ea. add'l minute. Records date back to 1975. Databases include property appraisal, building permits, tax collection, permit hearings, and others. Contact Jerry Kiernan at 305-596-8148 for information. Second, appraiser records are available free online at www.co.miami-dade.fl.us/pa/record.htm. Search by name, address, folio or map. Third, recorder records are available free online at www.metro-dade.com/clerk/public-records.

Duval
Criminal Records
www.coj.net/pub/clerk/default.htm
Online access requires a $100.00 setup fee, but no access charges. For more information, call Leslie Peterson at 904-630-1212 x5115. Also, court docket sheets are available free at the Clerk of Circuit Court website at www.coj.net/officialrecords.

Property Appraiser, Real Estate, Liens, Recordings
www.ci.jax.fl.us
Online access to the Clerk of Circuit Court and City of Jacksonville Official Records (a grantor/grantee index) is available free at www2.coj.net/officialrecords. Also, the County Property Appraiser offers free access to property records for the County and City of Jacksonville at http://pawww.coj.net/pub/property/lookup.htm. Also, records on County Property (Tax Collector) database are available free online at www2.coj.net/realestate. Also, limited property records on Jacksonville Public Data Depot database are available free online at www.ci.jax.fl.us/pub/depot.htm#prop.

Escambia
Criminal Records, Property Appraiser, Real Estate, Liens, Recordings, Marriage, Probate Records
www.clerk.co.escambia.fl.us
Online access to the Clerk of Court Public Records and criminal records database is available free at www.clerk.co.escambia.fl.us/public_records.html. This includes grantor/grantee index and marriage, traffic and court records. Also, online access to the tax collector's Property Tax Inquiry database is available free online at www.co.escambia.fl.us/ectc/taxiq.html. Also, search the property appraiser real estate records at www.clerk.co.escambia.fl.us/public_records.html.

Gadsden
Civil Cases, Criminal Records
www.clerk.co.gadsden.fl.us
Online access to county clerk records requires a written request sent to the Clerk of the Court. The subscription fee varies, dependent on the level of service. Records date back to 1985. For information, call 850-875-8629. Also, access to the official records index is available free at www.clerk.co.gadsden.fl.us/OfficialRecords. Index records go back to 1985.

Gilchrist
Civil Cases, Criminal Records
http://circuit8.org
Access to the circuit-wide criminal quick lookup is available at http://circuit8.org/golem/gencrim.html. Account and password is required; restricted usage.

Real Estate, Property Appraiser
www.co.gilchrist.fl.us/cophone
Online access to the property appraiser database is available free at www.ice-systems.net/~gilchrist/PublicPropertySearch.htm.

Hernando
Civil Cases, Criminal Records, Property Appraiser, Real Estate, Liens, Marriage Records
www.co.hernando.fl.us/ccc
Access to the remote online system requires $100 setup, $25 per month and $.10 per minute. Index and docket information is available

for felony and misdemeanor records. A fax back service is available for $1-$1.25 per page. Contact Bob Piercy for more information; call 352-754-4201. Lending agency information available. Also, the county now offers 2 levels of the Public Inquiry System Property Appraiser Real Estate database - Easy Search & Real Time Search - free online at www.co.hernando.fl.us/pa/propsearch.htm.

Highlands
Civil Cases, Criminal and Probate Records
http://jud10.flcourts.org
Online access to county clerk records is available free at www.clerk.co.highlands.fl.us/index_new.html. Also includes, small claims, probate, and tax deeds.

Property Appraiser, Real Estate, Liens, Recordings
www.clerk.co.highlands.fl.us
Property Appraiser records are available free online at www.appraiser.co.highlands.fl.us/search.html; Real Estate Property Records and Tangible Personal Property records are available. Online access to deeds, mortgages, judgments from the county recording database are available free at www.clerk.co.highlands.fl.us/owa_highlands/cgi-bin/instrument_search.form. Records go back to 1983. Also, online access to the county tax collector database is available free at www.collector.co.highlands.fl.us/search/index.html.

Hillsborough
Civil Cases, Criminal Records, Property Appraiser, Real Estate, Liens, Probate
www.hillsclerk.com
Property records are available free online at www.hcpafl.org/disclaimer.html. Select to receive owner information, also legal, sales, value summaries. The County also offers access to county court, real estate, and lien records through a fee online service. Court, Probate, traffic and domestic records included. Access is $.25 per minute or $5.00 per month, whichever is greater, plus a $50.00 one-time set-up fee with software. Contact the help desk at 813-276-8100 X 7000 for more information.

Indian River
Civil Cases, Criminal Records, Property Appraiser, Real Estate, Liens, Vital Records
http://indian-river.fl.us
Appraiser information is free, but only some of the recording information is. Appraiser records are available free online at http://indian-river.fl.us/realestate/search.html. Online access to recording indexes on the Clerk of the Circuit Court database is available free at http://bdc.co.indian-river.fl.us. Records go back to 1983. Full real estate, lien and court and vital records are available from the Clerk of the Circuit Court at the fee site, subscription is $200 per month. For information about free and fee access, call Gary at 561-567-8000 x216.

Jackson
Real Estate, Liens, Recording, Marriage, Death, Probate
www.jacksoncountyclerk.com
Online access to the Clerk of Circuit Court Official Records database is available free at www.jacksoncountyclerk.com/records.html. Images will go back to 5/1996.

Lake
Civil Cases, Criminal Records, Property Appraiser, Real Estate, Liens, Marriage, Recording
www.lakecountyclerk.org
Online access to Clerk of Court Records is available free at www.lakecountyclerk.org/services.asp?subject=Online_Court_Records. County civil records go back to 1985; Circuit records go back to 9/1984. The new county clerk official records database is available free online at www.lakecountyclerk.org/services.asp?subject=Online_Official_Records. Records go as far back as 1974. Includes court records. Also, records on the County Property Assessor database are available free online at www.lcpafl.org/agreement.asp. Also, marriage records back to 11/2000 are available at www.lakecountyclerk.org/departments.asp?subject=Marriage_Licenses.

Lee
Civil Cases, Criminal Records
www.leeclerk.org
The fee system has been replaced by free Internet access at the web site. Registration is required. Online records go back to 1988. Call 941-335-2975 for more information. Includes traffic, felony, misdemeanor, civil, small claims and probate.

Property Appraiser, Real Estate, Occupational Licenses
www.leetc.com
Online access to the appraiser database is available free at www.property-appraiser.lee.fl.us, or the tax roll database at www.leetc.com/Taxes/default.asp. Also, access to the county "license" database is available at www.leetc.com/OccupationalLicense/default.asp.

Leon
Civil Cases, Criminal and Probate Records
www.co.leon.fl.us/court/court.htm
Remote online access system, CHIPS, costs $50 for setup with an annual fee of $120. System includes civil and traffic indexes as of 12/99 as well as property appraiser, tax assessor, probate and domestic data. Call Terry Turner at 941-741-4003 for more information. Also, you may search "High Profile Cases" (re: Election 2000) at www.clerk.leon.fl.us under "Official Records Search."

Property Appraiser, Real Estate, Liens, Marriage Records
www.clerk.leon.fl.us
Real Estate, lien, and marriage records from the County Clerk are available free online at www.clerk.leon.fl.us. Lending agency information is also available. Also, Property Appraiser database records are available at www.co.leon.fl.us/propappr.prop.htm.

Levy
Civil Cases, Criminal Records, Real Estate, Liens, Recordings
http://circuit8.org or www.levyclerk.com
Online access to the Clerk of Circuit Court recording records is available free at www.levyclerk.com/Public_Records/Public_Records.html. Access to the circuit-wide criminal quick lookup is available at http://circuit8.org/golem/gencrim.html. Account and password is required; restricted usage.

Manatee
Civil Cases, Criminal Records
www.clerkofcourts.com
Civil records - dockets and indexes - from the clerk's office are available free on the Internet at the web site. Documents available as of Summer, 2001. Criminal records are on the Clerk of Circuit Courts' database, see below.

Appraiser, Real Estate, Liens, Probate, Vital Records
www.co.manatee.fl.us
Several options exist. Real estate and recordings are available free from the Clerk of Circuit Court and Comptroller's database at www.clerkofcourts.com/PubRec/RecordedDocs/ormain.htm. Also, Property Appraiser records are available free online at www.manateepao.com. On the third county online system, real estate and vital records are available at no fee to view, but you are limited to 2 hours access. Lending agency information is available. Call Martha Pope at 941-741-4051 for information.

Marion
Civil Cases, Property Appraiser, Real Estate, Liens, Marriage Records
www.marioncountyclerk.org
Online access to county clerk civil records is available free online at www.marioncountyclerk.org/Courts/factsweb.htm. Search by name or case number. The site's time default field must be used. Also, records on the County Clerk of Court Recordings database are available free online at www.marioncountyclerk.org. Also, records on the Marion County Property Appraiser database are available online free at www.propappr.marion.fl.us.

Martin
Civil Cases, Criminal Records, Property Appraiser, Real Estate, Liens, Recordings
www.martin.fl.us/GOVT/co/clerk
Several options exist. The county dial-up online system provides civil records from 1987 as well as probate, criminal, domestic and traffic records. The docket is listed. There is a setup fee and minimal charges. Call Cindy Johnson at 318-965-2336 for more information. Also, online access to the clerk of the circuit court recordings database is available free online at http://clerk-web.martin.fl.us/wb_or1. Includes small claims, recordings, and other document types. Also, records on the county property appraiser database are available free online at http://paoweb.martin.fl.us/L1.php3?Page=searches. The county tax collector data files are available free online at www.martin.fl.us/GOVT/co/tax/search.

Okaloosa
Civil Cases, Criminal Records, Property Appraiser, Real Estate, Liens, Recordings, Vital Records
www.clerkofcourts.cc
Several databases are available. Access to the full online system requires a monthly fee of $100.00. Searching is by name or case number, No addresses listed. Records also include probate, traffic and domestic records. Lending agency information is available. Both felony and misdemeanor indexes can be searched. For more information, contact Don Howard at 850-689-5821. Also, civil records are available free on the Internet at www.clerkofcourts.cc/civsearch/civilsearch.asp. Records go back to 1/86. Also, the county clerk is planning to place criminal records free on the Internet at www.clerkofcourts.cc/orsearch/contract.htm. Also, online access to land records is available free at www.clerkofcourts.cc/orsearch/orframe.asp. Access to marriage records is available free at

www.clerkofcourts.cc/marsearch/marriage.asp. Property Appraiser records are available free online at
http://propertyappraiser.co.okaloosa.fl.us/property_search.asp.

Orange
Civil Cases, Criminal Records, Property Appraiser, Real Estate, Liens, Marriage Records
http://orangeclerk.ocfl.net
The Teleclerk countywide remote online system requires a $100 one-time fee and $30 per month for unlimited online time. System also includes criminal, probate, traffic and domestic records. For more information, call 407-836-2060. Also, Real Estate, Lien, and Marriage records on the county Comptroller database are available free at www.occompt.com/records/or.htm. Lending Agency information is available. Also, property records on the Property Appraiser database are available free at www.ocpafl.org/docs/disclaimer.html. At this main site, click on "Record Searches." Also search Tangible Personal Property records and residential sales.

Osceola
Civil Cases
www.ninja9.net or www.osceolaclerk.com
Online access to court records on the Clerk of Circuit Court database is available free at www.osceolaclerkcourt.org/search.htm. Includes party index and case summary searching.
Real Estate, Property Appraiser
www.osceolaclerk.com
Online access to the county Clerk of Circuit Court database features court records only at this time; see www.osceolaclerkcourt.org. While property appraiser records are soon to be available free online at www.property-appraiser.com/records.htm, you may currently purchase property data from the county information system database. For information, call 407-343-3700. Data is delivered in 8mm data cartridges, CD-ROM, or 3.5" diskettes. Fees vary; tax roll data is available for $75.00. Also, land records may be available online at www.osceolaclerkrecording.org.

Palm Beach
Criminal Records
www.pbcountyclerk.com
Access to the countywide criminal online system requires $145 setup and $65 per month fees. Records also include probate, traffic and domestic. Contact Ms. Kokollari at 561-355-4277 for information. Also, online access to the 15th judicial circuit records is available at http://web3172.co.palm-beach.fl.us/aemasp/default.asp. Registration and password is required.
Property Appraiser, Real Estate, Liens, Recording, Marriage
www.co.palm-beach.fl.us
Online access to the clerk of circuit court recording database is available free at www.pbcountyclerk.com/official_records/disclaimer.html. Records go back to 1968; includes marriage records 1979 to present. Name search marriage records online at www.pbcountyclerk.com/servlets/MainServlet?fn=MS. Also, records on the county Property Appraiser database are available free online at www.co.palm-beach.fl.us/papa.

Pasco
Criminal Records
www.jud6.org
Access to the countywide criminal online system requires a $100 deposit, $50 annual fee and $10 monthly minimum. There is a $.10 per screen charge. The system is open 24 hours daily. Search by name or case number. Call 352-521-4201 for more information.
Property Appraiser, Real Estate, Liens, Marriage Records
http://pascogov.com
Several options are available. Access to real estate, liens, and marriage records requires $25 annual fee plus a $50 deposit. Billing rate is $.05 per minute, $.03 evenings. For information, call 352-521-4529. There is a fax back service. Lending agency information is available. Also, property records on the county Property Appraiser database are available free at http://appraiser.pascogov.com. Sales data and maps are also available. And, search tax records free at http://taxcollector.pascogov.com/search/prclsearch.asp.

Pinellas
Civil Cases, Criminal Records
www.jud6.org
Access to the countywide remote online system requires a $60 fee plus $.05 per screen. Indexes go back to 1972. Contact Sue Maskeny at 727-464-3779 for information. Includes probate and traffic records.
Property Appraiser, Real estate, Liens, Judgments

http://clerk.co.pinellas.fl.us/recsonl.htm
Assessor/property records are available free online at www.pao.co.pinellas.fl.us/search2.html. Also, the county clerk of circuit court's recordings are available free online at http://clerk.co.pinellas.fl.us/ori.htm.

Polk
Civil Cases, Criminal Records, Property Appraiser, Real Estate, Liens, Marriage Records
www.polk-county.net/clerk/clerk.html or http://jud10.flcourts.org
Several options are available. Online access to the complete database requires a $150 setup fee and $.15 per minute charge with a $50 minimum per quarter. Call 863-534-7575 for more information. Second, case index information back to 1990 is available free from the County Clerk's web site at www.polk-county.net/clerk/clerk.html. You may also search by name or document type for deeds, mortgages, plats, and resolutions. For copies of documents, call 863-534-4524. Fee is $1.00 per page. Also, property records from the County Property Appraiser database are available at www.polkpa.org.

Putnam
Civil Cases, Criminal Records, Real Estate, Liens, Tax Assessor
www.co.putnam.fl.us/clerkofcourt
Access to the countywide online system requires a $400 setup fee and $40 monthly charge plus $.05 per minute over 20 hours. Criminal records go back to 1972. System includes civil and real property records back to 10/1983. For info, call 904-329-0353.

Santa Rosa
Property Appraiser
www.srcpa.org
Property records are available free online. At the main Property Appraiser page, click on "Record Search."

Sarasota
Civil Cases, Criminal Records, Property Appraiser, Real Estate, Liens, Marriage
www.clerk.co.sarasota.fl.us
Civil case records from the Clerk of the Circuit Court database are available free online at www.clerk.co.sarasota.fl.us/civilapp/civilinq.asp. Probate court records are available at www.clerk.co.sarasota.fl.us/probapp/probinq.asp. Criminal cases are available at www.clerk.co.sarasota.fl.us/crimdisclaim.htm. Online access to the Clerk of Circuit Court recordings database is available at www.clerk.co.sarasota.fl.us/online.htm. Includes civil, criminal, and traffic court indexes. Marriage licenses may be searched free by groom/bride name, license number, and date of application or ceremony. Also, records on the Property Appraiser database are available free online at http://204.193.117.141/scpa_recs.htm.

Seminole
Civil Cases, Property Appraiser, Real Estate, Liens, Recordings
www.18thcircuit.state.fl.us or www.seminoleclerk.org
Property appraisal records are available free online at http://ntweb.scpafl.org:8080/owa/owa/seminole_county_selection?. Also, online access to the county clerk of circuit court's recordings and court records database is available free at www.seminoleclerk.org/officialrecords. Search by name, case number or document type.

St. Johns
Criminal Records
www.co.st-johns.fl.us
Access to the countywide criminal online system requires a $200 setup fee plus a monthly fee of $50. Searching is by name or case number. Call Mark Dearing at 904-823-2333 x361 for more information.
Property Appraiser, Real Estate, Liens, Recordings, Civil Cases, Probate
www.co.st-johns.fl.us
Online access to the county Clerk of Circuit Court recording database is available free at www.co.st-johns.fl.us/Const-Officers/Clerk-of-Court/doris/searchdocs.asp. Search by name, parcel ID, instrument type. Includes civil and probate records, UCCs. Also, Property Appraiser records on the Parcel Inquiry System are available free at www.co.st-johns.fl.us/Prop-App/parcel_search.html.

St. Lucie
Property Appraiser
www.stlucieco.gov
Property appraiser records are available free online at www.paslc.org. Click on the "real property database" or "interactive map."

Suwannee
Civil Cases, Criminal Records, Real Estate, Liens, Recordings, Property Tax
www.suwanneeclerkofcourt.com
Online access to County Clerk of Circuit Court records database is available free at www.suwanneeclerkofcourt.com/court/kiosk.html.
Also, search the tax collector database free at www.suwanneecountytax.com/collectmax/collect30.asp.

Union
Criminal Records
http://circuit8.org
Access to the circuit-wide criminal quick lookup is available at http://circuit8.org/golem/gencrim.html. Account and password is
required; restricted usage.

Volusia
Civil Cases, Criminal Records, Property Appraiser, Real Estate, Liens, Vital Records
http://www.clerk.org
Volusia County's Clerk of Circuit Court offers real estate, lien, civil, probate, traffic and vital records on its commercial site, and
criminal records back to 1988. The initial set up fee is $125, with a flat monthly fee of $25. For more information, call 904-822-5710.
Also, property records are available free online at www.clerk.org/publicrecords/or.tshtml. Records go back to 3/1996; will soon have
documents back to 1990.

Walton
Civil Cases, Criminal Records, Real Estate, Liens, Vital Records
www.co.walton.fl.us/clerk/
Records on the County Clerk database are available free online at www.co.walton.fl.us. The system includes probate, traffic, domestic
and criminal data. This has taken the place of the commercial system.

Federal Courts in Florida...

US District Court - Middle District of Florida
Home Page: www.flmd.uscourts.gov
PACER: Sign-up number is 800-676-6856. Access fee is $.60 per minute. Toll-free access: 888-815-8701. Local access: 813-301-
5820. Case records are available back to 1989-90. Records purged 3 years after case closed. New records available online after 1 day.
Fort Myers Division Counties: Charlotte, Collier, De Soto, Glades, Hendry, Lee.
Jacksonville Division Counties: Baker, Bradford, Clay, Columbia, Duval, Flagler, Hamilton, Nassau, Putnam, St. Johns, Suwannee, Union.
Ocala Division Counties: Citrus, Lake, Marion, Sumter.
Orlando Division Counties: Brevard, Orange, Osceola, Seminole, Volusia.
Tampa Division Counties: Hardee, Hernando, Hillsborough, Manatee, Pasco, Pinellas, Polk, Sarasota.

US Bankruptcy Court - Middle District of Florida
Home Page: www.flmb.uscourts.gov
PACER: Sign-up number is 800-676-6856. Access fee is $.60 per minute. Cases back to 1981. New records available after 1 week.
PACER Internet Access: www.flmb.uscourts.gov/cgi/foxweb.dll/usbc/webpacer.
Jacksonville Division Counties: Baker, Bradford, Citrus, Clay, Columbia, Duval, Flagler, Hamilton, Marion, Nassau, Putnam, St.
Johns, Sumter, Suwannee, Union, Volusia.
Orlando Division Counties: Brevard, Lake, Orange, Osceola, Seminole.
Tampa Division Counties: Charlotte, Collier, De Soto, Glades, Hardee, Hendry, Hernando, Hillsborough, Lee, Manatee, Pasco,
Pinellas, Polk, Sarasota.

US District Court - Northern District of Florida
Home Page: www.flnd.uscourts.gov
PACER: Sign-up number is 800-676-6856. Access fee is $.60 per minute. Toll-free access: 800-844-0479. Local access: 850-942-
8898. Case records are available back to 1992. Records are purged three years after case closed. New records available after 2 days.
Gainesville Division Counties: Alachua, Dixie, Gilchrist, Lafayette, Levy. Records for cases prior to July 1996 are maintained at the
Tallahassee Division.

Panama City Division Counties: Bay, Calhoun, Gulf, Holmes, Jackson, Washington.
Pensacola Division Counties: Escambia, Okaloosa, Santa Rosa, Walton.
Tallahassee Division Counties: Franklin, Gadsden, Jefferson, Leon, Liberty, Madison, Taylor, Wakulla.

US Bankruptcy Court - Northern District of Florida

PACER: Sign-up number is 904-435-8475. Access fee is $.60 per minute. Toll-free access: 888-765-1751. Local access: 904-444-0189. Case records are available back to September 1985. New civil records available online after 2 days.
Pensacola Division Counties: Escambia, Okaloosa, Santa Rosa, Walton.
Tallahassee Division Counties: Alachua, Bay, Calhoun, Dixie, Franklin, Gadsden, Gilchrist, Gulf, Holmes, Jackson, Jefferson, Lafayette, Leon, Levy, Liberty, Madison, Taylor, Wakulla, Washington.

US District Court - Southern District of Florida

Home Page: www.netside.net/usdcfls
PACER: Sign-up number is 800-676-6856. Access fee is $.60 per minute. Toll-free access: 800-372-8846. Local access: 305-536-7265. Case records are available back to August 1990. New records available online after 1 day.
PACER Internet Access: http://pacer.flsd.uscourts.gov.
Fort Lauderdale Division Counties: Broward.
Fort Pierce Division Counties: Highlands, Indian River, Martin, Okeechobee, St. Lucie.
Key West Division Counties: Monroe.
Miami Division Counties: Dade.
West Palm Beach Division Counties: Palm Beach.

US Bankruptcy Court - Southern District of Florida

Home Page: www.flsb.uscourts.gov
PACER: Sign-up number is 800-676-6856. Access fee is $.60 per minute. Toll-free access: 888-443-0081. Local access: 305-536-7492, 305-536-7493, 305-536-7494, 305-536-7495, 305-536-7496. Case records are available back to 1986. Records are purged every six months. New civil records are available online after 1 day.
PACER Internet Access: http://pacer.flsb.uscourts.gov.
Miami Division Counties: Broward, Dade, Highlands, Indian River, Martin, Monroe, Okeechobee, Palm Beach, St. Lucie. Cases may also be assigned to Fort Lauderdale or to West Palm Beach.

Editor's Choice for Florida

Alcohol, Beverage & Tobacco Delinquencies Database
http://fcn.state.fl.us/oraweb/owa/dbprabt2.Qry_ABT_Menu
Arrest Warrants (Active) Database
http://polksheriff.org/wanted/warrants.html
Arrests Database
www.hcso.tampa.fl.us/pub/default.asp?/Online/sname01
Delinquent Taxes Database
www2.coj.net/delinquent/
Inmate Escape Information Database
www.dc.state.fl.us/EscapedInmates/inmatesearch.asp
Inmate Release Information Database
www.dc.state.fl.us/InmateReleases/inmatesearch.asp
Inmates Database
www.dc.state.fl.us/ActiveInmates/inmatesearch.asp
Sex Offenders Database
www.fdle.state.fl.us/sexual_predators/
Supreme Court Opinions
www.law.ufl.edu/opinions/supreme/

Capital:	Atlanta
	Fulton County
Time Zone:	EST
Number of Counties:	159

Home Page   www.state.ga.us

Attorney General

www.ganet.org/ago

Archives   www.sos.state.ga.us/
archives

State Level...Major Agencies

Corporation Records, Limited Partnership Records, Limited Liability Company Records

Secretary of State, Corporation Division, 315 W Tower, #2 ML King Drive, Atlanta, GA 30334-1530; 404-656-2817, 404-651-9059 (Fax), 8AM-5PM.

www.sos.state.ga.us/corporations

Online: Records are available from the corporation database on the Internet site above or at www.ganet.org/services/corp/corpsearch.shtml. The corporate database can be searched by entity name or registered agent for no fee. Online multiple records are available for a fee determined by number of records retrieved. Major credit cards accepted. There's a $10.00 charge for a Certificate of Existence (Good Standing) or certified copy of Corporate Charter. Other services include name reservation, filing procedures, downloading of forms/applications.

Trademarks/Servicemarks

Secretary of State, Trademark Division, 2 Martin Luther King, Room 315, W Tower, Atlanta, GA 30334; 404-656-2861, 404-657-6380 (Fax), 8AM-5PM.

www.sos.state.ga.us/corporations/trademarks.htm

Online: A record database is searchable from the web site.

Uniform Commercial Code

Superior Court Clerks' Cooperative Authority, 1875 Century Blvd, #100, Atlanta, GA 30345; 404-327-9058, 404-327-7877 (Fax), 9AM-5PM.

www.gsccca.org

Online: Online access is available for regular, ongoing requesters. There is a monthly charge of $9.95 and a $.25 fee per image. Billing is monthly. The system is open 24 hours daily. The online service also includes real estate indexes and images. Minimum baud rate is 9600; 28.8 is supported. Information from 01/01/95 forward is available. Call 800-304-5175 or 404-327-9058 for a subscription package.

Legislation Records

General Assembly of Georgia, State Capitol, Atlanta, GA 30334; 404-656-5040 (Senate), 404-656-5015 (House), 404-656-2370 (Archives), 404-656-5043 (Fax), 8:30AM-4:30PM.

www.legis.state.ga.us/

Online: The Internet site listed above has bill information. Also, you can search at www.ganet.org/services/leg.

State Level...Occupational Licensing

Architect .... www.sos.state.ga.us/plb/architects/search.htm
Athletic Agent .... www.sos.state.ga.us/plb/agent/search.htm
Athletic Trainer .... www.sos.state.ga.us/plb/trainer/search.htm
Auctioneer/ Auction Dealer .... www.sos.state.ga.us/plb/auctioneer/search.htm
Bank .... www.ganet.org/dbf/other_institutions.html
Barber/ Barber Shop License .... www.sos.state.ga.us/plb/barber_cosmet/search.htm
Cardiac Technician .... www.medicalboard.state.ga.us/licensure_cert.html
Charity .... www.sos.state.ga.us/securities/charitysearch.htm
Check Casher/Seller .... www.ganet.org/dbf/other_institutions.html
Chiropractor .... www.sos.state.ga.us/plb/chiro/search.htm
Conditioned Air Contractor .... www.sos.state.ga.us/plb/construct/search.htm
Cosmetologist .... www.sos.state.ga.us/plb/barber_cosmet/search.htm
Counselor .... www.sos.state.ga.us/plb/counselors/search.htm
Credit Union .... www.ganet.org/dbf/other_institutions.html
Dental Hygienist .... www.sos.state.ga.us/plb/dentistry/search.htm
Dentist .... www.sos.state.ga.us/plb/dentistry/search.htm
Dietitian .... www.sos.state.ga.us/plb/dietitians/search.htm
EDP - Electronic Data Processors .... www.ganet.org/dbf/other_institutions.html
Electrical Contractor .... www.sos.state.ga.us/plb/construct/search.htm
Embalmer .... www.sos.state.ga.us/plb/funeral/search.htm
Engineer .... www.sos.state.ga.us/plb/pels/search.htm
Esthetician .... www.sos.state.ga.us/plb/barber_cosmet/search.htm
Family Therapist .... www.sos.state.ga.us/plb/counselors/search.htm
Forester .... www.sos.state.ga.us/plb/foresters/search.htm
Funeral Director/Apprentice/Establishment .... www.sos.state.ga.us/plb/funeral/search.htm
General Contractor .... www.sos.state.ga.us/plb/construct/search.htm
Geologist .... www.sos.state.ga.us/plb/geologists/search.htm
Hearing Aid Dealer/Dispenser .... www.sos.state.ga.us/plb/hearingaid/search.htm
Holding Company/Representative Offices .... www.ganet.org/dbf/other_institutions.html
Insurance Agent .... www.inscomm.state.ga.us/main.consumers.agentsearch.html
Interior Designer .... www.sos.state.ga.us/plb/architects/search.htm
Landscape Architect .... www.sos.state.ga.us/plb/landscape/search.htm
Low Voltage Contractor .... www.sos.state.ga.us/plb/construct/search.htm
Manicurist .... www.sos.state.ga.us/plb/barber_cosmet/search.htm
Marriage Counselor .... www.sos.state.ga.us/plb/counselors/search.htm
Medical Doctor .... www.medicalboard.state.ga.us/licensure_cert.html
Mortgage Institution .... www.ganet.org/dbf/mortgage.html
Nail Care .... www.sos.state.ga.us/plb/barber_cosmet/search.htm
Nuclear Pharmacist .... www.sos.state.ga.us/plb/pharmacy/search.htm

Nurse (Registered) .... www.sos.state.ga.us/plb/rn/search.htm
Nurse-LPN .... www.sos.state.ga.us/plb/lpn/search.htm
Nursing Home Administrator .... www.sos.state.ga.us/plb/nursinghome/search.htm
Occupational Therapist/Assistant .... www.sos.state.ga.us/plb/ot/search.htm
Optician, Dispensing .... www.sos.state.ga.us/plb/opticians/search.htm
Optometrist .... www.sos.state.ga.us/plb/optometry/search.htm
Osteopathic Physician .... www.medicalboard.state.ga.us/licensure_cert.html
Paramedic .... www.medicalboard.state.ga.us/licensure_cert.html
Pharmacist .... www.sos.state.ga.us/plb/pharmacy/search.htm
Pharmacy School, Clinic Researcher .... www.sos.state.ga.us/plb/pharmacy/search.htm
Physical Therapist/Assistant .... www.sos.state.ga.us/plb/pt/search.htm
Physician Assistant .... www.medicalboard.state.ga.us/licensure_cert.html
Plumber Journeyman .... www.sos.state.ga.us/plb/construct/search.htm
Plumbing Contractor .... www.sos.state.ga.us/plb/construct/search.htm
Podiatrist .... www.sos.state.ga.us/plb/podiatry/search.htm
Poison Pharmacist .... www.sos.state.ga.us/plb/pharmacy/search.htm
Private Detective .... www.sos.state.ga.us/plb/detective/search.htm
Psychologist .... www.sos.state.ga.us/plb/psych/search.htm
Public Accountant-CPA .... www.sos.state.ga.us/plb/acancy/search.htm
Respiratory Care Practitioner .... www.medicalboard.state.ga.us/licensure_cert.html
Retail, Hospital Wholesale Manufacturer .... www.sos.state.ga.us/plb/pharmacy/search.htm
School Librarian .... www.sos.state.ga.us/plb/librarians/search.htm
Security Guard .... www.sos.state.ga.us/plb/detective/search.htm
Social Worker .... www.sos.state.ga.us/plb/counselors/search.htm
Speech Pathologist/Audiologist .... www.sos.state.ga.us/plb/speech/search.htm
Surveyor .... www.sos.state.ga.us/plb/pels/search.htm
Used Car Dealer/ Parts Distributor .... www.sos.state.ga.us/plb/usedcar/search.htm
Utility Contractor .... www.sos.state.ga.us/plb/construct/search.htm
Veterinarian/Veterinary Technician/Facility .... www.sos.state.ga.us/plb/veterinary/search.htm
Waste Water Industrial/Lab Analyst .... www.sos.state.ga.us/plb/water/search.htm
Waste Water Sys. Operator/Operator Class 1-3 .. www.sos.state.ga.us/plb/water/search.htm
Waste Water Treatment/Dist.System Operator ... www.sos.state.ga.us/plb/water/search.htm
Water Operator Class 1-3 .... www.sos.state.ga.us/plb/water/search.htm

County Level...Courts, Recorders & Assessors

Court Administrator, 244 Washington St SW, Suite 550, Atlanta, GA, 30334; 404-656-5171; www.georgiacourts.org/aoc/index.html

Editor's Note: Cobb County has has Internet access to records, but there is no online access available statewide, although one is being planned.

The Georgia Superior Court Clerk's Cooperative Authority (GSCCCA) at http://www2.gsccca.org/search offers access on a subscription basis. The system includes a UCC Index with records back to 1/1995; Real Estate Deed Index back to 1/1999; Notary Public Index and Plat Index. Subscription is $9.95 per month, per user, for unlimited use, and $.25 for each page printed. You may submit UCC Certified Search requests on-line. The charge for certified searches is $10 per debtor name.

Clayton
Real Estate, UCC, Notary
www.co.clayton.ga.us/superior_court/clerk_of_courts

Online access to Real Estate, UCC, and Notary records is available free at www.co.clayton.ga.us/superior_court/clerk_of_courts. Also, see www2.gsccca.org for online access to Deed and UCC indexes.

Cobb
Civil Cases, Criminal Records, Real Estate, Grantor/Grantee
www.cobbgasupctclk.com

Property records on the County Superior Court Clerk web site are available free online at www.cobbgasupctclk.com/index.htm. Search by name, address, land description, instrument type, or book & page. You may also search court records. Data is updated every Friday. Also, see www2.gsccca.org for online access to Deed and UCC indexes.

Dougherty
Civil Cases, Criminal Records
www.dougherty.ga.us/dococlk.htm

Access to civil and criminal court docket data is available free at the web site. The same system permits access to probate, UCC, tax, deeds, and death certificate records.

Real Estate, Personal Property, Tax Records
www.albany.ga.us

Records on the Dougherty County and City of Albany Tax Department database are available free online at www.albany.ga.us/docotax.htm. Also, see www2.gsccca.org for online access to Deed and UCC indexes.

Fayette
Assessor, Real Estate
www.admin.co.fayette.ga.us

Records on the County Assessor database are available free online at www.admin.co.fayette.ga.us/property/propsearch.asp. Also, see www2.gsccca.org for online access to Deed and UCC indexes.

Gwinnett
Civil Cases, Criminal Records
www.gwinnettcourts.com/courts/Supcourt.htm

Online access to the court case party index is available free online at www.gwinnettcourts.com/misc/casendx.htm. Search by name or case number.

Property
Records on the County Property database are available free online at www.akanda.com/publicaccess/gwinprof.htm. Also, see www2.gsccca.org for online access to Deed and UCC indexes.

Houston
Assessor, Real Estate
www.houstoncountyga.com

Online access to the assessor's Mapguide database is available free at www.assessor.houstoncountyga.org. The Autodesk MapGuide viewer is available to download. Also see www2.gsccca.org for online access to Deed and UCC indexes.

Oglethorpe
UCC, Real Estate
www.gsccca.org

UCC and real estate records are available online from the Oglethorpe County Clerk for a monthly subscription fee of $9.95 plus $.25 per printed page. Guest accounts are available. For information and to open an account, call 404-327-9058. Also, see www2.gsccca.org for online access to Deed and UCC indexes.

Federal Courts in Georgia...

US District Court - Middle District of Georgia

Home Page: www.gamd.uscourts.gov
PACER: Sign-up number is 800-676-6856. Access fee is $.60 per minute. Toll-free access: 888-234-3839. Local access: 912-752-8170. Case records are available back to January 1991. Records are purged never. New records are available online after 1-2 days.
PACER Internet Access: http://pacer.gamd.uscourts.gov.
Albany/Americus Division Counties: Baker, Ben Hill, Calhoun, Crisp, Dougherty, Early, Lee, Miller, Mitchell, Schley, Sumter, Terrell, Turner, Webster, Worth. Ben Hill and Crisp were transfered from the Macon Division as of October 1, 1997.
Athens Division Counties: Clarke, Elbert, Franklin, Greene, Hart, Madison, Morgan, Oconee, Oglethorpe, Walton. Closed cases before April 1997 are located in the Macon Division.
Columbus Division Counties: Chattahoochee, Clay, Harris, Marion, Muscogee, Quitman, Randolph, Stewart, Talbot, Taylor.
Macon Division Counties: Baldwin, Ben Hill, Bibb, Bleckley, Butts, Crawford, Crisp, Dooly, Hancock, Houston, Jasper, Jones, Lamar, Macon, Monroe, Peach, Pulaski, Putnam, Twiggs, Upson, Washington, Wilcox, Wilkinson.Athens Division cases closed before April 1997 are also located here.
Thomasville Division Counties: Brooks, Colquitt, Decatur, Grady, Seminole, Thomas.
Valdosta Division Counties: Berrien, Clinch, Cook, Echols, Irwin, Lanier, Lowndes, Tift.

US Bankruptcy Court - Middle District of Georgia

Home Page: www.gamb.uscourts.gov
PACER: Sign-up number is 800-676-6856. Access fee is $.60 per minute. Toll-free access: 800-546-7343. Local access: 912-752-3551. Case records are available back to March 1990 (some back to 1985). Records are purged except last 12 months. New civil records are available online after 1 day.
PACER Internet Access: http://pacer.gamb.uscourts.gov.
Columbus Division Counties: Berrien, Brooks, Chattahoochee, Clay, Clinch, Colquitt, Cook, Decatur, Echols, Grady, Harris, Irwin, Lanier, Lowndes, Marion, Muscogee, Quitman, Randolph, Seminole, Stewart,Talbot, Taylor, Thomas, Tift.
Macon Division Counties: Baldwin, Baker, Ben Hill, Bibb, Bleckley, Butts, Calhoun, Clarke, Crawford, Crisp, Dooly, Dougherty, Early, Elbert, Franklin, Greene, Hancock, Hart, Houston, Jasper, Jones, Lamar, Lee, Macon, Madison, Miller, Mitchell, Monroe, Morgan, Oconee, Oglethorpe,Peach, Pulaski, Putnam, Schley, Sumter, Terrell, Turner, Twiggs, Upson, Walton, Washington, Webster, Wilcox, Wilkinson, Worth.

US District Court - Northern District of Georgia

Home Page: www.gand.uscourts.gov
PACER: Sign-up number is 800-676-6856. Access fee is $.60 per minute. Toll-free access: 800-801-6932. Local access: 404-730-9668. Case records are available back to August 1992. Records are purged on a varied schedule. New records are available online after 1 day.
PACER Internet Access: http://pacer.gand.uscourts.gov.
Atlanta Division Counties: Cherokee, Clayton, Cobb, De Kalb, Douglas, Fulton, Gwinnett, Henry, Newton, Rockdale.
Gainesville Division Counties: Banks, Barrow, Dawson, Fannin, Forsyth, Gilmer, Habersham, Hall, Jackson, Lumpkin, Pickens, Rabun, Stephens, Towns, Union, White.
Newnan Division Counties: Carroll, Coweta, Fayette, Haralson, Heard, Meriwether, Pike, Spalding, Troup.
Rome Division Counties: Bartow, Catoosa, Chattooga, Dade, Floyd, Gordon, Murray, Paulding, Polk, Walker, Whitfield.

US Bankruptcy Court - Northern District of Georgia

Home Page: www.ganb.uscourts.gov
PACER: Sign-up number is 800-676-6856. Access fee is $.60 per minute. Toll-free access: 800-436-8395. Local access: 404-730-3264. Case records are available back to August 1986. Records are purged never. New civil records are available online after 2 days.
Electronic Filing: Only law firms and practicioners may file documents electronically. Anyone can search online; however, searches only include those cases which have been filed electronically. Use http://ecf.ganb.uscourts.gov/cgi-bin/PublicCaseFiled-Rpt.pl to search. Electronic filing information is available online at http://ecf.ganb.uscourts.gov.
Atlanta Division Counties: Cherokee, Clayton, Cobb, DeKalb, Douglas, Fulton, Gwinnett, Henry, Newton, Rockdale.
Gainesville Division Counties: Banks, Barrow, Dawson, Fannin, Forsyth, Gilmer, Habersham, Hall, Jackson, Lumpkin, Pickens, Rabun, Stephens, Towns, Union, White.

Newnan Division Counties: Carroll, Coweta, Fayette, Haralson, Heard, Meriwether, Pike, Spalding, Troup.
Rome Division Counties: Bartow, Catoosa, Chattooga, Dade, Floyd, Gordon, Murray, Paulding, Polk, Walker, Whitfield.

US District Court - Southern District of Georgia

Home Page: www.gasd.uscourts.gov
PACER: Sign-up number is 800-676-6856. Access fee is $.60 per minute. Toll-free access: 800-801-6934. Local access: 912-650-4046. Case records are available back to June 1995. New records are available online after 1 day.
PACER Internet Access: http://pacer.gasd.uscourts.gov.
Augusta Division Counties: Burke, Columbia, Glascock, Jefferson, Lincoln, McDuffie, Richmond, Taliaferro, Warren, Wilkes.
Brunswick Division Counties: Appling, Camden, Glynn, Jeff Davis, Long, McIntosh, Wayne.
Dublin Division Counties: Dodge, Johnson, Laurens, Montgomery, Telfair, Treutlen, Wheeler.
Savannah Division Counties: Bryan, Chatham, Effingham, Liberty.
Statesboro Division Counties: Bulloch, Candler, Emanuel, Evans, Jenkins, Screven, Tattnall, Toombs.
Waycross Division Counties: Atkinson, Bacon, Brantley, Charlton, Coffee, Pierce, Ware.

US Bankruptcy Court - Southern District of Georgia

Home Page: www.gasb.uscourts.gov
PACER: Sign-up number is 800-676-6856. Access fee is $.60 per minute. Toll-free access: 800-259-8679. Local access: 706-722-9776. Use of PC Anywhere v4.0 suggested. Case records are available back to August 1986. Records are purged annually. New records are available online after.
PACER Internet Access: http://pacer.gasb.uscourts.gov.
Augusta Division Counties: Bulloch, Burke, Candler, Columbia, Dodge, Emanuel, Evans, Glascock, Jefferson, Jenkins, Johnson, Laurens, Lincoln, McDuffie, Montgomery, Richmond, Screven, Taliaferro, Tattnall, Telfair, Toombs, Treutlen, Warren, Wheeler, Wilkes.
Savannah Division Counties: Appling, Atkinson, Bacon, Brantley, Bryan, Camden, Charlton, Chatham, Coffee, Effingham, Glynn, Jeff Davis, Liberty, Long, McIntosh, Pierce, Ware, Wayne.

Editor's Choice for Georgia

Here are some additional sites recommended for this state.

Constitution Text
www.law.emory.edu/GEORGIA/gaconst.html
Inmates & Offenders Database
www.dcor.state.ga.us/OffenderQuery/asp/OffenderQueryForm.asp
Lobbyist Expenditures Database
www.accessatlanta.com/partners/ajc/reports/lobbyists/search.html
Sex Offenders Database
www.state.ga.us/gbi/disclaim.html
State Codes Search Form
http://gnsun1.ganet.state.ga.us/services/ocode/ocgsearch.htm

Capital:	Honolulu		Home Page	www.state.hi.us
Time Zone:	Honolulu County			
Time Zone:	HT		Attorney General	www.state.hi.us/ag
Number of Counties:	4		Archives	www.state.hi.us/dags/archives

State Level...Major Agencies

Criminal Records

Hawaii Criminal Justice Data Center, Liane Moriyama, Administrator, 465 S King St, Room 101, Honolulu, HI 96813; 808-587-3106, 8AM-4PM.

www.state.hi.us/hcjdc

The sexual offender registration list may be searched freely at http://www.ehawaiigov.org/HI_SOR/.

Corporation Records, Fictitious Name, Limited Partnership Records, Assumed Name, Trademarks/Servicemarks, Limited Liability Company Records, Limited Liability Partnerships

Business Registration Division, PO Box 40, Honolulu, HI 96810 (Courier: 1010 Richard St, 1st Floor, Honolulu, HI 96813); 808-586-2727, 808-586-2733 (Fax), 7:45AM-4:30PM.

www.businessregistrations.com

Online: Online access is available through the Internet or via modem dial-up at 808-587-4800. There are no fees, the system is open 24 hours. For assistance during business hours, call 808-586-1919. Also, business names searching is available free online at www.ehawaiigov.com. Tax license searching is available free at www.ehawaiigov.org/serv/taxpayer. Search by name, ID number of DBA name.

Legislation Records

Hawaii Legislature, 415 S Beretania St, Honolulu, HI 96813; 808-587-0700 (Bill # and Location), 808-586-6720 (Clerk's Office-Senate), 808-586-6400 (Clerk's Office-House), 808-586-0690 (State Library), 808-587-0720 (Fax), 7AM-6PM.

www.capitol.hawaii.gov

Online: To dial online for current year bill information line, call 808-296-4636. Or, access the information through the Internet site. There is no fee.

State Level...Occupational Licensing

Acupuncturist.. www.ehawaiigov.org/serv/pvl
Architect.. www.ehawaiigov.org/serv/pvl
Auction... www.ehawaiigov.org/serv/pvl
Barber Shop/Barber/Barber Apprentice............. www.ehawaiigov.org/serv/pvl
Beauty Operator.. www.ehawaiigov.org/serv/pvl
Cemetery... www.ehawaiigov.org/serv/pvl
Chiropractor.. www.ehawaiigov.org/serv/pvl
Collection Agency.. www.ehawaiigov.org/serv/pvl
Condominium Hotel Operator/Managing Agent.. www.ehawaiigov.org/serv/pvl
Contractor... www.ehawaiigov.org/serv/pvl
Dentist/Dental Hygienist................................. www.ehawaiigov.org/serv/pvl
Electrician .... www.ehawaiigov.org/serv/pvl
Electrologist.. www.ehawaiigov.org/serv/pvl
Elevator Mechanic .... www.ehawaiigov.org/serv/pvl
Emergency Medical Personnel.......................... www.ehawaiigov.org/serv/pvl
Employment Agency .... www.ehawaiigov.org/serv/pvl
Engineer .... www.ehawaiigov.org/serv/pvl
General Contractor.. www.ehawaiigov.org/serv/pvl
Guard Agency .... www.ehawaiigov.org/serv/pvl
Hearing Aid Dealer/Fitter .... www.ehawaiigov.org/serv/pvl
Insurance Adjuster .... www.ehawaiigov.org/serv/hils
Insurance Agent .... www.ehawaiigov.org/serv/hils
Insurance Solicitor .... www.ehawaiigov.org/serv/hils
Land Surveyor... www.ehawaiigov.org/serv/pvl
Landscape Architect.. www.ehawaiigov.org/serv/pvl
Lobbyist... www.state.hi.us/ethics/noindex/pubrec.htm
Marriage & Family Therapist............................ www.ehawaiigov.org/serv/pvl
Massage Establishment/Massage Therapist .... www.ehawaiigov.org/serv/pvl
Mechanic... www.ehawaiigov.org/serv/pvl
Medical Doctor .... www.ehawaiigov.org/serv/pvl
Mortgage Broker/Solicitor................................ www.ehawaiigov.org/serv/pvl
Motor Vehicle Broker/Dealer/Salesperson.......... www.ehawaiigov.org/serv/pvl
Motor Vehicle Repair Dealer .... www.ehawaiigov.org/serv/pvl
Naturopathic Physician..................................... www.ehawaiigov.org/serv/pvl
Nurse... www.ehawaiigov.org/serv/pvl
Nursing Home Administrator .... www.ehawaiigov.org/serv/pvl
Occupational Therapist .... www.ehawaiigov.org/serv/pvl
Optician, Dispensing... www.ehawaiigov.org/serv/pvl
Optometrist.. www.odfinder.org/LicSearch.asp
Osteopathic Physician .... www.ehawaiigov.org/serv/pvl
Pest Control Field Representative/Operator .... www.ehawaiigov.org/serv/pvl
Pharmacist/Pharmacy.. www.ehawaiigov.org/serv/pvl
Physical Therapist... www.ehawaiigov.org/serv/pvl
Physician Assistant .... www.ehawaiigov.org/serv/pvl
Plumber .... www.ehawaiigov.org/serv/pvl
Podiatrist .... www.ehawaiigov.org/serv/pvl

Port Pilot .... www.ehawaiigov.org/serv/pvl
Private Detective/Detective Agency................... www.ehawaiigov.org/serv/pvl
Psychologist.. www.ehawaiigov.org/serv/pvl
Public Accountant-CPA...................................... www.ehawaiigov.org/serv/pvl
Real Estate Broker/Salesperson......................... www.ehawaiigov.org/serv/pvl
Social Worker .... www.ehawaiigov.org/serv/pvl
Speech Pathologist/Audiologist .... www.ehawaiigov.org/serv/pvl
Time Share .... www.ehawaiigov.org/serv/pvl
Travel Agency... www.ehawaiigov.org/serv/pvl
Veterinarian.. www.ehawaiigov.org/serv/pvl

County Level...Courts, Recorders & Assessors

Administrative Director of Courts, Judicial Branch, 417 S King St, Honolulu, HI, 96813; 808-539-4900; www.state.hi.us/jud

Editor's Note: Online access to Circuit Court and family court records first became available free in mid-2000 at http://state.hi.us/jud. Search by name or case number.

Hawaii
Civil Cases, Criminal Records
www.state.hi.us/jud/trials1.htm
Online access to Circuit Court and family court records is available free at http://166.122.201.51/hod/judstart.htm. Search by name or case number. Records go back to 1984.

Honolulu
Civil Cases, Criminal Records
www.state.hi.us/jud/trials1.htm
Online access to Circuit Court & family court records is available free at http://166.122.201.51/hod/judstart.htm. Search by name or case number. Records go back to 1984.

Bureau of Conveyances
Property
Property records on the Honolulu Property Information database are available at http://caro.esri.com/honolulu/prperty.htm.

Kauai
Civil Cases, Criminal Records
www.state.hi.us/jud/trials1.htm
Online access to Circuit Court & family court records is available free at http://166.122.201.51/hod/judstart.htm. Search by name or case number. Records go back to 1984.

Maui
Civil Cases, Criminal Records
www.state.hi.us/jud/trials1.htm
Online access to Circuit Court & family court records is available free at http://166.122.201.51/hod/judstart.htm. Search by name or case number. Records go back to 1984.

Federal Courts in Hawaii...

US District Court - District of Hawaii

Home Page: www.hid.uscourts.gov
PACER: Sign-up number is 800-676-6856. Access fee is $.60 per minute. Case records are available back to October 1991. Records are purged never. New civil records are available online after 1 day. New criminal records are available online after 3 days.
Honolulu Division Counties: All counties.

US Bankruptcy Court - District of Hawaii

Home Page: www.hib.uscourts.gov
PACER: Sign-up number is 800-676-6856. Access fee is $.60 per minute. Use of PC Anywhere v4.0 suggested. Case records are available back to 1987. Records are purged varies. New civil records are available online after 1 day.
Honolulu Division Counties: All counties.

Editor's Choice for Hawaii

Here are some additional sites recommended for this state.

Attorney General Opinions
www.hsba.org/Hawaii/Admin/Ag/agindex.htm
Campaign Finance Database
http://la2.sdrdc.com/hi96
Constitution Text
www.hawaii.gov/lrb/con/condoc.html
Disciplinary Board Opinions
www.hsba.org/Hawaii/Admin/Disc/disc.htm
Legislative Bills & Documents Database
www.capitol.hawaii.gov/site1/docs/docs.asp?press1=docs
Sex Offenders Database
www.ehawaiigov.org/HI_SOR/
Supreme Court & Appellate Courts Opinions
www.hsba.org/Hawaii/Court/cour.htm

Capital:	Boise Ada County	Home Page	www.state.id.us
Time Zone:	MST/PST	Archives	www.state.id.us/ishs
Number of Counties:	44	Attorney General	www.state.id.us/ag

State Level...Major Agencies

Corporation Records, Limited Partnerships, Trademarks/Servicemarks, Limited Liability Company Records, Assumed Name

Secretary of State, Corporation Div, PO Box 83720, Boise, ID 83720-0080 (Courier: 700 W Jefferson, Boise, ID 83720); 208-334-2301, 208-334-2847 (Fax), 8AM-5PM.
www.idsos.state.id.us

Online: There are 2 systems. To subscribe to PAIS, you must pre-pay. An initial deposit of $25 is requested. There is a monthly subscription of $10.00 and an online usage charge of $.10 per minute. The system is available from 8AM-5PM M-F. This system offers an excellent array of reports and information. Business Entity Searches at www.accessidaho.org/apps/sos/corp/search.html is a free Internet service open 24 hours daily.

Uniform Commercial Code, Federal Tax Liens, State Tax Liens

UCC Division, Secretary of State, PO Box 83720, Boise, ID 83720-0080 (Courier: 700 W Jefferson, Boise, ID 83720); 208-334-3191, 208-334-2847 (Fax), 8AM-5PM.
www.idsos.state.id.us

Online: AccessIdaho at www.accessidaho.org is the official state site. There is a free limited search, but the professional searchers should subscribe to the commercial service at this site. There is a $75 annual fee and possible transaction fees.

Sales Tax Registrations

Revenue Operations Division, Records Management, PO Box 36, Boise, ID 83722 (Courier: 800 Park, Boise, ID 83722); 208-334-7660, 208-334-7792 (Records Management), 208-334-7650 (Fax), 8AM-5:00PM.
www.state.id.us/tax/index.htm

Online: E-mail requests are accepted at rmcmichael@tax.state.id.us.

Driver Records

Idaho Transportation Department, Driver's Services, PO Box 34, Boise, ID 83731-0034 (Courier: 3311 W State, Boise, ID 83703); 208-334-8736, 208-334-8739 (Fax), 8:30AM-5PM.
www2.state.id.us/itd/dmv/ds.htm

Online: Idaho offers online access (CICS) to the driver license files through its portal provider, Access Idaho. Fee is $5.50 per record. For more information, call 208-332-0102 or visit www.accessidaho.org.

Vehicle Ownership, Vehicle Identification

Idaho Transportation Department, Vehicle Services, PO Box 34, Boise, ID 83731-0034 (Courier: 3311 W State St, Boise, ID 83707); 208-334-8773, 208-334-8542 (Fax), 8:30AM-5PM. www2.state.id.us/itd/dmv/vs.htm

Online: Idaho offers online and batch access to registration and title files through its portal provider, Access Idaho. Records are $4.00 each plus an additional convenience fee. For more information, call 208-332-0102.

Legislation Records

Legislative Services Office, Research and Legislation, PO Box 83720, Boise, ID 83720-0054 (Courier: 700 W Jefferson, Lower Level, East, Boise, ID 83720); 208-334-2475, 208-334-2125 (Fax), 8AM-5PM. www.state.id.us/legislat/legislat.html

Online: Statutes, bill information, and subject are available from the web site. They also will answer questions via e-mail. At kford@lso.state.id.us.

State Level...Occupational Licensing

Attorney... www2.state.id.us/isb/roster_search.htm
Bank... http://finance.state.id.us/industry/bank_info.asp
Collection Agency/Collector............................... http://finance.state.id.us/industry/statutes_confin.asp?Chapter=CAA
Consumer Loans & Credit Sale www2.state.id.us/finance/icc/icclist.htm
Credit Union.. http://finance.state.id.us/industry/creditunion_section.asp
Dentist/Dental Hygienist.................................... www2.state.id.us/isbd/isbdqry.htm
Electrical Inspector/Contractor/Apr/ Journeyman www2.state.id.us/dbs
Engineer www2.state.id.us/ipels/pelsnumb.htm
Finance Company.. www2.state.id.us/finance/icc/icclist.htm
Guide... www2.state.id.us/oglb/oglbhome.htm
Investment Advisor
... http://finance.state.id.us/industry/securities_resources.asp?resource=IARR
Lobbyist... www.idsos.state.id.us/elect/lobbyist/lobinfo.htm
Mortgage Broker/Banker/Mortgage Company..... http://finance.state.id.us/industry/mortgage_section.asp
Optometrist.. www.arbo.org/nodb2000/licsearch.asp
Oral Surgeon... www2.state.id.us/isbd/isbdqry.htm
Orthodontist... www2.state.id.us/isbd/isbdqry.htm
Outfitter... www2.state.id.us/oglb/oglbhome.htm
Public Accountant-CPA or LPA.......................... www2.state.id.us/boa/HTM/license.htm
Savings & Loan Association................................ http://finance.state.id.us/industry/bank_section.asp
Securities Broker/Dealers Seller & Issuer........... http://finance.state.id.us/industry/securities.asp
Surveyor www2.state.id.us/ipels/pelsnumb.htm
Trust Company .... www2.state.id.us/finance/idbklst.htm#trust

County Level...Courts, Recorders & Assessors

Administrative Director of Courts, Supreme Court Building, 451 W State St, Boise, ID, 83720; 208-334-2246; http://www2.state.id.us/judicial

Editor's Note: There is no statewide computer system offering external access. ISTARS is a statewide intra-court/intra-agency system run and managed by the State Supreme Court. All counties are on ISTARS, and all courts provide public access terminals on-site.

Canyon

Assessor, Property

Online access to the Assessor and Treasurer's databases requires registration and monthly fees. For subscription information, email clane@canyoncounty.org or call 208-454-7401.

Kootenai

Civil Cases, Criminal Records

www.co.kootenai.id.us/court
Online access to court documents is available free at www.co.kootenai.id.us/court/default.asp.

Property, Recording, Unclaimed Property

www.co.kootenai.id.us/default.asp
Online access to the county mapping/recording database is available free at www.co.kootenai.id.us/publicinfo/default.asp. Click on "Search."

Federal Courts in Idaho...

US District Court - District of Idaho

Home Page: www.id.uscourts.gov
PACER: Sign-up number is 208-334-9342. Access fee is No charge. Case records are available back to January 1990. Records are purged varies. New civil records are available online after 2 days. New criminal records are available online after 1 day.
Opinions Online: Court opinions are available online at www.id.uscourts.gov.
Other Online Access: You can search records on the Internet using RACER. Currently the system is free and requires free registration. Simply visit www.id.uscourts.gov/wconnect/wc.dll?usdc_racer~main.
Boise Division Counties: Ada, Adams, Blaine, Boise, Camas, Canyon, Cassia, Elmore, Gem, Gooding, Jerome, Lincoln, Minidoka, Owyhee, Payette, Twin Falls, Valley, Washington.
Coeur d' Alene Division Counties: Benewah, Bonner, Boundary, Kootenai, Shoshone.
Moscow Division Counties: Clearwater, Latah, Lewis, Nez Perce.
Pocatello Division Counties: Bannock, Bear Lake, Bingham, Bonneville, Butte, Caribou, Clark, Custer, Franklin, Fremont, Idaho, Jefferson, Lemhi, Madison, Oneida, Power, Teton.

US Bankruptcy Court - District of Idaho

Home Page: www.id.uscourts.gov
PACER: Sign-up number is 208-334-9342. Access fee is No charge. Case records are available back to September 1990. Records are purged immediately when case closed. New civil records are available online after 1 day.
Opinions Online: Court opinions are available online at www.id.uscourts.gov.
Other Online Access: You can search records on the Internet using RACER. Currently the system is free and requires free registration. Visit www.id.uscourts.gov/wconnect/wc.dll?usbc_racer~main. Fednet also available; to access, dial 208-334-9476.
Boise Division Counties: Ada, Adams, Blaine, Boise, Camas, Canyon, Cassia, Elmore, Gem, Gooding, Jerome, Lincoln, Minidoka, Owyhee, Payette, Twin Falls, Valley, Washington.
Coeur d' Alene Division Counties: Benewah, Bonner, Boundary, Kootenai, Shoshone.
Moscow Division Counties: Clearwater, Idaho, Latah, Lewis, Nez Perce.
Pocatello Division Counties: Bannock, Bear Lake, Bingham, Bonneville, Butte, Caribou, Clark, Custer, Franklin, Fremont, Jefferson, Lemhi, Madison, Oneida, Power, Teton.

Editor's Choice for Idaho

Inmates Listing
www.adasheriff.org/jailrost/arresta-g.htm
Pesticide Data Database
www.kellysolutions.com/ID

Capital: Springfield Sangamon County	Home Page www.state.il.us
Time Zone: CST	Attorney General www.ag.state.il.us
Number of Counties: 102	Archives www.sos.state.il.us/depts/ archives/arc_home.html

State Level...Major Agencies

Criminal Records

Illinois State Police, Bureau of Identification, 260 N Chicago St, Joliet, IL 60432-4075; 815-740-5164, 8AM-4PM M-F.

www.state.il.us/isp/isphpage.htm

Online: Online access costs $7.00 per name. Upon signing an interagency agreement with ISP and establishing a $200 escrow account, users can submit inquiries over modem. Replies with convictions are returned by mail. Clear records can be returned via e-mail, by request. Modem access is available from 7AM-4PM M-F, excluding holidays. Users must utilize LAPLINK version 6.0 or later. For more information on the Modem Porgram, call 815-740-5164.

Corporation Records, Limited Partnership Records, Trade Names, Assumed Name, Limited Liability Company Records

Department of Business Services, Corporate Department, Howlett Bldg, 3rd Floor, Copy Section, Springfield, IL 62756 (Courier: 501 S 2nd St, Springfield, IL 62756); 217-782-7880, 217-782-4528 (Fax), 8AM-4:30PM.

www.sos.state.il.us

Online: The web site gives free access to records, except the web does not offer not-for-profit records. Search Corporate/LLC records at www.cyberdriveillinois.com/departments/business_services/corpstart.html. A commercial access program is also available. Potential users must submit in writing the purpose of the request. Submit to: Sharon Thomas, Dept. of Business Srvs, 330 Howlett Bldg, Springfield, IL 62756. Also, call 217-782-4104 for more information. Fees vary.

Legislation Records

Illinois General Assembly, State House, House (or Senate) Bills Division, Springfield, IL 62706; 217-782-3944 (Bill Status Only), 217-782-7017 (Index Div-Older Bills), 217-782-5799 (House Bills), 217-782-9778 (Senate Bills), 217-524-6059 (Fax), 8AM-4:30PM.

www.legis.state.il.us

Online: The Legislative Information System is available for subscription through a standard modem. The sign-up fee is $500.00 which includes 100 free minutes of access. Thereafter, access time is billed at $1.00 per minute. The hours of availability are 8 AM - 10 PM when in session and 8 AM - 5 PM when not in session, M-F. Contact Craig Garret at 217- 782-4083 to set-up an account. The Internet site offers free access; the state has a disclaimer that says the site should not be relied upon as official records of action.

State Level...Occupational Licensing

Architect.. www.dpr.state.il.us/licenselookup/default.asp
Athletic Trainer .... www.dpr.state.il.us/licenselookup/default.asp
Auctioneer .... www.obre.state.il.us/lookup/
Bank.. www.obre.state.il.us/CBT/REGENTY/BTREG.HTM
Barber... www.dpr.state.il.us/licenselookup/default.asp
Check Printer.. www.obre.state.il.us/CBT/REGENTY/BTREG.HTM
Chiropractor... www.dpr.state.il.us/licenselookup/default.asp
Collection Agency.. www.dpr.state.il.us/licenselookup/default.asp
Controlled Substance .... www.dpr.state.il.us/licenselookup/default.asp
Corporate Fiduciary .... www.obre.state.il.us/CBT/REGENTY/BTREG.HTM
Cosmetologist .... www.dpr.state.il.us/licenselookup/default.asp
Dentist/Dental Hygienist................................ www.dpr.state.il.us/licenselookup/default.asp
Detection of Deception Examiner.................... www.dpr.state.il.us/licenselookup/default.asp
Dietitian/Nutrition Counselor......................... www.dpr.state.il.us/licenselookup/default.asp
Employee Leasing Company............................ www.state.il.us/INS/elc.htm
Engineer .... www.dpr.state.il.us/licenselookup/default.asp
Engineer, Structural .... www.dpr.state.il.us/licenselookup/default.asp
Environmental Health Practitioner .... www.dpr.state.il.us/licenselookup/default.asp
Esthetician... www.dpr.state.il.us/licenselookup/default.asp
Funeral Director/Embalmer............................. www.dpr.state.il.us/licenselookup/default.asp
HMO .... www.state.il.us/INS/mmcchart.pdf
Interior Designer.. www.dpr.state.il.us/licenselookup/default.asp
Landscape Architect.. www.dpr.state.il.us/licenselookup/default.asp
Lead Contractors.. http://app.idph.state.il.us/Envhealth/Lead/Leadcnt.asp
Lead Risk Assessor/Inspector/Supervisor........... http://app.idph.state.il.us/Envhealth/lead/Leadinsp.asp
Lead Training Providers.................................. http://app.idph.state.il.us/Envhealth/lead/Leadinsp.asp
Liquor License (Retail, Distributor, Mfg) .... www.state.il.us/distributors/search.htm
Lobbyist... www.cyberdriveillinois.com/cgi-bin/index/lobbysrch.s
Long Term Care Insurance Company................. www.state.il.us/INS/longtermcareframe.htm
Marriage & Family Therapist........................... www.dpr.state.il.us/licenselookup/default.asp
Medical Corporation .... www.dpr.state.il.us/licenselookup/default.asp
Medical Doctor/Physician's Assistant .... www.dpr.state.il.us/licenselookup/default.asp
Mortgage Banker/Broker................................. www.obre.state.il.us/RESFIN/liclistc.pdf
Nail Technician... www.dpr.state.il.us/licenselookup/default.asp
Naprapath .... www.dpr.state.il.us/licenselookup/default.asp
Nurse.. www.dpr.state.il.us/licenselookup/default.asp
Nursing Home Administrator .... www.medicare.gov/Nursing/Overview.asp
Occupational Therapist .... www.dpr.state.il.us/licenselookup/default.asp
Optometrist.. www.dpr.state.il.us/licenselookup/default.asp
Osteopathic Physician .... www.dpr.state.il.us/licenselookup/default.asp
Pawnbroker.. www.obre.state.il.us/CBT/REGENTY/BTREG.HTM
Pharmacist/Pharmacy..................................... www.dpr.state.il.us/licenselookup/default.asp
Physical Therapist.. www.dpr.state.il.us/licenselookup/default.asp
Podiatrist .... www.dpr.state.il.us/licenselookup/default.asp
Private Detective.. www.dpr.state.il.us/licenselookup/default.asp
Private Security Contractor.............................. www.dpr.state.il.us/licenselookup/default.asp

Professional Counselor/Clinical Prof. Counselor. www.dpr.state.il.us/licenselookup/default.asp
Psychologist.. www.dpr.state.il.us/licenselookup/default.asp
Public Accountant-CPA...................................... www.dpr.state.il.us/licenselookup/default.asp
Real Estate Appraiser/Broker/Salesperson.......... www.obre.state.il.us/lookup/
Roofer... www.dpr.state.il.us/licenselookup/default.asp
Shorthand Reporter .... www.dpr.state.il.us/licenselookup/default.asp
Social Worker .... www.dpr.state.il.us/licenselookup/default.asp
Speech-Language Pathologist/Audiologist .... www.dpr.state.il.us/licenselookup/default.asp
Surveyor .... www.dpr.state.il.us/licenselookup/default.asp
Timeshare/Land Sales .... www.obre.state.il.us/lookup/
Trust Company .... www.obre.state.il.us/CBT/REGENTY/BTREG.HTM
Veterinarian... www.dpr.state.il.us/licenselookup/default.asp
Wholesale Drug Distributor .... www.dpr.state.il.us/licenselookup/default.asp

County Level...Courts, Recorders & Assessors

Administative Office of Courts, 222 N LaSalle 13th Floor, Chicago, IL, 60601; 312-793-3250;

Editor's Note: While there is no statewide public online system available, a number of Illinois Circuit
Courts offer online access.

Adams
Civil Cases, Criminal Records
www.co.adams.il.us
Online access to 8th Circuit Clerk of Court records is available free at www.circuitclerk.co.adams.il.us. Search by name, case or
docket number.

Bureau
Civil Cases, Criminal Records
www.bccirclk.gov
Online access to judicial circuit records is available to local attorney firms and retrievers. The service is free. Call the Clerk's office for
details, 815-872-0027.

Champaign
Civil Cases, Criminal Records
Access to the remote online system called PASS requires a setup fee and annual user fee. Online case records go back to 1992.
Contact Jo Kelly at 217-384-3767 for subscription information.

Cook
Civil Cases, Criminal Records
www.cookcountyclerkofcourt.org
Online case searching for limited case information, called case snapshots, is available free online at
www.cookcountyclerkofcourt.org/Terms/terms.html. Search by name, case number or court date. Information included is parties (up
to 3), attorneys, case type, the filing date, the ad damnum (amount of damages sought), division and district, and the most current
court date. Phone inquiries to court to check status only. Phone record requests can be directed to the Computer Center at 312-603-
7586. Misdemeanor records only.

Property Tax Records
www.assessor.co.cook.il.us
Records on the County Assessor Residential Assessment Search database are available free online at
www.assessor.co.cook.il.us/starsearch.html. Database is offered as a tax assessment comparison service.

De Kalb

Civil Cases, Criminal Records

Court planning to offer online access. Call 1-800-307-1100 for more information.

Real Estate, Liens

The DeKalb County online system requires a $350 subscription fee, with a per minute charge of $.25, $.50 if printing. Records date back to 1980. Lending agency information is available. For further information, contact Sheila Larson at 815-895-7152.

Du Page

Real Estate, Liens, Tax Assessor Records

www.co.dupage.il.us.org

For access to the Du Page County database, one must lease a live interface telephone line from a carrier to establish a connection. Additionally, there is a fee of $.05 per transaction. Records date back to 1977. For info, contact Fred Kieltcka at 630-682-7030.

Grundy

Civil Cases, Criminal Records

Online access to judicial circuit records should be available in 2001 for local attorney firms and retrievers. The service is free. Call the Court Clerk's office at 815-941-3256 for details.

La Salle

Civil Cases

Online access to Judicial Circuit records should be available in 2001 for local attorney firms and retrievers. The service is free. Call the Clerk's office at 815-434-8671 for details.

Real Estate, Assessor

www.lasallecounty.org/Final/contents2.htm

Assessor records on the County Assessor database are available free online at www.lasallecounty.org/cidnet/asrpfull.htm. Also, 1999 & 2000 assessment data can be accessed online at www.lasallecounty.org/contents3.htm.

Macon

Civil Cases, Criminal Records

www.court.co.macon.il.us

Access to court records is available free online at the web site. Docket information is viewable since 04/96. Search by name or case number. Online access to criminal records is open 24 hours daily. Docket information from 04/96 forward is searchable.

McHenry

Civil Cases, Criminal Records

www.mchenrycircuitclerk.org

Access to records on the remote online system requires a $750 license fee plus $50 per month. Records date back to 1990. Civil, criminal, probate, traffic, and domestic records are available. For more information, call 815-334-4193.

Assessor/Treasurer

Records on the County Treasurer Inquiry site are available free online at http://209.172.155.14/cidnet.publictre1.htm.

McLean

Assessor/Treasurer

www.mclean.gov

Online access to the county Tax Bill Information Lookup database is available free at www.mclean.gov/TaxLookupMainFirst.asp. No name searching; parcel number or street name and city required. Also, access to the Township of Normal assessor database is available free at www.normaltownship.org/Assessor/ParcelSearch.php. No name searching; parcel number or address required.

Montgomery

Civil Cases, Criminal Records

www.courts.montgomery.k12.il.us

Online access to court records is available at www.courts.montgomery.k12.il.us/CaseInfo.htm. Search by name or case number.

Ogle

Civil Cases, Criminal Records

www.oglecounty.org

Online access is available through a private company service at www.judici.com. Permission to use the system and sign-up is through the court, or email subscribe@judici.com.

Rock Island
Civil Cases, Criminal Records
www.co.rock-island.il.us
Access to records on the remote online system requires a $200 setup fee plus a $1.00 per minute for access. Civil, criminal, probate, traffic, and domestic records can be accessed by name or case number.

Stark
Unclaimed Funds
www.starkcourt.org
Online access to the county clerk of courts unclaimed funds database is available at www.starkcourt.org/cgi-bin/starkcrt/pdfarchive/uf_pdflist.cgi. File is in pdf format.

Wayne
Assessor, Property Records
http://assessor.wayne.il.us/Index.html
Records on the Wayne Township Assessor Office database are available free online at http://assessor.wayne.il.us/OPID.html. Also, an advanced search feature (fee) is available for subscribers. This includes legal, assessment, sales history, buildings and other information.

Federal Courts in Illinois...

US District Court - Central District of Illinois

Home Page: www.ilcd.uscourts.gov
PACER: Sign-up number is 800-676-6856. Access fee is $.60 per minute. Toll-free access: 800-258-3678. Local access: 217-492-4997. Case records are available back to 1995. Records are purged after 5-7 years. New records are available online after 1 day.
PACER Internet Access: http://pacer.ilcd.uscourts.gov.
Danville/Urbana Division Counties: Champaign, Coles, Douglas, Edgar, Ford, Iroquois, Kankakee, Macon, Moultrie, Piatt, Vermilion.
Peoria Division Counties: Bureau, Fulton, Hancock, Knox, Livingston, McDonough, McLean, Marshall, Peoria, Putnam, Stark, Tazewell, Woodford.
Rock Island Division Counties: Henderson, Henry, Mercer, Rock Island, Warren.
Springfield Division Counties: Adams, Brown, Cass, Christian, De Witt, Greene, Logan, Macoupin, Mason, Menard, Montgomery, Morgan, Pike, Sangamon, Schuyler, Scott, Shelby.

US Bankruptcy Court - Central District of Illinois

Home Page: www.ilcb.uscourts.gov
PACER: Sign-up number is 800-676-6856. Access fee is $.60 per minute. Toll-free access: 800-454-9893. Local access: 217-492-4260. Case records are available back to 1989-90. Records are purged immediately when case is closed. New civil records are available online after 2 days.
Danville Division Counties: Champaign, Coles, Douglas, Edgar, Ford, Iroquois, Kankakee, Livingston, Moultrie, Piatt, Vermilion.
Peoria Division Counties: Bureau, Fulton, Hancock, Henderson, Henry, Knox, Marshall, McDonough, Mercer, Peoria, Putnam, Rock Island, Stark, Tazewell, Warren, Woodford.
Springfield Division Counties: Adams, Brown, Cass, Christian, De Witt, Greene, Logan, Macon, Macoupin, Mason, McLean, Menard, Montgomery, Morgan, Pike, Sangamon, Schuyler, Scott, Shelby.

US District Court - Northern District of Illinois

Home Page: www.ilnd.uscourts.gov
PACER: Sign-up number is 800-676-6856. Access fee is $.60 per minute. Toll-free access: 800-621-7029. Local access: 312-408-7777. Case records are available back to 1988. Records are purged varies. New records are available online after 1-2 days.

PACER Internet Access: If you are a registered PACER subscriber, you can access this court through the Internet at http://pacer.ilnd.uscourts.gov.
Chicago (Eastern) Division Counties: Cook, Du Page, Grundy, Kane, Kendall, Lake, La Salle, Will.
Rockford Division Counties: Boone, Carroll, De Kalb, Jo Daviess, Lee, McHenry, Ogle, Stephenson, Whiteside, Winnebago.

US Bankruptcy Court - Northern District of Illinois

Home Page: www.ilnb.uscourts.gov
PACER: Sign-up number is 800-676-6856. Access fee is $.60 per minute. Toll-free access: 888-541-1078. Local access: 312-408-5101. Use of PC Anywhere v4.0 suggested. Case records are available back to July 1, 1993. Records are purged never. New civil records are available online after 1 day.
Other Online Access: You can search using RACER on the Internet. Currently the system is free but a fee has been approved and may be applied in the future. Visit http://207.41.17.23/wconnect/wc.dll?usbcn_racer~main to log on.
Chicago (Eastern) Division Counties: Cook, Du Page, Grundy, Kane, Kendall, La Salle, Lake, Will.
Rockford Division Counties: Boone, Carroll, De Kalb, Jo Daviess, Lee, McHenry, Ogle, Stephenson, Whiteside, Winnebago.

US District Court - Southern District of Illinois

Home Page: www.ilsd.uscourts.gov
PACER: Sign-up number is 800-676-6856. Access fee is $.60 per minute. Toll-free access: 800-426-7523. Local access: 618-482-9430. Case records are available back to 1985. Records are purged when deemed necessary. New civil records are available online after 1 day. New criminal records are available online after 1-2 days.
PACER Internet Access: http://pacer.ilsd.uscourts.gov.
Benton Division Counties: Alexander, Clark, Clay, Crawford, Cumberland, Edwards, Effingham, Franklin, Gallatin, Hamilton, Hardin, Jackson, Jasper, Jefferson, Johnson, Lawrence, Massac, Perry, Pope, Pulaski, Richland, Saline, Union, Wabash, Wayne, White, Williamson. Cases may also be allocated to the Benton Division.
East St Louis Division Counties: Bond, Calhoun, Clinton, Fayette, Jersey, Madison, Marion, Monroe, Randolph, St. Clair, Washington. Cases for these counties may also be allocated to the Benton Division.

US Bankruptcy Court - Southern District of Illinois

Home Page: www.ilsb.uscourts.gov
PACER: Sign-up number is 800-676-6856. Access fee is $.60 per minute. Toll-free access: 800-933-9148. Local access: 618-482-9114, 618-482-9115, 618-482-9116. Case records are available back to January 1989. Records are purged as deemed necessary. New civil records are available online after 1 day.
PACER Internet Access: http://pacer.ilsb.uscourts.gov.
Benton Division Counties: Alexander, Edwards, Franklin, Gallatin, Hamilton, Hardin, Jackson, Jefferson, Johnson, Massac, Perry, Pope, Pulaski, Randolph, Saline, Union, Wabash, Washington, Wayne, White, Williamson.
East St Louis Division Counties: Bond, Calhoun, Clark, Clay, Clinton, Crawford, Cumberland, Effingham, Fayette, Jasper, Jersey, Lawrence, Madison, Marion, Monroe, Richland, St. Clair.

Editor's Choice for Illinois

Campaign Finance Database
    www.voterinfonet.com/ethicsin.asp
Inmates Database
    www.idoc.state.il.us/inmates/search.htm
Schools Database
    www.copleynewspapers.com/rcard/
Sex Offenders Database
    http://samnet.isp.state.il.us/ispso2/sex_offenders/frames.htm
Veterans (Civil War) Database
    www.sos.state.il.us/cgi-bin/civilwar

Capital: Indianapolis
Marion County

Time Zone: EST/CST

Number of Counties: 92

Home Page www.state.in.us

Attorney General www.in.gov/attorneygeneral

Archives www.in.gov/icpr/webfile/
archives/homepage.html

State Level...Major Agencies

Corporation Records, Limited Partnerships, Fictitious Name, Assumed Name, Limited Liability Company Records, Limited Liability Partnerships

Corporation Division, Secretary of State, 302 W Washington St, Room E018, Indianapolis, IN 46204; 317-232-6576, 317-233-3387 (Fax), 8AM-5:30PM M-F.

www.state.in.us/sos

Online: This subscription service is available from the Access Indiana Information Network (AI) gateway on the Internet. There is no fee to view a partial record, but $1.00 to view a screen containing the registered agent and other information. Go to www.ai.org/.

Uniform Commercial Code

UCC Division, Secretary of State, 302 West Washington St, Room E-018, Indianapolis, IN 46204; 317-233-3984, 317-233-3387 (Fax), 8AM-5:30PM.

www.in.gov/sos/

Online: Searching is available via the Internet. Plans are underway to offer filing services also.

Driver Records

BMV-Driving Records, 100 N Senate Ave, Indiana Government Center North, Room N405, Indianapolis, IN 46204; 317-232-6000 x2, 8:15AM-4:30PM.

www.state.in.us/bmv

Online: Online access costs $5.00 per record. Access Indiana Information Network (AIIN) is the state owned interactive information and communication system which provides batch and interactive access to driving records. There is an annual $50.00 fee. For more information, call AIIN at 317-233-2010 or go to www.ai.org.

Vehicle Ownership, Vehicle Identification, Boat & Vessel Ownership, Boat & Vessel Registration

Bureau of Motor Vehicles, Records, 100 N Senate Ave, Room N404, Indianapolis, IN 46204; 317-233-6000, 8:15AM-4:45PM. www.state.in.us/bmv

Online: The Access Indiana Information network (AIIN) at 317-233-2010 is the state appointed vendor. The fee is $5.00 per record plus an annual fee of $50.00. Visit www.ai.org for more information.

Legislation Records

Legislative Services Agency, State House, 200 W Washington, Room 301, Indianapolis, IN 46204-2789; 317-232-9856, 8:15AM-4:45PM.

www.state.in.us

Online: All legislative information is available over the Internet. The Indiana Code is also available.

State Level...Occupational Licensing

Child Care Centers	www.ai.org/fssa/database/centers.html
Child Care Homes	www.ai.org/fssa/database/homes.html
Collection Agencies	www.state.in.us/serv/sos_securities
Hazardous Waste Facility/Handler	www.state.in.us/idem/olq/site_information/lists.html
Investment Advisor	www.state.in.us/serv/sos_securities
Loan Brokers	www.state.in.us/serv/sos_securities
Optometrist	www.arbo.org/nodb2000/licsearch.asp
Polygraph Examiner	www.indianapolygraphassociation.com
Securities Broker/Dealer	www.in.gov/serv/sos_securities
Securities Sales Agent	www.in.gov/serv/sos_securities
Solid Waste Facility	www.state.in.us/idem/olq/site_information/lists.html
Teacher	http://dew4.doe.state.in.us/LIC/license.html
Waste Tire Processor/Transporter	www.state.in.us/idem/olq/site_information/lists.html
Yard Waste Composting Facility	www.state.in.us/idem/olq/site_information/lists.html

County Level...Courts, Recorders & Assessors

State Court Administrator, 115 W Washington St Suite 1080, Indianapolis, IN, 46204; 317-232-2542; www.in.gov/judiciary/admin

Editor's Note: No online access computer system, internal or external, is available except for Marion County through CivicNet/Access Indiana Information Network, which is available on the Internet at www.civicnet.net. Account and password are required. No charge for civil court name searches. Fees range from $2.00 to $5.00 for civil case summaries, civil justice name searches, criminal case summaries, and party booking details.

Elkhart

Real Estate, Liens, Tax Assessor Records

www.elkhartcountygov.com/administrative

Access to Elkhart County records is available for an annual fee of $50 plus a minimum of $20 per month of use. The minimum fee allows for 2 hours access, and additional use is billed at $10 per hour. Lending agency information is available. For information, contact Nick Cenova at 219-535-6777.

Marion
Civil Cases, Criminal Records
Access to the remote online system is available via the Internet at www.civicnet.net. The setup fee is $50. Other fees vary by type of record or search. Criminal records go back to 1988.
Real Estate, Liens
www.indygov.net
Access to Marion County online records requires a $200 set up fee, plus an escrow balance of at least $100 must be maintained. Additional charges are $.50 per minute, $.25 display charge for first page; $.10 each add'l page. Records date back to 1987; images from 2/24/93. Federal tax liens and UCC information are available. For information, contact Mike Kerner at 317-327-4587.

Tippecanoe
Civil Cases, Criminal Records, Property Records
www.county.tippecanoe.in.us
Online access to court records through CourtView are available free online at http://court.county.tippecanoe.in.us/pa/pa.htm. Online access to property information on the county GIS-mapping site is available free at http://gis.county.tippecanoe.in.us/gis/app12/index.html.

Vanderburgh
Property Records
www.assessor.evansville.net
Records on the County Assessor Property database are available free online at www.assessor.evansville.net/disclaim.htm.

Wayne
Marriage
www.co.wayne.in.us/offices
Marriage records are being added irregularly to the web site at www.co.wayne.in.us/marriage/retrieve.cgi. Records are from 1811 forward, with recent years being added.

Federal Courts in Indiana...

US District Court - Northern District of Indiana
Home Page: www.innd.uscourts.gov
PACER: Sign-up number is 800-676-6856. Access fee is $.60 per minute. Toll-free access: 800-371-8843. Local access: 219-246-8200. Case records are available back to 1994. Records are purged as deemed necessary. New records available online after 2 days.
Fort Wayne Division Counties: Adams, Allen, Blackford, DeKalb, Grant, Huntington, Jay, Lagrange, Noble, Steuben, Wells, Whitley.
Hammond Division Counties: Lake, Porter.
Lafayette Division Counties: Benton, Carroll, Jasper, Newton, Tippecanoe, Warren, White.
South Bend Division Counties: Cass, Elkhart, Fulton, Kosciusko, La Porte, Marshall, Miami, Pulaski, St. Joseph, Starke, Wabash.

US Bankruptcy Court - Northern District of Indiana
Home Page: www.innb.uscourts.gov
PACER: Sign-up number is 800-676-6856. Access fee is $.60 per minute. Toll-free access: 888-917-2237. Local access: 219-968-2270. Case records are available back to 1992. Records are purged every 6 months. New civil records are available online after 2 days.
PACER Internet Access: http://pacer.innb.uscourts.gov.
Fort Wayne Division Counties: Adams, Allen, Blackford, DeKalb, Grant, Huntington, Jay, Lagrange, Noble, Steuben, Wells, Whitley.
Hammond at Gary Division Counties: Lake, Porter.
Hammond at Lafayette Division Counties: Benton, Carroll, Jasper, Newton, Tippecanoe, Warren, White.
South Bend Division Counties: Cass, Elkhart, Fulton, Kosciusko, La Porte, Marshall, Miami, Pulaski, St. Joseph, Starke, Wabash.

US District Court - Southern District of Indiana

Home Page: www.insd.uscourts.gov
PACER: There is no PACER access to this court.
Other Online Access: Searching online is currently free. Visit www.insd.uscourts.gov/casesearch.htm to search.
Evansville Division Counties: Daviess, Dubois, Gibson, Martin, Perry, Pike, Posey, Spencer, Vanderburgh, Warrick.
Indianapolis Division Counties: Bartholomew, Boone, Brown, Clinton, Decatur, Delaware, Fayette, Fountain, Franklin, Hamilton, Hancock, Hendricks, Henry, Howard, Johnson, Madison, Marion, Monroe, Montgomery, Morgan, Randolph, Rush, Shelby, Tipton, Union, Wayne.
New Albany Division Counties: Clark, Crawford, Dearborn, Floyd, Harrison, Jackson, Jefferson, Jennings, Lawrence, Ohio, Orange, Ripley, Scott, Switzerland, Washington.
Terre Haute Division Counties: Clay, Greene, Knox, Owen, Parke, Putnam, Sullivan, Vermillion, Vigo.

US Bankruptcy Court - Southern District of Indiana

Home Page: www.insb.uscourts.gov
PACER: Sign-up number is 317-229-3845. Access fee is $.60 per minute. NIBS system: First number is for Carbon Copy users and second is for Procomm users. Use of Carbon Copy Plus required. Case records are available back to 1988. Records are purged every 3 months. New civil records are available online after 2-3 days.
Other Online Access: You can search records online at www.insb.uscourts.gov/public/casesearch.asp. You may search using case number, party name, social security number and/or tax ID number. The system is currently free.
Evansville Division Counties: Daviess, Dubois, Gibson, Martin, Perry, Pike, Posey, Spencer, Vanderburgh, Warrick.
Indianapolis Division Counties: Bartholomew, Boone, Brown, Clinton, Decatur, Delaware, Fayette, Fountain, Franklin, Hamilton, Hancock, Hendricks, Henry, Howard, Johnson, Madison, Marion, Monroe, Montgomery, Morgan, Randolph, Rush, Shelby, Tipton, Union, Wayne.
New Albany Division Counties: Clark, Crawford, Dearborn, Floyd, Harrison, Jackson, Jefferson, Jennings, Lawrence, Ohio, Orange, Ripley, Scott, Switzerland, Washington.
Terre Haute Division Counties: Clay, Greene, Knox, Owen, Parke, Putnam, Sullivan, Vermillion, Vigo.

Editor's Choice for Indiana

Here are some additional sites recommended for this state.

Campaign Finance Database
www.indianacampaignfinance.com/search/start.htm
Circuit Court Records (1815-1855) Database
www.state.in.us/icpr/webfile/posey/podata.html
Constitution Text
www.law.indiana.edu/uslawdocs/inconst.html
Historical Markers Database
www.statelib.lib.in.us/www/ihb/marklist.html
Recycling Centers Database
www.state.in.us/idem/oppta/recycling/search
Sex Offenders Database
www.state.in.us//cji/html/sexoffender.html
State Code Text
www.ai.org/legislative/ic/code/index.html

Capital: Des Moines   Home Page   www.state.ia.us
              Polk County

Time Zone: CST   Attorney General   www.state.ia.us/
                                                                               government/ag

Number of Counties: 99   Archives   www.iowahistory.org

State Level...Major Agencies

Corporation Records, Limited Liability Company Records, Fictitious Name, Limited Partnership Records, Trademarks/Servicemarks

Secretary of State, Corporation Division, 2nd Floor, Hoover Bldg, Des Moines, IA 50319; 515-281-5204, 515-242-5953 (Fax), 8AM-4:30PM.

www.sos.state.ia.us

Online: The state offers the DataShare On-line System. Fees are $175.00 per year plus $.30 per minute. The system is open 5 AM to 8 PM daily. All records are available, including UCCs. Call 515-281-5204 and ask for Cheryl Allen for more information. Another online option is via the Internet. Access to information is free; however, the data is not as current as the DataShare System.

Uniform Commercial Code, Federal Tax Liens

UCC Division, Secretary of State, Hoover Bldg, 2nd Floor, Des Moines, IA 50319; 515-281-5204, 515-242-5953 (Other Fax Line), 515-242-6556 (Fax), 8AM-4:30PM.

www.sos.state.ia.us/business/services.html

Online: All information is available online at www.sos.state.ia.us/uccweb. There is no fee.

Legislation Records

Iowa General Assembly, Legislative Information Office, State Capitol, Des Moines, IA 50319; 515-281-5129, 8AM-4:30PM.

www.legis.state.ia.us

Online: Access is available through the Legislative Computer Support Bureau or through their web site.

State Level...Occupational Licensing

Acupuncturist... www.docboard.org/ia/find_ia.htm
Architect.. www.state.ia.us/government/com/prof/arch/archrost.htm
Bank.. www.idob.state.ia.us

Credit Union..www.iacudiv.state.ia.us/Public/fieldofmembership/membersearch.htm
Debt Management Company ....www.idob.state.ia.us/license/lic_default.htm
Delayed Deposit Service Business.....................www.idob.state.ia.us/license/lic_default.htm
Engineer ....www.state.ia.us/government/com/prof/engx/rosters.htm
Finance Company..www.idob.state.ia.us/license/lic_default.htm
Landscape Architect..www.state.ia.us/government/com/prof/lands/lanscros.htm
Medical Doctor ....www.docboard.org/ia/find_ia.htm
Money Transmitter...www.idob.state.ia.us/license/lic_default.htm
Mortgage Banker/Broker/Mortgage Loan Svc.....www.idob.state.ia.us/license/lic_default.htm
Notary Public..www.sos.state.ia.us/NotaryWeb
Optometrist..www.arbo.org/nodb2000/licsearch.asp
Osteopathic Physician ....www.docboard.org/ia/find_ia.htm
Public Accountant-CPA......................................www.state.ia.us/government/com/prof/acct/acctrost.htm
Real Estate Appraiser...www.state.ia.us/government/com/prof/realappr/approst.htm
Surveyor ....www.state.ia.us/government/com/prof/engx/rosters.htm
Trust Company ....www.idob.state.ia.us/license/lic_default.htm

County Level...Courts, Recorders & Assessors

State Court Administrator, State Capitol, Des Moines, IA, 50319; 515-281-5241; www.judicial.state.ia.us

Editor's Note: There is a statewide online computer system called the Iowa Court Information System (ICIS), which is for internal use only. There is no public access system.

Emmet
Real Estate
Online access to real estate records on the county database is available free at www.emmet.org/pmc. Also, the GIS mapping database may be searched. Includes parcel report, survey section grid, parcel maps, and more. Search the "Parcel Data" link by owner name, parcel ID, or address.

Polk
Property Records
www.co.polk.ia.us
Records on the Polk County assessor database is available free at www.co.polk.ia.us/departments/assessor/assessor.htm. Search by property or by sales.

Pottawattamie
Real Estate, Property Records
www.pottco.org
Records on the Pottawattamie County Courthouse/Council Bluffs property database are available free online. Search by owner name, address, or parcel number. Records of the Pottawattamie County Assessor "Residential Sales" database are available free online at www.pottco.org/htdocs/assessor.html.

Sioux
Tax Sale
www.court-house.co.sioux.ia.us
Online access to the Treasurer's delinquent tax list is available free at www.court-house.co.sioux.ia.us/pdf/taxlist.pdf.

Story
Assessor
www.storycounty.com/departments.html
Records on the county assessor database are available free online at www.storyassessor.org/pmc/query.asp.

Federal Courts in Iowa...

US District Court - Northern District of Iowa

Home Page: www.iand.uscourts.gov
PACER: Sign-up number is 800-676-5856. Access fee is $.60 per minute. Toll-free access: 888-845-4528. Local access: 319-362-3256. Case records are available back to November 1992. New records are available online after 1 day.
Cedar Rapids Division Counties: Benton, Cedar, Cerro Gordo, Grundy, Hardin, Iowa, Jones, Linn, Tama.
Dubuque Division Counties: Allamakee, Black Hawk, Bremer, Buchanan, Chickasaw, Clayton, Delaware, Dubuque, Fayette, Floyd, Howard, Jackson, Mitchell, Winneshiek.
Sioux City Division Counties: Buena Vista, Cherokee, Clay, Crawford, Dickinson, Ida, Lyon, Monona, O'Brien, Osceola, Plymouth, Sac, Sioux, Woodbury.

US Bankruptcy Court - Northern District of Iowa

PACER: Sign-up number is. Access fee is. New records are available online after.
PACER Internet Access: http://pacer.ianb.uscourts.gov.
Cedar Rapids Division Counties: Allamakee, Benton, Black Hawk, Bremer, Buchanan, Buena Vista, Butler, Calhoun, Carroll, Cedar, Cerro Gordo, Cherokee, Chickasaw, Clay, Clayton, Crawford, Delaware, Dickinson, Dubuque, Emmet, Fayette, Floyd, Franklin, Grundy, Hamilton, Hancock, Hardin,Howard, Humboldt, Ida, Iowa, Jackson, Jones, Kossuth, Linn, Lyon, Mitchell, Monona, O'Brien, Osceola, Palo Alto, Plymouth, Pocahontas, Sac, Sioux, Tama, Webster, Winnebago, Winneshiek, Woodbury, Worth, Wright.

US District Court - Southern District of Iowa

Home Page: www.iasd.uscourts.gov
PACER: Sign-up number is 800-676-6856. Access fee is $.60 per minute. Case records are available back to mid 1989. Records are purged every six months. New records are available online after 3 days.
PACER Internet Access: http://pacer.iasd.uscourts.gov.
Council Bluffs Division Counties: Audubon, Cass, Fremont, Harrison, Mills, Montgomery, Page, Pottawattamie, Shelby.
Davenport Division Counties: Henry, Johnson, Lee, Louisa, Muscatine, Scott, Van Buren, Washington.
Des Moines (Central) Division Counties: Adair, Adams, Appanoose, Boone, Clarke, Clinton, Dallas, Davis, Decatur, Des Moines, Greene, Guthrie, Jasper, Jefferson, Keokuk, Lucas, Madison, Mahaska, Marion, Marshall, Monroe, Polk, Poweshiek, Ringgold, Story, Taylor, Union, Wapello, Warren, Wayne.

US Bankruptcy Court - Southern District of Iowa

PACER: Sign-up number is 800-676-6856. Access fee is $.60 per minute. Toll-free access: 800-597-5917. Local access: 515-284-6466. Case records available back to June 1987. Records are purged every six months. New civil records available online after 1 day.
Des Moines Division Counties: Adair, Adams, Appanoose, Audubon, Boone, Cass, Clarke, Clinton, Dallas, Davis, Decatur, Des Moines, Fremont, Greene, Guthrie, Harrison, Henry, Jasper, Jefferson, Johnson, Keokuk, Lee, Louisa, Lucas, Madison, Mahaska, Marion, Marshall, Mills, Monroe,Montgomery, Muscatine, Page, Polk, Pottawattamie, Poweshiek, Ringgold, Scott, Shelby, Story, Taylor, Union, Van Buren, Wapello, Warren, Washington, Wayne.

Editor's Choice for Iowa

Here are some additional sites recommended for this state.

Appeals Court Opinions
www.judicial.state.ia.us/decisions/appeals/opinions
Retail Trade Statistics Database
www.profiles.iastate.edu/database/retail
Supreme Court Opinions
www.judicial.state.ia.us/decisions/supreme/opinions

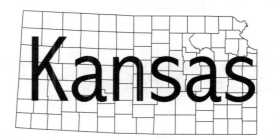

Capital:	Topeka Shawnee County	Home Page	www.state.ks.us
Time Zone:	CST/MST	Attorney General	www.ink.org/public/ksag
Number of Counties:	105	Archives	http://hs4.kshs.org

State Level...Major Agencies

Corporation Records, Limited Partnerships, Limited Liability Company Records

Secretary of State, Memorial Hall, 120 SW 10th Ave, 1st Floor, Topeka, KS 66612-1594; 785-296-4564, 785-296-4570 (Fax), 8AM-5PM.

http://okwww.kssos.org

Online: Corporate data can be ordered from the Information Network of Kansas (INK), a state sponsored interface at www.ink.org/public/corps. There is no fee to search or view records, but there is a fee to order copies of certificates or good standings. You must also subscribe to INK which entails an annual fee of $60.00 plus an initial subscription fee.

Uniform Commercial Code, Federal Tax Liens, State Tax Liens

UCC Division, Secretary of State, Memorial Hall, 120 SW 10th Ave, Topeka, KS 66612; 785-296-1849, 785-296-3659 (Fax), 8AM-5PM.

www.kssos.org/uccwelc.html

Online: Online service is provided the Information Network of Kansas (INK). The system is open 24 hours daily. There is an annual fee. Network charges are $.10 a minute unless access is through their Internet site - www.ink.org - which has no network fee. UCC records are $8.00 per record. This is the same online system used for corporation records. For more information, call INK at 800-4-KANSAS.

Driver Records, Accident Reports

Department of Revenue, Driver Control Bureau, PO Box 12021, Topeka, KS 66612-2021 (Courier: Docking State Office Building, 915 Harrison, 1st Floor, Topeka, KS 66612); 785-296-3671, 785-296-6851 (Fax), 8AM-4:45PM.

Online: Kansas has contracted with the Information Network of Kansas (INK) (800-452-6727) to service all electronic media requests of driver license histories. INK offers connection through an "800 number" or can be reached via the Internet - www.ink.org. The fee is $3.50 per record. There is an initial $75 subscription fee and an annual $60 fee to access records from INK. The system is open 24/7. Batch requests are available at 7:30 am (if ordered by 10PM the previous day).

Vehicle Ownership, Vehicle Identification

Division of Vehicles, Title and Registration Bureau, 915 Harrison, Rm 155, Topeka, KS 66612; 785-296-3621, 785-296-3852 (Fax), 7:30AM-4:45PM.

www.ink.org/public/kdor/kdorvehicle

Online: Online batch inquires are $3.00 per record; online interactive requests are $4.00 per record. See the Driving Records Section for a complete description of the Information Network of Kansas (800-452-6727), the state authorized vendor. There is an initial $75 subscription fee and an annual $60 fee to access records from INK.

Legislation Records

Kansas State Library, Capitol Bldg, 300 SW 10th Ave, Topeka, KS 66612; 785-296-2149, 785-296-6650 (Fax), 8AM-5PM.

www.ink.org

Online: The web site has bill information for the current session. The site also contains access to the state statutes.

State Level...Occupational Licensing

Athletic Trainer .... www.docboard.org/ks/df/kssearch.htm
Chiropractor.. www.docboard.org/ks/df/kssearch.htm
Insurance Company... www.ksinsurance.org/company/main.html
Lobbyist.. www.lobbyist.net/Kansas/KANLOB.htm
Medical Doctor .... www.docboard.org/ks/df/kssearch.htm
Mortician.. www.ink.org/public/ksbma/listings.html
Occupational Therapist/Assistant .... www.docboard.org/ks/df/kssearch.htm
Optometrist... www.odfinder.org/LicSearch.asp
Osteopathic Physician .... www.docboard.org/ks/df/kssearch.htm
Physical Therapist/Assistant.............................. www.docboard.org/ks/df/kssearch.htm
Physician Assistant .... www.docboard.org/ks/df/kssearch.htm
Podiatrist .... www.docboard.org/ks/df/kssearch.htm
Real Estate Appraiser... www.ink.org/public/kreab/appraisdir.html
Respiratory Therapist... www.docboard.org/ks/df/kssearch.htm

County Level...Courts, Recorders & Assessors

Judicial Administrator, Kansas Judicial Center, 301 SW 10th St, Topeka, KS, 66612; 785-296-4873; www.kscourts.org

Editor's Note: Commercial online access is available for District Court Records in 4 counties - Johnson, Sedgwick, Shawnee, and Wyandotte - through Access Kansas, part of the Information Network of Kansas (INK) Services. Franklin and Finney counties may be available in 2001. A user can access INK through their Internet site at www.ink.org or via a dial-up system. The INK subscription fee is $75.00, and the annual renewal fee is $60.00. There is no per minute connect charge, but there is a transaction fee. Other information from INK includes Drivers License, Title, Registration, Lien, and UCC searches. For additional information or a registration packet, call 800-4-KANSAS (800-452-6727).

Anderson
Civil Cases, Criminal Records
www.kscourts.org.dstcts/4dstct.htm
Current court calendars are available free online at www.kscourts.org/dstcts/4andckt.htm.

Coffey
Civil Cases, Criminal Records
www.kscourts.org/dstcts/4dstct.htm
Current court calendars are available free online at www.kscourts.org/dstcts/4codckt.htm.

Douglas
Civil Cases, Criminal Records
www.douglas-county.com/dcht.htm
Online access via Internet to district court records is available for a $180.00 annual fee and $60.00 set-up fee. For further information and registration, contact Beverly at 785-832-5299. All written requests must include a phone number. In person requests take 48 hours to process, if court does search.

Property Appraiser, Real Estate
www.douglas-county.com
Two non-government Internet sites provide free access to records from the Douglas County Assessor. Find County Property Appraiser records at www.douglas-county.com/value. Douglas County property valuations can be found at http://hometown.lawrence.com/valuation/valuation.cgi.

Franklin
Civil Cases, Criminal Records
www.kscourts.org/dstcts/4dstct.htm
Current court calendars are available free online at www.kscourts.org/dstcts/4frdckt.htm.

Johnson
Civil Cases, Criminal Records
www.jocoks.com/jococourts/index.htm
Index online through INK of Kansas. See www.ink.org for subscription information.

Property Appraiser
www.jocoks.com/appraiser
Records on the Johnson County Kansas Land Records database are available free online at www.jocoks.com/appraiser/disclaim.html. At the bottom of the Disclaimer page, click on "Yes" under "I understand and accept the above statement."

Osage
Civil Cases, Criminal Records
www.kscourts.org/dstcts/4dstct.htm
Current court calendars are available free online at www.kscourts.org/dstcts/4osdckt.htm.

Sedgwick
Civil Cases, Criminal Records
http://distcrt18.state.ks.us/
Access to the remote online system requires a $225 setup fee, $49 monthly fee and a small transaction fee. The system also includes probate, traffic, and domestic cases. For more information, call 316-383-7563.

Real Estate, Liens, Tax Assessor Records
www.co.sedgwick.ks.us/dept.htm
Records are available two ways. Records on the Sedgwick County online system are available for a set up fee of $225, with a $49 monthly fee, and a per transaction charge of $.03-$.04. Lending agency information is available. For information, call John Zukovich at 316-383-7384. A sex offender registry list is available on the Web at the county departments page. County Treasurer and Appraiser database records are available free online at www.co.sedgwick.ks.us/Appraiser/RealProperty.htm. Search by city, street numbers or name for property tax/appraisal information.

Shawnee
Civil Cases, Criminal Records
www.shawneecourt.org
Index online through INK of Kansas. See www.ink.org for subscription information. Also, online access to county court records is available free at www.shawneecourt.org/pa_inst.htm. Also, online access to court record images is available free at www.shawneecourt.org/img_temp.htm.

Wyandotte
Civil Cases, Criminal Records, Real Estate, Liens, Property Appraisal Records

County records are available online, and property tax records are available on the Internet. The online service requires a $20 set up fee, with a $5 monthly fee and $.05 each after the first 100 transactions. Lending agency information is available. For information, contact Louise Sachen at 913-573-2885. Records from the County Assessor Tax database are available free on the Internet at www.courthouseusa.com/wyanadd.htm. Search by street number and name, but no name searching.

Federal Courts in Kansas...

US District Court - District of Kansas

Home Page: www.ksd.uscourts.gov
PACER: Sign-up number is 800-676-6856. Access fee is $.60 per minute. Toll-free access: 800-898-3078. Local access: 913-551-6556. Case records are available back to 1991. Records are purged never. New civil records are available online after 2 days. New criminal records are available online after 3 days.
PACER Internet Access: http://pacer.ksd.uscourts.gov.
Kansas City Division Counties: Atchison, Bourbon, Brown, Cherokee, Crawford, Doniphan, Johnson, Labette, Leavenworth, Linn, Marshall, Miami, Nemaha, Wyandotte.
Topeka Division Counties: Allen, Anderson, Chase, Clay, Cloud, Coffey, Dickinson, Douglas, Franklin, Geary, Jackson, Jewell, Lincoln, Lyon, Marion, Mitchell, Morris, Neosho, Osage, Ottawa, Pottawatomie, Republic, Riley, Saline, Shawnee, Wabaunsee, Washington, Wilson, Woodson.
Wichita Division Counties: All counties in Kansas. Cases may be heard from counties in the other division.

US Bankruptcy Court - District of Kansas

Home Page: www.ksb.uscourts.gov
PACER: Sign-up number is 800-676-6856. Access fee is $.60 per minute. Toll-free access: 800-613-7052. Local access: 316-269-6258. Case records are available back to 1988. Records are purged every 6 months. New civil records are available online after 1 day.
PACER Internet Access: http://pacer.ksb.uscourts.gov.
Kansas City Division Counties: Atchison, Bourbon, Brown, Cherokee, Comanche, Crawford, Doniphan, Johnson, Labette, Leavenworth, Linn, Marshall, Miami, Nemaha, Wyandotte.
Topeka Division Counties: Allen, Anderson, Chase, Clay, Cloud, Coffey, Dickinson, Douglas, Franklin, Geary, Jackson, Jewell, Lincoln, Lyon, Marion, Mitchell, Morris, Neosho, Osage, Ottawa, Pottawatomie, Republic, Riley, Saline, Shawnee, Wabaunsee, Washington, Wilson, Woodson.
Wichita Division Counties: Barber, Barton, Butler, Chautauqua, Cheyenne, Clark, Comanche, Cowley, Decatur, Edwards, Elk, Ellis, Ellsworth, Finney, Ford, Gove, Graham, Grant, Gray, Greeley, Greenwood, Hamilton, Harper, Harvey, Haskell, Hodgeman, Jefferson, Kearny, Kingman, Kiowa,Lane, Logan, Mcpherson, Meade, Montgomery, Morton, Ness, Norton, Osborne, Pawnee, Phillips, Pratt, Rawlins, Reno, Rice, Rooks, Rush, Russell, Scott, Sedgwick, Seward, Sheridan, Smith, Stafford, Stanton, Stevens, Sumner, Thomas, Trego, Wallace, Wichita.

Editor's Choice for Kansas

Constitution Text
   http://skyways.lib.ks.us/kansas/KSL/Ref/GovDocs/Kan/State_Const/ks_const.html
Offenders Released Listing
   http://docnet.dc.state.ks.us/offenders/Offenders/releases.htm
Prison Escapees Listing
   http://docnet.dc.state.ks.us/escapees/index.htm
Supreme Court & Court of Appeals Opinions
   www.kscourts.org/kscases/wordsrch.htm

Capital:	Frankfort Franklin County	Home Page	www.state.ky.us
Time Zone:	EST/CST	Attorney General	www.law.state.ky.us
Number of Counties:	120	Archives	www.kdla.state.ky.us

State Level...Major Agencies

Corporation Records, Limited Partnerships, Assumed Name, Limited Liability Company Records

Secretary of State, Corporate Records, PO Box 718, Frankfort, KY 40602-0718 (Courier: 700 Capitol Ave, Room 156, Frankfort, KY 40601); 502-564-7330, 502-564-4075 (Fax), 8AM-4PM.

www.sos.state.ky.us

Online: The Internet site, open 24 hours, has a searchable database with over 340,000 KY businesses. The site also offers downloading of filing forms.

Uniform Commercial Code

UCC Division, Secretary of State, PO Box 1470, Frankfort, KY 40602-0718 (Courier: State Capitol Bldg, Rm 79, Frankfort, KY 40601); 502-564-2848, 502-564-5687 (Fax), 8AM-4:30PM.

www.sos.state.ky.us

Online: The Kentucky Lien Information Search System is offered free of charge at the web site. Search by debtor name, secured party name, location or date of filing, or county identification number.

Death, Marriage, Divorce Records

Department for Public Health, Vital Statistics, 275 E Main St - IE-A, Frankfort, KY 40621-0001; 502-564-4212, 502-227-0032 (Fax), 8AM-3PM.

http://publichealth.state.ky.us/vital.htm

Online: In cooperation with the University of Kentucky, there is a searchable index at http://ukcc.uky.edu:80/~vitalrec. This is for non-commercial use only. Death Records are from 1911 through 1992. The marriage index runs from 1973 through 1993. The divorce index is for 1973-1993.

Driver Records

Division of Driver Licensing, State Office Bldg, MVRS, 501 High Street, 2nd Floor, Frankfort, KY 40622; 502-564-6800 x2250, 502-564-5787 (Fax), 8AM-4:30PM.

www.kytc.state.ky.us

Online: This is a batch method for higher volume users. There is a minimum order of 150 requests per batch. Input received by 3 PM is available the next morning. Either the DL# or SSN is needed for ordering. The state will bill monthly. Fee is $3.00 per record.

Vehicle Ownership, Vehicle Identification

Department of Motor Vehicles, Division of Motor Vehicle Licensing, State Office Bldg, 3rd Floor, Frankfort, KY 40622; 502-564-4076 (Title History), 502-564-3298 (Other Requests), 502-564-1686 (Fax), 8AM-4:30PM.

www.kytc.state.ky.us

Online: Online access costs $2.00 per record. The online mode is interactive. Title, lien and registration searches are available. Records include those for mobile homes. For more information, contact Gale Warfield at 502-564-4076.

Legislation Records

Kentucky General Assembly, Legislative Research Commission, 700 Capitol Ave, Room 300, Frankfort, KY 40601; 502-372-7181 (Bill Status Only), 502-564-8100 x323 (Bill Room), 502-564-8100 x340 (LRC Library), 502-223-5094 (Fax), 8AM-4:30PM.

www.lrc.state.ky.us

Online: The web site has an extensive searching mechanism for bills, actions, summaries, and statutes.

State Level...Occupational Licensing

Architect .... http://kybera.com/roster.shtml
Check Seller/ Casher................ www.dfi.state.ky.us/banking/Compliance_Branch/financial_institutions_complianc.htm
Engineer .... http://kyboels.state.ky.us/roster.htm
Engineer/Land Surveyor Firm .. http://kyboels.state.ky.us/roster.htm
Geologist .... www.state.ky.us/agencies/finance/boards/geology/pages/geol.html
Loan Company .... www.dfi.state.ky.us/banking/Compliance_Branch/financial_institutions_complianc.htm
Mortgage Broker .... www.dfi.state.ky.us/aspscripts/mort_brokers.asp
Mortgage Loan Company .... www.dfi.state.ky.us/aspscripts/mort_company.asp
Optometrist............................... http://web.state.ky.us/GBC/LicenseSearch.asp?AGY=8
Physical Therapist/Assistant..... http://web.state.ky.us/gbc/LicenseSearch.asp?AGY=4
Public Accountant-CPA............ http://cpa.state.ky.us/Locate.html
Real Estate Broker/Sales Assoc.http://web.state.ky.us/krecweb/LicenseeLookUp.asp
Real Estate Broker Firm........... http://web.state.ky.us/krecweb/FirmLookUp.asp
Surveyor .... http://kyboels.state.ky.us/roster.htm

County Level...Courts, Recorders & Assessors

Administrative Office of Courts, 100 Mill Creek Park, Frankfort, KY, 40601; 502-573-2350; www.kycourts.net/aoc/default.htm

Editor's Note: There are statewide, online computer systems called SUSTAIN and KyCourts available for internal judicial/state agency use only. No courts offer online access.

Boone
Real Estate, Lines, UCCs, Assessor, Marriage
www.boonecountyclerk.com
Online access to the county clerk database is available through eCCLIX, a fee-based service; $200.00 sign-up and $65.00 monthly. Records go back to 1989; images to 1998. For information, see the web site or call 502-266-9445.

Boyd
Real Estate, Liens
Access to the County Clerk online records requires a $10 monthly usage fee. The system operates 24 hours daily; records date back to 1/1979. Lending agency information is available. For information, contact Maxine Selbee or Kathy Fisher at 606-739-5166.

Kenton
Property Appraiser
www.kentonpva.com
Online access to the county Property Valuation database is available free at www.kentonpva.com/pvacat/catsearch.htm.

Oldham
Real Estate, Liens, UCC, Assessor, Marriage
http://oldhamcounty.state.ky.us
Online access to the county clerk database is available through eCCLIX, a fee-based service; $200.00 sign-up and $65.00 monthly. Records go back, generally, to 1980. UCC images to 2/97. Real estate instruments back to 1/95. Marriages back to 1977. For information, call 502-222-9311. For information, see the web site or call 502-266-9445.

Warren
Real Estate, Liens, UCCs, Assessor, Marriage
http://warrencounty.state.ky.us
Online access to the county clerk database is available through eCCLIX, a fee-based service; $200.00 sign-up and $65.00 monthly. Records go back to 1989; images to 1998. For information, see the web site or call 502-266-9445.

Federal Courts in Kentucky...

US District Court - Eastern District of Kentucky
Home Page: www.kyed.uscourts.gov
PACER: Sign-up number is 800-676-6856. Access fee is $.60 per minute. Toll-free access: 800-361-0442. Local access: 606-233-2787. Case records are available back to September 1991. Records are purged never. New records are available online after 1 day.
PACER Internet Access: http://pacer.kyed.uscourts.gov.
Ashland Division Counties: Boyd, Carter, Elliott, Greenup, Lawrence, Lewis, Morgan, Rowan.
Covington Division Counties: Boone, Bracken, Campbell, Gallatin, Grant, Kenton, Mason, Pendleton, Robertson.
Frankfort Division Counties: Anderson, Carroll, Franklin, Henry, Owen, Shelby, Trimble.
Lexington Division Counties: Bath, Bourbon, Boyle, Clark, Estill, Fayette, Fleming, Garrard, Harrison, Jessamine, Lee, Lincoln, Madison, Menifee, Mercer, Montgomery, Nicholas, Powell, Scott, Wolfe, Woodford. Lee and Wolfe counties were part of the Pikeville Divisionbefore 10/31/92. Perry became part of Pikeville after 1992.
London Division Counties: Bell, Clay, Harlan, Jackson, Knox, Laurel, Leslie, McCreary, Owsley, Pulaski, Rockcastle, Wayne, Whitley.
Pikeville Division Counties: Breathitt, Floyd, Johnson, Knott, Letcher, Magoffin, Martin, Perry, Pike. Lee and Wolfe Counties were part of this division until 10/31/92, when they were moved to the Lexington Division.

US Bankruptcy Court - Eastern District of Kentucky
Home Page: www.kyeb.uscourts.gov
PACER: Sign-up number is 800-676-6856. Access fee is $.60 per minute. Toll-free access: 800-497-2777. Local access: 606-233-2777. Case records are available back to July 1992. Records are purged every six months. New civil records are available online after 1 day.
PACER Internet Access: http://pacer.kyeb.uscourts.gov.
Lexington Division Counties: Anderson, Bath, Bell, Boone, Bourbon, Boyd, Boyle, Bracken, Breathitt, Campbell, Carroll, Carter, Clark, Clay, Elliott, Estill, Fayette, Fleming, Floyd, Franklin, Gallatin, Garrard, Grant, Greenup, Harlan, Harrison, Henry, Jackson, Jessamine, Johnson,Kenton, Knott, Knox, Laurel, Lawrence, Lee, Leslie, Letcher, Lewis, Lincoln, Madison, Magoffin, Martin, Mason, McCreary, Menifee, Mercer, Montgomery, Morgan, Nicholas, Owen, Owsley, Pendleton, Perry, Pike, Powell, Pulaski, Robertson, Rockcastle, Rowan,Scott, Shelby, Trimble, Wayne, Whitley, Wolfe, Woodford.

US District Court - Western District of Kentucky

Home Page: www.kywd.uscourts.gov
PACER: Sign-up number is 800-676-6856. Access fee is $.60 per minute. Case records are available back to 1992. New records are available online after 1 day.
PACER Internet Access: http://38.244.24.105/webpacer.html.
Electronic Filing: Only law firms and practictioners may file cases electronically. Electronic filing information is available online at www.kywd.uscourts.gov/scripts/usdckyw/ecf/ecf.pl.
Bowling Green Division Counties: Adair, Allen, Barren, Butler, Casey, Clinton, Cumberland, Edmonson, Green, Hart, Logan, Metcalfe, Monroe, Russell, Simpson, Taylor, Todd, Warren.
Louisville Division Counties: Breckinridge, Bullitt, Hardin, Jefferson, Larue, Marion, Meade, Nelson, Oldham, Spencer, Washington.
Owensboro Division Counties: Daviess, Grayson, Hancock, Henderson, Hopkins, McLean, Muhlenberg, Ohio, Union, Webster.
Paducah Division Counties: Ballard, Caldwell, Calloway, Carlisle, Christian, Crittenden, Fulton, Graves, Hickman, Livingston, Lyon, McCracken, Marshall, Trigg.

US Bankruptcy Court - Western District of Kentucky

Home Page: www.kywb.uscourts.gov
PACER: Sign-up number is 800-676-6856. Access fee is $.60 per minute. Toll-free access: 800-263-9389. Local access: 502-627-5664. Case records are available back to July 1992. Records are purged every six months. New civil records are available online after 1-2 days.
PACER Internet Access: http://pacer.kywb.uscourts.gov.
Louisville Division Counties: Adair, Allen, Ballard, Barren, Breckinridge, Bullitt, Butler, Caldwell, Calloway, Carlisle, Casey, Christian, Clinton, Crittenden, Cumberland, Daviess, Edmonson, Fulton, Graves, Grayson, Green, Hancock, Hardin, Hart, Henderson, Hickman, Hopkins,Jefferson, Larue, Livingston, Logan, Lyon, Marion, Marshall, McCracken, McLean, Meade, Metcalfe, Monroe, Muhlenberg, Nelson, Ohio, Oldham, Russell, Simpson, Spencer, Taylor, Todd, Trigg, Union, Warren, Washington, Webster.

Editor's Choice for Kentucky

Here are some additional sites recommended for this state.

Atlas & Gazetteer Maps
www.uky.edu/KentuckyAtlas
Birth & Death Records Request Forms (Paper)
www.kdla.state.ky.us/arch/Bdvital.htm
Place Names Database
www.uky.edu/KentuckyPlaceNames/

Capital: Baton Rouge
               East Baton Rouge Parish

Time Zone: CST

Number of Parishes: 64

Home Page   www.state.la.us

Attorney General   www.ag.state.la.us

Archives   www.sec.state.la.us/archives/archives/
            archives-index.htm

State Level...Major Agencies

Corporation Records, Limited Partnership Records, Limited Liability Company Records, Trademarks/Servicemarks

Commercial Division, Corporation Department, PO Box 94125, Baton Rouge, LA 70804-9125 (Courier: 3851 Essen Lane, Baton Rouge, LA 70809); 225-925-4704, 225-925-4726 (Fax), 8AM-4:30PM.

www.sec.state.la.us

Online: There are 2 ways to go: free on the Internet or pay. Free but limited information is available on the web site; go to "Commercial Division, Corporations Section," then "Search Corporations Database." The pay system is $360 per year for unlimited access. Almost any communications software will work with up to a 14,400 baud rate. The system is open from 6:30 am to 11pm. For more information, call Brenda Wright at (225) 922-1475.

Uniform Commercial Code

Secretary of State, UCC Records, PO Box 94125, Baton Rouge, LA 70804-9125; 800-256-3758, 225-342-9011 (Fax).

www.sec.state.la.us/comm/ucc-index.htm

Online: An annual $400 fee gives unlimited access to UCC filing information. The dial-up service is open from 6:30 AM to 11 PM daily. Minimum baud rate is 9600. Most any software communications program can be configured to work. For further information, call Brenda Wright at 225-922-1475, or visit the web site.

Driver Records

Dept of Public Safety and Corrections, Office of Motor Vehicles, PO Box 64886, Baton Rouge, LA 70896 (Courier: 109 S Foster Dr, Baton Rouge, LA 70806); 877-368-5463, 225-925-6388, 225-925-6915 (Fax), 8AM-4:30PM.

www.dps.state.la.us/omv/home.html

Online: Online, interactive mode is available from 7 AM to 9:30 PM daily. There is a minimum order requirement of 2,000 requests per month. A bond or large deposit is required. Fee is $6.00 per record. For more information, call 225-925-6032. There are plans to convert to an Internet based system later in 2001.

Vehicle Ownership, Vehicle Identification

Department of Public Safety & Corrections, Office of Motor Vehicles, PO Box 64886, Baton Rouge, LA 70896 (Courier: 109 S Foster Dr, Baton Rouge, LA 70806); 225-922-6146, 877-368-5463, 225-925-3979 (Fax), 8AM-4PM.

www.dps.state.la.us/dmv/home.html

Online: Online access costs $6.00 per record. Minimum usage is 2,000 requests per month. The online system operates similar to the system for driving records. For more information: Dept. of Public Safety and Corrections, PO Box 66614, Baton Rouge, LA 70896; 225-925-6032.

Legislation Records

Louisiana House (Senate) Representative, State Capitol, 2nd Floor, PO Box 44486, Baton Rouge, LA 70804; 225-342-2456 (Information Help Desk), 225-342-2365 (Senate Documents (Room 205)), 225-342-6458 (House Documents (Room 207)), 800-256-3793 (General Information, In-state), 8AM-5PM.

www.legis.state.la.us

Online: The Internet site has a wealth of information about sessions and bills from 1997 forward.

State Level...Occupational Licensing

Acupuncturist	www.lsbme.org/bmeSearch/licenseesearch.asp
Athletic Trainer	www.lsbme.org/bmeSearch/licenseesearch.asp
Bank	www.ofi.state.la.us/newbanks.htm
Bond For Deed	www.ofi.state.la.us/newbfd.htm
Check Casher	www.ofi.state.la.us/newcheckcash.htm
Clinical Exercise Physiologist	www.lsbme.org/bmeSearch/licenseesearch.asp
Clinical Lab Personnel	www.lsbme.org/bmeSearch/licenseesearch.asp
Collection Agency	www.ofi.state.la.us/newcolagn.htm
Consumer Credit	www.ofi.state.la.us/newliclen.htm
Credit Repair	www.ofi.state.la.us/newcredrep.htm
Dental Hygienist	www.lsbd.org/fpDentistSearch.asp
Dentist	www.lsbd.org/dentistsearch.asp
Engineer	www.lapels.com/indv_reg.html
Insurance Agent/Broker	www.ldi.state.la.us/searchforms/searchform.asp
Insurance Agent-LHA/PC	www.ldi.state.la.us/searchforms/searchform.asp
Land Surveyor	www.lapels.com/indv_reg.html
Lenders	www.ofi.state.la.us/newliclen.htm
Lobbyist	www.ethics.state.la.us/lobs.htm
Medical Doctor	www.lsbme.org/bmeSearch/licenseesearch.asp
Midwife	www.lsbme.org/bmeSearch/licenseesearch.asp
Notary Public	www.sec.state.la.us/notary-pub/NTRINQ.htm
Notification Filers	www.ofi.state.la.us/newnotif.htm
Occupational Therapist/Technologist	www.lsbme.org/bmeSearch/licenseesearch.asp
Optometrist	www.odfinder.org/LicSearch.asp
Osteopathic Physician	www.lsbme.org/bmeSearch/licenseesearch.asp
Pawnbroker	www.ofi.state.la.us/newpawn.htm
Physician Assistant	www.lsbme.org/bmeSearch/licenseesearch.asp
Podiatrist	www.lsbme.org/bmeSearch/licenseesearch.asp
Radiologic Technologist, Private	www.lsbme.org/bmeSearch/licenseesearch.asp
Professional Counselor (LPC)	www.lpcboard.org/lpc_alpha_list.htm
Residential Mortgage Lenders/Brokers	www.ofi.state.la.us/newrml.htm

Respiratory Therapist/Technician .... www.lsbme.org/bmeSearch/licenseesearch.asp
Savings & Loan & Credit Union........................ www.ofi.state.la.us/newcus.htm
Solicitor.. www.ldi.state.la.us/searchforms/searchform.asp
Thrifts.. www.ofi.state.la.us/newthrift.htm
Vocational Rehabilitative Counselor .... www.lrcboard.org/licensee_database.asp
Wholesale Drug Distributor .... http://host.ntg.com/ldwdd/search.asp

County Level...Courts, Recorders & Assessors

Judicial Administrator, Judicial Council of the Supreme Court, 1555 Poydras St #1540, New Orleans, LA, 70112; 504-568-5747; www.lajao.org

Editor's Note: The online computer system, Case Management Information System (CMIS), is operating and its development continues. It is for internal use only; there is no plan to permit online public access. However, Supreme Court opinions are currently available.

Bossier Parish

Civil Cases, Criminal Records, Mortgage, Marriage Records

www.ebrclerkofcourt.org

Access to the Parish Clerk of Court online records requires a $100 setup fee and a $15 monthly minimum plus $.33 per minute if you view, $.50 if you print. Civil, criminal, probate (1988 forward), traffic and domestic index information is available by name or case number. Includes conveyance and mortgage record indexes from the previous 2 years to present. Also, marriage and court records from 1988 to present. Call the MIS Dept. at 225-389-5295 for more information.

Caddo Parish

Civil Cases, Criminal Records, Real Estate, Liens, Marriage

www.caddoclerk.com

Online access to civil records back to 1994 and name index back to 1984 are available through the county dial-up service. Registration and $50 set-up fee and $30 monthly usage fee is required. For information and sign-up, call 318-226-6918 or Susan Twohig at 318-226-6523. Online criminal name index goes back to 1980; minutes to 1984. Current calendar is also available. Mortgages and indirect conveyances date back to 1981; direct conveyances date back to 1914. Lending agency information available. Marriage licenses go back to 1937.

East Baton Rouge Parish

Civil Cases, Criminal Records

www.16thcircuit.org

There is no fee for remote online service, but a request to sign up must be on company letterhead and include indication of the business you are in. Fax requests to 816-851-3148. Call Becki Fortune at 816-881-3411 for information. Also, the court participates in a free Internet service at http://168.166.59.61/casenet/welcome.asp. Search by name, case number or filing date.

Real Estate, Liens

Access to online records requires a $100 set up fee with a $5 monthly fee and $.33 per minute of use. Four years worth of data is kept active on the system. Lending agency information is available. For information, contact Wendy Gibbs at 225-398-5295.

Iberia Parish

Civil Cases, Criminal Records, Real Estate, Liens, Marriage Records, Divorce Records

Access to the Parish online records requires a $50 monthly usage fee. Records date back to 1959. Lending agency information is available. For information, contact Mike Thibodeaux at 337-365-7282.

Jefferson Parish

Civil Cases, Criminal Records, Real Estate, Assessor, Marriage

www.clerkofcourt.co.jefferson.la.us

Online access to the clerk's JeffNet database is available by subscription; set-up fee is $200 plus $8.50 monthly and $.25 per minute. Mortgage and conveyance images go back to 1990; index to 1967. Marriage and assessor records go back to 1992. For information, visit www.clerkofcourt.co.jefferson.la.us/jeffnet.htm or call 504-364-2908.

Lafayette Parish
Civil Cases, Criminal Records, Real Estate, Liens
www.lafayetteparishclerk.com or www.lafayettecourthouse.com
Access to Parish online records requires a $100 set up fee plus $15 per month and $.50 per minute. Civil index goes back to 1986.
Conveyances date back to 1936; mortgages to 1948; other records to 1986. Lending agency information is available. For information,
contact Derek Comeaux at 337-291-6433 or Mike Prejean at 337-291-6232. Tax and UCC lien information is for this parish only.

Morehouse Parish
Real Estate, Liens
Remote online access will be available in 2001. The service and fees will be similar to the Lafayette Parish.

Orleans Parish
Civil Cases, Real Estate, Liens
www.orleanscdc.gov
Access to the Parish online records requires a set up fee and $300 deposit for 1,200 minutes of usage, plus $.25 per minute. Records
date back to 9/1987. Includes parish mortgage and conveyance indexes. No lending agency information is available. For information,
contact John Rabb at 504-592-9264.

St. Tammany Parish
Real Estate, Liens
http://stp.pa.st-tammany.la.us
Access to online records requires a $100 set up fee, plus $.30 per minute of use. Records date back to 1961; viewable images on
conveyances back to 1985; mortgages to 8/93. For information, contact Mark Cohn at 504-898-2890 or Christy Howell at 504-898-
2491. UCC lien information is with the Secretary of State.

Tangipahoa Parish
Civil Cases, Criminal Records, Real Estate, Liens, Recordings
www.tangiclerk.org
Access to Parish online records requires registration and a $55or $125 monthly fee. Record dates vary though most indexes go back to
1990. Lending agency information is available. For information, contact Alison Carona at 504-549-1611. Also, a mapping feature is
being developed that includes assessor basic information; access will be free.

Federal Courts in Louisiana...

US District Court - Eastern District of Louisiana
Home Page: www.laed.uscourts.gov
PACER: Sign-up number is 800-676-6856. Access fee is $.60 per minute. Toll-free access: 888-257-1175. Local access: 504-589-
6714. Case records are available back to 1989. Records are purged every six months. New records are available online after 1-2 days.
PACER Internet Access: http://pacer.laed.uscourts.gov.
New Orleans Division Counties: Assumption Parish, Jefferson Parish, Lafourche Parish, Orleans Parish, Plaquemines Parish, St.
Bernard Parish, St. Charles Parish, St. James Parish, St. John the Baptist Parish, St. Tammany Parish, Tangipahoa Parish, Terrebonne
Parish, Washington Parish.

US Bankruptcy Court - Eastern District of Louisiana
Home Page: www.laeb.uscourts.gov
PACER: Sign-up number is 800-676-6856. Access fee is $.60 per minute. Toll-free access: 800-743-2464. Local access: 504-589-
6761. Case records are available back to 1985. Records are purged every six months. New civil records available online after 2 days.
PACER Internet Access: http://pacer.laeb.uscourts.gov.
New Orleans Division Counties: Assumption Parish, Jefferson Parish, Lafourche Parish, Orleans Parish, Plaquemines Parish, St.
Bernard Parish, St. Charles Parish, St. James Parish, St. John the Baptist Parish, St. Tammany Parish, Tangipahoa Parish, Terrebonne
Parish, Washington Parish.

US District Court - Middle District of Louisiana

Home Page: www.lamd.uscourts.gov
PACER: Sign-up number is 800-676-6856. Access fee is $.60 per minute. Toll-free access: 800-616-8757. Local access: 225-389-3547. Case records are available back to October 1993. New records are available online after 1 day.
PACER Internet Access: http://pacer.lamd.uscourts.gov.
Baton Rouge Division Counties: Ascension Parish, East Baton Rouge Parish, East Feliciana Parish, Iberville Parish, Livingston Parish, Pointe Coupee Parish, St. Helena Parish, West Baton Rouge Parish, West Feliciana Parish.

US Bankruptcy Court - Middle District of Louisiana

Home Page: www.lamb.uscourts.gov
PACER: Sign-up number is 800-676-6856. Access fee is $.60 per minute. Case records are available back to May 15, 1992. New civil records are available online after 1 day.
PACER Internet Access: http://pacer.lamb.uscourts.gov.
Baton Rouge Division Counties: Ascension Parish, East Baton Rouge Parish, East Feliciana Parish, Iberville Parish, Livingston Parish, Pointe Coupee Parish, St. Helena Parish, West Baton Rouge Parish, West Feliciana Parish.

US District Court - Western District of Louisiana

Home Page: www.lawd.uscourts.gov
PACER: Sign-up number is 800-676-6856. Access fee is $.60 per minute. Toll-free access: 888-263-2679. Local access: 318-676-3958. Case records available back to 11/1993. Records are purged as deemed necessary. New records available online after 1 day.
PACER Internet Access: https://pacer.lawd.uscourts.gov.
Alexandria Division Counties: Avoyelles Parish, Catahoula Parish, Concordia Parish, Grant Parish, La Salle Parish, Natchitoches Parish, Rapides Parish, Winn Parish.
Lafayette Division Counties: Acadia Parish, Evangeline Parish, Iberia Parish, Lafayette Parish, St. Landry Parish, St. Martin Parish, St. Mary Parish, Vermilion Parish.
Lake Charles Division Counties: Allen Parish, Beauregard Parish, Calcasieu Parish, Cameron, Jefferson Davis, Vernon Parish.
Monroe Division Counties: Caldwell Parish, East Carroll Parish, Franklin Parish, Jackson Parish, Lincoln Parish, Madison Parish, Morehouse Parish, Ouachita Parish, Richland Parish, Tensas Parish, Union Parish, West Carroll Parish.
Shreveport Division Counties: Bienville Parish, Bossier Parish, Caddo Parish, Claiborne Parish, De Soto Parish, Red River Parish, Sabine Parish, Webster Parish.

US Bankruptcy Court - Western District of Louisiana

Home Page: www.lawb.uscourts.gov
PACER: Sign-up number is 800-676-6856. Access fee is $.60 per minute. Toll-free access: 888-523-1976. Local access: 318-676-4235. Case records are available back to 1992. New civil records are available online after 1 day.
PACER Internet Access: http://pacer.lawb.uscourts.gov.
Alexandria Division Counties: Avoyelles Parish, Catahoula Parish, Concordia Parish, Grant Parish, La Salle Parish, Natchitoches Parish, Rapides Parish, Vernon Parish, Winn Parish.
Lafayette-Opelousas Division Counties: Acadia Parish, Evangeline Parish, Iberia Parish, Lafayette Parish, St. Landry Parish, St. Martin Parish, St. Mary Parish, Vermilion Parish.
Lake Charles Division Counties: Allen Parish, Beauregard Parish, Calcasieu Parish, Cameron Parish, Jefferson Davis Parish.
Monroe Division Counties: Caldwell Parish, East Carroll Parish, Franklin Parish, Jackson Parish, Lincoln Parish, Madison Parish, Morehouse Parish, Ouachita Parish, Richland Parish, Tensas Parish, Union Parish, West Carroll Parish.
Shreveport Division Counties: Bienville Parish, Bossier Parish, Caddo Parish, Claiborne Parish, De Soto Parish, Red River Parish, Sabine Parish, Webster Parish.

Editor's Choice for

Campaign Finance Database
www.ethics.state.la.us/view.htm
Sex Offenders & Child Predators Database
www.lasocpr.lsp.org/Static/Search.htm
State Agencies Directory
www.state.la.us/otm/listings/telefone.htm

Capital: Augusta
                Kennebec County

Time Zone: EST

Number of Counties: 16

Home Page   www.state.me.us

Attorney General   www.state.me.us/ag

Archives   www.state.me.us/sos/arc

State Level...Major Agencies

Corporation Records, Limited Partnerships, Trademarks/Servicemarks, Assumed Name, Limited Liability Company, Limited Liability Partnerships

Secretary of State, Reports & Information Division, 101 State House Station, Augusta, ME 04333-0101; 207-624-7752, 207-624-7736 (Main Number), 207-287-5874 (Fax), 8AM-5PM.

www.state.me.us/sos/cec/corp

Online: The Internet site gives basic information about the entity including address, corp ID, agent, and status.

Birth/Death Records, Marriage Certificates

Maine Department of Human Services, Vital Records, 221 State St, Station 11, Augusta, ME 04333-0011; 207-287-3181, 207-287-1907 (Fax), 8AM-5PM.

www.state.me.us/dhs/welcome.htm

Online: Pre-1892 birth records are available at the Internet at www.state.me.us/sos/geneology/homepage.html. Both old and newer death records are available at www.state.me.us/sos/arc/geneology/homepage.html. Death History records from the Maine State Archives are also available at http://thor.ddp.state.me.us/archives.plsql/archdev.death_archinve.search_form. Marriage Certificate Records are available at www.state.me.us/sos/arc/geneology/homepage.html from 1892-1966 and 1976-1996. Marriage History records from the Maine State Archives are available at http://thor/ddp.state.me.us.

Driver Records

Bureau of Motor Vehicles, Driver License Services, 29 State House Station, Augusta, ME 04333-0029; 207-624-9000, 8AM-5PM.

www.state.me.us/sos/bmv

Online: Access is through InforME via the Internet. There is a $50.00 annual fee and records are $5.00 per request. Visit the web site for details and sign-up or call 207-621-2600. The state offers "Driver Cross Check" - a program of notification when activity occurs on a specific record.

Vehicle Ownership, Vehicle Identification

Department of Motor Vehicles, Registration Section, 29 State House Station, Augusta, ME 04333-0029; 207-624-9000 x52149, 207-287-5219 (Fax), 8AM-5PM M-T,TH-F; 8AM-4PM W.

www.state.me.us/sos/bmv/bmv.htm

Online: Maine offers online access to title and registration records via PC and modem. The system is open 24 hours daily. To set up an account, call 207-624-9264. Fee is $5.00 per record, annual registration is $50.00.

Legislation Records

Maine Legislature, 2 State House Station, Legislative Document Room, Augusta, ME 04333-0002; 207-287-1692 (Bill Status or LD #), 207-287-1408 (Document Room), 207-287-1456 (Fax), 8AM-5PM.

http://janus.state.me.us/legis/

Online: The web site offers bills, status, and access to text of state laws.

GED Certificates

Dept of Education, Attn: GED, 23 State House Station, Augusta, ME 04333; 207-624-6752, 207-624-6731 (Fax).

http://janus.state.me.us/education

Online: E-mail requests can be made by sending e-mail to: lisataylor@state&me.us

State Level...Occupational Licensing

Employee Leasing Company.............................. www.state.me.us/pfr/ins/emplease.htm
Health Maintenance Organization .... www.state.me.us/pfr/ins/inshmo.htm
Lobbyist... www.lobbyist.net/Maine/MAILOB.htm
Medical Doctor .... www.docboard.org/me/df/mesearch.htm
Notary Public.. www.state.me.us/sos/cec/rcn/notary/notlist.htm
Optometrist.. www.odfinder.org/LicSearch.asp
Osteopathic Physician/Resident/Intern............... www.docboard.org/me-osteo
Preferred Provider Organization .... www.state.me.us/pfr/ins/insppo.htm
Registration-ATV, Watercraft, Snowmobile .... www.state.me.us/ifw/index.html
Utilitization Review Entitity............................. www.state.me.us/pfr/ins/insmedur.htm

County Level...Courts, Recorders & Assessors

State Court Administrator, PO Box 4820, Portland, ME, 04112; 207-822-0792; www.courts.state.me.us

Editor's Note: Development of a statewide judicial computer system is in progress and will be available statewide sometime in the future. The system will be initially for judicial and law enforcement agencies and will not include public access in the near term. Some counties are online through a private vendor.

Barnstable
Civil Cases, Criminal Records
Online access to records on the Trial Courts Information Center web site is available to attorneys and law firms at www.ma-trialcourts.org. See state introduction for more information.

Cumberland
Assessor
Records on the Cape Elizabeth Town Assessor database are available free online at www.capeelizabeth.com/taxdata.html. Search by owner name, road and house number for Cape Elizabeth Town. Records on the Freeport Town Assessor property database are available free online at www.freeportmaine.com/assessordb/db.cgi.

Hancock
Real Estate, Lines, UCC, Recording
www.co.hancock.me.us/deeds2.html
Online access to the county registry of deeds database at www.registryofdeeds.com requires registration. Viewing of records back to 1790 is free, but $1.25 per page to print. Register online. This site has had hacker problems; site of the infamous 3-monkeys. For information, visit www.registryofdeeds.com or call 888-833-3979.

Kennebec
Assessor
Records on the Winslow Town Property Records database are available free online at www.winslowmaine.org. Records on the Town of Waterville Assessor's Database are available free at http://140.239.211.227/watervilleme/. User ID is required; registration is free.

Sagadahoc
Assessor
www.cityofbath.com
Records on the City of Bath Assessor database are available free online at www.cityofbath.com/assessing/INDEX.HTM.

York
Assessor
www.raynorshyn.com/yorknet
Records on the Town of York Assessor Database Lookup are available free online at www.raynorshyn.com/yorknet/accsel.cfm. Records on the Town of Eliot Assessor database are available free online at http://140.239.211.227/edliotme. Search by street name & number, map/block/lot/unit, or account number. Records on the Kennebunk Town Property Records database are available free online at www.Kennebunk.maine.org/assessing/database/database/html.

Federal Courts in Maine...

US District Court - District of Maine
Home Page: www.med.uscourts.gov
PACER: Sign-up number is 800-676-6856. Access fee is $.60 per minute. Toll-free access: 800-260-9774. Local access: 207-780-3392. Case records are available back to August 1991. Records are purged every 6 months. New records are available online after 1 day.
PACER Internet Access: https://pacer.med.uscourts.gov.
Bangor Division Counties: Aroostook, Franklin, Hancock, Kennebec, Penobscot, Piscataquis, Somerset, Waldo, Washington.
Portland Division Counties: Androscoggin, Cumberland, Knox, Lincoln, Oxford, Sagadahoc, York.

US Bankruptcy Court - District of Maine
Home Page: www.meb.uscourts.gov
PACER: Sign-up number is 800-676-6856. Access fee is $.60 per minute. Toll-free access: 800-733-8797. Local access: 207-780-3268, 207-780-3269. Case records are available back to December 1988. Records are purged every two years. New civil records are available online after 1 day.
PACER Internet Access: http://pacer.meb.uscourts.gov.
Bangor Division Counties: Aroostook, Franklin, Hancock, Kennebec, Knox, Lincoln, Penobscot, Piscataquis, Somerset, Waldo, Washington.
Portland Division Counties: Androscoggin, Cumberland, Oxford, Sagadahoc, York.

Editor's Choice for Maine

Constitution Text
    www.state.me.us/sos/arc/general/constit/conscont.htm
Statutes Text
    http://janus.state.me.us/legis/statutes/
Supreme Court Opinions
    www.courts.state.me.us/mescopin.home.html

Capital:	Annapolis Anne Arundel County	Home Page	www.mec.state.md.us
Time Zone:	EST	Attorney General	www.oag.state.md.us
Number of Counties:	23	Archives	www.mdarchives.state.md.us

State Level...Major Agencies

Criminal Records

Criminal Justice Information System, Public Safety & Correctional Records, PO Box 5743, Pikeville, MD 21282-5743 (Courier: 6776 Reisterstown Rd, Rm 200, Pikeville, MD 21208); 410-764-4501, 888-795-0011, 410-974-2169 (Fax), 8AM-3:30PM.

Online: The State Court Administrator's office has online access to criminal records from all state district courts, 3 circuit courts, and 1 city court. The system is available 24 hours daily. There is a one-time $50 fee to register and a $5.00 per hour fee. Land records may also be accessed. Call 410-260-1031 for a sign-up package.

Corporation Records, Limited Partnerships, Trade Names, Limited Liability Company Records, Fictitious Name, Limited Liability Partnerships

Department of Assessments and Taxation, Corporations Division, 301 W Preston St, Room 801, Baltimore, MD 21201; 410-767-1340, 410-767-1330 (Charter Information), 410-333-7097 (Fax), 8AM-4:30PM.

www.dat.state.md.us/bsfd

Online: The web site offers free searching for corporate name and trade name records. The site also includes real estate (cannot search by name) and UCC records.

Trademarks/Servicemarks

Secretary of State, Trademarks Division, State House, Annapolis, MD 21401; 410-974-5531 x2, 410-974-5527 (Fax), 9AM-5PM.

www.sos.state.md.us

Online: Online searching is available at the Internet site. Search can be by keyword in the description field, the service or product, the owner, the classification, or the mark name or keyword in the mark name. The site offers application forms to register, renew, or assign trade and service marks, and general information about registration. Click on "Trade & Service Marks."

Uniform Commercial Code, Federal Tax Liens, State Tax Liens

UCC Division, Department of Assessments & Taxation, 301 West Preston St, Baltimore, MD 21201; 410-767-1340, 410-333-7097 (Fax), 8AM-4:30PM.

www.dat.state.md.us/bsfd

Online: The Internet site offers free access to UCC index information. There is also a related site offering access to real property data for the whole state at www.dat.state.md.us/realprop.

Workers' Compensation Records

Workers Compensation Commission, 10 E Baltimore St, Baltimore, MD 21202; 410-864-5100, 410-864-5101 (Fax), 8AM-4:30PM. www.charm.net/~wcc

Online: Request for online hook-up must be in writing on letterhead. There is no search fee, but there is a $7.00 set-up fee, $5.00 monthly fee and a $.01-03 per minute connect fee assessed by Verizon or other provider. The system is open 24 hours a day to only in-state accounts. Write to the Commission at address above, care of Info. Technology Division, or call Lili Joseph at 410-864-5119.

Driver Records

MVA, Driver Records Unit, 6601 Ritchie Hwy, NE, Glen Burnie, MD 21062; 410-787-7758, 8:15AM-4:30PM.

Online: The network is available 6 days a week, twenty-four hours a day to qualified and bonded individuals and businesses. Access is through PC and modem at up to 9600 baud. The communication network is the Public Data Network (Bell Atlantic). Fee is $5.00 per record.

Vehicle Ownership, Vehicle Identification

Dept of Motor Vehicles, Vehicle Registration Div, Rm 204, 6601 Ritchie Hwy, NE, Glen Burnie, MD 21062; 410-768-7520, 410-768-7653 (Fax), 8:15AM-4:30PM.
www.mva.state.md.us

Online: The state offers vehicle and ownership data over the same online network utilized for driving record searches. Fee is $7.00 per record and line charges will be incurred. For more information, call 410-768-7234.

Legislation Records

Maryland General Assembly, Dept of Legislative Services, 90 State Circle, Annapolis, MD 21401-1991; 410-946-5400 (Bill Status Only), 410-946-5010, 800-492-7122 (In-state), 410-946-5405 (Fax), 8AM-5PM.
http://mlis.state.md.us

Online: The Internet site has complete information regarding bills and status.

State Level...Occupational Licensing

Architecture Partnership or Corporation .... www.dllr.state.md.us/query/arch.html
Barber.. www.dllr.state.md.us/query/barber.html
Charity... www.sos.state.md.us/sos/charity/html/search.html
Contractor.. www.dllr.state.md.us/query/home_imprv.html
Cosmetologist/Nail Tech/Esthetician/Makeup Artwww.dllr.state.md.us/query/cosmet.html
Engineer, Examining... www.dllr.state.md.us/query/stat_eng.html
Engineer, Professional...................................... www.dllr.state.md.us/query/prof_eng.html
Forester .... www.dllr.state.md.us/query/forester.html
Fundraising Counsel .... www.sos.state.md.us/sos/charity/html/psfrclist.html
Home Improvement Contractor/Salesperson .... www.dllr.state.md.us/query/home_imprv.html
HVACR Contractor... www.dllr.state.md.us/query/hvacr.html
Interior Designer.. www.dllr.state.md.us/query/cert_int_des.html
Land Surveyor.. www.dllr.state.md.us/query/land_surv.html
Landscape Architect... www.dllr.state.md.us/query/land_arch.html
Master Electrician.. www.dllr.state.md.us/query/master_elec.html
Medical Doctor .... www.docboard.org/md/df/mdsearch.htm
Optometrist.. www.arbo.org/nodb2000/licsearch.asp
Plumber .... www.dllr.state.md.us/query/plumb.html
Polygraph Examiner.. http://polygraph.org/states/mpa/Members.htm
Precious Metal & Gem Dealer/Secondhand .... www.dllr.state.md.us/query/sec_hand_deal.html
Professional Solicitor .... www.sos.state.md.us/sos/charity/html/psfrclist.html
Public Accountant-CPA..................................... www.dllr.state.md.us/query/cpa.html
Real Estate Agent .... www.dllr.state.md.us/query/Maryland.html

Real Estate Appraiser...www.dllr.state.md.us/query/real_est_app.html
Subcontractor...www.dllr.state.md.us/query/home_imprv.html

County Level...Courts, Recorders & Assessors

Court Administrator, Administrative Office of the Courts, 361 Rowe Blvd, Courts of Appeal Building, Annapolis, MD, 21401; 410-260-1400; www.courts.state.md.us

Editor's Note: An online computer system called the Judicial Information System (JIS) or (SJIS) provides access to civil and criminal case information from the following:

All District Courts - All civil and all misdemeanors

Circuit Courts Civil - All Circuit Courts are online through JIS except Montgomery and Prince George who have their own systems.

Circuit Courts Criminal - Three courts are on JIS - Anne Arundel, Carroll County and Baltimore City Court

Inquiries may be made to: the District Court traffic system for case information data, calendar information data, court schedule data, or officer schedule data; the District Court criminal system for case information data or calendar caseload data; the District Court civil system for case information data, attorney name and address data; the land records system for land and plat records. The one-time fee for JIS access is $50.00, which must be included with the application. There is a $5.00 per hr charge; $10.00 minimum per month. For additional information or to receive a registration packet, write or call Judicial Info Systems, Sec.Admin., 2661 Riva Rd., #900, Annapolis, MD 21401, 410-260-1031.

Federal Courts in Maryland...

US District Court - District of Maryland

Home Page: www.mdd.uscourts.gov
PACER: Sign-up number is 800-676-6856. Access fee is $.60 per minute. Toll-free access: 800-241-2259. Local access: 410-962-1812. Case records available back to October 1990. Records are purged every six months. New records available online after 1 day.
PACER Internet Access: http://pacer.mdd.uscourts.gov.
Opinions Online: Court opinions are available online at www.mdd.uscourts.gov.
Baltimore Division Counties: Allegany, Anne Arundel, Baltimore, City of Baltimore, Caroline, Carroll, Cecil, Dorchester, Frederick, Garrett, Harford, Howard, Kent, Queen Anne's, Somerset, Talbot, Washington, Wicomico, Worcester.
Greenbelt Division Counties: Calvert, Charles, Montgomery, Prince George's, St. Mary's.

US Bankruptcy Court - District of Maryland

Home Page: www.mdb.uscourts.gov
PACER: Sign-up number is 800-676-6856. Access fee is $.60 per minute. Toll-free access: 800-927-0474. Local access: 410-962-3211. Case records available back to mid 1991. Records are purged every six months. New civil records available online after 2 days.
PACER Internet Access: http://pacer.mdb.uscourts.gov.
Baltimore Division Counties: Anne Arundel, Baltimore, City of Baltimore, Caroline, Carroll, Cecil, Dorchester, Harford, Howard, Kent, Queen Anne's, Somerset, Talbot, Wicomico, Worcester.
Rockville Division Counties: Allegany, Calvert, Charles, Frederick, Garrett, Montgomery, Prince George's, St. Mary's, Washington.

Editor's Choice for Maryland

Government Phone Numbers Database
http://archive2.mdarchives.state.md.us/scripts/qpweb20fe/qntwfe20.dll/frame

Capital:	Boston		
	Suffolk County	Home Page	www.state.ma.us
Time Zone:	EST	Attorney General	www.ago.state.ma.us
Number of Counties:	14	Archives	www.state.ma.us/sec/arc

State Level...Major Agencies

Corporation Records, Trademarks/Servicemarks, Limited Liability Partnerships, Limited Partnership Records

Secretary of the Commonwealth, Corporation Division, One Ashburton Pl, 17th Floor, Boston, MA 02108; 617-727-9640 (Corporations), 617-727-2850 (Records), 617-727-8329 (Trademarks), 617-727-9440 (Forms request line), 617-742-4538 (Fax), 8:45AM-5PM.

www.state.ma.us/sec/cor/coridx.htm

Online: The agency offers "Direct Access." The annual subscription fee is $149.00 and there is a $.40 a minute access fee. System is available from 8 AM to 10 PM. This system also provides UCC record data. Call 617-727-7655 for a sign-up packet.

Uniform Commercial Code, State Tax Liens

UCC Division, Secretary of the Commonwealth, One Ashburton Pl, Room 1711, Boston, MA 02108; 617-727-2860, 900-555-4500 (Computer Prints), 900-555-4600 (Copies), 8:45AM-5PM.

www.state.ma.us/sec/

Online: "Direct Access" is available for $149 per year plus a $.40 per minute network fee. The system is open from 8 AM to 9:50 PM. Call 617-727-7655 to obtain information packet.

Vehicle Ownership, Vehicle Identification

Registry of Motor Vehicles, Customer Assistance-Mail List Dept., PO Box 199100, Boston, MA 02119-9100; 617-351-9384, 617-351-9524 (Fax), 8AM-4:30PM.

www.state.ma.us/rmv

Online: Searching is limited to Massachusetts based insurance companies and agents for the purpose of issuing or renewing insurance. This system is not open to the public. There is no fee, but line charges will be incurred.

Legislation Records

Massachusetts General Court, State House, Beacon St, Room 428 (Document Room), Boston, MA 02133; 617-722-2860 (Document Room), 9AM-5PM.

www.state.ma.us/legis.legis.htm

Online: The web site has bill information for the current session and the previous session.

State Level...Occupational Licensing

Alarm Installer	http://license.reg.state.ma.us/pubLic/licque.asp?color=red&Board=EL
Allied Health Professions	http://license.reg.state.ma.us/pubLic/licque.asp?color=red&Board=AH
Allied Mental Health Profs.	http://license.reg.state.ma.us/pubLic/licque.asp?query=personal&color=red&board=MH
Amusement Device Inspector	www.state.ma.us/dps/Lic_srch.htm
Architect	http://license.reg.state.ma.us/pubLic/licque.asp?color=red&Board=AR
Athletic Trainer	http://license.reg.state.ma.us/pubLic/licque.asp?color=red&Board=AH
Auctioneer School	www.state.ma.us/standards/auc-sch.htm
Audiologist	http://license.reg.state.ma.us/pubLic/licque.asp?color=red&Board=SP
Barber	http://license.reg.state.ma.us/pubLic/licque.asp?color=red&Board=BR
Barber Shop	http://license.reg.state.ma.us/pubLic/licque.asp?color=red&Board=BR
Boxer	www.state.ma.us/mbc/ranking.htm
Building Producer	www.state.ma.us/bbrs/mfg98.pdf
Chiropractor	http://license.reg.state.ma.us/pubLic/licque.asp?color=red&Board=CH
Concrete Technician	www.state.ma.us/bbrs/programs.htm
Concrete-Testing Laboratory	www.state.ma.us/bbrs/programs.htm
Construction Supervisor	www.state.ma.us/bbrs/cslsearch.htm
Cosmetologist/Hairdresser/Manicurist/Aesthetician	
	http://license.reg.state.ma.us/pubLic/licque.asp?color=red&Board=HD
Day Care Center	www.qualitychildcare.org/provider_search.htm
Dental Hygienist	http://license.reg.state.ma.us/pubLic/licque.asp?color=red&Board=DN
Dentist	http://license.reg.state.ma.us/pubLic/licque.asp?color=red&Board=DN
Dispensing Optician	http://license.reg.state.ma.us/pubLic/licque.asp?color=red&Board=DO
Educational Psychologist	http://license.reg.state.ma.us/pubLic/licque.asp?query=personal&color=red&board=MH
Electrician	http://license.reg.state.ma.us/pubLic/licque.asp?color=red&Board=EL
Electrologist	http://license.reg.state.ma.us/pubLic/licque.asp?color=red&Board=ET
Embalmer & Funeral Director	http://license.reg.state.ma.us/pubLic/licque.asp?color=red&Board=EM
Engineer	http://license.reg.state.ma.us/pubLic/licque.asp?color=red&Board=EN
Family Child Care Provider	www.qualitychildcare.org/provider_search.htm
Fire Protection Contr./Fitter	www.state.ma.us/dps/Lic_srch.htm
Firemen / Engineer	www.state.ma.us/dps/Lic_srch.htm
Gas Fitter	http://license.reg.state.ma.us/pubLic/licque.asp?color=red&Board=PL
Health Officer (Certified)	http://license.reg.state.ma.us/pubLic/licque.asp?color=red&Board=HO
HMO	www.state.ma.us/doi/Consumer/css_health_HMO.html
Hoisting Machinery Operator	www.state.ma.us/dps/Lic_srch.htm
Home Improvement Contr.	www.state.ma.us/bbrs/Hicsearch.htm
Inspector-Bldgs/Local Insp.	www.state.ma.us/bbrs/bocert.PDF
Inspector-Boilers/Pres. Vessels	www.state.ma.us/dps/Lic_srch.htm
Insurance Company	www.state.ma.us/doi/companies/companies_home.html

Land Surveyor	http://license.reg.state.ma.us/pubLic/licque.asp?color=red&Board=EN
Landscape Architect	http://license.reg.state.ma.us/pubLic/licque.asp?color=red&Board=LA
Lobbyist	www.state.ma.us/scripts/sec/pre/search.asp
Marriage & Family Therapist	http://license.reg.state.ma.us/pubLic/licque.asp?query=personal&color=red&board=MH
Medical Doctor	www.docboard.org/ma/df/masearch.htm
Mental Health Counselor	http://license.reg.state.ma.us/pubLic/licque.asp?query=personal&color=red&board=MH
Native Lumber Producer	www.state.ma.us/bbrs/lumber99.PDF
Nuclear Engineer/Operator	www.state.ma.us/dps/Lic_srch.htm
Nurse (LPN, RN, Midwife)	http://license.reg.state.ma.us/pubLic/licque.asp?color=red&Board=RN
Nursing Home Administrator	http://license.reg.state.ma.us/pubLic/licque.asp?color=red&Board=NH
Occupational Therapist/Assist.	http://license.reg.state.ma.us/pubLic/licque.asp?color=red&Board=AH
Oil Burner Tech/Contractor	www.state.ma.us/dps/Lic_srch.htm
Optician	http://license.reg.state.ma.us/pubLic/licque.asp?query=personal&color=red&board=DO
Optometrist	http://license.reg.state.ma.us/pubLic/licque.asp?color=red&Board=OP
Pharmacist	http://license.reg.state.ma.us/pubLic/licque.asp?color=red&Board=PH
Physical Therapist/Assistant	http://license.reg.state.ma.us/pubLic/licque.asp?color=red&Board=AH
Physician Assistant	http://license.reg.state.ma.us/pubLic/licque.asp?color=red&Board=AP
Pipefitter	www.state.ma.us/dps/Lic_srch.htm
Plumber	http://license.reg.state.ma.us/pubLic/licque.asp?color=red&Board=PL
Podiatrist	http://license.reg.state.ma.us/pubLic/licque.asp?color=red&Board=PD
Psychologist/Provider	http://license.reg.state.ma.us/pubLic/licque.asp?color=red&Board=PY
Public Accountant-CPA	http://license.reg.state.ma.us/pubLic/licque.asp?color=red&Board=PA
Radio/TV Repair Technician	http://license.reg.state.ma.us/pubLic/licque.asp?color=red&Board=TV
Real Estate Appraiser	http://license.reg.state.ma.us/pubLic/licque.asp?color=red&Board=RA
Real Estate Broker/Salesperson	http://license.reg.state.ma.us/pubLic/licque.asp?color=red&Board=RE
Refrigeration Tech/Contractor	www.state.ma.us/dps/Lic_srch.htm
Rehabilitation Therapist	http://license.reg.state.ma.us/pubLic/licque.asp?query=personal&color=red&board=MH
Respiratory Care Therapist	http://license.reg.state.ma.us/pubLic/licque.asp?color=red&Board=RC
Sanitarian	http://license.reg.state.ma.us/pubLic/licque.asp?color=red&Board=SA
Social Worker	http://license.reg.state.ma.us/pubLic/licque.asp?color=red&Board=SW
Speech-Language Pathologist	http://license.reg.state.ma.us/pubLic/licque.asp?color=red&Board=SP
Veterinarian	http://license.reg.state.ma.us/pubLic/licque.asp?color=red&Board=VT
Water Facilities/Operator	http://license.reg.state.ma.us/pubLic/licque.asp?color=red&Board=DW

County Level...Courts, Recorders & Assessors

Chief Justice for Administration and Management, 2 Center Plaza, Room 540, Boston, MA, 02108; 617-742-8575; www.state.ma.us/courts/admin/index.html

Editor's Note: Online access to records on the statewide Trial Courts Information Center web site is available to attorneys and law firms at www.ma-trialcourts.org. Contact Peter Nylin by email at nylin_p@jud.state.ma.us. Site is updated daily.

Agawam Town in Hampden County
Property Assessment Data

www.agawam.ma.us
Online access to Property Assessment Data at www.patriotproperties.com/agawam/Default.asp?br=exp&vr=5.

Andover Town in Essex County
Assessor

Property tax records on the Assessor's database are available free online at www.town.andover.ma.us/assess/values.htm.

Arlington Town in Middlesex County
Assessor

www.town.arlington.ma.us/arthalli.htm
Online access to the town assessor database is available free at http://arlserver.town.arlington.ma.us/property.html.

Barnstable County
Real Estate, Liens

www.bcrd.co.barnstable.ma.us
Access to County records requires a $50 annual fee, plus $.50 per minute of use. Records date back to 1976. Lending agency information is available. For information, contact Janet Hoben at 508-362-7733.

Barnstable Town in Barnstable County
Assessor

www.town.barnstable.ma.us
Town of Barnstable Assessor records are available free online at
http://town.barnstable.ma.us/Information_01/Assessment/asse_online_db.htm. Email questions or comments to
webadm@town.barnstable.ma.us or call the Assessing Dept. at 508-862-4022.

Berkshire County
Real Estate, Liens

Access to the County records requires an on-time $100 signup and $.50 per minute of use. System provides access to all three District Recorder's records; records date back to 1985. Searchable indexes: recorded land, plans, registered land. Lending agency information available. For information, contact Sharon Henault at 413-443-7438.

Boston City in Suffolk County
Assessor

www.ci.boston.ma.us/assessing
Records on the City of Boston Assessor database are available free online at www.ci.boston.ma.us/assessing/search.asp.

Bristol County
Real Estate, Liens

Access to County records requires a $100 set up fee and $.50 per minute of use. All three districts are on this system; the record dates vary by district. Lending agency information is available. For information, contact Rosemary at 508-993-2605.

Brookline Town in Norfolk County

Assessor

www.town.brookline.ma.us/Assessors

Records on the Town of Brookline Assessors database are available free online at www.town.brookline.ma.us/Assessors/property.asp.

Cambridge City in Middlesex County

Assessor

www2.ci.cambridge.ma.us/assessor

Records on the City of Cambridge Assessor database are available free online at www2.ci.cambridge.ma.us/assessor/index.html.

Dedham Town in Norfolk County

Assessor

Property records on the Assessor's database are available free online at http://data.visionappraisal.com/dedhamma. Registration is required for full access; registration is free.

Essex County

Real Estate, Liens

www.lawrencedeeds.com

Access to the Essex County online records requires a $25 deposit, with a $.25 per minute charge for use. Records date back to 1981. Lending agency information is available. For information, contact David Burke at 978-683-2745. Records on the Essex County South Registry of Deeds database are available free on the Internet at http://207.244.88.10/deedsonline.asp. Images start 1/1992; records back to 1/1984. Search by grantee/grantor, town & date, street, or book & page.

Falmouth Town in Barnstable County

Assessor

www.town.falmouth.ma.us

Records on the Town of Falmouth Assessor database are available free by experiment on the Internet at www.town.falmouth.ma.us/propinq.html. Provides owner, address, and valuation only.

Hampden County

Real Estate, Liens

Access to County online records requires a $50 annual fee and $.50 per minute of use. Records date back to 1965. Lending agency information is available. Searchable indexes are bankruptcy (from PACER), unregistered land site and registered land site. For information, contact Donna Brown at 413-748-7945.

Hampshire County

Real Estate, Liens

Access to County Register of Deeds online records requires a $100 annual fee and $.50 per minute of use, $.60 for out-of-state. Records date back to 9/2/1986. Lending agency information is available. For information, contact MaryAnn Foster at 413-584-3637.

Holden Town in Worcester County

Real Estate, Property Tax

http://140.239.211.227/HOLDENMA

Online access to the Town Assessor's database is available free at http://140.239.211.227/HOLDENMA. Registration required; sign-up is free.

Holyoke City in Hampden County

Tax Assessor

www.ci.holyoke.ma.us/

Online access to property valuations on the tax assessor database is available free at www.ci.holyoke.ma.us/Assesment.asp.

Leominster City in Worcester County

Assessor

Property tax records on the Assessor's database are available free online at http://140.239.211.227/leominsterma. User ID is required; registration is free.

Lowell City in Middlesex County
Assessor
Property tax records on the Assessor's database are available free online at http://140.239.211.227/LowellMA.

Mashpee Town in Barnstable County
Assessor
www.capecod.net/mashpee
Records on the Town of Mashpee Assessor database are available free online at www.capecode.net/mashpee/assess.

Medford City in Middlesex County
Assessor
www.medford.org/gov/cityhall/assess.htm
Records on the City Assessor database are available free online at www.medford.org/gov/cityhall/assess.htm#data.

Middlesex County (South)
Real Estate, Liens
Access to the LandTrack online system with Southern District records requires a $100 annual fee, plus $.50 per minute of use. Lending agency information is available as is a fax back service for documents. For info, contact Grace Abruzzio at 617-494-4510.

Middlesex County (North)
Real Estate, Liens
www.tiac.net/users/nmrd
Access to the Telesearch online system with North District records requires a $100 set up fee, plus $50 deposit, and $.20 per minute of use. Wang software is $95. Records date back to 1976. Fax back service available. For info, contact customer service: 978-458-8474.

Natick Town in Middlesex County
Property
Records on the Town of Natick Property database are available free online at http://univers.akanda.com/ProcessSearch.asp?cmd=Natick.

New Bedford City in Bristol County
Property, Assessor
www.ci.new-bedford.ma.us/Nav3.htm
Online access to the assessor's property database is available free at www.ci.new-bedford.ma.us/Assessors/RealPropertyLookup.htm.

Newton City in Middlesex County
Assessor
www.ci.newton.ma.us
Records on the City of Newton Fiscal 1998 Assessment database are available free at www.ci.newton.ma.us/GIS/Assessors/Default.asp. Data represents market value as of 1/1/1997.

Norfolk County
Real Estate, Liens
Access to county online records requires a $25 set up fee, plus $1 fee for the first minute and $.50 per minute thereafter per session. The system is only accessible in Massachusetts. Lending agency information is available. For info, contact Pam at 781-461-6116.

Plymouth County
Real Estate, Liens
Access to Online Titleview for Plymouth County records requires a usage charge of $.60 per minute of use. Records date back to 1971. Lending agency information is available. A fax back service is $3 plus $1 per page in county, $4 plus $1 per page, outside. For information, call 508-830-9287.

Provincetown Town in Barnstable County
Assessor
www.provincetowngov.org
Records on the Provincetown Assessor database are available free online at www.provincetowngov.org/assessor.html.

Reading Town in Middlesex County
Assessor
www.ci.reading.ma.us/depts.htm
Records on the Town of Reading Assessor database are available free online at www.ziplink.net/~reading1/assessor.htm.

Suffolk County
Real Estate, Liens, Deeds
Searches on the Registry of Deeds site are free; real estate/liens on the county online system is not. Access to the County online system requires a written request submitted to Paul R Tierney, Register of Deeds, POB 9660, Boston MA 02114. Online charges are $.50 per minute of use. A fax back service is available. Records on the County Registry of Deeds database are available free on the Internet at www.suffolkdeeds.com/search/default.asp. Search by name, corporation, and grantor/grantee. Recorded land records begin 1979; Registered land, 1983.

Swampscott Town in Essex County
Assessor, Real Estate
www.swampscott.org/government.htm
Online access to the Assessor's Property Valuation List FY-2000 is available free at www.swampscott.org/assessor%20file.xls. This is a lengthy MS-Excel file. Search the name column: Contol+F then enter name information, then "Find Next."

Waltham City in Middlesex County
Assessor
www.city.waltham.ma.us
Records on the City of Waltham Assessor database are available free online at www.city.waltham.ma.us/assessors/caveat.htm.

Watertown Town in Middlesex County
Assessor
Records on the Watertown Town Online Assessed Values site are available free online at www.townonline.com/watertown/realestate/assessments/index.html.

Wayland Town in Middlesex County
Assessor
www.wayland.ma.us/townadministration.html
Property tax records on the Assessor's database are available free online at www.wayland.ma.us/assess-reval99.htm. Also, the read only tax assessor information is available through a private company's site at www.mypropertyrecords.com/univers.

Wellesley Town in Norfolk County
Assessor
www.ci.wellesley.ma.us/town/index.html
Property tax records on the Assessor's database are available free online at www.ci.wellesley.ma.us/asr/index.html.

West Boylston Town in Worcester County
Assessor
www.westboylston.com
Online access to the town assessor Valuations Listings is available free at www.westboylston.com/ASSESS/Assessors1.htm. Files are searchable by street and include owner names.

Westfield City in Hampden County
Assessor
www.ci.westfield.ma.us
Property tax records on the Assessor's database are available free online at www.ci.westfield.ma.us/realest/rea00.htm.

Worcester City in Worcester County
Real Estate, Liens
Access to the "Landtrack System" for Worcester District records requires a $50 annual fee plus $.25 per minute of use. Index records date back to 1966. Images are viewable from 1974 onward. Lending agency info is available. Fax back service is available for $.50 per page. For information, contact Joe Ursoleo at 508-798-7713 X233.

Worcester County
Real Estate, Liens
www.state.ma.us/nwrod
Access to the "Northfield" online service requires $50 annually, plus $.25 per minute of use. Records date back to 1983. Viewable images are available back to 1995. Lending agency information is available. A fax back service is available. For information, contact Ruth Piermarini at 978-342-2637.

Yarmouth Town in Barnstable County
Assessor
www.Yarmouthcapecod.org
Records on the Assessor's database are available free online at http://140.239.211.227/yarmouthma. User ID number is required to access the full database; registration is free. Non-registered users can access a limited set of data.

Federal Courts in Massachusetts...

US District Court - District of Massachusetts
Home Page: www.mad.uscourts.gov
PACER: Sign-up number is 800-676-6856. Access fee is $.60 per minute. Toll-free access: 888-399-4639. Local access: 617-223-4294. Case records available back to January 1990. Records are purged every 12 months. New records are available online after 1 day.
PACER Internet Access: http://pacer.mad.uscourts.gov.
Boston Division Counties: Barnstable, Bristol, Dukes, Essex, Middlesex, Nantucket, Norfolk, Plymouth, Suffolk.
Springfield Division Counties: Berkshire, Franklin, Hampden, Hampshire.
Worcester Division Counties: Worcester.

US Bankruptcy Court - District of Massachusetts
Home Page: www.mab.uscourts.gov
PACER: Sign-up number is 800-676-6856. Access fee is $.60 per minute. Toll-free access: 888-201-3571. Local access: 617-565-7593, 617-565-7594, 617-565-6021, 617-565-6022, 617-565-6023. Case records are available back to April 1, 1987. Records are purged every 12 months. New civil records are available online after 1 day.
PACER Internet Access: http://pacer.mab.uscourts.gov.
Boston Division Counties: Barnstable, Bristol, Dukes, Essex (except towns assigned to Worcester Division), Nantucket, Norfolk (except towns assigned to Worcester Division), Plymouth, Suffolk, and the following towns in Middlesex: Arlington, Belmont, Burlington, Everett,Lexington, Malden, Medford, Melrose, Newton, North Reading, Reading, Stoneham, Wakefield, Waltham, Watertown, Wilmington, Winchester and Woburn.
Worcester Division Counties: Berkshire, Franklin, Hampden, Hampshire, Middlesex (except the towns assigned to the Boston Division), Worcester and the following towns: in Essex-Andover, Haverhill, Lawrence, Methuen and North Andover; in Norfolk-Bellingham, Franklin, Medway, Millis and Norfolk.

Editor's Choice for Massachusetts

Constitution Text
www.state.ma.us/legis/const.htm
Employment Statistics Listing
www.detma.org/lmi/local/local.htm
Software Industry Database
www.swcouncil.org/search.stm

Capital:	Lansing Ingham County	Home Page	www.state.mi.us
Time Zone:	EST/CST	Attorney General	www.ag.state.mi.us
Number of Counties:	83	Archives	www.sos.state.mi.us/ history/archive

State Level...Major Agencies

Criminal Records

Michigan State Police, Ident. Section, Criminal Justice Information Center, 7150 Harris Dr, Lansing, MI 48913; 517-322-5531, 517-322-0635 (Fax), 8AM-5PM.

www.msp.state.mi.us

Online: Online access is limited to businesses that are ongoing requesters. Access is via the Internet, credit cards are required. To set up an account, call 517-322-5546.

Driver Records

Department of State Police, Record Look-up Unit, 7064 Crowner Dr, Lansing, MI 48918; 517-322-1624, 517-322-1181 (Fax), 8AM-4:45PM.

www.sos.state.mi.us/dv

Online: Online ordering is available on an interactive basis. The system is open 7 days a week. Ordering is by DL or name and DOB. An account must be established and billing is monthly. Access is also available from the Internet. Fee is $6.55 per record. For more information, call Carol Lycos at 517-322-1591.

Vehicle Ownership, Vehicle Identification, Boat & Vessel Ownership, Boat & Vessel Registration

Department of State Police, Record Look-up Unit, 7064 Crowner Dr, Lansing, MI 48918; 517-322-1624, 517-322-1181 (Fax), 8AM-4:45PM.

www.sos.state.mi.us/dv

Online: Online searching is single inquiry and requires a VIN or plate number. A $25,000 surety bond is required. Fee is $6.55 per record. Direct dialup or Internet access is offered. For more information, call Carol Lycos at 517-322-1591.

Vital Statistics

Department of Community Health, Vital Records Requests, PO Box 30721, Lansing, MI 48909 (Courier: 3423 Martin Luther King, Jr Blvd, Lansing, MI 48909); 517-335-8656 (Instructions), 517-335-8666 (Request Unit), 517-321-5884 (Fax), 8AM-5PM.

www.mdch.state.mi.us/Pha/Osr/vitframe.htm

Online: Records may be ordered from the web site. Step-by-step instructions given, use of credit card required.

Legislation Records

Michigan Legislature Document Rm, State Capitol, POB 30036, Lansing, MI 48909 (Courier: North Capitol Annex, Lansing, MI 48909); 517-373-0169, 8:30AM-5PM.

www.michiganlegislature.org

Online: Access is available from their Internet site. Adobe Acrobat Reader is required. Information available includes status of bills, bill text, joint resolution text, journals, calendars, session and committee schedules, and Michigan complied laws.

State Level...Occupational Licensing

Architect	www.cis.state.mi.us:8020/public/lic_reg$.startup
Athletic Control	www.cis.state.mi.us:8020/public/lic_reg$.startup
Aviation Medical Examiners	www.mdot.state.mi.us/aero/resources/ame.htm
Barber	www.cis.state.mi.us:8020/public/lic_reg$.startup
Carnival-Amusement	www.cis.state.mi.us:8020/public/lic_reg$.startup
Cemetery	www.cis.state.mi.us:8020/public/lic_reg$.startup
Child Caring Institution	www.cis.state.mi.us/brs/cwl/cwllist.htm
Child Welfare Agency (Child Placing Agency)	www.cis.state.mi.us/brs/cwl/cwllist.htm
Chiropractor	www.cis.state.mi.us/bhser/lic/exams/examapp.htm
Collection Manager	www.cis.state.mi.us:8020/public/lic_reg$.startup
Community Planner-Professional	www.cis.state.mi.us:8020/public/lic_reg$.startup
Cosmetologist	www.cis.state.mi.us:8020/public/lic_reg$.startup
Counselor	www.cis.state.mi.us/bhser
Dental Assistant	www.cis.state.mi.us/bhser/lic/exams/rdaexam.htm
Dentist	www.cis.state.mi.us/bhser/lic/exams/denspex.htm
Emergency Medical Service	www.cis.state.mi.us/bhser/lic/exams/exems.htm
Employment Agency	www.cis.state.mi.us:8020/public/lic_reg$.startup
Forensic Polygraph Examiner	www.cis.state.mi.us:8020/public/lic_reg$.startup
Hearing Aid Dealer	www.cis.state.mi.us:8020/public/lic_reg$.startup
Marriage & Family Therapist	www.cis.state.mi.us/bhser/lic/exams/mftex.htm
Medical Doctor	www.cis.state.mi.us/bhser/lic/exams/usmleex.htm
Mortuary Science	www.cis.state.mi.us:8020/public/lic_reg$.startup
Notary Public	www.sos.state.mi.us/greatse/notaries/notaries.html
Nurse	www.cis.state.mi.us/bhser/lic/exams/exnurse.htm
Nurse Aide Registration Program	www.cis.state.mi.us/bhser/lic/exams/excna.htm
Nursing Home Administrator	www.cis.state.mi.us:8020/public/lic_reg$.startup
Optometrist	www.cis.state.mi.us/bhser/lic/exams/optex.htm
Osteopathic Physician	www.cis.state.mi.us/bhser/lic/exams/usmleex.htm
Pharmacist	www.cis.state.mi.us/bhser/lic/exams/phnaex.htm
Physical Therapist	www.cis.state.mi.us/bhser/lic/exams/ptexam.htm
Physician Assistant	www.cis.state.mi.us/bhser
Pilot Examiner	www.mdot.state.mi.us/aero/resources/dpe.htm
Podiatric Medicine & Surgery	www.cis.state.mi.us/bhser/lic/exams/podex.htm
Psychologist	www.cis.state.mi.us/bhser/lic/exams/psycex.htm
Public Accountant-CPA	www.cis.state.mi.us:8020/public/lic_reg$.startup
Real Estate	www.cis.state.mi.us:8020/public/lic_reg$.startup
Sanitarian	www.cis.state.mi.us/bhser/lic/exams/sanex.htm
Social Worker	www.cis.state.mi.us:8020/public/lic_reg$.startup

Social Worker .... www.cis.state.mi.us./bhser
Veterinarian.. www.cis.state.mi.us./bhser/lic/exams/vetex.htm
Veterinary Technician .... www.cis.state.mi.us./bhser/lic/exams/vtecex.htm

County Level...Courts, Recorders & Assessors

State Court Administrator, 309 N. Washington Sq, PO Box 30048, Lansing, MI, 48909; 517-373-2222; www.supremecourt.state.mi.us

Editor's Note: There is a wide range of online computerization of the judicial system from "none" to "fairly complete," but there is no statewide court records network. Some Michigan courts provide public access terminals in clerk's offices, and some courts are developing off-site electronic filing and searching capability, A few offer remote online to the public. The Criminal Justice Information Center (CJIC), the repository for MI criminal record info, offers online access, but the requester must be a business. Results are available in seconds; fee is $5.00 per name. For more information, call 517-322-5546.

Crawford
Civil Cases, Criminal Records
www.Circuit46.org
Online access to court case records (open or closed cases for 90 days only) is available free at www.circuit46.org/Cases/cases.html.

Eaton
Assessor, Tax Records
www.co.eaton.mi.us/cntsrv/online.htm
Two levels of service are available on the County Online Data Service site. For free information, click on the Free Limited Public Information on the main page; then, on the Access System Page, at "User" enter PUBLIC. For "password," enter PUBLIC. The more sophisticated, restricted "Enhanced Records Access" requires registration, a password, and an associated fee. Access fees are billable monthly and can be prepaid to cover usage for any length of time.

Ingham
Assumed Business Names
www.ingham.org/rd/rodindex.htm
County DBA and co-partnership listings are available free online at www.ingham.org/CL/dbalists.htm.

Jackson
Real Estate, Liens
Access to county online records requires pre-payment and $1 per minute of use (this may be revised). Records date back to 1985. Indexes include grantor/grantee, deeds, mortgage information. Lending agency information is available. Vital records will be added to the system when it is upgraded. For information, contact Mindy at 517-768-6682.

Kalkaska
Civil Cases, Criminal Records
www.Circuit46.org
Online access to court case records (open or closed cases for 90 days only) is available free at www.circuit46.org/Cases/cases.html.

Kent
Assessor
www.co.kent.mi.us/dept.htm
Records on the Walker City Assessing Dept. database are available free online at www.ci.walker.mi.us/Services/Assessor/AssessingData/DataIntro.html. In most cases, sales and permit histories go back to 1993. Database contains residential assessment and structural information. Also, records on the Alpine Charter Township Assessment database are available free online at http://alpine.data-web.net. Search by parcel number or street name.

Livingston
Real Estate, Liens, Tax Assessor Records
Access to County online records is available for occasional users, and a dedicated line is available for $1200 for professional users. Annual fee for occasional use is $400, plus $.000043 per second. Records date back to 1984. Lending agency information is available. For information, contact Judy Eplee at 517-546-2530.

Macomb
Business Registration, Death Records
www.co.macomb.mi.us
Business registration information - owner name, address, type and filing date - is available free online at http://macomb.mcntv.com/businessnames. Search by full or partial company name. County death records are available free online at http://macomb.mcntv.com/deathrecords. Search by name or apx. date. Also, County Recorder records are available from a private online source at www.landaccess.com; Fees and registration required. Also, Clinton Township Assessor records are available free online at www.clintontownship.com/assprd.htm. Enter user name: "clintwp" and password "assessor".

Montcalm
Real Estate, Liens
Two online options are available. To view the index, the monthly fee is $250. To view both the index and document image, the monthly fee is $650. Records date back to 1/1/1988. Lending agency information is available. For information, contact Laurie Wilson at 517-831-7321.

Oakland
Real Estate
County Recorder records are accessible through a private online service at www.landaccess.com; Fees and registration are required.

Otsego
Civil Cases, Criminal Records
www.Circuit46.org
Online access to court case records (closed cases for 90 days only) is available free at www.circuit46.org/Cases/cases.html.

Saginaw
Assessor
Records on the Saginaw Charter Township Assessor's Property Data Page are available free online at www.sagtwp.org/pt_scripts/search.cfm. Search by address, tax roll number, or owner name.

Wayne
Assessor
Records on the City of Dearborn Residential Property Assessment Database are available free online at http://dev.todaylink.net/asp/cityofdearborn/dbnCitySearch.asp. Search by street name and number.

Editor's Choice for Michigan

Campaign Finance Database
www.sos.state.mi.us/election/cfr/cfr_onln.html
Crime Statistics Database
www.state.mi.us/msp/crd/ucrstats/crime_reports.htm
Laws Database
http://michiganlegislature.org/law
Sex Offenders Database
www.mipsor.state.mi.us

Federal Courts in Michigan...

US District Court - Eastern District of Michigan

Home Page: www.mied.uscourts.gov
PACER: Sign-up number is 800-676-6856. Access fee is $.60 per minute. Toll-free access: 800-229-8015. Local access: 313-234-5376. Case records are available back to 1988. New records are available online after 2 days.
PACER Internet Access: http://pacer.mied.uscourts.gov.
Ann Arbor Division Counties: Jackson, Lenawee, Monroe, Oakland, Washtenaw, Wayne. Civil cases in these counties are assigned randomly to the Detroit, Flint or Port Huron Divisions. Case files are maintained where the case is assigned.
Bay City Division Counties: Alcona, Alpena, Arenac, Bay, Cheboygan, Clare, Crawford, Gladwin, Gratiot, Huron, Iosco, Isabella, Midland, Montmorency, Ogemaw, Oscoda, Otsego, Presque Isle, Roscommon, Saginaw, Tuscola.
Detroit Division Counties: Macomb, St. Clair, Sanilac. Civil cases for these counties are assigned randomly among the Flint, Ann Arbor and Detroit divisions. Port Huron cases may also be assigned here. Case files are kept where the case is assigned.
Flint Division Counties: Genesee, Lapeer, Livingston, Shiawassee. This office handles all criminal cases for these counties. Civil cases are assigned randomly among the Detroit, Ann Arbor and Flint divisions.

US Bankruptcy Court - Eastern District of Michigan

Home Page: www.mieb.uscourts.gov
PACER: Sign-up number is 800-676-6856. Access fee is $.60 per minute. Case records are available back to October 1, 1992. New civil records are available online after 1-2 days.
PACER Internet Access: http://pacer.mieb.uscourts.gov.
Bay City Division Counties: Alcona, Alpena, Arenac, Bay, Cheboygan, Clare, Crawford, Gladwin, Gratiot, Huron, Iosco, Isabella, Midland, Montmorency, Ogemaw, Oscoda, Otsego, Presque Isle, Roscommon, Saginaw, Tuscola.
Detroit Division Counties: Jackson, Lenawee, Macomb, Monroe, Oakland, Sanilac, St. Clair, Washtenaw, Wayne.
Flint Division Counties: Genesee, Lapeer, Livingston, Shiawassee.

US District Court - Western District of Michigan

Home Page: www.miw.uscourts.gov
PACER: Sign-up number is 800-676-6856. Access fee is $.60 per minute. Toll-free access: 800-547-6398. Local access: 616-732-2765. Case records are available back to September 1989. Records are purged never. New records are available online after 1-2 days.
PACER Internet Access: http://pacer.miwd.uscourts.gov.
Grand Rapids Division Counties: Antrim, Barry, Benzie, Charlevoix, Emmet, Grand Traverse, Ionia, Kalkaska, Kent, Lake, Leelanau, Manistee, Mason, Mecosta, Missaukee, Montcalm, Muskegon, Newaygo, Oceana, Osceola, Ottawa, Wexford. The Lansing and Kalamazoo Divisions also handle casesfrom these counties.
Kalamazoo Division Counties: Allegan, Berrien, Calhoun, Cass, Kalamazoo, St. Joseph, Van Buren. Also handle cases from the counties in the Grand Rapids Division.
Lansing Division Counties: Branch, Clinton, Eaton, Hillsdale, Ingham. Also handle cases from the counties in the Grand Rapids Division.
Marquette-Northern Division Counties: Alger, Baraga, Chippewa, Delta, Dickinson, Gogebic, Houghton, Iron, Keweenaw, Luce, Mackinac, Marquette, Menominee, Ontonagon, Schoolcraft.

US Bankruptcy Court - Western District of Michigan

Home Page: www.miw.uscourts.gov
PACER: Sign-up number is 800-676-6856. Access fee is $.60 per minute. Toll-free access: 800-526-0342. Local access: 616-732-2739. Case records are available back to September 1989. Records are purged six months after case closed. New civil records are available online after 1 day.
PACER Internet Access: http://pacer.miwb.uscourts.gov.
Grand Rapids Division Counties: Allegan, Antrim, Barry, Benzie, Berrien, Branch, Calhoun, Cass, Charlevoix, Clinton, Eaton, Emmet, Grand Traverse, Hillsdale, Ingham, Ionia, Kalamazoo, Kalkaska, Kent, Lake, Leelanau, Manistee, Mason, Mecosta, Missaukee, Montcalm, Muskegon, Newaygo,Oceana, Osceola, Ottawa, St. Joseph, Van Buren, Wexford.
Marquette Division Counties: Alger, Baraga, Chippewa, Delta, Dickinson, Gogebic, Houghton, Iron, Keweenaw, Luce, Mackinac, Marquette, Menominee, Ontonagon, Schoolcraft.

Capital: St. Paul
                  Ramsey County

Time Zone: CST

Number of Counties: 87

Home Page   www.state.mn.us

Archives   www.mnhs.org

Attorney General   www.ag.state.mn.us

State Level...Major Agencies

Corporation Records, Limited Liability Company Records, Assumed Name, Trademarks/Servicemarks, Limited Partnerships

Business Records Services, Secretary of State, 180 State Office Bldg, 100 Constitution Ave, St Paul, MN 55155-1299; 651-296-2803 (Information), 651-297-7067 (Fax), 8AM-4:30PM.

www.sos.state.mn.us

Online: The Internet site permits free look-ups of "business" names. The program is called Direct Access and is available 24 hours. There is an annual subscription fee of $50.00. Records are $1-4, depending on item needed. Call 651-297-9096 for information.

Uniform Commercial Code, Federal Tax Liens, State Tax Liens

UCC Division, Sec. of State, 180 State Office Bldg, St Paul, MN 55155-1299; 651-296-2803, 651-297-5844 (Fax), 8AM-4:30PM.

www.sos.state.mn.us

Online: There is a free look-up available from the web site. A comprehensive commercial program called Direct Access is available 24 hours. There is a subscription fee is $50.00 per year, plus $3.00 per UCC search or $4.00 per business search. Call 651-297-9097 for more information.

Driver Records

Driver & Vehicle Services, Records Section, 445 Minnesota St, #180, St Paul, MN 55101; 651-296-6911, 8AM-4:30PM.

www.dps.state.mn.us/dvs/index.html

Online: Online access costs $2.50 per record. Online inquiries can be processed either as interactive or as batch files (overnight) 24 hours a day, 7 days a week. Requesters operate from a "bank." Records are accessed by either DL number or full name and DOB. Call 651-297-1714 for more information.

Vehicle Ownership, Vehicle Identification

Driver & Vehicle Services, Records Section, 445 Minnesota St, St Paul, MN 55101; 651-296-6911 (Information), 8AM-4:30PM.

www.dps.state.mn.us/dvs/index.html

Online: Online access costs $2.50 per record. There is an additional monthly charge for dial-in access. The system is the same as described for driving record requests. It is open 24 hours a day, 7 days a week. Lien information is included. Call 651-297-1714 for more information.

Legislation Records

Minnesota Legislature, State Capitol, House-Room 211, Senate-Room 231, St Paul, MN 55155; 651-296-2887 (Senate Bills), 651-296-6646 (House Bill Status), 651-296-2314 (House Bill Copies), 651-296-2146 (House info), 651-296-1563 (Fax), 8AM-5PM.

www.leg.state.mn.us

Online: Information available through the Internet site includes full text of bills, status, previous 4 years of bills, and bill tracking.

State Level...Occupational Licensing

Acupuncturist	www.docboard.org/mn/df/mndf.htm
Architect	www.aelslagid.state.mn.us/lic.html
Athletic Trainer	www.docboard.org/mn/df/mndf.htm
Bingo Hall	www.gcb.state.mn.us/
Chiropractor	www.mn-chiroboard.state.mn.us/main-licensing.htm
Crematory	www.health.state.mn.us/divs/hpsc/mortsci/finda.htm
Engineer	www.aelslagid.state.mn.us/lic.html
Funeral Establishment	www.health.state.mn.us/divs/hpsc/mortsci/finda.htm
Gambling Equipment Distributor/Mfg	www.gcb.state.mn.us/
Geologist	www.aelslagid.state.mn.us/lic.html
Interior Designer	www.aelslagid.state.mn.us/lic.html
Landscape Architect	www.aelslagid.state.mn.us/lic.html
Lobbyist	www.cfboard.state.mn.us/lobby/index.html
Lottery (Retail)	www.lottery.state.mn.us/retailer/lookup.html
Medical Doctor	www.docboard.org/mn/df/mndf.htm
Midwife	www.docboard.org/mn/df/mndf.htm
Liquor Store	www.dps.state.mn.us/alcgamb/alcenf/liquorlic/liquorlic.html
Optometrist	www.odfinder.org/LicSearch.asp
Gambling Organization	www.gcb.state.mn.us/
Physical Therapist	www.docboard.org/mn/df/mndf.htm
Physician Assistant	www.docboard.org/mn/df/mndf.htm
Political Candidates	www.cfboard.state.mn.us/legcand.html
Respiratory Care Practitioner	www.docboard.org/mn/df/mndf.htm
Soil Scientist	www.aelslagid.state.mn.us/lic.html
Surgeon	www.docboard.org/mn/df/mndf.htm
Surveyor	www.aelslagid.state.mn.us/lic.html
Teacher	http://cfl.state.mn.us/licen/licinfo.html
Underground Storage Tank Contractor/Supvr	www.pca.state.mn.us/cleanup/ust.html#certification

County Level...Courts, Recorders & Assessors

State Court Adminstrator, 135 Minnesota Judicial Center, 25 Constitution Ave, St Paul, MN, 55155; 651-296-2474; www.courts.state.mn.us

Editor's Note: There is an online system in place that allows internal and external access. Some criminal information is available online from St Paul through the Bureau of Criminal Apprehension (BCA), 1246 University Ave, St. Paul, MN 55104. Additional information is available from BCA by calling 651-642-0670.

Anoka
Real Estate, Tax Assessor Records
www2.co.hennepin.mn.us
Access to the County online records requires an annual fee of $35 and a $25 monthly fee and $.25 per transaction. Records date back to 1995. Lending agency information is available. For information, contact Pam LeBlanc at 763-323-5424.

Carver
Property Tax Records
www.co.carver.mn.us
Records on the County Property Tax Information database are available free online at www.co.carvr.mn.us/Prop_Tax/default.asp. Information is updated bi-monthly.

Clay
Real Estate
www.co.clay.mn.us/
The county online GIS mapping service provides property record searching, but by parcel number only. County Recorder records may be available at the web site in the near future.

Dakota
Real Estate, Assessor
www.co.dakota.mn.us
Records on the County Real Estate Inquiry database are available free online at
www.co.dakota.mn.us/assessor/real_estate_inquiry.htm. Information includes address, value, taxes, last sale price, building details.

Hennepin
Real Estate, Liens
www2.co.hennepin.mn.us
Three options are available. Access to Hennepin County online records requires a $35 annual fee with a charge of $5 per hour from 7AM-7PM, or $4.15 per hour at other times. Records date back to 1988. Only UCC & lending agency information is available. Property tax info is at the Treasurer office. For information, contact Jerry Erickson at 612-348-3856. Records on the County Property Information Search database are available free on the Internet at www2.co.hennepin.mn.us/pins/main.htm. An Automated phone system is also available; 612-348-3011.

Sherburne
Real Estate, Tax Assessor Records
www.co.sherburne.mn.us
Records from the county tax assessor database are available free online at
www.hometimes.com/Communities/Taxes/TaxSearch/Shurburne/index.html.

St. Louis
Real Estate, Property Tax
Online access to the Auditor and Recorder's tax records for tax professionals database is available by subscription. Fee is $100 quarterly; password provided. For information or sign-up, contact Pam Palen at 218-726-2380 or email to palenp@co.st-louis.mn.us or visit www.co.st-louis.mn.us/auditorsoffice/subscription.pdf.

Stearns
Real Estate, Tax Assessor Records
Records from the county tax assessor database are available free online at
www.hometimes.com/Communities/Taxes/TaxSearch/index.html.

Washington
Real Estate, Liens, Tax Assessor
www.co.washington.mn.us
Access to county online records requires a $250 set up fee; no fees apply to Recorder office information. Records date back 3 years. Lending agency information is available, but UCC information is on a separate system. For information, contact Larry Haseman at 651-430-6423. Also, online access to property tax records is available free at
https://washington.mn.ezgov.com/ezproperty/review_search.jsp; property ID or address required.

Federal Courts in Minnesota...

US District Court - District of Minnesota

Home Page: www.mnd.uscourts.gov
PACER: Sign-up number is 800-676-6856. Access fee is $.60 per minute. Toll-free access: 800-818-8761. Local access: 612-664-5170. Case records are available back to February 1990. New records are available online after 1 day.
PACER Internet Access: http://pacer.mnd.uscourts.gov.
Duluth Division Counties: Aitkin, Becker*, Beltrami*, Benton, Big Stone*, Carlton, Cass, Clay*, Clearwater*, Cook, Crow Wing, Douglas*, Grant*, Hubbard*, Itasca, Kanabec, Kittson*, Koochiching, Lake, Lake of the Woods*, Mahnomen*, Marshall*, Mille Lacs, Morrison, Norman*, Otter*,Tail, Pennington*, Pine, Polk*, Pope*, Red Lake*, Roseau*, Stearns*, Stevens*, St. Louis, Todd*, Traverse*, Wadena*, Wilkin*. From March 1, 1995, to 1998, cases from the counties marked with an asterisk (*) were heard here.Before and after that period, cases were and are allocated between St. Paul and Minneapolis.
Minneapolis Division Counties: All counties not covered by the Duluth Division. Cases are allocated between Minneapolis and St Paul.
St Paul Division Counties: All counties not covered by the Duluth Division. Cases are allocated between Minneapolis and St Paul.

US Bankruptcy Court - District of Minnesota

Home Page: www.mnb.uscourts.gov
PACER: Sign-up number is 800-676-6856. Access fee is $.60 per minute. Case records are available back to January 1993. Records are purged up to April 1996. New civil records are available online after 1 day.
Electronic Filing: Electronic filing information is available online at www.mnb.uscourts.gov/cgi-bin/mnb-500-file.pl.
Other Online Access: You can search records using the Internet. Searching is currently free. Visit www.mnb.uscourts.gov/cgi-bin/mnb-500-main.pl.
Duluth Division Counties: Aitkin, Benton, Carlton, Cass, Cook, Crow Wing, Itasca, Kanabec, Koochiching, Lake, Mille Lacs, Morrison, Pine, St. Louis. A petition commencing Chapter 11 or 12 proceedings may initially be filed in any of the four divisons, but may be assigned toanother division.
Fergus Falls Division Counties: Becker, Beltrami, Big Stone, Clay, Clearwater, Douglas, Grant, Hubbard, Kittson, Lake of the Woods, Mahnomen, Marshall, Norman, Otter Tail, Pennington, Polk, Pope, Red Lake, Roseau, Stearns, Stevens, Todd, Traverse, Wadena, Wilkin. A petition commencingChapter 11 or 12 proceedings may be filed initially in any of the four divisions, but may then be assigned to another division.
Minneapolis Division Counties: Anoka, Carver, Chippewa, Hennepin, Isanti, Kandiyohi, McLeod, Meeker, Renville, Sherburne, Swift, Wright. Initial petitions for Chapter 11 or 12 may be filed initially at any of the four divisions, but may then be assigned to a judge in another division.
St Paul Division Counties: Blue Earth, Brown, Chisago, Cottonwood, Dakota, Dodge, Faribault, Fillmore, Freeborn, Goodhue, Houston, Jackson, Lac qui Parle, Le Sueur, Lincoln, Lyon, Martin, Mower, Murray, Nicollet, Nobles, Olmsted, Pipestone, Ramsey, Redwood, Rice, Rock, Scott,Sibley, Steele, Wabasha, Waseca, Washington, Watonwan, Winona, Yellow Medicine. Cases from Benton, Kanabec, Mille Lacs, Morrison and Pine may also be heard here. A petition commencing Chapter 11 or 12 proceedings may be filed initially with any of thefour divisions, but may then be assigned to another division.

Editor's Choice for Minnesota

Constitution Text
   www.house.leg.state.mn.us/cco/rules/mncon/preamble.htm
Offenders Database
   http://info.doc.state.mn.us/publicviewer/
State Employee Contact Information Directory
   www.state.mn.us/dir/index.html
Statutes & Laws Text
   www.leg.state.mn.us/leg/statutes.htm
Supreme Court Opinions
   http://156.99.5.29/opinions/sc/current/sccur.html

Mississippi

Capital:	Jackson Hinds County	Home Page	www.state.ms.us
Time Zone:	CST	Archives	www.mdah.state.ms.us
Number of Counties:	82	Attorney General	www.ago.state.ms.us

State Level...Major Agencies

Corporation Records, Limited Partnership Records, Limited Liability Company Records, Trademarks/Servicemarks

Corporation Commission, Secretary of State, PO Box 136, Jackson, MS 39205-0136 (Courier: 202 N Congress, Suite 601, Jackson, MS 39201); 601-359-1633, 800-256-3494, 601-359-1607 (Fax), 8AM-5PM.

www.sos.state.ms.us

Online: The system is called "CorpSnap" and is available from the Internet. There is no fee to view records, including officers and registered agents.

Uniform Commercial Code, Federal Tax Liens

Business Services Division, Secretary of State, PO Box 136, Jackson, MS 39205-0136 (Courier: 202 N Congress St, Suite 601, Union Planters Bank Bldg, Jackson, MS 39201); 601-359-1633, 800-256-3494, 601-359-1607 (Fax), 8AM-5PM.

www.sos.state.ms.us

Online: The PC system is called "Success" and is open 24 hours daily. There is a $250 set-up fee and usage fee of $.10 per screen. Users can access via the Internet to avoid any toll charges. Customers are billed quarterly. For more information, call Burrell Brown at 601-359-1633.

Workers' Compensation Records

Workers Compensation Commission, PO Box 5300, Jackson, MS 39296-5300 (Courier: 1428 Lakeland Dr, Jackson, MS 39216); 601-987-4200, 8AM-5PM.

www.mwcc.state.ms.us

Online: The First Report of Injury is available via the web. There is no fee, but users must register.

Driver Records

Department of Public Safety, Driver Records, PO Box 958, Jackson, MS 39205 (Courier: 1900 E Woodrow Wilson, Jackson, MS 39216); 601-987-1274, 8AM-5PM.

Online: Both interactive and batch delivery is offer for high volume users only. Billing is monthly. Hook-up is through the Advantis System, fees apply. Lookup is by name only-not by driver license number. Fee is $7.00 per record. For more information, call 601-987-1337.

Legislation Records

Mississippi Legislature, PO Box 1018, Jackson, MS 39215 (Courier: New Capitol, 3rd Floor, Jackson, MS 39215-1018); 601-359-3229 (Senate), 601-359-3358 (House), 8:30AM-5PM.
www.ls.state.ms.us
Online: The Internet site has an excellent bill status and measure information program. Data includes current and the previous year.

Voter Registration

Secretary of State, Elections Division,; 800-829-6786, 601-359-5019 (Fax), 8AM-5PM.
www.sos.state.ms.us
Online: County Voter Rolls are available to download free online at www.sos.state.ms.us/elections/voter_registration_downloads/voter_reg_main.html. Individual county files are in delimited text and may be downloaded to a database program.

State Level...Occupational Licensing

Architect	www.archbd.state.ms.us/aroster.htm
Attorney	www.mslawyer.com/index.html
Attorney Firm	www.mslawyer.com/LawFirms/
Dental Hygienist	http://dsitspe01.its.state.ms.us/msbde/hygienist.nsf
Dentist/Dental Radiologist	http://dsitspe01.its.state.ms.us/msbde/dassist.nsf
Engineer	http://dsitspe01.its.state.ms.us/pepls/EngSurveyors.nsf
General Contractor	www.msboc.state.ms.us/Search.cfm
HMO	www.doi.state.ms.us/hmolist.pdf
Insurance Company	www.doi.state.ms.us/compdir.html
Landscape Architect	www.archbd.state.ms.us/lroster.htm
Lobbyist	www.sos.state.ms.us/elections/Lobbyists/Lobbyist_Dir.html
Long Term Care Insurance Company	www.doi.state.ms.us/ltclist.html
Notary Public	www.sos.state.ms.us/busserv/notaries/NotarySearch.html
Optometrist	www.odfinder.org/LicSearch.asp
Surveyor	http://dsitspe01.its.state.ms.us/pepls/EngSurveyors.nsf

County Level...Courts, Recorders & Assessors

Court Administrator, Supreme Court, Box 117, Jackson, MS, 39205; 601-359-3697; www.mssc.state.ms.us

Editor's Note: A statewide online computer system is in use internally for court personnel. There are plans underway to make this system available to the public. For further details, call Susan Anthony at 601-354-7449.

Hinds
Real Estate, Assessor, Grantor/Grantee, Judgments
www.co.hinds.ms.us
Online access to the county clerk database is available free at www.co.hinds.ms.us/pgs/apps/gindex.asp. Chose to search general index, land roll, judgments, acreage, subdivision, and condominiums.

Madison
Real Estate, Tax Assessor Records
http://mcatax.com
Records from the county Assessor office are available free online. At www.mcatax.com/mcasearch.asp, click on "Search The Database." Records include parcel number, address, legal description, value information, and tax district.

Rankin

Real Estate, Tax Assessor Records

www.rankincounty.org

Records on the county Land Roll database are available free online at www.rankincounty.org/TA/interact_LandRoll.asp.

Federal Courts in Mississippi...

US District Court - Northern District of Mississippi

Home Page: www.msnd.uscourts.gov

PACER: Sign-up number is 800-676-6856. Access fee is $.60 per minute. Toll-free access: 888-227-0558. Local access: 662-236-4706. Case records are available back to 1990. Records are purged every six months. New records are available online after 1 day.

PACER Internet Access: http://pacer.msnd.uscourts.gov.

Opinions Online: Court opinions are available online at http://sunset.backbone.olemiss.edu/~llibcoll/ndms.

Aberdeen-Eastern Division Counties: Alcorn, Attala, Chickasaw, Choctaw, Clay, Itawamba, Lee, Lowndes, Monroe, Oktibbeha, Prentiss, Tishomingo, Winston.

Clarksdale/Delta Division Counties: Bolivar, Coahoma, De Soto, Panola, Quitman, Tallahatchie, Tate, Tunica.

Greenville Division Counties: Carroll, Humphreys, Leflore, Sunflower, Washington.

Oxford-Northern Division Counties: Benton, Calhoun, Grenada, Lafayette, Marshall, Montgomery, Pontotoc, Tippah, Union, Webster, Yalobusha.

US Bankruptcy Court - Northern District of Mississippi

Home Page: www.msnb.uscourts.gov

PACER: Sign-up number is 800-676-6856. Access fee is $.60 per minute. Toll-free access: 888-372-5709. Local access: 662-369-9805, 622-369-9854. Case records are available back to April 1, 1987. Records are purged every 6 months. New civil records are available online after 2 days.

Aberdeen Division Counties: Alcorn, Attala, Benton, Bolivar, Calhoun, Carroll, Chickasaw, Choctaw, Clay, Coahoma, De Soto, Grenada, Humphreys, Itawamba, Lafayette, Lee, Leflore, Lowndes, Marshall, Monroe, Montgomery, Oktibbeha, Panola, Pontotoc, Prentiss, Quitman, Sunflower,Tallahatchie, Tate, Tippah, Tishomingo, Tunica, Union, Washington, Webster, Winston, Yalobusha.

US District Court - Southern District of Mississippi

Home Page: www.mssd.uscourts.gov

PACER: Sign-up number is 800-676-6856. Access fee is. Toll-free access: 800-839-6425. Local access: 601-965-5141. Case records are available back to 1992. New records are available online after 2 days.

Biloxi-Southern Division Counties: George, Hancock, Harrison, Jackson, Pearl River, Stone.

Hattiesburg Division Counties: Covington, Forrest, Greene, Jefferson Davis, Jones, Lamar, Lawrence, Marion, Perry, Walthall.

Jackson Division Counties: Amite, Copiah, Franklin, Hinds, Holmes, Leake, Lincoln, Madison, Pike, Rankin, Scott, Simpson, Smith.

Meridian Division Counties: Clarke, Jasper, Kemper, Lauderdale, Neshoba, Newton, Noxubee, Wayne.

Vicksburg Division Counties: Adams, Claiborne, Issaquena, Jefferson, Sharkey, Warren, Wilkinson, Yazoo.

US Bankruptcy Court - Southern District of Mississippi

PACER: Sign-up number is 800-676-6856. Access fee is $.60 per minute. Toll-free access: 800-223-1078. Local access: 601-965-6103. Use of PC Anywhere V4.0 recommended. Case records available back to 1986. New civil records available online after 1 day.

Biloxi Division Counties: Clarke, Covington, Forrest, George, Greene, Hancock, Harrison, Jackson, Jasper, Jefferson Davis, Jones, Kemper, Lamar, Lauderdale, Lawrence, Marion, Neshoba, Newton, Noxubee, Pearl River, Perry, Stone, Walthall, Wayne.

Jackson Division Counties: Adams, Amite, Claiborne, Copiah, Franklin, Hinds, Holmes, Issaquena, Jefferson, Leake, Lincoln, Madison, Pike, Rankin, Scott, Sharkey, Simpson, Smith, Warren, Wilkinson, Yazoo.

Editor's Choice for Mississippi

Attorney General Opinions

www.agopin.state.ms.us

State Employee e-mail Listing

www.its.state.ms.us/email

Capital:	Jefferson City			Home Page
	Cole County			www.state.mo.us
Time Zone:	CST		Attorney General	www.ago.state.mo.us
Number of Counties:	114		Archives	http://mosl.sos.state.mo.us/
				rec-man/arch.html

State Level...Major Agencies

Corporation Records, Fictitious Name, Limited Partnership Records, Assumed Name, Trademarks/Servicemarks, Limited Liability Companies

Secretary of State, Corporation Services, PO Box 778, Jefferson City, MO 65102 (Courier: 600 W Main, Jefferson City, MO 65101); 573-751-4153, 573-751-5841 (Fax), 8AM-5PM.

http://mosl.sos.state.mo.us

Online: Searching can be done from the Internet site. The corporate name, the agent name or the charter number is required to search. The site will indicate the currency of the data. Many business entity type searches are available.

Driver Records

Department of Revenue, Driver and Vehicle Services Bureau, PO Box 200, Jefferson City, MO 65105-0200 (Courier: Harry S Truman Bldg, 301 W High St, Room 470, Jefferson City, MO 65105); 573-751-4300, 573-526-4769 (Fax), 7:45AM-4:45PM.

www.dor.state.mo.us/mvdl/drivers

Online: Online access costs $1.25 per record. Online inquiries can be put in Missouri's "mailbox" any time of the day. These inquiries are then picked up at 2 AM the following morning, and the resulting MVR's are sent back to each customer's "mailbox" approximately two hours later.

Legislation Records

Legislative Library, 117A State Capitol, Jefferson City, MO 65101; 573-751-4633 (Bill Status Only), 8:30AM-4:30PM.

www.moga.state.mo.us

Online: The web site offers access to bills and statutes. One can search or track bills by key words, bill number, or sponsors.

State Level...Occupational Licensing

Architect..http://showme.ded.state.mo.us/dynded/pronline.form1
Athletic Trainer http://showme.ded.state.mo.us/dynded/pronline.form1
Audiologist (Clinical).......................................http://showme.ded.state.mo.us/dynded/pronline.form1
Barber/ Barber Instructor/Schools/Shops http://showme.ded.state.mo.us/dynded/pronline.form1
Boxer..http://showme.ded.state.mo.us/dynded/pronline.form1
Chiropractor..http://showme.ded.state.mo.us/dynded/pronline.form1
Combined Speech/Clinical Audiologist http://showme.ded.state.mo.us/dynded/pronline.form1
Cosmetologist/Instructor/School/Shop http://showme.ded.state.mo.us/dynded/pronline.form1
Dental Hygienist http://showme.ded.state.mo.us/dynded/pronline.form1
Dentist...http://showme.ded.state.mo.us/dynded/pronline.form1
Drug Distribution..http://showme.ded.state.mo.us/dynded/pronline.form1
Embalmer http://showme.ded.state.mo.us/dynded/pronline.form1
Engineer http://showme.ded.state.mo.us/dynded/pronline.form1
Funeral Director/Establishment.......................http://showme.ded.state.mo.us/dynded/pronline.form1
Funeral Preneed ProviderSeller........................http://showme.ded.state.mo.us/dynded/pronline.form1
Interpreter for the Deaf....................................http://showme.ded.state.mo.us/dynded/pronline.form1
Landfill...www.dnr.state.mo.us/deq/swmp/availpub.htm
Landscape Architect/Corp./or/Partnership http://showme.ded.state.mo.us/dynded/pronline.form1
Manicurist http://showme.ded.state.mo.us/dynded/pronline.form1
Medical Doctor http://showme.ded.state.mo.us/dynded/pronline.form1
Nurse/ Nurse-LPN http://showme.ded.state.mo.us/dynded/pronline.form1
Occupational Therapist/Assistant http://showme.ded.state.mo.us/dynded/pronline.form1
Optometrist...http://showme.ded.state.mo.us/dynded/pronline.form1
Osteopathic Physician http://showme.ded.state.mo.us/dynded/pronline.form1
Pharmacist/Pharmacy Intern/Tech/Pharmacy http://showme.ded.state.mo.us/dynded/pronline.form1
Physical Therapist...http://showme.ded.state.mo.us/dynded/pronline.form1
Physician Assistant http://showme.ded.state.mo.us/dynded/pronline.form1
Podiatrist/ Podiatrist Temporary.......................http://showme.ded.state.mo.us/dynded/pronline.form1
Podiatrist/Ankle...http://showme.ded.state.mo.us/dynded/pronline.form1
Professional Counselor...................................http://showme.ded.state.mo.us/dynded/pronline.form1
Professional Nurse ....www.ecodev.state.mo.us/pr/nursingdown.html
Psychologist..http://showme.ded.state.mo.us/dynded/pronline.form1
Public Accountant-CPA/Partnership...................http://showme.ded.state.mo.us/dynded/pronline.form1
Real Estate Appraiser......................................http://showme.ded.state.mo.us/dynded/pronline.form1
Real Estate Broker/Sales Agent........................http://showme.ded.state.mo.us/dynded/pronline.form1
Respiratory Care Practitioner http://showme.ded.state.mo.us/dynded/pronline.form1
Social Worker (Clinical) http://showme.ded.state.mo.us/dynded/pronline.form1
Speech-LanguagePathologist/Audiologist http://showme.ded.state.mo.us/dynded/pronline.form1
Surveyor http://showme.ded.state.mo.us/dynded/pronline.form1
Transfer Station ....www.dnr.state.mo.us/deq/swmp/tranlist.htm
Veterinarian/ Veterinary Technician...................http://showme.ded.state.mo.us/dynded/pronline.form1
Waste Tire End User/Hauler/Processor/Site ....www.dnr.state.mo.us/deq/swmp/tireend.htm
Waste Tire Hauler...www.dnr.state.mo.us/deq/swmp/tirehaul.htm
Waste Tire Processor ....www.dnr.state.mo.us/deq/swmp/tireend.htm
Waste Tire Site ....www.dnr.state.mo.us/deq/swmp/tirelist.htm
Wrestler..http://showme.ded.state.mo.us/dynded/pronline.form1

County Level...Courts, Recorders & Assessors

State Court Administrator, 2112 Industrial Dr., PO Box 104480, Jefferson City, MO, 65109; 573-751-4377; www.osca.state.mo.us

Editor's Note: Missouri Casenet, a limited but growing online system, is available at http://casenet.osca.state.mo.us/casenet. The system includes 27 counties (with 16 more projected) as well as the Eastern, Western, and Southern Appellate Courts, the Supreme Court, and Fine Collection Center.

Andrew
Civil Cases, Criminal Records
Participates in the free state online court record system at http://casenet.osca.state.mo.us/casenet.

Barton
Civil Cases, Criminal Records
Participates in the free state online court record system at http://casenet.osca.state.mo.us/casenet.

Benton
Civil Cases, Criminal Records
www.positech.net/~dcourt
Court dockets and judgments from the circuit clerk's web site are available free at http://208.154.254.51:5061. The court will only indicate if subject is on probation or has open case. For criminal searches contact Jefferson City Highway Patrol.

Boone
Civil Cases, Criminal Records
Participates in the free state online court record system at http://casenet.osca.state.mo.us/casenet.
Real Estate, Liens, Vital Statistics, UCC
www.showmeboone.com/
Online access to the County Recorder database is available free at www.showmeboone.com/RECORDER.

Buchanan
Civil Cases, Criminal Records
Participates in the free state online court record system at http://casenet.osca.state.mo.us/casenet. Case.net records go back to 1992.

Callaway
Civil Cases, Criminal Records
www.osca.state.mo.us
Participates in the free state online court record system at http://casenet.osca.state.mo.us/casenet.

Carter
Civil Cases, Criminal Records
Participates in the free state online court record system at http://casenet.osca.state.mo.us/casenet.

Cass
Real Estate, Liens
www.casscounty.com/cassfr.htm
Access to county online records via modem requires a $250 monthly fee plus $.10 per minute after 90 minutes usage. Records date back to 1990. Images are viewable and can be printed, $1.00 each. Prepaid fax accounts available. For information, contact Sandy Gregory at 816-380-8117.

Cedar
Civil Cases, Criminal Records
Participates in the free state online court record system at http://casenet.osca.state.mo.us/casenet.

Clay
Civil Cases, Criminal Records
www.circuit7.net/
Online access to civil records on the 7th Judicial Circuit database is available free at www.circuit7.net/publicaccess/default.htm. Includes traffic and criminal records.

Cole
Civil Cases, Criminal Records
Participates in the free state online court record system at http://casenet.osca.state.mo.us/casenet.

Dade
Civil Cases, Criminal Records
Participates in the free state online court record system at http://casenet.osca.state.mo.us/casenet.

Franklin
Civil Cases, Criminal Records
Participates in the free state online court record system at http://casenet.osca.state.mo.us/casenet.

Gasconade
Civil Cases, Criminal Records
Participates in the free state online court record system at http://casenet.osca.state.mo.us/casenet.

Greene
Divorce
Records for divorces that occurred 1837 to 1920 in Greene County are available free online at http://userdb.rootsweb.com/divorces.

Grundy
Civil Cases, Criminal Records
Participates in the free state online court record system at http://casenet.osca.state.mo.us/casenet.

Harrison
Civil Cases, Criminal Records
Participates in the free state online court record system at http://casenet.osca.state.mo.us/casenet.

Howell
Civil Cases, Criminal Records
Participates in the free state online court record system at http://casenet.osca.state.mo.us/casenet. Online records go back to 8/2000.

Jackson
Criminal Records
www.16thcircuit.org
Participates in the free state online court record system at http://casenet.osca.state.mo.us/casenet.
Property, Tax Assessor
www.co.jackson.mo.us
Records from the county tax assessor database are available free at the web site. Click on "Tax Search." Search by owner name, address, street, or neighborhood. Property owner records on the Kansas City Neighborhood Network are available free online at www.kcmo-net.org/cgi-bin/db2www/realform.d2w/report.

Jasper
Civil Cases, Criminal Records
Participates in the free state online court record system at http://casenet.osca.state.mo.us/casenet. Online records go back to 7/2000.

Mercer
Civil Cases, Criminal Records
Participates in the free state online court record system at http://casenet.osca.state.mo.us/casenet. Online records go back to 3/2000.

Montgomery
Civil Cases, Criminal Records
Participates in the free state online court record system at http://casenet.osca.state.mo.us/casenet.

Oregon
Civil Cases, Criminal Records
Participates in the free state online court record system at http://casenet.osca.state.mo.us/casenet.

Osage
Civil Cases, Criminal Records
Participates in the free state online court record system at http://casenet.osca.state.mo.us/casenet.

Pemiscot
Civil Cases, Criminal Records
Participates in the free state online court record system at http://casenet.osca.state.mo.us/casenet.

Platte
Civil Cases, Criminal Records
Participates in the free state online court record system at http://casenet.osca.state.mo.us/casenet.

Putnam
Civil Cases, Criminal Records
Participates in the free state online court record system at http://casenet.osca.state.mo.us/casenet.

Reynolds
Civil Cases, Criminal Records
Access to civil records is available free at http://casenet.osca.state.mo.us/casenet. At the web site, select the judicial district, then search by name, case # or date.

Shannon
Civil Cases, Criminal Records
Participates in the free state online court record system at http://casenet.osca.state.mo.us/casenet.

St. Charles
Civil Cases, Criminal Records
Participates in the free state online court record system at http://casenet.osca.state.mo.us/casenet..
Assessor
www.win.org/county/codepts.htm
Records on the county Property Assessment database are available free online at www.win.org/library/library_office/assessment.

St. Louis City
Civil Cases
Remote access is through MoBar Net and is open only to attorneys. Call 314-535-1950 for more information.

Vernon
Civil Cases, Criminal Records
Participates in the free state online court record system at http://casenet.osca.state.mo.us/casenet. Records go back to 9/2000.

Warren
Civil Cases, Criminal Records
Participates in the free state online court record system at http://casenet.osca.state.mo.us/casenet.

Federal Courts in Missouri...

US District Court - Eastern District of Missouri

Home Page: www.moed.uscourts.gov
PACER: Sign-up number is 800-676-6856. Access fee is $.60 per minute. Toll-free access: 800-533-8105. Local access: 314-539-3857. Case records are available back to 1992. Records are purged never. New records are available online after 4-5 days.
PACER Internet Access: http://pacer.moed.uscourts.gov.
Cape Girardeau Division Counties: Bollinger, Butler, Cape Girardeau, Carter, Dunklin, Madison, Mississippi, New Madrid, Pemiscot, Perry, Reynolds, Ripley, Scott, Shannon, Stoddard, Wayne.
Hannibal Division Counties: Adair, Audrain, Chariton, Clark, Knox, Lewis, Linn, Macon, Marion, Monroe, Montgomery, Pike, Ralls, Randolph, Schuyler, Scotland, Shelby.
St Louis Division Counties: Crawford, Dent, Franklin, Gasconade, Iron, Jefferson, Lincoln, Maries, Phelps, St. Charles, Ste. Genevieve, St. Francois, St. Louis, Warren, Washington, City of St. Louis.

US Bankruptcy Court - Eastern District of Missouri

Home Page: www.moeb.uscourts.gov
PACER: Sign-up number is 800-676-6856. Access fee is $.60 per minute. Toll-free access: 888-577-1668. Local access: 314-425-6935. Case records available back to 1/ 1991. Records are purged every six months. New civil records are available online after 1 day.
PACER Internet Access: http://pacer.moeb.uscourts.gov.
St Louis Division Counties: Adair, Audrain, Bollinger, Butler, Cape Girardeau, Carter, Chariton, Clark, Crawford, Dent, Dunklin, Franklin, Gasconade, Iron, Jefferson, Knox, Lewis, Lincoln, Linn, Macon, Madison, Maries, Marion, Mississippi, Monroe, Montgomery, New Madrid, Pemiscot,Perry, Phelps, Pike, Ralls, Randolph, Reynolds, Ripley, Schuyler, Scotland, Scott, Shannon, Shelby, St. Charles, St. Francois, St. Louis, St.Louis City, Ste. Genevieve, Stoddard, Warren, Washington, Wayne.

US District Court - Western District of Missouri

PACER: Sign-up number is 800-676-6856. Access fee is $.60 per minute. Toll-free access: 888-205-2527. Local access: 816-512-5110. Case records available back to May 1, 1989. Records are purged as deemed necessary. New records available online after 1 day.
PACER Internet Access: http://pacer.mowd.uscourts.gov.
Electronic Filing: Only law firms and practioners may file cases electronically. Anyone may search online; however, the search only includes cases which have been filed electronically. To conduct a search, visit http://ecf.mowd.uscourts.gov/cgi-bin/PublicCaseFiled-Rpt.pl Electronic filing information is available online at http://ecf.mowd.uscourts.gov.
Jefferson City-Central Division Counties: Benton, Boone, Callaway, Camden, Cole, Cooper, Hickory, Howard, Miller, Moniteau, Morgan, Osage, Pettis.
Joplin-Southwestern Division Counties: Barry, Barton, Jasper, Lawrence, McDonald, Newton, Stone, Vernon.
Kansas City-Western Division Counties: Bates, Carroll, Cass, Clay, Henry, Jackson, Johnson, Lafayette, Ray, St. Clair, Saline.
Springfield-Southern Division Counties: Cedar, Christian, Dade, Dallas, Douglas, Greene, Howell, Laclede, Oregon, Ozark, Polk, Pulaski, Taney, Texas, Webster, Wright.
St Joseph Division Counties: Andrew, Atchison, Buchanan, Caldwell, Clinton, Daviess, De Kalb, Gentry, Grundy, Harrison, Holt, Livingston, Mercer, Nodaway, Platte, Putnam, Sullivan, Worth.

US Bankruptcy Court - Western District of Missouri

PACER: Sign-up number is 800-676-6856. Access fee is. New records are available online after.
PACER Internet Access: http://pacer.mowb.uscourts.gov/bc/index.html.
Kansas City-Western Division Counties: Andrew, Atchison, Barry, Barton, Bates, Benton, Boone, Buchanan, Caldwell, Callaway, Camden, Carroll, Cass, Cedar, Christian, Clay, Clinton, Cole, Cooper, Dade, Dallas, Daviess, De Kalb, Douglas, Gentry, Greene, Grundy, Harrison, Henry, Hickory, Holt,Howard, Howell, Jackson, Jasper, Johnson, Laclede, Lafayette, Lawrence, Livingston, McDonald, Mercer, Miller, Moniteau, Morgan, Newton, Nodaway, Oregon, Osage, Ozark, Pettis, Platte, Polk, Pulaski, Putnam, Ray, Saline, St. Clair, Sullivan, Taney, Texas,Vernon, Webster, Worth, Wright.

Editor's Choice for Missouri

Death Statistics Database
www.health.state.mo.us/BobCOD/allcodd.html

Capital: Helena
                Lews & Clark County   Home Page   www.mt.gov

Time Zone: MST   Attorney General   www.doj.state.mt.us/ago

Number of Counties: 56   Archives   www.his.state.mt.us

State Level...Major Agencies

Uniform Commercial Code, Federal Tax Liens

Business Services Bureau, Secretary of State, Rm 260, PO Box 202801, Helena, MT 59620-2801 (Courier: State Capital, 2nd Fl, Helena, MT 59620); 406-444-3665, 406-444-3976 (Fax), 8AM-5PM.

www.state.mt.us/sos

Online: The online system costs $25 per month plus $.50 per page if copies of filed documents are requested. A prepaid account is required. The system is open 24 hours daily. This commercial access is available via the Internet. The system will only return an exact match to the name submitted.

Legislation Records

State Legislature of Montana, State Capitol, Rm 110, PO Box 201706, Helena, MT 59620-1706; 406-444-3064, 406-444-3036 (Fax), 8AM-5PM.

www.leg.state.mt.us

Online: Information is available on the Internet. Committee minutes back to 1999 are available on the Internet. Exhibits from 1999 forward are available on CD-ROM.

State Level...Occupational Licensing

Editor's Note: E-mail addresses are listed for those agencies that accept verification requests via e-mail.

Appraiser .... compolrea@state.mt.us
Architect .... compolarc@state.mt.us
Athletic Event/ Atheltic Event Timekeeper .... compolath@state.mt.us
Barber/ Barber Instructor .... compolbar@state.mt.us
Boxer/Boxing Judge/Manager/Promoter .... compolath@state.mt.us
Boxing Corner Person/Second .... compolath@state.mt.us
Cemetery .... compolfnr@state.mt.us
Chemical Dependency Counselor .... compolcdc@state.mt.us
Chiropractor .... compolchi@state.mt.us
Construction Blaster .... compolbbc@state.mt.us

Cosmetologist/Cosmetology Instructor/School .... compolcos@state.mt.us
Crematory/Crematory Operator/Technician .... compolfnr@state.mt.us
Dental Assistant/ Dental Hygienist.................... compolden@state.mt.us
Dentist/Denturist .... compolden@state.mt.us
Electrician .... compolele@state.mt.us
Electrologist.. compolcos@state.mt.us
Engineer .... compolpel@state.mt.us
Esthetician.. compolcos@state.mt.us
Funeral Director.. compolfnr@state.mt.us
Hearing Aid Dispenser..................................... compolhad@state.mt.us
Land Surveyor.. compolpel@state.mt.us
Landscape Architect... compollar@state.mt.us
Lobbyist.. www.lobbyist.net/Montana/MONLOB.htm
Manicurist .... compolcos@state.mt.us
Mortician/Mortuary.. compolfnr@state.mt.us
Nurse-RN & LPN... compolnur@state.mt.us
Nursing... compolnur@state.mt.us
Occupational Therapist .... compolotp@mt.gov
Optometrist...................................... www.odfinder.org/LicSearch.asp
Outfitter.. compolout@state.mt.us
Pharmacist.. compolpha@state.mt.us
Physical Therapist.. compolptp@state.mt.us
Plumber .... compolplu@state.mt.us
Private Investigator .... compolpsp@state.mt.
Private Security Guard .... compolpsp@state.mt.
Psychologist.. compolpsy@state.mt.us
Radiologic Technologist................................... compolrts@state.mt.us
Referee .... compolath@state.mt.us
Respiratory Care Practitioner .... compolrcp@state.mt.us
Sanitarian .... compolsan@state.mt.us
Security Alarm Installer/ Security Company .... compolpsp@state.mt.
Speech Pathologist/Audiologist .... compolslp@state.mt.us
Surveyor .... compolpel@state.mt.us
Underground Storage Tank Inspector................. www.deq.state.mt.us/rem/tsb/ess/enfLicensedComplianceInspectors.pdf
Underground Storage Tank Installer/Remover .... www.deq.state.mt.us/rem/tsb/ess/installation_closure.asp
Veterinarian.. compolvet@state.mt.us
Wrestler.. compolath@state.mt.us

County Level...Courts, Recorders & Assessors

Court Administrator, Justice Building, 215 N Sanders, Room 315 (PO Box 203002), Helena, MT, 59620; 406-444-2621;

Editor's Note: There is no statewide internal or external online computer system available. Those courts with computer systems use them for internal purposes only.

Search for a for a Montana property owner by name and county on the Montana Cadastral Mapping Project GIS mapping database at http://gis.doa.state.mt.us/cadastral/textsearch.html.

Lewis and Clark
Civil Cases, Criminal Records
www.co.lewis-clark.mt.us
Will accept e-mail record requests to jwright@co.lewis-clark.mt.us..
Real Estate, Liens, Recording
www.co.lewis-clark.mt.us
Currently, the Records Department is in the processing of automating their recording and filing procedures. This automation will include document imaging. Available is the GIS map and parcel search at www.co.lewis-clark.mt.us/gis/atlas/index.html.

Yellowstone
Assessor, Tax Records, Grantor/Grantee
www.co.yellowstone.mt.us/clerk
Online access to the county clerk & recorder records are available free online at www.co.yellowstone.mt.us/clerk. Also, access to the tax assessor records is available free at www.co.yellowstone.mt.us/gis.

Federal Courts in Montana...

US District Court - District of Montana
PACER: Sign-up number is 800-676-6856. Access fee is $.60 per minute. Toll-free access: 800-305-5235. Local access: 406-452-9851. Case records are available back to 1992. Records are purged never. New records are available online after 5 days.
Billings Division Counties: Big Horn, Carbon, Carter, Custer, Dawson, Fallon, Garfield, Golden Valley, McCone, Musselshell, Park, Petroleum, Powder River, Prairie, Richland, Rosebud, Stillwater, Sweet Grass, Treasure, Wheatland,Wibaux, Yellowstone, Yellowstone National Park.
Butte Division Counties: Beaverhead, Deer Lodge, Gallatin, Madison, Silver Bow.
Great Falls Division Counties: Blaine, Cascade, Chouteau, Daniels, Fergus, Glacier, Hill, Judith Basin, Liberty, Phillips, Pondera, Roosevelt, Sheridan, Teton, Toole, Valley.
Helena Division Counties: Broadwater, Jefferson, Lewis and Clark, Meagher, Powell.
Missoula Division Counties: Flathead, Granite, Lake, Lincoln, Mineral, Missoula, Ravalli, Sanders.

US Bankruptcy Court - District of Montana
Home Page: www.mtb.uscourts.gov
PACER: Sign-up number is 800-676-6856. Access fee is $.60 per minute. Toll-free access: 800-716-4305. Local access: 406-782-1051. Use of PC Anywhere v4.0 suggested. Case records are available back to 1986. New civil records available online after 1 day.
Butte Division Counties: All counties in Montana.

Editor's Choice for Montana

Constitution & Laws Text
http://leg.state.mt.us/services/legal/laws.htm
Interactive County Map
www.co.yellowstone.mt.us/maps/static.asp
Parole Violators At Large Listing
www2.state.mt.us/bopp/parole_violators_at_large.htm
River Information Database
http://nris.state.mt.us/scripts/esrimap.dll?name=MRIS2&Cmd=INST
State Employee & Agency Telephone Numbers Database
www.state.mt.us/statedir/
Topographic Maps
http://nris.state.mt.us/scripts/esrimap.dll?name=LocMap&Cmd=Map

Capital:	Lincoln Lancaster County	Home Page	www.state.ne.us
Time Zone:	CST/MST	Attorney General	www.nol.org/home/ago
Number of Counties:	93	Archives	www.nebraskahistory.org

State Level...Major Agencies

Corporation Records, Limited Liability Company Records, Limited Partnerships, Trade Names, Trademarks/Servicemarks

Secretary of State, Corporation Commission, 1305 State Capitol Bldg, Lincoln, NE 68509; 402-471-4079, 402-471-3666 (Fax), 8AM-5PM.

www.nol.org.home/SOS

Online: The state has designated Nebrask@ Online (800-747-8177) to facilitate online retrieval of records. Access is through both a dial-up system and the Internet; however an account and payment is required. The state Internet site has general information only.

Uniform Commercial Code, Federal Tax Liens

UCC Division, Secretary of State, PO Box 95104, Lincoln, NE 68509 (Courier: 1301 State Capitol Bldg, Lincoln, NE 68509); 402-471-4080, 402-471-4429 (Fax), 7:30AM-5PM.

www.nol.org/home/SOS

Online: Access is outsourced to Nebrask@ Online. The system is available 24 hours daily. There is an annual $50 fee and a $.12 per minute access charge. The access charge can be avoided by using their Internet site at www.nol.org. Call 800-747-8177 for more information.

Sales Tax Registrations

Revenue Department, Revenue Operations Division, PO Box 94818, Lincoln, NE 68509-4818 (Courier: 301 Centennial Mall South, Lincoln, NE 68509); 402-471-5695, 402-471-5608 (Fax), 8AM-5PM.

www.nol.org/revenue

Information is available through Nebrask@ Online (402-471-7810). This is a commercial service with annual fee and monthly download fees.

Birth Certificates

NE Health & Human Services System, Vital Statistics Section, PO Box 95065, Lincoln, NE 68509-5065 (Courier: 301 Centennial Mall S, 3rd Floor, Lincoln, NE 68509); 402-471-2871, 8AM-5PM.

www.hhs.state.ne.us/ced/cedindex.htm

Online: Records may be ordered online from the Internet site.

Workers' Compensation Records

Workers' Compensation Court, PO Box 98908, Lincoln, NE 68509-8908 (Courier: State Capitol, 13th Floor, Lincoln, NE 68509); 402-471-6468, 800-599-5155 (In-state), 402-471-2700 (Fax), 8AM-5PM.

www.nol.org/workcomp

Online: Access to orders and decisions is available from the web site.

Driver Records

Department of Motor Vehicles, Driver & Vehicle Records Division, PO Box 94789, Lincoln, NE 68509-4789 (Courier: 301 Centennial Mall, S, Lincoln, NE 68509); 402-471-4343, 8AM-5PM.

www.nol.org/home/dmv/driverec.htm

Online: Nebraska outsources all online and tape record requests through Nebrask@ Online (800-747-8177). The system is interactive and open 24 hours a day, 7 days a week. Fee is $3.00 per record. There is an annual fee of $50.00 and a $.40 per minute connect fee or $.12 if through the Internet.

Vehicle Ownership, Vehicle Identification, Boat & Vessel Ownership

Department of Motor Vehicles, Driver & Vehicle Records Division, PO Box 94789, Lincoln, NE 68509-4789 (Courier: 301 Centennial Mall, S, Lincoln, NE 68509); 402-471-3918, 8AM-5PM.

www.nol.org/home/DMV

Online: Electronic access is through Nebrask@ Online. There is a start-up fee and line charges are incurred in addition to the $1.00 per record fee. The system is open 24 hours a day, 7 days a week. Call 800-747-8177 for more information.

Legislation Records

Clerk of Legislature Office, PO Box 94604, Lincoln, NE 68509-4604 (Courier: State Capitol, 1445 K Street, Room 2018, Lincoln, NE 68509); 402-471-2271, 402-471-2126 (Fax), 8AM-5PM.

www.unicam.state.ne.us

Online: The web site features the state statutes, legislative bills for the present session and a legislative journal. You can search by bill number or subject.

State Level...Occupational Licensing

Appraiser, Real Estate..http://dbdec.nrc.state.ne.us/appraiser/docs/list.html
Alcohol/Drug Testing..www.hhs.state.ne.us/lis/lis.asp
Architect...www.nol.org/home/NBOP/roster.html
Asbestos ....www.hhs.state.ne.us/lis/lis.asp
Assisted Living Facility..www.nlc.state.ne.us/docs/pilot/pubs/h.html
Athletic Trainer ....www.hhs.state.ne.us/lis/lis.asp
Attorney...www.nebar.com/directory/dir.asp
Bank...www.ndbf.org/banks.htm
Center for Developmentally Disabled.................www.nlc.state.ne.us/docs/pilot/pubs/h.html
Chiropractor..www.hhs.state.ne.us/lis/lis.asp
Collection Agency..www.nol.org/home/SOS/Collections/col-agn.htm
Cosmetology Salon...www.hhs.state.ne.us/lis/lis.asp
Cosmetology School...www.hhs.state.ne.us/lis/lis.asp
Credit Union..www.ndbf.org/culist.htm
Debt Management Agency ....www.nol.org/home/SOS/Collections/debtlist.htm
Delayed Deposit Service ....www.ndbf.org/ddslist.htm
Dentist/Dental Hygienist....................................www.hhs.state.ne.us/lis/lis.asp
Engineer ....www.nol.org/home/NBOP/roster.html
Environmental Health Specialist ....www.hhs.state.ne.us/lis/lis.asp
Exterminator..www.kellysolutions.com/ne/
Funeral Establishment...www.hhs.state.ne.us/lis/lis.asp
Health Clinic & Emergency Medical Care..........www.hhs.state.ne.us/lis/lis.asp
Hearing Aid Dispenser/Fitter ....www.hhs.state.ne.us/lis/lis.asp
Home Health Agency ....www.nlc.state.ne.us/docs/pilot/pubs/h.html
Hospice...www.nlc.state.ne.us/docs/pilot/pubs/h.html
Hospital ....www.nlc.state.ne.us/docs/pilot/pubs/h.html
Investment Advisor/Advisor Representative ....www.ndbf.org/secsearch.htm
Liquor Vendor ....www.nol.org/home/NLCC/nlccsearch.html
Lobbyist..www.lobbyist.net/Nebraska/NEBLOB.htm
Massage Therapy School....................................www.hhs.state.ne.us/lis/lis.asp
Medical Nutrition Therapy.................................www.hhs.state.ne.us/lis/lis.asp
Mental Health Center...www.hhs.state.ne.us/lis/lis.asp
Nurse...www.hhs.state.ne.us/lis/lis.asp
Nursing Home..www.hhs.state.ne.us/lis/lis.asp
Occupational Therapist ....www.hhs.state.ne.us/lis/lis.asp
Optometrist..www.hhs.state.ne.us/lis/lis.asp
Pesticide Applicator/Dealer...............................www.kellysolutions.com/ne/
Pharmacist/Pharmacy...www.hhs.state.ne.us/lis/lis.asp
Physical Therapist..www.hhs.state.ne.us/lis/lis.asp
Physician/ Physician Assistant...........................www.hhs.state.ne.us/lis/lis.asp
Plainclothes Investigator ....www.nol.org/home/SOS/Privatedetectives/pilist.htm
Podiatrist ....www.hhs.state.ne.us/lis/lis.asp
Polygraph Examiner, Private ....www.nol.org/home/SOS/Polygraph/polypri.htm
Polygraph Examiner, Public ....www.nol.org/home/SOS/Polygraph/polypub.htm
Private Detective...www.nol.org/home/SOS/Privatedetectives/pdlist.htm

Psychologist .... www.hhs.state.ne.us/lis/lis.asp
Public Accountant-CPA...................................... www.nol.org/home/BPA/license
Radiographer .... www.hhs.state.ne.us/lis/lis.asp
Respiratory Care .... www.hhs.state.ne.us/lis/lis.asp
Securities Agent/Broker/Dealer......................... www.ndbf.org/secsearch.htm
Substance Abuse Treatment Center .... www.nlc.state.ne.us/docs/pilot/pubs/h.html
Swimming Pool Operator .... www.hhs.state.ne.us/lis/lis.asp
Veterinarian... www.hhs.state.ne.us/lis/lis.asp
Voice Stress Examiner .... www.nol.org/home/SOS/Polygraph/voice.htm
Water Operator .... www.hhs.state.ne.us/lis/lis.asp

County Level...Courts, Recorders & Assessors

Court Administrator, PO Box 98910, Lincoln, NE, 68509-8910; 402-471-2643; http://court.nol.org/aoc

Editor's Note: Online access to District and County courts is being tested. For more information, call John Cariotto at 402-471-2643. Currently, Douglas county offers remote online access.

Nebrask@online offers online access to Secretary of State's UCC database; registration and usage fee required. Visit www.nol.org/home/SOS/htm/services.htm for information.

Dodge
Real Estate
www.registerofdeeds.com
Online access to Register of Deeds mortgages database is available at the web site. Registration is required. The site is under development.

Douglas
Assessor
Property tax records on the county assessor database are available free online at www.co.douglas.ne.us/dept.assessor/framevalinfo.htm. There is no name searching.

Lancaster
Real Estate, Liens, Grantor/Grantee, Assessor, Treasurer
www.ci.lincoln.ne.us/co_agenc.htm
Online access to the county on-line deeds search is available free at www.ci.lincoln.ne.us/cnty/deeds/deeds.htm. Also, access to the assessor database is available at www.ci.lincoln.ne.us/cnty/assess/property.htm. Treasurer information is also here. Also, search property information free on the map server site at http://ims.ci.lincoln.ne.us/isa/parcel.

Sarpy
Real Estate
www.sarpy.com
Records on the county Property Lookup database are available free online at www.sarpy.com/boe/capslookup.htm.

Federal Courts in Nebraska...

US District Court - District of Nebraska

Home Page: www.ned.uscourts.gov
PACER: Sign-up number is 800-676-6856. Access fee is $.60 per minute. Toll-free access: 800-252-9724. Local access: 402-221-4797. Case records are available back to late 1990. Records are purged every year. New records are available online after 2 days.
PACER Internet Access: http://pacer.ned.uscourts.gov.
Lincoln Division Counties: Nebraska cases may be filed in any of the three courts at the option of the attorney, except that filings in the North Platte Division must be during trial session.
North Platte Division Counties: Nebraska cases may be filed in any of the three courts at the option of the attorney, except that filings in the North Platte Division must be during trial session. Some case records may be in the Omaha Division as well as the Lincoln Division.
Omaha Division Counties: Nebraska cases may be filed in any of the three courts at the option of the attorney, except that filings in the North Platte Division must be during trial session.

US Bankruptcy Court - District of Nebraska

PACER: Sign-up number is 800-676-6856. Access fee is $.60 per minute. Toll-free access: 800-788-0656. Local access: 402-221-4882. Case records are available back to September 1989. Records are purged every six months. New civil records are available online after 3 days.
PACER Internet Access: http://pacer.neb.uscourts.gov.
Lincoln Division Counties: Adams, Antelope, Boone, Boyd, Buffalo, Butler, Cass, Clay, Colfax, Fillmore, Franklin, Gage, Greeley, Hall, Hamilton, Harlan, Holt, Howard, Jefferson, Johnson, Kearney, Lancaster, Madison, Merrick, Nance, Nemaha, Nuckolls, Otoe, Pawnee, Phelps, Platte,Polk, Richardson, Saline, Saunders, Seward, Sherman, Thayer, Webster, Wheeler, York. Cases from the North Platte Division may also be assigned here.
North Platte Division Counties: Arthur, Banner, Blaine, Box Butte, Brown, Chase, Cherry, Cheyenne, Custer, Dawes, Dawson, Deuel, Dundy, Frontier, Furnas, Garden, Garfield, Gosper, Grant, Hayes, Hitchcock, Hooker, Keith, Keya Paha, Kimball, Lincoln, Logan, Loup, McPherson, Morrill,Perkins, Red Willow, Rock, Scotts Bluff, Sheridan, Sioux, Thomas, Valley. Cases may be randomly allocated to Omaha or Lincoln.
Omaha Division Counties: Burt, Cedar, Cuming, Dakota, Dixon, Dodge, Douglas, Knox, Pierce, Sarpy, Stanton, Thurston, Washington, Wayne.

Editor's Choice for Nebraska

Here are some additional sites recommended for this state.

State Government Phone Numbers Database
http://vmhost.cdp.state.ne.us:97/phsearch.html
Supreme Court & Appeals Court Opinions
http://court.nol.org/opinions/opinindex.htm

Capital:	Carson City Carson City County	Home Page	www.silver.state.nv.us
Time Zone:	PST	Attorney General	http://ag.state.nv.us
Number of Counties:	17	Archives	http://dmla.clan.lib.nv.us/ docs/nsla

State Level...Major Agencies

Corporation Records, Limited Partnerships, Limited Liability Company Records, Limited Partnership Records

Secretary of State, Records, 101 N Carson, #3, Carson City, NV 89701-4786; 775-684-5708, 702-486-2880 (Las Vegas Ofc.:), 702-486-2888 (Las Vegas Ofc fax:), 775-684-5725 (Fax), 8AM-5PM.

www.sos.state.nv.us

Online: Online access is offered on the Internet site for no charge. You can search by corporate name, resident agent, corporate officers, or by file number.

Uniform Commercial Code, Federal Tax Liens, State Tax Liens

UCC Department, Sec. of State, 200 N Carson St, Carson City, NV 89701-4069; 775-684-5708, 775-684-5630 (Fax), 8AM-5PM.

www.sos.state.nv.us

Online: This is a PC dial-up system. The fee is $24.50 per hour or $10.75 per hour on an 800 number for unlimited access. There is a $50.00 minimum deposit. The system is up from 7 AM to 5 PM. Call 775-684-5704 and ask for Tom Horgan.

Driver Records

Department of Motor Vehicles and Public Safety, Records Section, 555 Wright Way, Carson City, NV 89711-0250; 775-684-4590, 800-992-7945 (In-state), 8AM-5PM.

The state has an FTP type online system available for high volume users. All files received by 5:30 PM are processed and returned at 6:30 PM. Call 775-684-4742 for details.

Legislation Records

Nevada Legislature, 401 S Carson St, Carson City, NV 89701-4747; 775-684-6827 (Bill Status Only), 775-684-6800 (Main Number), 775-684-6835 (Publications), 775-684-6600 (Fax), 8AM-5PM.

www.leg.state.nv.us

Online: Bills and bill status information is available via this agency's web site. Legislative bills, hearings, journals are searchable online for years 1997, 1999, and 2001.

State Level...Occupational Licensing

Architect	www.state.nv.us/nsbaidrd/adact1.htm
Carpentry Contractor	http://nscb.tecxprs.com
Chiropractor	www.state.nv.us/chirobd/dcactive.htm
Dental Hygienist	www.nvdentalboard.org/databaseRDH.html
Dentist	www.nvdentalboard.org/databaseDDS.html
Engineer	http://nevada7.natinfo.net/boe/rost_home.htm
Floor & Carpet Layer	http://nscb.tecxprs.com
Glazier Contractor	http://nscb.tecxprs.com
Heating & Air Conditioning Mechanic	http://nscb.tecxprs.com
Insulation Installer Contractor	http://nscb.tecxprs.com
Interior Designer	www.state.nv.us/nsbaidrd/idact2.htm
Lobbyist	www.lobbyistdirectory.com/Nevada/NEVLOB.htm
Monitor Well Driller	http://ndwr.state.nv.us/Engineering/welldrill.htm
Optometrist	www.arbo.org/nodb2000/licsearch.asp
Painter	http://nscb.tecxprs.com
Painter/Paper Hanger	http://nscb.tecxprs.com
Plasterer/Drywall Installer	http://nscb.tecxprs.com
Plumber	http://nscb.tecxprs.com
Residential Designer	www.state.nv.us/nsbaidrd/rdact1.htm
Roofer	http://nscb.tecxprs.com
Surveyor	http://nevada7.natinfo.net/boe/rost_home.htm
Water Well Driller	http://ndwr.state.nv.us/Engineering/welldrill.htm

Editor's Choice for Nevada

Here are some additional sites recommended for this state.

Law Text
www.leg.state.nv.us/law1.htm
Supreme Court Opinions
www.leg.state.nv.us/scd/index.html
Various Forms (Paper)
http://silversource.state.nv.us/

County Level...Courts, Recorders & Assessors

Supreme Court of Nevada, Administrative Office of the Courts, Capitol Complex, 201 S Carson St, Carson City, NV, 89701; 775-684-1700;

Editor's Note: Some Nevada Courts have internal online computer systems, but only Clark County has online access available to the public. A statewide court automation system has been with implemented, but there are no plans to make this system available to the public.

Online access to Assessor, Treasurer, Recorder and other county databases requires registration with goverNet, 208-522-1225. Sliding monthly and per-hit fees apply. Counties online are Churchill, Clark, Elko, Esmeralda, Eureka, Lander, Mineral, Nye, Pershing, Storey, Washoe, and White Pine. System includes access to Secretary of State's Corporation, Partnership, UCC, Fictitious Name, and Federal Tax Lien records.

Clark

Civil Cases, Criminal and Probate Records

http://co.clark.nv.us
Records from the court are available free online at http://courtgate.coca.co.clark.nv.us:8490. Search by case number or party name. Probate also available. *More*

Real Estate, Liens, Property Assessor, UCC, Fictitious Names, Vital Records, Marriage

www.co.clark.nv.us/assessor/Disclaim.htm
Property records, assessor maps, manufactured housing and road documents on the county Assessor database are available free online at www.co.clark.nv.us/assessor/Disclaim.htm. Search by parcel number, owner name, address, map, book & page. Marriage records are available online at www.co.clark.nv.us/recorder/mar_srch.htm. Real estate, UCC and Vital records are available free online at www.co.clark.nv.us/recorder/recindex.htm. The county fictitious names database can be searched at http://sandgate.co.clark.nv.us:8498/clarkcounty/clerk/clerkSearch.html.

Douglas

Assessor, Real Estate

www.recorder.co.douglas.nv.us
Property records on the Assessor's database are available free online at www.co.douglas.nv.us/databases/assessors.

Federal Courts in Nevada...

US District Court - District of Nevada

Home Page: www.nvd.uscourts.gov
PACER: There is no PACER access to this court.
Las Vegas Division Counties: Clark, Esmeralda, Lincoln, Nye.
Reno Division Counties: Carson City, Churchill, Douglas, Elko, Eureka, Humboldt, Lander, Lyon, Mineral, Pershing, Storey, Washoe, White Pine.

US Bankruptcy Court - District of Nevada

Home Page: www.nvb.uscourts.gov
PACER: Sign-up number is 800-676-6856. Access fee is $.60 per minute. Case records are available back to September 1993. Records are purged every 16 months. New civil records are available online after 1 day.
PACER Internet Access: http://pacer.nvb.uscourts.gov.
Other Online Access: You can search records on the Internet using RACER. Currently the system is free and requires free registration. Simply visit http://207.221.188.71/wconnect/wc.dll?usbc_racer~main.
Las Vegas Division Counties: Clark, Esmeralda, Lincoln, Nye.
Reno-Northern Division Counties: Carson City, Churchill, Douglas, Elko, Eureka, Humboldt, Lander, Lyon, Mineral, Pershing, Storey, Washoe, White Pine.

New Hampshire

Capital: Concord
                  Merrimack County

Time Zone: EST

Number of Counties: 10

Home Page   www.state.nh.us

Archives   www.state.nh.us/state

Attorney General   www.state.nh.us/nhdoj

State Level...Major Agencies

Driver Records

Department of Motor Vehicles, Driving Records, 10 Hazen Dr, Concord, NH 03305; 603-271-2322, 8:15AM-4:15PM.

www.state.nh.us/dmv

Online: Online access is offered for approved commercial accounts. The system is open 22 hours a day. Searches are by license number or by name and DOB. Fee is $7.00 per record. For more information, call Chuck DeGrace at 603 271-2314.

Legislation Records

New Hampshire State Library, 20 Part St, Concord, NH 03301; 603-271-2239, 603-271-2205 (Fax), 8AM-4:30PM.

www.state.nh.us/gencourt/iegencourt.html

Online: Information can be viewed from the web site.

State Level...Occupational Licensing

Architect .... www.state.nh.us/jtboard/arlist.htm
Bank .... http://webster.state.nh.us/banking/banking.html
Credit Union .... http://webster.state.nh.us/banking/banking.html
Engineer .... www.state.nh.us/jtboard/pe.htm
Forester .... www.state.nh.us/jtboard/forlist.htm
Lobbyist... www.lobbyist.net/NewHamps/NEWLOB.htm
Marital Mediator.. www.state.nh.us/marital/mediators.html
Natural Scientist .... www.state.nh.us/jtboard/ns.htm
Optometrist.. www.odfinder.org/LicSearch.asp
Surveyor .... www.state.nh.us/jtboard/lsis.htm

County Level...Courts, Recorders & Assessors

Administrative Office of the Courts, Supreme Court Bldg, Noble Dr, Concord, NH, 03301; 603-271-2521; www.state.nh.us/courts/home.htm

Editor's Note: There is no remote online computer access available.

Concord City in Merrimack County
Assessor

Records on the city assessor database are available free online at http://140.239.211.227/ConcordNH. Registration is required; no charge.

Derry Town in Rockingham County
Assessor

http://derrytax.4nh.com
Records on the Derry Tax Assessment database are available free online at http://derrytax.4nh.com.

Grafton
Real Estate, Liens

Access to the County dial-up service requires a $100 set up fee and $40 per month access fee. Two years of data are kept on system; prior years on CD. Lending agency information is available. A fax-back service is available in-state only. For further information, call 603-787-6921.

Laconia City in Belknap County
Assessor

http://data.visionappraisal.com/LaconiaNH
Property records on the Town assessor database are available free online at http://data.visionappraisal.com/LaconiaNH. Registration is required for full access; registration is free.

Lebanon City in Grafton County
Assessor

Records from the city assessor database are available free online at http://140.239.211.227/LebanonNH. Registration is required; no charge.

Merrimack County Registry of Deeds
Real Estate

www.nhdeeds.com
Records on the county Registry of Deeds database are available free online at www.nhdeeds.com.

Portsmouth City in Rockingham County
Assessor

Records from the Portsmouth Assessed Property Values database are available free online at www.portsmouthnh.com/realestate/index.htm.

Raymond Town in Rockingham County
Assessor

Records on the Town assessor database are available free online at http://140.239.211.227/raymondNH. Registration is required, no charge.

Salem Town in Rockingham
Assessor

www.ci.salem.nh.us/
Records from the Town database are available free online at http://data.visionappraisal.com/SalemNH. Registration is required, no charge.

Federal Courts in New Hampshire...

US District Court - District of New Hampshire

Home Page: www.nhd.uscourts.gov

PACER: Sign-up number is 800-676-6856. Access fee is $.60 per minute. Toll-free access: 800-361-7205. Local access: 603-226-7737. http://pacer.nhd.uscourts.gov. Case records are available back to 1980. Records are purged every two years. New records are available online after 1 day.

PACER Internet Access: http://pacer.nhd.uscourts.gov.

Concord Division Counties: Belknap, Carroll, Cheshire, Coos, Grafton, Hillsborough, Merrimack, Rockingham, Strafford, Sullivan.

US Bankruptcy Court - District of New Hampshire

Home Page: www.nhb.uscourts.gov

PACER: Sign-up number is 800-676-6856. Access fee is $.60 per minute. Toll-free access: 800-610-9325. Local access: 603-666-7923, 603-666-7948. Case records are available back to 1989. Records are purged every six months. New civil records are available online after 2 days.

PACER Internet Access: http://pacer.nhb.uscourts.gov.

Manchester Division Counties: Belknap, Carroll, Cheshire, Coos, Grafton, Hillsborough, Merrimack, Rockingham, Strafford, Sullivan.

Editor's Choice for New Hampshire

Here are some additional sites recommended for this state.

Constitution Text
www.state.nh.us/constitution/constitution.html
Sex Offenders Listing
www.wmur.com/sexoffenders
State Agency/Employee Telephone Number Directory
www.state.nh.us/das/gens/tele/

New Jersey

Capital: Trenton
               Mercer County

Time Zone: EST

Number of Counties: 21

Home Page   www.state.nj.us

Attorney General   www.state.nj.us/lps

Archives   www.state.nj.us/state/
darm/archives.html

State Level...Major Agencies

Corporation Records, Limited Liability Company Records, Fictitious Name, Limited Partnerships

Division of Revenue, Business Support Services Bureau, PO 308, Trenton, NJ 08625 (Courier: 225 W State St, 3rd Fl, Trenton, NJ 08608); 609-292-9292, 8:30AM-5PM.

www.state.nj.us/njbgs

Online: Records are available from the New Jersey Business Gateway Service (NJBGS) web site at www.state.nj.us/njbgs. There is no fee to browse the site to locate a name; however fees are involved for copies or status reports.

Driver Records

Motor Vehicle Services, Driver History Abstract Unit, PO Box 142, Trenton, NJ 08666; 609-292-6500, 888-486-3339 (In-state only), 609-292-7500 (Suspensions), 8AM-5PM.

www.state.nj.us/mvs

Online: Fee is $4.00 per record. Access is limited to insurance, bus and trucking companies, parking authorities, and approved vendors. There is a minimum of 100 requests per quarter. For more information, call 609-984-7771.

Vehicle Ownership, Vehicle Identification, Boat & Vessel Ownership, Boat & Vessel Registration

Motor Vehicle Services, Certified Information Unit, PO Box 146, Trenton, NJ 08666; 609-292-6500, 888-486-3339 (In-state).

www.state.nj.us/mvs

Online: Limited online access is available for insurance companies, bus and trucking companies, highway/parking authorities, and approved vendors for these businesses. Participation requires a minimum of 100 requests per calendar quarter at $4.00 per request. Call 609-684-7771 for more information.

Legislation Records

New Jersey State Legislature, State House Annex, PO Box 068, Room B01, Trenton, NJ 08625-0068; 609-292-4840 (Bill Status Only), 609-292-6395 (Copy Room), 800-792-8630 (In State Only), 609-777-2440 (Fax), 8:30AM-5PM.

www.njleg.state.nj.us

Online: The web site is a good source of information about bills. All statutes are online, also.

State Level...Occupational Licensing

Acupuncturist... www.state.nj.us/lps/ca/bme/acupdir.htm
Chiropractor... www.state.nj.us/lps/ca/chiro/chirofrm.htm
Court Reporter.. www.state.nj.us/lps/ca/short/shortdir.htm
Dentist/Dental Hygienist................................. www.state.nj.us/lps/ca/dentistry/dentdir.htm
Electrical Contractor...................................... www.state.nj.us/lps/ca/electric/elecdir.htm
Embalmer.. www.state.nj.us/lps/ca/mort/mortdir.htm
Engineer... www.state.nj.us/lps/ca/nonmed.htm
Funeral Practitioner....................................... www.state.nj.us/lps/ca/mort/mortdir.htm
Hearing Aid Dispenser/Fitter............................ www.state.nj.us/lps/ca/hear/heardir.htm
Lobbyist.. www.lobbyist.net/NewJerse/NEWLOB.htm
Marriage Counselor.. www.state.nj.us/lps/ca/marriage/pcdir.htm
Mortician.. www.state.nj.us/lps/ca/mort/mortdir.htm
Occupational Therapist/Therapist Assistant........ www.state.nj.us/lps/ca/occup/otdir.htm
Optometrist.. www.state.nj.us/lps/ca/optometry/optomet.htm
Pharmacist.. www.state.nj.us/lps/ca/pharm/pharmdir.htm
Physician.. www.state.nj.us/lps/ca/bme/medfrm.htm
Plumber - Master Plumber.............................. www.state.nj.us/lps/ca/plumber/plumdir.htm
Podiatrist.. www.state.nj.us/lps/ca/bme/podfrm.htm
Professional Counselor.................................... www.state.nj.us/lps/ca/marriage/pcdir.htm
Psychologist... www.state.nj.us/lps/ca/psyfrm.htm
Respiratory Care Practitioner........................... www.state.nj.us/lps/ca/respcare/respdir.htm
Shorthand Reporter.. www.state.nj.us/lps/ca/short/shortdir.htm
Speech-Language Pathologist/Audiologist.......... www.state.nj.us/lps/ca/aud/auddir.htm
Surveyor... www.state.nj.us/lps/ca/nonmed.htm
Veterinarian... www.state.nj.us/lps/ca/vetmed/vetdir.htm

County Level...Courts, Recorders & Assessors

Administrative Office of the Courts, RJH Justice Complex, Courts Bldg 7th Floor, CN 037, Trenton, NJ, 08625; 609-984-0275; www.judiciary.state.nj.us

Editor's Note: Online computer access is available through the ACMS, AMIS, and FACTS systems.

ACMS (Automated Case Management System) contains data on all active civil cases statewide from the Law Division-Civil Part, Chancery Division-Equity Part, the Special Civil Part for 21 counties, and the Appellate Division.

AMIS (Archival Management Information System) contains closed case information.

FACTS (Family Automated Case Tracking System) contains information on dissolutions from all counties. The fee is $1.00 per minute of use. For further information and/or an Inquiry System Guidebook containing hardware and software requirements and an enrollment form, write to: Superior Court Clerk's Office, Electronic Access Program, 25 Market St, CN971, Trenton NJ 08625, FAX 609-292-6564, or call 609-292-4987

Atlantic
Real Estate
www.atlanticcountyclerk.org
Property records for communities along the Jersey Shore in Atlantic county are available free online at
www.philly.com/packages/njshore/lookup.htm. Site is sponsored by the Philadelphia Inquirer. Search by clicking on community

name, then search by owner name, owner's city/state, address, or property value range.

Cape May
Real Estate
www.co.cape-may.nj.us/CLERKCMC.HTM
Property records for communities along the Jersey Shore in Cape May county are available free online at www.philly.com/packages/njshore/lookup.htm. Site is sponsored by the Philadelphia Inquirer. Search by clicking on community name, then search by owner name, owner's city/state, address, or property value range.

Gloucester
Real Estate, Recording
www.co.gloucester.nj.us
County Recorder records are accessible through a private online service at www.landaccess.com; Fees and registration are required.

Ocean
Property Tax, Real Estate
www.oceancountyclerk.com
Land records on the County Clerk database are available free online at www.oceancountyclerk.com/search.htm. Search by parties, document or instrument type, or township. Also, property records for communities along the Jersey Shore in Ocean County are available free online at www.philly.com/packages/njshore/lookup.htm. Site is sponsored by the Philadelphia Inquirer. Tax records for Ocean county are also available on the taxrecords.com web site at http://oc.taxrecords.com.

Federal Courts in New Jersey...

US District Court - District of New Jersey

Home Page: www.njuscourts.org
PACER: Sign-up number is 800-676-6856. Access fee is $.60 per minute. Toll-free access: 888-297-9938. Local access: 609-989-0590. Case records are available back to May 1991. Records are purged never. New records are available online after 1 day.
PACER Internet Access: http://pacer.njd.uscourts.gov.
Opinions Online: Court opinions are available online at http://lawlibrary.rutgers.edu/fed/search.html.
Camden Division Counties: Atlantic, Burlington, Camden, Cape May, Cumberland, Gloucester, Salem.
Newark Division Counties: Bergen, Essex, Hudson, Middlesex, Monmouth, Morris, Passaic, Sussex, Union. Monmouth County was transferred from Trenton Division in late 1997; closed cases remain in Trenton.
Trenton Division Counties: Hunterdon, Mercer, Ocean, Somerset, Warren. Monmouth County was transferred to Newark and Camden Division in late 1997; closed Monmouth cases remain in Trenton.

US Bankruptcy Court - District of New Jersey

Home Page: www.njuscourts.org
PACER: Sign-up number is 800-676-6856. Access fee is $.60 per minute. Toll-free access: 800-253-1597. Local access: 973-645-3555. Case records are available back to 1991. Records are purged every 6 months. New civil records are available online after 1 day.
PACER Internet Access: http://pacer.njb.uscourts.gov.
Camden Division Counties: Atlantic, Burlington (partial), Camden, Cape May, Cumberland, Gloucester, Salem.
Newark Division Counties: Bergen, Essex, Hudson, Morris, Passaic, Sussex. Also Elizabeth, Springfield and Hillside townships in Union County.
Trenton Division Counties: Burlington (partial), Hunterdon, Mercer, Middlesex, Monmouth, Ocean, Somerset, Warren, Union except the townships of Elizabeth, Hillside and Springfield.

Editor's Choice for New Jersey

Parole Eligibility Notices Listing
www.state.nj.us/parole/elig.htm
Schools & School Officials Database
www.state.nj.us/njded/directory/toc.htm

Capital:	Santa Fe		Home Page
	Santa Fe County		www.state.nm.us
Time Zone:	MST	Attorney General	www.ago.state.nm.us
Number of Counties:	33	Archives	www.state.nm.us/cpr

State Level...Major Agencies

Corporation Records, Limited Liability Company Records

New Mexico Public Regulation Commission, Corporate Department, PO Box 1269, Santa Fe, NM 87504-1269 (Courier: 1120 Paseo de Peralta, Pera Bldg 4th Fl, Rm 413, Santa Fe, NM 87501); 505-827-4502 (Main Number), 800-947-4722 (In-state Only), 505-827-4510 (Good Standing), 505-827-4513 (Copy Request), 505-827-4387 (Fax), 8AM-12:00: 1PM-5PM.

www.nmprc.state.nm.us

Online: There is no charge to view records at the Internet site, www.nmprc.state.nm.us/ftq.htm. Records can be searched by company name or by director name.

Uniform Commercial Code

UCC Division, Secretary of State, State Capitol North, Santa Fe, NM 87503; 505-827-3610, 505-827-3611 (Fax), 8AM-5PM.

www.sos.state.nm.us/ucc/ucchome.htm

Online: The web site permits searches and a form to use to order copies of filings. You can also request records via e-mail.

Driver Records

Motor Vehicle Division, Driver Services Bureau, PO Box 1028, Santa Fe, NM 87504-1028 (Courier: Joseph M. Montoya Bldg, 1100 S St. Francis Dr, 2nd Floor, Santa Fe, NM 87504); 505-827-2234, 505-827-2267 (Fax), 8AM-5PM.

www.state.nm.us/tax/mvd

Online: New Mexico Technet is the state authorized vendor for access. The costs are $2.50 per record for interactive, $1.50 per record for batch, plus a $.25 per minute network fee. The system is open 24 hours a day, batch requesters must wait 24 hours. Call 505-345-6555 for more information.

Vehicle Ownership, Vehicle Identification, Boat & Vessel Ownership, Boat & Vessel Registration

Motor Vehicle Division, Vehicle Services Bureau, PO Box 1028, Santa Fe, NM 87504-1028 (Courier: Joseph M. Montoya Bldg, 1100 S St. Francis Dr, 2nd Floor, Santa Fe, NM 87504); 505-827-4636, 505-827-1004, 505-827-0395 (Fax), 8AM-5PM.

www.state.nm.us/tax/mvd   *more*

Online: Records are available, for authorized users, from the state's designated vendor New Mexico Technet. Cost is $2.50 per record plus a $.25 per minute network charge. There is a $35.00 set-up fee, also. Call 505-345-6555 for more information.

Legislation Records

Legislative Council Service, State Capitol Bldg, Room 411, Santa Fe, NM 87501; 505-986-4600, 505-986-4350 (Bill Room During Session Only), 505-986-4610 (Fax), 8AM-5PM.

http://legis.state.nm.us

Online: The Internet site is a complete source of information about bills and legislators. There are also links to other NM state agencies and NM statutes.

State Level...Occupational Licensing

Architect	www.nmbea.org/People/Aroster.htm
Clinical Nurse Specialist	www.state.nm.us/nursing/lookup.html
Contractor	http://66.87.10.169/pub/index.cfm
Engineer	www.state.nm.us/pepsboard/roster.htm
Hemodialysis Technician	www.state.nm.us/nursing/lookup.html
Journeyman	http://66.87.10.169/pub/index.cfm
Liquefied Petroleum Gas (LPG)	www.newmexlicense.org/pub/index.cfm
Lobbyist	http://web.state.nm.us/LOBBY/LOB.htm
LP Gas Licensee	http://66.87.10.169/pub/index.cfm
LPN	www.state.nm.us/nursing/lookup.html
Medical Doctor	www.docboard.org/nm
Medication Aide	www.state.nm.us/nursing/lookup.html
Nurse	www.state.nm.us/nursing/lookup.html
Nurse Anesthetist	www.state.nm.us/nursing/lookup.html
Nurse-RN	www.state.nm.us/nursing/lookup.html
Optometrist	www.odfinder.org/LicSearch.asp
Physician Assistant	www.docboard.org/nm
Psychologist	www.rld.state.nm.us/b&c/psychology/lcnssrch.asp
Surveyor	www.state.nm.us/pepsboard/roster.htm

County Level...Courts, Recorders & Assessors

Administrative Office of the Courts, Supreme Court Building Room 25, Santa Fe, NM, 87503; 505-827-4800; www.nmcourts.com.aoc.htm

Editor's Note: The www.nmcourts.com web site offers free access to District and Magistrate Court case information. In general, records are available from June 1997 forward.

Also, a commercial online service is available for the Metropolitan Court of Bernalillo County. There is a $35.00 set up fee, a connect time fee based on usage. The system is available 24 hours a day. Call 505-345-6555 for more information.

Bernalillo

Civil Cases, Criminal Records
www.cabq.gov/cjnet/dst2alb
Online access available through New Mexico Technet. There is a setup fee and an access fee. Records go back 7 years. Call 505-345-6555 for information.

Real Estate
www.berncotreasurer.com
Records on the county Records Search page are available free online at
www.berncotreasurer.com/ProcessSearch.asp?cmd=NewSearch.

Dona Ana

Assessor, Liens, Real Estate
www.co.dona-ana.nm.us
Records on the Real Property database are available free online at www.co.dona-ana.nm.us/newpages/assr/search.html.

San Juan

Real Estate, Assessor
www.co.san-juan.nm.us
Online access to county real estate tax data is available free at www.co.san-juan.nm.us/InfoSJC/ProfilePublicAccess.asp.

Federal Courts in New Mexico...

US District Court - District of New Mexico

Home Page: www.nmcourt.fed.us
PACER: Sign-up number is 800-676-6856. Access fee is $.60 per minute. Case records are available back to 1990. Records are purged every six months. New records are available online after 2 weeks.
Electronic Filing: See Internet site for information about electronic filing. You must register to use the system. Electronic filing information is available online at www.nmcourt.fed.us/dcdocs (Click on ACE Filing).
Albuquerque Division Counties: All counties in New Mexico. Cases may be assigned to any of its three divisions.

US Bankruptcy Court - District of New Mexico

Home Page: www.nmcourt.fed.us
PACER: Sign-up number is 800-676-6856. Access fee is $.60 per minute. Toll-free access: 888-821-8813. Local access: 505-248-6518. Case records are available back to July 1, 1991. New civil records are available online after 1 day.
Albuquerque Division Counties: All counties in New Mexico.

Editor's Choice for New Mexico

Here are some additional sites recommended for this state.

Attorney General Opinions
www.ago.state.nm.us/Opinions/legal_opinions.html
Department of Labor Forms (Paper)
www3.state.nm.us/dol/dol_form.html
State Agency Phone Listing
www.state.nm.us/state/phone_idx.html
State Employee e-mail Database
www3.state.nm.us/email/

Capital:	Albany		Home Page
	Albany County		www.state.ny.us
Time Zone:	EST	Attorney General	www.oag.state.ny.us
Number of Counties:	62	Archives	www.sara.nysed.gov

State Level...Major Agencies

Corporation Records, Limited Partnership Records, Limited Liability Company Records, Limited Liability Partnerships

Division of Corporations, Department of State, 41 State St, Albany, NY 12231; 518-473-2492 (General Information), 900-835-2677 (Corporate Searches), 518-474-1418 (Fax), 8AM-4:30PM.

www.dos.state.ny.us

Online: A commercial account can be set up for direct access. Fee is $.75 per transaction through a drawdown account. There is an extensive amount of information available including historical information. Also, the Division's corporate and business gentility database may be accessed via the Internet without charge. Historical information is not available, nor is it real time. The Internet files are updated weekly.

Driver Records

Department of Motor Vehicles, MV-15 Processing, 6 Empire State Plaza, Rm 430, Albany, NY 12228; 518-474-0774, 8AM-5PM.

www.nydmv.state.ny.us

Online: NY has implemented a "Dial-In Inquiry" system which enables customers to obtain data online 24 hours a day. The DL# or name, DOB and sex are required to retrieve. If the DOB and sex are not entered, the system defaults to a limited group of 5 records. The fee is $5.00 per record. For more information, call 518-474-4293.

Vehicle Ownership, Vehicle Identification, Boat & Vessel Ownership, Boat & Vessel Registration

Department of Motor Vehicles, MV-15 Processing, 6 Empire State Plaza, Room 430, Albany, NY 12228; 518-474-0710, 518-474-8510, 8AM-5PM.

www.nydmv.state.ny.us

Online: New York offers plate, VIN and ownership data through the same network discussed in the Driving Records Section. The system is interactive and open 24 hours a day, with the exception of 10 hours on Sunday. The fee is $5.00 per record. Call 518-474-4293 for more information.

Legislation Records

NY Senate Document Room, State Capitol, State Street Rm 317, Albany, NY 12247; 518-455-2312 (Senate Document Room), 518-455-3216, 9AM-5PM.

www.senate.state.ny.us

Online: Both the Senate (www.senate.state.ny.us) and the Assembly (www.assembly.state.ny.us) have web sites to search for a bill or specific bill text. A much more complete system is the LRS online system. This offers complete state statutes, agency rules and regulations, bill text, bill status, summaries, and more. For more information, call Barbara Lett at 800-356-6566.

State Level...Occupational Licensing

Acupuncturist/Assistant .... www.op.nysed.gov/opsearches.htm#nme
Architect.. www.op.nysed.gov/opsearches.htm#nme
Athletic Trainer .... www.op.nysed.gov/opsearches.htm#nme
Attorney
    . . . www.courts.state.ny.us/webdb/wdbcgi.exe/apps/INTERNETDB.attyreghome.show
Audiologist .... www.op.nysed.gov/opsearches.htm#nme
Chiropractor.. www.op.nysed.gov/opsearches.htm#nme
Court Reporter .... www.op.nysed.gov/opsearches.htm#nme
Dentist/ Dental Assistant/Dental Hygienist......... www.op.nysed.gov/opsearches.htm#nme
Dietitian .... www.op.nysed.gov/opsearches.htm#nme
Engineer .... www.op.nysed.gov/opsearches.htm#nme
HMO www.ins.state.ny.us/tocol4.htm
Insurance Company... www.ins.state.ny.us/tocol4.htm
Interior Designer .... www.op.nysed.gov/opsearches.htm#nme
Landscape Architect... www.op.nysed.gov/opsearches.htm#nme
Lobbyist.. www.nylobby.state.ny.us/lobbysearch.html
Massage Therapist .... www.op.nysed.gov/opsearches.htm#nme
Medical Doctor .... www.op.nysed.gov/opsearches.htm#nme
Midwife.. www.op.nysed.gov/opsearches.htm#nme
Nurse – Nurse LPN - RPN .... www.op.nysed.gov/opsearches.htm#nme
Nutritionist .... www.op.nysed.gov/opsearches.htm#nme
Occupational Therapist/Assistant .... www.op.nysed.gov/opsearches.htm#nme
Ophthalmic Dispenser.. www.op.nysed.gov/opsearches.htm#nme
Optometrist... www.op.nysed.gov/opsearches.htm#nme
Pharmacist .... www.op.nysed.gov/opsearches.htm#nme
Physical Therapist/Assistant............................... www.op.nysed.gov/opsearches.htm#nme
Physician/ Physician Assistant............................ www.op.nysed.gov/opsearches.htm#nme
Podiatrist .... www.op.nysed.gov/opsearches.htm#nme
Psychiatrist .... www.ptofview.com/nyspa/search/
Psychologist.. www.op.nysed.gov/opsearches.htm#nme
Public Accountant-CPA...................................... www.op.nysed.gov/opsearches.htm#nme
Respiratory Therapist/Therapy Technician .... www.op.nysed.gov/opsearches.htm#nme
Social Worker .... www.op.nysed.gov/opsearches.htm#nme
Specialist Assistant .... www.op.nysed.gov/opsearches.htm#nme
Speech Pathologist/Audiologist .... www.op.nysed.gov/opsearches.htm#nme
Surveyor .... www.op.nysed.gov/opsearches.htm#nme
Teacher... www.highered.nysed.gov/tcert/ocvsintro.htm
Veterinarian.. www.op.nysed.gov/opsearches.htm#nme

County Level...Courts, Recorders & Assessors

Office of Administration, Empire State Plaza, Agency Plaza #4, Suite 2001, Albany, NY, 12223; 518-473-1196; www.courts.state.ny.us

Editor's Note:　Civil case information from the 13 largest counties is available through DataCase, a database index of civil case information publicly available at terminals located at Supreme and County courts. In addition to the civil case index, DataCase also includes judgment docket and lien information, New York County Clerk system data, and the New York State attorney registration file. Remote access is also available at a fee of $1.00 per minute. Call 800-494-8981 for more remote access information.

Albany
Naturalizations
www.albanycounty.com/departments
Online access to the clerk's naturalization records from 1821-1991 are available free online at www.albanycounty.com/online/online.asp. Volunteers are adding records.

Bronx
Real Estate, Liens, Tax Assessor Records
Two options are available. Access to Bronx County online records - including Boroughs of Brooklyn, Queens, Staten Island, Bronx, Manhattan - requires a $250 monthly fee and $5 per transaction fee. Records are kept 2-5 years. For information, contact Richard Reskin at 718-935-6523. Also, property assessment rolls from NYC's Dept. of Finance are available free online at www.ci.nyc.ny.us/html/dof/html/asmt.html. Search by borough, block and lot number. Tax reports are also available, with enrollment required.

Cattaraugus
Real Estate, Tax Assessor Records
Records on the City of Olean assessor database are available free online at www.cityofolean.com/Assessor/main.htm.

Kings
Real Estate, Liens, Tax Assessor Records
There are two options. The fee service supports the Boroughs of Brooklyn, Queens, Staten Island, Bronx, and Manhattan. There is a $250 monthly fee and a $5.00 fee per transaction. Records are kept 2-5 years. Search by name, grantor/grantee, and address. For information, contact Richard Reskin at 718-935-6523. Also, property assessment rolls from NYC's Dept. of Finance are available free online at www.ci.nyc.ny.us/html/dof/html/asmt.html. Search by borough, block and lot number. Tax reports are also available, with enrollment required.

Monroe
Civil Cases, Criminal Records, Land Records, Liens, Divorce, UCCs
www.clerk.co.monroe.ny.us/
Online access to the county clerk database are available online at www.clerk.co.monroe.ny.us. Includes mortgages, deeds, court records; free registration. Land records back to 1984. Liens, judgments, UCCS go back to 5/1989. Court records - civil, felony, divorce - back to June 1993. Earlier microfilm images are being added as time permits. Also, access to their remote online system requires $.50 per minute of usage. Fax back is available for $.50 per page. Call Tom Fiorilli 716-428-5151 for more information.

New York
Real Estate, Liens, Tax Assessor Records
Two options are available. Access to New York County online records - including Boroughs of Brooklyn, Queens, Staten Island, Bronx, and Manhattan - requires a $250 monthly fee and $5 per transaction fee. Records are kept 2-5 years. For information, contact Richard Reskin at 718-935-6523. Also, property assessment rolls from NYC's Dept. of Finance are available free online at www.ci.nyc.ny.us/html/dof/html/asmt.html. Search by borough, block and lot number. Tax reports are also available, with enrollment required.

Putnam
Real Estate, Recording
County Recorder records are accessible through a private online service at www.landaccess.com; Fees and registration are required.

Queens
Real Estate, Liens, Tax Assessor Records
Two options are available. Access to Queens County online records - including Boroughs of Brooklyn, Queens, Staten Island, Bronx, Manhattan - requires a $250 monthly fee and $5 per transaction fee. Records are kept 2-5 years. For information, contact Richard Reskin at 718-935-6523. Also, property assessment rolls from NYC's Dept. of Finance are available free online at www.ci.nyc.ny.us/html/dof/html/asmt.html. Search by borough, block and lot number. Tax reports are also available, with enrollment required.

Richmond
Real Estate, Liens, Tax Assessor Records
Two options are available. Access to Richmond-Staten Is. online records - including Boroughs of Brooklyn, Queens, Staten Island, Bronx, and Manhattan - requires a $250 monthly fee and $5 per transaction fee. Records are kept 2-5 years. For further information, contact Richard Reskin at 718-935-6523. Property assessment rolls from NYC's Dept. of Finance are available free online at www.ci.nyc.ny.us/html/dof/html/asmt.html. Search by borough, block and lot number. Tax reports are also available, with enrollment required.

Rockland
Civil Cases, Criminal Records, Real Estate, Liens
www.rocklandcountyclerk.com
Online access is the county clerk's expanding list of records is available free at the web site. Click on "Index to all records." System includes criminal index since 1982 plus civil judgments, real estate records, tax warrants. Images back to 6/96 are viewable, and more are being added. Call Paul Pipearto at 845-638-5221 for more information. Also, criminal index computer search available at OCA; see state introduction.

Schenectady
Real Estate, Tax Assessor Records
www.scpl.org
Records for approximately 2/5 of the county property assessments are available free online on the library database at www.scpl.org/assessments.

Steuben
Tax Assessor Records
Access to Town of Erwin Real Property Assessment Roll is available free online at www.pennynet.org/erwin/er95tax.htm.

Tompkins
Tax Assessor Records
www.co.tompkins.ny.us/assessment
1999 records on the county Division of Assessment database are available free online at a mirror site: http://md2020.hypermart.net/tentative.html. (this URL may change in 2001 - see the main assessor page.)

Ulster
Civil Cases, Criminal Records, Real Estate, Liens, Property Tax, Voter Registration
www.co.ulster.ny.us
Two options exist. Access to county online records requires a $33.33 or $44.55 monthly fee and a commitment to one year of service. Land Records date back to 1984. Includes county court records back to 7/1987. Lending agency information is available. For information, contact Valerie Harris at 914-340-5300. Also, the Ulster County Parcel Viewer at www.maphost.com/ulster provides free access to tax parcel information. Search by GIS map, parcel ID number, street

Wyoming
Real Estate, Recording
County Recorder records are accessible through a private online service at www.landaccess.com; Fees and registration are required.

Federal Courts in New York...

US District Court - Eastern District of New York

Home Page: www.nyed.uscourts.gov
PACER: Sign-up number is 800-676-6856. Access fee is $.60 per minute. Toll-free access: 888-331-4965. Local access: 718-246-2494. Case records are available back to January 1, 1990. Records are purged never. New records are available online after 1 day.
PACER Internet Access: http://pacer.nyed.uscourts.gov.
Electronic Filing: Only law firms and practitioners may file cases electronically. Anyone can search online; however only cases filed electronically are included in the search. To search, visit http://ecf.nyed.uscourts.gov/cgi-bin/PublicCaseFiled-Rpt.pl. Electronic filing information is available online at http://ecf.nyed.uscourts.gov.
Brooklyn Division Counties: Kings, Queens, Richmond. **Hauppauge Division** Counties: Suffolk.

US Bankruptcy Court - Eastern District of New York

PACER: Sign-up number is 800-676-6856. Access fee is $.60 per minute. Toll-free access: 800-263-7790. Local access: 718-488-7012. Case records are available back to 1991. Records are purged every year. New civil records are available online after 3 days.
PACER Internet Access: http://pacer.nyeb.uscourts.gov.
Brooklyn Division Counties: Kings, Queens, Richmond. Kings and Queens County Chapter 11 cases may also be assigned to Westbury. Other Queens County cases may be assigned to Westbury Division. Nassau County Chapter 11 cases may be assigned here.
Hauppauge Division Counties: Suffolk. Suffolk County Chapter 11 cases may also be assigned to Westbury Division. Nassau County Chapter 11 cases may be assigned here. Other cases for western Suffolk County may also be assigned to Westbury Division.
Westbury Division Counties: Nassau. Chapter 11 cases for Nassau County may also be assigned to the Brooklyn or Hauppauge Divisions. Kings and Suffolk County Chapter 11 cases may be assigned here. Any Queens County cases may be assigned here. Non-Chapter 11 cases from western. Suffolk County may also be assigned here.

US District Court - Northern District of New York

Home Page: www.nynd.uscourts.gov
PACER: Sign-up number is 800-676-6856. Access fee is $.60 per minute. Toll-free access: 800-480-7525. Local access: 315-448-0537. Case records are available back to June 1991. New records are available online after 2 days.
Albany Division Counties: Albany, Clinton, Columbia, Essex, Greene, Rensselaer, Saratoga, Schenectady, Schoharie, Ulster, Warren, Washington.
Binghamton Division Counties: Broome, Chenango, Delaware, Franklin, Jefferson, Lewis, Otsego, St. Lawrence, Tioga.
Syracuse Division Counties: Cayuga, Cortland, Fulton, Hamilton, Herkimer, Madison, Montgomery, Onondaga, Oswego, Tompkins.
Utica Division Counties: Oneida.

US Bankruptcy Court - Northern District of New York

Home Page: www.nynb.uscourts.gov
PACER: Sign-up number is 800-676-6856. Access fee is $.60 per minute. Toll-free access: 800-390-8432. Local access: 518-431-0175. Case records are available back to 1992. New civil records are available online after 48 hours.
Other Online Access: A system called CHASER is available on the Internet at http://pacer.nynb.uscourts.gov/bc/chs.html.
Albany Division Counties: Albany, Clinton, Essex, Franklin, Fulton, Jefferson, Montgomery, Rensselaer, Saratoga, Schenectady, Schoharie, St. Lawrence, Warren, Washington.
Utica Division Counties: Broome, Cayuga, Chenango, Cortland, Delaware, Hamilton, Herkimer, Lewis, Madison, Oneida, Onondaga, Otsego, Oswego, Tioga, Tompkins.

US District Court - Southern District of New York

Home Page: www.nysd.uscourts.gov
PACER: Sign-up number is 800-676-6856. Access fee is $.60 per minute. Case records are available back to early 1990. Records are purged every six months. New records are available online after 1 day.
Opinions Online: Selected rulings are searchable online using CourtWeb. To download and view copies of rulings you must have Adobe Acrobat Reader. Court opinions are available online at www.nysd.uscourts.gov/courtweb.
New York City Division Counties: Bronx, New York. Some cases from the counties in the White Plains Division are also assigned to the New York Division.
White Plains Division Counties: Dutchess, Orange, Putnam, Rockland, Sullivan, Westchester. Some cases may be assigned to New York Division.

US Bankruptcy Court - Southern District of New York

Home Page: www.nysb.uscourts.gov
PACER: Sign-up number is 800-676-6856. Access fee is $.60 per minute. Case records are available back to June 1991. Records are purged every six months. New civil records are available online after 2 days.
PACER Internet Access: http://pacer.nysb.uscourts.gov.
Electronic Filing: Only law firms and practitioners may file cases electronically. Anyone can search online; however only cases filed electronically are included in the search. To search, visit http://ecf.nysb.uscourts.gov/cgi-bin/PublicCaseFiled-Rpt.pl. Electronic filing information is available online at http://ecf.nysb.uscourts.gov.
New York Division Counties: Bronx, New York.
Poughkeepsie Division Counties: Columbia, Dutchess, Greene, Orange, Putnam, Sullivan, Ulster.
White Plains Division Counties: Rockland, Westchester.

US District Court - Western District of New York

Home Page: www.nywd.uscourts.gov
PACER: Sign-up number is 800-676-6856. Access fee is $.60 per minute. Toll-free access: 877-233-5848. Local access: 716-551-3333. Case records are available back to 1992. Records are purged never. New civil records are available online after 1 day. New criminal records are available online after 2 days.
PACER Internet Access: http://pacer.nywd.uscourts.gov.
Buffalo Division Counties: Allegany, Cattaraugus, Chautauqua, Erie, Genesee, Niagara, Orleans, Wyoming. Prior to 1982, this division included what is now the Rochester Division.
Rochester Division Counties: Chemung, Livingston, Monroe, Ontario, Schuyler, Seneca, Steuben, Wayne, Yates.

US Bankruptcy Court - Western District of New York

Home Page: www.nywb.uscourts.gov
PACER: Sign-up number is 800-676-6856. Access fee is $.60 per minute. Toll-free access: 800-450-8052. Local access: 716-551-3152, 716-551-3153, 716-551-3154, 716-551-3155. Case records are available back to August 1987. Records are purged never. New civil records are available online after 1 day.
PACER Internet Access: http://pacer.nywb.uscourts.gov.
Buffalo Division Counties: Allegany, Cattaraugus, Chautauqua, Erie, Genesee, Niagara, Orleans, Wyoming.
Rochester Division Counties: Chemung, Livingston, Monroe, Ontario, Schuyler, Seneca, Steuben, Wayne, Yates.

Editor's Choice for New York

Here are some additional sites recommended for this state.

Election Results Listing
www.elections.state.ny.us/elections/election.htm
Inmates Database
http://nysdocs.docs.state.ny.us:84/kinqw00
Naturalization Records (1812-1996) Database
http://userdb.rootsweb.com/naturalization
Personal Injury Awards Listing
www.nylj.com/awards
State Employee & Agency Phone Numbers Directory
www.ogs.state.ny.us/telecom

North Carolina

Capital:	Raleigh Wake County	Home Page	www.ncgov.com
Time Zone:	EST	Attorney General	www.jus.state.nc.us
Number of Counties:	100	Archives	www.ah.dcr.state.nc.us

State Level...Major Agencies

Corporation Records, Limited Partnerships, Limited Liability Company Records, Trademarks/Servicemarks

Secretary of State, Corporations Section, PO Box 29622, Raleigh, NC 27626-0622 (Courier: 2 S Salisbury, Raleigh, NC 27603); 919-807-2251 (Corporations), 919-807-2164 (Trademarks), 919-807-2039 (Fax), 8AM-5PM.

www.secretary.state.nc.us

Online: Access is currently available through a dial-up system. There is an initial registration fee of $185 and a charge of $.02 each time the "enter key" is pushed. To register, call Bonnie Elek at (919) 807-2196. Also, the web site offers a free search of status and registered agent by corporation name. The trademark database is not available online.

Uniform Commercial Code, Federal Tax Liens

UCC Division, Sec. of State, Raleigh, NC 27626-0622 (Courier: 2 South Salisbury St, Raleigh, NC 27603-5909); 919-807-2111, 919-807-2120 (Fax), 7:30AM-5PM.

www.secretary.state.nc.us/UCC

Online: Free access is available at http://ucc.secstate.state.nc.us. Search by ID number or debtor name. The state is preparing to offer a FTP system for ongoing commercial requesters. Call 919-807-2196 for more information.

Driver Records

Division of Motor Vehicles, Driver's License Section, 1100 New Bern Ave, Raleigh, NC 27697; 919-715-7000, 8AM-5PM.

www.dmv.dot.state.nc.us

Online: To qualify for online availability, a client must be an insurance agent or insurance company support organization. The mode is interactive and is open from 7 AM to 10 PM. The DL# and name are needed when ordering. Records are $5.00 each. A minimum $500 security deposit is required.

Legislation Records

North Carolina General Assembly, State Legislative Bldg, 16 W. Jones Street, 1st Fl, Raleigh, NC 27603; 919-733-7779 (Bill Numbers), 919-733-3270 (Archives), 919-733-5648 (Order Desk), 8:30AM-5:30PM.

www.ncleg.net

Online: The Internet site has copies of bills, status, and state statutes.

State Level...Occupational Licensing

Architect	www.ncbarch.org/cgi ncbarch/ncbarch_licdb/ncbarch/architects/query_form
Banking Division	www.banking.state.nc.us/banks.htm
Check Cashers	www.banking.state.nc.us/checkcas.htm
Chiropractor	www.ncchiroboard.org/public/licensed_chiros.html
Consumer Financers	www.banking.state.nc.us/cf.htm
Electrical Contractor/Inspector	www.ncbeec.org/LicSearch.asp
Engineer	www.member-base.com/ncbels/public/searchdb.asp
Fire Sprinkler Contractor/Inspector	www.nclicensing.org/OnlineReg.htm
Heating Contractor	www.nclicensing.org/OnlineReg.htm
Lobbyist	www.secretary.state.nc.us/lobbyists/Lsearch.asp
Medical Doctor/Physician	www.docboard.org/nc/df/ncsearch.htm
Mortgage Division	www.banking.state.nc.us/mbb.htm
Nurse/ Nurse-LPN	www.docboard.org/nc/df/ncsearch.htm
Occupational Therapist/ Therapist Assistant	www.ncbot.org/fpdb/otimport.html
Optometrist	www.ncoptometry.org/verify/index.asp
Osteopathic Physician	www.docboard.org/nc/df/ncsearch.htm
Physician Assistant	www.docboard.org/nc/df/ncsearch.htm
Plumber	www.nclicensing.org/OnlineReg.htm
Provisional Occupational Therapist/Assistant	www.ncbot.org/fpdb/otimport.html
Public Accountant-CPA	http://ndsips01.sips.state.nc.us/cpabd/search_the_database.htm
Real Estate Broker/Dealer/Firm	http://ndsips01.sips.state.nc.us/NCREC/search.asp
Surveyor	www.member-base.com/ncbels/public/searchdb.asp

County Level...Courts, Recorders & Assessors

Administrative Office of the Courts, Justice Bldg, 2 E Morgan St, Raleigh, NC, 27602; 919-733-7107; www.aoc.state.nc.us

Editor's Note: Access active criminal calendars on a county or statewide basis at www.aoc.state.nc.us/ www/public/html/calendars.html. Historical information is not available.

Alleghany
Real Estate, Grantor/Grantee
www.allcorod.com
Online access to the Register of Deeds database is available free at www.allcorod.com/cgi-bin/viewer/date.sh. Records go back to 12/1988. Also, search for property information on a GIS mapping site at www.webgis.net/Alleghany.

Anson
Assessor, Real Estate
www.co.anson.nc.us/servicesf0.htm
Records on the county Online Tax Inquiry System are available free online at www.co.anson.nc.us/pubcgi/taxinq.

Buncombe
Assessor, Real Estate
www.buncombecounty.org

Online access to property information is available free on the GIS mapping site at http://199.90.58.245/property. Click on "Search methods" and search by owner name. Also, records from the county assessor are available free online from a private company at www.propex.com/main_taxrecds.htm.

Burke
Real Estate, Assessor
www.co.burke.nc.us
Online access to the property information is available free on the GIS mapping site at www.webgis.net/burke.

Cabarrus
Assessor, Real Estate
www.co.cabarrus.nc.us
Records on the county GIS map server database are available free online at www.co.cabarrus.nc.us/pages/gis/applications.htm. Click on the county map to enter, then search at the bottom of the query page.

Caldwell
Assessor, Real Estate
Records on the county GIS map server site are available free online at http://maps.co.caldwell.nc.us. Click on "Start Spatial-data Explorer" then find query field at bottom of next page.

Catawba
Assessor, Real Estate
www.co.catawba.nc.us
Records on the Catawba County Geographic Information System database are available free online at www.gis.catawba.nc.us/maps/public.htm. Click on map area; zoom in to find the parcel on the map, or search using query fields.

Cleveland
Real Estate, Assessor
www.clevelandcounty.com
Online access to property information on a GIS mapping site is available free at www.webgis.net/Cleveland.

Craven
Assessor, Real Estate
Records on the County Assessor database are available free online at http://gismaps.cravencounty.com/taxinfo.htm.

Dare
Assessor, Real Estate
www.co.dare.nc.us
Records on the county Property Inquiry database are available free online at www.co.dare.nc.us/interactive/setup.htm.

Davidson
Assessor, Real Estate
www.co.davidson.nc.us
Records on the county Tax Department database are available free online at www.co.davidson.nc.us/asp/taxsearch.asp.

Durham
Property Records
http://199.72.142.253
Property records are available on the GIS map server; however, there is no name searching.

Forsyth
Real Estate
Online access to the county Geo-Data Explorer database is available free online at http://maps.co.forsyth.nc.us. Address and Parcel ID searching only. Includes Board of Adjustment and building permit records. Also, Register of Deed records are available on CD-ROM.

Franklin
Real Property
www.co.franklin.nc.us
Online access to the county spatial data explorer database is available free at www.co.franklin.nc.us/docs/frame_tax.htm. Search the GIS map or click on "text search" for name searching.

Guilford
Recorder, Assessor, Property, UCC, Vital Statistics
www.co.guilford.nc.us/
Online access to the county tax department database is available www.co.guilford.nc.us/egov/index.html.

Harnett
Real Estate, Grantor/Grantee
www.harnett.org/departments/rod.html
County real estate and property tax information is available free online at http://152.34.178.4/nc32.

Haywood
Real Estate
Records on the Land Records Search database are available free online at www.undersys.com/haywood/haywood.html. Search will result in a map showing the parcel and owner, parcel number, and deed book & page information.

Mecklenburg
Assessor, Real Estate
Records on the GIS map server are available free online at http://maps.co.mecklenburg.nc.us/taxgis/disclaimer.htm.

Moore
Real Estate, Liens, Grantor/Grantee, Vital Statistics, DD214, Property Tax
www.co.moore.nc.us
Online access to the recorder's Online Public Records (OPR) database is available free at http://rod.co.moore.nc.us/nc32. Also, access to county Tax Information System (TIS) data is available free online to registrants and subject to approval at www.co.moore.nc.us/property/TIS/Taxpayer%20Information%20Login.htm. For information, contact Kay Ingram at 910-947-6306.

Randolph
Real Property
www.co.randolph.nc.us
Online access to the county GIS database is available free at www.co.randolph.nc.us/gis.htm. In the "Search functions" on the map page, click on "parcel owner."

Rowan
Real Estate, Recording
www.co.rowan.nc.us/rod
Online access to the Register of Dees land records database is available free at http://rod.co.rowan.nc.us. Records go back to 1975; financing statements back to 1993; images back to 6/2000.

Stanly
Real Estate, Assessor
www.co.stanly.nc.us
Online access to the county Property database is available free on the GIS mapping site at www.webgis.net/stanly. Provides parcel ID and tax numbers, owner, address, year, land and building values.

Wake
Real Estate, Assessor
Records from the County Department of Revenue are downloadable by township for free at http://web.co.wake.nc.us/revenue/realdata2.html. Also, Online access to Town of Cary property information is available free at a GIS mapping site at www.webgis.net/cary.

Wilson

Assessor, Real Estate, Voter Records

www.wilson-co.com

Records on the county Tax Administrator database are available free online at www.wilson-co.com/wctax.html. Records on the county registered voter database are available at www.wilson-co.com/wcbe_search.cfm.

Federal Courts in North Carolina...

US District Court - Eastern District of North Carolina

Home Page: www.nced.uscourts.gov
PACER: Sign-up number is 800-676-6856. Access fee is $.60 per minute. Toll-free access: 800-995-0313. Local access: 919-856-4768. Case records are available back to 1989. Records are purged when deemed necessary. New records are available online after 3 days.
Elizabeth City Division Counties: Bertie, Camden, Chowan, Currituck, Dare, Gates, Hertford, Northampton, Pasquotank, Perquimans, Tyrrell, Washington.
Greenville-Eastern Division Counties: Beaufort, Carteret, Craven, Edgecombe, Greene, Halifax, Hyde, Jones, Lenoir, Martin, Pamlico, Pitt.
Raleigh Division Counties: Cumberland, Franklin, Granville, Harnett, Johnston, Nash, Vance, Wake, Warren, Wayne, Wilson.
Wilmington Division Counties: Bladen, Brunswick, Columbus, Duplin, New Hanover, Onslow, Pender, Robeson, Sampson.

US Bankruptcy Court - Eastern District of North Carolina

Home Page: www.nceb.uscourts.gov
PACER: Sign-up number is 800-676-6856. Access fee is $.60 per minute. Toll-free access: 800-565-2105. Local access:. Use of PC Anywhere v4.0 suggested. Case records are available back to 1992. Records are purged two years. New civil records are available online after 1 day.
Other Online Access: RACER is available on the Intenet at http://pacer.nceb.uscourts.gov.
Raleigh Division Counties: Franklin, Granville, Harnett, Johnston, Vance, Wake, Warren.
Wilson Division Counties: Beaufort, Bertie, Bladen, Brunswick, Camden, Carteret, Chowan, Columbus, Craven, Cumberland, Currituck, Dare, Duplin, Edgecombe, Gates, Greene, Halifax, Hertford, Hyde, Jones, Lenoir, Martin, Nash, New Hanover, Northampton, Onslow, Pamlico, Pasquotank,Pender, Perquimans, Pitt, Robeson, Sampson, Tyrrell, Washington, Wayne, Wilson.

US District Court - Middle District of North Carolina

Home Page: www.ncmd.uscourts.gov
PACER: Sign-up number is 800-676-6856. Access fee is $.60 per minute. Toll-free access: 800-372-8820. Local access: 336-332-6010. Case records are available back to September 1991. Records are purged never. New records are available online after 2 days.
PACER Internet Access: http://pacer.ncmd.uscourts.gov.
Greensboro Division Counties: Alamance, Cabarrus, Caswell, Chatham, Davidson, Davie, Durham, Forsyth, Guilford, Hoke, Lee, Montgomery, Moore, Orange, Person, Randolph, Richmond, Rockingham, Rowan, Scotland, Stanly, Stokes, Surry, Yadkin.

US Bankruptcy Court - Middle District of North Carolina

Home Page: www.ncmb.uscourts.gov
PACER: Sign-up number is 800-676-6856. Access fee is $.60 per minute. Toll-free access: 800-417-3571. Local access: 336-333-5389. Case records are available back to 1992. Records are purged every two years. New civil records are available online after 1 day.
PACER Internet Access: http://pacer.ncmb.uscourts.gov.
Greensboro Division Counties: Alamance, Cabarrus, Caswell, Chatham, Davidson, Davie, Durham, Guilford, Hoke, Lee, Montgomery, Moore, Orange, Person, Randolph, Richmond, Rockingham, Rowan, Scotland, Stanly.
Winston-Salem Division Counties: Forsyth, Stokes, Surry, Yadkin.

US District Court - Western District of North Carolina

Home Page: www.ncwd.uscourts.gov
PACER: Sign-up number is 800-676-6856. Access fee is. Toll-free access: 888-509-2865. Local access: 704-350-7426. Case records are available back to 1991. New records are available online after 2 days.

PACER Internet Access: http://pacer.ncwd.uscourts.gov.
Asheville Division Counties: Avery, Buncombe, Haywood, Henderson, Madison, Mitchell, Transylvania, Yancey.
Bryson City Division Counties: Cherokee, Clay, Graham, Jackson, Macon, Swain.
Charlotte Division Counties: Anson, Gaston, Mecklenburg, Union.
Shelby Division Counties: Burke, Cleveland, McDowell, Polk, Rutherford.
Statesville Division Counties: Alexander, Alleghany, Ashe, Caldwell, Catawba, Iredell, Lincoln, Watauga, Wilkes.

US Bankruptcy Court - Western District of North Carolina

Home Page: www.ncbankruptcy.org
PACER: Sign-up number is 800-676-6856. Access fee is $.60 per minute. Toll-free access: 800-324-5614. Local access: 704-344-6121, 704-344-6122, 705-344-6123, 705-344-6124. Case records are available back to 1992. Records are purged every 2 years. New civil records are available online after 1 day.
Other Online Access: You can search records using the Internet. Searching is currently free. Visit www.ncbankruptcy.org/view.html to search. You can search for creditors at www.ncbankruptcy.org/creditor.htm.
Charlotte Division Counties: Alexander, Alleghany, Anson, Ashe, Avery, Buncombe, Burke, Caldwell, Catawba, Cherokee, Clay, Cleveland, Gaston, Graham, Haywood, Henderson, Iredell, Jackson, Lincoln, Macon, Madison, McDowell, Mecklenburg, Mitchell, Polk, Rutherford, Swain,Transylvania, Union, Watauga, Wilkes, Yancey.

Editor's Choice for North Carolina

Here are some additional sites recommended for this state.

Constitution Text
    http://statelibrary.dcr.state.nc.us/nc/stgovt/preconst.htm
Crime Database
    www.charlotte.com/crime
Impaired Driving Database
    http://web1-sun.aoc.state.nc.us/data/dwi/index.html
Sex Offenders Database
    http://sbi.jus.state.nc.us/cgi-bin/hsrun.hse/SOR/SOR/SOR.htx;start=HS_SORSearchFrames
Shipwrecks Database
    www.2isystems.com/wreck/index.htm
Statutes Text
    www.ncga.state.nc.us/statutes/statutes.html

North Dakota

Capital:	Bismark	Home Page	www.state.nd.us
	Burleigh County	Attorney General	www.ag.state.nd.us
Time Zone:	CST	Archives	www.state.nd.us/hist/sal.htm
Number of Counties:	53		

State Level...Major Agencies

Uniform Commercial Code, Federal Tax Liens, State Tax Liens

UCC Division, Secretary of State, 600 E Boulevard Ave Dept 108, Bismarck, ND 58505-0500; 701-328-3662, 701-328-4214 (Fax), 8AM-5PM.

www.state.nd.us/sec

Online: Sign-up for access to the Central Indexing System includes an annual subscription $120 fee and a one-time $50.00 registration fee. The $7.00 fee applies, but documents will not be certified. Searches include UCC-11 information listing, farm product searches, and a general information Public Search.

Birth, Death, Marriage Certificates

ND Department of Health, Vital Records, State Capitol, 600 E Blvd, Dept 301, Bismarck, ND 58505-0200; 701-328-2360, 701-328-1850 (Fax), 7:30AM-5PM.

www.health.state.nd.us/ndhd/admin/vital/

Online: Records may be ordered online from the Internet site, $7.00 per name.

Driver Records

Department of Transportation, Driver License & Traffic Safety Div., 608 E Boulevard Ave, Bismarck, ND 58505-0780; 701-328-2603, 701-328-2435 (Fax), 8AM-5PM.

www.state.nd.us/dot

Online: The system is interactive and is open 24 hours daily. Fee is $3.00 per record, requester must be approved. For more information, call 701-328-4790.

Boat & Vessel Ownership, Boat & Vessel Registration

North Dakota Game & Fish Department, 100 N Bismarck Expressway, Bismarck, ND 58501; 701-328-6335, 701-328-6352 (Fax), 8AM-5PM.

www.state.nd.us/gnf

Online: There is a free public inquiry system on the home page. One can also search lottery hunting permit applications.

Legislation Records

North Dakota Legislative Council, State Capitol, 600 E Boulevard Ave, Bismarck, ND 58505; 701-328-2916, 701-328-2900 (Secretary of State), 701-328-2992 (Sec of State fax), 8AM-5PM.

www.state.nd.us/lr

Online: Their Internet site offers an extensive array of legislative information at no charge, including proposed and enacted legislation since 1997. Also, one may e-mail requests for information.

GED Certificates

Department of Public Instruction, GED Testing, 600 E Blvd Ave, Bismarck, ND 58505-0440; 701-328-2393, 701-328-4770 (Fax), 8AM-4:30PM.

www.dpi.state.nd.us

Online: One may request records via e-mail at JMarcell@mail.dpi.state.nd.us. There is no fee, unless a transcript is ordered.

Hunting License Information, Fishing License Information

ND Game & Fish Department, 100 N Bismarck Expressway, Bismarck, ND 58501-5095; 701-328-6300, 701-328-6335 (Licensing), 701-328-6352 (Fax), 8AM-5PM.

www.state.nd.us/gnf

Online: One can search to see if a person has been chosen (lottery) for a specific hunt or passed hunter safety.

State Level...Occupational Licensing

Asbestos Abatement Contractor/Project Planner	www.health.state.nd.us/ndhd/environ/ee/rad/asb/
Asbestos Abatement Inspector/Monitor/Supvr.	www.health.state.nd.us/ndhd/environ/ee/rad/asb/
Asbestos Worker/Designer	www.health.state.nd.us/ndhd/environ/ee/rad/asb/
Attorney	www.court.state.nd.us/court/lawyers/index/frameset.htm
Bank	www.state.nd.us/bank/Bank%20List.htm
Charitable Solicitation	www.state.nd.us/sec/charitableorganizationsearch.htm
Collection Agency	www.state.nd.us/bank/Collection%20Agencies.htm
Consumer Finance Company	www.state.nd.us/bank/Finance%20Companies.htm
Contractor/General Contractor	www.state.nd.us/sec/contractorsearch.htm
Credit Union	www.state.nd.us/bank/Credit%20Union%20List.htm
Livestock Agent	www.state.nd.us/agr/agents.html
Livestock Auction Market	www.state.nd.us/agr/markets.html
Livestock Dealer	www.state.nd.us/agr/dealers.html
Lobbyist	www.state.nd.us/sec/RegLobbyists/lobbyistregmnu.htm
Medical Doctor	www.docboard.org/nd
Money Broker Company	www.state.nd.us/bank/Money%20Brokers.htm
Optometrist	http://home.ctctel.com/ndsbopt/ods.htm
Pesticide Applicator/Dealer	www.ag.ndsu.nodak.edu/aginfo/pesticid/cert_info.htm
Physician Assistant	www.docboard.org/nd
Public Accountant-CPA	www.state.nd.us/ndsba
Public Accounting Firm	www.state.nd.us/ndsba
Trust Company	www.state.nd.us/bank/Trust%20Companies.htm

County Level...Courts, Recorders & Assessors

State Court Administrator, North Dakota Judiciary, 600 E Blvd, 1st Floor Judicial Wing, Dept. 180, Bismarck, ND, 58505-0530; 701-328-4216; www.ndcourts.com or www.court.state.nd.us

Editor's Note: A statewide computer system for internal purposes is in operation in most counties. You may now search North Dakota Supreme Court dockets and opinions at www.ndcourts.com. Search by docket number, party name, or anything else that may appear in the text. Records are from 1991 forward. Email notification of new opinions is also available.

The North Dakota Recorders Information Network (NDRIN) is a electronic central repository for ten participating counties. Burleigh, Cass, Dunn, McLean, Stark and Ward currently offer internet access. Other counties participating in the system are McKenzie, Richland, Walsh, and Williams. There is a $200 set-up fee and a choice of two monthly plans: $500 per month for unlimited access, or $100 with $1.00 charge per image printed. Register or request information via the web site at www.ndrin.com.

Federal Courts in North Dakota...

US District Court - District of North Dakota

Home Page: www.ndd.uscourts.gov
PACER: Sign-up number is 800-676-6856. Access fee is $.60 per minute. Toll-free access: 800-407-4453. Local access: 701-530-2367. Case records are available back to October 1990. Records are purged never. New records are available online after 1 day.
Bismarck-Southwestern Division Counties: Adams, Billings, Bowman, Burleigh, Dunn, Emmons, Golden Valley, Grant, Hettinger, Kidder, Logan, McIntosh, McLean, Mercer, Morton, Oliver, Sioux, Slope, Stark.
Fargo-Southeastern Division Counties: Barnes, Cass, Dickey, Eddy, Foster, Griggs, La Moure, Ransom, Richland, Sargent, Steele, Stutsman. Rolette County cases prior to 1995 may be located here.
Grand Forks-Northeastern Division Counties: Benson, Cavalier, Grand Forks, Nelson, Pembina, Ramsey, Towner, Traill, Walsh.
Minot-Northwestern Division Counties: Bottineau, Burke, Divide, McHenry, McKenzie, Mountrail, Pierce, Renville, Rolette, Sheridan, Ward, Wells, Williams. Case records from Rolette County prior to 1995 may be located in Fargo-Southeastern Division.

US Bankruptcy Court - District of North Dakota

Home Page: www.ndb.uscourts.gov
PACER: Sign-up number is 800-676-6856. Access fee is $.60 per minute. Toll-free access: 800-810-4092. Local access: 701-297-7164. Case records are available back to 1990. New civil records are available online after 1 day.
PACER Internet Access: http://pacer.okwd.uscourts.gov.
Fargo Division Counties: All counties in North Dakota.

Editor's Choice for North Dakota

Legislators Database
www.state.sd.us/state/legis/lrc/historical/HistoryMenu.cfm
Supreme Court Opinions
www.court.state.nd.us/Court/Opinions.htm

Capital: Columbus
Franklin County

Time Zone: EST

Number of Counties: 88

Home Page www.state.oh.us

Attorney General www.ag.state.oh.us

Archives www.ohiohistory.org/ar_tools.html

State Level...Major Agencies

Corporation Records, Fictitious Name, Limited Partnership Records, Assumed Name, Trademarks/Servicemarks, Limited Liability Company

Secretary of State, Attn: Customer Service, 30 E Broad St, 14th Floor, Columbus, OH 43266-0418; 877-767-3453, 614-466-3910, 614-466-3899 (Fax), 8AM-5PM.

www.state.oh.us/sos

Online: The agency has a free Internet search available for a number of business and corporation records, also includes UCC and campaign finance.

Uniform Commercial Code

UCC Division, 14th Floor, Secretary of State, 30 E Broad St, State Office Tower, Columbus, OH 43215; 877-767-3453, 614-466-3126, 614-466-2892 (Fax), 8AM-5PM.

www.state.oh.us/sos

Online: The Internet site offers free online access to records.

Death Records

Ohio Department of Health, Bureau of Vital Statistics, PO Box 15098, Columbus, OH 43215-0098 (Courier: 35 E Chestnut, 6th Floor, Columbus, OH 43215); 614-466-2531, 614-466-6604 (Fax), 7:45AM-4:30PM.

www.odh.state.oh.us/Birth/birthmain.htm

Online: The Ohio Historical Society Death Certificate Index Searchable Database at www.ohiohistory.org/dindex/search.cfm permits searching by name, county, index. Data is available from 1913 to 1937 only.

Driver Records

Department of Public Safety, Bureau of Motor Vehicles, 1970 W Broad St, Columbus, OH 43223-1102; 614-752-7600, 8AM-5:30PM M-T-W; 8AM-4:30PM TH-F.

www.ohio.gov/odps

Online: The system is called "Defender System" and is suggested for requesters who order 100 or more motor vehicle reports per day in batch mode. Turnaround is in 4-8 hours. The DL# or SSN and name are needed when ordering. Fee is $2.00 per record. For more information, call 614-752-7692.

Vehicle Ownership, Vehicle Identification

Bureau of Motor Vehicles, Motor Vehicle Title Records, 1970 W Broad St, Columbus, OH 43223-1102; 614-752-7671, 614-752-8929 (Fax), 7:30AM-4:45PM.

www.state.oh.us/odps/division/bmv/bmv/html

Online: Ohio offers online access through AAMVAnet. All requesters must comply with a contractual agreement prior to release of data, which complies with DPPA regulations. Fee is $2.00 per record. Call 614-752-7692 for more information.

Legislation Records

Ohio House of Representatives, 77 S High Street, Columbus, OH 43266 (Courier: Ohio Senate, State House, Columbus, OH 43215); 614-466-8842 (In-State Only), 614-466-9745 (Out-of-State), 614-466-3357 (Clerk's Office), 614-644-8744 (Fax), 8:30AM-5PM.

www.legislature.state.oh.us

Online: The Internet site offers access to bill text, status, and enactment.

State Level...Occupational Licensing

Accounting Firm	www.state.oh.us/acc/search.html
Architect	www.state.oh.us/scripts/arc/query.asp
Athletic Trainer	www.state.oh.us/scripts/pyt/query.asp
Barber School	www.state.oh.us/brb/barbsch.htm
Chiropractor	http://156.63.245.111/index.html
Clinical Nurse Specialist	www.state.oh.us/scripts/nur/query.asp
Coil Cleaner	www.state.oh.us/com/liquor/liquor13.htm
Cosmetic Therapist	www.state.oh.us/scripts/med/license/Query.stm
Counselor	www.state.oh.us/scripts/csw/query.asp
Dental Assistant Radiologist	www.state.oh.us/scripts/den/query.stm
Dental Hygienist	www.state.oh.us/scripts/den/query.stm
Dentist	www.state.oh.us/scripts/den/query.stm
Employer of Executive Agency Lobbyist	www.jlec-olig.state.oh.us/agent_search_form.cfm
Employer of Legislative Agent	www.jlec-olig.state.oh.us/agent_search_form.cfm
Engineer	www.peps.state.oh.us/index.html
Executive Agency Lobbyist	www.jlec-olig.state.oh.us/agent_search_form.cfm
Insurance Agent	www.ohioinsurance.gov/ConsumServ/ocs/agentloc.htm
Landscape Architect	www.state.oh.us/scripts/arc/query.asp
Legislative Agent	www.jlec-olig.state.oh.us/agent_search_form.cfm
Liquor Distributor	www.state.oh.us/com/liquor/liquor14.htm
Liquor License	www.state.oh.us/com/liquor/phone.txt
Lottery Retailer	www.ohiolottery.com/frameset/games/retailer.html
Massage Therapist	www.state.oh.us/scripts/med/license/Query.stm
Medical Doctor	www.state.oh.us/scripts/med/license/Query.stm
Nurse Anesthetist	www.state.oh.us/scripts/nur/query.asp
Nurse Midwife	www.state.oh.us/scripts/nur/query.asp

Nurse Practioner .... www.state.oh.us/scripts/nur/query.asp
Nurse-RN & LPN... www.state.oh.us/scripts/nur/query.asp
Occupational Therapist/Assistant .... www.state.oh.us/scripts/pyt/query.asp
Optometrist.. www.state.oh.us/scripts/opt/query.asp
Optometrist-Diagnostic or Therapeutic.............. www.state.oh.us/scripts/opt/query.asp
Osteopathic Doctor... www.state.oh.us/scripts/med/license/Query.stm
Physical Therapist/Assistant............................. www.state.oh.us/scripts/pyt/query.asp
Physician Assistant .... www.state.oh.us/scripts/med/license/Query.stm
Podiatrist .... www.state.oh.us/scripts/med/license/Query.stm
Polygraph Examiner... http://polygraph.org/states/oape/directory.htm
Psychologist.. www2.state.oh.us/psy/query.asp
Public Accountant-CPA..................................... www.state.oh.us/acc/search.html
Real Estate Sales Agent .... www.ohiorealtors.org/search/locate.html
Respiratory Therapist/Student Therapist............. www.state.oh.us/scripts/rsp/query.asp
School Psychologist.. www2.state.oh.us/psy/query.asp
Social Worker .... www.state.oh.us/scripts/csw/query.asp
Surveyor .... www.peps.state.oh.us/index.html
Teacher/Teacher's Aide .... www.ode.state.oh.us/tp/certifact.htm

County Level...Courts, Recorders & Assessors

Administrative Director, Supreme Court of Ohio, 30 E Broad St, 3rd Fl, Columbus, OH, 43266-0419; 614-466-2653; www.sconet.state.oh.us

Editor's Note: There is no statewide computer system, though a number of counties offer online access.

Ashland
Real Estate, Auditor
Property records on the county Auditor's database are available free online at www.ashlandcoauditor.org/ashland208/landrover.asp.

Ashtabula
Real Estate, Auditor
www.co.ashtabula.oh.us/
Property records on the county Auditor's database are available free online at http://216.28.192.48/ashtabula208/LandRover.asp.

Athens
Civil Cases, Criminal Records
www.athenscountycpcourt.org
Online access to the CP court records is available free at the web site.

Butler
Civil Cases, Criminal Records
www.butlercountyclerk.org
Online access to County Clerk of Courts records is available free at http://38.155.160.5/pa/pa.urd/pamw6500-display.

Probate, Voter Records
www.butlercountyohio.org/recorder
County voter records are available at www.butlercountyohio.org/elections. County probate records are available at www.butlercountyohio.org/probate/estate.cfm. Search the Estate or Guardianship databases.

Clermont
Property Records
Records from the county Property database are available free online at http://clermont.akanda.com.

Columbiana
Real Estate, Auditor
www.columbianacntyauditor.org
Property records on the county Auditor's database are available free online at
www.columbianacntyauditor.org/columbv208/LandRover.asp.

Coshocton
Civil Cases, Criminal Records
www.coshoctonmunicipalcourt.com
Online access to court records is available at the web site. Search by name, case number, attorney, and date.

Cuyahoga
Civil Cases, Criminal Records
www.garfieldhts.org/court
Online access is limited to current dockets; search by name, date or case number at http://docket.garfieldhts.org.
Auditor/Assessor
www.cuyahoga.oh.us/auditor/approg/Default.asp
Online access to the County Auditor Property Information database is available free at the web site.

Darke
Real Estate
Property records on the Darke County database are available free online at www.darkecountyrealestate.org. County Recorder records
are accessible through a private online service at www.landaccess.com; Fees and registration are required.

Delaware
Real Estate, Auditor
www.co.delaware.oh.us
The Delaware Appraisal Land Information System Project (DALIS) maps with County Auditor records are available free online. At
main site, click on "GIS mapping" in the left-hand menu bar, then select a search method. Once parcel is identified on the map, click
on "identify" then on parcel map to get parcel information, values, sales, and building information. Also, access to auditor's property
information is available free at www.delawarecountyauditor.org/delaware208/LandRover.asp.

Franklin
Civil Cases, Criminal Records
www.franklincountyclerk.com
Access records via the web site. Java-enable web browser required. Online access to probate court records is available free at
www.co.franklin.oh.us/probate/ProbateSearch.html.

Property, Auditor, Unclaimed Funds, Marriage
www.co.franklin.oh.us/
Online access to the County Auditor database is available free at http://209.190.72.70/realestate/LandRover.asp. Search the auditor's
database of unclaimed property at http://209.190.72.69/auditor/fiscal_services/unclaimed_funds.html. Also, search marriage records
online at www.co.franklin.oh.us/probate/PBMLSearch.html.

Gallia
Property, Real Estate
http://galliaauditor.ddti.net
Property records on the county auditor real estate database are available free online at http://galliaauditor.ddti.net. Click on "attributes"
for property information; click on "sales" to search by real estate attributes.

Greene

Civil Cases, Criminal Records

www.co.greene.oh.us/clerk.htm

Online access to clerk of court records is available free at http://198.30.12.229/pa/pa.htm. Search by name or case number.

Real Estate, Auditor

www.co.greene.oh.us/recorder.htm

Records on the county Internet Map Server are available free online at www.co.greene.oh.us/gismapserver.htm. Click on "Click here to enter. Server Site #1." Data includes owner, address, valuation, taxes, sales data, and parcel ID number.

Hamilton

Civil Cases, Criminal Records

www.courtclerk.org

Records from the court clerk are available free online at the web site. Civil index goes back to 1991. Criminal index back to 1986.

Real Estate, Liens

www.hcro.org

Access to county online records requires a $100 escrow account, plus $1 per connection and $.30 per minute. Records date back to 6/1988. Lending agency information is available. For information, contact Vicky Jones at 513-946-4571.

Hardin

Property

www.co.hardin.oh.us

Property records from the county database are available at the web site. Click on "Real Estate Internet Inquiry."

Knox

Civil Cases, Criminal Records

www.knoxcountyclerk.org

Search court index, dockets, calendars free online at www.knoxcountycpcourt.org. Search by name or case number.

Property

www.knoxcountyauditor.org

Records on the county auditor database are available free online at www.knoxcountyauditor.org/knox208/LandRover.asp.

Lake

Civil Cases, Criminal Records

www.lakecountyohio.org/clerk

Online access to court records, docket sheets, and quick index are available free at http://web2.lakecountyohio.org/clerk/search.htm. Includes domestic and appeals cases.

Real Estate, Auditor, Recordings, Liens

www.lakecountyrecorder.org

Online access to the Recorder's Document Index database is available free at http://web2.lakecountyohio.org/recorders/search/index.asp. Records go back to 1986. Also, access to the treasurer and auditor's real estate databases is available free at www.lake.iviewauditor.com. Click on "by attribute."

Lawrence

Civil Cases, Criminal Records

www.lawrencecountyclkofcrt.org

Online access to court records is available free at the web site.

Real Estate, Liens

Access to County Recorder records requires a $600-700 set-up fee, plus a $150 monthly fee. Mortgage records date back to 1988 and deeds to 1986. Only federal tax liens are online; the Clerk of Court keeps state liens. UCC liens date back to 1989. Lending agency information is available. Call 740-533-4314 for more information.

Logan

Real Estate, Auditor

Records on the County Auditor's database are available free online at www2.co.logan.oh.us/logan208/LandRover.asp.

Lorain
Civil Cases, Criminal Records
www.loraincountycpcourt.org
The web site offers free access to indices and dockets for civil, criminal and domestic relationship cases.

Real Estate, Liens, Auditor
www.loraincounty.com/government/
Online access to the county assessor database is available free at www.loraincounty.com/recorder/register. Free registration is required. Also, records on the County Auditor's database are available free online at www.loraincountyauditor.org/lorain208/LandRover.asp.

Lucas
Civil Cases, Criminal Records
www.maumee.org/court/court.htm
Online access to the interactive web court system database is available free at www.maumee.org/court/courtsystem/index.html.

Real Estate, Auditor
ww.co.lucas.oh.us
Property records on the County Auditor's Real Estate Information System (AREIS) database are available free online at www.co.lucas.oh.us/Real_Estate. User ID is required; registration is free.

Madison
Real Estate, Auditor
www.co.madison.oh.us/elected.htm
Records on the County Auditor's database are available free online at www.co.madison.oh.us/auditor/iViewW3/iViewW3.asp. Also, County Recorder records are accessible through a private online service at www.landaccess.com; Fees and registration are required.

Mahoning
Real Estate, Auditor
www.mahoningcountyauditor.org
Property records on the County Auditor's database are available free online at www.mahoningcountyauditor.org/maho208/LandRover.asp.

Marion
Real Estate, Auditor
www.co.marion.oh.us
Online access to the county auditor real estate database is available free at www.co.marion.oh.us. Click on "Real Estate Inquiry."

Medina
Civil Cases, Criminal Records
www.medinamunicipalcourt.org
Access to the online system requires Procomm Plus. There are no fees. Search by either name or case number. The computer access number is 330-723-4337. For more information, call Rich Armstrong at ext. 230.

Real Estate, Auditor
www.recorder.co.medina.oh.us
Online access to indexes 1983 to present on the County Recorder database is available free at the web site. Click on "Indexes" and use "View" as user name and password. Also, online access to property records on the Medina County Auditor database are available free online at www.medinacountyauditor.org - "Public Records."

Mercer
Real Estate, Auditor
www.mercercountyohio.org
Property records on the County Auditor - Real Estate Department database are available free online at www.mercercountyohio.org/auditor/RealEstate/PcardInq/category.htm.

Montgomery
Civil Cases, Criminal Records
www.clerk.co.montgomery.oh.us
Online access to the Courts countywide PRO system is available free at www.clerk.co.montgomery.oh.us/pro/index.cfm. Address mail requests to Montgomery County Clerk of Court. Online access to criminal and traffic records is the same as civil.
Property
www.mctreas.org
Property records on the county treasurer real estate tax information database are available free online at www.mctreas.org.

Muskingum
Real Estate, Assessor
www.muskingumcountyauditor.org
Records on the county assessor database are available free online at www.muskingumcountyauditor.org/realestate/LandRover.asp.

Preble
Real Estate, Auditor
Property records on the County Auditor's database are available free online at www.preblecountyauditor.org/preble208/LandRover.asp.

Richland
Real Estate, Auditor
Property records from the County Auditor database are available free online at www.richlandcountyauditor.org. Also, County Recorder records are accessible through a private online service at www.landaccess.com; Fees and registration are required.

Scioto
Civil Cases, Criminal Records
www.sciotocountycpcourt.org
Online access to court records is available free at www.sciotocountycpcourt.org/search.htm. Search by court calendar, quick index, general index or docket sheet.

Summit
Real Estate, Auditor, Property Tax
http://summitoh.net/
Tax map information from the County Auditor is available free online at http://scids.summitoh.net/taxmapsinternet, also property appraisal and tax information at www.summitoh.net:85/summit/pawsmain.html. Access to the full document images database requires registration, password and one-time $150.00 fee. Call Summit County Data Center Help Desk at 330-643-2698 for information and sign-up.

Stark
Civil Cases, Criminal Records
www.starkclerk.org
Online access to the county online case docket database is available free at www.starkclerk.org/docket/index.html.

Trumbull
Civil Cases, Criminal Records
www.clerk.co.trumbull.oh.us
Online access to court records is available free at www.clerk.co.trumbull.oh.us/search/search.htm. Records go back to May, 1996.
Auditor/Assessor
Records on the County Auditor Real Estate web site are available free online at www.co.auditor.trumbull.oh.us/trumv208/LandRover.asp. Click on "Press here to start property search" to enter the database query page.

Tuscarawas
Real Estate
www.co.tuscarawas.oh.us
County real estate records are available free online at www.co.tuscarawas.oh.us/Auditor/realsearch.htm. Also, the county list of Unclaimed Funds may be searched at www.co.tuscarawas.oh.us/Auditor/Unclaimed%20Funds.htm.

Van Wert
Real Estate, Recording
County Recorder records are accessible through a private online service at www.landaccess.com; Fees and registration are required.

Warren
Real Estate, Auditor
www.co.warren.oh.us
Online access to the county auditor database is available free at www.co.warren.oh.us/auditor/index.htm. Click on Warren County Property Information Search at the bottom of this web page.

Washington
Civil Cases, Criminal Records
www.mariettacourt.com
Online access to courts records is to be available free at the web site. Online access to criminal records is the same as

Wood
Civil Cases, Criminal Records
Records from the Perryburg Muni. Court are available free by remote online. Civil and criminal indexes go back to 1988. Contact Judy Daquano at 419-872-7906 for information.

Wyandot
Real Estate, Auditor
www.co.wyandot.oh.us/
Online access to the Auditor's real estate database is available free at www.co.wyandot.oh.us/auditor/default.html. Click on "Real estate Internet Inquiry."

Federal Courts in Ohio...

US District Court - Northern District of Ohio

Home Page: www.ohnd.uscourts.gov
PACER: Sign-up number is 800-676-6856. Access fee is $.60 per minute. Toll-free access: 800-673-4409. Local access: 216-522-3669. Many cases prior to the indicated dates are also online. Case records are available back to January 1, 1990. Records are purged never. New records are available online after 1 day.
PACER Internet Access: http://pacer.ohnd.uscourts.gov.
Electronic Filing: Only law firms and practictioners may file cases electronically. Anyone can search online; however, the search results only include cases that were filed electronically. To search, visit http://ecf.ohnd.uscourts.gov/cgi-bin/PublicCaseFiled-Rpt.pl. Electronic filing information is available online at http://ecf.ohnd.uscourts.gov.
Akron Division Counties: Carroll, Holmes, Portage, Stark, Summit, Tuscarawas, Wayne. Cases filed prior to 1995 for counties in the Youngstown Division may be located here.
Cleveland Division Counties: Ashland, Ashtabula, Crawford, Cuyahoga, Geauga, Lake, Lorain, Medina, Richland. Cases prior to July 1995 for the counties of Ashland, Crawford, Medina and Richland are located in the Akron Division. Cases filed prior to 1995 from the counties in the Youngstown Division may be located here.
Toledo Division Counties: Allen, Auglaize, Defiance, Erie, Fulton, Hancock, Hardin, Henry, Huron, Lucas, Marion, Mercer, Ottawa, Paulding, Putnam, Sandusky, Seneca, Van Wert, Williams, Wood, Wyandot.
Youngstown Division Counties: Columbiana, Mahoning, Trumbull. This division was reactivated in the middle of 1995. Older cases will be found in Akron or Cleveland.

US Bankruptcy Court - Northern District of Ohio

Home Page: www.ohnb.uscourts.gov
PACER: Sign-up number is 800-676-6856. Access fee is $.60 per minute. Toll-free access: 800-579-5735. Local access: 330-489-4779. Case records are available back to January 1985. Records are purged only up to September 1990. New civil records are available online after 2 days.
Akron Division Counties: Medina, Portage, Summit.

Canton Division Counties: Ashland, Carroll, Crawford, Holmes, Richland, Stark, Tuscarawas, Wayne.
Cleveland Division Counties: Cuyahoga, Geauga, Lake, Lorain.
Toledo Division Counties: Allen, Auglaize, Defiance, Erie, Fulton, Hancock, Hardin, Henry, Huron, Lucas, Marion, Mercer, Ottawa, Paulding, Putnam, Sandusky, Seneca, Van Wert, Williams, Wood, Wyandot.
Youngstown Division Counties: Ashtabula, Columbiana, Mahoning, Trumbull.

US District Court - Southern District of Ohio

PACER: Sign-up number is 800-676-6856. Access fee is $1.00 per minute. Toll-free access: 800-710-4939. Local access: 614-469-6990, 614-469-7460. Case records are available back to June January 1994. Records are purged never. New records are available online after 1 day.
PACER Internet Access: http://pacer.ohsd.uscourts.gov.
Cincinnati Division Counties: Adams, Brown, Butler, Clermont, Clinton, Hamilton, Highland, Lawrence, Scioto, Warren.
Columbus Division Counties: Athens, Belmont, Coshocton, Delaware, Fairfield, Fayette, Franklin, Gallia, Guernsey, Harrison, Hocking, Jackson, Jefferson, Knox, Licking, Logan, Madison, Meigs, Monroe, Morgan, Morrow, Muskingum, Noble, Perry, Pickaway, Pike, Ross, Union, Vinton,Washington.
Dayton Division Counties: Champaign, Clark, Darke, Greene, Miami, Montgomery, Preble, Shelby.

US Bankruptcy Court - Southern District of Ohio

PACER: Sign-up number is 800-676-6856. Access fee is $.60 per minute. Toll-free access: 800-793-7003. Local access: 937-225-7561. Case records are available back to 1990. Records are purged every six months. New civil records available online after 1 day.
PACER Internet Access: http://pacer.ohsb.uscourts.gov.
Cincinnati Division Counties: Adams, Brown, Clermont, Hamilton, Highland, Lawrence, Scioto and a part of Butler.
Columbus Division Counties: Athens, Belmont, Coshocton, Delaware, Fairfield, Fayette, Franklin, Gallia, Guernsey, Harrison, Hocking, Jackson, Jefferson, Knox, Licking, Logan, Madison, Meigs, Monroe, Morgan, Morrow, Muskingum, Noble, Perry, Pickaway, Pike, Ross, Union, Vinton,Washington.
Dayton Division Counties: Butler, Champaign, Clark, Clinton, Darke, Greene, Miami, Montgomery, Preble, Shelby, Warren; parts of Butler County are handled by Cincinnati Division.

Editor's Choice for Ohio

Here are some additional sites recommended for this state.

Death Records (1913-1937) Database
www.ohiohistory.org/dindex/search.cfm
Dog Licenses Database
www.butlercountyohio.org/auditor/dl_search.cfm
Dog Tags Database
www.co.hardin.oh.us/
Guardianship/Mental Health Database
www.butlercountyohio.org/probate/guardian.cfm
Inmates & Offenders Database
www.drc.state.oh.us/cfdocs/inmate/search.htm
Laws, Rules & Constitution Text
www.state.oh.us/ohio/ohiolaws.htm
State Employee Phone Numbers Directory
www.state.oh.us/scripts/phone/query.asp

Capital:	Oklahoma City	Home Page	www.state.ok.us
	Oklahoma County		
Time Zone:	CST	Attorney General	www.oag.state.ok.us
Number of Counties:	77	Archives	www.odl.state.ok.us

State Level...Major Agencies

Uniform Commercial Code

UCC Recorder, Oklahoma County Clerk, 320 R.S. Kerr Ave, County Office Bldg, Rm 105, Oklahoma City, OK 73102; 405-713-1521, 405-713-1810 (Fax), 8AM-5PM.

www.oklahomacounty.org/countyclerk

Online: Records of all UCC financing statements may be viewed free on the Internet at www.oklahomacounty.org/coclerk/default.htm. Neither certified searches nor record requests are accepted at the web.

Legislation Records

Oklahoma Legislature, State Capitol, Bill Status Info-Rm B-30, Copies-Rm 310, Oklahoma City, OK 73105; 405-521-5642 (Bill Status Only), 405-521-5515 (Bill Distribution), 405-528-2546 (Bills in Progress), 405-521-5507 (Fax), 8:30AM-4:30PM.

www.lsb.state.ok.us

Online: The web page provides a variety of legislative information including searching by topic or bill number.

State Level...Occupational Licensing

Accounting Firm .... www.state.ok.us/~oab/firms.html
Athletic Trainer/ Trainer Apprentice .... http://medbd.netplus.net/physrch.html
Consumer Finance Company .... www.okdocc.state.ok.us/introSL.htm
Credit Services Organization .... www.okdocc.state.ok.us/introCSO.htm
Dental Hygienist .... www.state.ok.us/~dentist
Dentist/ Dental Assistant.................................... www.state.ok.us/~dentist
Dietitian/Provisional Licensed Dietitian .... http://medbd.netplus.net/physrch.html
Electrologist.. http://medbd.netplus.net/physrch.html
Engineer .... www.okpels.org/rosters.htm
Health Spa .... www.okdocc.state.ok.us/introSpa.htm

Lobbyist.. www.state.ok.us/~ethics/lobbyist.html
Medical Doctor .... http://medbd.netplus.net/physrch.html
Mortgage Banker .... www.okdocc.state.ok.us/introMB.htm
Occupational Therapist/Assistant .... http://medbd.netplus.net/physrch.html
Optometrist... www.odfinder.org/LicSearch.asp
Osteopathic Physician .... www.docboard.org/ok/df/oksearch.htm
Pawnbroker... www.okdocc.state.ok.us/introPB.htm
Perfusionist.. http://medbd.netplus.net/physrch.html
Physical Therapist/Assistant.............................. http://medbd.netplus.net/physrch.html
Physician Assistant .... http://medbd.netplus.net/physrch.html
Podiatrist .... http://medbd.netplus.net/physrch.html
Precious Metal & Gem Dealer........................... www.okdocc.state.ok.us/introPMD.htm
Private Investigator/ Investigator Agency............ www.opia.com/searches/search.html
Public Accountant-CPA....................................... www.state.ok.us/~oab/twotier.html
Rent to Own Dealer .... www.okdocc.state.ok.us/introRTO.htm
Respiratory Care Practitioner .... http://medbd.netplus.net/physrch.html
Surveyor .... www.okpels.org/rosters.htm

County Level...Courts, Recorders & Assessors

Administrative Director of Courts, 1915 N Stiles #305, Oklahoma City, OK, 73105; 405-521-2450; www.oscn.net

Editor's Note: Free Internet access is available for eight District Courts and all Appellate courts. Both civil and criminal records are available. The counties are Canadian, Cleveland, Comanche, Garfield, Oklahoma, Payne, Rogers, and Tulsa.

One can search the Oklahoma Supreme Court Network from the Internet site at www.oscn.net by single cite or multiple cite (no name searches).

Case information is available in bulk form for downloading to computer. For information, call the Administrative Director of Courts, 405-521-2450.

Canadian
Civil Cases, Criminal Records
Access to court dockets is available free online at www.oscn.net/pinpoint3/applications/dockets/start.asp.

Cleveland
Civil Cases, Criminal Records
Access to court dockets is available free online at www.oscn.net/pinpoint3/applications/dockets/start.asp.

Comanche
Civil Cases, Criminal Records
Access to court dockets is available free online at www.oscn.net/pinpoint3/applications/dockets/start.asp.

Garfield
Civil Cases, Criminal Records
Access to court dockets is available free online at www.oscn.net/pinpoint3/applications/dockets/start.asp.

Garvin

Civil Cases, Criminal Records

Civil case information is available free online at www.idocket.com.

Oklahoma

Civil Cases, Criminal Records

www.oscn.net/pinpoint3/applications/dockets/start.asp
Access to court dockets is available free online at www.oscn.net/pinpoint3/applications/dockets/start.asp.

Real Estate, Assessor, Grantor/Grantee, UCC

www.oklahomacounty.org
Assessor and property information on the county assessor database are available free online at
www.oklahomacounty.org/assessor/disclaim.htm. Real estate, UCC, grantor/grantee records on the county clerk database are available
free online at www.oklahomacounty.org/coclerk.

Payne

Civil Cases, Criminal Records

Access to court dockets is available free online at www.oscn.net/pinpoint3/applications/dockets/start.asp.

Rogers

Civil Cases, Criminal Records

Access to court dockets is available free online at www.oscn.net/pinpoint3/applications/dockets/start.asp.

Tulsa

Civil Cases, Criminal Records

Access to court dockets is available free online at www.oscn.net/pinpoint3/applications/dockets/start.asp.

Federal Courts in Oklahoma...

US District Court - Eastern District of Oklahoma

PACER: Sign-up number is 800-676-6856. Access fee is $.60 per minute. Case records are available back to 1996. Records are
purged never. New records are available online after 1 day.
Muskogee Division Counties: Adair, Atoka, Bryan, Carter, Cherokee, Choctaw, Coal, Haskell, Hughes, Johnston, Latimer, Le Flore,
Love, McCurtain, McIntosh, Marshall, Murray, Muskogee, Okfuskee, Pittsburg, Pontotoc, Pushmataha, Seminole, Sequoyah,
Wagoner.

US Bankruptcy Court - Eastern District of Oklahoma

Home Page: www.okeb.uscourts.gov
PACER: Sign-up number is 800-676-6856. Access fee is $.60 per minute. Toll-free access: 877-377-1220. Local access: 918-756-
4812. Case records are available back to 1986. Records are purged every six months. New civil records available online after 1 day.
PACER Internet Access: http://pacer.okeb.uscourts.gov.
Okmulgee Division Counties: Adair, Atoka, Bryan, Carter, Cherokee, Choctaw, Coal, Haskell, Hughes, Johnston, Latimer, Le Flore,
Love, Marshall, McCurtain, McIntosh, Murray, Muskogee, Okfuskee, Okmulgee, Pittsburg, Pontotoc, Pushmataha, Seminole,
Sequoyah, Wagoner.

US District Court - Northern District of Oklahoma

PACER: Sign-up number is 800-676-6856. Access fee is $.60 per minute. Toll-free access: 888-881-0574. Local access: 918-699-
4742. Case records are available back to 1992. New records are available online after 1 day.
PACER Internet Access: http://pacer.oknd.uscourts.gov.
Tulsa Division Counties: Craig, Creek, Delaware, Mayes, Nowata, Okmulgee, Osage, Ottawa, Pawnee, Rogers, Tulsa, Washington.

US Bankruptcy Court - Northern District of Oklahoma

Home Page: www.oknb.uscourts.gov
PACER: Sign-up number is 800-676-6856. Access fee is $.60 per minute. Toll-free access: 800-790-0860. Local access: 918-699-4001. Use of PC Anywhere V4.0 recommended. Case records are available back to 1990. Records are purged never. New civil records are available online after 1 day.
Other Online Access: RACER is available at http://216.61.234.1/wconnect/wc.dll?usbcn_racer~main~~PUID=NOBILL.
Tulsa Division Counties: Craig, Creek, Delaware, Mayes, Nowata, Osage, Ottawa, Pawnee, Rogers, Tulsa, Washington.

US District Court - Western District of Oklahoma

Home Page: www.okwd.uscourts.gov
PACER: Sign-up number is 800-676-6856. Access fee is $.60 per minute. Toll-free access: 888-699-7068. Local access: 405-231-4531. Case records are available back to 1991. Records are purged never. New records are available online after 2 days.
PACER Internet Access: http://pacer.okwd.uscourts.gov.
Oklahoma City Division Counties: Alfalfa, Beaver, Beckham, Blaine, Caddo, Canadian, Cimarron, Cleveland, Comanche, Cotton, Custer, Dewey, Ellis, Garfield, Garvin, Grady, Grant, Greer, Harmon, Harper, Jackson, Jefferson, Kay, Kingfisher, Kiowa, Lincoln, Logan, McClain, Major, Noble,Oklahoma, Payne, Pottawatomie, Roger Mills, Stephens, Texas, Tillman, Washita, Woods, Woodward.

US Bankruptcy Court - Western District of Oklahoma

PACER: Sign-up number is 800-676-6856. Access fee is $.60 per minute. Case records are available back to May 1, 1992. Records are purged every six months. New civil records are available online after 1 dday.
Other Online Access: RACER is also available for records filed after January 1, 1995. Visit http://download.citrix.com to download the necessary software. Call the clerk's office for more information.
Oklahoma City Division Counties: Alfalfa, Beaver, Beckham, Blaine, Caddo, Canadian, Cimarron, Cleveland, Comanche, Cotton, Custer, Dewey, Ellis, Garfield, Garvin, Grady, Grant, Greer, Harmon, Harper, Jackson, Jefferson, Kay, Kingfisher, Kiowa, Lincoln, Logan, Major, McClain, Noble,Oklahoma, Payne, Pottawatomie, Roger Mills, Stephens, Texas, Tillman, Washita, Woods, Woodward.

Editor's Choice for Oklahoma

Here are some additional sites recommended for this state.

Constitution Text
http://oklegal.onenet.net/okcon/index.html
Sex Offenders Listing
www.kwtv.com/crime/sex_offenders/sex-offenders-map.htm

Capital:	Salem		Home Page
	Marion County		www.state.or.us
Time Zone:	PST	Attorney General	www.doj.state.or.us
Number of Counties:	36	Archives	http://arcweb.sos.state.or.us

State Level...Major Agencies

Criminal Records

Oregon State Police, Unit 11, Identification Services Section, PO Box 4395, Portland, OR 97208-4395 (Courier: 3772 Portland Rd NE, Bldg C, Salem, OR 97303); 503-378-3070, 503-378-2121 (Fax), 8AM-5PM.

www.osp.state.or.us

Online: A web based site is available for requesting and receiving criminal records. Use of this site is ONLY for high vol. requesters who must be pre-approved. Results are posted as "No Record" or "In Process" which means a record will be mailed in 14 days. Use the "open records" link to get into the proper site. Fee is $12.00 per record. Call 503-373-1808, ext 230 to receive the application, or visit the web site.

Corporation Records, Limited Partnership Records, Trademarks/Servicemarks, Fictitious Name, Assumed Name, Limited Liability Company Records

Corporation Division, Public Service Building, 255 Capital St NE, #151, Salem, OR 97310-1327; 503-986-2200, 503-378-4381 (Fax), 8AM-5PM.

Online: A commercial dial-up system is available. Call 503-229-5133 for details. Also, the complete database can be purchased with monthly updates via e-mail, call 503-986-2343.

Uniform Commercial Code, Federal Tax Liens, State Tax Liens

UCC Division, Secretary of State, 255 Capitol St NE, Suite 151, Salem, OR 97310-1327; 503-986-2200, 503-373-1166 (Fax).

www.sos.state.or.us/corporation/ucc/ucc.htm

Online: UCC index information can be obtained for free from the web site. You can search by debtor name or by lien number. You can also download forms from here.

Legislation Records

Oregon Legislative Assembly, State Capitol-Information Services, State Capitol, Rm 49, Salem, OR 97310; 503-986-1180 (Current Bill Information), 503-373-0701 (Archives), 503-373-1527 (Fax), 8AM-5PM.

www.leg.state.or.us

Online: Text and histories of measures can be found at the Internet site for no charge.

State Level...Occupational Licensing

Appraiser, Real Estate.. www.oda.state.or.us/aclb/search.html
Architect.. www.architect-board.state.or.us/A-B.htm
Architectural Firms .... www.architect-board.state.or.us/ARFirms.htm
Audiologist .... http://bspa.ohd.hr.state.or.us
Bakery.. www.oda.state.or.us/cgi/fm/food_safety/Search.html
Bank... www.cbs.state.or.us/external/dfcs/banking/regagent.htm
Building Official.. www.cbs.state.or.us/external/imd/database/bcd/licensing/index.html
Check & Money Order Seller .... www.oregondfcs.org/e_commerce/m_tran/m_tran.htm
Christmas Tree Grower....................................... www.oda.state.or.us/cgi/fm/nursery/Search.html
Collection Agency.. www.oregondfcs.org/ca/ca.htm
Construction Contractor/Subcontractor .... www.ccb.state.or.us/newq_start.htm
Consumer Finance Company.............................. www.cbs.state.or.us/external/dfcs/cf/cfdatabase/search_main.htm
Credit Service Organization .... www.oregondfcs.org/cso/cso.htm
Credit Union.. www.cbs.state.or.us/external/dfcs/cu/cuagents.htm
Dairy .... www.oda.state.or.us/cgi/fm/food_safety/Search.html
Debt Consolidation Agency............................... www.cbs.state.or.us/external/dfcs/dca/lic_dca.htm
Electrical Installation .... www.cbs.state.or.us/external/imd/database/bcd/licensing/index.html
Engineering Geologist.. www.open.org/~osbge/registrants.htm
Florist.. www.oda.state.or.us/cgi/fm/nursery/Search.html
Food Exporter.. www.oda.state.or.us/cgi/fm/food_safety/Search.html
Food Processing Facility/Storage Facility .... www.oda.state.or.us/cgi/fm/food_safety/Search.html
Geologist .... www.open.org/~osbge/registrants.htm
Greenhouse Grower of Herbaceous Plants .... www.oda.state.or.us/cgi/fm/nursery/Search.html
Inspector, Structural/Mechanical .... www.cbs.state.or.us/external/imd/database/bcd/licensing/index.html
Insurance Adjuster/Agent/Consultant .... www.cbs.state.or.us/external/imd/database/inslic/main.htm
Insurance Agency... www.cbs.state.or.us/external/imd/database/inslic/agency_main.htm
Insurance Company.. www.cbs.state.or.us/external/imd/database/inslic/comp_main.htm
Investment Advisor .... www.cbs.state.or.us/external/imd/database/lear/adviser_search_main.htm
Landscape Business .... www.ccb.state.or.us/lcbmenu.htm
Landscaper... www.oda.state.or.us/cgi/fm/nursery/Search.html
Limited Pump Installation Contractor .... www.cbs.state.or.us/external/imd/database/bcd/licensing/index.html
Limited Sign Contractor .... www.cbs.state.or.us/external/imd/database/bcd/licensing/index.html
Lobbyist... www.lobbyist.net/Oregon/ORELOB.htm
Manufactured Housing Construction .... www.cbs.state.or.us/external/imd/database/bcd/licensing/index.html
Massage Therapists.. http://pws.prserv.net/usinet.bholzma/LMTList.html
Medical Doctor/Surgeon.................................... www.docboard.org/or/df/search.htm
Money Transmitter... www.oregondfcs.org/e_commerce/m_tran/m_tran.htm
Mortgage Banker/Broker/Lender .... www.cbs.state.or.us/external/imd/database/lear/search_main.htm
Nursery Dealer... www.oda.state.or.us/cgi/fm/nursery/Search.html
Nursery Stock/Collectors of Native Plants .... www.oda.state.or.us/cgi/fm/nursery/Search.html
Optometrist.. www.odfinder.org/LicSearch.asp
Osteopathic Physician .... www.docboard.org/or/df/search.htm
Pawnbroker.. www.cbs.state.or.us/external/dfcs/pawn/pawnshop.htm
Plans Examiner.. www.cbs.state.or.us/external/imd/database/bcd/licensing/index.html
Plumber .... www.cbs.state.or.us/external/imd/database/bcd/licensing/index.html
Psychologist/ Psychologist Associate .... www.obpe.state.or.us/licensee_applicant.htm

Public Accountant-CPA...................................... www.boa.state.or.us/search.htm

Retail Food Establishment .... www.oda.state.or.us/cgi/fm/food_safety/Search.html

Speech Language Pathologist .... http://bspa.ohd.hr.state.or.us

Trust Company .... www.cbs.state.or.us/external/dfcs/banking/regagent.htm

Veterinarian.. www.oda.state.or.us/cgi/fm/vet_book/Search.html

County Level...Courts, Recorders & Assessors

Court Administrator, Supreme Court Building, 1163 State St, Salem, OR, 97310; 503-986-5500; www.ojd.state.or.us

Editor's Note: Online computer access is available through the Oregon Judicial Information Network (OJIN). OJIN Online includes almost all cases filed in the Oregon state courts. Generally, the OJIN database contains criminal, civil, small claims, probate, and some, but not all, juvenile records. However, it does not contain any records from municipal nor county courts. There is a one-time setup fee of $295.00, plus a monthly usage charge (minimum $10.00) based on transaction type, type of job, shift, and number of units/pages (which averages $10-13 per hour). For further information and/or a registration packet, write to: Oregon Judicial System, Information Systems Division, ATTN: Technical Support, 1163 State Street, Salem OR 97310, or call 800-858-9658.

Benton
Real Estate
www.co.benton.or.us

The County is developing a Geographic Information System Internet site for viewing property information at www.co.benton.or.us/irm/gis/GISpage.htm. A law enforcement case system may soon offer open case data.

Deschutes
Real Estate, Tax Assessor Records
http://recordings.co.deschutes.or.us

To access records on the Deschutes County "Assessor Inquiry System" web site, click on DIAL on the menu bar. Tax information, assessment, appraisal details, ownership, sales information, transaction histories, account histories, land use records, and lot numbers are available for no fee.

Lane
Assessor, Real Estate
Property records on the County Tax Map site are available at www.co.lane.or.us/taxmap/TaxMapSelect.asp.

Linn
Assessor, Real Estate
www.co.linn.or.us

Records on the County Property Records database are available free online at the web site.

Multnomah
Real Property
http://metromap.metro-region.org/public

Records on the County Metromap database are available free online at the web site. No name searching.

Tillamook
Assessor, Real Estate
www.co.tillamook.or.us/gov/clerk/default.htm

Assessment and taxation records on the County Property database are available free online at www.co.tillamook.or.us/Documents/Search/query.asp.

Washington
Real Estate
www.co.washington.or.us
Records on County GIS Intermap database are available free online at www.co.washington.or.us/gisaps/cfdocs/gisweb/par_2.htm.
General Recording Office information is available at www.co.washington.or.us/deptmts/at/recordng/record.htm.

Federal Courts in Oregon...

US District Court - District of Oregon

Home Page: www.ord.uscourts.gov
PACER: Sign-up number is 800-676-6856. Access fee is $.60 per minute. Case records are available back to September 1988. Records are purged never. New records are available online after 1 day.
Electronic Filing: Only law firms and practitioners may file cases electronically. Anyone can search online; however, the search results only include cases which were filed electronically. To search, visit http://ecf.ord.uscourts.gov/cgi-bin/PublicCaseFiled-Rpt.pl. Electronic filing information is available online at http://ecf.ord.uscourts.gov.
Eugene Division Counties: Benton, Coos, Deschutes, Douglas, Lane, Lincoln, Linn, Marion.
Medford Division Counties: Curry, Jackson, Josephine, Klamath, Lake. Court set up in April 1994; Cases prior to that time were tried in Eugene.
Portland Division Counties: Baker, Clackamas, Clatsop, Columbia, Crook, Gilliam, Grant, Harney, Hood River, Jefferson, Malheur, Morrow, Multnomah, Polk, Sherman, Tillamook, Umatilla, Union, Wallowa, Wasco, Washinton, Wheeler, Yamhill.

US Bankruptcy Court - District of Oregon

Home Page: www.orb.uscourts.gov
PACER: Sign-up number is 800-676-6856. Access fee is $.60 per minute. Toll-free access: 800-610-9315. Local access: 503-326-5650. Case records are available back to 1989. Records are purged every six months. New records are available online after 1 day.
PACER Internet Access: http://pacer.orb.uscourts.gov.
Eugene Division Counties: Benton, Coos, Curry, Deschutes, Douglas, Jackson, Josephine, Klamath, Lake, Lane, Lincoln, Linn, Marion.
Portland Division Counties: Baker, Clackamas, Clatsop, Columbia, Crook, Gilliam, Grant, Harney, Hood River, Jefferson, Malheur, Morrow, Multnomah, Polk, Sherman, Tillamook, Umatilla, Union, Wallowa, Wasco, Washington, Wheeler, Yamhill.

Editor's Choice for Oregon

Here are some additional sites recommended for this state.

Genealogical Information Database
http://159.121.115.13/databases/searchgeneal.html
Legislative Measures & Statutes Search Form
www.leg.state.or.us:8765/
State Employees Database
www.state.or.us/cgi-bin/employee.html
Statutes (Revised) Text
http://landru.leg.state.or.us/ors/

Capital:	Harrisburg Dauphin County	Home Page	www.state.pa.us
Time Zone:	EST	Attorney General	www.attorneygeneral.gov
Number of Counties:	67	Archives	www.phmc.state.pa.us

State Level...Major Agencies

Criminal Records

State Police Central Repository, 1800 Elmerton Ave, Harrisburg, PA 17110-9758; 717-783-9944, 717-783-9973, 717-705-8840 (Fax), 8:15AM-4:15PM.

www.pwp.state.pa.us

Record checks are available for approved agencies through the Internet on the Pennsylvania Access to Criminal Histories (PATCH). This is a commercial system, the same $10.00 fee per name applies. Go to http://patch.statep.pa.us or call 717-705-1768.

Driver Records

Department of Transportation, Driver Record Services, PO Box 68695, Harrisburg, PA 17106-8695 (Courier: 1101 S Front Street, Harrisburg, PA 17104); 717-391-6190, 800-932-4600 (In-state only), 7:30AM-4:30PM.

www.dmv.state.pa.us

Online: The online system is available to high volume requesters only. Fee is $5.00 per record. Call 717-787-7154 for more information. The sale of records over the Internet is strictly forbidden.

Legislation Records

Pennsylvania General Assembly, Legislative Reference Bureau, Main Capitol Bldg, Room 641, Harrisburg, PA 17120; 717-787-2342 (History Room), 717-787-5320 (House Bills), 717-787-6732 (Senate Bills), House-8:30AM-4:30PM/Senate-8:30AM-5PM.

www.legis.state.pa.us

Online: Free access to bill text is available at the Electronic Bill Room found at the web page by selecting "Session Information."

State Level...Occupational Licensing

Athletic Agent.................. www.dos.state.pa.us/sac/agents.html
Bank............................... www.banking.state.pa.us/PA_Exec/Banking/organiz.htm#exambureau
Credit Union.................... http://sites.state.pa.us/PA_Exec/Banking/resource/cufrm.pdf
Education Specialist......... http://tcp.ed.state.pa.us/tcsmainJS.asp
Insurance Company.......... www.insurance.state.pa.us/html/licensed.html
Lobbyist........................... www.lobbyist.net/Pennsylv/PENLOB.htm
Optometrist...................... www.arbo.org/nodb2000/licsearch.asp
Savings Association .... www.banking.state.pa.us/PA_Exec/Banking/organiz.htm#exambureau
Trust Company .... www.banking.state.pa.us/PA_Exec/Banking/organiz.htm#exambureau

County Level...Courts, Recorders & Assessors

Administrative Office of Pennsylvania Courts, PO Box 719, Mechanicsburg, PA, 17055; 717-795-2000; www.courts.state.pa.us

Editor's Note: The state's 550 magisterial district courts are served by a statewide, automated case management system; online access to the case management system is not available. However, public access to statutorily authorized information is available from the Special Courts, filing offices of Appellate Courts, and from the AOPC. The courts are considering ways to implement a unified, statewide system in the criminal division of the Courts of Common Pleas.

                 The Infocon County Access System provides direct dial-up access to court and real estate record information for 15 counties - Armstrong, Bedford, Blair, Butler, Clarion, Clinton, Erie, Franklin, Huntingdon, Juaniata, Lawrence, Mercer, Mifflin, Pike, and Potter. Set up entails a $25.00 base set-up fee plus $25.00 per county. The monthly usage fee minimum is $25.00, plus time charges. For Information, call Infocon at 814-472-6066.

Allegheny
Civil Cases
www.county.allegheny.pa.us
Online access to prothonotary civil records is available free at http://prothonotary.county.allegheny.pa.us/allegheny/welcome.htm.
Search by case number.
Assessor
www2.county.allegheny.pa.us/realestate/
Online access to the certified values database is available free at the web site.

Armstrong
Real Estate, Tax Liens, Marriage, Probate Records
Access is available through a private company. For information, call Infocon at 814-472-6066.

Beaver
Real Estate
www.co.beaver.pa.us
Online access to the Recorder's digitized images database is to be available free at www.co.beaver.pa.us/Recorder/index.htm.
Historical documents will be added.

Bedford
Civil Cases, Criminal Records, Tax Liens, Real Estate, Assessor, Probate, Marriage Records
www.bedford.net/regrec/home.html
Access is available through a private company. For information, call Infocon at 814-472-6066.

Berks
Civil Cases, Vital Records, Probate
www.berksrecofdeeds.com
Online access to the Registry of Wills' databases is available free at www.berksregofwills.com including county marriage, estate, birth and death records. Estate and marriage records are current.

Blair
Civil Cases, Criminal Records, Tax Liens, Real Estate, Marriage, Probate Records
Access is available through a private company. For information, call Infocon at 814-472-6066.

Bucks
Criminal Records, Assessor, Real Estate, Tax Lien, Probate Records
Access to County records requires a Sprint ID number and payment of $24 annual Sprint fee, plus $.60 per minute of use. Records date back to 1980. Lending agency and Register of Wills data is available. For information, contact Jack Morris at 215-348-6579.

Butler
Criminal Records, Marriage, Probate Records
Access is available through a private company. For information, call Infocon at 814-472-6066.

Chester
Criminal Records, Assessor, Tax Lien, Real Estate, Vital Statistics, Probate Records
www.chesco.org/gengovt.html
Internet access to countywide records including court records requires a sign-up and credit card payment. Application fee is $50. There is a $10.00 per month minimum (no charge for no activity); and $.10 each transaction beyond 100. Sign-up and/or logon at http://epin.chesco.org. County data is also available as reports, labels, magnetic tape, and diskette. Also, genealogical and older vital statistics are available free at www.chesco.org/archives.

Clarion
Criminal Records, Tax Liens, Assessor, Real Estate, Voter Registration Records
Access is available through a private company. For information, call Infocon at 814-472-6066.

Clinton
Civil Cases, Criminal Records, Tax Liens, Real Estate, Probate Records
Access is available through a private company. For information, call Infocon at 814-472-6066.

Delaware
Civil Cases, Criminal Records, Assessor, Deeds, Real Estate Records
www.co.delaware.pa.us
Online access to the public access system is available free - temporarily - at www2.co.delaware.pa.us/pa/default.htm. No criminal records. For more information, call 610-891-4675. Secondly, access to County online records is free by dialing 610-566-1507. Records go back to 1990. For information, call Data Processing at 610-891-4675. Also, property tax records are available free on the Internet at http://taxrecords.com.

Erie
Criminal Records, Real Estate, Marriage, Probate
www.eriecountygov.org/cor
Access is available through a private company. For information, call Infocon at 814-472-6066.

Franklin
Real Estate, Tax Liens, Probate Records
Access is available through a private company. For information, call Infocon at 814-472-6066.

Huntingdon
Civil Cases, Criminal Records, Tax Liens, Real Estate, Marriage, Probate
Access is available through a private company. For information, call Infocon at 814-472-6066.

Juniata
Real Estate, Marriage, Probate
Access is available through a private company. For information, call Infocon at 814-472-6066.

Lancaster
Civil Cases, Criminal Records, Assessor, Real Estate, Tax Lien Records
www.co.lancaster.pa.us
Two online resources are available. Access to County online records requires $25 monthly plus $.18 per minute of use. This system holds 5 years data. It uses Windows. Lending agency and Register of Wills information is available. For information, contact Nancy Malloy at 717-299-8252. Assessor records on the County GIS database are available free on the Internet at www.co.lancaster.pa.us/GIS/disclaimer.html. Click on "Lancaster. Search" then choose municipality; then "Go." Search by parcel number, owner name, address, or map.

Lawrence
Civil Cases, Criminal Records, Tax Liens, Real Estate, Assessor, Marriage, Probate
Access is available through a private company. For information, call Infocon at 814-472-6066.

Lehigh
Criminal Records, Assessor, Real Estate, Tax Lien, Marriage Records
www.lccpa.org/
Access to the countywide criminal online system is open 24 hours daily; there are set-up and monthly usage fees. Records go back to 1984. Lending agency information is available. Call Lehigh City Computer Svcs Dept at 610-782-3286 for more information.

Mercer
Criminal Records, Tax Liens, Real Estate, Assessor
www.mcc.co.mercer.pa.us/LOCRULES.htm
Access is available through a private company. For information, call Infocon at 814-472-6066.

Mifflin
Civil Cases, Criminal Records, Tax Liens, Real Estate, Assessor, Probate Records
Access is available through a private company. For information, call Infocon at 814-472-6066.

Montgomery
Criminal Records
www.montcopa.org
Court and other records are available free online at www1.montcopa.org. The system is experimental and may or may not be adapted full time. A pay service, offering remote dial-up, is also available. For info, call the helpdesk at 610-292-4931. There is a $10 registration fee plus $.15 per minute of usage.

Assessor, Real Estate, Tax Liens
www.montcopa.org
Two online sources are available. Access to County online records requires a $10 sign up fee plus $.15 per minute of use. Records date back to 1990. Lending agency and prothonotary information are available on the system. For information or to sign up, contact Berkheimer Assoc. at 800-360-8989. Also, records on the County PIR database are available free on the Internet at www.montcopa.org/reassessment/boahome0.htm. Click on "Instructions" to learn how to use the search features, and then search by parcel number, name, address, or municipality.

Philadelphia
Civil Cases
Access to 1st Judicial District Civil Trial records are available free online at http://dns2.phila.gov:8080. Search by name, judgment and docket information.

Pike
Civil Cases, Criminal Records, Tax Liens, Probate
Access is available through a private company. For information, call Infocon at 814-472-6066.

Potter
Civil Cases, Criminal Records, Real Estate, Tax Liens, Assessor, Probate Records
Access is available through a private company. For information, call Infocon at 814-472-6066.

Washington
Civil Cases, Criminal Records, Assessor, Real Estate Records
www.co.washington.pa.us/
Recordings are available on the county online system. Records date back to 1952. Register of Wills information and lending agency information is also available. For information, call 724-228-6766. Court records are to be online as of Summer, 2001.

Westmoreland
Criminal Records, Real Estate, Tax Lien Records
The online system costs $100 setup plus $20 per month minimum fee, and a per minute charge of $.50 after 40 minutes. The system also includes civil, criminal, prothonotary indexes. Recorder information dates back to 1957. No tax lien information is available, only UCC liens. For information, call 724-830-3874.

York
Criminal Records
Access to the remote online system is available for criminal records from mid-1988 forward and civil cases. Usage fee is $.75 per minute plus a $200.00 setup fee. For more information, call 717-771-9321 or 717-771-9235.

Property Information
www.york-county.org
Parcel numbers are available to the public on the website under "Assessment Office."

Federal Courts in Pennsylvania...

US District Court - Eastern District of Pennsylvania
Home Page: www.paed.uscourts.gov
PACER: Sign-up number is 215-597-5710. Access fee is $.60 per minute. Toll-free access: 800-458-2993. Local access: 215-597-0258. Case records are available back to July 1, 1990. Records are purged never. New records are available online after 1 day.
PACER Internet Access: http://pacer.paed.uscourts.gov.
Electronic Filing: Anyone may submit civil and criminal documents in electronic form; however, you must first fill out the application available on the web site. Electronic filing information is available online at www.paed.uscourts.gov/us01003.shtml.
Opinions Online: Court opinions are available online at www.paed.uscourts.gov/contents.shtml.
Allentown/Reading Division Counties: Berks, Lancaster, Lehigh, Northampton, Schuylkill.
Philadelphia Division Counties: Bucks, Chester, Delaware, Montgomery, Philadelphia.

US Bankruptcy Court - Eastern District of Pennsylvania
Home Page: www.paeb.uscourts.gov
PACER: Sign-up number is 800-676-6856. Access fee is $.60 per minute. Toll-free access: 888-381-2921. Local access: 215-597-3501. Case records are available back to 1988. Records are purged every 6 months. New civil records are available online after 1 day.
PACER Internet Access: http://pacer.paeb.uscourts.gov.
Philadelphia Division Counties: Bucks, Chester, Delaware, Montgomery, Philadelphia.
Reading Division Counties: Berks, Lancaster, Lehigh, Northampton, Schuylkill.

US District Court - Middle District of Pennsylvania

Home Page: www.pamd.uscourts.gov
PACER: Sign-up number is 800-676-6856. Access fee is $.60 per minute. Toll-free access: 800-658-8381. Local access: 570-347-8286, 570-341-0569. Case records available back to May 1989. Records are purged never. New records available online after 1 day.
PACER Internet Access: http://pacer.pamd.uscourts.gov.
Harrisburg Division Counties: Adams, Cumberland, Dauphin, Franklin, Fulton, Huntingdon, Juniata, Lebanon, Mifflin, York.
Scranton Division Counties: Bradford, Carbon, Lackawanna, Luzerne, Monroe, Pike, Susquehanna, Wayne, Wyoming.
Williamsport Division Counties: Cameron, Centre, Clinton, Columbia, Lycoming, Montour, Northumberland, Perry, Potter, Snyder, Sullivan, Tioga, Union.

US Bankruptcy Court - Middle District of Pennsylvania

Home Page: www.paeb.uscourts.gov
PACER: Sign-up number is 800-676-6856. Access fee is $.60 per minute. Toll-free access: 800-882-6899. Local access: 717-782-3727. Use of PC Anywhere v4.0 suggested. Case records are available back to August 1986. Records are purged never. New civil records are available online after 1 day.
PACER Internet Access: http://pacer.paeb.uscourts.gov.
Harrisburg Division Counties: Adams, Centre, Cumberland, Dauphin, Franklin, Fulton, Huntingdon, Juniata, Lebanon, Mifflin, Montour, Northumberland, Perry, Schuylkill, Snyder, Union, York.
Wilkes-Barre Division Counties: Bradford, Cameron, Carbon, Clinton, Columbia, Lackawanna, Luzerne, Lycoming, Monroe, Pike, Potter, Schuylkill, Sullivan, Susquehanna, Tioga, Wayne, Wyoming.

US District Court - Western District of Pennsylvania

Home Page: www.pawd.uscourts.gov
PACER: Sign-up number is 800-676-6856. Access fee is $.60 per minute. Toll-free access: 800-770-4745. Local access: 412-644-6374. Case records are available back to 1989. Records are purged never. New records are available online after 1 day.
PACER Internet Access: http://pacer.pawd.uscourts.gov.
Erie Division Counties: Crawford, Elk, Erie, Forest, McKean, Venango, Warren.
Johnstown Division Counties: Bedford, Blair, Cambria, Clearfield, Somerset.
Pittsburgh Division Counties: Allegheny, Armstrong, Beaver, Butler, Clarion, Fayette, Greene, Indiana, Jefferson, Lawrence, Mercer, Washington, Westmoreland.

US Bankruptcy Court - Western District of Pennsylvania

Home Page: www.pawb.uscourts.gov
PACER: Sign-up number is 800-676-6856. Access fee is $.60 per minute. Toll-free access: 800-795-2829. Local access: 412-355-2588. Case records are available back to 1991. Records are purged every six months. New civil records available online after 1 day.
PACER Internet Access: http://pacer.pawb.uscourts.gov.
Erie Division Counties: Clarion, Crawford, Elk, Erie, Forest, Jefferson, McKean, Mercer, Venango, Warren.
Pittsburgh Division Counties: Allegheny, Armstrong, Beaver, Bedford, Blair, Butler, Cambria, Clearfield, Fayette, Greene, Indiana, Lawrence, Somerset, Washington, Westmoreland.

Editor's Choice for Pennsylvania

Constitution Text
www.state.pa.us/PA_Constitution.html
Government Officials & Employees Directory
http://papower.state.pa.us/PAPower/Blue/Search.asp
Inmates Database
www.cor.state.pa.us/locator.htm
Local Government Officials Contact Information Database
http://papower.state.pa.us/PAPower/Blue/Search.asp

Rhode Island

Capital: Providence   Home Page   www.state.ri.us
                Providence County

Time Zone: EST   Attorney General   www.riag.state.ri.us

Number of Counties: 5   Archives   www.state.ri.us/archives

State Level...Major Agencies

Corporation Records, Fictitious Name, Limited Partnerships, Limited Liability Company Records, Limited Liability Partnerships, Not For Profit Entities

Secretary of State, Corporations Division, 100 N Main St, Providence, RI 02903-1335; 401-222-3040, 401-222-1356 (Fax), 8:30AM-4:30PM.

www.sec.state.ri.us

Online: Search both active and inactive entities through the web "Corporations Database Page" at www.corps.state.ri.us. Forms are also available from the web site.

Legislation Records

Secretary of State, State House, Room 38, Public Information Center, Providence, RI 02903; 401-222-3983 (Bill Status Only), 401-222-2473 (State Library), 401-222-1356 (Fax), 8:30AM-4:30PM.

www.sec.state.ri.us

Online: The site search http://dirac.rilin.state.ri.us/BillStatus/webclass1.asp provides two means to search enactments and measures by keywords or bill numbers.

State Level...Occupational Licensing

Acupuncturist.. www.health.state.ri.us/l2k/license.htm
Asbestos Abatement Worker www.health.state.ri.us/l2k/license.htm
Athletic Trainer www.health.state.ri.us/l2k/license.htm
Audiologist www.health.state.ri.us/l2k/license.htm
Barber.. www.health.state.ri.us/l2k/license.htm
Cable Installer.. www.crb.state.ri.us/search.asp
Chimney Sweep .... www.crb.state.ri.us/search.asp
Chiropractor.. www.health.state.ri.us/l2k/license.htm

Clinical Histologic Technician http://63.72.31.182
Clinical Lab Scientist/Lab Technician http://63.72.31.182
Clinical Lab Scientist/Election Microscopy http://63.72.31.182
Clinical Lab Scientist-Cytogenetic..................... http://63.72.31.182
Contractor, Residential Building .... www.crb.state.ri.us/search.asp
Dentist.. www.health.state.ri.us/l2k/license.htm
Dietitian/Nutritionist....................................... www.health.state.ri.us/l2k/license.htm
Electrologist.. www.health.state.ri.us/l2k/license.htm
Embalmer www.health.state.ri.us/l2k/license.htm
Emergency Medical Technician......................... www.health.state.ri.us/l2k/license.htm
Funeral Director.. www.health.state.ri.us/l2k/license.htm
Hearing Aid Dispenser..................................... www.health.state.ri.us/l2k/license.htm
Lobbyist... www.lobbyist.net/RhodeIsl/RHOLOB.htm
Marriage Therapist www.health.state.ri.us/l2k/license.htm
Medical Doctor .... www.docboard.org/ri/df/search.htm
Midwife... www.health.state.ri.us/l2k/license.htm
Notary Public.. www.corps.state.ri.us/notaries/notaries.htm
Nurse/ Nursing Assistant................................. www.health.state.ri.us/l2k/license.htm
Nursing Home Administrator www.health.state.ri.us/l2k/license.htm
Occupational Therapist www.health.state.ri.us/l2k/license.htm
Optometrist... www.arbo.org/nodb2000/licsearch.asp
Osteopathic Physician .... www.docboard.org/ri/df/search.htm
Pharmacy.. www.health.state.ri.us/l2k/license.htm
Physical Therapist... www.health.state.ri.us/l2k/license.htm
Podiatrist www.health.state.ri.us/l2k/license.htm
Prosthetist... www.health.state.ri.us/l2k/license.htm
Psychologist.. www.health.state.ri.us/l2k/license.htm
Respiratory Care Practitioner www.health.state.ri.us/l2k/license.htm
Sanitarian www.health.state.ri.us/l2k/license.htm
Security Alarm Installer .... www.crb.state.ri.us/search.asp
Social Worker www.health.state.ri.us/l2k/license.htm
Speech Pathologist www.health.state.ri.us/l2k/license.htm
Tattoo Artist www.health.state.ri.us/l2k/license.htm
Underground Sprinkler Installer .... www.crb.state.ri.us/search.asp
Veterinarian.. www.health.state.ri.us/l2k/license.htm

County Level...Courts, Recorders & Assessors

Court Administrator, Supreme Court, 250 Benefit St, Providence, RI, 02903; 401-222-3272; www.courts.state.ri.us

Editor's Note: The Superior (civil, criminal, family) and Appellate courts are online internally for court personnel only. There are plans to place criminal record data on the Internet. For more information, call Tracy Williams at 401-222-3000.

Exeter Town in Washington County

Assessor

www.town.exeter.ri.us

Records on the Town of Exeter assessor database are available free online at http://140.239.211.227/Exeter_RI.

Johnston Town in Providence County

Probate

http://johnston-ri.com/probate.asp

Probate records on the Town of Johnson lookup database are available free online at the web site.

Middletown Town in Newport County

Assessor

Records on the Town of Middletown assessor database are available free online at http://140.239.211.227/MiddletownRI.

Portsmouth Town in Newport County

Assessor

Records on the Town of Portsmouth assessor database are available free online at http://140.239.211.227/PortsmouthRI.

South Kingstown Town in Washington County

Real Estate, Assessor

www.southkingstownri.com

Online access to the property values database is available free at www.southkingstownri.com/code/propvalues_search.cfm.

Federal Courts in Rhode Island...

US District Court - District of Rhode Island

PACER: Sign-up number is 800-676-6856. Access fee is $.60 per minute. Toll-free access: 888-421-6861. Local access: 401-528-5145. Case records are available back to December 1988. Records are purged never. New records are available online after 2 days.
Providence Division Counties: All counties in Rhode Island.

US Bankruptcy Court - District of Rhode Island

Home Page: www.rib.uscourts.gov
PACER: Sign-up number is 800-676-6856. Access fee is $.60 per minute. Toll-free access: 800-610-9310. Local access: 401-528-4062. Case records are available back to 1990. Records are purged every three years. New civil records available online after 1 day.
PACER Internet Access: http://204.17.81.145/cgi-bin/webbill/bkplog.html.
Providence Division Counties: All counties in Rhode Island.

Editor's Choice for Rhode Island

Here are some additional sites recommended for this state.

Constitution Text
www.sec.state.ri.us/rihist/riconst.htm
State Police Homepage
www.risp.state.ri.us/
State Police Phone Numbers Listing
www.risp.state.ri.us/directo.htm
Statutes Text
www.rilin.state.ri.us/Statutes/Statutes.html

South Carolina

Capital:	Columbia Richland County	Home Page	www.state.sc.us
Time Zone:	EST	Attorney General	www.scattorneygeneral.org
Number of Counties:	46	Archives	www.state.sc.us/scdah

State Level...Major Agencies

Criminal Records

South Carolina Law Enforcement Division (SLED), Criminal Records Section, PO Box 21398, Columbia, SC 29221 (Courier: 4400 Broad River Rd, Columbia, SC 29210); 803-896-7043, 803-896-7022 (Fax), 8:30AM-5PM.

www.sled.state.sc.us

Online: SLED offers commercial access to criminal record history from 1960 forward on the web site. Fees are $25.00 per screening or $8.00 if for a charitable organization. Credit card ordering accepted. Visit the web site or call 803-896-7219 for details.

Corporation Records, Trademarks/Servicemarks, Limited Partnerships, Limited Liability Company Records

Corporation Division, Capitol Complex, PO Box 11350, Columbia, SC 29211 (Courier: Edgar A. Brown Bldg, Room 525, Columbia, SC 29201); 803-734-2158, 803-734-2164 (Fax), 8:30PM-5PM.

Online: Their program is called Direct Access. Information available includes corporate names, registered agents and addresses, date of original filings, and dates of amendments or merger filings. The system is open 24 hours daily and there are no fees. The system permits the retrieval of documents by fax return. For more information, call Jody Steigerwalt at 803-734-2345.

Uniform Commercial Code

UCC Division, Secretary of State, PO Box 11350, Columbia, SC 29211 (Courier: Edgar Brown Bldg, 1205 Pendelton St #525, Columbia, SC 29201); 803-734-1961, 803-734-2164 (Fax), 8:30AM-5PM.

www.scsos.com/ucc.htm

Online: "Direct Access" is open 24 hours daily, there are no fees. Inquiry is by debtor name. The system provides for copies to be faxed automatically. Call 803-734-2345 for registration information.

Driver License Information, Driver Records

Division of Motor Vehicles, Driver Records Section, PO Box 1498, Columbia, SC 29216-0028 (Courier: 955 Park St, Columbia, SC 29201); 803-737-4000, 803-737-1077 (Fax), 8:30AM-5PM.

www.state.sc.us/dps/dmv

Online: The online system offers basic driver data, for a 3 year or a 10 year record. This is a single inquiry process. Network charges will be incurred as well as initial set-up and a security deposit. The system is up between 8 AM and 7 PM. Fee is $2.00 per record. Access is through the AAMVAnet (IBMIN), which requesters much "join." Call Libby Thomasson at 803-737-1546 for further information.

Legislation Records

South Carolina Legislature, 937 Assembly St Rm 220, Columbia, SC 29201; 803-734-2060, 803-734-2145 (older bills), 9AM-5PM. www.leginfo.state.sc.us

Online: Bill text and status data can be found at the web site.

State Level...Occupational Licensing

Accounting Practitioner-AP http://167.7.126.243/Lookup/Cpa.asp
Animal Health Technician http://167.7.126.243/lookup/vet.asp
Architect http://167.7.126.243/Lookup/Architects.asp
Architecture Partnership/Corporation http://167.7.126.243/Lookup/Architects.asp
Attorney .... www.scbar.org/lawyer_directory.asp
Auctioneer http://167.7.126.243/Lookup/Auctioneers.asp
Audiologist http://167.7.126.243/Lookup/Speech.asp
Barber/ Barber Instructor http://167.7.126.243/lookup/barbers.asp
Chiropractor http://167.7.126.243/lookup/Chiropractic.asp
Contractor, General & Mechanical http://167.7.126.243/Lookup/Contractors.asp
Cosmetologist http://167.7.126.243/lookup/cosmetology.asp
Dentist http://167.7.126.243/Lookup/Dentistry.asp
Engineer http://167.7.126.243/Lookup/Engineers.asp
Forester http://167.7.126.243/Lookup/Foresters.asp
Geologist http://167.7.126.243/Lookup/Geologists.asp
Hair Care Specialist http://167.7.126.243/lookup/barbers.asp
Landscape Architect .... www.dnr.state.sc.us/water/envaff/prolicense/prolicense.html
Lobbyist .... www.lpitr.state.sc.us/reports/ethrpt.htm
Manicurist http://167.7.126.243/lookup/barbers.asp
Manufactured House Manufacturer http://167.7.126.243/Lookup/Mh.asp
Marriage & Family Therapist http://167.7.126.243/lookup/Counselors.asp
Medical Doctor http://167.7.126.243/Lookup/Medical.asp
Nurse/ LPN Nurse http://167.7.126.243/lookup/nurses.asp
Occupational Therapist/Assistant http://167.7.126.243/Lookup/OT.asp
Optician http://167.7.126.243/Lookup/Opticians.asp
Optometrist http://167.7.126.243/Lookup/Optometry.asp
Pharmacist/Pharmacy Store http://167.7.126.243/lookup/pharmacy.asp
Physical Therapist http://167.7.126.243/Lookup/PT.asp
Podiatrist http://167.7.126.243/Lookup/Podiatry.asp
Professional Counselor http://167.7.126.243/lookup/Counselors.asp
Psycho-Educational Specialist http://167.7.126.243/lookup/Counselors.asp
Psychologist http://167.7.126.243/Lookup/SW.asp
Public Accountant-CPA http://167.7.126.243/Lookup/Cpa.asp
Residential Home Builder http://167.7.126.243/Lookup/ResidentialBuilders.asp
Shampoo Assistant http://167.7.126.243/lookup/barbers.asp
Social Worker http://167.7.126.243/Lookup/SW.asp
Soil Classifier .... www.dnr.state.sc.us/water/envaff/prolicense/prolicense.html
Speech-Language Pathologist http://167.7.126.243/Lookup/Speech.asp
Surveyor http://167.7.126.243/Lookup/Engineers.asp
Veterinarian http://167.7.126.243/lookup/vet.asp

County Level...Courts, Recorders & Assessors

Court Administration, 1015 Sumter St, 2nd Floor, Columbia, SC, 29201; 803-734-1800; www.judicial.state.sc.us

Editor's Note: The Judicial Department is developing a statewide court case management system. Only Charleston County offers Internet access to court records at present.

Beaufort
Property Records, Assessor
www.co.beaufort.sc.us
Online access to the public records search database is available free online at http://rodweb.co.beaufort.sc.us; also, search county property information at the GIS mapping database at http://maps.co.beaufort.sc.us. A fuller records subscription service requiring registration, fees, and logon is under development.

Charleston
Civil Cases, Criminal Records
www3.charlestoncounty.org
Access to civil records (from 1988 forward), judgments and lis pendens are available free online at www3.charlestoncounty.org/connect. The Internet offers access to records from 04/92 forward. Search by name or case number. There is no fee.

Greenville
Real Property
www.greenvillecounty.org
Records on the Real Property Search database are available free online at www.greenvillecounty.org/vrealpr24/clrealprop.asp.

Greenwood
Property Records
www.akanda.com/grnwood
Records on the County Parcel Search database are available free online at www.akanda.com/grnwood/Search/search.htm. An interactive map is included.

Lexington
Tax Assessor
www.lex-co.com/my_lex.html
Online access to county Reassessment Information is available free at www.lex-co.com/my_lex.html. Click on "Assessment Information."

Federal Courts in South Carolina...

US District Court - District of South Carolina

Home Page: www.scd.uscourts.gov
PACER: Sign-up number is 800-676-6856. Access fee is $.60 per minute. Toll-free access: 800-831-6162. Local access: 803-765-5871. Case records are available back to January 1990. Records are purged never. New records are available online after 1 day.
PACER Internet Access: http://pacer.scd.uscourts.gov.
Opinions Online: Court opinions are available online at www.law.sc.edu/dsc/dsc.htm.
Anderson Division Counties: Anderson, Oconee, Pickens.
Beaufort Division Counties: Beaufort, Hampton, Jasper.
Charleston Division Counties: Berkeley, Charleston, Clarendon, Colleton, Dorchester, Georgetown.
Columbia Division Counties: Kershaw, Lee, Lexington, Richland, Sumter.
Florence Division Counties: Chesterfield, Darlington, Dillon, Florence, Horry, Marion, Marlboro, Williamsburg.
Greenville Division Counties: Greenville, Laurens.
Greenwood Division Counties: Abbeville, Aiken, Allendale, Bamberg, Barnwell, Calhoun, Edgefield, Fairfield, Greenwood, Lancaster, McCormick, Newberry, Orangeburg, Saluda.
Spartanburg Division Counties: Cherokee, Chester, Spartanburg, Union, York.

US Bankruptcy Court - District of South Carolina

Home Page: www.scb.uscourts.gov
PACER: Sign-up number is 800-676-6856. Access fee is $.60 per minute. Toll-free access: 800-410-2988. Local access: 803-765-5965. Case records are available back to November 1988. Records are purged never. New civil records are available online after 1 day.
PACER Internet Access: http://pacer.scb.uscourts.gov.
Columbia Division Counties: All counties in South Carolina.

Editor's Choice for South Carolina

Here are some additional sites recommended for this state.

Constitution Text
www.lpitr.state.sc.us/reports/sccnst00.htm
Sex Offenders Database
www.scattorneygeneral.com/public/registry.html

Capital:	Pierre Hughes County	Home Page	www.state.sd.us
Time Zone:	CST/MST	Attorney General	www.state.sd.us/attorney/ attorney.html
Number of Counties:	66	Archives	www.state.sd.us/deca/ cultural/archives.htm

State Level...Major Agencies

Uniform Commercial Code, Federal Tax Liens

UCC Division, Secretary of State, 500 East Capitol, Pierre, SD 57501-5077; 605-773-4422, 605-773-4550 (Fax), 8AM-5PM.

www.state.sd.us/sos/sos.htm

Online: Dakota Fast File is the filing and searching service available from the web site. This is a commercial service that requires registration and a $360 fee per year. A certified search is also available.

Vital Statistics

South Dakota Department of Health, Vital Records, 600 E Capitol, Pierre, SD 57501-2536; 605-773-4961, 605-773-5683 (Fax), 8AM-5PM.

www.state.sd.us/doh/VitalRec/index.htm

Online: You can search free at the web site for birth records over 100 years old. You can order recent (less than 100 years) birth records at the web site, for a fee.

Driver Records

Dept of Commerce & Regulation, Office of Driver Licensing, 118 W Capitol, Pierre, SD 57501; 605-773-6883, 605-773-3018 (Fax), 8AM-5PM.

www.state.sd.us/dcr/dl/sddriver.htm

The system is open for batch requests 24 hours a day. There is a minimum of 250 requests daily. It generally takes 10 minutes to process a batch. The current fee is $4.00 per record and there are some start-up costs. For more information, call 605-773-6883.

Legislation Records

South Dakota Legislature, Capitol Bldg - Legislative Research Council, 500 E Capitol Ave, Pierre, SD 57501; 605-773-3251, 605-773-4576 (Fax), 8AM-5PM.

http://legis.state.sd.us

Online: Information is available at their web site at no charge. The site is very thorough and has enrolled version of bills.

State Level...Occupational Licensing

Animal Remedy	www.state.sd.us/doa/das/hp-af-ar.htm
Architect	www.state.sd.us/dcr/engineer/Roster/index.cfm
Assessor	www.state.sd.us/dcr/engineer/Roster/index.cfm
Auctioneer	www.state.sd.us/dcr/realestate/roster/index.cfm
Chiropractor	prill@mitchell.com
Counselor	www.state.sd.us/dcr/counselor/roster.htm
Engineer	www.state.sd.us/dcr/engineer/Roster/index.cfm
Engineer-Petroleum Environmental	www.state.sd.us/dcr/engineer/Roster/index.cfm
Fertilizer	www.state.sd.us/doa/das/hp-fert.htm
Home Inspector	www.state.sd.us/dcr/realestate/roster/index.cfm
Landscape Architect	www.state.sd.us/dcr/engineer/Roster/index.cfm
Lobbyist	www.lobbyist.net/SouthDak/SOULOB.htm
Marriage & Family Therapist	www.state.sd.us/dcr/counselor/roster.htm
Optometrist	www.odfinder.org/LicSearch.asp
Pesticide Applicator	www.state.sd.us/doa/das
Pesticide Dealer	www.state.sd.us/doa/das
Petroleum Release Remedictor	www.state.sd.us/dcr/engineer/Roster/index.cfm
Plumber	www.state.sd.us/dcr/plumbing/
Real Estate Broker/Salesperson	www.state.sd.us/dcr/realestate/roster/index.cfm
Real Estate Property Manager	www.state.sd.us/dcr/realestate/roster/index.cfm
Real Estate Time Share	www.state.sd.us/dcr/realestate/roster/index.cfm
Remediator	www.state.sd.us/dcr/engineer/Roster/index.cfm
Surveyor	www.state.sd.us/dcr/engineer/Roster/index.cfm
Waste Water Collection System Operator	www.state.sd.us/denr/databases/operator/index.cfm
Waste Water Treatment Plant Operator	www.state.sd.us/denr/databases/operator/index.cfm
Water Distributor	www.state.sd.us/denr/databases/operator/index.cfm
Water Treatment Plant Operator	www.state.sd.us/denr/databases/operator/index.cfm

County Level...Courts, Recorders & Assessors

State Court Administrator, State Capitol Building, 500 E Capitol Av, Pierre, SD, 57501; 605-773-3474; www.state.sd.us/state/judicial

Editor's Note: There is no statewide online access computer system currently available. Larger courts are being placed on computer systems at a rate of 4 to 5 courts per year. Access is intended for internal use only. Smaller courts place their information on computer cards that are later sent to Pierre for input by the state office.

Federal Courts in South Dakota...

US District Court - District of South Dakota

Home Page: www.sdd.uscourts.gov

PACER: Sign-up number is 800-676-6856. Access fee is $.60 per minute. Case records are available back to 1991. Records are purged every six months. New records are available online after 1 day.

PACER Internet Access: http://pacer.sdd.uscourts.gov.

Opinions Online: Court opinions are available online at www.sdbar.org/opinions/dsindex.htm.

Other Online Access: You can search records on the Internet using RACER. Currently the system is free and requires free registration. Simply visit http://207.222.24.8/wconnect/wc.dll?usdc_racer~main.

Aberdeen Division Counties: Brown, Butte, Campbell, Clark, Codington, Corson, Day, Deuel, Edmunds, Grant, Hamlin, McPherson, Marshall, Roberts, Spink, Walworth. Judge Battey's closed case records are located at the Rapid City Division.

Pierre Division Counties: Buffalo, Dewey, Faulk, Gregory, Haakon, Hand, Hughes, Hyde, Jackson, Jerauld, Jones, Lyman, Mellette, Potter, Stanley, Sully, Todd, Tripp, Ziebach.

Rapid City Division Counties: Bennett, Custer, Fall River, Harding, Lawrence, Meade, Pennington, Perkins, Shannon. Judge Battey's closed cases are located here.

Sioux Falls Division Counties: Aurora, Beadle, Bon Homme, Brookings, Brule, Charles Mix, Clay, Davison, Douglas, Hanson, Hutchinson, Kingsbury, Lake, Lincoln, McCook, Miner, Minnehaha, Moody, Sanborn, Turner, Union, Yankton.

US Bankruptcy Court - District of South Dakota

Home Page: www.sdb.uscourts.gov

PACER: Sign-up number is 800-676-6856. Access fee is $.60 per minute. Toll-free access: 800-261-3167. Local access: 605-330-4342. Case records are available back to October 1, 1991. Records are purged never. New civil records are available online after 1 day.

PACER Internet Access: http://pacer.sdb.uscourts.gov.

Pierre Division Counties: Bennett, Brown, Buffalo, Butte, Campbell, Clark, Codington, Corson, Custer, Day, Deuel, Dewey, Edmunds, Fall River, Faulk, Grant, Gregory, Haakon, Hamlin, Hand, Harding, Hughes, Hyde, Jackson, Jerauld, Jones, Lawrence, Lyman, Marshall, McPherson, Meade,Mellette, Pennington, Perkins, Potter, Roberts, Shannon, Spink, Stanley, Sully, Todd, Tripp, Walworth, Ziebach.

Sioux Falls Division Counties: Aurora, Beadle, Bon Homme, Brookings, Brule, Charles Mix, Clay, Davison, Douglas, Hanson, Hutchinson, Kingsbury, Lake, Lincoln, McCook, Miner, Minnehaha, Moody, Sanborn, Turner, Union, Yankton.

Editor's Choice for South Dakota

Here are some additional sites recommended for this state.

Prison Escapees Listing
www.state.sd.us/state/executive/corrections/wanted.htm

Statutes & Constitution Text
www.state.sd.us/state/legis/lrc/statutes/lrcmenu.htm

Various Government Forms (Paper)
www.state.sd.us/forms/forms.cfm

Capital:	Nashville	Home Page	www.state.tn.us
	Davidson County		
Time Zone:	CST/EST	Attorney General	www.attorneygeneral.state.tn.us
Number of Counties:	95	Archives	www.state.tn.us/sos/statelib/ techsvs

State Level...Major Agencies

Corporation Records, Limited Partnership Records, Fictitious Name, Assumed Name, Limited Liability Company Records

Division of Business Svcs; Corporations, Department of State, 312 Eighth Ave. N, 6th Fl, Nashville, TN 37243; 615-741-2286, 615-741-7310 (Fax), 8AM-4:30PM.

www.state.tn.us/sos

Online: There is a free online search at www.tennesseeanytime.org/sosname. Intended for business name availability; details are given on existing entities.

Trademarks/Servicemarks, Trade Names

Secretary of State, Trademarks/Tradenames Division, 312 8th Ave North, 6th Fl, Nashville, TN 37243-0306; 615-741-0531, 615-741-7310 (Fax), 8AM-4:30PM.

www.state.tn.us/sos/service.htm

Online: The Internet provides a record search of Tennessee Trademarks, newest records are 3 days old.

Uniform Commercial Code, State Tax Liens, Federal Tax Liens

Division Of Business Services, Secretary of State, 312 Eighth Ave N, 6th Fl, Nashville, TN 37243; 615-741-3276, 615-741-7310 (Fax), 8AM-4:30PM.

www.state.tn.us/sos

Online: Free access at http://ndweb.state.tn.us/cgi-bin/nd_CGI_50/ietm/PgUCCSearch.

Birth Certificates, Death, Marriage, Divorce Records

Tennessee Department of Health, Office of Vital Records, 421 5th Ave North, 1st floor, Nashville, TN 37247; 615-741-1763, 615-741-0778 (Credit card order), 615-726-2559 (Fax), 8AM-4PM.

www.state.tn.us/health/vr

Online: Records may be ordered online at the web site, but are returned by mail. The Cleveland (Tennessee) Public Library staff and volunteers have published the 1914-1925 death records of thirty-three counties at www.state.tn.us/statelib/pubsvs/death.htm#index. The records of children under two years of age have been omitted from this project.

Legislation Records

Tennessee General Assembly, Office of Legislative Information Services, Rachel Jackson Bldg, 1st Floor, Nashville, TN 37243; 615-741-3511 (Status), 615-741-0927 (Bill Room), 8AM-4:30PM.

www.legislature.state.tn.us

Online: Bill information can be viewed at the Internet site. The Tennessee Code is also available from the web page.

State Level...Occupational Licensing

Accounting Firm www.state.tn.us/cgi-bin/commerce/roster2.pl
Alarm Contractor www.state.tn.us/cgi-bin/commerce/roster2.pl
Alcohol & Drug Abuse Counselor http://170.142.76.180/cgi-bin/licensure.pl
Architect.. www.state.tn.us/cgi-bin/commerce/roster2.pl
Athletic Trainer http://170.142.76.180/cgi-bin/licensure.pl
Auctioneer/ Auctioneer Firm............................ www.state.tn.us/cgi-bin/commerce/roster2.pl
Barber/Barber School/Shop/Technician www.state.tn.us/cgi-bin/commerce/roster2.pl
Boxing & Racing www.state.tn.us/cgi-bin/commerce/roster2.pl
Chiropractor... http://170.142.76.180/cgi-bin/licensure.pl
Collection Agent/Collections Manager www.state.tn.us/cgi-bin/commerce/roster2.pl
Contractor.. www.state.tn.us/cgi-bin/commerce/roster2.pl
Cosmetologist/ Cosmetology School/Shop www.state.tn.us/cgi-bin/commerce/roster2.pl
Counselor & Marriage/Family Therapist http://170.142.76.180/cgi-bin/licensure.pl
Dental Hygienist http://170.142.76.180/cgi-bin/licensure.pl
Dentist/ Dental Assistant.................................... http://170.142.76.180/cgi-bin/licensure.pl
Dispensing Optician.. http://170.142.76.180/cgi-bin/licensure.pl
Electrology... http://170.142.76.180/cgi-bin/licensure.pl
Embalmer www.state.tn.us/cgi-bin/commerce/roster2.pl
Emergency Medical Service http://170.142.76.180/cgi-bin/licensure.pl
Engineer www.state.tn.us/cgi-bin/commerce/roster2.pl
Funeral & Burial Director/Apprentice www.state.tn.us/cgi-bin/commerce/roster2.pl
Funeral & Burial Cemetery/Establishment www.state.tn.us/cgi-bin/commerce/roster2.pl
Geologist www.state.tn.us/cgi-bin/commerce/roster2.pl
Hearing Aid Dispenser....................................... http://170.142.76.180/cgi-bin/licensure.pl
Home Improvement.. www.state.tn.us/cgi-bin/commerce/roster2.pl
Insurance Agent/ Insurance Firm www.state.tn.us/cgi-bin/commerce/roster2.pl
Interior Designer... www.state.tn.us/cgi-bin/commerce/roster2.pl
Landscape Architect/ Landscape Architect Firm . www.state.tn.us/cgi-bin/commerce/roster2.pl
Lobbyist... www.state.tn.us/tref/lobby/lobby.htm
Marital & Family Therapist................................ http://170.142.76.180/cgi-bin/licensure.pl
Massage Therapist http://170.142.76.180/cgi-bin/licensure.pl
Medical Doctor http://170.142.76.180/cgi-bin/licensure.pl
Medical Laboratory Personnel http://170.142.76.180/cgi-bin/licensure.pl
Motor Vehicle Dealer//SalespersonAuction www.state.tn.us/cgi-bin/commerce/roster2.pl
Nurse-RN & LPN... http://170.142.76.180/cgi-bin/licensure.pl
Nursery/ Nursery Plant Dealer........................... www.state.tn.us/agriculture/regulate/regulat1.html
Nursing Home Administrator http://170.142.76.180/cgi-bin/licensure.pl
Optometrist.. www.arbo.org/nodb2000/licsearch.asp
Osteopathic Physician http://170.142.76.180/cgi-bin/licensure.pl

Personnel Leasing www.state.tn.us/cgi-bin/commerce/roster2.pl
Pharmacist/Pharmacy Researcher/Pharmacy www.state.tn.us/cgi-bin/commerce/roster2.pl
Physical Therapist/Assistant.............................. http://170.142.76.180/cgi-bin/licensure.pl
Physician Assistant http://170.142.76.180/cgi-bin/licensure.pl
Podiatrist http://170.142.76.180/cgi-bin/licensure.pl
Polygraph Examiner.. www.state.tn.us/cgi-bin/commerce/roster2.pl
Private Investigator/Private Investigative Co....... www.state.tn.us/cgi-bin/commerce/roster2.pl
Psychologist.. http://170.142.76.180/cgi-bin/licensure.pl
Public Accountant-CPA.................................... www.state.tn.us/cgi-bin/commerce/roster2.pl
Race Track.. www.state.tn.us/cgi-bin/commerce/roster2.pl
Real Estate Appraiser.. www.state.tn.us/cgi-bin/commerce/roster2.pl
Real Estate Broker/Sales Agent/Firm www.state.tn.us/cgi-bin/commerce/roster2.pl
Respiratory Care Practitioner http://170.142.76.180/cgi-bin/licensure.pl
Security Guard/Trainer/Security Company.......... www.state.tn.us/cgi-bin/commerce/roster2.pl
Social Worker http://170.142.76.180/cgi-bin/licensure.pl
Speech Pathologist/Audiologist http://170.142.76.180/cgi-bin/licensure.pl
Time Share Agent www.state.tn.us/cgi-bin/commerce/roster2.pl
Veterinarian.. http://170.142.76.180/cgi-bin/licensure.pl
X-ray Operator/Technologist http://170.142.76.180/cgi-bin/licensure.pl

County Level...Courts, Recorders & Assessors

Administrative Office of the Courts, 511 Union St (Nashville City Center) #600, Nashville, TN, 37243-0607; 615-741-2687; www.tsc.state.tn.us

Editor's Note: There is currently no statewide, online computer system available, internal or external. The Tennessee Administrative Office of Courts (AOC) has provided computers and CD-ROM readers to state judges, and a computerization project (named TnCIS) to implement statewide court automation started in January 1997.

Davidson
Criminal Records, Property Records
www.nashville.org
Records from the Metropolitan Nashville and Davidson County Criminal Court database are available free online at www.nashville.org/ccrt. Search the criminal court dockets by date. Also, the City of Nashville sponsors an Internet site at www.police.nashville.org/justice/default.asp. Also, Property records on the Metropolitan Planning Commission City of Nashville database are available free online at www.nashville.org/mpc/maps/index.html. Click on "Go straight to maps."

Hamilton
Civil Cases, Criminal Records
www.hamiltontn.gov/courts/sessions/default.htm
Online access to current court dockets is available free at www.hamiltontn.gov/courts/CircuitClerk/dockets/default.htm.
Online access to court dispositions and court dates is available free at www.hamiltontn.gov/courts/CriminalClerk/default.htm.

Real Estate
www.hamiltontn.gov/register
Two sources for records exist. The County Register of Deeds subscription service is available online for $50 per month and $1.00 per fax page. Search by name, address, or book & page. For further information, call 423-209-6560. Also, unofficial property records are available free online from a private company at http://216.205.78.218/Samples/HamiltonSearch.html. Site is under construction.

Knox

Real Property

Real property records are available free online through a private company at http://216.205.78.218/samples/KnoxSearch.html. Site may be under construction.

Shelby

Property Records

www.assessor.shelby.tn.us/page1.cfm

Property records on the assessor database are available free online at www.assessor.shelby.tn.us/page1.cfm.

Sumner

Property, Recording

www.deeds.sumnertn.org

Online access to the Register of Deeds website requires a $25.00 set-up fee and $50.00 monthly user fee. For information, call the Registrar at 615-452-3892 or download the User Agreement from the website.

Wilson

Real Estate, Liens, Recording

www.register.co.wilson.tn.us

Online access to the Register of Deeds database requires a $10 registration fee then $25.00 per month usage fee. Includes indexes and images back to 11/1999, expanding to include 1994.

Federal Courts in Tennessee...

US District Court - Eastern District of Tennessee

PACER: Sign-up number is 800-676-6856. Access fee is. Toll-free access: 800-869-1265. Local access: 423-545-4647. Case records are available back to 1994. Records are purged never. New records are available online after 1 day.
PACER Internet Access: http://pacer.tned.uscourts.gov.
Chattanooga Division Counties: Bledsoe, Bradley, Hamilton, McMinn, Marion, Meigs, Polk, Rhea, Sequatchie.
Greeneville Division Counties: Carter, Cocke, Greene, Hamblen, Hancock, Hawkins, Johnson, Sullivan, Unicoi, Washington.
Knoxville Division Counties: Anderson, Blount, Campbell, Claiborne, Grainger, Jefferson, Knox, Loudon, Monroe, Morgan, Roane, Scott, Sevier, Union.
Winchester Division Counties: Bedford, Coffee, Franklin, Grundy, Lincoln, Moore, Van Buren, Warren.

US Bankruptcy Court - Eastern District of Tennessee

Home Page: www.tneb.uscourts.gov
PACER: Sign-up number is 800-676-6856. Access fee is $.60 per minute. Toll-free access: 888-833-9512. Local access: 423-752-5131, 423-752-5133, 423-752-5134, 423-752-5135, 423-752-5136, 423-752-5137. Case records are available back to January 1986. Records are purged as deemed necessary. New civil records are available online after 1 day.
PACER Internet Access: http://pacer.tneb.uscourts.gov.
Chattanooga Division Counties: Bedford, Bledsoe, Bradley, Coffee, Franklin, Grundy, Hamilton, Lincoln, Marion, McMinn, Meigs, Moore, Polk, Rhea, Sequatchie, Van Buren, Warren.
Knoxville Division Counties: Anderson, Blount, Campbell, Carter, Claiborne, Cocke, Grainger, Greene, Hamblen, Hancock, Hawkins, Jefferson, Johnson, Knox, Loudon, Monroe, Morgan, Roane, Scott, Sevier, Sullivan, Unicoi, Union, Washington.

US District Court - Middle District of Tennessee

PACER: Sign-up number is 800-676-6856. Access fee is $.60 per minute. Toll-free access: 800-458-2994. Local access: 615-736-7164. Case records are available back three years. Records are purged every year. New records are available online after 1 day.
PACER Internet Access: http://pacer.tnmd.uscourts.gov.
Columbia Division Counties: Giles, Hickman, Lawrence, Lewis, Marshall, Maury, Wayne.
Cookeville Division Counties: Clay, Cumberland, De Kalb, Fentress, Jackson, Macon, Overton, Pickett, Putnam, Smith, White.
Nashville Division Counties: Cannon, Cheatham, Davidson, Dickson, Houston, Humphreys, Montgomery, Robertson, Rutherford, Stewart, Sumner, Trousdale, Williamson, Wilson.

US Bankruptcy Court - Middle District of Tennessee

Home Page: www.tnmb.uscourts.gov
PACER: Sign-up number is 615-736-5577. Access fee is $.60 per minute. Case records are available back to September 1989. Records are purged never. New civil records are available online after 1 day.
PACER Internet Access: http://pacer.tnmb.uscourts.gov.
Other Online Access: You can search all cases on the Internet clicking on "Database Access" and then choosing "NIBS case information" from the pop-up menu on the main page.
Nashville Division Counties: Cannon, Cheatham, Clay, Cumberland, Davidson, De Kalb, Dickson, Fentress, Giles, Hickman, Houston, Humphreys, Jackson, Lawrence, Lewis, Macon, Marshall, Maury, Montgomery, Overton, Pickett, Putnam, Robertson, Rutherford, Smith, Stewart, Sumner,Trousdale, Wayne, White, Williamson, Wilson.

US District Court - Western District of Tennessee

Home Page: www.tnwd.uscourts.gov
PACER: Sign-up number is 800-676-6856. Access fee is $.60 per minute. Toll-free access: 800-407-4456. Local access: 901-495-1259. Case records are available back to 1993. Records are purged as deemed necessary. New records are available online after 2 days.
Jackson Division Counties: Benton, Carroll, Chester, Crockett, Decatur, Gibson, Hardeman, Hardin, Haywood, Henderson, Henry, Lake, McNairy, Madison, Obion, Perry, Weakley.
Memphis Division Counties: Dyer, Fayette, Lauderdale, Shelby, Tipton.

US Bankruptcy Court - Western District of Tennessee

Home Page: www.tnwb.uscourts.gov
PACER: Sign-up number is 800-676-6856. Access fee is $.60 per minute. Toll-free access: 800-406-0190. Local access: 901-544-4336. Case records are available back to 1989. Records are purged never. New civil records are available online after 2 days.
Jackson Division Counties: Benton, Carroll, Chester, Crockett, Decatur, Gibson, Hardeman, Hardin, Haywood, Henderson, Henry, Lake, Madison, McNairy, Obion, Perry, Weakley.
Memphis Division Counties: Dyer, Fayette, Lauderdale, Shelby, Tipton.

Editor's Choice for Tennessee

Here are some additional sites recommended for this state.

Constitution Text
www.state.tn.us/sos/bluebook/tnconst.htm
Death Statistics Database
http://web.utk.edu/~chrg/hit/main/SPOT/frames/SPOT/data/DS1/A/mortfinc.htm
State Employee Telephone Numbers Database
http://ndweb.state.tn.us/cgi-bin/nd_CGI_50/agda/PgMainSearch

Capital: Austin
                Travis County

Time Zone: CST/MST

Number of Counties: 254

Home Page   www.state.tx.us

Archives   www.tsl.state.tx.us

Attorney General   www.oag.state.tx.us

State Level...Major Agencies

Criminal Records

Crime Records Service, Correspondence Section, PO Box 15999, Austin, TX 78761-5999 (Courier: 5805 N Lamar, Austin, TX 78752); 512-424-5079, 8AM-5PM.

http://records.txdps.state.tx.us/dps/default.cfm

Online: Records can be pulled from the web site. Requesters must establish an account and have a pre-paid bank to work from. The fee established by the Department (Sec. 411.135(b)) is $3.15 per request plus a $.57 handling fee when credit purchased.

Corporation Records, Fictitious Name, Limited Partnership Records, Limited Liability Company Records, Assumed Name, Trademarks/Servicemarks

Secretary of State, Corporation Section, PO Box 13697, Austin, TX 78711-3697 (Courier: J Earl Rudder Bldg, 1019 Brazos, B-13, Austin, TX 78701); 512-463-5555 (Information), 512-463-5578 (Copies), 512-463-5709 (Fax), 8AM-5PM.

www.sos.state.tx.us

Online: There are 2 online methods available. Dial-up access is available M-TH from 7 AM to 8 PM (6PM on Fridays). There is a $3.00 fee for each record searched (secured party searches are $10.00). Filing procedures and forms are available from the web site or from 900-263-0060 ($1.00 per minute). General corporation information is available at no fee at http://open.cpa.state.tx.us from the State Comptroller's office.

Uniform Commercial Code, Federal Tax Liens

UCC Section, Secretary of State, PO Box 13193, Austin, TX 78711-3193 (Courier: 1019 Brazos St, Rm B-13, Austin, TX 78701); 512-475-2705, 512-475-2812 (Fax), 8AM-5PM.

www.sos.state.tx.us/function/ucc/cover.htm

Online: Direct dial-up is open 7 AM to 6 PM. The fee is $3.00 per search, $10.00 for a secured party search. General information and forms can be found at the web site.

Sales Tax Registrations

Controller of Public Accounts, PO Box 13528, Austin, TX 78711-3528 (Courier: LBJ Office Bldg, 111 E 17th St, Austin, TX 78774); 800-252-5555, 800-252-1386 (Searches), 512-475-1610 (Fax), 8AM-5PM.

www.window.state.tx.us

Online: Go to http://aixtcp.cpa.state.tx.us/star/ to search 16,000+ documents by index or collection. This office makes general corporation information available at http://open.cpa.state.tx.us. There is no fee.

Vital Statistics

Texas Department of Health, Bureau of Vital Statistics, PO Box 12040, Austin, TX 78711-2040 (Courier: 1100 W 49th St, Austin, TX 78756-3191); 512-458-7111, 512-458-7506 (Fax), 8AM-5PM.

www.tdh.state.tx.us/bvs

Online: The birth database 1950-present of the Department of Health is available at http://userdb.rootsweb.com/tx/birth/summary/search.cgi. As of March 2000, Birth Indexes from 1926-1995 are available at http://userdb.rootsweb.com/tx/birth/general/search.cgi. Search by surname, given name, county, year and gender. The death records database is available at http://userdb.rootsweb.com/tx/death/search.cgi?. As of March 2000, Death Indexes from 1964-1998 are available. You may search by surname, given name, county, year or gender. The marriage records database 1966-1997 is available at http://userdb.rootsweb.com/tx/marriage/search.cgi. Search by husband or wife name, county, or year. The divorce records database 1968-1997 is available at http://userdb.rootsweb.com/tx/divorce/search.cgi. Search by spouse name, county, or year.

Vehicle Ownership, Vehicle Identification

Department of Transportation, Vehicle Titles and Registration, 40th St and Jackson, Austin, TX 78779-0001; 512-465-7611, 512-465-7736 (Fax), 8AM-5PM.

www.dot.state.tx.us

Online: Online access is available for pre-approved accounts. A $200 deposit is required, there is a $23 charge per month and $.12 fee per inquiry. Searching by name is not permitted. For more information, contact Production Data Control.

Legislation Records

Legislative Reference Library, PO Box 12488, Austin, TX 78711-2488 (Courier: State Capitol Building, 2N.3, 1100 Congress, Austin, TX 78701); 512-463-1252 (Bill Status), 512-463-0252 (Senate Bill Copies), 512-463-1144 (House Bill Copies), 512-475-4626 (Fax), 8AM-5PM.

www.lrl.state.tx.us

Online: The web is a thorough searching site of bills and status.

State Level...Occupational Licensing

Audiologist	www.tdh.state.tx.us/hcqs/plc/speech.htm
Banking Representative Offices	www.banking.state.tx.us/asp/rep/lookup.asp
Banks, State Chartered	www.banking.state.tx.us/asp/bank/lookup.asp
Barber School	www.tsbbe.state.tx.us/schoolr.htm
Check Sellers	www.banking.state.tx.us/asp/soc/lookup.asp
Chiropractor	www.tbce.state.tx.us
Currency Exchange	www.banking.state.tx.us/asp/cex/lookup.asp
Dentist/Dental Hygienist/Dental Lab	www.tsbde.state.tx.us/dbsearch
Dietitian	www.tdh.state.tx.us/hcqs/plc/dtrost.txt
ECA	http://160.42.108.3/ems_web/blh_html_page1.htm
Emergency Medical Technician	http://160.42.108.3/ems_web/blh_html_page1.htm
Foreign Bank Agencies	www.banking.state.tx.us/asp/fba/lookup.asp
Funeral Facility/Preneed Funeral Home	www.banking.state.tx.us/asp/pfc/lookup.asp
Health Facility	www.ecptote.state.tx.us/serv/verification/ftverif.php
Hearing Instrument Dispenser/Fitter	www.tdh.state.tx.us/hcqs/plc/fdhi.htm
Insurance Adjuster	www.tdi.state.tx.us/general/forms/colists.html
Insurance Agency	www.tdi.state.tx.us/general/forms/colists.html
Insurance Agent	www.tdi.state.tx.us/general/forms/agentlists.html

Insurance Company.. www.tdi.state.tx.us/general/forms/colists.html
Lobbyist.. www.lobbyist.net/Texas/TEXLOB.htm
Marriage & Family Therapist............................ www.tdh.state.tx.us/hcqs/plc/mft.htm#rosters
Massage Therapist/School/Instructor/Business ... www.tdh.state.tx.us/hcqs/plc/mtrost.txt
Medical Doctor .... www.docboard.org/tx/df/txsearch.htm
Medical Physicist.. www.tdh.state.tx.us/hcqs/plc/mprost.txt
Occupational Therapist/Assistant .... www.ecptote.state.tx.us/serv/verification/otverif.php
Optometrist... www.odfinder.org/LicSearch.asp
Orthotics/Prosthetics Facility............................. www.tdh.state.tx.us/hcqs/plc/op_fac.htm
Orthotist/Prosthetist .... www.tdh.state.tx.us/hcqs/plc/oprost.txt
Paramedic... http://160.42.108.3/ems_web/blh_html_page1.htm
Perpetual Care Cemetery.................................... www.banking.state.tx.us/asp/pcc/lookup.asp
Pharmacist.. www.tsbp.state.tx.us/dbsearch/pht_search.asp
Pharmacy.. www.tsbp.state.tx.us/dbsearch/phy_search.asp
Physical Therapist/Assistant.............................. www.ecptote.state.tx.us/serv/verification/ptverif.php
Polygraph Examiner .... http://polygraph.org/states/tape/members_roster.htm
Polygraph Examiners of Sex Offenders............... www.tdh.state.tx.us/hcqs/plc/csp.htm
Prepaid Funeral Permit Holder .... www.banking.state.tx.us/asp/pfc/lookup.asp
Professional Counselor...................................... www.tdh.state.tx.us/hcqs/plc/lpcrost.txt
Radiologic Technologist/ Radiology Technician.. www.tdh.state.tx.us/hcqs/plc/mrtrost.txt
Real Estate Broker/Inspector/Salesperson........... www.trec.state.tx.us/publicinfo
Respiratory Care Practitioner .... www.tdh.state.tx.us/hcqs/plc/rcrost.txt
Sex Offender Treatment Provider....................... www.tdh.state.tx.us/hcqs/plc/csotrost.txt
Social Worker .... www.tdh.state.tx.us/hcqs/plc/lsw/lsw_default.htm#roster
Speech-Language Pathologist .... www.tdh.state.tx.us/hcqs/plc/speech.htm
Trust Company .... www.banking.state.tx.us/asp/trustco/lookup.asp

County Level...Courts, Recorders & Assessors

Office of Court Administration, PO Box 12066, Austin, TX, 78711; 512-463-1625; www.courts.state.tx.us

Editor's Note: Statewide appellate court case information is searchable for free on the Internet at www.info.courts.state.tx.us/appindex/appindex.exe. An increasing number of individual county courts also offer online access to their records.

Two private companies offer online access to various Texas Counties.

1. TaxNetUSA - Assessor, Real Estate (63 Texas Counties)

www.taxnetusa.com

Appraisal district and property information records for 63 Texas counties on the TaxNetUSA site are available on the Internet. The information comes in two packages: basic/free and advanced. In addition, TaxNetUSA offers assessor/collector information records for 6 Texas counties. All counties on the Texas TaxNetUSA system are listed below, either as basic-free, advanced search only, or assessor/collector information.

Online search: At the TaxNetUSA site, user chooses "advanced search subscribers login" (fee service) or "Appraisal Districts Online Basic Search" (no fee). For a basic search, use the pull down menu in the county field to select the county to search. Select county and click go. At the county Assessor/Tax site, follow the directions for that county. Generally, but in varying degrees from county to county, the basic search allows you to access general property information: name, address, valuation, etc., and you may search by parcel number, owner name, or address. Depending on the county, more "detailed" information may be available.

TaxNetUSA's Advanced Search Information (fee) allows most counties to be searched by any combination of the following criteria: owner name, property location, city, school district, subdivision, mapsco page, land area, class, tax board code, tax value, deed date and more. Fees vary. All Texas counties online: $3000. Per year; 5 counties: $399; 1 county: $225. Signup at www.taxnetusa.com/infoform.htm.

TaxNetUSA Texas counties with appraisal district information online **no fee:**

Archer	Bandera	Bastrop	Brazoria
Bee	Brazos	Caldwell	Cameron
Chambers	Clay	Collin	Dallas
Denton	Ellis	ElPaso	Erath
Fannin	Franklin	Galveston	Grayson
Gregg	Guadalupe	Hardin*	Harrison
Hays	Henderson	Hidalgo	Hill
Hood	Jack	Jefferson	Johnson
Kaufman	Kleberg	Limestone	Lubbock
McLennan*	Montgomery	Nacogdoches	Nueces
Rockwall	Rusk	San Patricio	Smith*
Swisher*	Tarrant	Taylor	Travis
Van Zandt	Victoria	Webb	Wichita*
Wilbarger	Williamson	Wise	Zapata

     * Counties that do NOT offer **Advanced**

TaxNetUSA Texas counties with Assessor/tax records **Advanced (fee) only:**

Fort Bend	Harris	Hunt
Navarro	Parker	Potter-Randall

TaxNetUSA Texas counties that offer **Assessor/Collector information:**

Hidalgo	Johnson	Kaufman	Lubbock	Taylor	Travis

2. TXCOUNTYDATA - Assessor, Real Estate (46 Texas Counties)

www.txcountydata.com

Assessor and property information records for 46 Texas counties on the TXCOUNTYDATA site are available on the Internet for no fee. All counties on this Texas system are listed below.

Online search: At the TXCOUNTYDATA site, click on "County Search" then use the pull down menu in the county field to select the county to search. Select county and click go. The County Info page for each county lists the Appraiser, mailing address, phone, fax, web site, e-mail. Generally, you can search any county account, owner name, address, or property ID number. Search allows you to access owner address, property address, legal description, taxing entities, exemptions, deed, account, abstract/subdivision, neighborhood, valuation info, and/or building attributes.

Counties with Assessor/tax records online **no fee:**

Anderson	Angelina	Aransas	Atascosa
Austin	Bastrop	Blanco	Brazoria
Brazos	Brown	Burleson	Burnet
Caldwell	Calhoun	Coleman	Comanche
Fannin	Ft. Bend	Gillespie	Hays
Hunt	Kendall	Kerr	Kimble
Lamb	Liberty	Limestone	Llano
Lubbock	Madison	Maverick	Milam
Montgomery	Newton	Nueces	Rockwall
San Jacinto	Somervell	Swisher	Upshur
Victoria	Waller	Washington	Wharton
Wilson	Wood		

Bell
Assessor, Property Tax
TexasTax provides two methods of access to County records. Access to "Advanced Search" records requires a login and subscription fee. Subs are allowed in monthly increments. Advanced Search includes full data, maps, and Excel spreadsheet. For information, see www.texastax.com/bell/subscriptioninfo.asp. Records on "Quick Search - FREE" at www.texastax.com/bell/index/asp allows access to these County records: tax ID number, owner, parcel address, land value data. Search FREE by tax ID number, address, name, city or value. View details.

Bexar
Civil Cases, Criminal Records
www.co.bexar.tx.us/dclerk
Access to the remote online system requires a $100 setup fee, plus a $25 monthly fee, plus inquiry fees. Call Jennifer Mann at 210-335-0212 for more information.
Property Tax, Assessor
www.bcad.org/home.htm
Online access to the county Central Appraisal District database is available free at www.bcad.org/property.htm.

Brazoria
Assessor, Property Tax
www.brazoriacad.org
Online access to the county Central Appraisal District database is available free at www.brazoriacad.org/search.htm. Also, see notes at beginning of section.

Brooks
Civil Cases, Criminal Records
Case information is available free online at www.idocket.com.

Caldwell
Assessor, Property Tax
www.caldwellcad.org
Online access to the county Appraisal District database is available free at www.caldwellcad.org/search.htm. Search real estate or personal property. Also, see notes at beginning of section.

Cameron
Civil Cases, Criminal Records
Online access is available 24 hours daily. The $125 setup fee includes software, there is a $30 monthly access fee also. For more information, call Eric at 956-544-0838 X475.

Collin
Civil Cases, Criminal Records
Online is available 7am to 7pm M-Sat, 6 to 6 on Sun. The access fee is $.12 a minute, there is a monthly minimum of $31.13. Procomm Plus is suggested. Subscribers also receive fax call-back service. Call Patty Ostrom at 972-548-4503 for subscription information.

Comal
Civil Cases, Criminal Records
www.co.comal.tx.us
Online access to county judicial records is available free at www.co.comal.tx.us/Search/judsrch.htm. Search by either party name. Online access to criminal judicial records is available free at www.co.comal.tx.us/Search/judsrch.htm. Search by defendant name.

Dallas
Criminal Records
www.dallascounty.org
Public Access System allows remote access at $1.00 per minute to these and other court and public records. Will invoice to your telephone bill. Access number is 900-263-INFO. ProComm Plus is recommended. Searching is by name or case number. Call the Public Access Administrator at 214-653-6807 for more information.

Dallas Property Tax, Voter Registration
Access to the County Voter Registration Records is available free online at www.openrecords.org/records/voting/dallas_voting. Search by name or partial name. Also, online access to the Central Appraisal District database is available free at www.dallascad.org. Business personal property searches are to be available. Also, see note at beginning of section.

Denton
Civil Cases, Criminal Records
www.co.denton.tx.us/dept/District_Clerk/dcl.htm
Civil searches available on the web site at no charge. Search by name or cause number. Criminal searches are available on the web site at no charge. Records are available from 1994 forward. Access also includes sheriff bond and jail records.

Eastland
Civil Cases, Criminal Records
Case information is available free online at www.idocket.com.

Fort Bend
Civil Cases, Criminal Records
www.co.fort-bend.tx.us/distclerk/index.htmlOnline searching available through a 900 number service. The access fee is $.55 per minute plus a deposit. Call 281-341-4522 for information. Criminal records from 1987 are available on the same online system.

Real Estate, Liens, Assessor, UCC, Marriage, Death, Birth Records
www.co.fort-bend.tx.us
Online access to the county clerk database is available free at
www.co.fort-bend.tx.us/admin_of_justice/County_Clerk/index_info_research.htm. Search the property index by name, or the plat index. And, search county UCCs, probate and court records. Also, for full records, their fee remote system is available, including images. Access fee is $.25 per minute plus set-up. For information, contact Diane Shepard at 281-341-8664. Also, see note at beginning of section for add'l fee service for tax records.

Galveston
Civil Cases, Criminal Records
Access to the GCNET remote online service requires a $200 escrow account plus a $.25 per minute fee. Fax back service is available. For more information, call Robert Dickinson at 409-770-5115.
Real Estate, Liens, Assessor Records
www.galvestoncad.org/
Several sources exist. 1) Access to County online records requires $200 escrow deposit, $25 monthly fee, plus $.25 per minute. Index records date back to 1965; image documents to 1/95. Lending agency information and fax back services are available. For information, contact Robert Dickinson at 409-770-5115. 2) Online access to the Central Appraisal District database is available free at www.galvestoncad.org/search.htm. 3) Also, see note at beginning of section.

Grayson
Civil Cases, Criminal Records
www.co.grayson.tx.us
Online access to court records is available free online at http://209.151.115.130:3004/judsrch.asp. Also includes criminal records, sheriffs' bail, and sheriff's jail searching.

Gregg
Civil Cases, Criminal Records
www.co.gregg.tx.us/Gregg_DC.html
Online access to county judicial records is available free at www.co.gregg.tx.us/judsrch.htm. Search by name, cause #, status. Also includes jail and bond search.

Guadalupe
Civil Cases, Criminal Records
www.co.guadalupe.tx.us/districtclerk.htm
Online access to court case information from 1990 forward is available at www.idocket.com; subscription required.

Property Tax, Assessor

www.guadalupecad.org/

Online access to the county Appraisal District database is available free at www.guadalupecad.org/gadname.html. Name search here, but other methods are allowed at the web site above. Also, see note at beginning of section.

Harris

Civil Cases, Criminal Records

www.hcdistrictclerk.com

The online subscriber fee site requires a $150 deposit, possible training fees, and $10 monthly fee plus per minute usage charges. The system includes probate, misdemeanor and traffic. Also, civil court general information is available on the Internet at www.ccl.co.harris.tx.us/civil/default.htm. Also, Internet access to criminal records is available to qualified JIMs subscribers at www.co.harris.tx.us/subscriber/cb/submenu.htm. Records include felonies and A & B class misdemeanors.

Real Estate, Liens, Assessor, Voter, UCC, Assumed Name, Grantor/Grantee, Vital Statistics

www.co.harris.tx.us/cclerk

Two sources for County Clerk information exist. Access to the County online subscription service requires a $300 deposit and $40 per hour of use. For info, call Ken Peabody at 713-755-7151. Also, free access to records is available from the web site. Assumed Name records are found at http://63.101.65.71/CoolICE/AssumeNames/an_inquiry. UCC filings are at http://63.101.65.71/CoolICE/UniformCode/uc_inquiry. Real Property at http://63.101.65.71/CoolICE/RealProperty/rp_inquiry and www.hcad.org/Records. Vital statistics are available at http://63.101.65.71/CoolICE/VitalStats/vs_inquiry; marriage at http://63.101.65.71/CoolICE/MarriageLic/ma_inquiry. Also, search the Assessor-Collector database free at www.tax.co.harris.tx.us/dbsearch.htm.

Jefferson

Civil Cases, Criminal Records

www.co.jefferson.tx.us

Online access to the civil records index is available at www.co.jefferson.tx.us/dclerk/civil_index/main.htm. Search by defendant or plaintiff by year 1985 to present. Search results are not certified unless done by the court itself. Online access to the criminal records index is available at www.co.jefferson.tx.us/dclerk/criminal_index/main.htm.

Johnson

Assessor, Property Tax

www.johnsoncad.com/search.htm

Records from the County Appraiser are available fee online at the web site. Also, see note at beginning of section.

Kendall

Assessor, Property Tax

www.kendallcad.org/

Online access to the county Appraisal District is available at the web site. Also, see note at beginning of section.

Lamar

Death Records

Cemetery records in Lamar County are available free online at http://userdb.rootsweb.com/cemeteries/TX/Lamar.

Lubbock

Assessor, Property Tax, Voter Registration

http://tax.co.lubbock.tx.us

For assessor and property tax information, see notes at beginning of section. Voter registration records from the County Assessor/Collector database are available free online at www.lubbocktax.com/registration.

McCulloch

Civil Cases, Criminal Records

Civil case information is available free online at www.idocket.com.

Midland

Civil Cases, Criminal Records

www.co.midland.tx.us/DC/default.asp

Online access to the district Clerk database is available free at www.co.midland.tx.us/DC/Database/search.asp.

Nacogdoches
Property Tax
Online access to the county Central Appraisal District Appraisal Roll from TaxNetUSA is available free at www.taxnetusa.com/nacogdoches.

Navarro
Civil Cases, Criminal Records
Civil case information is available free online at www.idocket.com.

Newton
Assessor, Property Tax, Death
Death records in this county may be accessed over the Internet at www.jas.net/jas.htm (click on historical commission). Assessor, Property Tax: see note at beginning of section.

Nueces
Civil Cases, Criminal Records
www.co.nueces.tx.us/districtclerk/
Online access to District Court records are available free online at the web site. Search by name, company, or cause number.
Assessor, Property Tax
www.co.nueces.tx.us
Records from the County Appraiser are available fee online at www.nuecescad.org/nueces3.html. Also: notes at beginning of section.

Potter
Civil Cases, Criminal Records
www.co.potter.tx.us/districtclerk
Civil case information from 1988 forward is available free online at www.idocket.com.
Assessor, Property Tax
www.prad.org
Two sources exist. Records on the Potter-Randall Appraisal District database are available free online at www.prad.org/search.html. Records periodically updated; for current tax information call Potter (806-342-2600) or Randall (806-665-6287). See note at beginning of section for "Advanced" fee service.

Randall
Civil Cases, Criminal Records
www.randallcounty.org
Civil case information is available free online at www.idocket.com.
Assessor, Property Tax
Two sources exist. Randall County records are combined online with Potter County; see Potter County for access information. Also, see notes at beginning of section.

Tarrant
Civil Cases, Criminal Records
www.tarrantcounty.com
Access to the remote online system requires a $50 setup that includes software. The per minute fee is $.05 plus $25 per month. Call Mr. Hinojosa at 817-884-1419 for more information.
Property Tax, Assessor
www.tad.org
Online access to the county Appraisal District Property data is available free at www.tad.org/Datasearch/datasearch.htm. Also, see note at beginning of section.

Taylor
Assessor, Property Tax
www.taylorcad.org
Online access to the county Central Appraisal District database is available free at www.taylorcad.org/tayname.html. Search is by name, but other methods are available via the web site listed above. Also, see note at beginning of section.

Tom Green

Civil Cases, Criminal Records

http://justice.co.tom-green.tx.us
Online access to civil case records back to 1994 is available online at the web site.

Travis

Assessor, Property Tax

www.traviscad.org/
Online access to the Central Appraisal District database is available free at www.traviscad.org/search.htm. Also search business personal property. Also, See note at beginning of section.

Webb

Appraiser, Property Tax

www.webbcad.org
Online access to the county Central Appraisal District database is available at www.webbcad.org/search1.htm. Also, See note at beginning of section.

Williamson

Assessor, Property Tax

TexasTax provides free access to County tax assessor information online at www.texastax.com/search/default.asp?County=williamson. Also, see note at beginning of section.

Federal Courts in Texas...

US District Court - Eastern District of Texas

Home Page: www.txed.uscourts.gov
PACER: Sign-up number is 800-676-6856. Access fee is $.60 per minute. Toll-free access: 888-837-7816. Local access: 903-590-1104. Case records are available back to 1992. Records are purged once per year. New records are available online after 1 day.
PACER Internet Access: http://pacer.txed.uscourts.gov.
Beaumont Division Counties: Delta*, Fannin*, Hardin, Hopkins*, Jasper, Jefferson, Lamar*, Liberty, Newton, Orange, Red River. Counties marked with an asterisk are called the Paris Division, whose case records are maintained here.
Marshall Division Counties: Camp, Cass, Harrison, Marion, Morris, Upshur.
Sherman Division Counties: Collin, Cooke, Denton, Grayson.
Texarkana Division Counties: Angelina, Bowie, Franklin, Houston, Nacogdoches, Polk, Sabine, San Augustine, Shelby, Titus, Trinity, Tyler.
Tyler Division Counties: Anderson, Cherokee, Gregg, Henderson, Panola, Rains, Rusk, Smith, Van Zandt, Wood.

US Bankruptcy Court - Eastern District of Texas

Home Page: www.txeb.uscourts.gov
PACER: Sign-up number is 800-676-6856. Access fee is $.60 per minute. Toll-free access: 800-466-1681. Local access: 903-590-1220. Case records are available back to 1989. Records are purged every six months. New civil records available online after 1 day.
PACER Internet Access: http://pacer.txeb.uscourts.gov.
Beaumont Division Counties: Angelina, Hardin, Houston, Jasper, Jefferson, Liberty, Nacogdoches, Newton, Orange, Polk, Sabine, San Augustine, Shelby, Trinity, Tyler.
Marshall Division Counties: Camp, Cass, Harrison, Marion, Morris, Upshur.
Plano Division Counties: Collin, Cooke, Delta, Denton, Fannin, Grayson, Hopkins, Lamar, Red River.
Texarkana Division Counties: Bowie, Franklin, Titus.
Tyler Division Counties: Anderson, Cherokee, Gregg, Henderson, Panola, Rains, Rusk, Smith, Van Zandt, Wood.

US District Court - Northern District of Texas

Home Page: www.txnd.uscourts.gov
PACER: Sign-up number is 800-676-6856. Access fee is $.60 per minute. Toll-free access: 800-684-2393. Local access: 214-767-8918. Case records are available back to June 1991. Records are purged once per year. New records are available online after 1 day.
PACER Internet Access: https://pacer.txnd.uscourts.gov.

Abilene Division Counties: Callahan, Eastland, Fisher, Haskell, Howard, Jones, Mitchell, Nolan, Shackelford, Stephens, Stonewall, Taylor, Throckmorton.
Amarillo Division Counties: Armstrong, Briscoe, Carson, Castro, Childress, Collingsworth, Dallam, Deaf Smith, Donley, Gray, Hall, Hansford, Hartley, Hemphill, Hutchinson, Lipscomb, Moore, Ochiltree, Oldham, Parmer, Potter, Randall, Roberts, Sherman, Swisher, Wheeler.
Dallas Division Counties: Dallas, Ellis, Hunt, Johnson, Kaufman, Navarro, Rockwall.
Fort Worth Division Counties: Comanche, Erath, Hood, Jack, Palo Pinto, Parker, Tarrant, Wise.
Lubbock Division Counties: Bailey, Borden, Cochran, Crosby, Dawson, Dickens, Floyd, Gaines, Garza, Hale, Hockley, Kent, Lamb, Lubbock, Lynn, Motley, Scurry, Terry, Yoakum.
San Angelo Division Counties: Brown, Coke, Coleman, Concho, Crockett, Glasscock, Irion, Menard, Mills, Reagan, Runnels, Schleicher, Sterling, Sutton, Tom Green.
Wichita Falls Division Counties: Archer, Baylor, Clay, Cottle, Foard, Hardeman, King, Knox, Montague, Wichita, Wilbarger, Young.

US Bankruptcy Court - Northern District of Texas

Home Page: www.txnb.uscourts.gov
PACER: Sign-up number is 800-676-6856. Access fee is $.60 per minute. Toll-free access: 888-225-1738. Local access: 214-753-2134. You can search PACER using the Internet at https://pacer.txnb.uscourts.gov. Case records are available back to 1994. Records are purged every six months. New civil records are available online after 1 day.
PACER Internet Access: https://pacer.txnb.uscourts.gov.
Amarillo Division Counties: Armstrong, Briscoe, Carson, Castro, Childress, Collingsworth, Dallam, Deaf Smith, Donley, Gray, Hall, Hansford, Hartley, Hemphill, Hutchinson, Lipscomb, Moore, Ochiltree, Oldham, Parmer, Potter, Randall, Roberts, Sherman, Swisher, Wheeler.
Dallas Division Counties: Dallas, Ellis, Hunt, Johnson, Kaufman, Navarro, Rockwall.
Fort Worth Division Counties: Comanche, Erath, Hood, Jack, Palo Pinto, Parker, Tarrant, Wise.
Lubbock Division Counties: Bailey, Borden, Brown, Callahan, Cochran, Cooke, Coleman, Concho, Crockett, Crosby, Dawson, Dickens, Eastland, Fisher, Floyd, Gaines, Garza, Glasscock, Hale, Haskell, Hockley, Howard, Irion, Jones, Kent, Lamb, Lubbock, Lynn, Menard, Mills, Mitchell,Motley, Nolan, Reagan, Runnels, Schleicher, Scurry, Shackelford, Stephens, Sterling, Stonewall, Sutton, Taylor, Terry, Throckmorton, Tom Green, Yoakum.
Wichita Falls Division Counties: Archer, Baylor, Clay, Cottle, Foard, Hardeman, King, Knox, Montague, Wichita, Wilbarger, Young.

US District Court - Southern District of Texas

Home Page: www.txs.uscourts.gov
PACER: Sign-up number is 800-676-6856. Access fee is $.60 per minute. Toll-free access: 800-998-9037. Local access: 713-250-5046. Case records are available back to June 1990. Records are purged every six months. New records are available online after 1 day.
PACER Internet Access: http://pacer.txs.uscourts.gov.
Brownsville Division Counties: Cameron, Willacy.
Corpus Christi Division Counties: Aransas, Bee, Brooks, Duval, Jim Wells, Kenedy, Kleberg, Live Oak, Nueces, San Patricio.
Galveston Division Counties: Brazoria, Chambers, Galveston, Matagorda.
Houston Division Counties: Austin, Brazos, Colorado, Fayette, Fort Bend, Grimes, Harris, Madison, Montgomery, San Jacinto, Walker, Waller, Wharton.
Laredo Division Counties: Jim Hogg, La Salle, McMullen, Webb, Zapata.
McAllen Division Counties: Hidalgo, Starr.
Victoria Division Counties: Calhoun, De Witt, Goliad, Jackson, Lavaca, Refugio, Victoria.

US Bankruptcy Court - Southern District of Texas

Home Page: www.txs.uscourts.gov
PACER: Sign-up number is 800-676-6856. Access fee is $.60 per minute. Toll-free access: 800-998-9037. Local access: 713-250-5046. Case records are available back to June 1, 1991. Records are purged every six months. New civil records are available online after 1-3 days.
PACER Internet Access: http://pacer.txs.uscourts.gov.
Corpus Christi Division Counties: Aransas, Bee, Brooks, Calhoun, Cameron, Duval, Goliad, Hidalgo, Jackson, Jim Wells, Kenedy, Kleberg, Lavaca, Live Oak, Nueces, Refugio, San Patricio, Starr, Victoria, Willacy.Files from Brownsville, Corpus Christi, and McAllen are maintained here.

Houston Division Counties: Austin, Brazoria, Brazos, Chambers, Colorado, De Witt, Fayette, Fort Bend, Galveston, Grimes, Harris, Jim Hogg*, La Salle*, Madison, Matagorda, McMullen*, Montgomery, San Jacinto, Walker,Waller, Wharton, Webb* Zapata*. Open case records for the counties marked with an asterisk are being moved to the Laredo Division.

San Antonio Division Counties: Atascosa, Bandera, Bexar, Comal, Dimmit, Edwards, Frio, Gonzales, Guadalupe, Karnes, Kendall, Kerr, Kinney, Maverick, Medina, Real, Terrell, Uvalde, Val Verde, Wilson, Zavala.

US District Court - Western District of Texas

Home Page: www.txwd.uscourts.gov
PACER: Sign-up number is 800-676-6856. Access fee is $.60 per minute. Toll-free access: 888-869-6365. Local access: 210-472-5256. Case records are available back to 1994. Records are purged every six months. New records are available online after 1 day.
PACER Internet Access: http://pacer.txwd.uscourts.gov.
Austin Division Counties: Bastrop, Blanco, Burleson, Burnet, Caldwell, Gillespie, Hays, Kimble, Lampasas, Lee, Llano, McCulloch, Mason, San Saba, Travis, Washington, Williamson.
Del Rio Division Counties: Edwards, Kinney, Maverick, Terrell, Uvalde, Val Verde, Zavala.
El Paso Division Counties: El Paso.
Midland Division Counties: Andrews, Crane, Ector, Martin, Midland, Upton.
Pecos Division Counties: Brewster, Culberson, Hudspeth, Jeff Davis, Loving, Pecos, Presidio, Reeves, Ward, Winkler.
San Antonio Division Counties: Atascosa, Bandera, Bexar, Comal, Dimmit, Frio, Gonzales, Guadalupe, Karnes, Kendall, Kerr, Medina, Real, Wilson.
Waco Division Counties: Bell, Bosque, Coryell, Falls, Freestone, Hamilton, Hill, Leon, Limestone, McLennan, Milam, Robertson, Somervell.

US Bankruptcy Court - Western District of Texas

Home Page: www.txwb.uscourts.gov
PACER: Sign-up number is 800-676-6856. Access fee is $.60 per minute. Toll-free access: 888-372-5708. Local access: 210-472-6262. Case records are available back to May 1, 1987. Records are purged every 6-8 months. New civil records are available online after 1 day.
PACER Internet Access: http://pacer.txwb.uscourts.gov.
Electronic Filing: Electronic filing information is available online at http://ecf.txwb.uscourts.gov.
Austin Division Counties: Bastrop, Blanco, Burleson, Burnet, Caldwell, Gillespie, Hays, Kimble, Lampasas, Lee, Llano, Mason, McCulloch, San Saba, Travis, Washington, Williamson.
El Paso Division Counties: El Paso.
Midland/Odessa Division Counties: Andrews, Brewster, Crane, Culberson, Ector, Hudspeth, Jeff Davis, Loving, Martin, Midland, Pecos, Presidio, Reeves, Upton, Ward, Winkler.
Waco Division Counties: Bell, Bosque, Coryell, Falls, Freestone, Hamilton, Hill, Leon, Limestone, McLennan, Milam, Robertson, Somervell.

Editor's Choice for Texas

Cemetery Records Database
http://userdb.rootsweb.com/cemeteries/TX/Lamar/
Death Index (1964-1998) Listing
www.rootsweb.com/~txwinkle/deathindex.htm
Marriage Records (1841-1910) Database
http://userdb.rootsweb.com/marriages/TX/Lamar/
Missing Persons Listing
www.txdps.state.tx.us/mpch/bulletina-c.htm
Motion Dockets (Circuit Court) Listing
www.hamiltontn.gov/courts/CircuitClerk/dockets/motion.htm
Probate Index (1891-1949) Listing
www.rootsweb.com/~txector/prob_ector.htm
Sex Offenders Database
http://records.txdps.state.tx.us/so_caveats.cfm

Capital: Salt Lake City
Salt Lake County

Time Zone: MST

Number of Counties: 29

Home Page www.state.ut.us

Archives
www.archives.state.ut.us

Attorney General http://attorneygeneral.utah.gov

State Level...Major Agencies

Corporation Records, Limited Liability Company Records, Fictitious Name, Limited Partnership Records, Assumed Name, Trademarks/Servicemarks

Commerce Department, Corporate Division, PO Box 146705, Salt Lake City, UT 84114-6705 (Courier: 160 E 300 S, 2nd fl, Salt Lake City, UT 84111); 801-530-4849 (Call Center), 801-530-6205 (Certified Records), 801-530-6034 (Non-Certified), 801-530-6363 (Cert. Of Existence), 801-530-6111 (Fax), 8AM-5PM.

www.commerce.state.ut.us

Online: A business entity/principle search service is available on the eUtah web site at www.state.ut.us/egov_services/services.html. Basic information (name, address, agent) is free, detailed data is a available for minimal fees, but registration is required. The eUtah web site also offers an Unclaimed Property search page.

Uniform Commercial Code

Department of Commerce, UCC Division, Box 146705, Salt Lake City, UT 84114-6705 (Courier: 160 E 300 South, Heber M Wells Bldg, 2nd Floor, Salt Lake City, UT 84111); 801-530-4849, 801-530-6438 (Fax), 8AM-5PM.

www.commerce.state.ut.us

Online: User fee is $10.00 per month. There is no additional fee at this time; however, the state is considering a certification fee. The system is open 24 hours daily and is the same system used for corporation records. Call 801-530-6643 for details. The web site also provides details of the "Datashare" program. E-mail requests are accepted at orders@br.state.ut.us.

Vehicle Ownership, Vehicle Identification, Boat & Vessel Ownership, Boat & Vessel Registration

State Tax Commission, Motor Vehicle Records Section, 210 North 1950 West, Salt Lake City, UT 84134; 801-297-3507, 801-297-3578 (Fax), 8AM-5PM.

Online: Motor Vehicle Dept. Driver records are available online, also titles, liens, and registration searches are available at www.state.ut.us/egov_services/services.html; registration is required.

Legislation Records

Utah Legislature, Research and General Counsel, 436 State Capitol, Salt Lake City, UT 84114; 801-538-1588 (Bill Room), 801-538-1032 (Older Passed Bills), 801-538-1712 (Fax), 8AM-5PM.

www.le.state.ut.us

Online: Web site contains bill information and also the Utah Code.

State Level...Occupational Licensing

Accounting Firm .... www.commerce.state.ut.us/dopl/current.htm
Acupuncturist.. www.commerce.state.ut.us/dopl/current.htm
Alarm Company/Agent/Response Runner .... www.commerce.state.ut.us/dopl/current.htm
Analytical Laboratory.. www.commerce.state.ut.us/dopl/current.htm
Animal Euthanasia Agency................................ www.commerce.state.ut.us/dopl/current.htm
Arbitrator, Alternate Dispute Resolution .... www.commerce.state.ut.us/dopl/current.htm
Architect.. www.commerce.state.ut.us/dopl/current.htm
Athletic Judge .... www.commerce.state.ut.us/dopl/current.htm
Bank .... www.dfi.state.ut.us/Banks.htm
Boxer.. www.commerce.state.ut.us/dopl/current.htm
Building Inspector/Inspector Trainee .... www.commerce.state.ut.us/dopl/current.htm
Building Trades .... www.commerce.state.ut.us/dopl/current.htm
Chiropractor.. www.commerce.state.ut.us/dopl/current.htm
Clinical Social Worker .... www.commerce.state.ut.us/dopl/current.htm
Consumer Lender... www.dfi.state.ut.us/consumer.htm
Contractor... www.commerce.state.ut.us/dopl/current.htm
Controlled Substance Precursor Distributor .... www.commerce.state.ut.us/dopl/current.htm
Cosmetologist/Barber.. www.commerce.state.ut.us/dopl/current.htm
Cosmetologist/Barber Apprentice .... www.commerce.state.ut.us/dopl/current.htm
Cosmetologist/Barber Instructor .... www.commerce.state.ut.us/dopl/current.htm
Cosmetologist/Barber School .... www.commerce.state.ut.us/dopl/current.htm
Credit Union.. www.dfi.state.ut.us/CreditUn.htm
Deception Detection Examiner/Intern................. www.commerce.state.ut.us/dopl/current.htm
Dental Hygienist .... www.commerce.state.ut.us/dopl/current.htm
Dental Hygienist with Local Anesthesia .... www.commerce.state.ut.us/dopl/current.htm
Dentist.. www.commerce.state.ut.us/dopl/current.htm
Dietitian .... www.commerce.state.ut.us/dopl/current.htm
Electrician/Electrician Apprentice .... www.commerce.state.ut.us/dopl/current.htm
Electrologist.. www.commerce.state.ut.us/dopl/current.htm
Employee Leasing Company.............................. www.commerce.state.ut.us/dopl/current.htm
Engineer .... www.commerce.state.ut.us/dopl/current.htm
Environmental Health Specialist/Trainee........... www.commerce.state.ut.us/dopl/current.htm
Escrow Agent.. www.dfi.state.ut.us/OtherInt.htm
Funeral Service Establishment .... www.commerce.state.ut.us/dopl/current.htm
Health Care Assistant....................................... www.commerce.state.ut.us/dopl/current.htm
Health Facility Administrator .... www.commerce.state.ut.us/dopl/current.htm
Hearing Aid Specialist .... www.commerce.state.ut.us/dopl/current.htm
Hearing Instrument Intern .... www.commerce.state.ut.us/dopl/current.htm
Hospital or Institutional Pharmacy.................... www.commerce.state.ut.us/dopl/current.htm
Industrial Loan.. www.dfi.state.ut.us/IndustLn.htm
Journeyman Electrician .... www.commerce.state.ut.us/dopl/current.htm
Journeyman Plumber.. www.commerce.state.ut.us/dopl/current.htm
Landscape Architect... www.commerce.state.ut.us/dopl/current.htm
Manufactured Housing Dealer & Salesperson..... www.commerce.state.ut.us/dopl/current.htm
Marriage & Family Therapist or Trainee .... www.commerce.state.ut.us/dopl/current.htm
Massage Technician or Apprentice .... www.commerce.state.ut.us/dopl/current.htm

Master Electrician... www.commerce.state.ut.us/dopl/current.htm
Mediator, Alternate Dispute Resolution .... www.commerce.state.ut.us/dopl/current.htm
Medical Doctor/Surgeon.................................... www.commerce.state.ut.us/dopl/current.htm
Mortgage Lenders .... www.dfi.state.ut.us/mortgage.htm
Naturopath.. www.commerce.state.ut.us/dopl/current.htm
Naturopathic Physician...................................... www.commerce.state.ut.us/dopl/current.htm
Negotiator, Alternate Dispute Resolution .... www.commerce.state.ut.us/dopl/current.htm
Nuclear Pharmacy.. www.commerce.state.ut.us/dopl/current.htm
Nurse / Nurse-LPN .... www.commerce.state.ut.us/dopl/current.htm
Nurse Midwife... www.commerce.state.ut.us/dopl/current.htm
Occupational Therapist/Assistant .... www.commerce.state.ut.us/dopl/current.htm
Optometrist... www.commerce.state.ut.us/dopl/current.htm
Osteopathic Physician .... www.commerce.state.ut.us/dopl/current.htm
Out-of-State Mail Service Pharmacy.................. www.commerce.state.ut.us/dopl/current.htm
Pharmaceutical Facility/Teaching Organization .. www.commerce.state.ut.us/dopl/current.htm
Pharmaceutical Dog Trainer .... www.commerce.state.ut.us/dopl/current.htm
Pharmaceutical Researcher/Manufacturer........... www.commerce.state.ut.us/dopl/current.htm
Pharmaceutical Wholesaler/Distributor .... www.commerce.state.ut.us/dopl/current.htm
Pharmacist/ Pharmacy Technician/Intern .... www.commerce.state.ut.us/dopl/current.htm
Pharmacy Branch/Retail.................................... www.commerce.state.ut.us/dopl/current.htm
Physical Therapist... www.commerce.state.ut.us/dopl/current.htm
Physician Assistant .... www.commerce.state.ut.us/dopl/current.htm
Plumber, Apprentice .... www.commerce.state.ut.us/dopl/current.htm
Podiatrist .... www.commerce.state.ut.us/dopl/current.htm
Pre-Need Provider/Sales Agent .... www.commerce.state.ut.us/dopl/current.htm
Private Probation Provider .... www.commerce.state.ut.us/dopl/current.htm
Professional Counselor/ Counselor Trainee .... www.commerce.state.ut.us/dopl/current.htm
Psychologist.. www.commerce.state.ut.us/dopl/current.htm
Public Accountant-Certificate Holder/CPA......... www.commerce.state.ut.us/dopl/current.htm
Radiology Technologist/Practical Technician...... www.commerce.state.ut.us/dopl/current.htm
Real Estate Broker/Agent.................................. www.commerce.state.ut.us/re/lists/agntbrkr.txt
Real Estate Appraiser.. www.commerce.state.ut.us/re/lists/apprais.txt
Real Estate Establishment................................. www.commerce.state.ut.us/dopl/current.htm
Recreational Therapist .... www.commerce.state.ut.us/dopl/current.htm
Recreational Vehicle Dealer.............................. www.commerce.state.ut.us/dopl/current.htm
Residential Journeyman Electrician/Elect.Traineewww.commerce.state.ut.us/dopl/current.htm
Residential Journeyman Plumber or Apprentice.. www.commerce.state.ut.us/dopl/current.htm
Residential Master Electrician .... www.commerce.state.ut.us/dopl/current.htm
Residential Mortgage Broker............................. www.commerce.state.ut.us/re/lists/agntbrkr.txt
Respiratory Care Practitioner .... www.commerce.state.ut.us/dopl/current.htm
Sanitarian .... www.commerce.state.ut.us/dopl/current.htm
Security Company.. www.commerce.state.ut.us/dopl/current.htm
Security Officer, Armed Private/ Unarmed .... www.commerce.state.ut.us/dopl/current.htm
Shorthand Reporter .... www.commerce.state.ut.us/dopl/current.htm
Social Service Aide/Worker .... www.commerce.state.ut.us/dopl/current.htm
Social Work Trainee .... www.commerce.state.ut.us/dopl/current.htm
Social Worker... www.commerce.state.ut.us/dopl/current.htm
Speech Pathologist/Audiologist .... www.commerce.state.ut.us/dopl/current.htm

Structural Engineer .... www.commerce.state.ut.us/dopl/current.htm
Substance Abuse Counselor .... www.commerce.state.ut.us/dopl/current.htm
Surveyor .... www.commerce.state.ut.us/dopl/current.htm
Veterinarian/ Veterinary Intern .... www.commerce.state.ut.us/dopl/current.htm
Veterinary Pharmaceutical Outlet..................... www.commerce.state.ut.us/dopl/current.htm

County Level...Courts, Recorders & Assessors

Court Administrator, 450 South State Street, Salt Lake City, UT, 84114; 801-578-3800; http://courtlink.utcourts.gov

Editor's Note: Case information from all Utah District Court locations is available through XChange. Fees include $25.00 registration and $30.00 per month plus $.10 per minute for usage, over 120 minutes. Information about XChange and the subscription agreement can be found at http://courtlink.utcourts.gov/howto/access or call 801-238-7877. Records go back 7 to 10 years.

Davis
Real Estate, Liens
www.co.davis.ut.us
Access to the county land records database requires written registration and $15.00 per month fee plus $.10 per transaction. Records go back to 1981. For information and sign-up, contact Janet at 801-451-3347.

Salt Lake
Assessor
www.co.slc.ut.us
Two sources are available. Records on the county Truth-In-Tax Information web site are available free online at www.co.slc.ut.us/valnotice. Also, Assessor, real estate, appraisal, abstracts, and GIS mapping are available for $150.00 fee on the online system at http://rec.co.slc.ut.us/polaris/default.cfm. Search by GIS, name, or property information. Register online or call 801-468-3013.

Tooele
Property Tax
www.co.tooele.ut.us
Online access to the property information database may be operational at www.co.tooele.ut.us/taxinfo.html.

Uintah
Property
www.co.uintah.ut.us/recorder/rec.htm
Online access to the county recorder's land records is available free at www.co.uintah.ut.us/recorder/landinfo.html.

Utah
Real Estate, Liens, Assessor
www.co.utah.ut.us
Online access to the land records database and also map searching is available free at www.co.utah.ut.us/omninet/land. Indexes go back to 1978; parcel indexes back to 1981. Document images go back to 1994. Building and GIS information is also available online.

Wasatch
Real Property
www.co.wasatch.ut.us/d/
The county GIS Dept. plans to have "metadata" (property information) available free online from its GIS site at www.co.wasatch.ut.us/d/dpgis.html.

Weber

Real Estate

www.co.weber.ut.us

Property records on the County Parcel Search site are available free online at www.co.weber.ut.us/netapps/Parcel/main.htm.

Federal Courts in Utah...

US District Court - District of Utah

Home Page: www.utd.uscourts.gov

PACER: Sign-up number is 800-676-6856. Access fee is $.60 per minute. Toll-free access: 800-314-3423. Local access: 801-524-4221. http://pacer.utd.uscourts.gov. Case records are available back to July 1, 1989. Records are never purged. New records are available online after 1 day.

PACER Internet Access: http://pacer.utd.uscourts.gov.

Division Counties: All counties in Utah. Although all cases are heard here, the district is divided into Northern and Central Divisions. The Northern Division includes the counties of Box Elder, Cache, Rich, Davis, Morgan and Weber, and the Central Division includes all other counties.

US Bankruptcy Court - District of Utah

Home Page: www.utb.uscourts.gov

PACER: Sign-up number is 800-676-6856. Access fee is $.60 per minute. Toll-free access: 800-718-1188. Local access: 801-524-5760. Case records are available back to January 1985. Records are purged after 12 months. New civil records are available online after 2 days or more.

PACER Internet Access: http://pacer.utb.uscourts.gov.

Opinions Online: Court opinions are available online at www.utb.uscourts.gov/OPINIONS/opin.htm.

Division Counties: All counties in Utah. Although all cases are handled here, the court divides itself into two divisions. The Northern Division includes the counties of Box Elder, Cache, Rich, Davis, Morgan and Weber, and the Central Division includes the remaining counties. Court is held once per week in Ogden for Northern cases.

Editor's Choice for Utah

Here are some additional sites recommended for this state.

Constitution Text
www.le.state.ut.us/~code/const/const.htm
Statutes & Constitution Text
www.le.state.ut.us/~code/code.htm

| Capital: | Montpelier | | Home Page | www.state.vt.us |
| | Washington County | | | |

| Time Zone: | EST | | Attorney General | www.state.vt.us/atg |
| Number of Counties: | 14 | | Archives | http://vermont-archives.org |

State Level...Major Agencies

Corporation Records, Limited Liability Company Records, Limited Liability Partnerships, Limited Partnerships, Trademarks/Servicemarks

Secretary of State, Corporation Division, 109 State St, Montpelier, VT 05609-1101 (Courier: 81 River St, Heritage Bldg, Montpelier, VT 05602); 802-828-2386, 802-828-2853 (Fax), 7:45AM-4:30PM.

www.sec.state.vt.us/soshome.htm

Online: Corporate and trademark records can be accessed from the Internet for no fee. All records are available except for LPs, LLCs, and Farm Product Liens (however, all of these records will eventually be up). Also, the web site offers a "Trade Name Finder."

Uniform Commercial Code

UCC Division, Secretary of State, 81 River St, Drawer 4, Montpelier, VT 05609-1101; 802-828-2386, 802-828-2853 (Fax), 7:45AM-4:30PM.

www.sec.state.vt.us/corps/corpindex.htm

Online: Searches are available from the Internet site. You can search by debtor or business name, there is no fee.

Driver Records, Driver License Information

Department of Motor Vehicles, DI - Records Unit, 120 State St, Montpelier, VT 05603-0001; 802-828-2050, 802-828-2098 (Fax), 7:45AM-4:30PM.

www.aot.state.vt.us/dmv/dmvhp.htm

Online: Online access costs $4.00 per 3 year record. The system is called "GovNet." Two methods are offered-single inquiry and batch mode. The system is open 24 hours a day, 7 days a week (except for file maintenance periods). Only the license number is needed when ordering, but it is suggested to submit the name and DOB also.

Legislation Records

Vermont General Assembly, State House-Legislative Council, 115 State Street, Drawer 33, Montpelier, VT 05633; 802-828-2231, 802-828-2424 (Fax), 8AM-4:30PM.

www.leg.state.vt.us

Online: The web site offers access to bill information.

State Level...Occupational Licensing

Accounting Firm .... www.sec.state.vt.us/seek/lrspseek.htm
Acupuncturist... www.sec.state.vt.us/seek/lrspseek.htm
Appraiser .... www.sec.state.vt.us/seek/lrspseek.htm
Architect .... www.sec.state.vt.us/seek/lrspseek.htm
Auctioneer .... www.sec.state.vt.us/seek/lrspseek.htm
Barber.. www.sec.state.vt.us/seek/lrspseek.htm
Boxing Manager/Promoter .... www.sec.state.vt.us/seek/lrspseek.htm
Chiropractor.. www.sec.state.vt.us/seek/lrspseek.htm
Cosmetologist .... www.sec.state.vt.us/seek/lrspseek.htm
Dental Hygienist/Dentist/ Dental Assistant......... www.sec.state.vt.us/seek/lrspseek.htm
Dietitian .... www.sec.state.vt.us/seek/lrspseek.htm
Embalmer.. www.sec.state.vt.us/seek/lrspseek.htm
Engineer .... www.sec.state.vt.us/seek/lrspseek.htm
Esthetician.. www.sec.state.vt.us/seek/lrspseek.htm
Funeral Director... www.sec.state.vt.us/seek/lrspseek.htm
Hearing Aid Dispenser....................................... www.sec.state.vt.us/seek/lrspseek.htm
Lobbyist... www.sec.state.vt.us/seek/lbylseek.htm
Manicurist .... www.sec.state.vt.us/seek/lrspseek.htm
Marriage & Family Therapist............................. www.sec.state.vt.us/seek/lrspseek.htm
Medical Doctor/Surgeon.................................... www.docboard.org/vt/df/vtsearch.htm
Mental Health Counselor, Clinical .... www.sec.state.vt.us/seek/lrspseek.htm
Naturopathic Physician...................................... www.sec.state.vt.us/seek/lrspseek.htm
Notary Public.. www.sec.state.vt.us/seek/not_seek.htm
Nurse/Nurse Practitioner/LNA .... www.sec.state.vt.us/seek/lrspseek.htm
Nursing Home Administrator .... www.sec.state.vt.us/seek/lrspseek.htm
Occupational Therapist .... www.sec.state.vt.us/seek/lrspseek.htm
Optician... www.sec.state.vt.us/seek/lrspseek.htm
Optometrist... www.sec.state.vt.us/seek/lrspseek.htm
Osteopathic Physician .... www.sec.state.vt.us/seek/lrspseek.htm
Pharmacist/ Pharmacy.. www.sec.state.vt.us/seek/lrspseek.htm
Physical Therapist/Assistant............................... www.sec.state.vt.us/seek/lrspseek.htm
Physician Assistant .... www.docboard.org/vt/df/vtsearch.htm
Podiatrist .... www.docboard.org/vt/df/vtsearch.htm
Private Investigator .... www.sec.state.vt.us/seek/lrspseek.htm
Psychoanalyst/ Psychologist............................... www.sec.state.vt.us/seek/lrspseek.htm
Psychotherapist .... www.sec.state.vt.us/seek/lrspseek.htm
Public Accountant-CPA...................................... www.sec.state.vt.us/seek/lrspseek.htm
Racing Promoter .... www.sec.state.vt.us/seek/lrspseek.htm
Radiologic Technologist .... www.sec.state.vt.us/seek/lrspseek.htm
Real Estate Appraiser.. www.sec.state.vt.us/seek/lrspseek.htm
Real Estate Broker/Agent/Salesperson............... www.sec.state.vt.us/seek/lrspseek.htm
Security Guard.. www.sec.state.vt.us/seek/lrspseek.htm
Social Worker, Clinical .... www.sec.state.vt.us/seek/lrspseek.htm
Surveyor .... www.sec.state.vt.us/seek/lrspseek.htm
Tattooist .... www.sec.state.vt.us/seek/lrspseek.htm
Veterinarian.. www.sec.state.vt.us/seek/lrspseek.htm

County Level...Courts, Recorders & Assessors

Administrative Office of Courts, Court Administrator, 109 State St, Montpelier, VT, 05609-0701; 802-828-3278; www.state.vt.us/courts

Editor's Note: There is no online computer access to the public; however, some courts offer calendar data over the Internet.

Federal Courts in Vermont...

US District Court - District of Vermont

Home Page: www.vtd.uscourts.gov
PACER: Sign-up number is 800-676-6856. Access fee is $.60 per minute. Toll-free access: 800-263-9396. Local access: 802-951-6623. Case records are available back to January 1991. Records are purged never. New records are available online after 1 day.
Burlington Division Counties: Caledonia, Chittenden, Essex, Franklin, Grand Isle, Lamoille, Orleans, Washington. However, cases from all counties in the state are assigned randomly to either Burlington or Brattleboro. Brattleboro is a hearing location only, not listed here.
Rutland Division Counties: Addison, Bennington, Orange, Rutland, Windsor, Windham. However, cases from all counties in the state are randomly assigned to either Burlington or Brattleboro. Rutland is a hearing location only, not listed here.

US Bankruptcy Court - District of Vermont

Home Page: www.vtb.uscourts.gov
PACER: Sign-up number is 800-676-6856. Access fee is $.60 per minute. Toll-free access: 800-260-9968. Local access: 802-776-2006. Case records are available back to 1992 (limited information prior). Records are purged never. New civil records are available online after 1 day.
PACER Internet Access: http://pacer.vtb.uscourts.gov.
Rutland Division Counties: All counties in Vermont.

Editor's Choice for Vermont

Here are some additional sites recommended for this state.

> **Department of Aging & Disabilities Homepage**
>   www.dad.state.vt.us/
> **Inmates & Offenders Database**
>   http://public.doc.state.vt.us/cgi-bin/public.cgi
> **Statutes & Constitution Text**
>   www.leg.state.vt.us/statutes/statutes.htm
> **Tax Filing Forms (Paper)**
>   www.state.vt.us/tax/download.htm

Capital:	Richmond	Home Page	www.state.va.us
	Richmond City County		
Time Zone:	EST	Attorney General	www.oag.state.va.us
Number of Counties:	95	Archives	www.lva.lib.va.us

State Level...Major Agencies

Criminal Records

Virginia State Police, CCRE, PO Box 85076, Richmond, VA 23261-5076 (Courier: 7700 Midlothian Turnpike, Richmond, VA 23235); 804-674-2084, 804-674-2277 (Fax), 8AM-5PM.

www.vsp.state.va.us/

Online: Certain entities, including screening companies, are entitled to online access. The system is ONLY available to IN-STATE accounts. Fees are same as manual submission with exception of required software package purchase. The system is windows oriented, but will not handle networks. The PC user must be a stand alone system. There is a minimum usage requirement of 25 requests per month. Turnaround time is 24-72 hours. Fee is $15.00 per record.

Corporation Records, Limited Liability Company Records, Fictitious Name, Limited Partnership Records

State Corporation Commission, Clerks Office, PO Box 1197, Richmond, VA 23218-1197 (Courier: Tyler Bldg, 1st Floor, 1300 E Main St, Richmond, VA 23219); 804-371-9733, 804-371-9133 (Fax), 8:15AM-5PM.

www.state.va.us/scc/division/clk/index.htm

Online: There is a dial-up system, called Direct Access, for registered accounts. There are no fees. A wealth of information is available on this system. For more details, call 804-371-9819 or visit www.state.va.us/scc/division/clk/diracc.htm. Download the application from the web site.

Uniform Commercial Code, Federal Tax Liens

UCC Division, State Corporation Commission, PO Box 1197, Richmond, VA 23218-1197 (Courier: 1300 E Main St, 1st Floor, Richmond, VA 23219); 804-371-9733, 804-371-9744 (Fax), 8:15AM-5PM.

www.state.va.us/scc/division/clk/index.htm

Online: This is a free, non-Internet service. Accounts must be registered. This is the same system used for corporation records. Call 804-371-9819 and ask for a registration packet.

Driver Records

Motorist Records Services, Attn: Records Request Work Center, PO Box 27412, Richmond, VA 23269; 804-367-0538, 8:30AM-5:30PM M-F; 8:30AM-12:30PM S.

www.dmv.state.va.us *continued*

Online: Online service is provided by the Virginia Information Providers Network (VIPNet). Online reports are provided via the Internet on an interactive basis 24 hours daily. There is a $50 annual administrative fee and records are $5.00 each. Go to www.vipnet.org for more information or call 804-786-4718.

Vehicle Ownership, Vehicle Identification

Motorist Records Services, Customer Records Request Section, PO Box 27412, Richmond, VA 23269; 804-367-0538, 8:30AM-5:30PM M-F; 8:30AM-12:30PM S.

www.dmv.state.va.us

Online: The online system, managed by the Virginia Information Providers Network (VIPNet), is an interactive system open 24 hours daily. There is an annual $50 administration fee and records are $5.00 each. All accounts must be approved by both the DMV and VIPNet. Contact Rodney Willett at 804-786-4718 to request an information use agreement application. The URL is www.vipnet.org.

Boat & Vessel Ownership, Boat & Vessel Registration

Game & Inland Fisheries Dept, 4010 W Broad St, Richmond, VA 23230-1528; 804-367-6135, 804-367-1064 (Fax), 8:15AM-5PM.

www.dgif.state.va.us

Online: The VA boat registration database may be searched on the web at www.vipnet.org. There is both a free service and a more advanced pay service, but both require a subscription which is $50.00 a year. Other motor vehicle records are available.

Legislation Records

House of Delegates, Information & Public Relations, PO Box 406, Richmond, VA 23218 (Courier: 1st Floor, State Capitol Bldg, 9th and Grace Streets, Richmond, VA 23219); 804-698-1500, 877-391-3228 (Toll Free), 804-786-3215 (Fax), 8AM-5PM.

http://legis.state.va.us/vaonline/v.htm

Online: Information can be found on the web site. There is no fee.

State Level...Occupational Licensing

Accountants/Accountant Business/Sponsor .... www.dpor.state.va.us/regulantlookup/
Acupuncturist .... www.vipnet.org/dhp/cgi-bin/search_publicdb.cgi
Air Conditioning Contractor .... www.dpor.state.va.us/regulantlookup/
Architect .... www.dpor.state.va.us/regulantlookup/
Asbestos Related Occupation .... www.dpor.state.va.us/regulantlookup/
Auctioneer .... www.dpor.state.va.us/regulantlookup/
Barber .... www.dpor.state.va.us/regulantlookup/
Boxer .... www.dpor.state.va.us/regulantlookup/
Branch Pilot .... www.dpor.state.va.us/regulantlookup/
Carpenter .... www.dpor.state.va.us/regulantlookup/
Cemetery Company .... www.dpor.state.va.us/regulantlookup/
Chiropractor .... www.vipnet.org/dhp/cgi-bin/search_publicdb.cgi
Clinical Nurse Specialist .... www.vipnet.org/dhp/cgi-bin/search_publicdb.cgi
Contractor .... www.dpor.state.va.us/regulantlookup/
Cosmetologist/Cosmetology School/Business ..... www.dpor.state.va.us/regulantlookup/
Dentist/Dental Hygienist .... www.vipnet.org/dhp/cgi-bin/search_publicdb.cgi
Electrical Contractor .... www.dpor.state.va.us/regulantlookup/
Embalmer .... www.vipnet.org/dhp/cgi-bin/search_publicdb.cgi
Engineer .... www.dpor.state.va.us/regulantlookup/
Funeral Director .... www.vipnet.org/dhp/cgi-bin/search_publicdb.cgi
Gas Fitter .... www.dpor.state.va.us/regulantlookup/
Geologist .... www.dpor.state.va.us/regulantlookup/

Hearing Aid Specialist .... www.dpor.state.va.us/regulantlookup/
Heating & AC Mechanic/Contractor .... www.dpor.state.va.us/regulantlookup/
Interior Designer .... www.dpor.state.va.us/regulantlookup/
Landscape Architect .... www.dpor.state.va.us/regulantlookup/
Lead-Related Occupation .... www.dpor.state.va.us/regulantlookup/
Lobbyist .... www.soc.state.va.us/databa.htm
Marriage & Family Therapist .... www.vipnet.org/dhp/cgi-bin/search_publicdb.cgi
Medical Doctor .... www.vipnet.org/dhp/cgi-bin/search_publicdb.cgi
Medical Equipment Supplier .... www.vipnet.org/dhp/cgi-bin/search_publicdb.cgi
Nail Technician .... www.dpor.state.va.us/regulantlookup/
Nurse-LPN .... www.dhp.state.va.us/nurse/lpn.htm
Nurse/Nurse-RN/ Nurse Aide .... www.vipnet.org/dhp/cgi-bin/search_publicdb.cgi
Nursing Home Administrator/Preceptor .... www.vipnet.org/dhp/cgi-bin/search_publicdb.cgi
Occupational Therapist .... www.vipnet.org/dhp/cgi-bin/search_publicdb.cgi
Optician .... www.dpor.state.va.us/regulantlookup/
Optometrist www.arbo.org/nodb2000/licsearch.asp
Osteopathic Physician .... www.vipnet.org/dhp/cgi-bin/search_publicdb.cgi
Pharmacist/Pharmacy .... www.vipnet.org/dhp/cgi-bin/search_publicdb.cgi
Physical Therapist .... www.vipnet.org/dhp/cgi-bin/search_publicdb.cgi
Physician .... www.vipnet.org/dhp/cgi-bin/search_publicdb.cgi
Plumber .... www.dpor.state.va.us/regulantlookup/
Podiatrist .... www.vipnet.org/dhp/cgi-bin/search_publicdb.cgi
Polygraph Examiner .... www.dpor.state.va.us/regulantlookup/
Property Association .... www.dpor.state.va.us/regulantlookup/
Psychologist, Clinical, Applied, School .... www.vipnet.org/dhp/cgi-bin/search_publicdb.cgi
Public Accountant-CPA .... www.dpor.state.va.us/regulantlookup/
Real Estate Agent/Business/School .... www.dpor.state.va.us/regulantlookup/
Real Estate Appraiser Individual/Business .... www.dpor.state.va.us/regulantlookup/
Respiratory Care Practitioner .... www.vipnet.org/dhp/cgi-bin/search_publicdb.cgi
Social Worker, Clinical .... www.vipnet.org/dhp/cgi-bin/search_publicdb.cgi
Soil Scientist .... www.dpor.state.va.us/regulantlookup/
Speech Pathologist/Audiologist .... www.vipnet.org/dhp/cgi-bin/search_publicdb.cgi
Substance Abuse Treatment Practitioner .... www.vipnet.org/dhp/cgi-bin/search_publicdb.cgi
Surveyor .... www.dpor.state.va.us/regulantlookup/
Veterinarian/ Veterinary Technician .... www.vipnet.org/dhp/cgi-bin/search_publicdb.cgi
Waste Management Facility Operator .... www.dpor.state.va.us/regulantlookup/
Waste Water Works Operator .... www.dpor.state.va.us/regulantlookup/
Wrestler .... www.dpor.state.va.us/regulantlookup/

Editor's Choice for Virginia

Constitution Text
http://legis.state.va.us/vaonline/li1.htm
State Code Search Form
http://leg1.state.va.us/000/src.htm
Violent Sex Offenders Database
http://sex-offender.vsp.state.va.us/cool-ICE

County Level...Courts, Recorders & Assessors

Executive Secretary, Administrative Office of Courts, 100 N 9th St 3rd Fl, Supreme Court Bldg, Richmond, VA, 23219; 804-786-6455; www.courts.state.va.us

Editor's Note: Two online, statewide public access computer system are available. The first is the Law Office Public Access System (LOPAS). The system allows remote access to the court case indexes and abstracts from most of the state's courts. In order to determine which courts are on LOPAS, you must obtain an ID and password (instructions below), and search on the system. A summary list of included courts is not available. Searching is by specific court; there is no combined index.

The system contains opinions from the Supreme Court and the Court of Appeals as well as criminal and civil case information from Circuit and District Courts. The number of years of information provided varies widely from court to court, depending on when the particular court joined the Courts Automated Information System (CAIS). There are no sign-up or other fees to use LOPAS. Access is granted on a request-by-request basis. Anyone wishing to establish an account or receive information on LOPAS must contact Ken Mittendorf, Director of MIS, Supreme Court of Virginia, 100 N 9th St, Richmond VA 23219 or by phone at 804-786-6455 or Fax at 804-786-4542.

Virginia also has the "Circuit Court Case Information Pilot Project," which includes free access to records from these Circuit Courts: Arlington, Augusta, Bedford, Botetourt, Carroll, Chesapeake City, Danville City, Dickenson, Fauquier, Floyd, Franklin City, Fredericksburg City, Gloucester, Hampton City, Henry, Hopewell City, Isle of Wight, King George, Louisa, Martinsville City, Nelson, Newport News City, Norfolk City, Nottoway, Orange, Petersburg City, Pulaski, Radford City, Richmond City, Roanoke City, Rockingham, Russell, Tazewell, Warren, Waynesboro City, Williamsburg/James City, Winchester, Wise, York.

Arlington
Civil Cases, Criminal Records
http://158.59.15.115/arlington/
Online access is available free at http://208.210.219.132/courtinfo/vacircuit/select.jsp?court=. For information about the statewide online system, LOPAS, see start of this section.
Real Estate, Assessor
Property records on the County assessor database are available free at www.co.arlington.va.us/REAssessments/Scripts/DreaDefault.asp.

Augusta
Civil Cases, Criminal Records
Online access is available free at http://208.210.219.132/courtinfo/vacircuit/select.jsp?court=. For information about the statewide online system, LOPAS, see start of this section.

Bedford
Civil Cases, Criminal Records
Online access is available free at http://208.210.219.132/courtinfo/vacircuit/select.jsp?court=. For information about the statewide online system, LOPAS, see start of this section.
Property Tax
County real estate records on the Bedford County Commissioner of the Revenue site are available free online at http://208.206.84.33/realestate2. Records on the City of Bedford (www.ci.bedford.va.us) Property Tax database are available free online at www.ci.bedford.va.us/taxf.shtml. Search by name, address or tax map reference number.

Botetourt
Civil Cases, Criminal Records
Online access is available free at http://208.210.219.132/courtinfo/vacircuit/select.jsp?court=. For information about the statewide online system, LOPAS, see start of this section.

Carroll
Civil Cases, Criminal Records
Online access is available free at http://208.210.219.132/courtinfo/vacircuit/select.jsp?court=. For information about the statewide online system, LOPAS, see start of this section.
Real Estate
Online access to Carroll county property information is available free on the GIS mapping site at http://arcims.webgis.net/webgis/carroll_grayson. No name searching at this time. Access to Town of Hillsville property information is available on the GIS mapping site at http://arcims.webgis.net/webgis/hillsville.

Chesapeake City
Civil Cases, Criminal Records
Online access is available free at http://208.210.219.132/courtinfo/vacircuit/select.jsp?court=. For information about the statewide online system, LOPAS, see start of this section.

Danville City
Civil Cases, Criminal Records
Online access is available free at http://208.210.219.132/courtinfo/vacircuit/select.jsp?court=. For information about the statewide online system, LOPAS, see start of this section.
Real Estate, Liens
Access to Danville City online records is free; signup is required. Records date back to 1993. Lending agency information is available. For information, contact Leigh Ann Thomas at 804-799-5168.

Dickenson
Civil Cases, Criminal Records
Online access is available free at http://208.210.219.132/courtinfo/vacircuit/select.jsp?court=. For information about the statewide online system, LOPAS, see start of this section.

Fairfax
Real Estate, Property Tax
www.co.fairfax.va.us
Records on the Dept. of Tax Administration Real Estate Assessment database are available free online at www.co.fairfax.va.us/dta/re/notice.asp. Also, the Automated Information System operates Monday-Saturday 7AM-7PM at 703-222-6740. Hear about property descriptions, assessed values and sales prices. Fax-back service is available.

Fauquier
Civil Cases, Criminal Records
http://co.fauquier.va.us/services/ccc/index.html
Online access is available free at http://208.210.219.132/courtinfo/vacircuit/select.jsp?court=. For information about the statewide online system, LOPAS, see start of this section.

Floyd
Civil Cases, Criminal Records
Online access is available free at http://208.210.219.132/courtinfo/vacircuit/select.jsp?court=. For information about the statewide online system, LOPAS, see start of this section.
Real Estate
Online access to county property information is available free at the GIS mapping site at http://arcims.webgis.net/webgis/floyd/default.asp. No name searching at this time.

Franklin City
Civil Cases, Criminal Records
Online access is available free at http://208.210.219.132/courtinfo/vacircuit/select.jsp?court=. For information about the statewide

online system, LOPAS, see start of this section.

Fredericksburg City
Civil Cases, Criminal Records
Online access is available free at http://208.210.219.132/courtinfo/vacircuit/select.jsp?court=. For information about the statewide online system, LOPAS, see start of this section.

Gloucester
Civil Cases, Criminal Records
www.co.gloucester.va.us
Online access is available free at http://208.210.219.132/courtinfo/vacircuit/select.jsp?court=. For information about the statewide online system, LOPAS, see start of this section.

Grayson
Real Estate
Online access to Grayson county property information is available free on the GIS mapping site at http://arcims.webgis.net/webgis/carroll_grayson. No name searching at this time.

Hampton City
Civil Cases, Criminal Records
Online access is available free at http://208.210.219.132/courtinfo/vacircuit/select.jsp?court=. For information about the statewide online system, LOPAS, see start of this section.

Henry
Civil Cases, Criminal Records
Online access is available free at http://208.210.219.132/courtinfo/vacircuit/select.jsp?court=. For information about the statewide online system, LOPAS, see start of this section.
Real Estate, Assessor
http://henrycounty.neocom.net
Online access to county property information is available free at the GIS mapping site at www.webgis.net/henry.

Hopewell City
Civil Cases, Criminal Records
Online access is available free at http://208.210.219.132/courtinfo/vacircuit/select.jsp?court=. For information about the statewide online system, LOPAS, see start of this section.

Isle of Wight
Civil Cases, Criminal Records
Online access is available free at http://208.210.219.132/courtinfo/vacircuit/select.jsp?court=. For information about the statewide online system, LOPAS, see start of this section.

James City
Civil Cases, Criminal Records
Online access is available free at http://208.210.219.132/courtinfo/vacircuit/select.jsp?court=. For information about the statewide online system, LOPAS, see start of this section.
Real Estate
www.regis.state.va.us/jcc/public/index.htm
Records on the James City County Property Information database are available free online at the web site.

King George
Civil Cases, Criminal Records
Online access is available free at http://208.210.219.132/courtinfo/vacircuit/select.jsp?court=. For information about the statewide online system, LOPAS, see start of this section.

Louisa
Civil Cases, Criminal Records
Online access is available free at http://208.210.219.132/courtinfo/vacircuit/select.jsp?court=. For information about the statewide online system, LOPAS, see start of this section.

Martinsville City
Civil Cases, Criminal Records
Online access is available free at http://208.210.219.132/courtinfo/vacircuit/select.jsp?court=. For information about the statewide online system, LOPAS, see start of this section.

Montgomery
Real Estate, Property Tax
Access to the county Tax Parcel Information System database is available free online at www.webgis.net/montgomery/index.htm. Select what to search and click next. Records on the Town of Blackburg GIS site are available free online at www.webgis.net/blacksburg. Use map or enter an owner name. Find owner name, address, land or building values.

Nelson
Civil Cases, Criminal Records
Online access is available free at http://208.210.219.132/courtinfo/vacircuit/select.jsp?court=. For information about the statewide online system, LOPAS, see start of this section.

Newport News City
Civil Cases, Criminal Records
Online access is available free at http://208.210.219.132/courtinfo/vacircuit/select.jsp?court=. For information about the statewide online system, LOPAS, see start of this section.
Assessor, Real Estate
www.newport-news.va.us
Online access to the City's "Real Estate on the Web" database is available free at http://216.54.20.244/reisweb1. Search by address or parcel number; new "advanced search" may include name searching.

Norfolk City
Civil Cases, Criminal Records
Online access is available free at http://208.210.219.132/courtinfo/vacircuit/select.jsp?court=. For information about the statewide online system, LOPAS, see start of this section.
Real Estate, Assessor
http://206.246.226.47/RealEstate
Records on the City of Norfolk Real Estate Property Assessment database are available free online at http://206.246.226.47/RealEstate/search.html.

Nottoway
Civil Cases, Criminal Records
Online access is available free at http://208.210.219.132/courtinfo/vacircuit/select.jsp?court=. For information about the statewide online system, LOPAS, see start of this section.

Orange
Civil Cases, Criminal Records
Online access is available free at http://208.210.219.132/courtinfo/vacircuit/select.jsp?court=. For information about the statewide online system, LOPAS, see start of this section.

Petersburg City
Civil Cases, Criminal Records
Online access is available free at http://208.210.219.132/courtinfo/vacircuit/select.jsp?court=. For information about the statewide online system, LOPAS, see start of this section.

Pittsylvania
Real Estate
See Danville City for Real Estate and Lien records online for Danville City.

Prince William
Property Records
www.pwcgov.org/ccourt
Records on the county Property Information database are available free online at www.pwcgov.org/realestate/LandRover.asp.

Pulaski
Civil Cases, Criminal Records
www.pulaskicircuitcourt.com
Online access to court records is available free at http://records.pulaskicircuitcourt.com/splash.jsp. Registration required; search by name, document type or number. Also, online access is available free at http://208.210.219.132/courtinfo/vacircuit/select.jsp?court=.

Radford City
Civil Cases, Criminal Records
Online access is available free at http://208.210.219.132/courtinfo/vacircuit/select.jsp?court=. For information about the statewide online system, LOPAS, see start of this section.

Richmond City
Civil Cases, Criminal Records
www.ncsc.dni.us/court/richmond/richmond.htm
Online access is available free at http://208.210.219.132/courtinfo/vacircuit/select.jsp?court=. For information about the statewide online system, LOPAS, see start of this section.

Roanoke City
Civil Cases, Criminal Records
www.co.roanoke.va.us
Online access is available free at http://208.210.219.132/courtinfo/vacircuit/select.jsp?court=. For information about the statewide online system, LOPAS, see start of this section.
Property Records
Online access to Roanoke City property records is available free at www.webgis.net/RoanokeCity.

Rockingham
Civil Cases, Criminal Records
Online access is available free at http://208.210.219.132/courtinfo/vacircuit/select.jsp?court=. For information about the statewide online system, LOPAS, see start of this section.

Russell
Civil Cases, Criminal Records
Online access is available free at http://208.210.219.132/courtinfo/vacircuit/select.jsp?court=. For information about the statewide online system, LOPAS, see start of this section.

Tazewell
Civil Cases, Criminal Records
Online access is available free at http://208.210.219.132/courtinfo/vacircuit/select.jsp?court=. For information about the statewide online system, LOPAS, see start of this section.

Warren
Civil Cases, Criminal Records
www.courts.state.va.us/courts/circuit/warren/home.html
Online access is available free at http://208.210.219.132/courtinfo/vacircuit/select.jsp?court=. For information about the statewide online system, LOPAS, see start of this section.

Washington

Real Estate, Assessor

Online access to Town of Abington property information is available free on the GIS mapping site at www.webgis.net/abingdon.

Waynesboro City

Civil Cases, Criminal Records

Online access is available free at http://208.210.219.132/courtinfo/vacircuit/select.jsp?court=. For information about the statewide online system, LOPAS, see start of this section.

Winchester City

Civil Cases, Criminal Records

www.winfredclerk.com
Online access is available free at http://208.210.219.132/courtinfo/vacircuit/select.jsp?court=. For information about the statewide online system, LOPAS, see start of this section.

Wise

Civil Cases, Criminal Records

Online access is available free at http://208.210.219.132/courtinfo/vacircuit/select.jsp?court=. Also, court indexes are available at www.courtbar.org. Registration and a fee is required. Records go back to June, 2000.

Assessor, Real Estate, Liens, Probate, Marriage Records

www.courtbar.org
Includes City of Norton. Premium User fee is $395 annually or $39 per month. Genealogists have two plans: the 150-year marriage and probate database is $99 annually or $10 per month. Database index and images include the Court's orders, land documents from 1970 including links to real estate tax assessments, fifty-year real estate transfer histories, tax maps, plat maps, delinquent taxes, and permit images, probate and marriage records, with recent document images from probate. Access the judgment lien index for the past 20 years; UCC-1 indices for the past five years. Also, property information is available free at http://arcims.webgis.net/webgis/wise.

Wythe

Real Estate

Online access to property information is available at the GIS mapping site at http://arcims.webgis.net/webgis/wythe. No name searching at this time.

York

Civil Cases, Criminal Records

Online access is available free at http://208.210.219.132/courtinfo/vacircuit/select.jsp?court=. For information about the statewide online system, LOPAS, see start of this section.

Property Records

www.yorkcounty.gov/circuitcourt
Property records from the County GIS site are available free online at http://206.246.204.37.

Federal Courts in Virginia...

US District Court - Eastern District of Virginia

Home Page: www.vaed.uscourts.gov
PACER: Sign-up number is 800-676-6856. Access fee is $.60 per minute. Toll-free access: 800-852-5186. Local access: 703-299-2158. Case records are available back to June 1990. New records are available online after 1 day.
PACER Internet Access: http://pacer.vaed.uscourts.gov.
Alexandria Division Counties: Arlington, Fairfax, Fauquier, Loudoun, Prince William, Stafford, City of Alexandria, City of Fairfax, City of Falls Church, City of Manassas, City of Manassas Park.
Newport News Division Counties: Gloucester, James City, Mathews, York, City of Hampton, City of Newport News, City of Poquoson, City of Williamsburg.
Norfolk Division Counties: Accomack, City of Chesapeake, City of Franklin, Isle of Wight, City of Norfolk, Northampton, City of Portsmouth, City of Suffolk, Southampton, City of Virginia Beach.

Richmond Division Counties: Amelia, Brunswick, Caroline, Charles City, Chesterfield, Dinwiddie, Essex, Goochland, Greensville, Hanover, Henrico, King and Queen, King George, King William, Lancaster, Lunenburg, Mecklenburg, Middlesex, New Kent, Northumberland, Nottoway, City ofPetersburg, Powhatan, Prince Edward, Prince George, Richmond, City of Richmond, Spotsylvania, Surry, Sussex, Westmoreland, City of Colonial Heights, City of Emporia, City of Fredericksburg, City of Hopewell.

US Bankruptcy Court - Eastern District of Virginia

Home Page: www.vaeb.uscourts.gov
PACER: Sign-up number is 800-676-6856. Access fee is $.60 per minute. Toll-free access: 800-890-2858. Local access: 703-557-6272. Use of PC Anywhere v4.0 suggested. Case records are available back to mid 1989. Records are purged never. New civil records are available online after 1 day.
Electronic Filing: Electronic filing information is available online at http://ecf.vaeb.uscourts.gov.
Other Online Access: You can search records using the Internet. Searching is currently free. To search by name - www.vaeb.uscourts.gov/home/SearchNM.html. To search by case number - www.vaeb.uscourts.gov/home/SearchCSNUM.html. More options available from main site.
Alexandria Division Counties: City of Alexandria, Arlington, Fairfax, City of Fairfax, City of Falls Church, Fauquier, Loudoun, City of Manassas, City of Manassas Park, Prince William, Stafford.
Norfolk Division Counties: Accomack, City of Cape Charles, City of Chesapeake, City of Franklin, Gloucester, City of Hampton, Isle of Wight, James City, Matthews, City of Norfolk, Northampton, City of PoquosonCity of Portsmouth, Southampton, City of Suffolk,City of Virginia Beach, City of Williamsburg, York.
Richmond Division Counties: Amelia, Brunswick, Caroline, Charles City, Chesterfield, City of Colonial Heights, Dinwiddie, City of Emporia, Essex, City of Fredericksburg, Goochland, Greensville, Hanover, Henrico, City of Hopewell, King and Queen, King George, King William,Lancaster, Lunenburg, Mecklenburg, Middlesex, New Kent, Northumberland, Nottoway, City of Petersburg, Powhatan, Prince Edward, Prince George, Richmond, City of Richmond, Spotsylvania, Surry, Sussex, Westmoreland.

US District Court - Western District of Virginia

Home Page: www.vawd.uscourts.gov
PACER: Sign-up number is 800-676-6856. Access fee is. Toll-free access: 888-279-7848. Local access: 540-857-5140, 540-857-2290, 540-857-2288. Case records available back to Mid 1990. Records are purged never. New records available online after 1 day.
PACER Internet Access: http://pacer.vawd.uscourts.gov.
Abingdon Division Counties: Buchanan, City of Bristol, Russell, Smyth, Tazewell, Washington.
Big Stone Gap Division Counties: Dickenson, Lee, Scott, Wise, City of Norton.
Charlottesville Division Counties: Albemarle, Culpeper, Fluvanna, Greene, Louisa, Madison, Nelson, Orange, Rappahannock, City of Charlottesville.
Danville Division Counties: Charlotte, Halifax, Henry, Patrick, Pittsylvania, City of Danville, City of Martinsville, City of South Boston.
Harrisonburg Division Counties: Augusta, Bath, Clarke, Frederick, Highland, Page, Rockingham, Shenandoah, Warren, City of Harrisonburg, City of Staunton, City of Waynesboro, City of Winchester.
Lynchburg Division Counties: Amherst, Appomattox, Bedford, Buckingham, Campbell, Cumberland, Rockbridge, City of Bedford, City of Buena Vista, City of Lexington, City of Lynchburg.
Roanoke Division Counties: Alleghany, Bland, Botetourt, Carroll, Craig, Floyd, Franklin, Giles, Grayson, Montgomery, Pulaski, Roanoke, Wythe, City of Covington, City of Clifton Forge, City of Galax, City of Radford, City of Roanoke, City of Salem.

US Bankruptcy Court - Western District of Virginia

Home Page: www.vawb.uscourts.gov
PACER: Sign-up number is 800-676-6856. Access fee is $.60 per minute. Toll-free access: 800-248-0329. Local access: 540-434-8373. Use of PC Anywhere v4.0 suggested. Case records are available back to March 1986. Records are purged never. New civil records are available online after 1 day.
Harrisonburg Division Counties: Alleghany, Augusta, Bath, City of Buena Vista, Clarke, City of Clifton Forge, City of Covington, Frederick, City of Harrisonburg, Highland, City of Lexington, Page, Rappahannock, Rockbridge, Rockingham, Shenandoah, City of Staunton, Warren, City ofWaynesboro, City of Winchester.
Lynchburg Division Counties: Albemarle, Amherst, Appomattox, Bedford, City of Bedford, Buckingham, Campbell, Charlotte, City of Charlottesville, Culpeper, Cumberland, City of Danville, Fluvanna, Greene, Halifax, Henry, Louisa, City of Lynchburg, Madison, City of Martinsville,Nelson, Orange, Patrick, Pittsylvania, City of South Boston.
Roanoke Division Counties: Bland, Botetourt, City of Bristol, Buchanan, Carroll, Craig, Dickenson, Floyd, Franklin, City of Galax, Giles, Grayson, Lee, Montgomery, City of Norton, Pulaski, City of Radford, Roanoke, City of Roanoke, Russell, City of Salem, Scott, Smyth, Tazewell,Washington, Wise, Wythe.

Capital: Olympia
Thurston County

Time Zone: PST

Number of Counties: 39

Home Page http://access.wa.gov

Attorney General www.wa.gov/ago

Archives www.secstate.wa.gov/archives

State Level...Major Agencies

Criminal Records

Washington State Patrol, Identification Section, PO Box 42633, Olympia, WA 98504-2633 (Courier: 3000 Pacific Ave. SE #204, Olympia, WA 98501); 360-705-5100, 8AM-5PM.

www.wa.gov/wsp/wsphome.htm

Online: The State Court Administrator's office maintains a database of criminal records in their JIS-Link. Records do not include arrests unless case is filed. There is a $100.00 set-up fee and a $25.00 per hour access charge. Call 360-357-2407 for packet. WSP offers access through a system called WATCH, which can be accessed from their web site. The fee is $10.00. The exact DOB and exact spelling of the name is required. Credit cards are accepted for payment. To set up a WATCH account, call (360) 705-5100 or e-mail to criminhis@wsp.gov.

Corporation Records, Trademarks/Servicemarks, Limited Partnerships, Limited Liability Company Records

Secretary of State, Corporations Division, PO Box 40234, Olympia, WA 98504-0234 (Courier: Dolliver Bldg, 801 Capitol Way South, Olympia, WA 98501); 360-753-7115, 360-664-8781 (Fax), 8AM-4PM.

www.secstate.wa.gov/corps/

Online: From the Dept of Licensing; subscription is $18 per month, access is $60 per hour plus line charges of $.09-37 per minute. A $200 deposit is required to start. Hours are from 5 AM to 9 PM. Call Darla at 360-664-1530 for more information. A free, non-commercial look-up service is provided at the web site. Information is updated weekly. Also, the Department of Revenue has a non-commercial use site for tax license and registration at http://dov.wa.gov/prd.

Trade Names

Master License Service, Business & Professions Div, PO Box 9034, Olympia, WA 98507-9034 (Courier: 405 Black Lake Blvd, Olympia, WA 98507); 360-664-1400, 900-463-6000 (Trade Name Search), 360-753-9668 (Fax), 8AM-5PM.

www.wa.gov/dol

Online: This is the same system for corporation and UCC records. A deposit is required (depends on usage), access is $60 per hour plus a $.09-.37 phone charge. Hours are 5 AM to 9 PM daily. Call Field Access at 360-664-1400 to set up a contractual agreement.

Uniform Commercial Code, Federal Tax Liens

Department of Licensing, UCC Records, PO Box 9660, Olympia, WA 98507-9660 (Courier: 405 Black Lake Blvd, Olympia, WA 98502); 360-664-1530, 360-586-1404 (Fax), 8AM-5PM.

www.wa.gov/dol/bpd/uccfront.htm

Online: Subscription fee is $18.00 per month. Online access costs $60.00 per hour. There is a deposit of $200 required which is replenished at end of the month. Line charges will vary from $.09 to.37 per minute. Hours are from 5 AM to 9 PM. Call Darla at 360-664-1530 for more information.

Sales Tax Registrations

Revenue Department, Taxpayer Services, PO Box 47498, Olympia, WA 98504-7478 (Courier: 415 Gen Admin Bldg, Olympia, WA 98501); 360-786-6100, 800-647-7706, 360-664-0456 (Fax), 8AM-5PM.

www.dor.wa.gov

Online: The agency provides a state business records database with free access on the Internet. Lookups are by owner names, DBAs, and tax reporting numbers. Results show a myriad of data.

Vehicle Ownership, Vehicle Identification, Boat & Vessel Ownership, Boat & Vessel Registration

Department of Licensing, Vehicle Records, PO Box 2957, Olympia, WA 98507-2957 (Courier: 1125 S Washington MS-48001, Olympia, WA 98504); 360-902-3780, 360-902-3827 (Fax), 8AM-5PM.

www.wa.gov/dol

Online: This is a commercial subscription service. All accounts must be pre-approved. Access is via the Internet. Known as IVIPS, the system processes the same as the phone search. A $25.00 deposit is required and there is a $.04 fee per hit. For more information, call 360-902-3760.

Legislation Records

Washington Legislature, State Capitol-Legislative Info Center, PO Box 40600, Olympia, WA 98504-0600; 360-753-5000 (Information), 800-562-6000 (Local Only), 360-786-7573 (Bill Room), 360-786-1293 (Fax), 9AM-5PM.

www.leg.wa.gov

Online: The web site offers bill text and status look-up.

Hunting License Information, Fishing License Information

Department of Fish & Wildlife, Attn: Public Disclosure Officer, 600 Capitol Way, N, Olympia, WA 98501-1091; 360-902-2253, 360-902-2171 (Fax), 8AM-5PM.

www.wa.gov/wdfw

Online: You may send an e-mail request; check the web site for the exact address.

State Level...Occupational Licensing

Cosmetologist/Instructor/School https://wws2.wa.gov/dol/profquery
Crematory https://wws2.wa.gov/dol/profquery
Electrician/Electrical Administrator/Contractor .. https://wws2.wa.gov/lni/bbip/contractor.asp
Embalmer https://wws2.wa.gov/dol/profquery
Employment Agency https://wws2.wa.gov/dol/profquery
Engineer .... www.wa.gov/dol/bpd/pliseng.htm
Engineers https://wws2.wa.gov/dol/profquery/LicenseeSearch.asp
Esthetician/ Esthetician Instructor https://wws2.wa.gov/dol/profquery
Funeral Director/Establishment https://wws2.wa.gov/dol/profquery
General Contractor https://wws2.wa.gov/lni/bbip/contractor.asp
Geologist https://wws2.wa.gov/dol/profquery
Insurance Company .... www.insurance.wa.gov/tableofcontents/annualreptins.htm
Land Surveyor https://wws2.wa.gov/dol/profquery/LicenseeSearch.asp
Landscape Architect https://wws2.wa.gov/dol/profquery/LicenseeSearch.asp
Limousine Carrier https://wws2.wa.gov/dol/profquery
Liquor Store .... www.liq.wa.gov/services/storesearch.asp
Manicurist/ Manicurist Instructor https://wws2.wa.gov/dol/profquery
Manufactured Home Dealer https://wws2.wa.gov/dol/profquery
Mobile Home Travel Trailer Dealer https://wws2.wa.gov/dol/profquery
Notary Public https://wws2.wa.gov/dol/profquery
Optometrist www.arbo.org/nodb2000/licsearch.asp
Plumber https://wws2.wa.gov/lni/bbip/contractor.asp
Private Investigative Agency https://wws2.wa.gov/dol/profquery
Private Investigator, Armed or Unarmed https://wws2.wa.gov/dol/profquery
Real Estate Appraiser https://wws2.wa.gov/dol/profquery
Real Estate Broker/Sales https://wws2.wa.gov/dol/profquery
Salon/Shop https://wws2.wa.gov/dol/profquery
Scrap Processor https://wws2.wa.gov/dol/profquery
Security Guard https://wws2.wa.gov/dol/profquery
Snowmobile Dealer https://wws2.wa.gov/dol/profquery
Surveyor .... www.wa.gov/dol/bpd/plisls.htm
Tow Truck Operator https://wws2.wa.gov/dol/profquery
Travel Agency/Seller of Travel https://wws2.wa.gov/dol/profquery
Vehicle Dealer/Transporter/Manufacturer https://wws2.wa.gov/dol/profquery
Vehicle Dealer, Miscellaneous https://wws2.wa.gov/dol/profquery
Wrecker https://wws2.wa.gov/dol/profquery
Wrestler https://wws2.wa.gov/dol/profquery

County Level...Courts, Recorders & Assessors

Court Administrator, Temple of Justice, PO Box 41174, Olympia, WA, 98504; 360-357-2121; www.courts.wa.gov

Editor's Note: Appellate, Superior, and District Court records are available online. The Superior Court Management Information System (SCOMIS), the Appellate Records System (ACORDS) and the District/Municipal Court Information System (DISCIS) are on the Judicial Information System's JIS-Link. Case records available through JIS-Link from 1977 include criminal, civil, domestic, probate, and judgments. JIS-Link is generally available

24-hours daily. Equipment requirements are a PC running Windows or MS-DOS. There is a one-time installation fee of $100.00 per site, and a connect time charge of $25.00 per hour (approximately $.42 per minute). For additional information and/or a registration packet, contact: JISLink Coordinator, Office of the Administrator for the Courts, 1206 S Quince St., PO Box 41170, Olympia WA 98504-1170, 360-357-2407 or visit the web site at www.courts.wa.gov/jislink.

Clark
Real Estate, Liens, Vital Statistics, Recording
www.co.clark.wa.us/auditor/
Online access to County Auditor's database is available at www.co.clark.wa.us/auditor/recording.htm. Court documents are excluded from this index.

Jefferson
Assessor, Real Estate
www.co.jefferson.wa.us/departments.htm
Online access to the "Recorded Document Search" database is available at www.co.jefferson.wa.us/_hidden/disclaimer.htm. Records on the County Property (Tax Parcel) Database Tool are also available as well as plats & survey images.

King
Real Estate, Liens, Marriage
www.metrokc.gov
Online access to the county recorder's database is available free at www.metrokc.gov/recelec/records. Also, property records on Dept. of Developmental and Environmental Resources database are available free online at www.metrokc.gov/ddes/gis/parcel. After the disclaimer page, search by parcel number, address, street intersection, or map.

Pierce
Civil Cases, Criminal Records
www.co.pierce.wa.us/abtus/ourorg/supct/abtussup.htm
Online Superior Court case information, inmates, attorneys, and scheduled proceedings is available free at www.co.pierce.wa.us/cfapps/linx/headerindex.cfm?source=search.cfm&activeTab=search. Also, a statewide index is available remotely online (see state introduction).

Assessor
Property records on County Assessor-Treasurer database are available free online at www.co.pierce.wa.us/CFApps/atr/TIMSNet/index.htm. After the disclaimer page, search by parcel number or site address.

Thurston
Assessor, Real Estate
Assessor and property information on Thurston GeoData database are available free online at www.geodata.org/scripts/esrimap.dll?name=TGCMAP&Cmd=Map.

Whatcom
Assessor, Real Estate
www.co.whatcom.wa.us
Online access to the assessor parcel database information system is available free at www.co.whatcom.wa.us/cgibin/db2www/assessor/search/RPSearch.ndt/disclaimer.

Yakima
Assessor, Real Estate
www.pan.co.yakima.wa.us
Assessor and property information on County Assessor database are available free online at www.co.yakima.wa.us/assessor/propinfo/asr_info.asp.

Federal Courts in Washington...

US District Court - Eastern District of Washington

Home Page: www.waed.uscourts.gov
PACER: Sign-up number is 800-676-6856. Access fee is $.60 per minute. Toll-free access: 888-372-5706. Local access: 509-353-2395. Case records available back to July 1989. Records are purged every six months. New records available online after 2-3 days.
PACER Internet Access: http://pacer.waed.uscourts.gov.
Spokane Division Counties: Adams, Asotin, Benton, Chelan, Columbia, Douglas, Ferry, Franklin, Garfield, Grant, Lincoln, Okanogan, Pend Oreille, Spokane, Stevens, Walla Walla, Whitman. Also, some cases from Kittitas, Klickitat and Yakima are heard here.
Yakima Division Counties: Kittitas, Klickitat, Yakima. Cases assigned primarily to Judge McDonald are here. Some cases from Kittitas, Klickitat and Yakima are heard in Spokane.

US Bankruptcy Court - Eastern District of Washington

Home Page: www.waeb.uscourts.gov
PACER: Sign-up number is 800-676-6856. Access fee is $.60 per minute. Toll-free access: 800-314-3430. Local access: 509-353-3289. Use of PC Anywhere V4.0 recommended. Case records available back to 1986. New civil records available online after 1 day.
Other Online Access: You can search records on the Internet using RACER. Currently the system is free and requires free registration. Simply visit http://204.227.177.194/wconnect/wc.dll?usbcn_racer~main.
Spokane Division Counties: Adams, Asotin, Benton, Chelan, Columbia, Douglas, Ferry, Franklin, Garfield, Grant, Kittitas, Klickitat, Lincoln, Okanogan, Pend Oreille, Spokane, Stevens, Walla Walla, Whitman, Yakima.

US District Court - Western District of Washington

Home Page: www.wawd.uscourts.gov
PACER: Sign-up number is 800-676-6856. Access fee is $.60 per minute. Toll-free access: 800-520-8604. Local access: 206-553-6127, 206-553-2288. Case records are available back to 1988. Records are purged never. New civil records are available online after 4 days. New criminal records are available online after 2 days.
PACER Internet Access: http://pacer.wawd.uscourts.gov.
Seattle Division Counties: Island, King, San Juan, Skagit, Snohomish, Whatcom.
Tacoma Division Counties: Clallam, Clark, Cowlitz, Grays Harbor, Jefferson, Kitsap, Lewis, Mason, Pacific, Pierce, Skamania, Thurston, Wahkiakum.

US Bankruptcy Court - Western District of Washington

Home Page: www.wawb.uscourts.gov
PACER: Sign-up number is 800-676-6856. Access fee is $.60 per minute. Toll-free access: 800-704-4492. Local access: 206-553-0060, 206-553-0061, 206-553-0062, 206-553-0063, 206-553-0064, 206-553-6127. Case records are available back to June 1995. Records are purged never. New civil records are available online after 2 days.
PACER Internet Access: http://pacer.wawb.uscourts.gov.
Seattle Division Counties: Clallam, Island, Jefferson, King, Kitsap, San Juan, Skagit, Snohomish, Whatcom.
Tacoma Division Counties: Clark, Cowlitz, Grays Harbor, Lewis, Mason, Pacific, Pierce, Skamania, Thurston, Wahkiakum.

Editor's Choice for Washington

Constitution Text
    www.wolfenet.com/~dhillis/con/constitution.htm
Inmates Database
    www.co.pierce.wa.us/cfapps/linx/HeaderIndex.cfm?source=Search.cfm&activeTab=Searc
Telephone Numbers Directory
    http://dial.wa.gov/

Capital:	Charleston	Home Page	www.state.wv.us
	Kanawha County		
Time Zone:	EST	Attorney General	www.state.wv.us/wvag
Number of Counties:	55	Archives	www.wvculture.org/
			history/wvsamenu.html

State Level...Major Agencies

Corporation Records, Limited Liability Company Records, Limited Partnerships, Trademarks/Servicemarks, Limited Liability Partnerships

Secretary of State, Corporation Division, State Capitol Bldg, Room W139, Charleston, WV 25305-0776; 304-558-8000, 304-558-0900 (Fax), 8:30AM-4:30PM.

www.state.wv.us/sos

Birth Certificates, Death Records

Bureau of Public Health, Vital Records, 350 Capitol St, Rm 165, Charleston, WV 25305-3701; 304-558-2931, 304-343-2169 (Fax), 8AM-4PM.

www.wvdhhr.org/bph/oehp/hsc

Online: Online ordering is available at www.vitalchek.com.

Driver License Information, Driver Records

Div. of Motor Vehicles, 1800 Kanawha Blvd, Bldg. 3, Rm 118, State Capitol Complex, Charleston, WV 25317; 304-558-0238, 304-558-0037 (Fax), 8:30AM-4:30PM.

www.state.wv.us/dmv

Online: Online access is available in either interactive or batch mode. The system is open 24 hours a day. Batch requesters receive return transmission about 3 AM. Users must access through AAMVAnet. A contract is required and accounts must pre-pay. Fee is $5.00 per record. For more information, call Lacy Morgan at (304) 558-3915.

Legislation Records

West Virginia State Legislature, State Capitol, Documents, Charleston, WV 25305; 304-347-4830, 800-642-8650 (Local), 8:30AM-4:30PM.

www.legis.state.wv.us

Online: The Internet site allows one to search for status and/or text of bills.

State Level...Occupational Licensing

Attorney...www.wvbar.org/BARINFO/mdirectory/index.htm
Lobbyist..www.lobbyist.net/WestVirg/WESLOB.htm
Optometrist...www.odfinder.org/LicSearch.asp
Public Accountant-CPA....................................www.state.wv.us/scripts/wvboa/default.cfm
Radiologic Technologist....................................www.state.wv.us/rtboe/RTLIST.pdf

County Level...Courts, Recorders & Assessors

Administrative Office, Supreme Court of Appeals, 1900 Kanawha Blvd, 1 E 100 State Capitol, Charleston, WV, 25305; 304-558-0145; www.state.wv.us/wvsca

Editor's Note: There is no statewide online computer system, internal or external. Most courts with a computer system use FORTUNE software; however, no external access is permitted. A number of Circuit Courts are now online through a private company. These courts are located in the counties of Hancock, Kanawha, Mineral, Nicholas, Ohio, and Putnam. The private company also provides record look-ups for WV Magistrate Courts, however, access is restricted. For information, call 800-795-8543 or visit www.swcg-inc.com/courts.htm.

Hancock
Civil Cases, Criminal Records
Limited online access to court records is available; see note at start of section.

Kanawha
Civil Cases, Criminal Records
Limited online access to court records is available; see note at start of section.

Mineral
Civil Cases, Criminal Records
Limited online access to court records is available; see note at start of section.

Monongalia
Assessor, Real Estate Records
Records on the County Parcel Search database are available free online at www.assessor.org/parcelweb. Search by a wide variety of criteria including owner name and address.

Nicholas
Civil Cases, Criminal Records
Limited online access to court records is available; see note at start of section.

Ohio
Civil Cases, Criminal Records
Limited online access to court records is available; see note at start of section.

Putnam
Civil Cases, Criminal Records
Limited online access to court records is available; see note at start of section.

Federal Courts in West Virginia...

US District Court - Northern District of West Virginia

Home Page: www.wvnd.uscourts.gov
PACER: Sign-up number is 800-676-6856. Access fee is $.60 per minute. Toll-free access: 888-513-7959. Local access: 304-233-7424. Case records available back to October 1994. Records are purged every 5 years. New records are available online after 1 day.
PACER Internet Access: http://pacer.wvnd.uscourts.gov.
Clarksburg Division Counties: Braxton, Calhoun, Doddridge, Gilmer, Harrison, Lewis, Marion, Monongalia, Pleasants, Ritchie, Taylor, Tyler.
Elkins Division Counties: Barbour, Grant, Hardy, Mineral, Pendleton, Pocahontas, Preston, Randolph, Tucker, Upshur, Webster.
Martinsburg Division Counties: Berkeley, Hampshire, Jefferson, Morgan.
Wheeling Division Counties: Brooke, Hancock, Marshall, Ohio, Wetzel.

US Bankruptcy Court - Northern District of West Virginia

Home Page: www.wvnb.uscourts.gov
PACER: Sign-up number is 800-676-6856. Access fee is $.60 per minute. Toll-free access: 800-809-3016. Local access: 304-233-2871. Case records are available back to early 1990. Records are purged never. New civil records are available online after 1 day.
PACER Internet Access: http://pacer.wvnb.uscourts.gov.
Wheeling Division Counties: Barbour, Berkeley, Braxton, Brooke, Calhoun, Doddridge, Gilmer, Grant, Hampshire, Hancock, Hardy, Harrison, Jefferson, Lewis, Marion, Marshall, Mineral, Monongalia, Morgan, Ohio, Pendleton, Pleasants, Pocahontas, Preston, Randolph, Ritchie, Taylor,Tucker, Tyler, Upshur, Webster, Wetzel.

US District Court - Southern District of West Virginia

Home Page: www.wvsd.uscourts.gov
PACER: Sign-up number is 800-676-6856. Access fee is $.60 per minute. Toll-free access: 800-650-2141. Local access: 304-347-5596. Case records are available back to 1991. New records are available online after 1 day.
PACER Internet Access: http://pacer.wvsd.uscourts.gov.
Other Online Access: You can search records online using RACER. Visit http://207.41.17.36/wc.dll?usdc_racer~main.
Beckley Division Counties: Fayette, Greenbrier, Raleigh, Sumners, Wyoming.
Bluefield Division Counties: McDowell, Mercer, Monroe.
Charleston Division Counties: Boone, Clay, Jackson, Kanawha, Lincoln, Logan, Mingo, Nicholas, Putnam, Roane.
Huntington Division Counties: Cabell, Mason, Wayne.
Parkersburg Division Counties: Wirt, Wood.

US Bankruptcy Court - Southern District of West Virginia

PACER: Sign-up number is 800-676-6856. Access fee is $.60 per minute. Case records are available back to 1988. Records are purged every 6 months. New civil records are available online after 1 day.
Other Online Access: Records are searchable online using RACER. Visit http://207.41.17.36/wconnect/wc.dll?usbc_racer~main.
Charleston Division Counties: Boone, Cabell, Clay, Fayette, Greenbrier, Jackson, Kanawha, Lincoln, Logan, Mason, McDowell, Mercer, Mingo, Monroe, Nicholas, Putnam, Raleigh, Roane, Summers, Wayne, Wirt, Wood, Wyoming.

Editor's Choice for West Virginia

Code Text
www.legis.state.wv.us/Code/toc1.html
Sex Offenders Database
www.wvstatepolice.com/sexoff/
State Governmetn Phone Numbers Database
www.state.wv.us/scripts/phone/default.cfm

Capital:	Madison		Home Page	www.state.wi.us
	Dane County		Archives	
Time Zone:	CST			www.shsw.wisc.edu/archives
Number of Counties:	72		Attorney General	www.doj.state.wi.us

State Level...Major Agencies

Criminal Records

Wisconsin Department of Justice, Crime Information Bureau, Record Check Unit, PO Box 2688, Madison, WI 53701-2688 (Courier: 123 W Washington Ave, Madison, WI 53703); 608-266-5764, 608-266-7780 (Online Questions), 8AM-4:30PM.

www.doj.state.wi.us

Online: The agency offers Internet access at http://wi-recordcheck.org. An account is required. Also, there is a free Internet service for access to the state's Circuit Courts' records. However, not all counties participate. Visit http://ccap.courts.state.wi.us.

Corporation Records, Limited Partnership Records, Limited Liability Company Records, Limited Liability Partnerships

Department of Financial Institutions, Division of Corporate & Consumer Services, PO Box 7846, Madison, WI 53707-7846 (Courier: 345 W Washington Ave, 3rd Floor, Madison, WI 53703); 608-261-7577, 608-267-6813 (Fax), 7:45AM-4:30PM.

www.wdfi.org

Online: Selected elements of the database ("CRIS" Corporate Registration System) are available online on the department's website at www.wdfi.org/corporations/crispix.

Uniform Commercial Code, Federal Tax Liens, State Tax Liens

Department of Financial Institutions, CCS/UCC, PO Box 7847, Madison, WI 53707-7847 (Courier: 345 W Washington Ave 3rd Fl, Madison, WI 53703); 608-261-9548, 608-264-7965 (Fax), 7:45AM-4:30PM.

www.wdfi.org

Online: There is free Internet access for most records. Some records may require a $1.00 fee. All requesters must be registered with a password.

Driver Records

Division of Motor Vehicles, Records & Licensing Section, PO Box 7995, Madison, WI 53707-7995 (Courier: 4802 Sheboygan Ave, Room 301, Madison, WI 53707); 608-266-2353, 608-267-3636 (Fax), 7:30AM-4:30PM.

www.dot.state.wi.us

Online: Commercial online access is available for high volume users only, fee is $3.00 per record. Call 608-266-2353 for more information.

Legislation Records

Wisconsin Legislative, Legislative Reference Bureau, PO Box 2037, Madison, WI 53701-2037 (Courier: 100 N. Hamilton Street, Madison, WI 53703); 608-266-0341, 800-362-9472 (Bill Status), 608-266-5648 (Fax), 7:45AM-4:30PM.

www.legis.state.wi.us

Online: Information on current bills is available over the Internet. There is a Folio Program to search text of previous session bills.

State Level...Occupational Licensing

Accountant	http://165.189.238.43/plsql/plsql/Search_Ind_Bdp
Accounting Firm	http://drlchq.state.wi.us/plsql/chq/cred_holder_query
Acupuncturist	http://165.189.238.43/plsql/plsql/Search_Ind_Health
Adjustment Service Company	www.wdfi.org/fi/lfs/licensee_lists
Aesthetics Establishment	http://drlchq.state.wi.us/plsql/chq/cred_holder_query
Aesthetics Instructor	http://165.189.238.43/plsql/plsql/Search_Ind_Bdp
Aesthetics Specialty School	http://drlchq.state.wi.us/plsql/chq/cred_holder_query
Architect	http://165.189.238.43/plsql/plsql/Search_Ind_Bdp
Architecural Corp	http://drlchq.state.wi.us/plsql/chq/cred_holder_query
Art Therapist	http://165.189.238.43/plsql/plsql/Search_Ind_Health
Auction Company	http://drlchq.state.wi.us/plsql/chq/cred_holder_query
Auctioneer	http://165.189.238.43/plsql/plsql/Search_Ind_Bdp
Audiologist	http://165.189.238.43/plsql/plsql/Search_Ind_Health
Bank	www.wdfi.org/fi/banks/licensee_lists/default.asp
Barber	http://165.189.238.43/plsql/plsql/Search_Ind_Bdp
Barber/Cosmetology Apprentice/Instructor/Mgr.	http://165.189.238.43/plsql/plsql/Search_Ind_Bdp
Barbering School	http://drlchq.state.wi.us/plsql/chq/cred_holder_query
Boxer	http://165.189.238.43/plsql/plsql/Search_Ind_Bdp
Boxing Club (Amateur or Professional)	http://drlchq.state.wi.us/plsql/chq/cred_holder_query
Boxing Show Permit	http://drlchq.state.wi.us/plsql/chq/cred_holder_query
Cemetery Authority/ Cemetery Warehouse	http://drlchq.state.wi.us/plsql/chq/cred_holder_query
Cemetery Salesperson/ Cemetery Preneed Seller	http://165.189.238.43/plsql/plsql/Search_Ind_Bdp
Charitable Organization	http://drlchq.state.wi.us/plsql/chq/cred_holder_query
Check Seller	www.wdfi.org/fi/lfs/licensee_lists
Chiropractor	http://165.189.238.43/plsql/plsql/Search_Ind_Health
Collection Agency	www.wdfi.org/fi/lfs/licensee_lists
Cosmetologist	http://165.189.238.43/plsql/plsql/Search_Ind_Bdp
Cosmetology School	http://drlchq.state.wi.us/plsql/chq/cred_holder_query
Credit Union/ Credit Service Organization	www.wdfi.org/fi/cu/chartered_lists/default.asp
Currency Exchange	www.wdfi.org/fi/lfs/licensee_lists
Dance Therapist	http://165.189.238.43/plsql/plsql/Search_Ind_Health
Debt Collector	www.wdfi.org/fi/lfs/licensee_lists
Dental Hygienist	http://165.189.238.43/plsql/plsql/Search_Ind_Health
Dentist	http://165.189.238.43/plsql/plsql/Search_Ind_Health
Designer of Engineering Systems	http://165.189.238.43/plsql/plsql/Search_Ind_Bdp
Dietitian	http://165.189.238.43/plsql/plsql/Search_Ind_Health
Drug Distributor/.Manufacturer	http://drlchq.state.wi.us/plsql/chq/cred_holder_query
Electrologist/ Electrology Instructor	http://165.189.238.43/plsql/plsql/Search_Ind_Bdp

Electrology Establishment/ Specialty School....... http://drlchq.state.wi.us/plsql/chq/cred_holder_query
Engineer/ Engineer in Training .... http://165.189.238.43/plsql/plsql/Search_Ind_Bdp
Engineering Corp... http://drlchq.state.wi.us/plsql/chq/cred_holder_query
Firearms Permit.. http://drlchq.state.wi.us/plsql/chq/cred_holder_query
Fund Raiser, Professional.................................. http://165.189.238.43/plsql/plsql/Search_Ind_Bdp
Fund Raising Counsel .... http://drlchq.state.wi.us/plsql/chq/cred_holder_query
Funeral Director/ Director Apprentice .... http://165.189.238.43/plsql/plsql/Search_Ind_Bdp
Funeral Establishment.. http://drlchq.state.wi.us/plsql/chq/cred_holder_query
Funeral Preneed Seller...................................... http://165.189.238.43/plsql/plsql/Search_Ind_Bdp
General Appraiser (Certified or Licensed).......... http://165.189.238.43/plsql/plsql/Search_Ind_Bdp
Geologist .... http://165.189.238.43/plsql/plsql/Search_Ind_Bdp
Geology Firm... http://drlchq.state.wi.us/plsql/chq/cred_holder_query
Hearing Instrument Specialist .... http://165.189.238.43/plsql/plsql/Search_Ind_Health
Home Inspector.. http://drlchq.state.wi.us/plsql/chq/cred_holder_query
Home Inspector.. http://165.189.238.43/plsql/plsql/Search_Ind_Bdp
Hydrologist .... http://165.189.238.43/plsql/plsql/Search_Ind_Bdp
Hydrology Firm.. http://drlchq.state.wi.us/plsql/chq/cred_holder_query
Insurance Company.. http://badger.state.wi.us/agencies/oci/dir_ins.htm
Insurance Premium Finance Company............... www.wdfi.org/fi/lfs/licensee_lists
Interior Designer.. http://drlchq.state.wi.us/plsql/chq/cred_holder_query
Interior Designer.. http://165.189.238.43/plsql/plsql/Search_Ind_Bdp
Investment Advisor/ Advisor Representative ...... www.wdfi.org/fi/securities/licensing/licensee_lists/default.asp
Land Surveyor... http://165.189.238.43/plsql/plsql/Search_Ind_Bdp
Landscape Architect... http://165.189.238.43/plsql/plsql/Search_Ind_Bdp
Loan Company.. www.wdfi.org/fi/lfs/licensee_lists
Loan Solicitor/Originator .... www.wdfi.org/fi/mortbank/default.htm
Lobbyist.. http://ethics.state.wi.us/Scripts/Lobbyists2000.asp
Manicuring Establishment/ Specialty School ...... http://drlchq.state.wi.us/plsql/chq/cred_holder_query
Manicurist/ Manicuring Instructor..................... http://165.189.238.43/plsql/plsql/Search_Ind_Bdp
Marriage & Family Therapist............................. http://165.189.238.43/plsql/plsql/Search_Ind_Health
Massage Therapist/Bodyworker .... http://165.189.238.43/plsql/plsql/Search_Ind_Health
Medical Doctor/Surgeon................................... http://165.189.238.43/plsql/plsql/Search_Ind_Health
Mobile Home & RV Dealer............................... www.wdfi.org/fi/lfs/licensee_lists
Mortgage Banker/Broker.................................. www.wdfi.org/fi/mortbank/default.htm
Motorcycle Dealer.. www.wdfi.org/fi/lfs/licensee_lists
Music Therapist... http://165.189.238.43/plsql/plsql/Search_Ind_Health
Nurse (Practical or Registered)......................... http://165.189.238.43/plsql/plsql/Search_Ind_Health
Nurse Midwife... http://165.189.238.43/plsql/plsql/Search_Ind_Health
Nursing Home Administrator .... http://165.189.238.43/plsql/plsql/Search_Ind_Bdp
Occupational Therapist/ Therapy Assistant......... http://165.189.238.43/plsql/plsql/Search_Ind_Health
Optometrist... http://165.189.238.43/plsql/plsql/Search_Ind_Health
Pay Day Lender... www.wdfi.org/fi/lfs/licensee_lists
Pharmacist/ Pharmacy...................................... http://165.189.238.43/plsql/plsql/Search_Ind_Health
Physical Therapist.. http://165.189.238.43/plsql/plsql/Search_Ind_Health
Physician Assistant .... http://165.189.238.43/plsql/plsql/Search_Ind_Health
Podiatrist .... http://165.189.238.43/plsql/plsql/Search_Ind_Health
Principal Lobbying Organization http://ethics.state.wi.us/Scripts/OEL2000.asp
Private Detective.. http://165.189.238.43/plsql/plsql/Search_Ind_Bdp

Private Detective Agency .... http://drlchq.state.wi.us/plsql/chq/cred_holder_query
Professional Counselor .... http://165.189.238.43/plsql/plsql/Search_Ind_Health
Psychologist .... http://165.189.238.43/plsql/plsql/Search_Ind_Health
Public Accountant .... http://165.189.238.43/plsql/plsql/Search_Ind_Bdp
Real Estate Appraiser/Broker/Salesperson .... http://165.189.238.43/plsql/plsql/Search_Ind_Bdp
Real Estate Business Entity .... http://drlchq.state.wi.us/plsql/chq/cred_holder_query
Residental Appraiser .... http://165.189.238.43/plsql/plsql/Search_Ind_Bdp
Respiratory Care Practitioner .... http://165.189.238.43/plsql/plsql/Search_Ind_Health
Sales Finance Company .... www.wdfi.org/fi/lfs/licensee_lists
Sales Finance Loan Company .... www.wdfi.org/fi/lfs/licensee_lists
Savings & Loan Sales Finance Company .... www.wdfi.org/fi/lfs/licensee_lists
Savings Institution .... www.wdfi.org/fi/savings_institutions/licensee_lists/default.asp
School Psychology Private Practice .... http://165.189.238.43/plsql/plsql/Search_Ind_Health
Securities Agent/Broker/Dealer .... www.wdfi.org/fi/securities/licensing/licensee_lists/default.asp
Security Guard .... http://165.189.238.43/plsql/plsql/Search_Ind_Bdp
Social Worker .... http://165.189.238.43/plsql/plsql/Search_Ind_Health
Soil Science Firm .... http://drlchq.state.wi.us/plsql/chq/cred_holder_query
Soil Scientist .... http://165.189.238.43/plsql/plsql/Search_Ind_Bdp
Speech Pathologist/Audiologist .... http://165.189.238.43/plsql/plsql/Search_Ind_Health
Time Share Salesperson .... http://165.189.238.43/plsql/plsql/Search_Ind_Bdp
Veterinarian/ Veterinary Technician .... http://165.189.238.43/plsql/plsql/Search_Ind_Health

County Level...Courts, Recorders & Assessors

Director of State Courts, Supreme Court, PO Box 1688, Madison, WI, 53701; 608-266-6828; www.courts.state.wi.us

Editor's Note: Wisconsin Circuit Court Access (WCCA) allows users to view circuit court case information at http://ccap.courts.state.wi.us/internetcourtaccess which is the Wisconsin court system web site. Data is available from all counties except Outagamie and Walworth. Searches can be conducted statewide or county by county. WCCA provides detailed information about circuit cases and for civil cases, the program displays judgment and judgment party information. WCCA also offers the ability to generate reports. In addition, public access terminals are available at each court. Due to statutory requirements, WCCA users will not be able to view restricted cases. There are probate records for all counties except Outagamie, Milwaukee and Walworth. Portage County offers probate records only online.

Brown
Real Estate
www.co.brown.wi.us/rod
Online access to Register of Deeds real estate records is available by subscription at
www.co.brown.wi.us/rod/LaredoTapestry/main.html. Registration and fees are required. A more sophisticated subscription system, named Laredo, offers full access to land records for firms operating in Wisconsin.

Dane
Assessor, Real Estate
www.co.dane.wi.us/regdeeds/rdhome.htm
Records on the geographic & land database are available free online at http://dc-web.co.dane.wi.us/dane. For fuller access, a subscription service is available. Also, parcel information is available free at http://dc-web.co.dane.wi.us/dane/html/parcelsearch.asp. Professional companies may register to use assessor/land record services at http://dc-web.co.dane.wi.us/dane/html/community.asp. Registration and login. Also, the City of Madison tax assessor database is accessible at www.ci.madison.wi.us/assessor/property.html.

Kenosha
Real Estate, Liens, Vital Records
The set-up fee is $500, plus $6.00 per hour usage fee. The system operates 24 hours daily; records date back to 5/1986. Federal tax liens are listed. Lending agency information is available. For further information, contact Joellyn Storz at 262-653-2511.

Manitowoc
Assessor, Real Estate
www.manitowoc.org/
Records on the City of Manitowoc Assessor database are available free online at http://assessor.manitowoc.org/default.htm.

Milwaukee
Criminal Records
www.co.milwaukee.wi.us/courts/court.htm
Court records are available free on the Internet at http://ccap.courts.state.wi.us/internetcourtaccess. Also, criminal case records on the Milwaukee Municipal Court Case Information System database are available free online at www.court.ci.mil.wi.us/home.asp.
Assessor, Real Estate
www.co.milwaukee.wi.us
Ownership, Property and Assessment data as well as sales data by year on the Milwaukee City (not county) Assessor Office database are available free online at www.ci.mil.wi.us/citygov/assessor/assessments.htm. Search by address.

Rock
Assessor, Real Estate
Records on the City of Janesville Assessor database are available free online at http://assessor.ci.janesville.wi.us/Assessor/query.asp.

Trempealeau
Real Estate, Assessor
www.tremplocounty.com
Online access to the county assessor's database is available free at www.tremplocounty.com/Search.

Winnebago
Assessor, Real Estate
Records on the City of Menasha Tax Roll Information database are available free online at http://my.athenet.net/~mencity/search.

Federal Courts in Wisconsin...

US District Court - Eastern District of Wisconsin

Home Page: www.wied.uscourts.gov
PACER: Sign-up number is 800-676-6856. Access fee is. Toll-free access: 877-253-4862. Local access: 414-297-3361. http://pacer.wied.uscourts.gov. Case records are available back to 1991. Records are purged never. New records are available online after 1 day.
PACER Internet Access: http://pacer.wied.uscourts.gov.
Milwaukee Division Counties: Brown, Calumet, Dodge, Door, Florence, Fond du Lac, Forest, Green Lake, Kenosha, Kewaunee, Langlade, Manitowoc, Marinette, Marquette, Menominee, Milwaukee, Oconto, Outagamie, Ozaukee, Racine, Shawano, Sheboygan, Walworth, Washington, Waukesha, Waupaca,Waushara, Winnebago.

US Bankruptcy Court - Eastern District of Wisconsin

Home Page: www.wieb.uscourts.gov
PACER: Sign-up number is 800-676-6856. Access fee is $.60 per minute. Toll-free access: 877-467-5537. Local access: 414-297-1400. Case records are available back to 1991. Records are purged aafter case is closed. New civil records are available online after 1-2 days.
PACER Internet Access: http://pacer.wieb.uscourts.gov.
Milwaukee Division Counties: Brown, Calumet, Dodge, Door, Florence, Fond du Lac, Forest, Green Lake, Kenosha, Kewaunee, Langlade, Manitowoc, Marinette, Marquette, Menominee, Milwaukee, Oconto, Outagamie, Ozaukee, Racine, Shawano, Sheboygan, Walworth, Washington, Waukesha, Waupaca,Waushara, Winnebago.

US District Court - Western District of Wisconsin

Home Page: www.wiw.uscourts.gov
PACER: Sign-up number is 800-676-6856. Access fee is $.60 per minute. Toll-free access: 800-372-8791. Local access: 608-264-5914. Case records are available back to 1990. Records are purged never. New records are available online after 1 day.
PACER Internet Access: http://pacer.wiwd.uscourts.gov.
Madison Division Counties: Adams, Ashland, Barron, Bayfield, Buffalo, Burnett, Chippewa, Clark, Columbia, Crawford, Dane, Douglas, Dunn, Eau Claire, Grant, Green, Iowa, Iron, Jackson, Jefferson, Juneau, La Crosse, Lafayette, Lincoln, Marathon, Monroe, Oneida, Pepin, Pierce, Polk,Portage, Price, Richland, Rock, Rusk, Sauk, Sawyer, St. Croix, Taylor, Trempealeau, Vernon, Vilas, Washburn, Wood.

US Bankruptcy Court - Western District of Wisconsin

Home Page: www.wiw.uscourts.gov/bankruptcy
PACER: Sign-up number is 800-676-6856. Access fee is $.60 per minute. Toll-free access: 800-373-8708. Local access: 608-264-5630. Case records are available back to April 1991. New civil records are available online after 1 day.
Eau Claire Division Counties: Ashland, Barron, Bayfield, Buffalo, Burnett, Chippewa, Clark, Douglas, Dunn, Eau Claire, Iron, Jackson, Juneau, La Crosse, Lincoln, Marathon, Monroe, Oneida, Pepin, Pierce, Polk, Portage, Price, Rusk, Sawyer, St. Croix, Taylor, Trempealeau, Vernon,Vilas, Washburn, Wood. Division has satellite offices in LaCrosse and Wausau.
Madison Division Counties: Adams, Columbia, Crawford, Dane, Grant, Green, Iowa, Jefferson, Lafayette, Richland, Rock, Sauk.

Editor's Choice for Wisconsin

Here are some additional sites recommended for this state.

Constitution Text
www.legis.state.wi.us/rsb/2wiscon.html
Statutes Text
www.legis.state.wi.us/rsb/stats.html

Capital: Cheyenne   Home Page
            Laramie County   www.state.wy.us

Time Zone: MST   Attorney General   http://attorneygeneral.state.wy.us

Number of Counties: 23   Archives   http://commerce.state.wy.us/
                                                                    cr/archives

State Level...Major Agencies

Corporation Records, Limited Liability Company Records, Limited Partnership Records, Fictitious Name, Trademarks/Servicemarks

Corporations Division, Secretary of State, State Capitol, Cheyenne, WY 82002; 307-777-7311, 307-777-5339 (Fax), 8AM-5PM.

http://soswy.state.wy.us

Online: Information is available through the Internet site listed above. You can search by corporate name or even download the whole file. Also, they have 2 pages of excellent searching tips.

Uniform Commercial Code, Federal Tax Liens

UCC Division, Secretary of State, The Capitol, Cheyenne, WY 82002-0020 (Courier: Capitol Bldg, RM 110, Cheyenne, WY 82002); 307-777-5372, 307-777-5988 (Fax), 8AM-5PM.

http://soswy.state.wy.us

Online: There is a $50 annual registration, a $20 monthly fee, and long distant access fees of between $3 and $6 per hour. A word of caution, if user fails to log off the "clock" still keeps ticking and user is billed! The system is open 24 hours daily except 1:30AM to 5AM Mon. through Sun., and 4PM to 6PM on Sunday.

Legislation Records

Wyoming Legislature, State Capitol, Room 213, Cheyenne, WY 82002; 307-777-7881, 8AM-5PM.

http://legisweb.state.wy.us

Online: The Internet site contains a wealth of information regarding the legislature and bills.

State Level...Occupational Licensing

Attorney	www.wyomingbar.org/setemp.asp
Bank	http://audit.state.wy.us/banking/banks.htm
Collection Agency	http://audit.state.wy.us/banking/CAB.htm
Engineer	www.wrds.uwyo.edu/wrds/borpe/roster/roster.html
Insurance Agent/Solicitor/Consultant	http://insurance.state.wy.us/
Insurance Claims Adjuster	http://insurance.state.wy.us/
Insurance Service Representatives	http://insurance.state.wy.us/
Lobbyist	www.lobbyist.net/Wyoming/WYOLOB.htm
Motor Club Agents	http://insurance.state.wy.us/
Optometrist	www.odfinder.org/LicSearch.asp
Preneed Agents	http://insurance.state.wy.us/
Public Accountant-CPA or CPA Firm	http://cpaboard.state.wy.us/search.cfm
Resident Insurance Broker	http://insurance.state.wy.us/
Resident Surplus Lines Broker	http://insurance.state.wy.us/
Savings & Loan Association	http://audit.state.wy.us/banking/fsb.htm
Surveyor	www.wrds.uwyo.edu/wrds/borpe/roster/roster.html
Travel & Baggage Agents	http://insurance.state.wy.us/

County Level...Courts, Recorders & Assessors

Court Administrator, 2301 Capitol Av, Supreme Court Bldg, Cheyenne, WY, 82002; 307-777-7480; www.courts.state.wy.us

Editor's Note: Wyoming's statewide case management system is for internal use only. Planning is underway for a new case management system that will ultimately allow public access.

Teton County
Real Estate, Liens, Recordings
www.tetonwyo.org/clerk/
Online access to the clerk's database of scanned images is available free at www.tetonwyo.org/clerk/query. Search for complete documents back to 7/1996; partial documents back to 4/1991.

Federal Courts in Wyoming...

US District Court - District of Wyoming

Home Page: www.ck10.uscourts.gov/wyoming/district
PACER: Sign-up number is 800-676-6856. Access fee is $.60 per minute. Toll-free access: 888-417-3560. Local access: 307-772-2808. Case records are available back to 1988. Records are purged once per year. New civil records are available online after 1-2 days. New criminal records are available online after 1 day.
PACER Internet Access: http://pacer.wyd.uscourts.gov.
Cheyenne Division Counties: All counties in Wyoming. Some criminal records are held in Casper.

US Bankruptcy Court - District of Wyoming

Home Page: www.wyb.uscourts.gov
PACER: Sign-up number is 800-676-6856. Access fee is $.60 per minute. Toll-free access: 888-804-5536. Local access: 307-772-2036. Case records are available back one year. Records are purged annually. New civil records are available online after 1 day.
Opinions Online: Court opinions are available online at www.wyb.uscourts.gov/opinion_search.htm.
Other Online Access: You can search records on the Internet using RACER. Currently the system is free and requires free registration. Simply visit www.wyb.uscourts.gov/wconnect/wc.dll?usbc_racer~main.
Cheyenne Division Counties: All counties in Wyoming.

Editor's Choice for Wyoming

Here are some additional sites recommended for this state.

Sex Offenders Listing
www.state.wy.us/~ag/dci/so/so_registration.html
State Government Officials Phone Listing
http://soswy.state.wy.us/director/dir-toc.htm

Other Recommended Government Web Sites

Editor's Tip: The sites for this chapter were submitted by and used with the permission of Alan M. Schlein. Mr. Schlein is the author of *Find It Online* (2000, 513 pages, $19.95). This excellent book can be purchased at a local bookstore or by calling 1-800-929-3811. The book contains more than 1,200 web site profiles and is an excellent resource guide for performing online research.

Editor's Choice --
Government Records Gateways

There are hundreds of web sites, called government gateways, that organize and link government sites. Some are simply collections of links. Others provide access to bulletin boards of specific government agencies so that you find and contact employees with specific knowledge. Guides are becoming increasingly important in light of the growing number of reports and publications that aren't printed any more, but simply posted online.

Here are some of the best government gateway sites:

Documents Center

www.lib.umich.edu/libhome/Documents.center/index.html

Documents Center is a clearinghouse for local, state, federal, foreign, and international government information. It is one of the more comprehensive online searching aids for all kinds of government information on the Internet. It's especially useful as a meta-site of meta-sites.

Federal Web Locator

www.law.vill.edu

This web locator is really two sites in one: a federal government web site and a separate site that tracks federal courts – both of which are browsable by category or by keywords. Together they provide links to thousands of government agencies and departments. In addition, this site has an excellent **State Web Locator** at www.infoctr.edu/swl and a **State Court Locator** at www.law.vill.edu/Locator/statecourt/index.htm. All four are top-notch resources.

FedLaw

http://fedlaw.gsa.gov

FedLaw is an extremely broad resource for federal legal and regulatory research containing 1600+ links to law-related information. It has very good topical and title indexes that group web links into hundreds of subjects. It is operated by the General Services Administration (GSA).

FedWorld Information Network

www.fedworld.gov

FedWorld is a massive collection of 14,000 files and databases of government sites, including bulletin boards that can help you identify government employees with expertise in a broad range of subjects. A surprising number of these experts will take the time to discuss questions from the general public.

GOVBOT – Government Search Engine

http://eden.cs.umass.edu/Govbot

Developed by the Center For Intelligent Information Retrieval, GOVBOT's searchable keyword index of government web sites is limited to sites with a top-level domain name ending in .gov or .mil.

INFOMINE: Scholarly Internet Resource Collections

http://lib-www.ucr.edu

INFOMINE provides collections of scholarly Internet resources, best for academics. Its government portion — Government INFOMINE — is easily searchable by subject. It has detailed headings and its resource listings are very specific. Since it's run by a university, some of its references are to limited to student use only.

US Federal Government Agencies Directory

www.lib.lsu.edu/gov/fedgov.html

This directory of federal agencies is maintained by Louisiana State University and links to hundreds of federal government Internet sites. It's divided by branch and agency and is very thorough, but focus on your target because it's easy to lose your way or become overwhelmed en route.

US Government Information

www-libraries.colorado.edu/ps/gov/us/federal.htm

This is a gem of a site and a good starting point. From the University of Colorado, it's not as thorough as the LSU site above, but still very valuable.

YAHOO! Government

www.yahoo.com/Government

Yahoo is one of the best known and most frequently-used general Internet engines. Its' subject approach is especially good for subjects like government. It is substantial, frequently updated, broad in scope and has sections for all levels of government.

Editor's Choice -- Online Government Resources

Your tax dollars are put to good and visible use here. A few of the government's web pages are excellent. Some can be used in lieu of commercial tools, but only if you have the time to invest.

A few of the top government sites – the Census and the Securities and Exchange Commission – are models of content and presentation. They are very deep, very thorough and easy to use. If only the rest of the federal government would follow suit. Unfortunately, the best of the federal government is just that: *the best*. Not all agencies maintain such detailed and relevant resources.

Following are the crown jewels of the government's collection, in ranked order:

Bureau of Transportation Statistics

www.bts.gov

The US Department of Transportation's enormous collection of information about every facet of transportation. There's a lot of valuable material here including the Transportation Statistics Annual Report. It also holds financial data for airlines and searchable databases containing information about fatal accidents and on-time statistics for airlines, which can be narrowed to your local airport.

Defense LINK – US Department of Defense (DOD)

www.defenselink.mil

This is the brand-name site for Pentagon-related information. There's a tremendous amount of data here, categorized by branch of service – including US troop deployments worldwide. But the really valuable information is on the DTIC site below.

Defense Technical Information Center (DTIC)

www.dtic.mil

The DTIC site is loaded with links and defense information – everything from contractors to weapon systems. It even includes recently de-classified information about the Gulf War. It is the best place to start for defense information. You can even find a list of all military-related contracts, including beneficiary communities and the kinds of contracts awarded.

IGnet: Internet. . . . for the Federal IG Community

www.ignet.gov

This is a truly marvelous collection of reports and information from the Inspector Generals of about sixty federal agency departments. Well worth checking when starting research on government-related matters.

Library of Congress (LOC)

www.loc.gov

An extraordinary collection of documents. **Thomas**, the Library's Congressional online center site (http://thomas.loc.gov/home/thomas2.html) provides an exhaustive collection of congressional documents, including bill summaries, voting records and the full Congressional Record, which is the official record of Congressional action. This LOC site also links to many international, federal, state and local government sites. You can also access the library's 4.8 million records online, some versions in full-text and some in abstract form. Though the Library's entire 27 million-item collection is not yet available online, the amount increases daily. In addition to books and papers, it includes an extensive images collection ranging from Frank Lloyd Wright's designs to the Dead Sea Scrolls to the world's largest online collection of baseball cards.

National Archives & Records Administration

www.nara.gov

A breathtaking collection of research online. The National Archives has descriptions of more than 170,000 documents related to the Kennedy assassination, for example. It also contains a world-class database holding descriptions of more than 95,000 records held by the Still Picture and Motion Picture, Sound and Video Branches. This site also links to the twelve Presidential Archives with their records of every person ever mentioned in Executive Branch correspondence. You can view an image of the original document.

National Technical Information Service (NTIS)

www.ntis.gov

The best place to find federal government reports related to technology and science. NTIS is the nation's clearinghouse for unclassified technical reports of government-sponsored research. NTIS collects, indexes, abstracts and sells US and foreign research – mostly in science and technology – as well as behavioral and social science data.

Superintendent of Documents Home Page (GPO)

www.access.gpo.gov/su_docs

The GPO is the federal government's primary information printer and distributor. All federally funded information from every agency is sent here, which makes the GPO's holdings priceless. Luckily, the GPO site is well-constructed and easy to use. For example, it has the full-text of the Federal Register, which lists all federal regulations and proposals, and full-text access to the Congressional Record. The GPO also produces an online version of the Congressional Directory, providing details on every congressional district, profiles of members, staff profiles, maps of every district and historical documents about Congress. EFOIA required all federal government resources to be computerized and available online by the end of 1999. This site will continue to expand over the next few years, as the number of materials go out of print and online.

US Census Bureau

www.census.gov

Without question, this is the US government's top site. It's saturated with information and census publications – at times overwhelmingly so – but worth every minute of your time. A few hours spent here is a worthwhile investment for almost anyone seeking to background a community, learn about business or find any kind of demographic information. You can search several ways: alphabetically by subject, by word, by location, and by geographic map. The only problem is the sheer volume of data.

One feature, the **Thematic Mapping System**, allows users to extract data from Census CD-ROMs and display them in maps by state or county. You can create maps on all kinds of subjects – for example, tracking violent crime to farm income by region.

The site also features the **Statistical Abstract of the US** in full text, with a searchable version at www.census.gov:80/stat_abstract.

The potential uses of census data are infinite. Marketers use it to find community information. Reporters search out trends by block, neighborhood or region. Educators conduct research. Businesses evaluate new business prospects. Genealogists trace family trees though full census data isn't available for 72 years from the date the census was taken. You can even use it to identify ideal communities in which to raise a family. The *San Jose Mercury News'* Jennifer LaFleur used it to find eligible bachelors in specific areas of San Jose for an article on which she was working.

US Securities & Exchange Commission (SEC)

www.sec.gov

This SEC site, which is first-rate and surpassed only by the Census site, is a must-stop place for information shopping on US companies. Its **EDGAR** database search site www.sec.gov/edaux/searches.htm is easy to use and provides access to documents that companies and corporations are required to file under regulatory laws.

The SEC site is a great starting point for information about specific companies and industry trends. The SEC requires all publicly held corporations and some large privately held corporations to disclose detailed financial information about their activities, plans, holdings, executives' salaries and stakes, legal problems and so forth.

White House

www.whitehouse.gov

This site wouldn't make this list if not for two features. One, a terrific list of federal government links called **Commonly Requested Federal Services** and two, a transcript of every official action the US President takes. Unfortunately, as with many government sites, its primary focus is in promoting itself.

More Nationwide Web Sites

Here are some additional recommended web sites for US information:

Appeals Court (7th Circuit) Opinions
www.findlaw.com/casecode/courts/7th.html

Autopsy Reports Database
www.med.jhu.edu/pathology/iad.htmlwww.med.jhu.edu/pathology/iad.html

Campaign Contributions Database
www.followthemoney.org/database/enter.html

Codes of Ordinances Texts
www.amlegal.com/alpeg004.htm

Constitution Text
www.findlaw.com/casecode/constitution/www.findlaw.com/casecode/constitution

Mayors Database
www.usmayors.org/USCM/search/database_search_form.html

Supreme Court Opinions
http://supct.law.cornell.edu/supct

Supreme Court Orders Database
http://www4.law.cornell.edu/php/orderinquiry.php3

US Code & Constitution Search Form
www.findlaw.com/casecode/code2.html

Editor's Choice -- State & Regional Resources

The federal government isn't the only government entity with valuable information online. Each of the fifty state governments and the US territories have a web presence. Some are top quality, like Texas and Florida. Others aren't as good. Here are some of the better regional sites:

Global Computing

www.globalcomputing.com/states.html

A solid collection of links on a variety of topics. This site is especially strong on state and local government topics.

Government Information Sharing Project

http://govinfo.kerr.orst.edu

This site, from the Oregon State University Library, is a great collection of online databases about everything from economics to demographics. It's particularly valuable because it has regional information on the economy and demographic breakdowns all the way down to the county level. Its content is sometimes outdated. Still, it's worthwhile for finding how federal money trickles down to localities and where state and local agencies spend tax dollars.

NASIRE - National Association of State Information Resource Executives

www.nasire.org

This site provides state-specific information on state-government innovations and is a companion to the NASIRE State Search site mentioned by Greg Notess in his book *Government Information on the Internet.*

USADATA

www.usadata.com/usadata/market

This is an innovative site for finding information about a particular region or part of the country. Data is not only sorted by region, but also by twenty subjects within each region.

Guam Web Sites

Here are few web sites that offer information about Guam:

Attorney General Homepage
http://www.justice.gov.gu/dol/default.htm
Code Search Form
http://www.guam.net/guamlaw/
Department of Revenue & Taxation Homepage
http://www.admin.gov.gu/revtax/index.html
Governor's Office Homepage
http://ns.gov.gu/webtax/govoff.html
Supreme Court Opinions
http://www.justice.gov.gu/supreme/OPNSpage.htm
Telephone Numbers Directory
http://gta.guam.net/
Territory Web Site Homepage
http://ns.gov.gu/

Private Company Sources

This Section Includes . . .

Company Information Index

◆ An index of the types of information provided by the companies profiled. Includes geographic area as well as the name of any proprietary databases or gateways.

Distribution Method Index

◆ An index of special distribution methods offered. Distribution methods include Internet, CD-ROM and more. Web sites for each company are included.

Private Company Profiles

◆ Full profiles of each company. Includes proprietary products, clientele restrictions, and contact information.

Trade Associations

◆ A listing of trade associations connected to the public information industry and their web sites.

Canadian Web Sites

◆ A listing of private (and government-sponsored) Canadian web sites.

Private Company Indexes

Company Information Index

The Company Information Index is designed to quickly and accurately direct you to the public information category you need.

Twenty-seven types of information found in online public record information are listed here. On the following pages are each specific category, listed in alphabetical order along with those companies that offer access to that public record information.

The Company Information Index indicates the geographic coverage - a particular state, national, or international - offered by a company.

The index also includes companies that maintain their own proprietary **database** and those that act as an interactive **gateways** to other databases.

After finding a potential company, we anticipate that you will usually refer to that company's individual profile, which will be found in the Private Company Profiles section.

27 Types of Public Record Information

Addresses/Telephone Numbers	Military Svc
Associations/Trade Groups	Mortgage
Aviation	News/Current Events
Bankruptcy	Patents
Corporate/Trade Name Data	Real Estate/Assessor
Credit Information	SEC/Other Financial
Criminal Information	Software/Training
Driver and/or Vehicle	Tenant History
Education/Employment	Trademarks
Environmental	Uniform Commercial Code
Foreign Country Information	Vessels
Genealogical Information	Vital Records
Legislation/Regulation	Voter Registration
Licenses/Registrations/Permits	Wills/Probate
Litigation/Judgments/Tax Liens	Workers Compensation

- In each of the following Public Record Information Categories, if a company listing includes a product name, then the company has a Database or serves as a Gateway.

- If there is no product name, then general search services are offered.

Address/Telephone Numbers

Address/Telephone Numbers Company	Product Name	Region
555-1212.com	555-1212.com	US
AcuSearch Services LLC		US
ADREM Profiles Inc		US
American Business Information	Consumer Sales Leads	US
American Business Information	Business Sales Leads	US
Ameridex Information Systems	SSDI & Live Index	US
Anybirthday.com	Anybithdate.com	US
ARISTOTLE	ARISTOTLE	US
Avantex Inc	FAA Data	US
BiblioData	BiblioData	US
Cambridge Statistical Research Associates		US
ChoicePoint Inc	Consumer Services	US
ChoicePoint, formerly CDB Infotek	Address Inspector	US
ChoicePoint, formerly DBT Online Inc	AutoTrackXP	US
Commercial Information Systems Inc		US
CompuServe	Phonefile	US
Daily Report, The	The Daily Report (Kern County Only)	CA
DataQuick		US
DCS Information Systems	AmeriFind (DNIS)	TX,US
Dun & Bradstreet	D & B Public Record Search	US
Equifax Credit Services	Investigation System	US
Everton Publishers	Everton's Online Search	US
Experian Information Solutions	File 1	US
Experian Online	Experian Online	US
First American Real Estate Solutions - Amerestate	PaceNet	KY, MI, OH
FlatRateInfo.com	QI National People Locator	US
Folks Finders Ltd		US
Gale Group Inc, The	GaleNet	US
Haines & Company Inc	Criss+Cross Plus, Directory	US
Hoovers Inc	Hoover's Company Profiles	US

Address/Telephone Numbers Company	Product Name	Region
Household Drivers Reports Inc (HDR Inc)		US
Information Inc		TN
Informus Corporation	IntroScan	US
Intellicorp Ltd		US
Interstate Data Corporation		US
Investigators Anywhere Resource Line	Resource Line	US
IQ Data Systems	IQ Data	US
KnowX	KnowX	US
Kompass USA Inc	Kompass.com	US, Itl
Law Bulletin Information Network	Access Plus	IL
LEXIS-NEXIS	B-Find, P-Find, P-Seek	US
Lloyds Maritime Information Services Inc		US
Logan Registration Service Inc		CA
Martindale-Hubbell	Martindale-Hubbell Law Directory	US, Itl
Merlin Information Services	Merlin Super Header	US
Merlin Information Services	National FlatRate	US
Merlin Information Services	National People Finder	US
Metro Market Trends Inc	Parcel Information Reporting System	FL, AL
Metronet	MetroNet, Cole's Directory	US
National Credit Information Network NCI	NCI Network	US
Nebrask@ Online	Nebrask@ Online	NE
Northwest Location Services	People Finder	WA
OPEN (Online Professional Electronic Network)	OPEN	US
Owens OnLine Inc		US
Pallorium Inc	Skiptrace America, People Finder CDs	US
Paragon Document Research		MN,ND,SD,MT, WI, US
Professional Services Bureau	PSB Database	LA, MS
Property Data Center Inc	Owner Phone Numbers	CO
PROTEC	Consta-Trac	US
Public Record Research Library	PRRS	US
Publook Information Service	Publook	OH
RC Information Brokers	MassData	MA
Search Company of North Dakota LLC	North Dakota Records	ND
Southeastern Public Records Inc.	Michigan/Georgia Public Records	MI, GA
Tax Analysts	The Tax Directory	US
Telebase	Dun & Bradstreet @ AOL	US

Address/Telephone Numbers Company	Product Name	Region
Telebase	Brainwave, I-Quest	US
TEXSEARCH		TX
United State Mutual Association	Retail Industry Theft Database	US
US SEARCH.com		US
USADATA.com	Marketing Portal	US
Westlaw Public Records	Business Finder/People Finder	US

Associations/Trade Groups

Associations/Trade Groups Company	Product Name	Region
Access Indiana Information Network		IN
Cal Info		CA,US
FOIA Group Inc		US
Gale Group Inc, The	GaleNet	US
Public Data Corporation		NY
Publook Information Service		OH
Tax Analysts		US
Virginia Information Providers Network		VA

Aviation

Aviation Company	Product Name	Region
Avantex Inc	FAA Data	US
Commercial Information Systems Inc	Aircraft Registrations	US
FlatRateInfo.com	US Aircraft	US
KnowX	KnowX	US
Landings.com	Landings.com	US
Merlin Information Services	National FlatRate	US
Motznik Computer Services Inc	Alaska Public Information Access System	AK
Pallorium Inc	Skiptrace America, People Finder CDs	US
US SEARCH.com		US
Westlaw Public Records	Aircraft Locator	US

Bankruptcy

BankruptcyCompany	Product Name	Region
Access Louisiana Inc		LA
ADREM Profiles Inc		US

BankruptcyCompany	Product Name	Region
Banko	BANKO	US
CaseStream.com	CaseAlert for Federal Courts	US
CCH Washington Service Bureau	SECnet	US
Chattel Mortgage Reporter Inc		US
ChoicePoint Inc	Legal Information	US
ChoicePoint, formerly CDB Infotek	Legal Information	US
Commercial Information Systems Inc		US
Conrad Grundlehner Inc	Conrad Grundlehner	DC, MD, NC, VA, WV
Court PC of Connecticut		CT,US
CourtClerk.com	Courtclerk.com	TN
CourtExpress.com (RIS Legal Svcs)	US Court Records	US
CourtH.com		TX
CourthouseDirect.com		US
CourtLink	Courtlink Classic, CaseStream	US
Diligenz LLC		US
Disclosure		US
Diversified Information Services Corp		AZ
Dun & Bradstreet	D & B Public Record Search	US
Equifax Credit Services	Investigation System	US
Experian Online	Experian Online Business Records Reports	US
FDR Research / Disclosure	Bankruptcy Filings & Reports	US
Fidelifacts		US
FlatRateInfo.com	QI	US
Golden Bear Information Services		CA
Haines & Company Inc		US
Hogan Information Services	Hogan Online	US
Intellicorp Ltd		US
Intranet Inc	Bankscan	TX
IQ Data Systems	IQ Data	US
J B Data Research Co.		ID, MT, ND, NV, OR, SD, UT, WA, WY
KnowX	KnowX	US
LEXIS-NEXIS	ALLBKT	US
LIDA Credit Agency Inc		US
Merlin Information Services	BANKO	US

BankruptcyCompany	Product Name	Region
Motznik Computer Services Inc	Alaska Public Information Access System	AK
National Credit Information Network NCI		IN, KY, OH
National Service Information		US
OPEN (Online Professional Electronic Network)	OPEN	US
OSO Grande Technologies	NM Fed Courts/LegalNet	NM
Paragon Document Research		MN,ND.SD.MT, WI, US
Professional Services Bureau		LA, MS
Public Data Corporation		NY
Record Information Services Inc	Bankruptcies	IL
San Diego Daily Transcript/San Diego Source	Filings	US
SEAFAX Inc		US
Search Company of North Dakota LLC	North Dakota Records	ND
Security Search & Abstract Co		PA,NJ,US
SKLD Information Services LLC		CO
Southeastern Public Records Inc.	Michigan/Georgia Public Records	MI, GA
Superior Information Services LLC	Superior Online	DC, DE, MD, NC, NJ, NY, PA, VA
TEXSEARCH		TX
The Todd Wiegele Research Co Inc		US
UCC Direct Services - AccuSearch Inc	AccuSearch	CA, IL, TX
UCC Retrievals		VA
Unisearch Inc		US
US Corporate Services		US
US SEARCH.com		US
Westlaw Public Records	Bankruptcy Records	US

Corporate/Trade Name Data

Corporate/Trade Name Company	Product Name	Region
Access Indiana Information Network	Premium Services	IN
Access Louisiana Inc	LA Corporate Data	LA
Accutrend Corporation	New Business Database	US
Better Business Bureau	Business Report	US
BNA, Inc (Bureau of National Affairs)	Corporate Law Daily	US
Bureau1 (Philippines)	Philippines Registries	Itl
Chattel Mortgage Reporter Inc		IL,US
ChoicePoint Inc	Legal Information	US

Corporate/Trade Name Company	Product Name	Region
ChoicePoint, formerly CDB Infotek	Corporate & Limited Partnerships	US
ChoicePoint, formerly DBT Online Inc	AutoTrackXP	US
Colorado Central Information System (CIS)	State of Colorado	CO
Commercial Information Systems Inc	Corporations & Limited Partnerships	CA,ID,OR,WA
Companies Online - Lycos	companiesonline.com	US
CorporateInfomation.com	Corporate/Trade Name Data	US
Court PC of Connecticut		CT
CourtH.com	Courthouse Research	TX
CourthouseDirect.com		TX
DataQuick		US
Derwent Information	Derwent World Patents Index, Patent Explorer	US
Dialog Corporation, The	Profound; DIALOG Web	US
Diligenz LLC	Diligenz.com	US
Diversified Information Services Corp		AZ
Dun & Bradstreet	D & B Public Record Search	US
eUtah	Business Entity List	UT
Experian Online	Experian Online Business Records Reports	US
FlatRateInfo.com	QI	US
Gale Group Inc, The	GaleNet	US
GuideStar	Charity Search	US
Hoovers Inc	Hoover's Company Profiles	US
Household Drivers Reports Inc (HDR Inc)	Corp Data	TX
Infomation-KS LLC		KS, MO
Information Network of Arkansas	Secretary of State	AR
Information Network of Kansas	Premium Services	KS
Interstate Data Corporation	CA Corporate Records	CA
IQ Data Systems	IQ Data	US
KnowX	KnowX	US
Kompass USA Inc	Kompass.com	US, Itl
KY Direct	Secretary of State	KY
LEXIS-NEXIS	ALLSOS	US
LLC Reporter	LLC Reporter	US
Merlin Information Services	Investigator's National New Business Filings	CA,US
Merlin Information Services	National FlatRate	US
Motznik Computer Services Inc	Alaska Public Information Access System	AK
National Credit Information Network NCI		IN, KY, OH
National Fraud Center		US

Corporate/Trade Name Company	Product Name	Region
National Service Information	NSI Online	IN, OH, WI, US
Nebrask@ Online	Nebrask@ Online	NE
OPEN (Online Professional Electronic Network)	OPEN	US
OSO Grande Technologies	New Mexico Technet	NM
Pallorium Inc	BusinessFinder America	US
Paragon Document Research		MN, US
Professional Services Bureau		LA, MS
Publook Information Service	Publook	OH
QuickInfo.net Information Services	QuickInfo.net	AZ, AR, GA, ID, NV, NM, OR, TX, UT, WY
SEAFAX Inc		US
Search Company of North Dakota LLC		ND
Search Network Ltd		IA,KS,US
Security Search & Abstract Co		PA,NJ,US
Superior Information Services LLC	Corporate Files	NY, PA
Tax Analysts	Exempt Organization Master List	US
Telebase	Brainwave, I-Quest	US
TEXSEARCH		TX,US
Thomson & Thomson		US
UCC Direct Services - AccuSearch Inc	AccuSearch	TX,CA,PA,IL,WA, OH,OR,MO
UCC Retrievals		VA
Unisearch Inc		US
US Corporate Services		US
US Corporate Services	MN Secretary of State Records	MN
US Document Services Inc		US
US Document Services Inc	Secretary of State	SC,NC
USADATA.com	Marketing Portal	US
VISTA Information Solutions	VISTACheck	US
West Group	Westlaw	US
Westlaw Public Records	Corporations and Partnerships	US

Credit Information

Credit Information Company	Product Name	Region
AcuSearch Services LLC		US
ADREM Profiles Inc		US

Credit Information Company	Product Name	Region
Agency Records		US
American Business Information	Consumer Sales Leads	US
American Business Information	Business Sales Leads	US
ChoicePoint, formerly CDB Infotek		US
Confi-Chek		US
CourthouseDirect.com		US
DAC Services	Transportation Employment/Security Guard History	US
Diligenz LLC		US
Dun & Bradstreet	Business Credit Information	US
Dun & Bradstreet	D & B Public Record Search	US
Equifax Credit Services	Credit Profile	US
Experian Information Solutions	File 1	US
Fidelifacts		US
Infomation-KS LLC		KS, MO
Informus Corporation		US
Intellicorp Ltd		US
iplace.com	Qspace, Consumer info	US
IQ Data Systems	IQ Data	US
LIDA Credit Agency Inc		US
National Credit Information Network NCI	NCI Network	US
NIB Ltd	BACAS, BcomM	US
OPEN (Online Professional Electronic Network)	OPEN	US
Owens OnLine Inc	Owens Online	US
Pallorium Inc		US
Paragon Document Research		US
PROTEC		US
RC Information Brokers		US
SEAFAX Inc	Business Reports	US
Southeastern Public Records Inc.		MI,GA
Telebase	Dun & Bradstreet @ AOL	US
Telebase	Brainwave, -Quest	US
TEXSEARCH		US
The Todd Wiegele Research Co Inc		US
Trans Union	Trans Union	US

Criminal Information

Criminal Information Company	Product Name	Region
AcuSearch Services LLC	CO Criminal Information	CO
AcuSearch Services LLC		US
ADREM Profiles Inc		US
Agency Records	ARI	CT
Agency Records	MN Court Convictions (15 yrs)	MN
Agency Records		US
Alacourt.com	Alacourt.com	AL
CaseStream.com	CaseAlert for Federal Courts	US
Chattel Mortgage Reporter Inc		US
ChoicePoint Inc	Legal Information	US
Commercial Information Systems Inc	Criminal Records	ID,OR,WA,CA
Confi-Chek	Confi-Chek Online	CA
Confi-Chek		US
Court PC of Connecticut	Superior Index	CT
CourtClerk.com	Courtclerk.com	TN
CourthouseDirect.com		US
CourtLink		TX, OR, WA, NC, MD, US
DAC Services	20/20 Insight	US
Daily Report, The	The Daily Report (Kern County Only)	CA
Daily Report, The	The Daily Report (Kern County Only)	CA
DataQuick		US
DCS Information Systems	Texas Systems	TX
Diligenz LLC		US
Felonies R Us	AR Felonies	AR
Fidelifacts	Fidelifacts Data Bank	NY
Folks Finders Ltd		US
Golden Bear Information Services		US
Hollingsworth Court Reporting Inc		US
Household Drivers Reports Inc (HDR Inc)	Criminal Record Data	TX
Infocon Corporation	INFOCON County Access System-15 counties	PA
Infomation-KS LLC		KS, MO
Information Inc		US
Information Inc	Arrest Database (Nashville)	TN
Information Network of Kansas	Sedgwick, Shawnee, Wyandotte Ctys	KS

Criminal Information Company	Product Name	Region
Informus Corporation		US
Intellicorp Ltd	Court, Inmate, & Booking Records	OH,MN,IN,KY,WI
Interstate Data Corporation		US
Interstate Data Corporation	Criminal	CA
J B Data Research Co.		MT
Juritas.com	Juritas	CA, DE, FL, IL, NJ, WA
LEXIS-NEXIS	LEXIS	US
Merlin Information Services	California Criminal	CA
Motznik Computer Services Inc	Alaska Public Information Access System	AK
National Credit Information Network NCI		IN, KY, OH
National Fraud Center	Bank Fraud/Insurance Fraud/Organized Crime	US, Itl
National Fraud Center	The Fraud Bulletin	US, Itl
National Fraud Center	Cellular Fraud Database	US
National Service Information		US
NC Recordsonline.com	ncrecordsonline.com	NC
Northwest Location Services		WA
OPEN (Online Professional Electronic Network)	Arrest Records	OH,IN,MI
OPEN (Online Professional Electronic Network)	OPEN	US
OSO Grande Technologies	NM Fed Courts/LegalNet	NM
Owens OnLine Inc		US
Pallorium Inc		US
Paragon Document Research		US
Professional Services Bureau		LA, MS
PROTEC		US
Search Company of North Dakota LLC	North Dakota Records	ND
Software Computer Group Inc	Circuit Express	WV
TEXSEARCH		TX
The Todd Wiegele Research Co Inc		US
United State Mutual Association	Retail Industry Theft Database	US
US SEARCH.com		US

Driver and/or Vehicle

Driver and/or Vehicle Company	Product Name	Region
Access Indiana Information Network	Premium Services	IN
AcuSearch Services LLC		US

ADREM Profiles Inc	ADREM	US
Agency Records	ARI	US
American Business Information	Consumer Sales Leads	US
American Driving Records	ADR	US
AutoDataDirect, Inc	ADD123	FL
Carfax	Vehicle History, Motor Vehicle Title Information	US
Chattel Mortgage Reporter Inc		US
ChoicePoint Inc	Insurance Services	US
ChoicePoint, formerly DBT Online Inc	AutoTrackXP	US
Commercial Information Systems Inc	Driver's License & Registration	ID,OR
Confi-Chek		US
DAC Services	Driving Records	US
DCS Information Systems	Texas Systems	TX
eUtah	TLR/MVR	UT
Experian Online	Experian Online	US
Explore Information Services	EARS	CO, FL, IA, KY, ME, MN, MO, NE, NH, OH, TN, UT, WI
Fidelifacts		US
Folks Finders Ltd		US
Household Drivers Reports Inc (HDR Inc)	Driver & Vehicle	TX
iiX (Insurance Information Exchange)	Motor Vehicle Reports	US
iiX (Insurance Information Exchange)	UDI-Undisclosed Drivers, VIN	US
Infomation-KS LLC		KS, MO
Information Network of Arkansas	INA	AR
Information Network of Kansas	Premium Services	KS
InforME - Information Resource of Maine	Bureau of Motor Vehicles Driver's Records	ME
Informus Corporation		US
Intellicorp Ltd		OH,US
IQ Data Systems	IQ Data	US
LIDA Credit Agency Inc		NY
Logan Registration Service Inc	Logan	CA, US
MDR/Minnesota Driving Records	MDR	US
Merlin Information Services	Trace Wizard National Residential Locator	US
Motznik Computer Services Inc	Alaska Public Information Access System	AK
National Credit Information Network NCI	NCI Network	US
Nebrask@ Online	Nebrask@ Online	NE

Northwest Location Services		WA,OR,ID
OPEN (Online Professional Electronic Network)	OPEN	US
OSO Grande Technologies	New Mexico Technet	NM
Pallorium Inc	Skiptrace America, People Finder CDs	US
Paragon Document Research		MN, CA, US
Professional Services Bureau		LA, MS
PROTEC		US
QuickInfo.net Information Services	QuickInfo.net	FL, ID, IA, LA, ME, MN, MS, MO, NC, OR, SD, TX, UT, WV, WI, WY
RC Information Brokers		US
Search Company of North Dakota LLC		ND
Texas Driving Record Express Service	Certified MVRs	TX
TEXSEARCH		TX
TML Information Services Inc	Driver Check	AL, AZ, CA, CT, FL, ID, KS, LA, MD, MI, MN, NE, NH, NY, NC, OH, PA, SC, VA, WV
TML Information Services Inc	Title File	AL, FL, SD
TML Information Services Inc	Auto-Search	AL, AZ, CT, DC, FL, ID, IN, KS, KY, LA, MA, MI, MN, MS, NC, ND, NE, NH, NJ, NY, OH, SC, VA, WI, WV
TML Information Services Inc	Driving Records	US
UCC Retrievals		VA
US Corporate Services		US
US Document Services Inc		US
Virginia Information Providers Network	VIPNet	VA

Westlaw Public Records	Motor Vehicle Records	AK, AL, CO, CT, DC, DE, FL, IA, ID, IL, KY, LA, MA, MD, ME, MI, MN, MO, MS, MT, ND, NE, NH, NM, NY, OH, SC, TN, UT, WI, WV, WY

Education/Employment

Education/Employment Company	Product Name	Region
ADREM Profiles Inc		US
Campus Direct	Campus Direct	US
ChoicePoint Inc		US
Credentials Inc	Degreechk	US
DAC Services		US
EdVerify Inc	EdVerify.com	US
Equifax Credit Services	Investigation System	US
Fidelifacts		US
LIDA Credit Agency Inc		NY
National Credit Information Network NCI		IN, KY, OH
National Student Clearinghouse	EnrollmentVerify, DegreeVerify	US
OPEN (Online Professional Electronic Network)		US
PROTEC		US
RC Information Brokers		US
TEXSEARCH		US
US SEARCH.com		US

Environmental

Environmental Company	Product Name	Region
Access Indiana Information Network		IN
BNA, Inc (Bureau of National Affairs)	Environment & Safety Library on the Web	US
Cal Info		CA,US
Canadian Law Book Inc		CD
Commercial Information Systems Inc	Hazardous Materials	OR,WA
DataQuick		US
Environmental Data Resources, Inc. (EDR)	NEDIS, Sanborn Maps	US

Environmental Company	Product Name	Region
FDR Research / Disclosure	State & Federal Agency Filings	US
Loren Data Corp	Commerce Business Daily	US
OSHA DATA		US
Public Data Corporation	Public Data	NY
Richland County Abstract Co		MN, ND
VISTA Information Solutions	VISTACheck	US
West Group	Westlaw	US

Foreign Country Information

Foreign Country Information Company	Product Name	Region
A.M. Best Company	Best's Insight Global	GB, Itl, CD
Ancestry	Ancestry.com	
BNA, Inc (Bureau of National Affairs)	International Trade Daily, WTO Reporter	Itl
Bureau1 (Philippines)		Itl
Burrelles Information Services	BIO	
Canadian Law Book Inc		CD
CorporateInfomation.com	Corporate/Trade Name Data	Itl
CountryWatch.com Inc.	countrywatch.com db	Itl
Derwent Information	Derwent World Patents Index, Patent Explorer	Itl
Dialog Corporation, The	Profound; DIALOG Web	
Diligenz LLC		Canada, Bahamas, PR, Guam
Disclosure	Laser D International/Worldscope Global	Itl
Gale Group Inc, The	GaleNet	Itl
Hoovers Inc	Foreign Country Information	
Investigators Anywhere Resource Line	Resource Line	
Kompass USA Inc	Kompass.com	
Lloyds Maritime Information Services Inc		
Offshore Business News & Research	Courts and Businesses	Bermuda, Caribbean
Owens OnLine Inc		
Pallorium Inc		Itl
SEAFAX Inc		
Tax Analysts	TAXBASE, The Ratx Directory	
Telebase	Brainwave, I-Quest	
The Search Company Inc		CD

Foreign Country Information Company	Product Name	Region
Thomson & Thomson	Worldwide Domain	
UMI - Bell & Howell Information & Learning		Itl
Vital Records Information	vitalrec.com	

Genealogical Information

Genealogical Information Company	Product Name	Region
American Business Information	Consumer Sales Leads	US
CourthouseDirect.com		US
Folks Finders Ltd		US
KY Direct		KY
RC Information Brokers		MA
Vital Records Information	vitalrec.com	US

Legislation/Regulation

Legislation/Regulation Company	Product Name	Region
Access Indiana Information Network	Free Services	IN
ARISTOTLE		US
Avantex Inc	FAA Data	US
BNA, Inc (Bureau of National Affairs)	Intl Trade Daily, WTO Reporter	US, Itl
Cal Info	Guide to State Statutes	US
Cal Info	Administrative Guide to State Regulations	US
Canadian Law Book Inc	Canada Statute Service	CD
CCH Washington Service Bureau		US
Congressional Information Service Inc	Current Issues Sourcefile	US
CourtH.com		TX
Dialog Corporation, The	Profound; DIALOG Web	US
Disclosure		US
FDR Research / Disclosure	State & Federal Agency Filings	US
FOIA Group Inc		US
Information Network of Kansas	Premium Services	KS
KY Direct	Legislature Searching Service	KY
LEXIS-NEXIS	Congressional Information Service	US
Loren Data Corp	Commerce Business Daily	US
OSHA DATA	OSHA Data Gateway	US
OSO Grande Technologies	New Mexico Technet	NM
Public Record Research Library	PRRS	US

Legislation/Regulation Company	Product Name	Region
SEAFAX Inc		US
Silver Plume		US
State Net	State Net	US
Tax Analysts	The OneDisc, TAXBASE	US
Thomas Legislative Information		US
Virginia Information Providers Network	VIPNet	VA
West Group	West CD-ROM Libraries	US
West Group	Westlaw	US

Licenses/Registrations/Permits

Licenses/Registrations/Permits Company	Product Name	Region
Access Indiana Information Network	Premium Services	IN
Accutrend Corporation	New Business Database	US
ADREM Profiles Inc		US
Bureau1 (Philippines)		Itl
ChoicePoint Inc	Information Services	US
Commercial Information Systems Inc	Professional Licenses	ID,OR,WA
Confi-Chek		US
CourtH.com		TX
Daily Report, The	The Daily Report (Kern County Only)	CA
Environmental Data Resources, Inc. (EDR)	NEDIS, Sanborn Maps	US
Fidelifacts		US
Information Inc		TN
Information Network of Arkansas	Secretary of State	AR
Interstate Data Corporation	CA Professional Licenses	CA
Investigators Anywhere Resource Line	Resource Line	US
KnowX	KnowX	US
KY Direct		KY
LEXIS-NEXIS	Professional Licensing Boards	CA, CT, FL, GE, IL, MA, MI, NE, NJ, NC, OH, PA, TX, VA, WI
Loren Data Corp		US
Merlin Information Services	CA Sales, Use Tax, Prof. Licenses, etc.	CA
Motznik Computer Services Inc	Alaska Public Information Access System	AK
Northwest Location Services	Business Licenses	WA
Publook Information Service		OH

Licenses/Registrations/Permits Company	Product Name	Region
QuickInfo.net Information Services	QuickInfo.net	FL, ID, IA, LA, MN, MS, MO, NV, NC, OR, TX, UT, WI, WY
Record Information Services Inc	Business Licenses, News Incorporations	Il
Search Company of North Dakota LLC	North Dakota Records	ND
Thomson & Thomson	US Full Copyright Search	US
Westlaw Public Records	Professional Licenses	AZ, CA, CO, CT, FL, GA, IL, IN, LA, MA, MD, MI, NJ, OH, PA, SC, TN, TX, VA, WI

Litigation/Judgments/Tax Liens

Litigation/Judgments/Tax Liens Company	Product Name	Region
Access Indiana Information Network	Premium Services	IN
Access Louisiana Inc		LA
AcuSearch Services LLC		CO, US
ADREM Profiles Inc		US
Alacourt.com	Alacourt.com	AL
Attorneys Title Insurance Fund	The Fund (40 counties)	FL
Banko	BANKO	US
BNA, Inc (Bureau of National Affairs)	Class Action Litigation Report	US
Cal Info		CA,US
Canadian Law Book Inc	Caselaw on Call	CD
Case Record Info Services	Judgment Lists	CA
CaseStream.com	CaseAlert for Federal Courts	US
CaseStream.com	Delaware Chancery DB	DE
Chattel Mortgage Reporter Inc		IL,US
ChoicePoint Inc	Legal Information	US
ChoicePoint, formerly CDB Infotek	Legal Information	US
Colorado Central Information System (CIS)	State of Colorado	CO
Commercial Information Systems Inc	Civil Records	ID, OR, WA, CA
Confi-Chek		US
Conrad Grundlehner Inc	Conrad Grundlehner	DC, MD, NC, VA, WV
Court PC of Connecticut	Superior Index	CT
Court PC of Connecticut		US

Litigation/Judgments/Tax Liens Company	Product Name	Region
CourtClerk.com	CourtClerk.com	TN
CourtExpress.com (RIS Legal Svcs)	US Court Records	US
CourtH.com	Courthouse Research	TX
CourthouseDirect.com		US
CourtLink	Courtlink Classic, CaseStream	US
Daily Report, The	The Daily Report (Kern County Only)	CA
Diligenz LLC		US
Diversified Information Services Corp		AZ
Dun & Bradstreet	D & B Public Record Search	US
Electronic Property Information Corp (EPIC)	OPRA-Erie, Monroe Counties	NY
Equifax Credit Services	Investigation System	US
FDR Research / Disclosure	State & Federal Agency Filings	US
Fidelifacts		US
FlatRateInfo.com	QI	US
Folks Finders Ltd		US
Golden Bear Information Services	Golden Bear	CA, NV, AZ, OR, WA
Hogan Information Services	Hogan Online	US
Hollingsworth Court Reporting Inc	Tenant Eviction/Public Record Report	AL, AR, FL, GA, IL, LA, MS, TN
Infocon Corporation	INFOCON County Access System-15 counties	PA
Information Network of Kansas	-Johnson, Sedgwick, Shawnee, Wyandotte	KS
Intranet Inc		TX
IQ Data Systems	IQ Data	US
J B Data Research Co.		MT
Juritas.com	Juritas	CA, DE, FL, IL, NJ, WA
KnowX	KnowX	US
KY Direct		KY
Law Bulletin Information Network	Access Plus-Central, North Counties	IL
LEXIS-NEXIS	LEXIS Law Publishing, Shepard's	US
LIDA Credit Agency Inc	LIDA	DE, NJ, NY, PA
Merlin Information Services	National FlatRate	US
Merlin Information Services	CA Civil Superior Indexes	CA
Motznik Computer Services Inc	Alaska Public Information Access System	AK
National Fraud Center		US
National Service Information		US

Litigation/Judgments/Tax Liens Company	Product Name	Region
Nebrask@ Online	Nebrask@ Online	NE
Northwest Location Services	Superior Courts	WA
Northwest Location Services		OR
OSO Grande Technologies	New Mexico Technet	NM
Paragon Document Research		US
Professional Services Bureau		LA, MS
PROTEC		US
Public Data Corporation	Public Data	NY
RC Information Brokers		MA
Record Information Services Inc	IL Records, Liens & Judgments	IL
Richland County Abstract Co	Judgment & Tax Liens	MN, ND
San Diego Daily Transcript/San Diego Source	San Diego Source	CA
Search Company of North Dakota LLC	North Dakota Records	ND
Search Network Ltd		IA,KS,US
Security Search & Abstract Co		PA,NJ,US
SKLD Information Services LLC		CO
Software Computer Group Inc	Circuit Express	WV
Southeastern Public Records Inc.	Michigan/Georgia Public Records	MI, GA
Superior Information Services LLC	Superior Online	DC, DE, MD, NC, NJ, NY, PA, VA
Telebase	LEXIS-NEXIS Caselow @AOL	US
TEXSEARCH		TX
The Todd Wiegele Research Co Inc		US
Thomson & Thomson		US
UCC Direct Services - AccuSearch Inc		CA, IL, TX
UCC Retrievals	Federal Tax Liens and UCCs	VA
Unisearch Inc		US
US Corporate Services		US
US Document Services Inc		SC,NC,US
US SEARCH.com		US
Westlaw Public Records	Lawsuits, Judgments, Liens	US

Military Service

Military Service Company	Product Name	Region
ADREM Profiles Inc		US
Ameridex Information Systems	Military DB	US

Military Service Company	Product Name	Region
Fidelifacts		US
Folks Finders Ltd		US
KnowX	KnowX	US
Military Information Enterprises Inc	Nationwide Locator Online	US

Mortgage Data

Mortgage Data	Product Name	Region
First American Real Estate Solutions - Amerestate	PaceNet	KY, MI, OH

News/Current Events

News/Current Events Company	Product Name	Region
Access Indiana Information Network		IN
American Business Information	Business Sales Leads	US
BiblioData	BiblioData	US
Bureau1 (Philippines)		Itl
Burrelles Information Services	BIO	US
CCH Washington Service Bureau		US
CompuServe	Quest Research Center	US
Congressional Information Service Inc	Government Periodicals Universe	US
Dialog Corporation, The	Profound LiveWire`	US
FDR Research / Disclosure	State & Federal Agency Filings	US
FOIA Group Inc		US
Hoovers Inc	Hoover's Company Profiles	US
Infomation-KS LLC		US
Loren Data Corp	Commerce Business Daily	US
SEAFAX Inc		US
Telebase	Brainwave, I-Quest	US
UMI - Bell & Howell Information & Learning		US

Patents

Patents Company	Product Name	Region
Aurigin Systems Inc.	Aurigin	US, Itl
Cal Info		US
Canadian Law Book Inc	Canadian Patent Reporter	CD

Patents Company	Product Name	Region
Derwent Information	Derwent World Patents Index, Patent Explorer	US
MicroPatent USA	WPS	US, Itl
QPAT	QPAT-WW	US, Itl
Telebase	Brainwave, I-Quest	US
Thomson & Thomson	Site Comber	US

Real Estate/Assessor

Real Estate/Assessor Company	Product Name	Region
ACS Inc	BRC	IL,OH,ME
American Business Information	Consumer Sales Leads	US
Attorneys Title Insurance Fund	The Fund (40 counties)	FL
Chattel Mortgage Reporter Inc		US
ChoicePoint Inc	Real Property	US
ChoicePoint, formerly CDB Infotek	Real Property Ownership & Transfers	US
Commercial Information Systems Inc	Real Estate Records	ID,NV,OR,WA
Confi-Chek		US
CourtH.com	Courthouse Research	TX
CourthouseDirect.com	Real Estate/Assessor	AZ, CA, FL, HI, IL, NY, OK, PA, TX, UT, WA
CourthouseDirect.com		US
DataQuick	DataQuick	US
DCS Information Systems	AmeriFind (DNIS)	TX,US
Diversified Information Services Corp	Real Property Records-Maricopa Cty	AZ
Electronic Property Information Corp (EPIC)	OPRA-Erie, Monroe Counties	NY
Environmental Data Resources, Inc. (EDR)	NEDIS, Sanborn Maps	US
Experian Online	Experian Online	US
First American Corporation, The	Real Estate Information	US
First American Real Estate Solutions	Real Property Database	LA, AZ, CA, CO, DC, DE, FL, GA, HI, IL, IN, LA, MA, MD, MI, MN, MS, NC, NJ, NM, NY, NV, OH, OK, OR, PA, SC, TN, TX, UT, VA, VI,
First American Real Estate Solutions - Amerestate	PaceNet, Prospect Services	KY, MI, OH

Real Estate/Assessor Company	Product Name	Region
FlatRateInfo.com	QI	US
Haines & Company Inc	Criss+Cross Plus	US
Hogan Information Services		US
IDM Corporation	Tax, Assessor and Recorders	US
Infocon Corporation	INFOCON County Access System-15 counties	PA
Information Network of Kansas	Premium Services	KS
iplace.com	e-neighborhoods, iplace	US
IQ Data Systems	IQ Data	US
KnowX	KnowX	US
Law Bulletin Information Network	Access Plus-Cook Cty	IL
LEXIS-NEXIS	ALLOWN	US
Merlin Information Services	National FlatRate	US
Merlin Information Services	CA Statewide Property	CA
Metro Market Trends Inc	Real Estate Activity Reporting System	FL, AL
Metronet	MetroNet, Cole's Directory	US
Motznik Computer Services Inc	Alaska Public Information Access System	AK
National Fraud Center		US
Northwest Location Services		WA
OPEN (Online Professional Electronic Network)	OPEN	US
Paragon Document Research		MN,ND,SD,MT
Plat System Services Inc	PropertyInfoNet™ (Minneapolis, St. Paul)	MN
Plat System Services Inc	System90, PID Directory (Minneapolis, St. Paul)	MN
Professional Services Bureau		LA, MS
Property Data Center Inc	Real Property Assessments, Taxes	CO
Public Data Corporation	Public Data	NY
QuickInfo.net Information Services	QuickInfo.net	FL, ID, IA, LA, MN, MS, MO, NV, NC, OR, TX, UT, WI, WY
Real Estate Guide, The	Real Estate Filing Guide	US
Record Information Services Inc	New Homeowners	IL
Richland County Abstract Co		MN, ND
Security Search & Abstract Co	Security Search, Title Plants	PA
Security Search & Abstract Co		US
SKLD Information Services LLC	New Homeowners List, Deeds, Loan Activity, Notice of Demand (13 Counties)	CO
Superior Information Services LLC	Real Estate Files	NY, NJ
The Search Company Inc	Property Ownership & Tenant Data	CD

Real Estate/Assessor Company	Product Name	Region
The Todd Wiegele Research Co Inc		US
The Todd Wiegele Research Co Inc	FASTRACT	WI
tnrealestate.com KAL Software	Tennessee Real Estate Data	TN
UCC Direct Services - AccuSearch Inc		CA, TX
US Document Services Inc		US
US SEARCH.com		US
USADATA.com	Marketing Portal	US
Western Regional Data Inc	WRDI's Lead Focus, Property Search	NV
Westlaw Public Records	Real Estate, Liens & Judgments	US

SEC/Other Financial

SEC/Other Financial Company	Product Name	Region
A.M. Best Company	Best Database Services	US
American Business Information	Business Sales Leads	US
CCH Washington Service Bureau	SECnet	US
Dialog Corporation, The	Profound; DIALOG Web	US
Disclosure	Compact D (US & Canada)	US, CD
FDR Research / Disclosure	Disclosure SEC Database	US
Fidelifacts		US
Hoovers Inc	Real-Time SEC Documents	US
Infomation-KS LLC		KS, MO
Pallorium Inc		US
SEAFAX Inc		US
Silver Plume	Insurance Industry Rates, Forms and Manuals, Reference & Research Material	US
Telebase	Brainwave, I-Quest	US

Software/Training

Software/Training Company	Product Name	Region
Canadian Law Book Inc		CD
Carfax	VINde (VIN Validity Check Program)	US
FOIA Group Inc	FOIA-Ware	US
National Fraud Center	NFC Online	US
Southeastern Public Records Inc.		MI,GA

Tenant History

Tenant History Company	Product Name	Region
Fidelifacts		US
Golden Bear Information Services	Golden Bear	CA, NV, AZ, OR, WA
Hogan Information Services		US
Hollingsworth Court Reporting Inc		AL, AR, FL, GA, IL, LA, MS, TN
LIDA Credit Agency Inc		NY
National Credit Information Network NCI	NCI Network	IN, KY, OH

Trademarks

Trademarks Company	Product Name	Region
Access Louisiana Inc	LA Corporate Data	LA
AcuSearch Services LLC		US
American Business Information		US
Cal Info		US
ChoicePoint, formerly DBT Online Inc	AutoTrackXP	US
CompuServe	Quest Research Center	US
CourthouseDirect.com		TX
Dialog Corporation, The	Profound; DIALOG Web	US
Disclosure		US
FDR Research / Disclosure	State & Federal Agency Filings	US
MicroPatent USA	TradeMark Checker, Mark Search Plus	US, Itl
Publook Information Service	Publook	OH
Telebase	Brainwave, I-Quest	US
Thomson & Thomson	US Full Trademark Search, Site Comber	US
Trademark Register, The	The Trademark Register	US
UCC Retrievals		US

Uniform Commercial Code

Uniform Commercial Code Company	Product Name	Region
Access Indiana Information Network	Premium Services	IN
Access Louisiana Inc	LA UCC	LA
ACS Inc	BRC	IL,OH,ME
Chattel Mortgage Reporter Inc	Chattel Mortgage Reporter (Cook County)	IL

Uniform Commercial Code Company	Product Name	Region
ChoicePoint Inc	Legal Information	US
ChoicePoint, formerly CDB Infotek	UCC	US
Colorado Central Information System (CIS)	State of Colorado	CO
Commercial Information Systems Inc	UCCs	CA,ID,OR,WA
Confi-Chek		US
Court PC of Connecticut		CT
CourthouseDirect.com		TX
Diligenz LLC	Diligenz.com	US
Dun & Bradstreet	D & B Public Record Search	US
Electronic Property Information Corp (EPIC)	OPRA-Erie, Monroe Counties	NY
Experian Online	Experian Online Business Records Reports	US
Hogan Information Services		US
Information Network of Kansas	Premium Services	KS
Intranet Inc		TX
IQ Data Systems	IQ Data	US
J B Data Research Co.		MT
KnowX	KnowX	US
KY Direct	UCC Index Search	KY
Law Bulletin Information Network	Access Plus-Cook County	IL
Law Bulletin Information Network		IL
LEXIS-NEXIS	ALLUCC	US
LIDA Credit Agency Inc		NY, US
Merlin Information Services	UCC Index	CA
Motznik Computer Services Inc	Alaska Public Information Access System	AK
National Credit Information Network NCI		IN, KY, OH
National Service Information		US
National Service Information	NSI Online	IN, OH, WI
Nebrask@ Online	Nebrask@ Online	NE
OPEN (Online Professional Electronic Network)	OPEN	US
OSO Grande Technologies	New Mexico Technet	NM
Paragon Document Research	Pdrlog	MN, US
Professional Services Bureau		LA, MS
Public Data Corporation	Public Data	NY
Publook Information Service	Publook	OH
Record Information Services Inc		IL
San Diego Daily Transcript/San Diego Source	San Diego Source	CA
Search Company of North Dakota LLC	ND UCC	ND

Uniform Commercial Code Company	Product Name	Region
Search Network Ltd	Search Network	IA,KS
Search Network Ltd		US
Security Search & Abstract Co		PA,NJ,US
Superior Information Services LLC	UCC Files	PA, NJ
The Todd Wiegele Research Co Inc		US
UCC Direct Services - AccuSearch Inc	AccuSearch	TX,CA,PA,IL,WA, OH,OR,MO
UCC Guide Inc, The	UCC Filing Guide	US
UCC Retrievals	Federal Tax Liens and UCCs	VA
Unisearch Inc	WALDO	CA, IL, WA, OH, IL
Unisearch Inc		US
US Corporate Services		US
US Corporate Services	WI UCCs	WI
US Document Services Inc		SC,NC,US
West Group	Westlaw	US

Vessels

Vessels Company	Product Name	Region
AutoDataDirect, Inc	ADD123	FL
FlatRateInfo.com	US Merchant Vessels	US
Intellicorp Ltd		US
KnowX	KnowX	US
LEXIS-NEXIS	USBoat	AL, AZ, AR, CO,CT,FL,GE,IA, ME,MD,MA,MS, MO,MN,MT,NE,N V,NH,NC,ND,OH ,OR,SC,UT,VA, WV,WI
Lloyds Maritime Information Services Inc	SEADATA, SeaSearcher	US, Itl
Motznik Computer Services Inc	Alaska Public Information Access System	AK
National Marine Fisheries Service	Vessel Documentation Data	US
Pallorium Inc	Skiptrace America, People Finder CDs	US
US Document Services Inc		US
US SEARCH.com		US
Virginia Information Providers Network	VIPNet	VA
Westlaw Public Records	Watercraft Locator	US

Vital Records

Vital Records Company	Product Name	Region
AcuSearch Services LLC		US
ADREM Profiles Inc		US
Ancestry	Ancestry.com	US, Itl
Ancestry	SSN Death Index	US
Bureau1 (Philippines)		Itl
Cambridge Statistical Research Associates	Death Master File	US
CourthouseDirect.com		TX
DCS Information Systems	Texas Systems (marriage/divorce)	TX
Folks Finders Ltd	Birth Index, Cemetery Internment, POW, MIA, Causalty Reports	US
Household Drivers Reports Inc (HDR Inc)	Vital Records	TX
Infocon Corporation	INFOCON County Access System-15 counties	PA
KnowX	KnoxX	US
KY Direct	Vital Statistics	KY
LIDA Credit Agency Inc		NY, US
Merlin Information Services	CA Brides and Grooms, Trace Wizard	CA, US
National Service Information		US
Northwest Location Services		WA
QuickInfo.net Information Services	QuickInfo.net	CO, NV, TX
RC Information Brokers	MassData	MA
Richland County Abstract Co		MN, ND
Search Company of North Dakota LLC		ND
Security Search & Abstract Co		US
Thomson & Thomson	US Title Availability Search, The deForest Report	US
US Document Services Inc		US
Vital Records Information	vitalrec.com	US
VitalChek Network	VitalChek	US

Voter Registration

Voter Registration Company	Product Name	Region
ARISTOTLE	ARISTOTLE	US
E-Merges.com	US Registered Voter File	AK,AR,CO,CT,DE,DC,LA,ME,MA,MI,NV,NH,NY,NC,OH,OK,RI,SC,SD,UT,VT,WI

Voter Registration Company	Product Name	Region
Haines & Company Inc		OH
Infocon Corporation	INFOCON County Access System-15 counties	PA
Infomation-KS LLC		KS, MO
Merlin Information Services	Trace Wizard National Residential Locator	US
Motznik Computer Services Inc	Alaska Public Information Access System	AK
National Credit Information Network NCI	NCI Network	US
Northwest Location Services		WA
Pallorium Inc	Skiptrace America, People Finder CDs	US
QuickInfo.net Information Services	QuickInfo.net	AK, AR, CO, DE, GA, KS, MI, NV, OH, OK, TX, UT

Wills/Probate

Wills/Probate Company	Product Name	Region
CourthouseDirect.com		TX
Electronic Property Information Corp (EPIC)	OPRA-Erie, Monroe Counties	NY
Folks Finders Ltd		US
Infomation-KS LLC		KS, MO
Richland County Abstract Co		MN, ND
Security Search & Abstract Co		US

Workers Compensation

Workers Compensation Company	Product Name	Region
ADREM Profiles Inc		US
Agency Records	20 yrs of Claims	FL
ChoicePoint Inc		US
Commercial Information Systems Inc		US
DAC Services	Claims and Injury Reports	AR, FL, IA, IL, KS, MA, MD, ME, MI, MS, ND, NE, OH, OK, OR, TX
DAC Services		US
Infomation-KS LLC		KS, MO
Information Network of Arkansas	INA	AR
Informus Corporation		US
Informus Corporation	Informus	MS
Intellicorp Ltd		US

Workers Compensation Company	Product Name	Region
National Credit Information Network NCI		IN, KY, OH
OPEN (Online Professional Electronic Network)		US
PROTEC		US
US Document Services Inc		US

Distribution Methods Index

We have indicated whether a company will sell its databases, offers CD-ROMs, sell its products via the Internet, etc. We have NOT indicated if the company will provide its services through traditional methods (by phone, mail or fax) because that is common practice for most firms.

The 14 Distribution Methods

Automated Telephone Look -Up	CD-ROM
Dial-Up (Other than Internet)	Disk
E-Mail	FTP
Gateway via Another Online Svc	Internet
Lists or Labels	Magnetic Tape
Microfilm-Microfiche	Publication/Directory
Software	Will Sell Database

Automated Telephone Look-Up

Automated Telephone Look-Up Company	Web Site
Agency Records	www.agencyrecords.com
Information Inc	www.members.aol.com/infomantn/info.html
Hoovers Inc	www.hoovers.com
Investigators Anywhere Resource Line	www.investigatorsanywhere.com/
Nebrask@ Online	www.nol.org

CD-ROM

CD-ROM Company	Web Site
A.M. Best Company	www.ambest.com
Accutrend Corporation	www.accutrend.com
Amerestate Inc	www.amerestate.com
ARISTOTLE	www.aristotle.org
Avantex Inc	www.avantext.com
Banko Inc	www.BANKO.com
Burrelles Information Services	http://burrelles.com
Cambridge Statistical Research Associates	

CD-ROM Company	Web Site
Congressional Information Service Inc	www.cispubs.com
Dialog Corporation, The	www.dialog.com
Disclosure	www.primark.com/pfid
Diversified Information Services Corp	www.discaz.com
First American Real Estate Solutions	www.firstAm.com
Gale Group Inc, The	www.gale.com
Haines & Company Inc	www.haines.com
Hoovers Inc	www.hoovers.com
IDM Corporation	www.idmcorp.com
InfoUSA	www.infousa.com
Interstate Data Corporation	www.cdrominvestigations.com
Kompass USA Inc	www.kompass-intl.com
Martindale-Hubbell	www.martindale.com
Merlin Information Services	www.merlindata.com
Metro Market Trends Inc	www.mmtinfo.com
MicroPatent USA	http://micropat.com
National Fraud Center	www.nationalfraud.com
OSHA DATA	www.oshadata.com
Real Estate Guide, The	www.eguides.com
Silver Plume	www.silverplume.iix.com
Southeastern Public Records Inc	www.instantimpact.com/spr
Tax Analysts	www.tax.org
Thomson & Thomson	www.thomson-thomson.com
UCC Guide Inc, The	www.eguides.com
UMI Company	www.umi.com
VISTA Information Solutions	www.vistainfo.com
West Group	www.westgroup.com
Western Regional Data Inc	www.wrdi.com

Dial-Up (Other than Internet)

Dial-Up (Other than Internet) Company	Web Site
AccuSearch Inc	www.accusearchinc.com
ACS Inc	
ADREM Profiles Inc	www.adpro.com
Agency Records	www.agencyrecords.com
Amerestate Inc	www.amerestate.com
American Driving Records	www.mvrs.com
Ameridex Information Systems	www.ameridex.com
Attorneys Title Insurance Fund	www.thefund.com

Dial-Up (Other than Internet) Company	Web Site
Aurigin Systems Inc	http://aurigin.com
Avert Inc	www.avert.com
Banko Inc	www.BANKO.com
Burrelles Information Services	http://burrelles.com
Cambridge Statistical Research Associates	
Carfax	www.carfax.com
CaseStream.com	www.CaseStream.com
CCH Washington Service Bureau	www.wsb.com
ChoicePoint Inc	www.choicepointinc.com
ChoicePoint, formerly CDB Infotek	www.cdb.com
ChoicePoint, Formerly DBT Online Inc	www.dbtonline.com
CIC Applicant Background Checks	www.hirecheck.com
Commercial Information Systems Inc	www.cis-usa.com
CompuServe	www.compuserve.com
Confi-Chek	www.confi-chek.com
Congressional Information Service Inc	www.cispubs.com
CourtH.com	www.courth.com
CourtLink	www.courtlink.com
DAC Services	www.dacservices.com
DataQuick	www.dataquick.com
Data-Trac Network Inc	www.DATA-TRAC.com
DCS Information Systems	www.dnis.com
Derwent Information	www.derwent.com
Dialog Corporation, The	www.dialog.com
Diversified Information Services Corp	www.discaz.com
Dun & Bradstreet	www.dnb.com
Electronic Property Information Corp (EPIC)	
Equifax Credit Services	www.equifax.com
Everton Publishers	www.everton.com
Experian Consumer Credit	www.experian.com
Experian Online	www.experian.com
Explore Information Services	www.exploredata.com
Federal Filings Inc	www.fedfil.com
FOIA Group Inc	www.FOIA.com
Gale Group Inc, The	www.gale.com
Golden Bear Information Services	
Haines & Company Inc	www.haines.com
Hogan Information Services	www.hoganinfo.com
Hollingsworth Court Reporting Inc	www.public-records.com
Hoovers Inc	www.hoovers.com

Dial-Up (Other than Internet) Company	Web Site
Household Drivers Reports Inc (HDR Inc)	www.hdr.com
IDM Corporation	www.idmcorp.com
Infocon Corporation	
Information Inc	www.members.aol.com/infomantn/info.html
Information Network of Kansas	www.ink.org
Informus Corporation	www.informus.com
InfoUSA	www.infousa.com
Insurance Information Exchange (iiX)	www.iix.com
Intellicorp Ltd	www.intellicorp.net
Interstate Data Corporation	www.cdrominvestigations.com
Investigators Anywhere Resource Line	www.investigatorsanywhere.com
KnowX	www.knowx.com
Law Bulletin Information Network	www.lawbulletin.com
LEXIS-NEXIS	www.lexis-nexis.com
Lloyds Maritime Information Services Inc	www.lmis.com
Logan Registration Service Inc	www.loganreg.com
Merlin Information Services	www.merlindata.com
MicroPatent USA	http://micropat.com
Motznik Computer Services Inc	www.motznik.com
National Credit Information Network NCI	www.wdia.com
National Fraud Center	www.nationalfraud.com
Nebrask@ Online	www.nol.org
New Mexico Technet	www.technet.nm.org
NIB	http://nib.com
Northwest Location Services	http://legallocate.com
OPEN (Online Professional Electronic Network)	www.openonline.com
OSHA DATA	www.oshadata.com
Pallorium Inc	www.pallorium.com
Plat System Services Inc	www.platsystems.com
Professional Services Bureau	
PROTEC	
Publook Information Service	http://publook.com
QPAT	www.qpat.com
Record Information Services Inc	www.public-record.com
RentGrow Inc	www.rentgrow.com
Screening Network, The	www.screeningnetwork.com
Search Network Ltd	http://searchnetworkltd.com
Software Computer Group Inc	www.swcg-inc.com
Southeastern Public Records Inc	www.instantimpact.com/spr
State Net	www.statenet.com

Dial-Up (Other than Internet) Company	Web Site
Superior Information Services LLC	www.superiorinfo.com
Telebase	www.telebase.com
The Registry	www.registrycheck.com
The Search Company Inc	www.thesearchcompany.com
Thomson & Thomson	www.thomson-thomson.com
TML Information Services Inc	www.tml.com
tnrealestate.com	www.tnrealestate.com
Trans Union	www.transunion.com
Trans Union Employment Screening Services Inc	http://tuess.com
UMI Company	www.umi.com
Unisearch Inc	www.unisearch.com
US Corporate Services	www.uscorpserv.com
US SEARCH.com	http://1800ussearch.com
VISTA Information Solutions	www.vistainfo.com
West Group	www.westgroup.com
Westlaw Public Records	www.westlaw.com

Disk

Disk Company	Web Site
A.M. Best Company	www.ambest.com
Amerestate Inc	www.amerestate.com
Attorneys Title Insurance Fund	www.thefund.com
Banko Inc	www.BANKO.com
Carfax	www.carfax.com
Congressional Information Service Inc	www.cispubs.com
Conrad Grundlehner Inc	www.superiorinfo.com
CourtLink	www.courtlink.com
DataQuick	www.dataquick.com
DataTech Research	
Diversified Information Services Corp	www.discaz.com
Dun & Bradstreet	www.dnb.com
Experian Online	www.experian.com
Explore Information Services	www.exploredata.com
FOIA Group Inc	www.FOIA.com
Haines & Company Inc	www.haines.com
Hogan Information Services	www.hoganinfo.com
IDM Corporation	www.idmcorp.com
InfoUSA	www.infousa.com
Intranet Inc	

Disk Company	Web Site
Lloyds Maritime Information Services Inc	www.lmis.com
Metro Market Trends Inc	www.mmtinfo.com
MicroPatent USA	http://micropat.com
National Fraud Center	www.nationalfraud.com
OSHA DATA	www.oshadata.com
Paragon Document Research	www.banc.com/pdrstore
Plat System Services Inc	www.platsystems.com
Professional Services Bureau	
Property Data Center Inc	www.pdclane.net
Public Data Corporation	www.pdcny.com
RC Information Brokers	
Record Information Services Inc	www.public-record.com
Richland County Abstract Co	
SKLD Information Services LLC	www.skld.com
Southeastern Public Records Inc	www.instantimpact.com/spr
Tax Analysts	www.tax.org
Todd Wiegele Research Co Inc	www.execpc.com/~research
Trans Union Employment Screening Services Inc	http://tuess.com
UCC Guide Inc, The	www.eguides.com
US Corporate Services	www.uscorpserv.com
VISTA Information Solutions	www.vistainfo.com
Western Regional Data Inc	www.wrdi.com

E-Mail

E-Mail Company	Web Site
Access Indiana Information Network	www.ai.org
Accufax	www.accufax-us.com
ADREM Profiles Inc	www.adpro.com
Anybirthday.com	www.anybirthdate.com/
Avert Inc	www.avert.com
Better Business Bureau	www.bbb.org
Cal Info	http://members.aol.com/calinfola/
CaseStream.com	www.CaseStream.com
Chattel Mortgage Reporter Inc	www.chattelmtg.com
CourtH.com	www.courth.com
Credentials LLC	www.degreechk.com
Diversified Information Services Corp	www.discaz.com
EdVerify Inc	http://edverify.com
Finder Group, The	

E-Mail Company	Web Site
FOIA Group Inc	www.FOIA.com
Folks Finders Ltd	www.pimall.com/folkfinders/folkfind.htm
Golden Bear Information Services	
Hollingsworth Court Reporting Inc	www.public-records.com
Intellicorp Ltd	www.intellicorp.net
Landlord Protection Agency	www.mnlpa.com
Law Bulletin Information Network	www.lawbulletin.com
Logan Registration Service Inc	www.loganreg.com
Loren Data Corp	www.LD.com
Metro Market Trends Inc	www.mmtinfo.com
MicroPatent USA	http://micropat.com
Military Information Enterprises Inc	www.militaryusa.com
National Credit Information Network NCI	www.wdia.com
Northwest Location Services	http://legallocate.com
Owens OnLine Inc	www.owens.com
Professional Services Bureau	
Publook Information Service	http://publook.com
RC Information Brokers	
Record Information Services Inc	www.public-record.com
Search Company of North Dakota LLC	
Southeastern Public Records Inc	www.instantimpact.com/spr
The Search Company Inc	www.thesearchcompany.com
Trans Union Employment Screening Services Inc	http://tuess.com
US SEARCH.com	http://1800ussearch.com
USADATA.com	www.usadata.com

FTP

FTP Company	Web Site
Attorneys Title Insurance Fund	www.thefund.com
CourtLink	www.courtlink.com
Hollingsworth Court Reporting Inc	www.public-records.com
Western Regional Data Inc	www.wrdi.com

Gateway via Another Online Service

Gateway via Another Online Service Company	Web Site
555-1212.com	www.555-1212.com
Access Indiana Information Network	www.ai.org
Access Louisiana	

Gateway via Another Online Service Company	Web Site
ACS Inc	
AcuSearch Services LLC	
American Driving Records	www.mvrs.com
Better Business Bureau	www.bbb.org
CaseStream.com	www.CaseStream.com
CIC Applicant Background Checks	www.hirecheck.com
CompuServe	www.compuserve.com
CorporateInfomation.com	http://corporateinformation.com
CourtLink	www.courtlink.com
DataTech Research	
Dialog Corporation, The	www.dialog.com
Explore Information Services	www.exploredata.com
Federal Filings Inc	www.fedfil.com
Folks Finders Ltd	www.pimall.com/folkfinders/folkfind.htm
Haines & Company Inc	www.haines.com
Household Drivers Reports Inc (HDR Inc)	www.hdr.com
Infocon Corporation	
Information Network of Arkansas	www.state.ar.us/ina/about_ina.html
Information Network of Kansas	www.ink.org
Insurance Information Exchange (iiX)	www.iix.com
Intellicorp Ltd	www.intellicorp.net
Interstate Data Corporation	www.cdrominvestigations.com
IQ Data Systems	www.iqdata.com
Logan Registration Service Inc	www.loganreg.com
Loren Data Corp	www.LD.com
MDR/Minnesota Driving Records	
Merlin Information Services	www.merlindata.com
Metro Market Trends Inc	www.mmtinfo.com
National Credit Information Network NCI	www.wdia.com
National Fraud Center	www.nationalfraud.com
Nebrask@ Online	www.nol.org
OPEN (Online Professional Electronic Network)	www.openonline.com
OSHA DATA	www.oshadata.com
Owens OnLine Inc	www.owens.com
RentGrow Inc	www.rentgrow.com
San Diego Daily Transcript/San Diego Source	www.sddt.com
Screening Network, The	www.screeningnetwork.com
Software Computer Group Inc	www.swcg-inc.com
State Net	www.statenet.com
Telebase	www.telebase.com

Gateway via Another Online Service Company	Web Site
Thomson & Thomson	www.thomson-thomson.com
TML Information Services Inc	www.tml.com
Trans Union Employment Screening Services Inc	http://tuess.com
US SEARCH.com	http://1800ussearch.com
USADATA.com	www.usadata.com
Virginia Information Providers Network	www.vipnet.org
VISTA Information Solutions	www.vistainfo.com
Vital Records Information	http://vitalrec.com
VitalChek Network	www.vitalchek.com
Westlaw Public Records	www.westlaw.com

Internet

Internet Company	Web Site
555-1212.com	www.555-1212.com
Access Indiana Information Network	www.ai.org
AccuSearch Inc	www.accusearchinc.com
Accutrend Corporation	www.accutrend.com
Anybirthday.com	www.anybirthday.com
Banko Inc	www.BANKO.com
Better Business Bureau	www.bbb.org
BiblioData	www.bibliodata.com
Carfax	www.carfax.com
CCH Washington Service Bureau	www.wsb.com
ChoicePoint, formerly CDB Infotek	www.cdb.com
ChoicePoint, Formerly DBT Online Inc	www.dbtonline.com
CIC Applicant Background Checks	www.hirecheck.com
Commercial Information Systems Inc	www.cis-usa.com
Companies Online	www.companiesonline.com
CompuServe	www.compuserve.com
Confi-Chek	www.confi-chek.com
Corporate Screening Services Inc	www.corporate-screening.com
CorporateInfomation.com	http://corporateinformation.com
CourtH.com	www.courth.com
CourtLink	www.courtlink.com
Credentials LLC	www.degreechk.com
Daily Report, The	www.thedailyreport.com
DataTech Research	
Data-Trac Network Inc	www.DATA-TRAC.com
DCS Information Systems	www.dnis.com

Internet Company	Web Site
Derwent Information	www.derwent.com
Dialog Corporation, The	www.dialog.com
Dun & Bradstreet	www.dnb.com
EdVerify Inc	http://edverify.com
Electronic Property Information Corp (EPIC)	
Equifax Credit Services	www.equifax.com
Everton Publishers	www.everton.com
Experian Consumer Credit	www.experian.com
Experian Online	www.experian.com
Explore Information Services	www.exploredata.com
Federal Filings Inc	www.fedfil.com
FlatRateInfo.com	www.flatrateinfo.com
FOIA Group Inc	www.FOIA.com
Golden Bear Information Services	
Hollingsworth Court Reporting Inc	www.public-records.com
Hoovers Inc	www.hoovers.com
Information Network of Arkansas	www.state.ar.us/ina/about_ina.html
Information Network of Kansas	www.ink.org
InfoUSA	www.infousa.com
Insurance Information Exchange (iiX)	www.iix.com
Investigators Anywhere Resource Line	www.investigatorsanywhere.com
IQ Data Systems	www.jim@iqdata.com
KnowX	www.knowx.com
Kompass USA Inc	www.kompass-intl.com
Landings.com	www.landings.com
Landlord Protection Agency	www.mnlpa.com
Law Bulletin Information Network	www.lawbulletin.com
Merlin Information Services	www.merlindata.com
MicroPatent USA	http://micropat.com
Military Information Enterprises Inc	www.militaryusa.com
National Credit Information Network NCI	www.wdia.com
National Marine Fisheries Service	www.st.nmfs.gov/st1/commercial/index.html
National Service Information	www.nsii.net
Nebrask@ Online	www.nol.org
New Mexico Technet	www.technet.nm.org
Northwest Location Services	http://legallocate.com
Offshore Business News & Research	www.offshorebusiness.com
Owens OnLine Inc	www.owens.com
Plat System Services Inc	www.platsystems.com
Property Data Center Inc	www.pdclane.net

Internet Company	Web Site
QPAT	www.qpat.com
QuickInfo.net Information Services	www.quickinfo.net
RC Information Brokers	
Real Estate Guide, The	www.eguides.com
Record Information Services Inc	www.public-record.com
Rental Research Services Inc	www.rentalresearch.com
RentGrow Inc	www.rentgrow.com
San Diego Daily Transcript/San Diego Source	www.sddt.com
Screening Network, The	www.screeningnetwork.com
SEAFAX Inc	www.seafax.com
Software Computer Group Inc	www.swcg-inc.com
Southeastern Public Records Inc	www.instantimpact.com/spr
Tax Analysts	www.tax.org
Telebase	www.telebase.com
Thomas Legislative Information	http://thomas.loc.gov
Thomson & Thomson	www.thomson-thomson.com
TML Information Services Inc	www.tml.com
tnrealestate.com	www.tnrealestate.com
UCC Guide Inc, The	www.eguides.com
Unisearch Inc	www.unisearch.com
Virginia Information Providers Network	www.vipnet.org
Vital Records Information	http://vitalrec.com
Western Regional Data Inc	www.wrdi.com
Westlaw Public Records	www.westlaw.com

Lists or Labels

Lists or Labels Company	Web Site
Accutrend Corporation	www.accutrend.com
Amerestate Inc	www.amerestate.com
Banko Inc	www.BANKO.com
CourtLink	www.courtlink.com
DataQuick	www.dataquick.com
Felonies R Us	
Folks Finders Ltd	www.pimall.com/folkfinders/folkfind.htm
Haines & Company Inc	www.haines.com
Hogan Information Services	www.hoganinfo.com
InfoUSA	www.infousa.com
Martindale-Hubbell	www.martindale.com
MDR/Minnesota Driving Records	

Lists or Labels Company	Web Site
Metro Market Trends Inc	www.mmtinfo.com
Paragon Document Research	www.banc.com/pdrstore
Plat System Services Inc	www.platsystems.com
Property Data Center Inc	www.pdclane.net
Record Information Services Inc	www.public-record.com
Search Company of North Dakota LLC	
Search Network Ltd	http://searchnetworkltd.com
Trans Union Employment Screening Services Inc	http://tuess.com
UCC Retrievals Inc	
US Corporate Services	www.uscorpserv.com
USADATA.com	www.usadata.com
VISTA Information Solutions	www.vistainfo.com
Western Regional Data Inc	www.wrdi.com

Magnetic Tape

Magnetic Tape Company	Web Site
A.M. Best Company	www.ambest.com
Accutrend Corporation	www.accutrend.com
Amerestate Inc	www.amerestate.com
ARISTOTLE	www.aristotle.org
Attorneys Title Insurance Fund	www.thefund.com
Banko Inc	www.BANKO.com
Congressional Information Service Inc	www.cispubs.com
Conrad Grundlehner Inc	www.superiorinfo.com
DataQuick	www.dataquick.com
Disclosure	www.primark.com/pfid/
Experian Online	www.experian.com
Explore Information Services	www.exploredata.com
Haines & Company Inc	www.haines.com
Hogan Information Services	www.hoganinfo.com
IDM Corporation	www.idmcorp.com
InfoUSA	www.infousa.com
Merlin Information Services	www.merlindata.com
Metro Market Trends Inc	www.mmtinfo.com
Nebrask@ Online	www.nol.org
Professional Services Bureau	
Public Data Corporation	www.pdcny.com
Silver Plume	www.silverplume.iix.com
SKLD Information Services LLC	www.skld.com

Magnetic Tape Company	Web Site
Southeastern Public Records Inc	www.instantimpact.com/spr
Todd Wiegele Research Co Inc	www.execpc.com/~research

Microfilm-Microfiche

Microfilm-Microfiche Company	Web Site
CCH Washington Service Bureau	www.wsb.com
Chattel Mortgage Reporter Inc	www.chattelmtg.com
Disclosure	www.primark.com/pfid/
First American Real Estate Solutions	www.firstAm.com
Gale Group Inc, The	www.gale.com
Paragon Document Research	www.banc.com/pdrstore
Search Network Ltd	http://searchnetworkltd.com
Todd Wiegele Research Co Inc	www.execpc.com/~research
UMI Company	www.umi.com
Western Regional Data Inc	www.wrdi.com

Publication/Directory

Publication/Directory Company	Web Site
BiblioData	www.bibliodata.com
Burrelles Information Services	http://burrelles.com
Cal Info	http://members.aol.com/calinfola
CCH Washington Service Bureau	www.wsb.com
Congressional Information Service Inc	www.cispubs.com
Daily Report, The	www.thedailyreport.com
DataTech Research	
Derwent Information	www.derwent.com
Disclosure	www.primark.com/pfid
Haines & Company Inc	www.haines.com
Hoovers Inc	www.hoovers.com
InfoUSA	www.infousa.com
Kompass USA Inc	www.kompass-intl.com
Law Bulletin Information Network	www.lawbulletin.com
LEXIS-NEXIS	www.lexis-nexis.com
Martindale-Hubbell	www.martindale.com
Military Information Enterprises Inc	www.militaryusa.com
Plat System Services Inc	www.platsystems.com
Real Estate Guide, The	www.eguides.com
Search Network Ltd	http://searchnetworkltd.com

Publication/Directory Company	Web Site
State Net	www.statenet.com
Tax Analysts	www.tax.org
UCC Guide Inc, The	www.eguides.com
US Corporate Services	www.uscorpserv.com

Software

Software Company	Web Site
Aurigin Systems Inc	http://aurigin.com
CIC Applicant Background Checks	www.hirecheck.com
Dialog Corporation, The	www.dialog.com
Dun & Bradstreet	www.dnb.com
FOIA Group Inc	www.FOIA.com
Haines & Company Inc	www.haines.com
Hoovers Inc	www.hoovers.com
InfoUSA	www.infousa.com
Metro Market Trends Inc	www.mmtinfo.com
MicroPatent USA	http://micropat.com
NIB	http://nib.com
PROTEC	
Record Information Services Inc	www.public-record.com
Southeastern Public Records Inc	www.instantimpact.com/spr
The Search Company Inc	www.thesearchcompany.com
Trans Union	www.transunion.com
Trans Union Employment Screening Services Inc	http://tuess.com
US Corporate Services	www.uscorpserv.com
USADATA.com	www.usadata.com
VISTA Information Solutions	www.vistainfo.com

Will Sell Database

Will Sell Database Company	Web Site
Hogan Information Services	www.hoganinfo.com
InfoUSA	www.infousa.com
Real Estate Guide, The	www.eguides.com
SKLD Information Services LLC	www.skld.com
UCC Guide Inc, The	www.eguides.com

Private Company Profiles

The following profiles of over 170 companies specializing in public records access are designed to give you an overview of the firms' expertise and online capabilities.

How to Read & Use the Profiles

You can get a good sense a company's orientation by reviewing its profile. Here are some tips:

- **What are the Clientele Restrictions?** Does the company permit casual (non-recurring) requesters? Is a signed agreement or contract required?

- **What National Organizations does the company belong to?** The organizations that the company belongs to, listed under Memberships, may indicate the nature and focus of their services and products.

- **What are the Proprietary Products or Gateways provided by the company?** Each entry for a company lists the name of the product; the information type according to the categories defined in the Information Index; and the geographic area in which the product is available.

- **Are There Any Special Distribution Methods?** We have indicated whether a company will sell its databases, offers CD-ROMs, sell its products via the Internet, etc. We have NOT indicated if the company will provide its services through traditional methods (by phone, mail or fax) because that is common practice for most firms.

You should note that some products cover very specific geography (e.g., Motznick in Alaska) or specific information types (e.g., ARISTOTLE) while others are sometimes vast conglomerations of various information types (e.g., ChoicePoint). You may want to use the same information in one or the other of these products depending upon the breadth or depth of your search requirements.

- **Are there any other special characteristics of the company?** Each company was invited to submit a short description of special capabilities. This Statement of Capabilities may mention a service or other detail that you are looking for, including for example the availability of an online ordering system.

- Some of the other information you should notice as you review a profile include:

  1. When was the firm was founded? This industry is fast growing with a lot of new entrants with special experience and skills.

  2. A World Wide Web address for service or product information.

Editor's Tip: Visit www.publicrecordsources.com for updated information about these and other companies.

Editor's Note

These profiles were developed from a questionnaire sent to each company. When necessary, we completed the information about companies from our own knowledge where they failed to provide adequate details. We have tried to be as accurate as possible, we do not of course guarantee the complete accuracy of every profile. Companies can, and do, change products, and change coverage areas.

To help you determine which vendor is best suited to your needs, we recommend reviewing "10 Questions to Ask an Online Vendor" in the Public Records Primer Section.

555-1212.com
164 South Park
San Francisco, Ca 94107-1809
415-288-2440
www.555-1212.com
support@555-1212.com
Clientele Restrictions: None reported
Products & Information Categories:
Proprietary Databases or Gateways:
Gateway Name: 555-1212.com
Addresses/Telephone Numbers (US)
Special Distribution Methods to Client: Internet
A powerful, free access, web site. Search the white pages, yellow pages, phone reverse look-up, e-mail reverse look-up, and the web site finder. This site ranks among the top 1000 sites on the web, visit-wise.

A.M. Best Company
Ambest Rd
Oldwick, NJ 08858-9988
908-439-2200; Fax: 908-439-3296
www.ambest.com
sales@ambest.com
Founded: 1899
Clientele Restrictions: Casual requesters permitted
Products & Information Categories:
Proprietary Databases or Gateways:
Database Name: Best Database Services
SEC/Other Financial (US)

Database Name: Best's Insight Global
Foreign Country Information (GB, Itl, Canada)
Special Distribution Methods to Client: CD-ROM, Disk, Magnetic Tape, Software
A.M. Best Company, known worldwide as The Insurance Information Source, was the first company to report on the financial condition of insurance companies. A.M. Best strives to perform a constructive and objective role in the insurance industry toward the prevention and detection of insurer solvency. The company's exclusive Best's Ratings are the original and most recognized insurer financial strength ratings. A.M. Best provides quantitative and qualitative evaluations, and offers information through more than 50 reference publications and services. Since its inception a century ago, A.M. Best has provided financial services to professionals with timely, accurate and comprehensive insurance information. A.M. Best's London office can be reached at 011-44-171-264-2260. A.M. Best International, also based in London, can be reached at 011-44-181-579-1091.

Access Indiana Information Network
10 W Market St #600
Indianapolis, IN 46204-2497
800-236-5446, 317-233-2010; Fax: 317-233-2011
www.ai.org
dnsadmin@ai.org
Founded: 1995
Memberships: NASIRE,
Clientele Restrictions: Subscription required
Products & Information Categories:
General: Environmental (IN)

Proprietary Databases or Gateways:
Gateway Name: Premium Services
Driver and/or Vehicle, Corporate/Trade Name Data, Licenses/Registrations/Permits, Uniform Commercial Code,
    Litigation/Judgments/Tax Liens (IN)
Gateway Name: Free Services
Legislation/Regulation (IN)
Special Distribution Methods to Client: E-Mail, Internet
AIIN (or AccessIndiana) is a comprehensive, one-stop source for electronic access to State of Indiana government
information. This network is owned by the state of Indiana. Access to the public records listed here requires a
subscription fee and per-use fee. Specialties include drivers records, vehicle title and lien information, vehicle
registration records, physician and nurse license verification, Secretary of State records (including UCC, lobbyist, and
corporation information) and information on the Indiana General Assembly. See the Internet site for more information.

Access Louisiana Inc
400 Travis St #504
Shreveport, LA 71101
800-489-5620, 318-227-9730
debois41@aol.com
Founded: 1981
Memberships: NPRRA, NFPA, PRRN,
Clientele Restrictions: None reported
Products & Information Categories:
General: Bankruptcy (LA)
Proprietary Databases or Gateways:
Gateway Name: LA UCC
Uniform Commercial Code (LA)
Gateway Name: LA Corporate Data
Corporate/Trade Name Data, Trademarks/Patents and Addresses/Telephone Numbers (LA)
Special Distribution Methods to Client:
Access Louisiana is a statewide legal research company with a physical presence in every Louisiana parish. Services
include: public records (UCC, accounts, receivable, state/federal tax liens, suits, chattel mortgages, bankruptcy
records), corporate filing/retrieval, court records and registered agent services. They have extensive knowledge of
where information is recorded and how to effectively retrieve Louisiana public records.

Accutrend Corporation
6021 S Syracuse Wy #111
Denver, CO 80111
800-488-0011, 303-488-0011; Fax: 303-488-0133
www.accutrend.com
info@accutrend.com
Founded: 1987
Memberships: DMA,
Clientele Restrictions: None reported
Products & Information Categories:
Proprietary Databases or Gateways:
Database Name: New Business Database
Licenses/Registrations/Permits and Corporate/Trade Name Data (US)
Special Distribution Methods to Client: CD-ROM, Internet, Lists/Labels, Magnetic Tape
Accutrend Corporation compiles a new business database monthly that contains 175 to 200 million new business
registrations, licenses and incorporations. Data is collected from all levels of government and is enhanced with
demographic overlays.

ACS Inc
PO Box 4889
Syracuse, NY 13221
315-437-1283; Fax: 315-437-3223
Clientele Restrictions: Signed agreement required, must be ongoing account
Products & Information Categories:
Proprietary Databases or Gateways:
Gateway Name: BRC
Real Estate/Assessor, Uniform Commercial Code (IL, OH, ME)
Special Distribution Methods to Client: Dial-Up (Other than Internet)
ACS specializes in online access to Recorders, County Clerks and Registers across the country. Fees are involved.
Online access capabilities will be expanding to MI and PA in the near future. Other states will follow.

AcuSearch Services LLC
PO Box 100613
Denver, CO 80250
303-756-9687; Fax: 303-756-9687
AcuSearch9@aol.com
Founded: 1997
Memberships: NAIS, NAPPS,
Clientele Restrictions: Casual requesters permitted
Products & Information Categories:
General: Addresses/Telephone Numbers (US)
Proprietary Databases or Gateways:
Gateway Name: CO Criminal Information
Criminal Information (CO)
Special Distribution Methods to Client:
AcuSearch specializes in locating and obtaining pertinent information for financial institutions, businesses and
individuals. Instant access to nationwide people, credit, and vehicle info. 24 hour turnaround time on all Colorado and
Washington criminal/civil, driving/plate records, and process service. They provide in depth investigation in trademark
matters. Owner Layla Flora is a Univ. of Colorado graduate and has extensive case investigation experience in civil and
criminal matters. Guarantees quality and professional service.

ADREM Profiles Inc
5461 W Waters Ave #900
Tampa, FL 33634
800-281-1250, 813-890-0334
www.adpro.com
adrem-sales@adpro.com
Founded: 1992
Memberships: SHRM, AIIP, PRRN, NPRRA, ASIS,
Clientele Restrictions: Signed agreement required, must be ongoing account
Products & Information Categories:
General: Bankruptcy (US)
Proprietary Databases or Gateways:
Gateway Name: ADREM
Driver and/or Vehicle (US)
Special Distribution Methods to Client: Automated Telephone Look-Up, Dial-Up (Other than Internet), E-Mail, FTP,
Gateway via Another Online Service

ADREM Profiles is an international, full service public records research and retrieval company. Their comprehensive retrieval network allows access to information repositories within the 3,347 counties and independent cities throughout the United States. A staff of over 1,500 field researchers provides access to all counties within the US as well as to the Bahamas, Bermuda, Canada, the Caribbean and Europe. Utilizing ADREM's information ordering system, ADREM Advantage, research requests may be sent and retrieved securely and swiftly via the Internet 24 hours a day, 7 days a week.

Agency Records
PO Box 310175
Newington, CT 06131
800-777-6655, 860-667-1490; Fax: 860-666-4247
www.agencyrecords.com
Founded: 1972
Clientele Restrictions: Signed Agreement Required
Products & Information Categories:
General: Credit Information (US)

Proprietary Databases or Gateways:
Database Name: ARI
Criminal Information (CT)

Database Name: MN Court Convictions (15 years)
Criminal Information (MN)

Database Name: FL Workers Compensation Claims (20 years)
Workers Compensation (FL)

Gateway Name: ARI
Driver and/or Vehicle (US)

Special Distribution Methods to Client: Automated Telephone Look-Up, Dial-Up (Other than Internet), Gateway via Another Online Service, Internet, Magnetic Tape
Agency Records or ARI is a business to business provider of public record information. They offer nationwide retrieval of driving records with instant access to MVRs for FL, AL, SC, NC, WV, NJ, NY, CT, VA, MS, NH, and ME. They also provide instant access to court convictions for Connecticut and Minnesota. They offer computer, fax and phone ordering as well as volume discounts. Public companies may be invoiced.

Alacourt.com
PO Box 8173
Mobile, AL 36689
877-799-9898, 334-633-5484
http://alacourt.com
info@alacourt.com
Parent Company: On-Line Information Services, Inc
Founded: 1990
Clientele Restrictions: Subscription required
Products & Information Categories:
Proprietary Databases or Gateways:
Gateway Name: Alacourt.com
Litigation/Judgments/Tax Liens, Criminal Information (AL)
Special Distribution Methods to Client: E-Mail, Internet
Alacourt.com is an Internet-browser driven way to access the Alabama Trial Court records. All currently active cases are maintained in the system as are disposed cases, some going back as far as the late 1970's. The courts included are civil circuit and district courts, criminal cases in circuit and district courts, domestic relations & child support, traffic, and small claims. The system includes outstanding alias warrants, trial court dockets, attorney case information, and

other features. Search results include case summaries, party & attorney names, dockets, judgments, claims, creditors & charges.

American Business Information
PO Box 27347
Omaha, NE 68127
800-555-5335, 402-930-3500; Fax: 402-331-0176
www.infousa.com
Parent Company: InfoUSA Inc
Memberships: ALA, DMA, SIIA, NACM, SLA,
Clientele Restrictions: Casual requesters permitted
Products & Information Categories:
General: Trademarks (US)
Proprietary Databases or Gateways:
Database Name: Business Sales Leads
Addresses/Telephone Numbers, Credit Information, Foreign Country Information, News/Current Events and
     SEC/Other Financial (US)
Database Name: Consumer Sales Leads
Addresses/Telephone Numbers, Credit Information, Driver and/or Vehicle, Genealogical Information and Real
     Estate/Assessor (US)
Special Distribution Methods to Client: CD-ROM, Database, Dial-Up (Other than Internet), Disk, Gateway via
Another Online Service, Internet, Lists/Labels, Magnetic Tape, Publication/Directory, Software
American Business Information, a division of InfoUSA, compiles business information from telephone directories and other public sources. Over the past 20+ years, they have provided services to over 2 million customers. They telephone verify every name in their database before they offer it for sale. They phone-verify address changes from the USPS NCOA program. Their info is available in a variety of ways including online (SalesLeadsUSA.com), CD-ROM, and by telephone (Directory Assistance Plus). A division produces the Pro-CD Disk and another operates Digital Directory Assistance. For business leads call 800-555-5335. For SalesLeads USA call 402-592-9000.

American Driving Records
PO Box 1970
Rancho Cordova, CA 95741-1970
800-766-6877, 916-456-3200
www.mvrs.com
sales@mvrs.com
Founded: 1986
Clientele Restrictions: Signed agreement required, must be ongoing account
Products & Information Categories:
Proprietary Databases or Gateways:
Gateway Name: ADR
Driver and/or Vehicle (US)
Special Distribution Methods to Client: Dial-Up (Other than Internet), Internet
American Driving Record (ADR) services include accessing driving records and registration information. Also, they provide special processing for the insurance industry with such products as automatic checking (ACH), calculating underwriting points, and ZapApp(tm) - an automated insurance application from the agency to the carrier. Driving records can be instant, same day or overnight, depending on the state.

Ameridex Information Systems
PO Box 51314
Irvine, CA 92619-1314
714-731-2546; Fax: 714-731-2116

www.ameridex.com
Founded: 1988
Clientele Restrictions: Registration required, must be ongoing account
Products & Information Categories:
Proprietary Databases or Gateways:
Database Name: SSDI/Live Index
Addresses/Telephone Numbers (US)

Database Name: Military
Military Service (US)

database Name: Nationwide Index
DOB/DEATH/SSN (US)
Special Distribution Methods to Client: Dial-Up (Other than Internet)
Ameridex presents several unique databases for people tracing on the Internet. Over 260 million names and 230 million with a date of birth are compiled from multiple public record sources. Speciality databases include a nationwide death index with supplements, an active military personnel database, and vital records (birth, marriage, divorce) for several states.

Ancestry
266 W Center St
Orem, UT 84057
801-431-5220
http://ancestry.com
Parent Company: MyFamily.com
Clientele Restrictions: Premium services require subscription

Proprietary Databases or Gateways:
Database Name: Ancestry.com
Vital Records, Foreign Country Information (US, Itl)

Database Name: SSN Death Index
Vital Records (US)
Special Distribution Methods to Client: Internet
Ancestry.com is one of the leading Family History genealogy web sites. Over 600 million records can be searched from literally thousands of databases. One may search by record type, or locality. Many free searches are available, to access the entrie system, a subscription is required. An editor's choice site.

Anybirthday.com
American Automated Systems
304 Navajo St
Louisville, OH 44641
330-455-2201
www.anybirthdate.com/
skeeles@AMERICANAUTOMATED.COM
Clientele Restrictions: None reported

Proprietary Databases or Gateways:
Database Name: AnyBirthdate.com
Addresses/Telephone Numbers (US)
Special Distribution Methods to Client: Dial-Up (Other than Internet), E-Mail, Internet
Find a birthday of most anyone. Anybirthday.com holds over 135,000,000 records each derived from non-privileged public access information sources. Access is free, there is no charge. They offer an e-mail reminder system also, to keep track of birthdays of friends, family, etc. Information found in the Anybirthday.com database can be found elsewhere by anyone with a simple knowledge of public record access. One may opt-out of their database.

ARISTOTLE
205 Pennsylvania Ave SE
(Administrative: 50 E St. SE)
Washington, DC 20003
800-296-2747, 202-543-8345; Fax: 202-543-6407
www.aristotle.org
postmaster@aristotle.org
Branch Offices:
San Francisco, CA, 415-440-1012; Fax: 415-440-2162
London, GB, 44 020-7881-2787; Fax: 44 020-7881-2701
Atlanta, GA, 404-350-9429; Fax: 404-352-5757
Founded: 1981
Clientele Restrictions: Casual requesters permitted
Products & Information Categories:
General: Legislation/Regulation - Political (US)
Proprietary Databases or Gateways:
Database Name: ARISTOTLE
Voter Registration and Addresses/Telephone Numbers (US)
Special Distribution Methods to Client: CD-ROM, Magnetic Tape
ARISTOTLE maintains a nationwide file of registered voters. Information obtained from 3,400 counties and municipalities is standardized and enhanced with listed phone number, postal correction and national change of address, census geography, and age and vote history. Twenty-six states have no significant restrictions on the commercial use of their voter registration information. ARISTOTLE also assists in the business operations of political campaigns.

Attorneys Title Insurance Fund
PO Box 628600
Orlando, FL 32862
800-336-3863, 407-240-3863; Fax: 407-888-2592
www.thefund.com
Founded: 1948
Memberships: ALTA, REIPA,
Clientele Restrictions: Signed agreement required, must be ongoing account
Products & Information Categories:
Proprietary Databases or Gateways:
Database Name: The Fund
Real Estate/Assessor, Litigation/Judgments/Tax Liens (FL-40 counties)
Special Distribution Methods to Client: Dial-Up (Other than Internet), Disk, FTP, Magnetic Tape
Although the primary business of The Fund (as they are called) is to issue title insurance, they offer access to over 100 million real estate records from nearly 40 major counties in FL. The Fund has 14 branch offices and is expanding to SC and IL. Online users can access public records including mortgages, deeds, liens, assessments, right-of-way data, and even judgment and divorce proceedings.

Aurigin Systems Inc.
10710 N Tantau Ave
Cupertino, CA 95014
408-873-8400; Fax: 408-257-9133
http://aurigin.com
jross@aurigin.com
Branch Offices:
Princeton, NJ, 609-734-4300; Fax: 609-734-4352

Founded: 1992
Memberships: AIPLA, ABA, LES,
Clientele Restrictions: None reported
Products & Information Categories:
Proprietary Databases or Gateways:
Database Name: Aurigin
Patents (US, Itl)
Special Distribution Methods to Client: Dial-Up (Other than Internet), Software
Aurigin, formally known as SmartPatents Inc, offers the Aurigin Aureka® System to manage a company's intellectual and innovation assets. Other important products are Aurigin Electronic Patents, indexed patents from the US Patent and Trademark Office, and the Aurigin Workbench, a desktop software application.

AutoDataDirect, Inc

2940 E. Park Ave #B
Tallahassee, FL 32301-3427
850-877-8804
www.add123.com
jtaylor@add123.com
Founded: 1999
Clientele Restrictions: Signed agreement required
Products & Information Categories:
Proprietary Databases or Gateways:
Gateway Name: ADD123
Driver and/or Vehicle, Vessels (FL)
Special Distribution Methods to Client: Internet
AutoDataDirect provides real time access to Florida motor vehicle, vessel and driver's license records. ADD's services are not available to individuals, but companies with a permissible use of personal information as described in the Federal Driver's Privacy Protection Act of 1994 are eligible for ADD's service. To determine if you are eligible to receive the vehicle records, please read the Federal Driver's Privacy Protection Act of 1994 which can be found at our Web site.

Avantex Inc

340 Morgantown Road
Reading, PA 19611
800-998-8857, 610-796-2385
www.avantext.com
dara@avantex.com
Founded: 1992
Clientele Restrictions: None reported
Products & Information Categories:
Proprietary Databases or Gateways:
Database Name: FAA Data
Aviation, Addresses/Telephone Numbers, Legislation/Regulations (US)
Special Distribution Methods to Client: CD-ROM
Avantext product line includes 6 powerful CDs for the aviation industry. The FAA Data CD includes a full listing of pilots and aircraft owners, schools, technicians, dealers and much more.

Banko

100 S. 5th St #300
Minneapolis, MN 55402
800-533-8897, 612-332-2427; Fax: 612-215-7498

www.banko.com
sales@banko.com
Parent Company: Dolan Media Inc
Founded: 1987
Memberships: ACA, ICA, NACM, NPRRA,
Clientele Restrictions: Casual requesters permitted
Products & Information Categories:
Proprietary Databases or Gateways:
Database Name: BANKO
Bankruptcy (US)

Database Name: BANKO
Litigation/Judgments/Tax Liens (US)
Special Distribution Methods to Client: CD-ROM, Dial-Up (Other than Internet), Disk, Internet, Lists/Labels, Magnetic Tape
Banko provides up to the minute information about bankruptcy suppression, tax liens, judgments with notification in a variety of electronic formats. Other divisions of Dolan Information includes Hogan Information, Probate Finder LLC, Accollaid, and Identify Guardian.

Better Business Bureau
4200 Wilson Blvd # 800
Arlington, VA 22203-1838
703-276-0100; Fax: 703-525-8277
www.bbb.org
webwork@MAIL.BBB.ORG
Clientele Restrictions: Agreement Required to Join
Products & Information Categories:
Proprietary Databases or Gateways:
Gateway Name: Business Report
Corporate/Trade Name Data (US)
Special Distribution Methods to Client: Dial-Up (Other than Internet), E-Mail, Internet
Business Reports are created and maintained by the BBB office where the business is located. Information reported includes time in business, complaint history, and information obtained through special Bureau investigations. Bureaus also have the option of reporting whether companies are Bureau members, or participate in any special Bureau programs, such as Alternative Dispute Resolution or BBBOnLine®. For additional information about the BBB reporting process, visit the BBB Help Desk online. If you desire a report from a BBB office that does not appear online, contact the office directly and request a verbal or printed copy of the report. Find BBB contact information on the "locate a BBB" page. BBB is creating a national database of reports -- see National Information Database -- with an expected completion in 2001. In the meantime, offices maintain their data on separate online databases, access from the web site listed above.

BiblioData
PO Box 61
Needham Heights, MA 02494
781-444-1154; Fax: 781-449-4584
www.bibliodata.com
ina@bibliodata.com
Founded: 1989
Clientele Restrictions: Casual requesters permitted
Products & Information Categories:
Proprietary Databases or Gateways:
Database Name: BiblioData

News/Current Events, Addresses/Telephone Numbers (US)
Special Distribution Methods to Client: Internet, Publication/Directory
BiblioData publishes informative newsletters directly related to the online industry and publish the Cyberskeptic's Guide to Internet Research. Their products are targeted for researchers and librarians.

BNA, Inc (Bureau of National Affairs)

1231 25th Street, NW
Washington, MD 20037
800-372-1033, 202-452-4200
http://web.bna.com
icustrel@bna.com
Branch Offices:
Rockville, MD, 800-372-1033; Fax: 800-253-0332
Founded: 1929
Clientele Restrictions: Must be ongoing account

Products & Information Categories:

Proprietary Databases or Gateways:
Gateway Name: Intl Trade Daily, WTO Reporter
International Trade Daily, WTO Reporter
International Trade Daily, WTO Reporter
International Trade Daily, WTO Reporter
Legislation/Regulation, Foreign Country Information (Itl)
Gateway Name: Environment & Safety Library on the Web
Environment & Safety Library on the Web
Environmental (US)
Gateway Name: Class Action Litigation Report
Litigation/Judgments/Tax Liens (US)
Gateway Name: Corporate Law Daily
Corporate/Trade Name Data (US)
Special Distribution Methods to Client: E-Mail, Internet, Publication/Directory
BNA is a leading publisher of print and electronic news and information, reporting on developments in health care, business, labor relations, law, economics, taxation, environmental protection, safety, and other public policy and regulatory issues. Its Class Action Litigation Report covers the most important developments in class action and multiparty litigation, in all subject areas. It monitors hard-to-find, significant litigation news acress all subject areas, including antitrust, consumer, employment, health care, mass torts, products and securities. The Report's timely notification is supplemented by analysis and practice pointers by outside experts and attorneys. Visit www.bna.com/new/ for additional products.

Bureau1 (Philippines)

Address not known at press time

www.bureau1.bigstep.com
bureau1@asia.com
Clientele Restrictions: Casual requesters permitted.

Products & Information Categories:

General: Corporate/Trade Name Data (Itl)
Proprietary Databases or Gateways:
Database Name: Philippines Registries
Corporate/Trade Name Data (Itl)
Special Distribution Methods to Client: E-Mail

They are a distributor of Philippine Public Record Information, and accept requests via email and the Internet. They can authenticate a wide variety of records, including: education, marriage, death, birth, certificates, driver's license, immigration, laws, muslim rules, patents, trademarks, affivadits, contracts, visas, investor information. They are also a source of Philippine news.

Burrelles Information Services

75 East Northfield Rd
Livingston, NJ 07039
800-631-1160, 973-992-6600
http://burrelles.com
info@burrelles.com
Clientele Restrictions: None reported
Products & Information Categories:
Proprietary Databases or Gateways:
Database Name: BIO
News/Current Events (US, Itl)
Special Distribution Methods to Client: CD-ROM, Dial-Up (Other than Internet), Publication/Directory
For over 100 years Burrelle's has been monitoring, organizing, and delivering media data to clients. Products include Press Clipping, NewsExpress, NewsAlert, Media Direcories, Broadcast Transcripts, and Web Clips. The BIO - Burrelle's Information Office, is software to receive and use information from Burrelle's.

Cal Info

316 W 2nd St #102
Los Angeles, CA 90012
213-687-8710; Fax: 213-687-8778
www.calinfo.net
admin@calinfo.net
Branch Offices:
Washington, DC, 202-667-9679; Fax: 202-967-9605
Founded: 1986
Memberships: AIIP, AALL,
Clientele Restrictions: None reported
Products & Information Categories:
General: Litigation/Judgments/Tax Liens (US, CA)
Proprietary Databases or Gateways:
Database Name: Guide to State Statutes
Legislation/Regulation (State Statutes) (US)
Database Name: Administrative Guide to State Regulations
Legislation/Regulation (US)
Special Distribution Methods to Client: E-Mail, Publication/Directory
Cal Info offers an information research and retrieval service that finds answers to questions that affect law firms and businesses every day. Their personnel are trained to search computerized databases as well as the more traditional information sources, including libraries, publishers, government agencies, courts, trade unions and associations. They provide company reports, financial data, product information, people information, journals and news stories, real estate information, legal research, public records research, government information and document retrieval.

Cambridge Statistical Research Associates

53 Wellesley
Irvine, CA 92612
800-327-2772, 949-250-8579
Founded: 1988

Clientele Restrictions: Must be ongoing account

Products & Information Categories:

General: Addresses/Telephone Numbers (US)

Proprietary Databases or Gateways:

Database Name: Death Master File

Vital Records (US)

Special Distribution Methods to Client: CD-ROM, Dial-Up (Other than Internet)

CSRA traces its origin to an actuarial and programming service established in 1979. In recent years, its efforts moved toward bringing large mainframe databases to the desktop computing platform, including CD-ROM. CSRA specializes in nationwide death index by name and Social Security Number, death auditing service, database consulting, genealogical and probate research, and address trace service.

Campus Direct

One Plymouth Meeting, #610

Plymought Meeting, PA 19462

800-889-4249

www.campusdirect.com/

sales@campusdirect.com

Parent Company: Student Advantage Inc

Founded: 1990

Clientele Restrictions: Registration required.

Products & Information Categories:

Proprietary Databases or Gateways:

Database Name: Campus Direct

Education/Employment (US)

Special Distribution Methods to Client: Internet

Student Advantage's Campus Direct® division is the nation's premier outsource provider of student information services to colleges and universities. Search the client schools list at the web site. Client schools utilize Campus Direct® as a means by which to provide particular services or as a coexisting backup system where services such as transcript fulfillment are already provided in-house. Campus Direct's knowledgeable staff and state-of-the-art Internet and telephone technologies enable colleges and universities to provide superior service for students and information requesters.

Canadian Law Book Inc

240 Edward St

Aurora, Ont L4G 3S9

800-263-3269, 905-841-6472; Fax: 905-841-5085

www.canadalawbook.ca/

bloney@canadalawbook.ca

Branch Offices:

Vancouver, BC, 604-844-7855; Fax: 604-844-7813

Founded: 1855

Products & Information Categories:

General: Foreign Country Information (Canada)

Proprietary Databases or Gateways:

Gateway Name: Canada Statute Service

Legislation/Regulation (Canada)

Gateway Name: Canadian Patent Reporter

Patents (Canada)

Gateway Name: Caselaw on Call

Litigation/Judgments/Tax Liens (Canada)

Special Distribution Methods to Client: Automated Telephone Look-Up, CD-ROM, Internet, Publication/Directory, Software

In Canada, dial 800-263-2037. Canada Law Book resources have expanded to encompass a broad collection of material from leading experts in the legal profession. They're empowered with the latest technological tools to enhance the delivery of the content. Get exactly the information you need, in the manner that suits you best.

Carfax

10304 Eaton Place, #500
Fairfax, VA 22030
703-934-2664; Fax: 703-218-2465
www.carfaxonline.com
subscribe@carfax.com
Parent Company: R.L. Polk
Founded: 1986
Memberships: AAMVA, DMA,
Clientele Restrictions: Casual requesters permitted
Products & Information Categories:
Proprietary Databases or Gateways:
Database Name: Vehicle History Service, Motor Vehicle Title Information
Driver and/or Vehicle (US)
Database Name: VINde (VIN Validity Check Program)
Software/Training (US)
Special Distribution Methods to Client: Dial-Up (Other than Internet), Disk, Internet
With the largest online vehicle history database (over one billion records), Carfax can generate a Vehicle History Report based on a VIN in less than one second. They collect data from a variety of sources including state DMVs and salvage pools. Reports include details from previous titles, city and state, odometer rollbacks, junk and flood damage, etc, reducing the risk of handling used vehicles with hidden problems that affect their value. Reports do not contain personal information on current or previous owners.

Case Record Info Services

33895 Cape Cove
Dana Point, CA 92629
949-248-5860; Fax:
jeancris@aol.com
Founded: 1994
Clientele Restrictions: Casual requesters permitted
Products & Information Categories:
Proprietary Databases or Gateways:
Database Name: Judgment Lists
Litigation/Judgments/Tax Liens (CA)
Special Distribution Methods to Client: Dial-Up (Other than Internet), Disk, Internet, Lists/Labels
Case Record Info Services provides judgment lists in California. Their data is used by bulk data providers, collection and mediation companies. They are also members of the American Arbitration Association. Note: The telephone number is to the residence of the principal.

CaseStream.com

489 Devon Park Dr, #206
Wayne, PA 19087
800-500-0888, 610-254-8282; Fax: 610-254-9672
www.CaseStream.com
Info@MarketSpan.com

Parent Company: MarketSpan Inc
Founded: 1997
Memberships: ABA,
Clientele Restrictions: Casual requesters permitted
Products & Information Categories:
Proprietary Databases or Gateways:
Database Name: CaseAlert for Federal Courts
Litigation/judgments/Tax Liens, Criminal (US)

Gateway Name: Delaware Chancery
Litigation/Judgments/Tax Liens (DE)

Database Name: CaseAlert for Federal Courts
Criminal Information, Bankruptcy (US)

Special Distribution Methods to Client: Dial-Up (Other than Internet), E-Mail
CaseStream products include; Alert! which notifies you each day of activity in federal civil cases of interest to you; Historical which gives leagl research on similar cases before the same federal judge; Docket Direct provides a fast and efficient means to retrieve federal civil or criminal docket on demand; and Delaware Chancery which provides a fully searchable database of the dockets in the Delaware Court of Chancery.

CCH Washington Service Bureau
655 15th Street NW #275
Washington, DC 20005
800-955-5219, 202-508-0600; Fax: 202-508-0694
www.wsb.com
custserv@wsb.com
Parent Company: Wolters Klower US
Founded: 1967
Clientele Restrictions: Signed Agreement Required
Products & Information Categories:
General: Legislation/Regulation (US)

Proprietary Databases or Gateways:
Database Name: SECnet
SEC/Other Financial, Bankrupcy (US)

Special Distribution Methods to Client: Dial-Up (Other than Internet), Internet, Microfilm/Microfiche,
Publication/Directory
CCH Washington Service Bureau, has been serving the information needs of lawyers, corporate executives, brokers, accountants, and government officials since its inception in 1967. The company offers a number of products and services in a variety of practice areas to the legal and business professional. CCH Washington Service Bureau provides expedited information retrieval on filings made with the Securities and Exchange Commission. A pioneer in the area of "sample" securities research, our experienced research staff uses in-house proprietary databases and a library of SEC filings dating back to 1979 to fulfill the most difficult research request. CCH Washington Service Bureau offers watch services which are tailored by the individual needs of each client. We also offer "filex" services, enabling clients to file documents with federal regulatory agencies.

Chattel Mortgage Reporter Inc
300 W Washington #808
Chicago, IL 60606
312-214-1048; Fax: 312-214-1054
www.accesscmr.com/cmr.htm
Branch Offices:
Springfield, IL, 217-544-6435; Fax: 217-544-6436
Founded: 1901

Memberships: NPRRA,
Clientele Restrictions: Casual requesters permitted
Products & Information Categories:
General: Real Estate/Assessor (US)

Proprietary Databases or Gateways:
Database Name: Chattel Mortgage Reporter-Cook County
Uniform Commercial Code (IL)

Special Distribution Methods to Client: E-Mail, Microfilm/Microfiche

CMR is a national public record service organization specializing in Illinois. They have more than 95 years of experience, with emphasis on public record research in Cook County, IL and the counties surrounding the Chicago area. For fast copy retrieval, their UCC database for Cook County is backed up by microfilm dating back to 1973.

ChoicePoint Inc
1000 Alderman Dr
Alpharetta, GA 30005
770-752-6000; Fax: 770-752-6005
www.choicepointinc.com
Founded: 1997
Memberships: AALL, ABI, ASIS,
Clientele Restrictions: Signed agreement required, must be ongoing account
Products & Information Categories:
General: Workers Compensation (US)

Proprietary Databases or Gateways:
Database Name: Legal Information
Corporation/Trade Name Data (US)

Database Name: Legal Information
Bankruptcy (US)

Database Name: Legal Information
Uniform Commercial Code (US)

Database Name: Real Property
Real Estate/Assessor (US)

Database Name: Legal Information
Litigation/Judgments/Tax Liens (US)

Database Name: Information Services
Licenses/Registrations/Permits (Physicians) (US)

Database Name: Consumer Services
Addresses/Telephone Numbers (US)

Gateway Name: Insurance Services
Driver and/or Vehicle (US)

Gateway Name: Legal Information
Criminal Information (US)

Special Distribution Methods to Client: Dial-Up (Other than Internet)

ChoicePoint is a leading provider of intelligence information to help businesses, governments, and individuals to better understand with whom they do business. ChoicePoint services the risk management information needs of the property and casualty insurance market, the life and health insurance market, and business and government, including asset-based lenders and professional service providers. The company, with many branch offices nationwide, was spun off/out from Equifax in 1997. They offer a variety of useful online products.

ChoicePoint, formerly CDB Infotek

6 Hutton Centre Dr #600
Santa Ana, CA 92707
800-427-3747, 714-708-2000; Fax: 714-708-1000
www.cdb.com
tony.mears@choicepointinc.com
Founded: 1997
Memberships: SIIA, NALV, NPRRA, ASIS, ACA, IRSG
Clientele Restrictions: Signed agreement required, must be ongoing account
Products & Information Categories:
General: Credit Information (US)

Proprietary Databases or Gateways:
Database Name: Real Property Ownership & Transfers
Real Estate/Assessor (US)

Database Name: Corporate & Limited Partnerships
Corporate/Trade Name Data (US)

Database Name: Uniform Commercial Code
Uniform Commerical Code (US)

Database Name: Legal Information
Bankruptcy and Litigation/Judgments/Tax Liens (US)

Database Name: Address Inspector
Addresses/Telephone Numbers (US)

Special Distribution Methods to Client: Dial-Up (Other than Internet), Internet
ChoicePoint (CDB Infotek) offers nationwide public records information, including instant access to more than 4 billion records and 1,600 targeted databases to efficiently locate people or businesses, conduct background research, identify assets, control fraud, conduct due diligence, etc. Subscribers learn search strategies at free, year-round seminars and have toll-free access to customer service representatives for help. ChoicePoint also offers direct marketing lists, monitoring services, hard copy document retrieval and high-volume processing services.

ChoicePoint, formerly DBT Online Inc

4530 Blue Lake Dr
Boca Raton, FL 33431
800-279-7710, 561-982-5000; Fax: 561-982-5872
www.dbtonline.com
Parent Company: DBT Online Inc
Founded: 1992
Clientele Restrictions: License required, must be ongoing account
Products & Information Categories:
Proprietary Databases or Gateways:
Database Name: AutoTrackXP
Addresses/Telephone Numbers, Real Estate/Assessor, Corporate/Trade Name Data (US)

Database Name: AutoTrackXP
Driver and/or Vehicle (US)

Special Distribution Methods to Client: Dial-Up (Other than Internet), Internet
ChoicePoint (DBT Online) offers nationwide public records information, including instant access to more than 4 billion records and 1,600 targeted databases to efficiently locate people or businesses, conduct background research, identify assets, control fraud, conduct due diligence, etc. Subscribers learn search strategies at free, year-round seminars and have toll-free access to customer service representatives for help. ChoicePoint also offers direct marketing lists, monitoring services, hard copy document retrieval and high-volume processing services.

Commercial Information Systems Inc

PO Box 69174
(4747 SW Kelly #110)
Portland, OR 97201-0174
800-454-6575, 503-222-7422; Fax: 503-222-7405
www.cis-usa.com
cis@cis-usa.com
Founded: 1991
Memberships: SIIA, NACM, NALI,
Clientele Restrictions: Casual requesters permitted

Products & Information Categories:

General: Addresses/Telephone Numbers (US)

Proprietary Databases or Gateways:
Database Name: Aircraft Registrations
Aviation (US)

Database Name: UCCs
Uniform Commercial Code (CA, ID, OR, WA)

Database Name: Corporations & Limited Partnerships
Corporate/Trade Name Data (CA, ID, OR, WA)

Database Name: Professional Licenses
Licenses/Registrations/Permits (ID, OR, WA)

Database Name: Real Estate Records
Real Estate/Assessor (ID, NV, OR, WA)

Database Name: Criminal & Civil Records
Criminal Information,Litigation/Judgments/Tax Liens (ID, OR, WA, CA)

Database Name: Fish & Wildlife Records
Licenses/Registrations/Permits (ID, OR, NV)

Database Name: Driver's License & Registration
Driver and/or Vehicle (ID, OR)

Database Name: Hazardous Materials
Environmental (OR, WA)

Special Distribution Methods to Client: Dial-Up (Other than Internet), Internet

Commercial Information Systems (CIS) is an online/on-site database of public records serving business and government entities. They provide direct access to selected public and private database records on a national level through special gateway relationships - for example, gateway access to OJIN (Oregon) and JIS (Washington) court records. The CIS integrated regional database aggregates, commingles and cross-matches records at the state level by name, address, city, state, ZIP Code, birth date, driver's license, vehicle plates and other identifiers with a search engine that allows a subscriber to return all related records on a common identifier. The CIS system is always available through a PC and modem. CIS provides the communication software. CIS also provides information on a manual retrieval basis, including credit bureau products and services as well as special data mining capabilities tailored to a clients' specific research or volume searching needs.

Companies Online - Lycos

400-2 Totten Pond Road
Waltham, MA 02451
781-370-2700; Fax: 781-370-3412
www.companiesonline.com
Parent Company: Lycos, Inc.
Founded: 1995

Products & Information Categories:

Proprietary Databases or Gateways:
Database Name: companiesonline.com
Corporate/Trade Name Data (US)
Special Distribution Methods to Client: Internet
Excellent Internet site with free searching on over 900,000 public and private companies. This is a partnership of Lycos and Dun & Bradstreet, using information from the latter.

CompuServe

PO Box 20212
Columbus, OH 43220
800-848-8199, 614-457-8600; Fax: 614-457-0348
www.compuserve.com
Parent Company: America Online Inc
Clientele Restrictions: Casual requesters permitted
Products & Information Categories:

Proprietary Databases or Gateways:
Gateway Name: Quest Research Center
Trademarks/Patents, News/Current Events (US)

Gateway Name: Phonefile
Addresses/Telephone Numbers (US)

Special Distribution Methods to Client: Dial-Up (Other than Internet), Internet
Now a subsidiary of AOL, CompuServe is available in 185 countries and provides comprehensive services for serious Internet online users at home, in the workplace, and globally. Business and professional resources, latest news and information, are but a few of CompuServe's powerful communications capabilities.

Confi-Chek

1816 19th St
Sacramento, CA 95814
800-821-7404, 916-443-4822
www.confi-chek.com
Founded: 1988
Memberships: ION,
Clientele Restrictions: Must be ongoing account
Products & Information Categories:
General: Litigation/Judgments/Tax Liens (US)

Proprietary Databases or Gateways:
Database Name: Confi-Chek Online
Criminal History (CA)

Special Distribution Methods to Client: Dial-Up (Other than Internet), Internet
Confi-Check provides instant access to national and local records throughout the US. They also offer asset services. Their web site has almost all state records. Dial-up and fax call-in services are also available.

Congressional Information Service Inc

4520 East-West Highway
Bethesda, MD 20814-3389
800-638-8380, 301-654-1550; Fax: 301-657-3203
www.cispubs.com
cisinfo@lexis-nexis.com
Parent Company: Lexis-Nexis
Founded: 1969
Clientele Restrictions: None reported

Products & Information Categories:

Proprietary Databases or Gateways:
Database Name: Current Issues Sourcefile
Legislation/Regulations (US)

Database Name: Government Periodicals Universe
News/Current Events (US)

Special Distribution Methods to Client: CD-ROM, Dial-Up (Other than Internet), Disk, Internet, Magnetic Tape, Publication/Directory

Congressional Information Service is an international publisher of reference, research, and current awareness information products and services. Many of their products deal with economic and demographic issues. Their multiple databases are offered in electronic format and through partners such as LEXIS-NEXIS.

Conrad Grundlehner Inc

8605 Brook Rd
McLean, VA 22102-1504
703-506-9648; Fax: 703-506-9580
www.superiorinfo.com
Founded: 1984
Memberships: SIIA, NPRRA,
Clientele Restrictions: License required

Products & Information Categories:

Proprietary Databases or Gateways:
Database Name: Conrad Grundlehner
Bankruptcy, Litigation/Judgments/Tax Liens (DC, MD, NC, VA, WV)

Special Distribution Methods to Client: Disk, Magnetic Tape

Conrad Grundlehner Inc (CGI) was among the first companies to use portable computers to collect legal data at courts and recording offices. The use of notebook computers combined with electronic transmission of data to the customer reduces the time between data collection and its availability to the customer. CGI's information processing expertise also allows it to provide a high degree of customized service to its customers. Data can be delivered in a wide variety of ways on a broad spectrum of media. Data is available online from www.superiorinfo.com.

CorporateInfomation.com

440 Wheelers Farms Road
Milford, CT 06460
800-232-0013, 203-783-4366
http://corporateinformation.com
regnery@wisi.com
Parent Company: The Winthrop Corporation
Clientele Restrictions: None Reported

Products & Information Categories:

Proprietary Databases or Gateways:
Database Name: Corporate/Trade Name Data
Corporate/Trade Name Data, Foreign Country Information (US, Itl)

Special Distribution Methods to Client: Internet

Features include: research a company; research a company's industry; research by country; and research by state among others. A very informative web site with much information available at no charge.

CountryWatch.com Inc.

Three Riverway #710
Houston, TX 77056
800-879-3885, 713-355-6500; Fax: 713-355-2008

www.countrywatch.com
subscribe@countrywatch.com
Founded: 2000
Clientele Restrictions: Casual requesters permitted
Products & Information Categories:

Proprietary Databases or Gateways:
Database Name: countrywatch.com db
Foreign Country Information (Itl)
Special Distribution Methods to Client: Internet
Countrywatch.com is a growing online publisher providing original content and aggregated news to customers needing real-time, quality, formatted political, economic, cultural/demographic and environmental information and data on each of the 191 countries of the world.

Court PC of Connecticut

PO Box 11081
Greenwich, CT 06831-1081
203-531-7866; Fax: 203-531-6899
http://courtpcofct.com
jel@courtpcofct.com
Founded: 1992
Memberships: NPRRA,
Clientele Restrictions: Casual requesters occasionally permitted
Products & Information Categories:
General: Bankruptcy (US, CT)

Proprietary Databases or Gateways:
Database Name: Superior Index
Litigation/Judgments/Tax Liens, Criminal Information (CT)
Special Distribution Methods to Client:
Court PC is Connecticut's comprehensive source of docket search information from Superior Court and US District Court cases. Their

Connecticut Superior Court database contains records of civil filings since 1985, family/divorce filings since 1989, and discloseable criminal convictions since 1991. Microfiche indexes supplement PACER data to provide complete USDC/CT civil and criminal searches from 1970 forward. Court PC also provides current corporation (also LPs and LLCs) and tax lien data from the Connecticut Secretary of State database.

CourtClerk.com

PO Box 1519
Dandridge, TN 37725
865-471-5501; Fax: 865-397-5900
www.courtclerk.com
rtucker@courtclerk.com
Clientele Restrictions: None reported
Products & Information Categories:

Proprietary Databases or Gateways:
Gateway Name: courtclerk.com
Bankruptcy, Crinimal Information, Litigation/Judgments/Tax Liens (TN)
Special Distribution Methods to Client:
CourtClerk.com serves as a gateway for docket searches by judge for TN general sessions courts and court clerks. SEC and Secretary of State features may be available. Three access plans are available, tailored to suit your needs.

CourtExpress.com (RIS Legal Svcs)
701 Pennsylvania Avenue NW
Washington, DC 20004-2608
800-542-3320, 202-737-7111; Fax: 202-737-3324
http://courtexpress.com
Parent Company: RIS Legal Services
Founded: 2000
Clientele Restrictions: Registration required
Products & Information Categories:
Proprietary Databases or Gateways:
Gateway Name: US Court Records
Bankruptcy, Litigation/Judgments/Tax Liens (US)
Special Distribution Methods to Client: E-Mail, Internet
CourtEXPRESS.com delivers powerful U.S. Court searching and document delivery features to your desktop. They cover most of the U.S. Federal District and Bankruptcy Courts, also providing searching from the U.S. Party Case Index from three files: civil, criminal and bankruptcy, which they call the National Locator Service or "NLS." Every step is easier and more productive than all other traditional searching methods. Rather than waiting online for results, CourtEXPRESS.com will alert you via Email when your search is done. Each member has access to their last 100 searches, including Due Diligence for Federal cases and Case Tracker for current cases. Other searches can be set up to repeat daily or weekly. Document ordering takes only seconds. Try either a Guest Quick Search or get a Private Guest Account.

CourtH.com
PO Box 70558
Houston, TX 77270-0558
800-925-4225, 713-683-0491; Fax: 713-683-0493
www.courth.com
orders@courth.com
Branch Offices:
Richmond, TX, 281-342-1777; Fax:
Parent Company: Right-of-Way Acquisition Services Inc
Founded: 1982
Memberships: NACM,
Clientele Restrictions: Casual requesters permitted
Products & Information Categories:
General: Bankruptcy (TX)
Proprietary Databases or Gateways:
Database Name: Courthouse Research
Corporate/Trade Name Data, Real Estate/Assessor, Litigation/judgments/Tax Liens (TX)
Special Distribution Methods to Client: Dial-Up (Other than Internet), E-Mail, Internet
Our Internet service provides access to 30 databases of public information from marriage records to property records to bankruptcies. Our proprietary database consists of public records from Harris, Montgomery, and Fort Bend counties. These records are easily searched on our web site.

CourthouseDirect.com
9800 Northwest Fwy #400
Houston, TX 77092
713-683-0314; Fax: 713-683-0493
http://courthousedirect.com
info@courthousedirect.com

Branch Offices:
Dallas, TX, ; Fax:
Richmond, TX, ; Fax:
Bryan/College Station, TX, ; Fax:
Founded: 1982
Memberships: NAR,
Clientele Restrictions: Subscription preferred; credit card requestors accepted
Products & Information Categories:
General: Litigation/Judgments/Tax Liens (US)

Proprietary Databases or Gateways:
Gateway Name: Real Estate/Assessor
Real Estate/Assessor (AZ, CA, FL, HI, IL, NY, OK, PA, TX, UT, WA)
Special Distribution Methods to Client: Internet
CourthouseDirect.com, a specialized Internet portal based in Houston, provides electronic document images of Deeds, Mortgages, Releases, IRS Liens, Assignments, and other county Real Property and Official Record filings via the internet. CourthouseDirect.com currently provides images for major counties in California, Florida, Arizona, Illinois, Michigan, New York, Oklahoma, and Texas. The current database contains 10 counties in Texas and 112 counties nationwide. CourthouseDirect.com expects to have images for 85% of the U. S. population online by the end of the year 2001. In addition to those listed above, other applications includes collections, geneology research, and litigation.

CourtLink
13427 NE 16th St, #100
Bellevue, WA 98005-2307
800-774-7317, 425-974-5000; Fax: 425-974-1419
www.courtlink.com
support@courtlink.com
Founded: 1986
Memberships: AALL, ABI, NACM, NAFE, SLA,
Clientele Restrictions: Casual requesters permitted
Products & Information Categories:
Proprietary Databases or Gateways:
Gateway Name: CourtLink Classic
Bankruptcy, Litigation/Judgments/Tax Liens (US)

Database Name: CaseStream
Bankruptcy, Litigation/Judgments/Tax Liens (US)

Special Distribution Methods to Client: Dial-Up (Other than Internet), Disk, E-Mail, FTP, Internet, Lists/Labels
CourtLink partners with courts throughout the country to help them grant electronic public access to docket information. CourtLink currently provides real-time electronic public access to over 700 federal, state and local courts nationwide. Users gain access to the complete federal system as well as a select number of local courts through a state-of-the-art electronic interface. There are many benefits that CourtLink can provide, including one central source of accessing multiple courts. Possible uses of the system include litigation history, employee screening, discovery, case management and background checks. Search results include case summaries, names of parties and attorneys, dockets, judgments, claims, creditors and charges. Over 80% of the 250 largest law firms in the country use CourtLink. Affialiate JusticeLink is now live in the State of Colorado. Colorado's e-filing implementation leads the nation as the first-ever statewide e-filing initiative. As of 2/2001, each of the state's civil courts will have the ability to accept legal filings electronically in civil, probate, water and domestic relations cases.

Credentials Inc
550 Frontage Road #3500
Northfield, IL 60093
847-446-7422; Fax: 847-446-7424
www.degreechk.com

tmckechney@degreechk.com
Founded: 1997
Clientele Restrictions: Casual requesters permitted
Products & Information Categories:
Proprietary Databases or Gateways:
Database Name: Degreechk
Education/Employment (US)
Special Distribution Methods to Client: E-Mail, Internet
Credentials Inc offers 24 hour, 365 day Internet access to degree verification from participating colleges and universities. All verification transactions are uniquely audit-trailed and confirmed to the user via fax or e-mail, often within the hour. In addition to online databases provided by participating schools, the system includes an off-line, archival search capability for degrees that are not included in the online database. This feature is important since most school databases only date back to the early or mid-1980s. A Preferred Client Package, which includes wholesale pricing and billing options, is available to the employment screening firms. All interactions with degreechk.com are fully encrypted. Other important security features are detailed on the web site. Growth in the number of school listed is expected; will broadcast e-mail notifications of new school additions to the Degreechk.com menu.

DAC Services
4500 S 129th E Ave
Tulsa, OK 74134
800-331-9175, 918-664-9991; Fax: 918-664-4366
www.dacservices.com
jeriw@dacservices.com
Founded: 1981
Memberships: SIIA, SHRM, AAMVA, ATA, PRRN,
Clientele Restrictions: Signed agreement required, must be ongoing account
Products & Information Categories:
General: Credit Information (US)
Proprietary Databases or Gateways:
Database Name: Transportation Employment History; Drug/Alcohol Test Results, Security Guard Employment
    History; Drug/Alcohol Test Results, Security Guard Employment History
Education/Employment (US)
Gateway Name: Driving Records
Driver and/or Vehicle (US)
Gateway Name: 20/20 Insight
Criminal Information (US)
Database Name: Claims and Injury Reports
Workers Compensation (AR, FL, IA, IL, KS, MA, MD, ME, MI, MS, ND, NE, OH, OK, OR, TX)
Special Distribution Methods to Client: Dial-Up (Other than Internet)
DAC has serviced employers and insurance businesses for more than 15 years, providing employment screening and underwriting/risk assessment tools. CDLIS contains summary information on more than 6,000,000 drivers. Customers request information by PC and modem via toll-free lines. Computer access is available through networks and mainframe-to-mainframe connections. Customers may opt to call or fax requests to their service representative toll-free.

Daily Report, The
310 H Street
Bakersfield, CA 93304-2914
661-322-3226; Fax: 661-322-9084
www.thedailyreport.com
staff@thedailyreport.com

Memberships: PRRN,
Clientele Restrictions: Casual requesters permitted
Products & Information Categories:
Proprietary Databases or Gateways:
Database Name: The Daily Report
Addresses/Telephone Numbers, Licenses/Registrations/Permits, Criminal Information, Litigation/Judgments/Tax Liens
  (CA-Kern County)
Special Distribution Methods to Client: Internet, Publication/Directory
The Daily Report is a legal newspaper, published continuously since August 21, 1907. Since publication began, the volume of information filed with the Courts and Hall of Records in Kern County has increased significantly. This website was developed in response to a growing need expressed by our subscribers to easily search for information filed in the Courts and Hall of Records pertinent to their specific needs. With The Daily Report, online subscribers can now browse for information filed with the Courts such as New Suits or Judgments and the Hall of Records, featuring most all recorded documents, including Notices of Default, Deeds, Maps, Liens and Oil and Gas leases. Other information such as Building Permits and business Licenses are also available through our specially designed search engine.

DataQuick
9620 Towne Centre Dr
San Diego, CA 92121
888-604-3282, 858-597-3100; Fax: 858-455-7406
www.dataquick.com
smorga@dataquick.com
Parent Company: Axiom Corporation
Founded: 1978
Memberships: REIPA,
Clientele Restrictions: Casual requesters permitted
Products & Information Categories:
Proprietary Databases or Gateways:
Database Name: DataQuick
Real Estate/Assessor (US)
Special Distribution Methods to Client: Dial-Up (Other than Internet), Disk, Lists/Labels, Magnetic Tape
A leading name in real property information products, DataQuick services the title, mortgage, real estate and insurance industries. They provide property details such as: ownership and address information; sale and loan details; characteristics such as sq footage etc.; and historical sales and data such as previous transactions for marketing and research purposes. They cover household development demographics and market trend data.

DCS Information Systems
500 N Central Expressway #280
Plano, TX 75074
800-394-3274, 972-422-3600; Fax: 972-422-3621
www.dcs-amerifind.com
carroll@dcs-amerifind.com
Founded: 1967
Memberships: IRSG, SIIA,
Clientele Restrictions: signed agreement required; business or government agencies only
Products & Information Categories:
Proprietary Databases or Gateways:
Database Name: AmeriFind (DNIS)
Addresses/Telephone Numbers, Real Estate/Assessor (US)

Database Name: Texas Systems
Driver and/or Vehicle, Criminal Convictions, Real Estate/Assessor, Vital Records (marriage & divorce) (TX)
Special Distribution Methods to Client: Dial-Up (Other than Internet), Internet
DCS' national products, DNIS and AmeriFind are very comprehensive national skip tracing, locating, fraud prevention and investigation tools. The TEXAS product provides comprehensive, up to date, information on Texas drivers and vehicle owners, with up to 12 years' history. These systems provide the users with search capabilities not available from other suppliers. DCS offers customized information solutions for large volume users. The new AmeriFind product is available via the internet.

Derwent Information

1725 Duke Street #250
Alexandria, VA 22314
800-337-9368, 703-706-4220; Fax: 703-838-5240
www.derwent.com
custserv@derwentus.com
Parent Company: The Thompson Corporation
Founded: 1952
Clientele Restrictions: None reported
Products & Information Categories:
Proprietary Databases or Gateways:
Database Name: Derwent World Patents Index, Patent Explorer
Derwent World Patent Index
Trademarks/Patents, Corporate/Trade Name Data (US)
Special Distribution Methods to Client: Dial-Up (Other than Internet), E-Mail, Internet, Publication/Directory
With offices in London, Japan, and Alexandria, Derwent provides access to the over 200,000 patents filed each year in the US alone while the European Patent office files around 80,000 patents a year. Derwent makes this information easily accessible by combining the world's patents on one searchable database. During our editorial process, a team of more than 350 specialist editors assess, classify and index patent documents to provide concise English language abstracts which are readily searched and easily understood. With a wide range of delivery options, Derwent ensures that companies are kept fully aware of the latest developments in today's fast moving markets.

Dialog Corporation, The

11000 Regency Parkway
Cary, NC 27511
800-334-2564, 919-468-6000; Fax: 919-461-7252
www.dialog.com
Founded: 1972
Clientele Restrictions: None reported
Products & Information Categories:
Proprietary Databases or Gateways:
Gateway Name: Profound; DIALOG Web
Foreign Country Information, Corporate/Trade Name Data, Trademarks, Legislation/Regulation, SEC/Other Financial
    (US,Itl)
Gateway Name: Profound LiveWire
News/Current Events (US)
Special Distribution Methods to Client: CD-ROM, Dial-Up (Other than Internet), Internet, Software
The Dialog Corporation provides comprehensive, authoritative sources of information to professionals worldwide. The company was created by the merger of MAID plc and Knight-Rider Information Inc. The Dialog Corporation's complete line of Internet, intranet, CD-ROM and Windows-based products and services have been designed to specifically address individual as well as enterprise-wide information solutions. They include DIALOGWeb, DataStar Web, DIALOG Select, Profound, DIALOG@Site, and Profound LiveWire.

Diligenz LLC

4629 168th St SE, #E
Lynnwood, WA 98037
800-858-5294, 425-741-0990
www.diligenz.com
search.department@diligenz.com
Memberships: NPPRA, PRRN, UAEL, CFA,
Clientele Restrictions: Sign-up required.

Products & Information Categories:

General: Bankruptcy (US)

Proprietary Databases or Gateways:
DB Name: Diligenz.com
Uniform Commercial Code, Corporate/Trade Name Data (US)

Special Distribution Methods to Client: CD-ROM, Dial-Up (Other than Internet), E-Mail, FTP, Internet

Diligenz provides databases of public records, especially to the search and retrieval of Uniform Commercial Code and Corporate information. Financial statements, continuations, amendments are also here. In addition, Diligenz also has available all records pertaining to corporate status, ownership interests, business credit and business licensing information. In order to offer on-line searches that are accurate, timely and cost effective, theyimmediately update their database. At this web site, they can offer rapid response and total reliability. The online search interface allows you to order and retrieve searches, and actually view and print documents online.

Disclosure

5161 River Rd
Bethesda, MD 20816
800-874-4337, 301-951-1300; Fax: 301-215-6004
www.primark.com/pfid/
researchcenter@primark.com
Parent Company: Primark Financial/Thomson Financial
Founded: 1968
Memberships: SIIA,
Clientele Restrictions: Casual requesters permitted

Products & Information Categories:

General: Trademarks (US)

Proprietary Databases or Gateways:
Database Name: Compact D
SEC/Other Financial (US)

Database Name: Compact D/Canada
SEC/Other Financial (Canada)

Database Name: Laser D International
Foreign Country Information (US, Itl)

Database Name: Worldscope Global
Foreign Country Information (US, Itl)

Special Distribution Methods to Client: CD-ROM, Internet, Magnetic Tape, Microfilm/Microfiche, Publication/Directory

At the website, click on "Products" then find "Disclosure." The Disclosure SEC Database consists of business and financial information on virtually all public companies in the United Statues - over 12,000 in all. This extensive coverage includes domestic and foreign companies listed on the national, regional and over-the-counter U.S. stock exchanges. The Database contains up to 200 data elements per company record and up to 15 years of annual and quarterly financial statement data. Data changes and updates are sourced from documents filed with the U.S. Securities and Exchange Commission (SEC) as well as company-supplied Annual Reports to Shareholders and other publicly available reports. The Database provides company profile information such as corporate addresses, officers and directors, financial statement data, full-text management's discussion and president's letters and current pricing, earnings and dividends data.

Diversified Information Services Corp

67 East Weldon #220
Phoenix, AZ 85012
602-532-0111; Fax: 602-532-0393
www.discaz.com
info@discaz.com
Founded: 1970
Memberships: ALTA,
Clientele Restrictions: Must be ongoing account
Products & Information Categories:
General: Bankruptcy (AZ)
Proprietary Databases or Gateways:
Database Name: Real Property Records
Real Estate/Assessor (AZ-Maricopa)
Special Distribution Methods to Client: CD-ROM, Dial-Up (Other than Internet), Disk, E-Mail, Gateway via Another Online Service
Diversified Information Services is owned by North American Title Agency, Old Republic Title Insurance Agency, Transnation Title, Lawyers Title of Arizona, Fidelity National Title Agency, Stewart Title & Trust of Phoenix, and Nations Title Agency.

Dun & Bradstreet

1 Diamond Hill Rd
Murray Hill, NJ 07974
800-234-3867, 908-665-5000
www.dnb.com
Branch Offices:
Murry Hill, NJ, 800-234-3867; Fax:
Memberships: NPRRA,
Clientele Restrictions: Casual requesters permitted
Products & Information Categories:
Proprietary Databases or Gateways:
Database Name: D & B Public Record Search
Addresses/Telephone Numbers, Bankruptcy, Corporate/Trade Name Data, Credit Information,
    Litigation/Judgments/Tax Liens and Uniform Commercial Code (US)
Database Name: Business Credit Information
Credit Information (US)
Special Distribution Methods to Client: Dial-Up (Other than Internet), Disk, Internet, Software
D&B isa leading provider of business information for credit, marketing, purchasing, and receivables management decisions worldwide. More than 100,000 companies rely on D&B to provide the insight they need to help build profitable, quality business relationships with their customers, suppliers and business partners. Dun & Bradstreet's Public Records Search database is one of the most extensive commercial public record information sites available. It is probably the only online database of corporate, UCC, litigation and tax lien information about businesses that covers all 50 states, the Virgin Islands, Puerto Rico and the District of Columbia. The 800 number listed above is for business credit information.

EdVerify Inc
880 Jupiter Park Drive, #3
Jupiter, FL 33458
877-338-3743; Fax: 516-746-9023
http://edverify.com
Founded: 1998
Clientele Restrictions: Signed agreement required, must be ongoing account
Products & Information Categories:
Proprietary Databases or Gateways:
Database Name: EdVerify.com
Education/Employment (US)
Special Distribution Methods to Client: E-Mail, Internet
EdVerify has automated education and enrollment verifications for every accredited post secondary school in the nation, and quickly responds to verification requests via the Internet. The company offers the exchange of data to high volume clients through an FTP "batch" transfer protocol or by an HTTPS real time, server-to-server protocol; and offers attractive pricing discounts to large accounts. EdVerify acts as the agent for educational institutions by consolidating Directory Information as defined by FERPA.

Electronic Property Information Corp (EPIC)
227 Alexander St #206
Rochester, NY 14607
716-454-7390; Fax: 716-486-0098
Founded: 1987
Clientele Restrictions: None reported
Products & Information Categories:
Proprietary Databases or Gateways:
Database Name: OPRA-Erie, Monroe Counties
Real Estate/Assessor, Uniform Commerical Code, Litigation/Judgments/Tax Liens and Wills/Probate (NY-Erie,
    Monroe Counties)
Database Name: OPRA
Bankruptcy (NY)
Special Distribution Methods to Client: Dial-Up (Other than Internet), Internet
EPIC provides online access to their proprietary database of all public records affecting real property in Erie and Monroe Counties, NY and bankruptcy records for New York's Western and Northern Districts. In addition to helping create abstracts and write title insurance, the database has been used for collections, asset search, and individual and business screening applications.

E-Merges.com
1756 Ebling Tl #2000
Annapolis, MD 21401-6614
410-353-6894; Fax: 801-437-3555
www.e-merges.com/
info@e-merges.com
Clientele Restrictions: None reported
Products & Information Categories:
Proprietary Databases or Gateways:
Database Name: US Registered Voter File
Voter Registration (AK,AR,CO,CT,DE,DC,LA,ME,MA,MI,NV,NH,NY,NC,OH,OK,RI,SC,SD,UT,VT,WI)
Special Distribution Methods to Client: CD-ROM, Database, Disk, Magnetic Tape

E-Merges provides voter registration records with date of birth for unrestricted use from AK, AR CO, CT, DE, DC, LA, ME, MA, MI, NV, NH, NY, NC, OH, OK, RI, SC, SD, UT, VT, and WI. They will sell by county, state, or entire file, which is updated annually and is internally compiled from 3600 towns and counties acreoss the USA.

Environmental Data Resources, Inc. (EDR)

3530 Post Rd
Southport, CT 06490
800-352-0050, 203-255-6606
www.edrnet.com
Founded: 1991
Clientele Restrictions: Casual requesters permitted
Products & Information Categories:
Proprietary Databases or Gateways:
Database Name: NEDIS, Sanborn Maps
Environmental, Licenses/Registratoins/Permits, and Real Estate/Assessor (US)
Special Distribution Methods to Client:
Environmental Data Resources, Inc. (EDR) is an information company specializing in providing data on environmental liabilities associated with companies and properties. EDR provides this data to environmental consulting firms, banks, insurance companies, law firms, corporations and accounting firms. EDR has compiled and organized more than 600 separate government databases, obtained at the federal, state and local levels, into an environmental database referred to as NEDIS, the National Environmental Data Information System.

Equifax Credit Services

1600 Peachtree St NW
Atlanta, GA 30309
888-202-4025, 404-885-8000
www.equifax.com
customer.care@equifax.com
Parent Company: Equifax Inc
Founded: 1899
Memberships: AAMVA,
Clientele Restrictions: Signed agreemnet required for Hoover's Online subscription
Products & Information Categories:
Proprietary Databases or Gateways:
Database Name: Credit Profile
Credit Information (US)
Database Name: Investigation System
Persona
Addresses/Telephone Numbers, Education/Employment, Bankruptcy, Litigation/Judgments/Tax Liens (US)
Special Distribution Methods to Client: Dial-Up (Other than Internet), Internet
Equifax is a leading provider of consumer and commercial financial information worldwide. The database includes information on almost 400 million consumers and businesses around the world.

eUtah

68 S Main St #200
Salt Lake City, UT 84101
877-588-3468, 801-983-0275; Fax: 801-983-0282
www.e-utah.org/
info@e-utah.org
Parent Company: Utah Electronic Commerce Council
Clientele Restrictions: Must be ongoing account

Products & Information Categories:

Proprietary Databases or Gateways:
Gateway Name: TLRIS/MVR
Driver and/or Vehicle (UT)

Gateway Name: Business Entity List
Corporate/Trade Name Data (UT)

Special Distribution Methods to Client: Internet
In the Salt Lake area, call 801-983-0275. You must be a registered user to access certain e-government services through e-utah. E-Gov Services are currently available are Business Entity Search, Business Certificate of Existence, Business Principals Search (by business entity name), Registered Principals Search (RPS) (by principal name), Business Name Availability Search (BNA), Vehicle Titles Liens and Registration System (TLRIS), Interactive Online Drivers License Search (MVR), Personalized Plate Lookup (vehicle license plates), Sample Plate Sales (vehicle license plates), and Hunting & Fishing Licenses Online. Eligible organizations may subscribe by visiting www.state.ut.us/eutah/nra.pdf.

Everton Publishers

PO Box 368
Logan, UT 84323
800-443-6325, 801-752-6022
www.everton.com
leverton@everton.com
Founded: 1947
Clientele Restrictions: None reported

Products & Information Categories:

Proprietary Databases or Gateways:
Database Name: Everton's Online Search
Addresses/Telephone Numbers (US)

Special Distribution Methods to Client: Dial-Up (Other than Internet), Internet
Everton has offered online access since 1990. The company publishes the Everton's Genealogical Helper magazine and The Handbook For Genealogists.

Experian Information Solutions

500 City Parkway West #205
Orange, CA 92868
888-397-3742
www.experian.com
pyoung@experian.com
Parent Company: Experian
Clientele Restrictions: Casual requesters permitted

Products & Information Categories:

Proprietary Databases or Gateways:
Database Name: File 1
Consumer File
Credit Information, Addresses/Telephone Numbers (US)

Special Distribution Methods to Client: Dial-Up (Other than Internet), Internet
As the consumer credit arm of Experian, data from Experian Information Solutions (formerly Experian Consumer Credit) may be used for a variety of purposes related to individuals, subject to permissible purposes. Individuals who need assistance with reports should call 888-397-3742.

Experian Online

505 City Parkway
Orange, CA 92868
800-831-5614
www.experian.com
pat.young@experian.com
Parent Company: Experian
Clientele Restrictions: None reported

Products & Information Categories:

Proprietary Databases or Gateways:
Database Name: Experian Online
Various Experian Databases
Addresses/Telephone Numbers, Driver and/or Vehicle, Real Estate/Assessor (US)
Database Name: Experian Online Business Records Reports
Uniform Commercial Code, Corporate/Trade Name Data, Bankruptcy (US)
Special Distribution Methods to Client: Dial-Up (Other than Internet), Disk, Internet, Magnetic Tape
Experian is an information solutions company. We help organisations to use information to reach new customers and to develop successful and long lasting customer relationships. We have built our business on the simple premise that commercial success is about getting close to customers. The more an organisation understands them, the more able it is to respond to their very individual needs and circumstances. This is the approach that we adopt in our own client relationships. It is also the underlying motivation behind everything we do as a company.

Explore Information Services

4920 Moundview Dr
Red Wing, MN 55066
800-531-9125, 651-385-2284; Fax: 651-385-2281
www.exploredata.com
explore.info@exploredata.com
Clientele Restrictions: Signed agreement required, must be ongoing account

Products & Information Categories:

Proprietary Databases or Gateways:
Database Name: EARS
Driver and/or Vehicle (CO, FL, IA, KY, ME, MN, MO, NE, NH, OH, TN, UT, WI)
Special Distribution Methods to Client: Dial-Up (Other than Internet), Disk, Internet, Magnetic Tape
Their Electronically Accessed Reunderwriting Service (EARS), is a database of driver information, including violation history, that can be customized for use by insurance industry clients. RiskAlert is a service that identifies all licensed drivers in a household.

FDR Research / Disclosure

5161 River Rd, Bldg 4
Bethesda, MD 20816
800-847-4337
www.disclosure.com
researchcenter@disclosure.com
Parent Company: Thomson Financial
Founded: 1987
Clientele Restrictions: Casual requesters permitted

Products & Information Categories:

General: Litigation/Judgments/Tax Liens (US)

Proprietary Databases or Gateways:
Database Name: Disclosure SEC Database
SEC/Other Financial (US)

Database Name: State & Federal Agency Filings
News/Current Events, Trademarks, Environmental, Legislation/Regulation, Litigation/Judgments/Tax Liens (US)

Database Name: Bankruptcy Filings & Reports
Bankruptcy (US)

Special Distribution Methods to Client: CD-ROM, E-Mail, Internet
FDR Research / Disclosure - formerly Federal Filings - is a nationwide research and retrieval company. Records and searches can be done on a state and federal basis at any court or agency around the country. Court services include monitoring companies for new cases and new pleadings in existing cases. SEC documents can also be ordered through our research centers. FDR Research has an extensive in-house collection of bankruptcy documents dating back to 1988 as well as other types of agency filings.

Felonies R Us

1423 W 3rd #21
Little Rock, AR 72201
501-376-4719; Fax: 501-376-4619
Founded: 1998
Clientele Restrictions: Must be ongoing account

Products & Information Categories:

Proprietary Databases or Gateways:
Database Name: AR Felonies
Criminal Information (AR)

Special Distribution Methods to Client: Lists/Labels
Felonies 'R' Us maintains an updated criminal database obtained from the Arkansas Administrative Office of the Courts. Able to run statewide searches, they retrieve documents desired by the client.

Fidelifacts

42 Broadway
New York, NY 10004
800-678-0007, 212-425-1520; Fax: 212-248-5619
www.fidelifacts.com
norton@fidelifacts.com
Founded: 1956
Memberships: EMA, SHRM, NCISS, ASIS, PRRN,
Clientele Restrictions: Casual requesters permitted

Products & Information Categories:

General: Bankruptcy (US)

Proprietary Databases or Gateways:
Database Name: Fidelifacts Data Bank
Criminal Information (NY)

Special Distribution Methods to Client:
Among the oldest companies engaged in the business of providing background reports on individuals for employment purposes and on companies, Fidelifacts has a network of investigators in offices around the country, and local personnel who examine public records in less populated areas. Fidelifacts specialty is conducting background investigations, reference checks, screening checks of job applicants and due diligence investigations. They also provide asset location services, skip tracing and other services on legal matters. Their in-house database lists 1,500,000 names of persons arrested, indicted, convicted, and otherwise had problems with the law. Data is primarily for metro New York area, but also includes SEC/NASD filings where unlawful activity may be a question. Note: their office is located 1/2 block from the NY State Office of Court Administration and they have personnel there on a daily basis.

First American Corporation, The

1 First American Way
Santa Ana, CA 92707
800-854-3643, 714-800-3000
http://firstam.com
jbandy@firstam.com
Branch Offices:
900+ offices in USA & abroad, ; Fax:
Products & Information Categories:
Proprietary Databases or Gateways:
Database Name: Real Estate Information
Real Estate/Assessor (US)

Special Distribution Methods to Client: Automated Telephone Look-Up, CD-ROM, Gateway via Another Online Service, Internet

First American Corp. is a leading provider of business information and related products and services. Their 3 primary business segments include: title insurance & services; real estate information & services, which includes mortgage and database information and services; and consumer information & services which provides automotive, subprime and direct-to-consumer credit reporting; residence and pre-employment screening (see CIC company profile), auto insurance tracking, property & casualty insurance, home warranties, investment advisory, and trust & banking services. Visit www.firstam.com for further information.

First American Real Estate Solutions

5601 E. La Palma Ave
Anaheim, CA 92807
800-345-7334, 714-701-2150
www.firstamres.com/
sales.res.ca@firstam.com
Parent Company: Formerly w/ Experian; now w/ First Amer. Financial
Clientele Restrictions: Casual requesters permitted
Products & Information Categories:
Proprietary Databases or Gateways:
Database Name: Real Property Database
Real Estate/Assessor (AL, AZ, CA, CO, DC, DE, FL, GA, HI, IL, IN, LA, MA, MD, MI, MN, MS, NC, NJ, NM, NY, NV, OH, OK, OR, PA, SC, TN, TX, UT, VA, VI, WA, WI)

Special Distribution Methods to Client: CD-ROM, Microfilm/Microfiche

Now independent of Experian Inc, First American Real Estate Solutions is now part of the First American Financial Corporation. They are a leading provider of real estate information from major counties in most US states. Call for specific coverage and access via online database, CD-ROM and microfiche information.

First American Real Estate Solutions - Amerestate

8160 Corporate Park Dr #200
Cincinnati, OH 45242
800-582-7300, 513-489-7300; Fax: 513-489-4409
www.firstamres.com
sales.res.ca@firstam.com
Branch Offices:
Columbus, OH, 614-277-9688; Fax: 614-277-9689
Detroit, MI, 248-348-8112; Fax: 248-348-8101
Cleveland, OH, 440-974-7863; Fax: 440-974-7935
Founded: 1980
Memberships: MBAA, NAR, REIPA,

Clientele Restrictions: Casual requesters permitted
Products & Information Categories:
Proprietary Databases or Gateways:
Database Name: PaceNet
Real Estate/Assessor, Mortgage Data and Addresses/Telephone Numbers (KY, MI, OH)

Database Name: PaceNet
Real Estate/Assessor (KY, MI, OH)

Special Distribution Methods to Client: CD-ROM, Dial-Up (Other than Internet), Disk, Lists/Labels, Magnetic Tape
Now part of First Am. Real Estate Solutions, Amerestate maintains databases of existing real estate ownership and gathers and verifies data from courthouse public records and other sources on all real estate sales. They collect most information manually, assuring accuracy, completeness and timely information. Property addresses are standardized and updated quarterly to current CASS standards required by the USPS. Amerestate has recently introduced PaceNet Mortgage Leads, a product specifically designed for those in the lending industry who want to target prospects for refinance, lines of credit or seconds.

FlatRateInfo.com
1033 Walnut #300
Boulder, CO 80302
888-259-6173
www.flatrateinfo.com
Parent Company: QuickInfo.net Information Services
Founded: 1999
Clientele Restrictions: Signed Agreement Required
Products & Information Categories:
Proprietary Databases or Gateways:
Database Name: QI National People Locator
Addresses/Telephone Numbers (US)

Database Name: QI
Bankruptcy, Litigation/Judgments/Tax Liens, Real Estate/Assessor, Fictious Business Names (US)

Database Name: US Merchant Vessels
Vessels (US)

Database Name: US Aircraft
Aviation (US)

Special Distribution Methods to Client: Internet
FlatRateInfo.com provides on-line access to nationwide databases to licensed professionals and qualified businesses with legitimate need for the information. FlatRateInfo.com is the source for accurate, up-to-date and highly searchable information for the investigative and collection industries. As the name implies, most of our databases are available at a flat rate, meaning no per-search fees. Available databases on FlatRateInfo.com include two national people locators; national bankruptcies, judgments and liens; national property; national fictitious business names; and the Social Security death index. At the heart of the FlatRateInfo.com system is the QI National People Locator, a powerful searching tool containing over 600 million records from most U.S residents, including social security number, current and previous addresses, date of birth and aliases. Paying for every single search you make on other systems can add up quickly into large research fees. With its unlimited searching subscriptions, FlatRateInfo.com is a great way to expand your nationwide searching ability. FlatRateInfo.com is the fastest and easiest way to retrieve valuable and up-to-date information from all 50 states. Call 888-259-6173 today to receive a free demo.

FOIA Group Inc
1090 Vermont Ave NW # 800
Washington, DC 20005
202-408-7028; Fax: 202-347-8419
www.foia.com

foia@foia.com
Founded: 1988
Memberships: ABA, SCIP,
Clientele Restrictions: Casual requesters permitted
Products & Information Categories:
General: Associations/Trade Groups (US)

Proprietary Databases or Gateways:
Database Name: FOIA-Ware
Software/Training (US)

Special Distribution Methods to Client: Dial-Up (Other than Internet), Disk, E-Mail, Internet, Software
FOIA specializes in the Freedom of Information Act and State Open Records Act protocols. They help prepare and file FOIA requests, monitor and review documents, and service the legal profession and others seeking information through the Act. They also offer agency and customer competitive research and surveys. FOIA Group attorneys provide whistleblower assistance.

Folks Finders Ltd
PO Box 880
Neoga, IL 62447
800-277-3318
www.pimall.com/folkfinders/folkfind.htm
wehuntum@aol.com
Parent Company: Lenco Corporation of Kentucky @ Paducah
Founded: 1970
Memberships: NAIS, ICFA, NFDA, PRRN,
Clientele Restrictions: Casual requesters permitted
Products & Information Categories:
General: Vital Records (US)

Proprietary Databases or Gateways:
Database Name: Birth Index, Cemetery Internment
Vital Records (US)

Database Name: Casualty Reports, POW, MIA
Vietnam/Korea/WWII Casualty Reports ()

Special Distribution Methods to Client: CD-ROM, Disk, E-Mail, Lists/Labels, Magnetic Tape
Folks Finders specializes in finding folks - MISSING PERSONS - that may not object to being located. Most service charges are based on a "NO FIND-NO FEE" philosophy. Categories of searches include no-name pension beneficiaries, health-science related studies, edidemiology research, and adoption searches. As part of their expertise, they obtain and provide vital records worldwide. They have begun "alternate identity" locating. They also market actual original certified "Celebrity" death certificates for the serious collector. The driving record product is called Locate MVRs Plus.

Gale Group Inc, The
27500 Drake Rd
Framington Hills, MI 48331-3535
800-877-4253, 248-699-4253
www.gale.com
galeord@gale.com
Branch Offices:
Cambridge, MA, ; Fax:
Woodbridge, CT, ; Fax:
Foster City, CA, ; Fax:
Parent Company: Thomson Corporation
Founded: 1998
Clientele Restrictions: Casual requesters permitted

Products & Information Categories:

Proprietary Databases or Gateways:

Database Name: GaleNet

Associations/Trade Groups, Addresses/Telephone Numbers, Foreign Country Information, Corporate/Trade Name Data (US, Itl)

Special Distribution Methods to Client: CD-ROM, Dial-Up (Other than Internet), Microfilm/Microfiche

As a major publisher of academic, educational, and business research companies serving libraries, educational institutions, and businesses in all major international markets, The Gale Group provides much of its material online through products such as Associations Unlimited, Biography and Genealogy Master Index, Brands and Their Companies, Gale Business Resources, and Peterson's Publications. It was formed Sept. '98 with the merger of Gale Research, Information Access Co., and Primary Source Material.

Golden Bear Information Services

8780 19th Street #140

Rancho Cucamonga, CA 91701

909-483-0778; Fax: 909-980-3922

gbelaura@earthlink.net

Clientele Restrictions: Casual requesters permitted

Products & Information Categories:

General: Criminal Information (US)

Proprietary Databases or Gateways:

Database Name: Golden Bear

Litigation/Judgments/Tax Liens, Tenant History (CA, NV, AZ, OR, WA)

Special Distribution Methods to Client: Dial-Up (Other than Internet), E-Mail, Internet

Golden Bear Information Services collects public records daily from local courthouses around the nation. Their trained researchers collect public record information from Criminal Records, Civil Judgments, Unlawful Detainers, Evictions and Bankruptcies. GB continues to be a leader in providing quality, accurate and timely data to agencies, with special emphasis on Criminal History Searches. GB delivers a work product that is accurate, fast and inexpensive. Over 80% of State Criminal Searches are delivered within 24 hours and over 95% completed within 48. Golden Bear is proud of their reputation and unsurpassed knowledge, dedication and service. As a large wholesaler of criminal and civil history searches to the Employment & Background Screening Industries, GB offers its superior work product directly to clients at wholesale prices. All searches are preformed at the records department of the court specified for both misdemeanor and felony violations. GB does not utilize any third party computer generated indices or CD-ROM services. Research is 100% on-site, guaranteed.

GuideStar

427 Scotland Street

Williamsburg, VA 23185

757-229-4631

www.guidestar.org

administrator@guidestar.org

Parent Company: Philanthropic Research Inc

Clientele Restrictions: None

Products & Information Categories:

Proprietary Databases or Gateways:

Database Name: Charity Search

Corporate/Trade Name Data (US)

Special Distribution Methods to Client: Internet

GuideStar is a searchable database of more than 640,000 non-profit organizations in the United States. Type a name in the Charity Search box to find your favorite charity, or use the Advanced Search to find a charity by subject, state, zip code, or other criteria.

Haines & Company Inc

8050 Freedom Ave
North Canton, OH 44720
800-843-8452, 330-494-9111; Fax: 330-494-3862
www.haines.com
criscros@haines.com
Branch Offices:
Atlanta, GA, 770-936-9308; Fax: 770-455-1799
San Francisco, CA, 510-471-6181; Fax: 510-471-4910
Chicago, IL, 847-352-8696; Fax: 847-352-8698
Founded: 1932
Memberships: NAR, REIPA, DMA,
Clientele Restrictions: Casual requesters permitted

Products & Information Categories:

General: Voter Registration (OH)

Proprietary Databases or Gateways:
Database Name: Criss+Cross Plus, Directory
Address/Telephone Numbers (US)

Database Name: Criss+Cross Plus
Real Estate/Assessor (US)

Special Distribution Methods to Client: CD-ROM, Dial-Up (Other than Internet), Disk, Lists/Labels, Magnetic Tape, Publication/Directory, Software

Varied products and full-service capabilities allow Haines & Company to satisfy the marketing and research needs of most industries. County Real Estate on CD-ROM has been noted for its ease of use, speed and marketing power. They also offer cross-reference directories in book form or on CD-ROM in 71 major markets, also business and residential lists on labels, manuscripts, CD-ROM, off the Internet or bulletin boards (24-hour turnaround time available). Using their target list or a customer-provided list, they can provide complete direct marketing services, graphic design, printing and database maintenance -- all in-house. In addition to the branches listed above, they have offices in St. Louis, MO (800-922-3846, fax 314-429-2121), Cincinnati, OH (800-582-1734, fax 513-831-4286), Los Angeles, CA (800-562-8262, fax 714-870-4651) and in Washington, DC (877-889-1027, fax 301-780-3673).

Hogan Information Services

14000 Quail Springs Parkway #4000
Oklahoma, OK 73134
405-302-6954; Fax: 405-302-6902
www.hoganinfo.com
Parent Company: Dolan Media
Founded: 1990
Clientele Restrictions: Signed agreement required, must be ongoing account

Products & Information Categories:

General: Litigation/Judgments/Tax Liens (US)

Proprietary Databases or Gateways:
Database Name: Hogan Online
Bankruptcy (US)

Database Name: Hogan Online
()

Special Distribution Methods to Client: Database, Dial-Up (Other than Internet), Disk, Lists/Labels, Magnetic Tape
Hogan Information Services provides high-quality national public record information to credit bureaus, bankcard issuers, collection agencies, retail institutions, and other businesses through the US. Hogan gathers public record information on laptop computers in over 8,000 courthouses nationwide for business to business applications. They

specialize in helping businesses make smarter decisions and manage risk by using public record information. The toll-free phone number for their employment screening services only is 888-834-6658.

Hollingsworth Court Reporting Inc

10761 Perkins Rd #A
Baton Rouge, LA 70810
225-769-3386; Fax: 225-769-1814
www.public-records.com
Nora@hcrinc.com
Founded: 1983
Memberships: NPRRA,
Clientele Restrictions: None reported

Products & Information Categories:
General: Tenant History (AL, AR, FL, GA, IL, LA, MS, TN)

Proprietary Databases or Gateways:
Database Name: Tenant Eviction/Public Record Report
Litigation/Judgments/Tax Liens (AL, AR, FL, GA, IL, LA, MS, TN)
Special Distribution Methods to Client: Dial-Up (Other than Internet), E-Mail, FTP, Internet
HCR offers regional public record information including access to 25 million records. They have judgment, lien & eviction information. They also process criminal record searches with a 48 hour turnaround time.

Hoovers Inc

1033 La Posada Drive #250
Austin, TX 78752
800-486-8666, 512-374-4500; Fax: 512-374-4505
www.hoovers.com
info@hoovers.com
Clientele Restrictions: Casual requesters permitted

Products & Information Categories:
Proprietary Databases or Gateways:
Database Name: Hoover's Company Profiles
Addresses/Telephone Numbers, Corporate/Trade Name Data, News/Current Events (US)

Database Name: Real-Time SEC Documents
SEC/Other Financial (US)

Database Name:
Foreign Country Information (Itl)
Special Distribution Methods to Client: CD-ROM, Dial-Up (Other than Internet), Internet, Publication/Directory, Software
Hoovers offers a wide range of company information, much for investing purposes. Their published materials are distributed electronically and in print, and they claim their databases are among the least expensive sources of information on operations, strategies, etc. of major US and global and private companies.

Household Drivers Reports Inc (HDR Inc)

902 S Friendswood Dr Suite F
Friendswood, TX 77546
800-899-4437, 281-996-5509; Fax: 281-996-1947
www.hdr.com
sthomas@hdr.com
Founded: 1989
Clientele Restrictions: Signed agreement required, must be ongoing account

Products & Information Categories:
General: Addresses/Telephone Numbers (TX)
Proprietary Databases or Gateways:
Database Name: Corp Data
Corporation/Trade Name Data (TX)
Database Name: Criminal Record Data
Criminal Information (TX)
Database Name: Driver & Vehicle
Driver and/or Vehicle (TX)
Database Name: Vital Records
Vital Records (TX)
Special Distribution Methods to Client: Dial-Up (Other than Internet)
Household Drivers Report Inc has been in the information business since 1989, at which time it pioneered its first online database. Subscribers can access the information available through HDR's online system with the slightest amount of information. The HDR system offers the unique capability of wildcard searches. With only a partial last name, plate, VIN or address, HDR can locate that person or business and identify a wealth of information. Information is updated weekly. HDR is an online, real time database system, providing results within minutes. They offer a "no-hit, no-charge" feature on their online searches as well as a competitive pricing structure. The system is available to qualified professionals in law enforcement, private investigation, insurance fraud investigation, business professionals and security investigations. HDR offers customize information solutions for large volume users. They operate strictly in compliance with state and federal laws. The HDR system allows access to the following: Texas: driver license records, vehicle registration records, business records, vehicle by manufacturer, automatic driver update report, criminal conviction records, sex offender records, marriage, death, divorce records; also,moving violation reports from various states. New databases are added periodically.

IDM Corporation
3550 W Temple St
Los Angeles, CA 90004
877-436-3282, 213-389-2793; Fax: 213-389-9569
www.idmcorp.com
Founded: 1989
Memberships: REIPA,
Clientele Restrictions: License required, must be ongoing account
Products & Information Categories:
Proprietary Databases or Gateways:
Database Name: Tax, Assessor and Recorders
Real Estate/Assessor (US)
Special Distribution Methods to Client: CD-ROM, Dial-Up (Other than Internet), Disk, Magnetic Tape
IDM Corporation is one of the largest source providers of real estate public records. They convert 900 tax/assessor counties and 500 recorder's counties to a uniform format. Their assessment files are updated once per year, and recorder's are updated weekly. Their business-to-business site is www.sitexdata.com, and their consumer site is www.smarthomebuy.com.

iiX (Insurance Information Exchange)
PO Box 30001
College Station, TX 77842-3001
800-683-8553; Fax: 979-696-5584
www.iix.com
Founded: 1966
Clientele Restrictions: Must be ongoing account
Products & Information Categories:

Proprietary Databases or Gateways:
Database Name: UDI-Undisclosed Drivers, VIN
Driver and/or Vehicle (US)
Gateway Name: Motor Vehicle Reports
Driver and/or Vehicle (US)
Special Distribution Methods to Client: Dial-Up (Other than Internet), Internet, Software
iiX is an established provider of information systems to the insurance industry. Their services and products include MVR, claims, undisclosed driver, and other underwriting services. Users still call this system AMS or AMSI. The Undisclosed Driver Information (UDI) and VIN are only available on Expressnet, the Internet ordering system. A new program offered by iiX is ExpressFill. Start with a phone number, and ExpressFill prefills information for that address for drivers, VINs and gives the option to order an MVR.

Infocon Corporation
PO Box 568
Ebensburg, PA 15931-0568
814-472-6066; Fax: 814-472-5019
Clientele Restrictions: Casual requesters permitted
Products & Information Categories:
Proprietary Databases or Gateways:
Gateway Name: INFOCON County Access System
Criminal Information, Vital Records, Voter Registration, Litigation/Judgments/Tax Liens, Real Estate/Assessor (PA-15
     counties)
Special Distribution Methods to Client: Dial-Up (Other than Internet)
The Infocon County Access System offers online access to civil, criminal, real estate, and vital record information in Pennsylvania counties of Armstrong, Bedford, Blair, Butler, Clarion, Clinton, Erie, Huntingdon, Lawrence, Mifflin, Potter, and Pike. Fees are involved, access is through a remote 800 number.

Infomation-KS LLC
PO Box 15491
Lenexa, KS 66285-5491
913-634-3175; Fax: 913-894-5045
www.infomationks.com
infoks@swbell.net
Founded: 2000
Memberships: NPPRA,
Clientele Restrictions: Casual requesters permitted; agreement required.
Products & Information Categories:
General: Corporate/Trade Name Data (KS, MO)
Special Distribution Methods to Client: E-Mail, Gateway via Another Online Service, Publication/Directory
Information-KS specializes in background research including criminal, civil actions, drivers' license records for Kansas and Missouri counties. Via their web site, you may request meta-searches of related public record provider sites. They also provide searches for archived materials.

Information Inc
PO Box 382
Hermitage, TN 37076
877-484-4636, 615-884-8000; Fax: 615-889-6492
http://hometown.aol.com/publicrecordstn
infomantn@aol.com
Founded: 1991
Memberships: PRRN, FOP,

Clientele Restrictions: Casual requesters permitted

Products & Information Categories:

General: Criminal Information (US)

Proprietary Databases or Gateways:

Database Name: Arrest Database

Criminal Information (TN-Nashville)

Special Distribution Methods to Client: Dial-Up (Other than Internet), E-Mail

Information Inc provides a real time criminal arrest database for Davidson County, TN. This includes all agencies in the 20th Judicial District of Tennessee. The database, updated weekly allows you to obtain results 24/7. Instant results let you know if there is more research to be done at the courthouse level, and often lets allows for the compilation of additional information such as former residences and license information. Free demos and audits are welcomed.

Information Network of Arkansas

425 West Capitol Ave #3565

Little Rock, AR 72201

800-392-6069, 501-324-8900

www.state.ar.us/ina/about_ina.html

info@ark.org

Founded: 1998

Clientele Restrictions: Signed agreement required, must be ongoing account

Products & Information Categories:

Proprietary Databases or Gateways:

Gateway Name: INA

Driver and/or Vehicle, Workers' Compensation (AR)

Gateway Name: Secretary of State

Corporate/Trade Name Data,Licenses/Registrations/Permits (AR)

Special Distribution Methods to Client: Internet

The Information Network of Arkansas was created by the Arkansas Legislature with the responsibility of assisting the state in permitting citizens to access public records. There is a fee for driving records, Nursing Registry, Lobbyist, and Workers' Comp record access, but none for Secretary of State Trademarks, Corporations, Banking and notaries. There may be fees for new record categories.

Information Network of Kansas

534 S Kansas Ave #1210

Topeka, KS 66603

800-452-6727, 785-296-5059; Fax: 785-296-5563

www.ink.org

Founded: 1991

Clientele Restrictions: Signed agreement required, must be ongoing account

Products & Information Categories:

Proprietary Databases or Gateways:

Gateway Name: Premium Services

Driver and/or Vehicle, Uniform Commercial Code, Corporate/Trade Name Data, Legislation/Regulations, Real Estate/Assessor (KS)

Gateway Name: Premium Services

Litigation/Judgments/Tax Liens (KS-Johnson, Sedgwick, Shawnee, Wyandotte)

Gateway Name: Premium Services

Criminal Information (KS- Sedgwick, Shawnee, Wyandotte)

Special Distribution Methods to Client: Dial-Up (Other than Internet), Internet

INK is the official source for electronic access to the State of Kansas government information. Access to public record information is a premium service and requires a subscription.

InforME - Information Resource of Maine

One Market Square #101
Augusta, ME 04330
877-463-3468, 207-621-2600
www.informe.org
info@informe.org

Products & Information Categories:

Proprietary Databases or Gateways:
Gateway Name: Bureau of Motor Vehicles Driver's Records
Driver and/or Vehicle (ME)

Special Distribution Methods to Client: Internet
InforME provides access to Maine's Bureau of Motor Vehicles Driver's Records on a subscription basis.

Informus Corporation

2001 Airport Rd #201
Jackson, MS 39208
800-364-8380, 601-664-1900
www.informus.com
info@informus.com
Parent Company: ChoicePoint
Founded: 1990
Clientele Restrictions: Signed agreement required, must be ongoing account

Products & Information Categories:

General: Criminal Information (US)

Proprietary Databases or Gateways:
Database Name: Informus
Workers Compensation (MS, US)

Gateway Name: IntroScan
Addresses/Telephone Numbers (US)

Special Distribution Methods to Client: Dial-Up (Other than Internet), Internet
Informus provides an online pre-employment screening and public record retrieval service. Online access is available through the Internet. Some searches provide instant information, depending on state and category.

Intellicorp Ltd

3659 Green Road #116
Beachwood, OH 44122
888-946-8355, 216-591-9032; Fax: 216-591-9578
www.intellicorp.net
info@intellicorp.net
Founded: 1996
Memberships: ASIS, SHRM,
Clientele Restrictions: Signed agreement required, must be ongoing account

Products & Information Categories:

General: Addresses/Telephone Numbers (US)

Proprietary Databases or Gateways:
Database Name: Court, Inmate, & Booking Records
Criminal Information (OH,MN,IN,KY,WI)

Special Distribution Methods to Client: Dial-Up (Other than Internet), E-Mail, Gateway via Another Online Service
Intellicorp is an Ohio-based company providing online access to public records and other information. Theirr online systems are being used by law enforcement agencies, businesses, and professional organizations throughout the

country. Their customers and markets include human resources, health care, insurance companies, investigators, financial, attorneys, government and general business needs for the information. All approved subscribers have been carefully screened and qualified under the company's enrollment process. By utilizing the latest technologies, Intellicorp can provide access to an array of information in a fast and cost efficient manner. Intellicorp is one of a select group of companies licensed to provide access to Arrest and Booking records from OH, MI, IN, MN and IL county sheriff's offices. Intellicorp's information products are made available through its secured online system, accessible via the Internet or by dial-up methods. With over 700 million records available immediately online and access to millions of other records from other sources, Intellicorp services provide access to the right information to make more informed decisions.

Interstate Data Corporation

113 Latigo Lane
Canon City, CO 81212
800-332-7999
www.cdrominvestigations.com
Founded: 1987
Clientele Restrictions: Must be ongoing account
Products & Information Categories:
Proprietary Databases or Gateways:
Gateway Name: CA Criminal
Criminal Information (CA)

Database Name: CA Professional Licenses
Licenses/Registration/Permits (CA)

Database Name: CA Corporate Records
Corporate/Trade Name Data (CA)

Special Distribution Methods to Client: CD-ROM, Dial-Up (Other than Internet)

Intertstate Data Corporation provides primary access to over 50 databases for the California area. Databases include professional licenses, Board of Equalization, fictitious business names, criminal and civil courts, and others. Features online and CD-ROM technology at competitive prices.

Intranet Inc

1321 Valwood Prky #420
Carrollton, TX 75006
800-333-8818, 903-593-9817; Fax: 903-593-8183
Clientele Restrictions: None reported
Products & Information Categories:
General: Litigation/Judgments/Tax Liens (TX)

Proprietary Databases or Gateways:
Database Name: Bankscan
Bankruptcy (TX)

Special Distribution Methods to Client: Disk
Intranet specializes in bankruptcy research and retrieval services for the state of Texas.

Investigators Anywhere Resource Line

PO Box 40970
Mesa, AZ 85274-0970
800-338-3463, 480-730-8088; Fax: 480-730-8103
www.investigatorsanywhere.com/
IONPRRN@IONINC.com
Parent Company: ION Incorporated
Founded: 1987

Memberships: ASIS, CII, ION, NALI, NAPPS, NCISS
Clientele Restrictions: Casual requesters permitted
Products & Information Categories:
Proprietary Databases or Gateways:
Database Name: Resource Line
Addresses/Telephone Numbers, Licenses/Registrations/Permits, Foreign Country Information (US, Itl)
Special Distribution Methods to Client: Automated Telephone Look-Up, Dial-Up (Other than Internet), Internet
Investigators Anywhere Resources' Resource Line service provides access to over 30,000 investigators, prescreened for excellence of service levels. Connect direct to the web page for 24 hour service. Callers are matched to appropriate investigators. No fee to the callers except for international and non-commercial projects.

iplace.com

Langhorne, PA
; Fax: 215-785-3200
www.iplace.com
info@iplace.com
Branch Offices:
Orange, CA, ; Fax:
San Francisco, CA, ; Fax:
Founded: 2000
Clientele Restrictions: Registration required.
Products & Information Categories:
General: Credit Information (US)
Proprietary Databases or Gateways:
DB Name: Qspace, Consumer info
Credit Information (US)
DB Name: e-neighborhoods, iplace
Real Estate/Assessor (US)
Special Distribution Methods to Client: Internet
iPlace, Inc., is a provider of personally relevant information about credit, home, neighborhood and other personal assets. The company's services, data, and technologies provide compelling information solutions, relationship building tools and transaction facilitation for more than 100,000 online and offline businesses. With its newly launched iPlace.com, the company introduced its proprietary infoStructure Technology™, enabling businesses to capture and deliver vital customer information while strengthening customer relationships via individually targeted communications.

IQ Data Systems
1401 El Camino Ave, 5th Fl
Sacramento, CA 95815
800-264-6517, 916-418-9000
www.iqdata.com
ballas@iqdata.com
Founded: 1996
Memberships: NPRRA,
Clientele Restrictions: Must be ongoing account
Products & Information Categories:
Proprietary Databases or Gateways:
Database Name: IQ Data
Uniform Commercial Code, Bankruptcy, Real Estate/Assessor, Litigation/Judgments/Tax Liens, Addresses/Telephone Numbers, Corporate/Trade Name Data (US)

Gateway Name: IQ Data
Driver and/or Vehicle, Credit Information (US)
Special Distribution Methods to Client: Internet
IQ Data Systems is a leading nationwide online public record information provider. Accurate, up-to-date cost effective and instant easy-to-access national data to verify information and identities, conduct background checks, locate people/business/assets, detect fraud, find criminal/civil/financial records, assist law enforcement and more. Empowering corporations, government agencies and individuals to maximize the use and value of public record information. IQ Data's cutting edge technology and proprietary databases direct its customers to make better, timely and more informed decisions.

J B Data Research Co.

333 Haggerty Ln #6
Bozeman, MT 59715
406-585-3323; Fax: 406-585-3323
www.eellis.net
jbdata@eellis.net
Founded: 1999
Clientele Restrictions: Casual requesters permitted.
Products & Information Categories:
General: Bankruptcy (ID, MT, ND, NV, OR, SD, UT, WA, WY)
Proprietary Databases or Gateways:
Database Name:
Bankruptcy (ID, MT, ND, NV, OR, SD, UT, WA, WY)
Special Distribution Methods to Client: Disk, E-Mail, Lists/Labels
J B Data Research can provide a quick 12-hour turnaround from their database of bankruptcy records from nine western states. They are also an expert document retrieval company in Southwest Montana.

Juritas.com

120 S State St, 2nd Fl
Chicago, IL 60603
888-877-9695, 312-424-0800; Fax: 312-424-0700
www.juritas.com
jparkman@juritas.com
Founded: 2000
Clientele Restrictions: Registration required.
Products & Information Categories:
Proprietary Databases or Gateways:
Database Name: Juritas
Criminal Information (CA, DE, FL, IL, NJ, WA)
Database Name: Juritas
Litigation/Judgments/Tax Liens (CA, DE, FL, IL, NJ, WA)
Special Distribution Methods to Client: Internet
The documents found on Juritas.com come directly from state and federal trial courts across the United States, and cover the 14 most litigated practice areas, including Antitrust, Personal Injury, Securities, Medical Malpractice, Tax, Insurance, Labor & Employment, Products Liability, White Collar Criminal, Environmental, Civil Rights, Intellectual Property and more.

KnowX

730 Peachtree St. #700
Atlanta, GA 30308
888-975-6699; Fax: 404-541-0260

www.knowx.com
support@knowx.com
Parent Company: ChoicePoint
Clientele Restrictions: Casual requesters permitted
Products & Information Categories:
Proprietary Databases or Gateways:
Database Name: KnowX
Addresses/Telephone Numbers, Vital Records, Real Estate/Assessor, Bankruptcy, Licenses/Registrations/Permits,
    Corporate/Trade Name Data, Military Svc, Aviation, Vessels, Litigation/Judgments/Tax Liens, Uniform
    Commercial Code (US (with limited Canadian))
Special Distribution Methods to Client: Dial-Up (Other than Internet), Internet
KnowX is one of the most comprehensive sources of public records available on the Internet, and as a subsidiary of
ChoicePoint, they have 40 offices nationwide. KnowX provides public records on aircraft ownership, bankruptcies,
business directories, partnerships, DBAs, DEAs, death records, Duns, judgments, liens, lawsuits, licensing, residencies,
real property foreclosures, tax records, property transfers, sales permits, stock ownership, UCC and watercraft records.
Often, they run promotions that offer free services.

Kompass USA Inc

1255 Route 70, #25s
Parkway 70 Plaza
Lakewood, NJ 08701
732-730-0340; Fax: 732-730-0342
www.kompass-intl.com
Clientele Restrictions: None Reported
Products & Information Categories:
Proprietary Databases or Gateways:
Database Name: Kompass.com
Addresses/Telephone Numbers, Corporate/Trade Name Data (US)

Database Name: Kompass.com
Foreign Country Information ()

Special Distribution Methods to Client: CD-ROM, Internet, Publication/Directory
The Kompass Worldwide Database contains access to 1.5 million companies, 23 million product and service
references, 600,000 trade and brand names, and 2.9 million executives' names. Many searches are free over the
Internet.

KY Direct

Dept.of Info. Systems, 101 Cold Harbor Drive
Frankfort, KY 40601
502-564-7284; Fax: 502-564-1598
www.kydirect.net/
bpuckett@mail.state.ky.us
Parent Company: Commonwealth of Kentucky
Founded: 2000
Products & Information Categories:
General: Litigation/Judgments/Tax Liens (KY)
Proprietary Databases or Gateways:
Gateway Name: Secretary of State
Corporate/Trade Name Data (KY)

Gateway Name: Vital Statistics
Vital Records (KY)

Gateway Name: Legislature Searching Service
Legislation/Regulation (KY)

Gateway Name: UCC Index Search
Uniform Commerical Code (KY)

Special Distribution Methods to Client: Internet, Lists/Labels, Publication/Directory

KY Direct is the Commonwealth of Kentucky's clearinghouse web site or the dissemination of state agency, Secretary of State information, and vital statistics. The site is new, so not all options (such as workers compensation records and driver histories) may be available. Site is a portal for the purchase of online records and online and print directories such as state agencies lists, resource directory, sex offenders lists, nuring registry, state agency telephone directory, agency forms, maps, and more.

Landings.com

545 Concord Ave
Cambridge, MA 02138
617-441-0455; Fax: 617-249-0630
www.landings.com/
landings-ops@landings.com
Clientele Restrictions: Sign-in Required

Products & Information Categories:

Proprietary Databases or Gateways:

Database Name: Landings.com
Aviation (US)

Special Distribution Methods to Client: Internet

Landings.com is the busiest and largest aviation website in the world. The web site is a portal to industry databases (FAA Regulations, AIM, SDRs, NTSB Briefs, N Numbers), flight planning, pilot weather, shop, links, training, everything that flies, news and advice.

Law Bulletin Information Network

415 N State
Chicago, IL 60610-4674
312-644-7800; Fax: 312-644-1215
www.lawbulletin.com
Founded: 1854
Memberships: NALFM, NPRRA, NFPA,
Clientele Restrictions: Casual requesters permitted

Products & Information Categories:

General: Uniform Commercial Code (IL)

Proprietary Databases or Gateways:

Database Name: Access Plus
Real Estate/Assessor (IL-Cook County)

Database Name: Access Plus
Litigation/Judgments/Tax Liens, (IL-Central, North Counties)

Database Name: Access Plus
Addresses/Telephone Numbers (IL)

Database Name: Access Plus
Uniform Commercial Code (IL-Cook County)

database Name: Access Plus
Court Dockets (IL-Cook County)

Special Distribution Methods to Client: Dial-Up (Other than Internet), E-Mail, Internet, Publication/Directory

The Law Bulletin Publishing Company's Information Network's primary product, AccessPlus, provides both online and access to Illinois Courts, vital public record information, UCCs, corporate documents, court dockets, realty sales, etc.

They offer other document retrieval services including licensed investigative services through an affiliated licensed, private investigation agency. These services can be requested online through the DocuServices product at www.lawbulletin.com.

LEXIS-NEXIS

PO Box 933
Dayton, OH 45401-0933
800-227-9597, 937-865-6800
www.lexis-nexis.com
Greg.Noble@lexis-nexis.com
Parent Company: Reed Elsevier Inc
Founded: 1973
Memberships: AALL, ATLA, NALA, ABI, NPRRA, SCIP
Clientele Restrictions: Signed Agreement Required
Products & Information Categories:

Proprietary Databases or Gateways:
Database Name: LEXIS Law Publishing, Shepard's
Litigation/Judgments/Tax Liens (US)

Database Name: USBoat
Vessels (AL, AZ, AR,
    CO,CT,FL,GE,IA,ME,MD,MA,MS,MO,MN,MT,NE,NV,NH,NC,ND,OH,OR,SC,UT,VA,WV,WI)

Database Name: Congressional Information Service
Legislation/Regulation (US)

Database Name: ALLBKT
Bankruptcy (US)

Database Name: ALLOWN
Real Estate/Assessor (US)

Database Name: ALLUCC
Uniform Commercial Code (US)

Database Name: ALLSOS
Corporate/Trade Name Data (US)

Database Name: B-Find, P-Find, P-Seek
Addresses/Telephone Numbers (US)

Database Name: Professional Licensing Boards
Licenses/Registrations/Permits (CA, CT, FL, GE, IL, MA,MI,NE,NJ,NC,OG,PA,TX,VA,WI)

Special Distribution Methods to Client: Dial-Up (Other than Internet), Gateway via Another Online Service, Publication/Directory
The LEXIS-NEXIS services offer one of the most comprehensive aggregations of public records available anywhere. Additionally, they compile and categorize these records so that you find the information you need faster and easier. With minimal effort, you can search one of the largest and faster growing public records collections in the United States. They offer industry-leading access to critical information such as real and personal property records; business and person locators; civil and criminal filings; Secretary of State records; liens, judgments, and UCC filings; jury verdicts and settlements; professional license, bankruptcy filings; and much more.

LIDA Credit Agency Inc

450 Sunrise Hwy
Rockville Centre, NY 11570
516-678-4600; Fax: 516-678-4611
Founded: 1920
Clientele Restrictions: Casual requesters permitted

Products & Information Categories:
General: Credit Information (US, NY)

Proprietary Databases or Gateways:
Database Name: LIDA
Litigation/Judgments/Tax Liens (DE, NJ, NY, PA)

Special Distribution Methods to Client:
LIDA's management averages more than 35 years in public record research, investigations and credit/financial reporting. Among their 17 member staff are five licensed and bonded private investigators. They specialize in Metro New York City, including the five boroughs and surrounding counties.

LLC Reporter
Frontier Law Center, 1107 W 6th Ave
Cheyenne, WY 82001
800-282-4552; Fax: 307-637-7445
www.llc-reporter.com
WDBagley@LLC-REPORTER.com
Founded: 1993
Clientele Restrictions: None Reported

Products & Information Categories:

Proprietary Databases or Gateways:
Database Name: LLC Reporter
Corporate/Trade Name Data (US)

Special Distribution Methods to Client: Internet, Publication/Directory
The Limited Liability Company Reporter is a national newsletter committed to assisting Lawyers, CPA's and Business Planners who need to stay current in a fast changing field. The Reporter Archive contains all issues of the Reporter from January 1, 1993 through December 31, 1999, accessible by a topic index and author index. The most recent events are found under Current LLC News. The authors are a coast-to-coast network of LLC practitioners and administrators who contribute their expertise.

Lloyds Maritime Information Services Inc
1200 Summer St
Stamford, CT 06905
800-423-8672, 203-359-8383; Fax: 203-358-0437
www.lmis.com
lmisusa@llplimited.com
Founded: 1986
Clientele Restrictions: Casual requesters permitted
Products & Information Categories:
General: Addresses/Telephone Numbers (US)

Proprietary Databases or Gateways:
Database Name: SEADATA
Vessels (US, Itl)
Database Name: SeaSearcher
Vessels (US, Itl)

Special Distribution Methods to Client: Dial-Up (Other than Internet), Disk
Lloyd's Maritime Information Services (LMIS) provides the maritime business community with access to the world's most authoritative, up-to-date and comprehensive source of computerized international maritime information, derived from the databases of it's two principles LLP Ltd. (now part of the Informa Group) and Lloyd's Register. This gives access to an unparalled range of information on the world commercial shipping fleet of vessels of 100gt and above (some 85,000+ vessels) and a vast resource for collecting, maintaining and verifying the data. The LMIS mission is to provide decision ready data. Data can be provided as a custom built service on CD Rom, diskette or via e-mail and can

also be accessed through a wide range of standard products such as the online systems SeaSearcher and SeaData and the PC databases AS+ and Fleet Information Database. The Market Intelligence Division of LMIS provides industry specific products for the oil and liner markets as well as producing the prestigious Lloyd's Shipping Economist magazine and offering ad-hoc consultancy services, forecasting and market research.

Logan Registration Service Inc
PO Box 161644
Sacramento, CA 95816
916-457-5787
www.loganreg.com
contact@loganreg.com
Founded: 1976
Memberships: NFIB,
Clientele Restrictions: Signed agreement required, must be ongoing account
Products & Information Categories:
General: Addresses/Telephone Numbers (CA)

Proprietary Databases or Gateways:
Gateway Name: Logan
Driver and/or Vehicle (CA,US)
Special Distribution Methods to Client: Dial-Up (Other than Internet), E-Mail
Logan has more than 25 years experience working with California driver and vehicle records. They are an online vendor that allows their DMV authorized clients to retrieve driver and vehicle registration records in seconds with a computer software program that is available free of charge. Clients are also able to access needed records via phone or fax.

Loren Data Corp
4640 Admiralty Way #430
Marina Del Rey, CA 90292
800-745-6736, 310-827-7400
www.LD.com
info@LD.com
Founded: 1987
Clientele Restrictions: Casual requesters permitted
Products & Information Categories:
General: Licenses/Registrations/Permits (US)

Proprietary Databases or Gateways:
Gateway Name: Commerce Business Daily
Environmental, Military Svc, News/Current Events, Legislation/Regulation (US)
Special Distribution Methods to Client: E-Mail
Loren Data Corp provides customers with access to government business, helping make bids and gain government contracts. They offer free access and e-mail based subscription services for their publication Commerce Business Daily, CBD.

Martindale-Hubbell
121 Chanlon Road
Providence, NJ 07974
800-526-4902, 908-464-6800; Fax: 908-464-3553
www.martindale.com
ccooper@martindale.com
Branch Offices:
London, GB, 44 20 7868 4885; Fax: 44 20 7868 4886
Parent Company: Reed Elsevier PLC Group

Founded: 1868
Clientele Restrictions: Casual requesters permitted
Products & Information Categories:
Proprietary Databases or Gateways:
Database Name: Martindale-Hubbell Law Directory (Attorneys and Law Firms)
Addresses/Telephone Numbers, Education/Employment (US, Itl)
Special Distribution Methods to Client: CD-ROM, Lists/Labels, Publication/Directory
Martindale-Hubbell's database is now regarded as the primary source for attorney and law firm information around the world. Their flagship product, Martindale-Hubbell Law Directory consists of more the 900,000 listings, organized by city, state, county, and province with extensive cross-references and indexes. Products are available in four media: hardbound print, CR-ROM, via LEXIS/NEXIS (a sister company) and Internet via the Martindale-Hubbell Lawyer Locator. Their data includes corporate law departments, legal-related services such as P.I.s, title search companies, law digests.

MDR/Minnesota Driving Records
1710 Douglas Dr. N #103
Golden Valley, MN 55422-4313
800-644-6877, 612-755-1164; Fax: 612-595-8079
Clientele Restrictions: Signed agreement required, must be ongoing account
Products & Information Categories:
Proprietary Databases or Gateways:
Database Name: MDR
Driver and/or Vehicle (MN)
Special Distribution Methods to Client: Lists/Labels
MDR provides an automated touch-tone call-in service for driver information in Minnesota, letting clients retrieve a record with a verbal response in less than one minute, followed by a fax hard copy within minutes. Service available 24 hours a day every day. The service is endorsed by the Minnesota Insurance Agents Assoc.

Merlin Information Services
215 S Complex Dr
Kalispell, MT 59901
800-367-6646, 406-755-8550; Fax: 406-755-8568
www.merlindata.com
Support@merlindata.com
Founded: 1991
Clientele Restrictions: Casual requesters permitted
Products & Information Categories:
Proprietary Databases or Gateways:
Database Name: CA Criminal Indexes, Brides and Grooms, Statewide Property, Civil Superior Indexes, Fictitious
    Business Names, Consumer affsirs, Many Other Licenses
Criminal Information, Vital Records, Real Estate/Assessor, Litigation/Judgments/Tax Liens,
    Licenses/Registrations/Permits (Professional Licenses) (CA)
Gateway Name: National FlateRate
Criminal Information (CA), Civil Indexes(CA), UCC, Aviation, vessels, Real Estate/Assessor,
    Litigation/Judgments/Tax Liens, Addresses/Telephone Numbers, Corporation/Trade Name Data, SSN & Death
    Records (US)
Database Name: Merlin Super Header
Addresses/Telephone Numbers, SSNs (US)
Gateway Name: Banko
Bankruptcy (US)

Database Name: CA Sales, Use Tax, Prof. Licenses, Alcohol Bev Control Lic
Licenses/Registrations/Permits (Professional Licenses) (CA)

Gateway Name: UCC Index
Uniform Commercial Code (Filing Index) (CA)

Database Name: Investigator's National New Business Filings
Corporation/Trade Name Data, Occupational Licenses/Business Registrations/Permits, News/Current Events (CA, US)

Database Name: National People Finder, National Credit Headers
Addresses/Telephone Numbers, Vital Records (US)

Database Name: Trace Wizard National Residential Locator
Addresses/Telephone Numbers, Vital Records, Driver and/or vehicle, Voter Registration, Credit Header Info (US)

Special Distribution Methods to Client: CD-ROM, Dial-Up (Other than Internet), Internet, Magnetic Tape

Merlin Information Services produces unique search and retrieval systems to search public record and proprietary information databases. Merlin specializes in new technology for combined media search and retrieval using both CD-ROM and the Internet. Merlin's proprietary databases and several national databases are available on the Internet at their web site. They also sell public record related CD-ROM products, produced by a number of other publishers, including voter registration records, DMV records, and Social Security death records. Their list of available gateways and databases is so exhaustive that this profile could not list the CA Fictitious Business Names Index, CA Corporations, Limited Partnerships, and Limited Liability Corporations, and National Bankruptcies Index.

Metro Market Trends Inc

PO Box 30042
Pensacola, FL 32503-1042
800-239-1668, 850-474-1398; Fax: 850-478-6249
www.mmtinfo.com
mmt@mmtinfo.com
Founded: 1990
Memberships: REIPA,
Clientele Restrictions: Casual requesters permitted

Products & Information Categories:

Proprietary Databases or Gateways:

Database Name: Real Estate Activity Reporting System
Real Estate/Assessor (FL, AL)

Gateway Name: Parcel Information Reporting System
Addresses/Telephone Numbers (FL, AL)

Special Distribution Methods to Client: CD-ROM, Disk, E-Mail, Lists/Labels, Magnetic Tape, Software

MMT Inc is a leading provider of real estate related information products and software for Florida and south Alabama. Real estate information products include tax roll databases, updated real estate sales information systems, market share reports, comparable sales reports, property owner mailing lists, and custom data runs for economic and financial analysis. Real estate software products include tax roll programs and real estate sales information programs that are licensed to other real estate information providers.

Metronet

500 City Parkway West #205
(Attn.: Pat Young)
Orange, CA 92868
888-397-3742
www.experian.com/experian_us.html
pat.young@experian.com
Parent Company: Experian
Founded: 1941
Memberships: DMA, ACA, ALA,

Clientele Restrictions: Casual requesters permitted

Products & Information Categories:

Proprietary Databases or Gateways:
Database Name: MetroNet, Cole's Directory
Addresses/Telephone Numbers, Real Estate/Assessor (US)

Special Distribution Methods to Client: Automated Telephone Look-Up, CD-ROM, Dial-Up (Other than Internet), Gateway via Another Online Service, Publication/Directory

MetroNet includes direct access to the electronic directory assistance databases of the Regional Bells (RBOC's). Regional editions of the MetroSearch CD-ROM products and call-in services are featured. At the US Experian web site, select "Subscriber" and click Metronet.

MicroPatent USA

250 Dodge Ave
East Haven, CT 06512
800-648-6787, 203-466-5055; Fax: 203-466-5054
http://micropat.com
info@micropat.com
Branch Offices:
London, UK, ; Fax:
Parent Company: Information Holdings Inc
Founded: 1989
Memberships: AALL, ATLA, AIPLA, INTA, NALA, NLG
Clientele Restrictions: Casual requesters permitted

Products & Information Categories:

Proprietary Databases or Gateways:
Database Name: WPS
Patents (US, Itl)

Database Name: TradeMark Checker, Mark Search Plus
Trademarks (US, Itl)

Special Distribution Methods to Client: CD-ROM, Dial-Up (Other than Internet), Disk, E-Mail, Internet, Software
MicroPatent is a global leader in the production and distribution of patent and trademark information. MicroPatent is committed to developing intellectual property systems with its sophisticated and talented programming staff. MicroPatent Europe is located in London, England.

Military Information Enterprises Inc

PO Box 17118
Spartanburg, SC 29301
800-937-2133, 864-595-0981; Fax: 864-595-0813
www.militaryusa.com
thelocator@aol.com
Founded: 1988
Memberships: SCALI,
Clientele Restrictions: Casual requesters permitted

Products & Information Categories:

Proprietary Databases or Gateways:
Database Name: Nationwide Locator Online
Military Svc (US)

Special Distribution Methods to Client: E-Mail, Internet, Publication/Directory
Military Information Enterprises specializes in current and former military locates and background checks, also military reunions and service verifications. They also publish books on locating people. The owner is a South Carolina licensed private investigator.

Motznik Computer Services Inc
8301 Briarwood St #100
Anchorage, AK 99518-3332
907-344-6254; Fax: 907-344-1759
www.motznik.com
sales@motznik.com
Founded: 1974
Memberships: NFIB,
Clientele Restrictions: Casual requesters permitted
Products & Information Categories:
Proprietary Databases or Gateways:
Database Name: Alaska Public Information Access System

Aviation, Vessels, Bankruptcy, Licenses/Registrations/Permits, Litigation/Judgments/Tax Liens, Criminal Information, Corporate/Trade Name Data, Uniform Commercial Code, Real Estate/Assessor, Voter Registration and Driver and/or Vehicle (AK)

Special Distribution Methods to Client: Dial-Up (Other than Internet)

Motznik Computer Services' product is a comprehensive online information research system that provides access to a wide selection of Alaska public files. Information that can be researched includes: tax liens, UCC, address, real property, Anchorage civil suits, commercial fishing vessels, judgments, motor vehicles, partnerships, bankruptcies, aircraft, permanent fund filing, businesses, Anchorage criminal cases and commercial fishing permits. MV data does not include driver's personal information.

National Credit Information Network NCI
PO Box 53247
Cincinnati, OH 45253
800-374-1400, 513-522-3832; Fax: 513-522-1702
www.wdia.com
Parent Company: WDIA Corporation
Founded: 1983
Clientele Restrictions: Signed agreement required; some searches available to non-members
Products & Information Categories:
General: Bankruptcy (IN, KY, OH)

Proprietary Databases or Gateways:
Database Name: NCI
Tenant History (IN, KY, OH)

Gateway Name: NCI Network

Credit Information, Addresses/Telephone Numbers, Voter Registration, Driver and/or Vehicle (US)

Special Distribution Methods to Client: Dial-Up (Other than Internet), E-Mail, Internet

National Credit Information Network (NCI) specializes in interfacing with credit and public record databases for online searches with immediate response time. Online ordering is available for setup and for searches using a credit card. Access is available through their Internet site. A variety of packages include applicant identity, SSNs, DMVs, education, reference and credential verification, criminal history, bankruptcy and civil history, workers comp claims, and more.

National Fraud Center
Four Horsham Business Center
300 Welsh Rd #200
Horsham, PA 19044
800-999-5658, 215-657-0800; Fax: 215-657-7071
www.nationalfraud.com
email@nationalfraud.com

Branch Offices:
Dallas, TX, ; Fax:
Minneapolis, MN, ; Fax:
San Francisco, CA, ; Fax:
Founded: 1981
Memberships: ASIS, IAAI, CII, IFS,
Clientele Restrictions: Casual requesters permitted
Products & Information Categories:
General: Litigation/Judgments/Tax Liens (US)

Proprietary Databases or Gateways:
Database Name: NFC Online
Software/Training, Publication/Directory (US, Itl)

Database Name: Bank Fraud/Insurance Fraud/Organized Crime
Criminal Information (US, Itl)

Database Name: The Fraud Bulletin
Criminal History (US)

Gateway Name: Cellular Fraud Database
Criminal Information (US)

Special Distribution Methods to Client: CD-ROM, Dial-Up (Other than Internet), Disk
National Fraud Center combines its diverse databases into a system: NFConline. They utilize a fraud prevention, an interdiction program, and risk management tools to discover and prevent fraud and risk. They also specialize in pro-active measures such as security policies, training, and installation of security devices to protect corporations from future losses.

National Marine Fisheries Service
Statistics & Economic Division (F/ST1)
1315 East-West Highway
Silver Spring, MD 20910

www.st.nmfs.gov/st1/commercial/index.html
Products & Information Categories:
Proprietary Databases or Gateways:
Database Name: Vessel Documentation Data
Vessels (US)
Special Distribution Methods to Client: Internet
This organization provides free searches to the US Coast Guard vessel database. Data is updated every quarter. Search by vessel number or name.

National Service Information
145 Baker St
Marion, OH 43301
800-235-0337, 740-387-6806
www.nsii.net
Branch Offices:
Indianpolis, IN, 317-266-0040; Fax: 317-266-8453
Founded: 1989
Memberships: NPRRA, REIPA,
Clientele Restrictions: Casual requesters permitted
Products & Information Categories:
General: Uniform Commercial Code (US)

Proprietary Databases or Gateways:
Database Name: NSI - Online
Corporate/Trade Name Data, Uniform Commercial Code (IN, OH, WI)
Special Distribution Methods to Client: Internet
National Service Information is engaged in the search, filing and document retrieval of public record information. Having offices in Marion, OH and Indianapolis, IN, they consider Ohio, Indiana and Kentucky their local market in addition to 4300 different jurisdictions they search nationwide. They recently unveiled a comprehensive database to allow clients to perform public record searches via the Web. Their web site allows you to perform state level UCC lien and corporate detail searches for Ohio, and state level UCCs for Indiana. NSI also provides the option of requesting copies of microfilmed UCC lien images.

National Student Clearinghouse

2191 Fox Mill Rd #300
Herndon, VA 20171-3019
703-742-7791; Fax: 703-742-7792
www.studentclearinghouse.com
service@studentclearinghouse.org
Clientele Restrictions: Registration required.

Products & Information Categories:

Proprietary Databases or Gateways:
Database Name: EnrollmentVerify, DegreeVerify
Education/Employment (US)
Special Distribution Methods to Client: FTP, Internet
They conveniently provide attendance, degree, and financial information about students of a wide number (2400+ or up to 80% of all students) of colleges and universities in the USA. Does not include addresses, SSN verification, or records "on hold" or "blocked."

NC Recordsonline.com

6525 Morrison Blvd #350
Charlotte, NC 28211
877-442-9600, 704-442-9600
www.ncrecordsonline.com
info@ncrecordsonline.com
Parent Company: RSM Group LLC
Clientele Restrictions: Casual requesters permitted

Products & Information Categories:

General: Criminal Information (NC)

Proprietary Databases or Gateways:
Gateway Name: ncrecordsonline.com
Criminal Information (NC)
Special Distribution Methods to Client: Gateway via Another Online Service, Internet
NCRecordsonline.com offers a reliable link to the North Carolina Administrative Office of the Courts criminal and civil mainframe. This allows high volume users, research firms, employment screeners, attorneys, PI's, bondsmen, paralegals, etc to log on from any computer and access the same criminal and civil index system that is used by the NC Clerk of Court, 24-hours a day, 7 days a week. NCRecordsonline.com lets its users bypass all state required set-up costs, long distance charges, and equipment fees associated with a direct connection. Payment options are available for both causal requestors and ongoing accounts.

Nebrask@ Online
301 South 13th #301
Lincoln, NE 68508
800-747-8177, 402-471-7810; Fax: 402-471-7817
www.nol.org
info@nol.org
Founded: 1992
Clientele Restrictions: Signed Agreement Required
Products & Information Categories:
Proprietary Databases or Gateways:
Gateway Name: Nebrask@ Online
Driver and/or Vehicle, Corporate/Trade Name Data and Uniform Commercial Code (NE)
Gateway Name: Nebrask@ Online
Litigation/Judgments/Tax Liens and Addresses/Telephone Numbers (NE)
Special Distribution Methods to Client: Automated Telephone Look-Up, Dial-Up (Other than Internet), Internet, Magnetic Tape
Nebrask@ Online is a State of Nebraska information system that provides electronic access to state, county, local, association and other public information. Some agency and association data is updated daily, weekly or monthly, Subscribers connect via 800 #, local #s, or the Internet 24-hours per day. There are sign-up and connect fees if not accessing via the Internet. Interactive access to premium services (those with a statutory fee) requires an annual subscription.

NIB Ltd
100 Canal Pointe Vlvd #114
Princeton, NJ 08540-7063
800-537-5528, 609-936-2937; Fax: 609-936-2859
www.nib.com
Info@nib.com
Parent Company: Bristol Investments LTD
Founded: 1993
Memberships: SIIA,
Clientele Restrictions: Signed agreement required, must be ongoing account
Products & Information Categories:
Proprietary Databases or Gateways:
Database Name: BACAS, BcomM
Credit Information (US)
Special Distribution Methods to Client: Dial-Up (Other than Internet), Software
NIB has been providing credit processing information to businesses for over 10 years. Courier is a combination of the 5 accessible credit reporting agencies. Other state-of-the-art products include BACAS and BcomM.

Northwest Location Services
PO Box 1345
Puyallup, WA 98371
253-848-7767; Fax: 253-848-4414
http://legallocate.com
Founded: 1990
Clientele Restrictions: None reported
Products & Information Categories:
General: Criminal Information (WA)

Proprietary Databases or Gateways:
Database Name: Superior Courts
Northwest Online
Statewide Court Filings (WA)

Database Name: Business Licenses
Licenses/Registration/Permits (WA)

Database Name: People Finder
Name/Address/SSN/DOB (WA)

Special Distribution Methods to Client: Dial-Up (Other than Internet), E-Mail, Internet

Serving investigative, legal and business professionals, Northwest Location Services specializes in witness location, skip tracing, asset research and other information services, with an eye on protecting privacy and the public safety. Licensed and bonded in Washington, they are allied with Northwest Online and Digital Research Company who produces CD-ROM database products for investigators, attorneys and collection agencies.

Offshore Business News & Research

123 SE 3rd Ave #173
Miami, FL 33131
305-372-6267; Fax: 305-372-8724
www.offshorebusiness.com
Parent Company: Offshore Business News & Research Inc
Founded: 1996
Clientele Restrictions: Casual requesters permitted

Products & Information Categories:

Proprietary Databases or Gateways:
Database Name:
Addresses/Telephone Numbers (Itl)

Special Distribution Methods to Client: Internet

OBNR supplies information on businesses and individuals involved in offshore finance and insurance. OBNR owns litigation databases covering Bermuda and the Cayman Islands. They offer 24 hour daily access, year around via the Internet. They publish investigative newsletters covering Bermuda and the Caribbean.

OPEN (Online Professional Electronic Network)

PO Box 549
Columbus, OH 43216-0549
888-381-5656, 614-481-6999; Fax: 614-481-6980
www.openonline.com
Founded: 1992
Memberships: ASIS, NCISS, NSA, SHRM,
Clientele Restrictions: Signed agreement required, must be ongoing account

Products & Information Categories:

General: Criminal Information (US)

Proprietary Databases or Gateways:
Database Name: OPEN
OPEN
Real Estate/Assessor, Bankruptcy, Uniform Commercial Code, Corporate/Trade Name Data, Addresses/Telephone
    Numbers, Credit Information, Driver and/or Vehicle, Criminal Information (US)

Gateway Name: Arrest Records
Criminal Information (OH,IN,MI)

Special Distribution Methods to Client: Dial-Up (Other than Internet), Gateway via Another Online Service

OPEN provides real-time, direct access to a large range of nationwide public records, such as driver records, arrest & conviction records, commercial & consumer credit reports, bankruptcies, liens and judgments. The service is subscription-based and is available to professionals and businesses for a variety of applications including background checks, skip-traces, verification of information such as addresses, phone numbers, SSNs, previous employment and educational background. OPEN provides free software, account start-up, and toll-free technical support with no monthly minimum.

OSHA DATA

12 Hoffman St
Maplewood, NJ 07040-1114
973-378-8011
www.oshadata.com
mcarmel@oshadata.com
Founded: 1991
Memberships: ASSE, AIHA,
Clientele Restrictions: Casual requesters permitted

Products & Information Categories:

General: Environmental (US)

Proprietary Databases or Gateways:
Gateway Name: OSHA Data Gateway
Legislation/Regulation (US)

Special Distribution Methods to Client: CD-ROM, Dial-Up (Other than Internet), Disk, Lists/Labels,
Publication/Directory, Software

OSHA DATA's database contains corporate regulator violation records for every business inspected since July 1972. Information includes not only OSHA data, but also wage and hour, EEOC, insurance, NLRB asbestos and other regulatory types. The database is updated quarterly. Consultation and software for the utilization of the data are available.

OSO Grande Technologies

5921 Jefferson NE
Albuquerque, NM 87109
505-345-6555; Fax: 505-345-6559
www.technet.nm.org
info@nm.net
Parent Company: New Mexico Technet
Founded: 1984
Clientele Restrictions: None reported

Products & Information Categories:

Proprietary Databases or Gateways:
Database Name: New Mexico Technet
Driver, Vehicle, Litigation/Judgments/Tax Liens, Corporate/Trade Name Data, UCC, Legislation/Regulation (NM)
Gateway Name: NM Fed Courts/LegalNet
Bankruptcy, Criminal Information (NM)

Special Distribution Methods to Client: Dial-Up (Other than Internet), Internet

Oso Grande Technologie is the for-profit portion of a self-supporting, non-profit corporation operating to provide management of a statewide computer network serving New Mexico, its state universities and statewide research, educational and economic-development interests. OGT serves as the primary connection point to the Internet for other Internet Service Providers, business, government and private users. OGT offers a full range of Internet services from dial-up to direct connections and web page services, to co-located services and New Mexico MVR requests. LegalNet provides legal resources; Oso Grande provides premium services.

Owens OnLine Inc

6501 N Himes Ave #104
Tampa, FL 33614
800-745-4656, 813-877-2008; Fax: 813-877-1826
www.owens.com
email@owens.com
Founded: 1987
Clientele Restrictions: Casual requesters permitted
Products & Information Categories:
General: Addresses/Telephone Numbers (US)

Proprietary Databases or Gateways:
Gateway Name: Owens OnLine
Credit Information (US, Itl)

Special Distribution Methods to Client: E-Mail, Gateway via Another Online Service, Internet
Owens OnLine specializes in international credit reports on businesses and individuals, and in international criminal checks. They provide worldwide coverage, with 9 million foreign credit reports online. Single orders are welcomed and there are no complex unit contracts.

Pallorium Inc

PO Box 155-Midwood Station
Brooklyn, NY 11230
212-969-0286; Fax: 212-858-5720
www.pallorium.com
pallorium@pallorium.com
Founded: 1979
Memberships: ION, WAD, NAIS, BOMP, ASIS, NCISS
Clientele Restrictions: Casual requesters permitted
Products & Information Categories:
General: SEC/Other Financial (US)

Proprietary Databases or Gateways:
Database Name: Skiptrace America
Addresses/Telephone Numbers, Driver and/or Vehicle, Vital Records and Voter Registration (US)
Database Name: People Finder
Aviation, Vessels, Driver and/or Vehicle, Vital Records and Voter Registration (US)
Database Name: Business Finder America
Corporate/Trade Name Data (US)

Special Distribution Methods to Client: Dial-Up (Other than Internet), Internet
Pallorium (PallTech Online) services are divided into three areas: the electronic mail system, which links all users (800 investigative/security professionals); the bulletin board system, which provides a forum for the free exchange of information among all approved subscribers (public or private law enforcement only); and the investigative support system, which provides investigative support to approved users. PallTech's searches include aircraft record locator, national financial asset tracker, bankruptcy filings locator, business credit reports, consumer credit reports, NCOA trace, criminal records, national vehicle records, current employment locator, NYC registered voters by address, court and governmental jurisdiction identifier, ZIP Code locator and more searches in the US, Canada, Israel and Hong Kong. New products of addresses and personal information for all states total more than five billion records.

Paragon Document Research

PO Box 65216
St Paul, MN 55165
800-892-4235, 651-222-6844
www.banc.com/pdrstore

pdrinc@mn.uswest.net
Parent Company: PDR Inc
Founded: 1991
Memberships: NAFE, NALA, NPRRA, PRRN, MSBA,
Clientele Restrictions: Signed agreement required for subscriber rates; casual requests permitted
Products & Information Categories:
General: Addresses/Telephone Numbers (MN, ND, SD, MT, WI, US)
Proprietary Databases or Gateways:
Database Name: Pdrlog
Uniform Commercial Code (US)
Special Distribution Methods to Client: Disk, Lists/Labels, Microfilm/Microfiche
Paragon Document Research's services include searches throughout state and county levels nationwide covering UCC and federal and state tax Liens, corporate documents, Bankruptcy filings, judgment searches, past and present litigation, searches for ownership of, and liens on DMV reports, aircraft/watercraft and vessel searches, assumed name searches, and name reservations. Registered Agent Services and weekly tax lien bulletin orders can be requested online through www.banc.com.

Plat System Services Inc
12450 Wayzata Blvd #108
Minnetonka, MN 55305-1926
612-544-0012; Fax: 612-544-0617
www.platsystems.com
Founded: 1961
Clientele Restrictions: Casual requesters permitted
Products & Information Categories:
Proprietary Databases or Gateways:
Database Name: System90, PID Directory
Real Estate/Assessor (MN- Minneapolis, St. Paul)

Database Name: PropertyInfoNet™
Addresses/Real Estate/Assessor (MN-Minneapolis and St Paul)
Special Distribution Methods to Client: Dial-Up (Other than Internet), Disk, Internet, Lists/Labels,
Publication/Directory
Plat System Services has a variety of services available including online services updated weekly, PID directories published annually, commercial sold reports monthly, residential sold reports monthly, custom reports updated weekly, and other monthly reports such as contract for deeds, and commercial buyers and sellers reports. They also offer mailing lists and labels, diskettes updated weekly, printed PLAT maps and PLAT books updated semi-annually. They provide computerized county plat maps.

Professional Services Bureau
315 S College #245
Lafayette, LA 70503
800-960-2214, 337-234-9933; Fax: 337-235-5318
www.tenstarcorporation.com
tenstarco@aol.com
Branch Offices:
Baton Rouge, LA, 800-864-5154; Fax: 225-273-8987
Jackson, MS, 800-864-5154; Fax: 225-273-8987
New Orleans, LA, 800-864-5154; Fax: 504-524-9727
Parent Company: Tenstar Corporation
Founded: 1989
Memberships: ION, NAIS, NAPPS, NPRRA, ACA,
Clientele Restrictions: Casual requesters permitted

Products & Information Categories:

General: Bankruptcy (LA, MS)

Proprietary Databases or Gateways:
Database Name: PSB Database
Addresses/Telephone Numbers, Credit Information, Social Security (Numbers), Criminal Information (LA)
Special Distribution Methods to Client: Dial-Up (Other than Internet), Disk, E-Mail, Magnetic Tape
Professional Services Bureau and On the Record specialize in research, retrieval, recording, corporate services, notary services, abstracting, process service, litigation support, paralegal services, court reporting, investigations, risk management and claims adjusting, and business office services. All services are statewide. In addition to the offices listed above, they have offices in Tupelo, MS. All 64 Louisiana parishes can be researched in about 48 hours; about 72 hours for Mississippi.

Property Data Center Inc

7100 E Bellevue #110
Greenwood Village, CO 80111
303-850-9586; Fax: 303-850-9637
www.pdclane.net
Founded: 1984
Memberships: NPRRA, REIPA, DMA, NAR,
Clientele Restrictions: Casual requesters permitted
Products & Information Categories:

Proprietary Databases or Gateways:
Database Name: Real Property Assessments, Taxes
Real Estate/Assessor (CO)

Database Name: Owner Phone Numbers
Addresses/Telephone Numbers (CO)

Special Distribution Methods to Client: Disk, Internet, Lists/Labels
Property Data Center's PDC database includes more than two million real property ownership and deed transfer records for the metro Denver area, plus counties of Adams, Arapahoe, Boulder,Clear Creek, Denver, Douglas, El Paso, Eagle, Elbert, Jefferson, Larimer, Mesa, Pitkin, Pueblo, Summit, Weld. Customized databases are accessible by owner, location, and indicators such as property value. They specialize in lender marketing data, new owners, sold comparables, mapping data and direct mail lists.

PROTEC

PO Box 54866
Cincinnati, OH 45254
800-543-7651, 513-528-4400; Fax: 513-528-4402
procaq007@fuse.net
Branch Offices:
Indianapolis, IN, 317-632-4264; Fax:
Cold Springs, KY, 999-241-2992; Fax:
Parent Company: World Search Group, Inc
Founded: 1964
Memberships: ACFE, EPIC, ICA, NCISS, WAD,
Clientele Restrictions: Casual requesters permitted
Products & Information Categories:

General: Credit Information (US)

Proprietary Databases or Gateways:
Database Name: Consta-Trac
Addresses/Telephone Numbers (US)
Special Distribution Methods to Client: Dial-Up (Other than Internet), Software

PROTEC has 35 years of concurrent exposure to the information highway, beginning its database system in 1979 using its own information. Since that beginning, they have remained unique in responsible information gathering, being useful in fraud detection and factual data gathering. Their newest and most successful database is "CONSTRA-TRAC" - a master compilation of over 700 record systems and special use cross-check histories from individuals, businesses, societies, and public record data.

Public Data Corporation

38 East 29th St
New York, NY 10016
212-519-3063; Fax: 212-519-3067
www.pdcny.com
Founded: 1988
Clientele Restrictions: Casual requesters permitted
Products & Information Categories:
General: Bankruptcy (NY)

Proprietary Databases or Gateways:
Database Name: Public Data
Real Estate/Assessor, Environmental, Litigation/Judgments/Tax Liens and Uniform Commercial Code (NY)
Special Distribution Methods to Client: Disk, Magnetic Tape
PDC maintains an online database of 60 million NYC real estate and lien records which are updated daily. Record include deed and mortgage recordings, bankruptcy judgments, federal tax liens and UCC filings. Searches can be ordered and received by e-mail thru the company's web site at www.pdcny.com.

Public Record Research Library

1971 E 5th Street #101
Tempe, AZ 85281
800-929-3811, 480-829-7475
www.brbpub.com
brb@brbpub.com
Parent Company: BRB Publications Inc
Founded: 1989
Memberships: PRRN, AIIP, AALL, SIIA,
Clientele Restrictions: Casual requesters permitted
Products & Information Categories:
Proprietary Databases or Gateways:
Database Name: PRRS
Addresses/Telephone Numbers, Legislation/Regulations (US)
Special Distribution Methods to Client: CD-ROM, Database, Disk, Internet, Lists/Labels, Publication/Directory
The Public Record Research Library is a series of in-depth databases formatted into books, CDs and online. BRB is recognized as the nation's leading research and reference publisher of public record related information. The principals of the parent company are directors of the Public Record Retriever Network, the nation's largest organization of public record professionals. Over 26,000 government and private enterprises are analyzed in-depth regarding regulations and access of public records and public information. The Public Record Research System (PRRS) is available on CD, the Internet and as a customized database.

Publook Information Service

PO Box 450
Worthington, OH 43085-0450
877-478-2566, 740-928-2035; Fax: 740-928-2036
http://publook.com
mail@publook.com
Founded: 1998

Clientele Restrictions: Signed Agreement Required
Products & Information Categories:
Proprietary Databases or Gateways:
Database Name: Publook
Uniform Commercial Code, Corporate/Trade Name Data, Addresses/Telephone Numbers, Trademarks/Patents, Licenses/Registrations/Permits (OH)
Special Distribution Methods to Client: Dial-Up (Other than Internet), E-Mail
Publook.com features immediate Internet web access to its proprietary databases of Ohio Secretary of State corporations, trade names, trademarks and UCC filings information. Search corporation, debtor names by keywords, search by debtor address, secured party name, secured party address, filing number. Search corporations by agent/business address, agent/business associate name, charter number. Information is updated weekly. No subscription fees, no charge if no hits, pay a flat fee per search that hits results.

QPAT
8000 Westpark Dr
McLean, VA 22102
800-326-1710, 703-442-0900; Fax: 703-893-5632
www.qpat.com
help@questal.orbit.com
Branch Offices:
Paris, FR, 33 (0)1 55 04 52 00; Fax:
Parent Company: Questal Orbit-France Telecom Group
Clientele Restrictions: License Agreement Required
Products & Information Categories:
Special Distribution Methods to Client: Dial-Up (Other than Internet), Internet
Qpat-WW has the full text of all US patents since 01/01/74, along with most European patents since 1987. Access is available through a subscription service.

QuickInfo.net Information Services
1033 Walnut #200
Boulder, CO 80302
888-259-6173, 303-381-2260; Fax: 303-381-2279
www.quickinfo.net
info@quickinfo.net
Founded: 1995
Clientele Restrictions: Signed Agreement Required
Products & Information Categories:
Proprietary Databases or Gateways:
Database Name: QuickInfo.net
Voter Registration (AK, AR, CO, DE, GA, KS, MI, NV, OH, OK, TX, UT)

Database Name: QuickInfo.net
Corporate/Trade Name Data (AZ, AR, GA, ID, NV, NM, OR, TX, UT, WY)

Database Name: QuickInfo.net
Driver and/or Vehicle (FL, ID, IA, LA, ME, MN, MS, MO, NC, OR, SD, TX, UT, WV, WI, WY)

Database Name: QuickInfo.net
Real Estate/Assessor (FL, ID, IA, LA, MN, MS, MO, NV, NC, OR, TX, UT, WI, WY)

Database Name: QuickInfo.net
Licenses/Registrations/Permits (FL, ID, IA, LA, MN, MS, MO, NV, NC, OR, TX, UT, WI, WY)

Database Name: QuickInfo.net
Vital Records (CO, NV, TX)
Special Distribution Methods to Client: CD-ROM, Internet

QuickInfo.Net is a governmental and business network for licensed professionals with a need for "highly searchable" access to critical public and proprietary information. The password-protected network takes you to county courthouses, state agencies, federal archives. Your agency or company will have easy, affordable and expert access to hundreds of millions of public records. Also, QuickInfo.Net is a leader in expanding the number of databases available to the public. Their databases are "word-indexed" to assure you're getting the best information. CD-Rom products available for some Colorado, Georgia and limited Southwestern states records.

RC Information Brokers

PO Box 1114
Framingham, MA 01701-0206
508-651-1126; Fax: 508-657-2414
psconnor@gis.net
Clientele Restrictions: Casual requesters permitted
Products & Information Categories:
General: Addresses/Telephone Numbers (US)

Proprietary Databases or Gateways:
Database Name: MassData
Addresses/Telephone Numbers and Vital Records (MA)
Special Distribution Methods to Client: Disk, E-Mail, Internet
RC Information Brokers provide "critical information support" to attorneys, licensed private investigators and other professionals. RCIB specializes in supporting attorneys seeking information on individuals for litigation, credit checks, internal financial investigations and background checks. Information support is also available for major financial centers outside the US, especially London. Specific proprietary databases include "MassData" compiled from various databases archived over the past 22 years on current and previous residents of Massachusetts. Turnaround time depends on specific needs and caseload. Locating Massachusetts individuals past and present including adoption cases is their specialty.

Real Estate Guide, The

PO Box 338
Ravena, NY 12143
800-345-3822
www.eguides.com
Parent Company: Ernst Publishing Company, LLC
Founded: 1995
Memberships: SIIA, REIPA, Joint Task Force,
Clientele Restrictions: None reported
Products & Information Categories:
Proprietary Databases or Gateways:
Database Name: Real Estate Filing Guide
Real Estate/Assessor (US)
Special Distribution Methods to Client: CD-ROM, Database, Internet, Publication/Directory
The Real Estate Recording Guide is recognized as the nation's leading reference service used by real estate documentation specialists for the purpose of accurately recording those documents in any of the 3,600 county recording offices nationwide. It is available in print, Internet and CD-ROM. Firms wishing to integrate this information with internal documentation systems may license the underlying databases. Ernst Publishing also publishes The UCC Filing Guide, The National Release Guide and The UCC Revised Article 9 Alert.

Record Information Services Inc

PO Box 894
Elburn, IL 60119
630-365-6490; Fax: 630-365-6524
www.public-record.com

jmetcalf@public-record.com
Founded: 1993
Clientele Restrictions: Casual requesters permitted
Products & Information Categories:
General: Uniform Commercial Code (IL)

Proprietary Databases or Gateways:
Database Name: IL Records
Litigation/Judgments/Tax Liens (IL)

Database Name: Bankruptcies
Bankruptcy (IL)

Database Name: Business Licenses, News Incorporations
Licenses/Registrations/Permits (IL)

Database Name: New Homeowners
Real Estate/Assessor (IL)

Special Distribution Methods to Client: Disk, E-Mail, Internet, Lists/Labels, Software
Record Information Services provides complete and timely public record data that is delivered through state-of-the-art technology. Custom reports are available upon request. They also provide local document retrieval in Northeast Illinois counties.

Richland County Abstract Co

POB 910
Wahpeton, ND 58074-0910
701-642-3781; Fax: 701-642-3852
Founded: 1922
Memberships: ALTA, MLTA, NDLTA,
Clientele Restrictions: Casual requesters permitted
Products & Information Categories:
General: Real Estate/Assessor (MN, ND)

Proprietary Databases or Gateways:
Database Name: Judgment & Tax Liens
Litigation/Judgments/Tax Liens (MN, ND)

Special Distribution Methods to Client: Disk
Richland County Abstract specializes in providing real estate information for the states of Minnesota and North Dakota.

San Diego Daily Transcript/San Diego Source

2131 Third Ave
San Diego, CA 92101
800-697-6397, 619-232-4381; Fax: 619-236-8126
www.sddt.com/notices/
leeanne.wonnacott@sddt.com
Clientele Restrictions: Casual requesters permitted
Products & Information Categories:

Proprietary Databases or Gateways:
Database Name: San Diego Source
Litigation/Judgments/Tax Liens and Uniform Commercial Code (CA)

Gateway Name: US Bankruptcy Court Filings
Bankruptcy (US)

Special Distribution Methods to Client: Internet
The San Diego Source is a leading California web site for public record information and business data. Site visitors can perform customized searches on one or more than fifteen databases. Links with Transcripts Online are provided.

SEAFAX Inc

PO Box 15340
Portland, ME 04112-5340
800-777-3533, 207-773-3533; Fax: 207-773-9564
www.seafax.com
Founded: 1985
Clientele Restrictions: Casual requesters permitted

Products & Information Categories:

General: Legislation/Regulation (US)

Proprietary Databases or Gateways:
Database Name: Business Reports
Credit Information (US)

Special Distribution Methods to Client: Internet

Seafax is the leading source of food industry-specific information, thus a valuable credit reporting resource to manage your exposure. Using Seafax, decision-makers access timely and accurate information 24/7. More than 1200 food producers, processors and distributors use Seafax services to minimize rick, save time and maximize profits using products like Supersearch to perform company, date or geography searches, or business report services like Seafax Credit Appraisal & Risk Index, bank & trade references, and unique financial data. Their Bankruptcy Creditor Index allow the identification of unsecured creditors of bankruptcies, receiverships and assignments. Other products include Agriwire and Agriscan Bulletin.

Search Company of North Dakota LLC

1008 E Capitol Ave
Bismarck, ND 58501-1930
701-258-5375; Fax: 701-258-5375
mkautzma@btigate.com
Founded: 1984
Memberships: PRRN,
Clientele Restrictions: Casual requesters permitted

Products & Information Categories:

Proprietary Databases or Gateways:
Database Name: North Dakota Records
Addresses/Telephone Numbers, Litigation/Judgments/Tax Liens, Licenses/Registrations/Permits, Criminal Information
    and Bankruptcy (ND)
Database Name: ND UCC
Uniform Commercial Code (ND)

Special Distribution Methods to Client: E-Mail, Lists/Labels

They will provide any and all city, county, state, or federal record searching or filing in North Dakota. Over 15 years of experience in all aspects of public record searching, retrieval, or filing.

Search Network Ltd

Two Corporate Place #210
1501 42nd St
West Des Moines, IA 50266-1005
800-383-5050, 515-223-1153
http://searchnetworkltd.com
lharken@searchnetworkltd.com
Branch Offices:
Topeka, KS, 800-338-3618; Fax: 785-235-5788
Founded: 1965
Memberships: NPRRA, PRRN,

Clientele Restrictions: Casual requesters permitted
Products & Information Categories:
General: Litigation/Judgments/Tax Liens (US, IA, KS)

Proprietary Databases or Gateways:
Database Name: Search Network
Uniform Commercial Code (IA, KS)
Special Distribution Methods to Client: Dial-Up (Other than Internet), Lists/Labels, Microfilm/Microfiche, Publication/Directory
In business since 1965, Search Network provides full service public record search information. The company maintains an on-site UCC database for Iowa and Kansas. Same day searches and copies are available as well as personal filing service for UCC and corporate documents. Since 1980, they have offered direct online access to their databases of UCC filing/records information in Iowa and Kansas

Security Search & Abstract Co
926 Pine St
Philadelphia, PA 19107
800-345-9494, 215-592-0660
www.securitysearchabstract.com
Founded: 1961
Clientele Restrictions: None reported
Products & Information Categories:
General: Bankruptcy (US, PA, NJ)

Proprietary Databases or Gateways:
Database Name: Security Search
Real Estate (PA)

Special Distribution Methods to Client:
Security Search & Abstract Co., Inc. provides comprehensive searches in Pennsylvania, New Jersey and Delaware. Security Search & Abstract Co., Inc. also provides title insurance in Pennsylvania and New Jersey. They have their own in-house title plant, housing the most complete collection of histories and duplicate records for Philadelphia-area properties dating back to 1950.

Silver Plume
4775 Walnut St #2B
Boulder, CO 80301
800-677-4442, 303-444-0695; Fax: 303-449-1199
www.silverplume.com
sales@silverplume.com
Founded: 1989
Clientele Restrictions: Signed Agreement Required
Products & Information Categories:
General: SEC/Other Financial (US)

Proprietary Databases or Gateways:
Database Name: Insurance Industry Rates, Forms and Manuals
Legislation/Regulations (US)
Special Distribution Methods to Client: CD-ROM, Internet, Magnetic Tape
Silver Plume is the leading provider of insurance-related reference and research material. Receive material in one subscription on CD-Rom or online.

SKLD Information Services LLC

720 S Colorado Blvd #1000N
Denver, CO 80246
800-727-6358, 303-820-0888; Fax: 303-260-6391
www.skld.com
sales@skld.com
Founded: 1961
Memberships: ATLA, DMA, National Association of Mortgage Brokers,
Clientele Restrictions: Casual requesters permitted but Agreement Required

Products & Information Categories:

General: Bankruptcy (CO)

Proprietary Databases or Gateways:
Database Name: New Homeowners List
Real Estate/Assessor (CO-13 counties)

Database Name: Deeds, Loan Activity, Notice of Demand
Real Estate/Assessor (CO-13 counties)

Special Distribution Methods to Client: Database, Disk, Magnetic Tape
SKLD Information Services maintains a complete database of public record information from documents recorded in 14 County Recorder offices in Colorado since 1990. Information is available to enhance existing databases, create new homeowner mailing lists, report on real estate loan transaction information, and mortgage marketing data. With archived county recorded documents and plat maps in their in-house microfilm library, SKLD can provide quick turnaround time for document and plat map retrieval. Reports available include: real estate loan activity reports, warranty deed/trust deed match, trust deed report, owner carry reports, notice of election and demand, and new homeowners lists.

Software Computer Group Inc

PO Box 3042
Charleston, WV 25331-3042
800-795-8543, 304-343-6480
www.swcg-inc.com
info@swcg-inc.com
Founded: 1975
Clientele Restrictions: Casual requesters permitted

Products & Information Categories:

Proprietary Databases or Gateways:
Gateway Name: Circuit Express
Criminal Information, Litigation/judgments/Tax Liens (WV)
Special Distribution Methods to Client: Dial-Up (Other than Internet), Internet
The Circuit Express product brings civil and criminal public information records from the Circuit Courts in West Virginia to you online. You can locate cases by name or case filing type. Not all counties are available. Fees include a sign-up fee, and monthly fee with connect charges. There is an additional system for magistrate courts; however, this service is only available to government agencies.

Southeastern Public Records Inc.

208 W Chicago Rd #4
Sturgis, MI 49091
616-659-8131; Fax: 616-659-1169
www.instantimpact.com/spr
jimbarfield@msn.com
Founded: 1993
Clientele Restrictions: Casual requesters permitted

Products & Information Categories:

General: Credit Information (MI, GA)

Proprietary Databases or Gateways:
Database Name: Michigan/Georgia Public Records
Addresses/Telephone Numbers, Bankruptcy, Litigation/Judgments/Tax Liens (MI)

Special Distribution Methods to Client: CD-ROM, Database, Dial-Up (Other than Internet), Disk, E-Mail, Internet, Magnetic Tape, Software

Southeastern Public Records can deliver bulk data up to 3,000,000 records within 48 hours of verifying customer specifications. Smaller batches of data available in 1 to 48 hours if needed. Verification of any judgment, tax lien, or bankruptcy at its original place of filing in all covered areas. All data is recorded from its original source by one of our certified collectors on software developed by us for that particular purpose. Our databases contain 15 years of historical data in Michigan and 10 years in Georgia. Our key personnel include: a full time onsite Internet/web specialist; full time onsite database development specialists; several full time personnel with extensive knowledge of legal recording, mortgages, major credit bureaus, and all civil public records at all levels.

State Net

2101 K Street
Sacramento, CA 95816
916-444-0840; Fax: 916-446-5369
www.statenet.com

Branch Offices:
Washington, DC, 202-638-7999; Fax: 202-638-7291
Tallahassee, FL, 850-205-7710; Fax: 850-205-7714
Springfield, IL, 217-522-1188; Fax: 217-522-1195

Founded: 1978

Clientele Restrictions: Casual requesters permitted

Products & Information Categories:

Proprietary Databases or Gateways:
Database Name: State Net
Legislation/Regulations (US)

Special Distribution Methods to Client: Dial-Up (Other than Internet), Publication/Directory

State Net delivers vital data, legislative intelligence and in-depth reporting for people who care about the actions of government. Based in Sacramento, CA, they were created by legislative experts who invented a computerized tracking system that has evolved into what they feel is the nation's leading source of legislative and regulatory information. State net monitors 100% of all pending bills and regulations in the 50 states and Congress. Successful government affairs managers from small state associations to giant Fortune 500 companies rely on them to report activity on their issues in the 50 states. Backed by a 29-year commitment to providing fast, accurate legislative information. State Net publishes a variety of online and print publications.

Superior Information Services LLC

300 Phillips Blvd #500
Trenton, NJ 08618-1427
800-848-0489, 609-883-7000
www.superiorinfo.com
lmartin@superiorinfo.com

Founded: 1987

Memberships: NPRRA, ICA, AALL, SLA, PRRN,

Clientele Restrictions: None reported

Products & Information Categories:

Proprietary Databases or Gateways:
Database Name: Superior Online

Litigation/Judgments/Tax Liens and Bankruptcy (DC, DE, MD, NC, NJ, NY, PA, VA)

Database Name: Corporate Files
Corporate/Trade Name Data (NY, PA, NJ)

Database Name: UCC Files
Uniform Commercial Code (PA, NJ)

Database Name: Real Estate Files
Real Estate/Assessor (NY (NYC), NJ)

Special Distribution Methods to Client: Dial-Up (Other than Internet)

Superior Information Services provides accurate, reliable and comprehensive information to a wide variety of clients including attorneys, investigators, financial institutions, financial underwriters, employment agencies, insurance claims departments, leasing companies, and government agencies. Their proprietary database searches all counties in the following states: NY, NJ, PA, DE, MD, DC, VA and NC. Their search engine uncovers filings under similar/misspelled names. Superior Information Services is the leading supplier of public record information in the Mid-Atlantic region.

Tax Analysts

6830 N Fairfax Dr
Arlington, VA 22213
800-955-3444, 703-533-4400; Fax: 703-533-4444
www.tax.org
cserve@tax.org
Founded: 1970
Clientele Restrictions: Casual requesters permitted

Products & Information Categories:

General: Associations/Trade Groups (US)

Proprietary Databases or Gateways:

Database Name: Exempt Organization Master List
Corporate/Trade Name Data (US)

Database Name: The Tax Directory
Addresses/Telephone Numbers (US)

Database Name: The OneDisc,TAXBASE
Legislation/Regulations (US)

Database Name: TAXBASE, The Ratx Directory
Foreign Country Information ()

Special Distribution Methods to Client: CD-ROM, Disk, Internet, Publication/Directory

Tax Analysts is a nonprofit organization dedicated to providing timely, comprehensive information to tax professionals at a reasonable cost. They are the leading electronic publisher of tax information. The Exempt Organization Master List contains information about more than 1.1 million not-for-profit organizations registered with the federal government. The Tax Directory contains information about 14,000 federal tax officials, 9000 private tax professionals and 8000 corporate tax professionals. Online databases include daily federal, state and international tax information as well as complete research libraries. Some products are available on DIALOG & LEXIS.

Telebase

1150 First Ave #820
King of Prussia, PA 19406
800-220-4664, 610-945-2420; Fax: 610-945-2460
www.telebase.com
Parent Company: Office Com Inc.
Founded: 1984
Memberships: SPA/IIA,
Clientele Restrictions: Casual requesters permitted

Products & Information Categories:

Proprietary Databases or Gateways:
Gateway Name: Brainwave, I-Quest
Corporate/Trade Name Data, Addresses/Telephone Numbers, News/Current Events, Credit Information, Trademarks, SEC/Other Financial,Foreign Country Information (US)
Gateway Name: LEXIS-NEXIS CaseLaw @AOL
Litigation/Judgments/Tax Liens (US)
Gateway Name: Dun & Bradstreet @ AOL
Credit Information, Addresses/Telephone Numbers (US)
Special Distribution Methods to Client: Dial-Up (Other than Internet), Gateway via Another Online Service, Internet
Telebase's Information Services are designed for people with little or no online searching experience and provide easy access to business information for sales prospecting, market analysis, competitive intelligence, product development, and other research. Several thousand sources, from over 450 databases, are available including credit reports, financial reports, company directories, magazines, newspapers, newswires, industry newsletters, etc. For a list of distribution partners visit www.telebase.com.

Texas Driving Record Express Service
7809 Easton / 7399 Gulf Freeway Plaza
Houston, TX 77017
800-671-2287, 713-641-5252
Parent Company: Ernest L Calderon dba CATS
Founded: 1992
Clientele Restrictions: License Agreement Required
Products & Information Categories:
General: Driver and/or Vehicle (TX)
Proprietary Databases or Gateways:
Gateway Name: Certified MVRs
Driver and/or Vehicle (TX)
Special Distribution Methods to Client:
Texas Driving Records Express provides driving records statewide in 1-7 days, also original/state-certified documents for ticket elimination, restoration of Texas driving privileges from TX Dept of Public Safety, employment requirements, current addresses.

TEXSEARCH
3529 Bennett Lane
Sherman, TX 75092
903-786-4636; Fax: 903-786-4636
www.texsearch.com
info@texsearch.com
Founded: 1998
Memberships: NAIS, PRRN, NNIC, TALI, ACI,
Clientele Restrictions: Casual requesters permitted
Products & Information Categories:
General: Addresses/Telephone Numbers (TX)
Special Distribution Methods to Client: E-Mail
TEXSEARCH, insured and licensed as a investigative company, specializes in public record searches in any county in Texas at the local, state and federal level. Services include court record searches/document retrieval, real estate, property ownership, asset/lien, UCC, motor vehicle ownership, credit reports, bankruptcy, employment or educational verification and driving records. TexSearch utilizes online records directly with the courts and in-house searches within Texas. The priority is to provide accurate information in an expedient, cost-effective manner. Their unique sliding scale offers volume discounts and package prices designed to meet specific needs. Results within 24 hours or less.

The Search Company Inc
1410-439 University Ave
Toronto, ON M5G 1Y8
800-396-8241, 416-979-5858
www.thesearchcompany.com
info@thesearchcompany.com
Founded: 1993
Clientele Restrictions: Must be ongoing account
Products & Information Categories:
General: Foreign Country Information (Canada)

Proprietary Databases or Gateways:
Database Name: Property Ownership & Tenant Data
Real Estate/Assessor (Canada)

Special Distribution Methods to Client: Dial-Up (Other than Internet), E-Mail, Software
The Search Company covers 2 distinct markets: 1) Canada wide public record retrieval; 2) Litigation related asset and corporate background reporting with or without a full narrative report, with analysis and opinion regarding the advisability of litigation.

The Todd Wiegele Research Co Inc
10425 W North Ave #331
Wauwatosa, WI 53226
800-754-7800, 414-607-0700; Fax: 414-607-0800
www.execpc.com/~research/
research@execpc.com
Founded: 1994
Memberships: PRRN, NACM, ANA, BHI, AWI, NAWCC
Clientele Restrictions: Casual requesters permitted
Products & Information Categories:
General: Real Estate/Assessor (US)

Proprietary Databases or Gateways:
Database Name: FASTRACT
Real Estate/Assessor (WI)

Special Distribution Methods to Client: Disk, Magnetic Tape, Microfilm/Microfiche
The Todd Wiegele Research Co is an agent for Old Republic National Title Insurance and specializes in mortgage closing services (within a 150-mile radius) and providing national title companies with searches in Milwaukee and Waukesha Counties. They have a centrally-located office for title closings and are fully covered by E&O insurance. Occupying more space in the Milwaukee County Courthouse than any other company, they have a next business day turnaround time and are located also on the Internet at www.currentowner.com. Other company names are Wiegele Title & Closing also CurrentOwner.com.

Thomas Legislative Information
101 Independence S.E.
Washington, DC 20540

http://thomas.loc.gov
thomas@loc.gov
Parent Company: Library of Congress
Products & Information Categories:
Proprietary Databases or Gateways:
Database Name: Thomas

Legislation/Regulation (US)
Special Distribution Methods to Client: Internet
Although technically a government site, we have posted in this section due to the tremendous information available to the public. Free Internet access to legislative information (including bill summary, status, and text), congressional record, and committee information. A giant plus is the ability to search by bill number or by key word/phrase.

Thomson & Thomson
500 Victory Rd
North Quincy, MA 02171-3145
800-692-8833, 617-479-1600
www.thomson-thomson.com
john.giaquinto@t-t.com
Branch Offices:
Antwerp, Belgium, 323-220-7211; Fax:
Montreal, Quebec, CANADA, 800-561-6240; Fax: 514-393-3854
Parent Company: The Thomson Corporation
Founded: 1922
Memberships: INTA, SIIA, AALL,
Clientele Restrictions: Casual requesters permitted
Products & Information Categories:
General: Litigation/Judgments/Tax Liens (US)
Proprietary Databases or Gateways:
Database Name: TRADEMARKSCAN
Trademarks and Foreign Country Information (US, Itl)

Database Name: Worldwide Domain
Foreign Country Information (US, Itl)

Gateway Name: Site Comber
Patents (US)

Database Name: US Full Trademark Search, Site Comber
Trademarks (US)

Database Name: US Full Copyright Search
Licenses/Registrations/Permits (US)

Database Name: US Title Availability Search
Vital Records (US)

Database Name: The deForest Report for Script Clearance
Vital Records (US)

Special Distribution Methods to Client: CD-ROM, Dial-Up (Other than Internet), Internet
Thomson & Thomson is a world leader in trademark, copyright and script clearance services, with over 75 years of experience and offices in the US, Canada, Europe and Japan. Accessing trademark records from more than 200 countries, T&T analysts provide reports to help clients determine if their proposed trademarks are available for use. Clients can perform their own trademark searches via Thomson & Thomson's TRADEMARKSCAN online databases. Thomson & Thomson also provides a complete offering of equally impressive copyright, title and script clearance services to help manage and protect your intellectual property assets.

TML Information Services Inc
116-55 Queens Blvd
Forest Hills, NY 11375
800-743-7891, 718-793-3737; Fax: 718-544-2853
www.tml.com
edarmody@tml.com
Founded: 1985

Memberships: AAMVA, IIAA, NAPIA, NETS,
Clientele Restrictions: Signed agreement required, must be ongoing account
Products & Information Categories:
Proprietary Databases or Gateways:
Gateway Name: Auto-Search
Driver and/or Vehicle (AL, AZ, CT, DC, FL, ID, IN, KS, KY, LA, MA, MI, MN, MS, NC, ND, NE, NH, NJ, NY, OH, SC, VA, WI, WV)
Gateway Name: Title File
Driver and/or Vehicle (AL, FL, SD)
Gateway Name: Driver Check
Driver and/or Vehicle (AL, AZ, CA, CT, FL, ID, KS, LA, MD, MI, MN, NE, NH, NY, NC, OH, PA, SC, VA, WV)
Gateway Name: Driving Records
Driver and/or Vehicle (US)
Special Distribution Methods to Client: Dial-Up (Other than Internet), Internet
TML Information Services specializes in providing access to motor vehicle information in an online, real-time environment. Their standardization format enables TML to offer several unique automated applications for instant access to multiple states' driver and vehicle information, including a touch-tone fax-on-demand service and a rule-based decision processing service for driver qualification for car rental. TML has online access to more than 200 million driver and vehicle records in more than 30 states and expects to add several more states soon. No third party use; professional license required.

tnrealestate.com KAL Software
PO Box 1375
Murfreesboro, TN 37133
615-907-8231
www.tnrealestate.com
sales@tnrealestate.com
Parent Company: Kal Software LLC
Founded: 1996
Clientele Restrictions: Casual requesters permitted
Products & Information Categories:
Proprietary Databases or Gateways:
Database Name: Tennessee Real Estate Data
Real Estate/Assessor (TN)
Special Distribution Methods to Client: Dial-Up (Other than Internet), Internet
Tnrealestate.com provides free searches to Tennessee real estate for 91 of 94 counties. Records reflect the tax assessor files and sales files.

Trademark Register, The
2100 National Press Building
Washington, DC 20045
202-347-2138; Fax: 202-347-4408
www.trademarkregister.com/
trademarks@erols.com
Memberships: ITA, SLA, NPC,
Products & Information Categories:
Proprietary Databases or Gateways:
Database Name: The Trademark Register
Trademarks (US)
Special Distribution Methods to Client: Internet, Publication/Directory

The Trademark Register is an annual volume consisting of over 1 million active trademarks in effect with the U.S. Patent and Trademark Office from 1884 to 2001. It was first published in 1958 when it contained approximately 200,000 registered trademarks. 43Rd edition has over 1 million active trademarks. Each trademark entry gives the date of registration or filling date, international class, registration or serial number. A daily subscription is offered for Internet access.

Trans Union

PO Box 2000
Chester, PA 19022
800-888-4213
www.transunion.com
Founded: 1969
Memberships: SIIA,
Clientele Restrictions: Signed agreement required, must be ongoing account

Products & Information Categories:

Proprietary Databases or Gateways:
Database Name: Trans Union Credit Data
Credit Information (US)

Special Distribution Methods to Client: Dial-Up (Other than Internet), Software

Trans Union is a primary source of credit information and offers risk and portfolio management services. They serve a broad range of industries that routinely evaluate credit risk or verify information about their customers. Their customers include financial and banking services, insurance agencies, retailers, collection agencies, communication and energy companies, and hospitals. They have strong relationships with every large and most medium and small credit grantors throughout the nation. Trans Union operates nationwide through a network of our own offices and independent credit bureaus. They also have many subsidiaries and divisions in the U.S. and abroad. The needs and desires of our customers and consumers directly shape Trans Union's products and services design. They have a competitive stance based on the highest levels of quality coupled with unmatched levels of service.

UCC Direct Services - AccuSearch Inc

PO Box 3248
2727 Allen Parkway, 10th Fl
Houston, TX 77253-3248
800-833-5778, 713-864-7639; Fax: 713-831-9891
www.accusearchinc.com
info@uccdirect.com
Branch Offices:
Sacramento, CA, 888-863-9241; Fax: 916-492-6655
Austin, TX, 800-884-0185; Fax: 512-323-9102
Chicago, IL, 847-853-0892; Fax: 847-853-0893
Founded: 1985
Memberships: NPRRA,
Clientele Restrictions: License required

Products & Information Categories:

General: Litigation/Judgments/Tax Liens (CA, IL, TX)

Proprietary Databases or Gateways:
Database Name: AccuSearch
Corporate/Trade Name, Uniform Commercial Code (TX,CA,PA,IL,WA,OH,OR,MO)

Database Name: AccuSearch
Bankruptcy (CA,IL,TX)

Special Distribution Methods to Client: Dial-Up (Other than Internet), Internet

UCC Direct - formerly AccuSearch - provides immediate access to UCC, corporate, charter, real property and bankruptcy search services via the Internet. Instantaneous access is available for each online database listed. Each online or over-the-phone search is followed by same-day mailing or faxing of the search report. They also performs any of the above searches for any county or state nationwide. Their Direct Access system allows multi-page, formatted reports which eliminates print screens, and selective ordering of UCC copies. AccuFile UCC Filing and & Portfolio Managemnet allows UCC filing electronically.

UCC Guide Inc, The
416 Broad St
Nevada City, CA 95959
800-345-3822
www.eguides.com
lrcanier@onemain.com
Parent Company: Ernst Publishing Company, LLC
Founded: 1992
Memberships: AIIP, SIIA, NPRRA,
Clientele Restrictions: None reported
Products & Information Categories:
Proprietary Databases or Gateways:
Database Name: Uniform Commercial Code Filing Guide
Uniform Commercial Code Filing Guide (US)
Special Distribution Methods to Client: CD-ROM, Database, Internet, Publication/Directory
The Uniform Comemrcial Code Filing Guide™ is a practical "How to" reference for the preparation, filing and searching of Article 9 Financing Statements nationwide. This Guide provides information re: fees, forms, facts for all 4,316 filing jurisidictions and is designed for the high-volume multi-juridiction filer. Included are sections hosting the Model Act, Filing Fundamentals, Purchase Money Secured Interest snd Definitions. Subscription is annual with quarterly updates; a newsletter is provided in non-updating months. The new Revised Article 9 Alert will assist filers and searchers to function in the new Revision environment. They also publish the Real Estate Recording Guide and National Release Guide and offers a database and web-based product, National Online Mortgage Assistance Database Program.

UCC Retrievals
7288-A Hanover Green Dr
Mechanicsville, VA 23111
804-559-5919; Fax: 804-559-5920
www.uccretrievals.com
mara-beth@uccretrievals.com
Founded: 1988
Memberships: NPRRA, PRRN,
Clientele Restrictions: Casual requesters permitted
Products & Information Categories:
General: Bankruptcy (VA)
Proprietary Databases or Gateways:
Database Name: Federal Tax Liens and UCCs
Litigation/judgments/Tax Liens and Uniform Commercial Code (VA)
Special Distribution Methods to Client:
UCC Retrievals specializes in searching UCC and federal tax liens in Virginia. They also file motor vehicle records, do corporate filings and retrievals, and assist with litigation. Their turnaround time is 24-48 hours.

UMI - Bell & Howell Information & Learning
PO Box 1346
Ann Arbor, MI 48106-1346
734-761-4700, 800-521-0600; Fax: 734-975-6486
www.umi.com

info@umi.com
Parent Company: Bell & Howell Inc.
Clientele Restrictions: Casual requesters permitted
Products & Information Categories:
General: News/Current Events (US)

Special Distribution Methods to Client: CD-ROM, Dial-Up (Other than Internet), Microfilm/Microfiche
Bell & Howell Information & Learning - formerly UMI - formerly operated DataTimes and now offers a number of useful electronic and print services with information on business, current events, technology innovations, including graphics, charts, photos. Their products are useful to libraries, researchers, scientists, schools, and competitive intelligence gathering. Products include ProQuest packages (includes newspapers) and IntellX.

Unisearch Inc
1780 Barnes Blvd SW
Tumwater, WA 98512-0410
800-722-0708, 360-956-9500
www.unisearch.com
Branch Offices:
Sacramento, CA, 800-769-1864; Fax: 800-769-1868
Salem, OR, 800-554-3113; Fax: 800-554-3114
St Paul, MN, 800-227-1256; Fax: 800-227-1263
Founded: 1991
Memberships: NPRRA, NRAI, PRRN,
Clientele Restrictions: Casual requesters permitted
Products & Information Categories:
General: Bankruptcy, Litigation/Judgments/Tax Liens (US)

Proprietary Databases or Gateways:
Database Name: WALDO
Uniform Commercial Code (CA, IL, WA, OH, WI)

Special Distribution Methods to Client: Dial-Up (Other than Internet), Internet
Unisearch is online with 40 states' UCC databases, providing instant access to current information available. They maintain a UCC microfilm library of AK, CA, ID, IL, MN, MT, NV, OH, OR, UT, WA, WI. In areas where computer access is not yet available, Unisearch also offers a complete range of corporate services, including Registered Agent service, on a national and international basis. Additional branch offices are in; Lawrence, KS (800-607-7751); Ohio (877-208-7783); and Reno, NV (800-260-1331).

United State Mutual Association
4500 S 129th E. Ave., #200
Tulsa, OK 74134
888-338-8762, 918-280-4088; Fax: 912-828-9141
www.usmutual.com
corporate@usmutual.com
Parent Company: Total Information Services Inc.
Founded: 1996
Memberships: ASIS, SHRM, NRF, NACS,
Clientele Restrictions: Agreement required
Products & Information Categories:
Proprietary Databases or Gateways:
Database Name: Retail Industry Theft Database
Criminal Information, Addresses/Telephone Numbers (US)

Special Distribution Methods to Client: Automated Telephone Look-Up, Dial-Up (Other than Internet), FTP, Gateway via Another Online Service, Internet

USMA provides reports from a mutual and proprietary database containing documented incidents of theft. Applicant searches against this database provides member companies with a powerful tool that helps improve the quality and efficiency of the employment screening process. USMA is the single most comprehensive source of employment screening products for human resource and loss prevention professionals. They provide unique access to background screening for retailers through automated phone, fax, web, dial-up and state-of-the-art call center services.

US Corporate Services

200 Minnesota Bldg, 46 E Fourth St
St Paul, MN 55101
800-327-1886, 651-227-7575
www.uscorpserv.com
info@uscorpserv.com
Branch Offices:
Portland, OR, 877-415-1822; Fax: 503-443-1056
Parent Company: Dolan Media Co
Founded: 1966
Memberships: NPRRA,
Clientele Restrictions: Casual requesters permitted
Products & Information Categories:
General: Bankruptcy (US)

Proprietary Databases or Gateways:
Database Name: MN Secretary of State Records
Corporation/Trade Name Data (MN)

Database Name: WI UCCs
Uniform Commerical Code (WI)

Special Distribution Methods to Client: Dial-Up (Other than Internet), Disk, Lists/Labels, Publication/Directory, Software
US Corporate Services is a full service UCC, tax lien, judgment, litigation and corporate search and filing firm. Their optical image library of Minnesota enables them to provide custom reports to their clients. They have nationwide correspondent relationships. Their turnaround time is 24-72 hours. They will invoice monthly; projects are generally billed by the number of names searched.

US Document Services Inc

PO Box 50486 (2817 Devine St #12)
Columbia, SC 29250
803-254-9193; Fax: 803-771-9905
www.us-doc-services.com
info@us-doc-services.com
Founded: 1990
Memberships: NPRRA, PRRN,
Clientele Restrictions: Casual requesters permitted
Products & Information Categories:
General: Uniform Commercial Code (US, SC, NC)

Proprietary Databases or Gateways:
Database Name: Secretary of State
Corporation/Trade Name Data (NC, SC)
Special Distribution Methods to Client:
US Document Services is a nationwide public record search and document retrieval company specializing in North Carolina and South Carolina. They offer UCC, tax lien, suit and judgment, bankruptcy and asset searches, and provide legal, financial and commercial clients with a wide variety of services including formation, qualification and registrations of corporations, etc. With an in-house South Carolina and North Carolina microfilm and online database,

they provide up-to-date results, with 48-hour turnarounds. They can also provide reports on DMVs, Workers Comp, watercraft and Real Estate transactions.

US SEARCH.com
5401 Beethoven St
Los Angeles, CA 90066
800-877-2410, 310-302-6300; Fax: 310-822-7898
http://1800ussearch.com
corporate@ussearch.com
Founded: 1995
Memberships: PIHRA, SHRM,
Clientele Restrictions: Casual requesters permitted
Products & Information Categories:
General: Addresses/Telephone Numbers (US)
Special Distribution Methods to Client: Dial-Up (Other than Internet), E-Mail
US SEARCH.com is one of the leading public record providers on the Internet. In addition to comprehensive locate and background reports on people and businesses, US SEARCH.com also provides nationwide data on Corporate & Limited Partnerships; Uniform Commerical Code; Employer ID Numbers; Bankruptcies, Liens and Judgments; Death Records; Real Property; Watercraft; Aircraft and Pilots. US SEARCH.com also offers On-Site Civil and Criminal Records Checks.

USADATA.com
292 Madison Ave, 3rd Fl
New York, NY 10017
800-599-5030, 212-326-8760; Fax: 212-679-8507
www.usadata.com
info@usadata.com
Founded: 1995
Clientele Restrictions: Casual requesters permitted
Products & Information Categories:
Proprietary Databases or Gateways:
Gateway Name: Marketing Portal
Corporate/Trade Name Data, Addresses/Telephone Numbers, Real Estate/Assessor (US)
Special Distribution Methods to Client: E-Mail, Lists/Labels, Software
USADATA.com's Marketing Information Portal (www.usadata.com) provides fast, easy access to the information you need to make critical business decisions. They provide mailing lists, research reports, consumer info, and helpful information gathering solutions. They draw data from the top names in syndicated consumer data on both a local and national level, including Mediamark Research Inc (MRI), Scarborough Research, Arbitron, Acxiom, Competitive Media Reporting (CMR) and National Decision Systems (NDS). Marketers, planners and media buyers can order reports on a pay-per-view basis from the website, or subscribe to unlimited Internet access.

Virginia Information Providers Network
1111 East Main Street #901
Richmond, VA 23219
877-482-3468, 804-786-4718; Fax: 804-786-6227
www.vipnet.org
webmaster@vipnet.org
Founded: 1996
Clientele Restrictions: Signed agreement required, must be ongoing account
Products & Information Categories:
General: Associations/Trade Groups (VA)

Proprietary Databases or Gateways:
Gateway Name: VIPNet
Driver and/or Vehicle, Vessels, Legislation/Regulation (VA)
Special Distribution Methods to Client: Internet
The Virginia Information Providers Network was created by the state of Virginia to streamline and enhance the ways in which citizens and businesses access government information. VIPNet premium services includes access to state motor vehicle records, vessel records, bill tracking service for lobbyists.

VISTA Information Solutions
5060 Shoreham Place
San Diego, CA 92122
800-733-7606, 858-450-6100
www.vistainfo.com
Founded: 1989
Memberships: SIIA, ABA,
Clientele Restrictions: None reported
Products & Information Categories:
Proprietary Databases or Gateways:
Database Name: VISTACheck
Environmental, Corporation/Trade Name Data (US)
Special Distribution Methods to Client: CD-ROM, Dial-Up (Other than Internet), Disk, Internet, Lists/Labels, Software
VISTAinfo, based in San Diego with offices in the U.S. and Canada, is an Internet real estate-based information provider to consumers, real estate professionals, environmental engineers, mortgage bankers, insurance, banking and legal industries. VISTAinfo helps its customers determine the desirability, financability, insurability and value of any property anywhere in the U.S. in moments, via the Web. VISTA is a premier provider of environmental risk information software and services and has exclusive endorsements by the American Bankers Association. Their myriad of products provide information to the environmental and insurance underwriting industries to assist with risk management. The VISTA environmental database includes environmental record information from more than 500 state and federal sources, and contains over 10 million records which are geo-coded.

Vital Records Information
Vital records Information

http://vitalrec.com
Corrections@vitalrec.com
Products & Information Categories:
Proprietary Databases or Gateways:
Gateway Name: vitalrec.com
Vital Records, Genealogical Information (US)

Gateway Name: vitalrec.com
Foreign Country Information ()
Special Distribution Methods to Client: Internet
Although primarily a links list, vitalrec.com is a gateway to extensive information, geneology especially.

VitalChek Network
4512 Central Pike
Hermitage, TN 37076
800-255-2414
www.vitalchek.com
vitals.comments@vitalchek.com

Clientele Restrictions: Casual requesters permitted

Products & Information Categories:

Proprietary Databases or Gateways:
Gateway Name: VitalChek
Vital Records (US)

Special Distribution Methods to Client:
VitalChek Network has a sophisticated voice and fax network setup to help people acquire certified copies of birth, death and marriage certificates and other vital records. VitalChek provides a direct access gateway to participating agencies at the state and local level.

West Group

620 Opperman Dr
Eagan, MN 55123
800-328-9352, 651-687-7000; Fax: 651-687-7302
www.westgroup.com
Founded: 1872
Memberships: SIIA,
Clientele Restrictions: Casual requesters permitted

Products & Information Categories:

Proprietary Databases or Gateways:
Database Name: West CD-ROM Libraries
Legislation/Regulations (US)

Database Name: Westlaw
Environmental, Legislation/Regulations, Corporate/Trade Name Data, Uniform Commercial Code (US)

Special Distribution Methods to Client: CD-ROM, Dial-Up (Other than Internet), Internet

West Group is one of the largest providers of information to US legal professionals. West Group includes renowned names such as Barclays, Bancroft Whitney, Clark Boardman Callaghan, Counterpoint, Lawyers Cooperative Publishing, West Publishing and Westlaw. Westlaw is a computer-assisted research service consisting of more than 9,500 legal, financial and news databases, including Dow Jones News/Retrieval. West Group produces a total of more than 3,800 products including 300 CD-ROMs.

Western Regional Data Inc

PO Box 20520
Reno, NV 89515
775-329-9544; Fax: 775-324-1652
wrdi@accutech.com
Founded: 1984
Memberships: NPRRA,
Clientele Restrictions: Casual requesters permitted

Products & Information Categories:

Proprietary Databases or Gateways:
Database Name: WRDI's Lead Focus, Property Search
Real Estate/Assessor (NV)

Special Distribution Methods to Client: CD-ROM, Disk, FTP, Internet, Lists/Labels, Microfilm/Microfiche

Western Regional Data (WDRI) gathers public record information from all 17 counties in Nevada and state agencies, making it available in one online system. The information includes property tax data, building permits, business licenses and other less well known types of public records. They have a new program called "Lead Focus" that makes available targeted mailing list data with more than 35 ways to pinpoint your market.

Westlaw Public Records

P.O. Box 64833 (620 Opperman Dr)
St. Paul, MN 55164
800-328-4880
www.westlaw.com
admin@WESTPUB.COM
Memberships: NPRRA,
Clientele Restrictions: Casual requesters permitted

Products & Information Categories:

General: Driver and/or Vehicle (US)

Proprietary Databases or Gateways:

Database Name: Bankruptcy Records
Bankruptcy (US)

Database Name: Corporations and Partnerships
Corporate/Trade Name Data (US)

Database Name: Lawsuits, Judgments, Liens
Litigation/Judgments/Tax Liens (US)

Database Name: Professional Licenses
Licenses/Regis./Permits (AZ, CA, CO, CT, FL, GA, IL, IN, LA, MA, MD, MI, NJ, OH, PA, SC, TN, TX, VA, WI)

Database Name: Real Estate, Liens & Judgments
Real Estate/Assessor, Litigation/Judgments/Tax Liens (US)

Database Name: UCCs
Uniform Commerical Code (US)

Database Name: Watercraft Locator/Aircraft Locator
Aviation/Vessels (US)

Database Name: Business Finder/People Finder
Addresses/Telephone Numbers (US)

Gateway Name: Motor Vehicle Records
Driver and/or Vehicle (AK, AL, CO, CT, DC, DE, FL, IA, ID, IL, KY, LA, MA, MD, ME, MI, MN, MO, MS, MT, ND, NE, NH, NM, NY, OH, SC, TN, UT, WI, WV, WY)

Special Distribution Methods to Client: Dial-Up (Other than Internet), Internet

Westlaw Public Records combines and links public records and courthouse documents with information from private sources to address the relationships between corporations, people and their assets. Banks, financial service companies, corporations, law firms and government agencies across the nation use their online and document retrieval services to obtain background data on businesses, locate assets and people, retrieve official public records and solve business problems. Westlaw Public Records was originally founded by a practicing attorney and a computer systems expert acquainted with the needs of government, legal and corporate customers.

Editor's Choice --
Trade Associations

There are many trade associations related to the public records industry. Below you will find a list of many of these associations. The companies profiled in our Private Company Profiles section (beginning on page 349), are often members of one or more of these associations.

Acronym	Organization	Web Site	Members
AALL	American Assn of Law Librarians	www.aallnet.org/index.asp	4600
AAMVA	American Assn of Motor Vehicle Administrators	www.aamva.org	1500
AAPL	American Assn of Professional Landmen	www.landman.org	7000
ABA	American Bar Assn	www.abanet.org/home.html	417000
ABA (2)	American Banking Assn	www.aba.com	470
ABFE	American Board of Forensic Examiners	www.acfe.com	12000
ABI	American Bankruptcy Institute	www.abiworld.org	6500
ABW	American Business Women	www.abwahq.org	80000
ACA	American Collectors Assn	www.collector.com	3500
ACFE	Assn of Certified Fraud Examiners	http://cfenet.com	20000
AFIO	Assn of Former Intelligence Officers	www.afio.com	2500
AICPA	Assn of Certified Public Accountants	www.aicpa.org/index.htm	330000
AIIP	Assn of Independent Information Professionals	www.aiip.org	750
AIPLA	American Intellectual Property Law Assn	www.aipla.org	10000
ALA	American Library Assn	www.ala.org	56800
ALTA	American Land Title Association	www.alta.org	2400
AMA	American Management Assn	www.amanet.org/index.htm	70000
APA (2)	American Psychological Assn	www.apa.org	155000
APG	Assn of Professional Genealogists	www.apgen.org	1000
ASIS	American Society for Industrial Security	www.asisonline.org	40000
ASLET	American Society of Law Enforcement Trainers	www.aslet.org	7000
ASSE	American Society of Safety Engineers	www.asse.org	35000
ATA	American Truckers Assn	www.trucking.org	4100
ATLA	Assn of Trial Lawyers of America	www.atlanet.org	56000
CII	Council of Intl Investigators	www.cii2.org	
DMA	Direct Marketing Assn	www.the-dma.org	4500

Acronym	Organization	Web Site	Members
EAE	Environmental Assessment Assn	www.iami.org/eaa.cfm	3500
EMA	Employment Management Assn	www.shrm.org/EMA	4200
EPIC	Evidence Photographers Intl Council	www.epic-photo.org	1000
FBINAA	FBI Natl Academy Assn	www.fbinaa.org	17000
IAAI	Intl Assn of Arson Investigators	www.fire-investigators.org	9000
IAHSS	Intl Assn of Healthcare Security & Safety	www.iahss.org	
IALEIA	Intl Assn of Law Enforcement Intelligence Analysts	www.ialeia.org	1000
IIAA	Independent Insurance Agents of America	www.iiaa.org	300000
INA	Intl Nanny Assn	www.nanny.org	
INOA	Intl Narcotics Officers Assn	www.ineoa.org	
INTA	Intl Trademark Assn	www.inta.org	
ION	Investigative Open Network	www.ioninc.com	500
IREM	Institute of Real Estate Management	www.irem.org	8600
LES	Licensing Executive Society	www.usa-canada.les.org	4700
MBAA	Mortgage Bankers Assn of America	www.mbaa.org	2700
NAC	Natl Assn of Counselors	http://nac.lincoln-grad.org	500
NACM	Natl Assn of Credit Managers	www.nacm.org	35000
NAFE	Natl Assn of Female Executives	www.nafe.com	150000
NAFI	Natl Assn of Fire Investigators	www.nafi.org	5000
NAHB	Natl Assn of Home Builders	www.nahb.com	197000
NAHRO	Natl Assn of Housing & Redvlp Officials	www.nahro.org	8500
NAIS	Natl Assn of Investigative Specialists	www.pimall.com/nais/nais.menu.html	3000
NALA	Natl Assn of Legal Assistants	www.nala.org	17000
NALFM	Natl Assn of Law Firm Marketers	www.legalmarketing.org	1000
NALI	Natl Assn of Legal Investigators	www.nali.com	800
NALSC	Natl Assn of Legal Search Consultants	www.nalsc.org	130
NAMSS	Natl Assn of Medical Staff Svcs	www.namss.org	4000
NAPIA	Natl Assn of Public Insurance Adjustors	www.napia.com	
NAPPS	Natl Assn of Professional Process Servers	www.napps.org/napps.htm	1100
NAR	Natl Assn of Realtors	www.realtor.com	805000
NAREIT	Natl Assn of Real Estate Investment Trusts	www.nareit.org	1080
NARPM	Natl Assn of Residential Property Managers	www.narpm.org	1400
NASA	Natl Assn of Screening Agencies	www.n-a-s-a.com	25
NASIR	Natl Assn of Security & Investgt Regulators	www.nasir.org	90
NAWBO	Natl Assn of Women Business Owners	www.nawbo.org/nawbo/nawbostart.nsf	3000
NCISS	Natl Council of Investigation & Security Sevices	www.nciss.org	
NCRA	Natl Court Reporters Assn	www.verbatimreporters.com	23
NDIA	Natl Defender Investigator Assn	www.ndia-inv.org	32000

Acronym	Organization	Web Site	Members
NFIB	Natl Federation of Independent Businesses	www.nfib.org	650
NFIP	Natl Flood Insurance Program	www.fema.gov/nfip	600000
NFPA	Natl Federation of Paralegal Assn	www.paralegals.org	
NGS	Natl Genealogical Society	www.ngsgenealogy.org	
NHEMA	Natl Home Equity Mortgage Assn	www.nhema.org	240
NHRA	Natl Human Resources Assn	www.humanresources.org	1500
NICA	Natl Insurance Claims Assn	www.gonatgo.com	
NLG	Natl Lawyers Guild	www.nlg.org	6000
NPPRA	Natl Public Record Research Assn	www.nprra.org	450
PBUS	Professional Bail Agents of the United States	www.pbus.com	
PIHRA	Professionals in Human Resources Assn	www.pihra.org	3500
PRRN	Public Record Retriever Network	www.brbpub.com	672
REIPA	Real Estate Information Providers Assn	www.reipa.org	
SCIP	Society of Competitive Intelligence Professionals	www.scip.org	6500
SFSA	Society of Former Special Agents of the FBI	www.socxfbi.org	7800
SHRM	Society of Human Resources Management	www.shrm.org	65000
SIIA	Software & Information Industry Association	www.siia.net	1200
SILA	Society of Insurance License Administrators	www.sila.org	
SLA	Special Libraries Assn	www.sla.org	14000
USFN	US Foreclosure Network	www.usfn.org	
WAD	World Assn of Detectives	www.wad.net	

Editor's Choice -- Canadian Web Sites

Here are some web sites that offer government and public record-related information for Canada and its provinces.

Attorneys & Law Firms Database
http://www.lexpert.ca/
Bills Listing
http://www.assembly.gov.nt.ca/Legislation/MainActs.html
Bills Listing
http://www.legis.gov.bc.ca/proceedings/bills.htm
Birth Records (1869-1898) Listing
http://www3.sympatico.ca/smplayter/ovs.births.html
Births (1872-1899) Database
http://www2.bcarchives.gov.bc.ca/cgi-bin/www2vsb
Business Licenses Database
http://www.gov.ab.ca/ma/cfml/buslic/buslic1.cfm
Calgary Property Database
http://www.fairshare.gov.calgary.ab.ca/mainproperty.htm
Civil Code Search Form
http://www.lexum.umontreal.ca/ccq/en/index.html
Companies Database
http://db.itt.gov.mb.ca/ITT/CIMIS/CIMISWeb.nsf
Corporations Database
http://strategis.ic.gc.ca/cgi-bin/sc_mrksv/corpdir/dataOnline/corpns_se
Death Records (1869-1923) Listing
http://www3.sympatico.ca/smplayter/ovs.deaths.html
Death Records (1872-1979) Database
http://www2.bcarchives.gov.bc.ca/cgi-bin/www2vsd
Governing Documents Text
http://canada.justice.gc.ca/Loireg/index_en.html
Governing Documents Text
http://www.gov.ab.ca/qp/indiv.html
Joint Stock Companies Database
http://www.gov.ns.ca/bacs/rjsc/search.stm
Land Grants (1870-1930) Database
http://www.archives.ca/exec/naweb.dll?fs&02011102&e&top&0
Lawyers Database
http://lawyers.martindale.com/canada
Lobbyist Listing
http://lobbyist.oico.on.ca/Integrity/RegistrationPublic.nsf/ApprovedByType?OpenView
Lobbyists Listing
http://lobbyist.oico.on.ca/Integrity/RegistrationPublic.nsf/ApprovedByType?OpenView
Marriage Records (1872-1924) Database

http://www2.bcarchives.gov.bc.ca/cgi-bin/www2vsm

Marriage Records (1873-1913) Listing

http://www3.sympatico.ca/smplayter/ovs.marriages.html

Patents Database

http://patents1.ic.gc.ca/intro-e.html

Post Offices Database

http://www.archives.ca/exec/naweb.dll?fs&02010902&e&top&0

Real Estate Agencies & Brokers Database

http://www.reca.ab.ca/asp/pubinqry.asp

Securities Companies Listing

http://www.osc.gov.on.ca/en/Market/registrants.html

Securities Database

http://www.bcsc.bc.ca/bcscdb/default.asp

Statutes Text

http://legis.acjnet.org/TNO/Loi/a_en.html

Supreme Court Opinions

http://www.lexum.umontreal.ca/csc-scc/en/index.html

Vehicle Recalls Listing

http://www.tc.gc.ca/securiteroutiere/Recalls/search_e.asp

Vital Statistics Homepage

http://www.gov.ns.ca/bacs/vstat/index.htm

Editor's Choice --
World Government Web Sites

In this section, we present web sites for the various governments of the world's countries. Use these as a starting point for international research projects.

Afghanistan
www.afghan-government.com

Albania
http://presidenca.gov.al

Andorra
www.andorra.ad/govern

Angola
www.angola.org/politics

Anguilla
www.gov.ai

Argentina
www.senado.gov.ar

Armenia
www.gov.am

Aruba
http://www.aruba.com/pages/governm.htm

Australia
www.fed.gov.au

Austria
www.parlament.gv.at

Azerbaijan
www.president.az

Bahrain
www.bma.gov.bh

Belarus
www.belarus.net/parliame

Belgium
http://belgium.fgov.be

Belize
www.belize.gov.bz

Bolivia

www.congreso.gov.bo

Botswana

www.gov.bw

Brazil

www.brasil.gov.br

Brunei

www.brunet.bn/homepage/gov/mibhom.htm

Bulgaria

www.government.bg

Cameroon

www.camnet.cm/celcom/homepr.htm

Canada

http://canada.gc.ca

Cape Verde

www.capeverdeusembassy.org/govtmain.html

Chile

www.congreso.cl

Colombia

www.presidencia.gov.co

Congo

www.rdcongo.gov.cd

Costa Rica

www.casapres.go.cr

Croatia

www.sabor.hr

Cyprus

www.pio.gov.cy

Czech Republic

www.psp.cz

Denmark

www.folketinget.dk

Dominican Republic

www.congreso.do

Ecuador

www.mmrree.gov.ec

Egypt

www.assembly.gov.eg

El Salvador

www.casapres.gob.sv

Estonia

www.rk.ee

Ethiopia

www.ethiopar.net

Finland
> www.eduskunta.fi

France
> www.assemblee-nat.fr

Gabon
> www.presidence-gabon.com

Gambia
> www.gambia.com

Georgia
> www.parliament.ge

Germany
> www.bundesregierung.de

Ghana
> www.ghana.com/republic/index.html

Greece
> www.primeminister.gr

Greenland
> www.gh.gl

Guatemala
> www.congreso.gob.gt

Haiti
> www.haiti.org

Hong Kong
> www.info.gov.hk

Hungary
> www.mkogy.hu

Iceland
> www.althingi.is

India
> http://alfa.nic.in

Indonesia
> www.deplu.go.id/english/govern1.htm

Iran
> www.netiran.com/statestructure.html

Ireland
> www.irlgov.ie

Israel
> www.knesset.gov.il

Italy
> www.parlamento.it

Japan
> www.sorifu.go.jp

Jordan
> www.nic.gov.jo

Kazakhstan
www.president.kz

Kenya
www.kenyastatehouse.go.ke

Kuwait
www.kna.org.kw

Kyrgyzstan
http://kabar.gov.kg

Laos
www.laoembassy.com

Latvia
www.latnet.lv/WWWsites/government

Lebanon
www.lp.gov.lb

Liechtenstein
www.firstlink.li

Lithuania
www.president.lt

Luxembourg
www.chd.lu

Macau
www.macau.gov.mo

Macedonia
www.gov.mk

Malaysia
www.parlimen.gov.my

Malta
www.magnet.mt

Mauritus
http://ncb.intnet.mu/govt/house.htm

Mexico
www.cddhcu.gob.mx

Micronesia
www.fsmgov.org

Mongolia
www.parl.gov.mn

Morocco
www.mincom.gov.ma

Mozambique
www.mozambique.mz

Namibia
www.republicofnamibia.com

Netherlands
www.parlement.nl

New Zealand
www.govt.nz

Nicaragua
www.asamblea.gob.ni

Norway
http://odin.dep.no

Oman
www.omanet.com

Pakistan
www.pak.gov.pk

Palestine
www.pal-plc.org

Panama
www.presidencia.gob.pa

Paraguay
www.camdip.gov.py

Peru
http://www.congreso.gob.pe

Philippines
www.opnet.ops.gov.ph

Poland
www.kprm.gov.pl

Qatar
www.islam.gov.qa

Romania
www.guv.ro

Russia
www.gov.ru

Saudia Arabia
www.saudinf.com

Senegal
www.primature.sn

Singapore
www.gov.sg

Slovakia
www.government.gov.sk

Slovenia
www.sigov.si

South Africa
www.gov.za

South Korea
www.gcc.go.kr

Spain
www.la-moncloa.es

Sri Lanka
   www.lk/Government.html

St. Kitts & Nevis
   www.stkittsnevis.net

Swaziland
   www.swazi.com/government

Sweden
   www.regeringen.se

Switzerland
   www.parlament.ch

Taiwan
   www.ey.gov.tw

Tanzania
   www.bungetz.org

Thailand
   www.thaigov.go.th

Togo
   www.republicoftogo.com

Trinidad & Tobago
   www.gov.tt

Turkey
   www.tbmm.gov.tr

Uganda
   www.uganda.co.ug/home.htm

Ukraine
   www.kmu.gov.ua

United Arab Emirates
   www.fedfin.gov.ae

United Kingdom
   www.open.gov.uk

Uruguay
   www.presidencia.gub.uy

Uzbekistan
   www.gov.uz

Vatican City
   www.vatican.va

Venezuela
   www.parlamento.gov.ve

Yugoslavia
   www.gov.yu

Zambia
   www.statehouse.gov.zm

Editor's Choice --
Legal Reference Web Sites

Use these sites to find out what common and obscure legal terms mean. Some of these sites focus on a particular area of law, such as fraud or divorce, while the majority of the sites listed focus on general law.

Bernstein's Dictionary of Bankruptcy Terminology
www.bernsteinlaw.com/publications/bankdict.html

Black's Law Dictionary
www.alaska.net/!winter/black_law_dictionary.html

Commercial Fraud Glossary
http://www.mc2consulting.com/fraudef.htm

Divorce Law Dictionary
www.divorcenet.com/dictionary.html

Duhaime's Law Dictionary
www.wwlia.org/diction.htm

Glossary of Legal Terms
http://mobar.org/media/gloss.htm

Glossary of Legal Terms II
www.wisbar.org/pbcg4.htm

Law.Com Legal Dictionary
http://dictionary.law.com

'Letric Law Library Lexicon
http://lectlaw.com//def.htm

Maritime Law Glossary
www.admiraltylaw.com/tetley/Glosind.htm

Nolo's Legal Encyclopedia
www.nolo.com/ChunkLR/LR.index.html

Oran's Dictionary of the Law
www.lawoffice.com/pathfind/orans/orans.asp

Webster's Dictionary of Legal, Lawful & Propaganda Terms
www.freedom-and-law.org

Notes

Notes

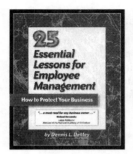

Facts on Demand Press

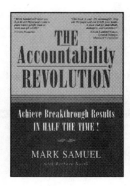

The Accountability Revolution

The Accountability Revolution is the "Emperor's New Clothes" for those who want to achieve and maintain dynamic, results oriented leadership. Samuel pulls no punches in revealing the flaws in today's accepted business thinking. He provides powerful strategies and practical tools that increase morale & productivity, reduce team conflicts, decrease turnover, increase performance ratings, and earn greater profits. *The Accountability Revolution* puts you and your company on the fast track to breakthrough results and greater success.

Mark Samuel • 1-889150-27-4 • Pub. Date 2001 • 248 pgs • $17.95

Organizing the Good Life

Organizing The Good Life is packed with tips on achieving a successful business and home life. It's a welcome source of support for the emotional drains of disorganization, work addiction and the nagging self-doubt that occurs when you forget you are in charge of creating the life you want. Celia's philosophy is truly unique. It's a workplace simplicity message for those who have too much to do — yet don't want to give up the good parts of "having it all."

Celia Rocks • 1-889150-26-6 • Pub. Date 2001 • 170 pgs. • $12.95

Criminal Records Book

Coming March, 2002!

Criminal records provide essential information used for employment screening, locating people, fraud detection and other investigative purposes. This book is the complete guide to accessing and utilizing criminal records housed at the federal, state and county level. Learn how to:

- determine where criminal records are stored.
- obtain records at each jurisdiction level.
- select a record vendor.
- legally access criminal records.

Derek Hinton • 1-889150-27-4 • Pub. Date 2002 • 320 pgs • $19.95

Available at Your Local Bookstore!

1-800-929-3811 • Facts on Demand Press • www.brbpub.com